Managing Internet Information Services

Managing Internet Information Services

Cricket Liu, Jerry Peek, Russ Jones,
Bryan Buus, and Adrian Nye

with Greg George, Neophytos Iacovou, Jeff LaCoursiere,
Paul Lindner, and Craig Strickland

O'Reilly & Associates, Inc.
103 Morris Street, Suite A
Sebastopol, CA 95472

Managing Internet Information Services
by Cricket Liu, Jerry Peek, Russ Jones, Bryan Buus, & Adrian Nye

Printed in the United States of America.

Editor: Adrian Nye

Production Editor: Ellen Siever

Printing History:

December 1994: First Edition.

This book is printed on acid-free paper with 85% recycled content, 15-20% post-consumer waste. O'Reilly & Associates is committed to using paper with the highest recycled content available consistent with high quality.

ISBN: 1-56592-062-7 [2/95]

Table of Contents

Preface .... *xxv*

1: Internet Service Concepts *1*

1.1 What Is the Internet? 1
1.1.1 What Does It Mean to Be on the Internet? 2
1.1.2 What Is on the Internet? 5
1.2 How Are Internet Services Structured? 7
1.3 What Is TCP/IP? 8
1.3.1 Protocols 8
1.3.2 The inetd Superserver 11
1.3.3 Standalone Servers 12
1.3.4 Naming 13
1.4 How Information Clients Talk to Information Servers 14

2: Introduction to Information Services *17*

2.1 An Overview of Internet Information Services 18
2.1.1 Mail-based Services 18
2.1.2 FTP 20
2.1.3 Telnet and Finger 20
2.1.4 Gopher 21
2.1.5 The World Wide Web 22

2.1.6 WAIS 24
2.2 What To Do with Internet Services 26
2.2.1 Internal Services 26
2.2.2 External Services 27
2.2.3 Can You Charge Money? 28
2.3 System and Network Requirements 29
2.3.1 Network Connection Type 30
2.3.2 Network Load 30
2.3.3 Computational Load 33
2.3.4 Disk Space 33
2.4 Human Requirements 34

3: Finger-, Inetd-, and Telnet-based Services 37

3.1 Finger-based Information Services 37
3.1.1 FIFOs for Smart Updating 39
3.2 Inetd-based Information Services 40
3.3 Telnet and Other Login-based Information Services 42
3.3.1 Security for Telnet and Inetd Services 43
3.3.2 Clients as Login Shells 43
3.3.3 Captured Shells as Login Shells 44
3.3.4 Starting X Clients in a Captured Shell 45
3.3.5 Customized Login and No Login Services 47
3.3.6 An Example: The Weather Underground 47
3.4 Other Possibilities 50

4: Setting Up an FTP Archive 51

4.1 What Is FTP Good For? 52
4.2 The FTP Server 53
4.2.1 inetd Configuration 53
4.2.2 The ftp User 55
4.2.3 Other Standard ftpd Command-Line Options 56
4.2.4 Domain Naming 56
4.2.5 Standard Aliases 57
4.3 The Filesystem 58
4.3.1 Anonymous FTP Directory Structure 58
4.3.2 passwd and group Files 58
4.3.3 File and Directory Permissions and Ownership 59
4.3.4 A Note on SunOS and Solaris 60

4.3.5 Optional Subdirectories ... 61
4.3.6 Sublogins ... 62
4.4 Testing and Debugging Your Archive ... 64
4.4.1 Connecting to the Archive ... 65
4.4.2 Using the Archive ... 67

5: The WU Archive FTP Daemon ... *69*

5.1 Compiling the WU Archive ftpd ... 70
5.2 New ftpd Command-Line Options ... 73
5.3 The ftpconversions File ... 73
5.4 The ftpaccess File ... 75
5.4.1 Defining Classes of Users ... 75
5.4.2 Denying Access ... 77
5.4.3 Limiting Access ... 78
5.4.4 Group Controls ... 80
5.4.5 Printing Information ... 82
5.4.6 Logging Information ... 85
5.4.7 Easier Navigation ... 87
5.4.8 Uploading Controls ... 88
5.5 The ftphosts File ... 89
5.6 Utility Programs ... 90
5.6.1 ftpcount ... 90
5.6.2 ftpwho ... 91
5.6.3 ftpshut ... 91
5.7 For More Information ... 92

6: Maintaining an FTP Archive ... *93*

6.1 Populating Your Archive ... 93
6.1.1 Standard Filename Extensions ... 94
6.2 Making Access Easier ... 95
6.2.1 Creating Links ... 95
6.2.2 Aliases and Search Paths ... 96
6.2.3 Printing Messages ... 98
6.2.4 ls-lR Files and Archie Support ... 99
6.3 Denying and Limiting User Access ... 102
6.3.1 Denying Access ... 102
6.3.2 Limiting Access ... 103
6.3.3 Hidden Directories ... 104

6.4 Monitoring Log Files ... 106
6.5 Reading Mail ... 107

7: *Creating an Internet Database Server with WAIS* ... *109*

7.1 What Is WAIS? ... 109
7.1.1 Using a WAIS Database ... 110
7.1.2 How Does WAIS Work? ... 111
7.2 Building WAIS ... 112
7.3 Testing and Installing WAIS ... 118
7.3.1 Running waisserver Under inetd ... 120
7.3.2 Running waisserver Standalone ... 121
7.3.3 Testing waisserver ... 122
7.4 Configuring waisserver ... 124
7.4.1 waisserver Run-Time Configuration ... 124
7.4.2 Server Security ... 125
7.4.3 WAIS and Firewalls ... 128

8: *Creating WAIS Sources with waisindex* ... *133*

8.1 Index Files ... 133
8.2 Relevance Ranking ... 136
8.3 A Table for the Impatient ... 138
8.4 Document Formats ... 138
8.4.1 Indexing Other File Types ... 141
8.4.2 Associating One File with Another ... 142
8.5 Other Command-Line Options ... 143
8.5.1 Naming Your Source ... 143
8.5.2 Exporting Your Source ... 144
8.5.3 Registering Your Source ... 144
8.5.4 Updating Existing Index Files ... 144
8.5.5 Indexing an Entire Directory Tree ... 145
8.5.6 Configuring Logging ... 145
8.5.7 Controlling Indexing ... 145
8.5.8 Saving Space ... 146
8.6 Customizing waisindex Operation ... 146
8.6.1 Selecting Words for waisindex to Ignore ... 147
8.6.2 Setting Up Synonyms ... 147
8.7 Updating Indexes ... 148
8.7.1 Indexing from Scratch Without Downtime ... 148

8.7.2 Adding to an Old Index ... 149
8.7.3 Indexes with Multiple Types ... 149

9: Gopher: Introduction ... 151

9.1 How Gopher Works: the Gopher Protocol ... 152
9.2 What Is Gopher+? ... 155
9.2.1 A Tour of Gopher+ Features ... 155
9.2.2 The Gopher+ Protocol ... 158
9.3 Selection of Server Software ... 159
9.3.1 Licensing of the Gopher 2.x Server ... 160
9.4 Variety of Client Software ... 161
9.5 The Gopher FAQ ... 162
9.6 Overview of Gopher Chapters ... 162

10: Gopher: Compiling the Server ... 163

10.1 Getting the Source Code ... 163
10.1.1 Extracting the Files ... 163
10.1.2 What's Here? ... 164
10.2 Precompilation Configuration ... 165
10.2.1 Modifying Makefile.config ... 165
10.2.2 Modifying conf.h ... 169
10.2.3 Optional Precompilation Setup ... 171
10.3 Compiling the Client and Server ... 174
10.3.1 Compilation Problems ... 175
10.4 Installing the Client and Server ... 176

11: Gopher: Managing the Server ... 179

11.1 Configuring the Server ... 179
11.1.1 Naming the Server: the Hostalias Token ... 179
11.1.2 Controlling Access: the Access Token ... 180
11.1.3 Global Attributes ... 182
11.1.4 Customizing the Access Denied Message: the BummerMsg Token ... 183
11.1.5 Recognizing a New Filename Extension ... 183
11.1.6 Excluding Files: the ignore Token ... 185
11.1.7 Other Gopher 2.x Tokens ... 186
11.2 Running the Server ... 187
11.2.1 Preparing the Data Directory ... 187

11.2.2 Recommended Command-Line Options 188
11.2.3 Starting gopherd Standalone 188
11.2.4 Using inetd 189
11.3 Testing Your Server 191
11.3.1 Ack! My Server Isn't Working! 192
11.4 Running gopherd as gopherls and gindexd 195
11.5 Making Sense of Gopher Logs 196
11.5.1 Summarizing Log Data 198
11.5.2 Rotating Logs 201
11.6 How to Register Your Gopher Server 202
11.6.1 Example 203
11.6.2 Server Name 204
11.6.3 Gopher Server Hostname 204
11.6.4 Gopher Port Number 204
11.6.5 Administrator's Email Address 204
11.6.6 Geographic Location 204

12: Gopher: Preparing Information 205

12.1 The Easy Stuff—Text Files and Directories 205
12.2 Menu Item Naming, Ordering, and Attributes 206
12.2.1 So, what's a .cap directory? 207
12.2.2 Gopher 2.x .names files 208
12.2.3 Gopher+ Multi-format Menu Items 210
12.2.4 Form and Abstract Attributes 210
12.3 Data Architecture 211
12.3.1 Menu Structure 211
12.3.2 Menu Item Names 212
12.3.3 Document Length and Format 212
12.3.4 Getting the Big Picture 213
12.4 File Types 215
12.4.1 Overriding the Default Type 217
12.4.2 Special Files 217
12.5 Chroot and Symbolic Links 219
12.5.1 Symbolic Links to Outside the Gopher Data Directory 220
12.5.2 Symbolic Links to Within the Gopher Data Directory 220
12.6 Converting an Existing FTP Structure 221

13: Gopher: Linking Services Together *223*

13.1 .Links Files 223
13.2 Linking to Data on Other Gopher Servers 225
13.3 Links to CSO Phone Books and Telnet Sites 227
13.3.1 Linking to a CSO Phone Book Server 227
13.3.2 The telnet Link Type (Including the TN3270 Type) 228
13.4 Links to FTP, WAIS, and Scripts 229
13.4.1 Links to FTP Archives 229
13.4.2 Links That Execute Scripts 232
13.4.3 Links That Do WAIS Searches 236

14: Gopher: Incorporating Databases *237*

14.1 Using WAIS Indexes 237
14.1.1 Placement of WAIS Data 237
14.1.2 Creating an Index 238
14.1.3 Using a Link to Incorporate WAIS indexes 239
14.1.4 WAIS Linking Using a .cap File 240
14.1.5 Pointing to a WAIS server 240
14.1.6 Using WAIS with a chrooted Server 241
14.1.7 Avoiding Indexing Unwanted Files 242
14.1.8 If Things Don't Work 243
14.2 Using NeXT Indexes 244
14.2.1 Building a NeXT Index 244
14.2.2 Including a NeXT Index 245
14.3 Serving WAIS and NeXT Indexes with gindexd 246
14.3.1 Creating and Placing Index Files 247
14.3.2 Creating a hostdata File 247
14.3.3 Running gindexd 248
14.3.4 Testing the gindexd Server 248
14.3.5 Linking to the gindexd Server 249
14.4 grep Indexes 249
14.5 Script Queries 250
14.5.1 Combining Shell Indexes and exec: Links 252
14.5.2 Security Concerns with Shell Indexes and exec: Links 254
14.6 Searching Multiple Indexes 255

15: Gopher: Veronica and Jughead 257

15.1 Registering Your Gopher Server with Veronica 258
15.2 Avoiding Veronica Registration 258
15.3 Running a Veronica Server 258
15.4 Local Links to Veronica Servers Using maltshop 259
15.5 Making a Local Veronica Using Jughead 259
15.5.1 Creating the Table 260
15.5.2 Building the Table and Index 261
15.5.3 Running the Server 261
15.5.4 Rereading the Index File 262
15.5.5 Linking to a Jughead Server 262

16: Gopher+ Forms and Other New Features 263

16.1 Gopher+ Forms 263
16.1.1 Types of Form Input 263
16.1.2 How to Use Ask Blocks 264
16.1.3 A Simple Example Form 265
16.1.4 Adding Default Values and Radio Boxes (Choose) 267
16.1.5 Adding Multiline Input (AskL) and Checkboxes (Select) 268
16.1.6 Saving the Output 270
16.1.7 Ask Forms That Return More Complicated Types 271
16.1.8 My Ask Block Doesn't Work! 273
16.2 Other Features of Gopher 2.0.16 275
16.2.1 The ADMIT1 Protocol 275
16.2.2 New Indexing Script 276
16.2.3 New Information-only Type 276
16.3 New Features in Gopher 2.1 276
16.3.1 User Authentication 276
16.3.2 Updated FTP Gateway 277
16.3.3 Virtual Documents 277

17: Introduction to the World Wide Web 279

17.1 What Is the Web Good For? 280
17.2 Basic Web Concepts 282
17.2.1 Hyperlinking 283
17.2.2 The HTML Tagging Language 284
17.2.3 The URL Concept 285

17.2.4 What Is a World Wide Web Browser? 286
17.2.5 What Is a World Wide Web Server? 287
17.2.6 HTTP 287
17.3 World Wide Web Servers and Browsers 288
17.3.1 Web Browsers 288
17.3.2 Web Servers 292
17.4 Future Directions 294
17.4.1 HTML Enhancements 294
17.4.2 Secure Transactions 296
17.4.3 Uniform Naming 296
17.4.4 Commercialization 297
17.5 Overview of Web Chapters 298

18: Setting Up a Web Server 299

18.1 Setting Up Basic Services 299
18.1.1 Installing a Precompiled Server 299
18.1.2 Compilation of NCSA HTTP 300
18.1.3 Site-Specific Configuration 302
18.1.4 Installing the Server 305
18.1.5 Starting the Server 305
18.1.6 Startup Under inetd 307
18.1.7 Mapping URLs to Documents 307
18.1.8 Testing Your HTTP Server 309
18.1.9 Setting Up Home Pages 309
18.1.10 Delegating Document Tree Management 310
18.1.11 Conventions for Public Access 311
18.1.12 Announcing Your Server 311
18.2 Web Server Maintenance 312
18.2.1 Updating HTML Documents 312
18.2.2 Managing the Log Files 313
18.2.3 Moving Directory Structures 313
18.2.4 Mirroring Documents and Servers 314
18.2.5 HTTP Logs and Log Analysis 315
18.3 Enabling More Features 318
18.3.1 Adding MIME Types 318
18.3.2 Enabling Server-Side Includes 320
18.3.3 Automatic Directory Indexing 321
18.4 Installation Summary 324

19: Authoring for the Web ... 325

19.1 HTML Overview ... 325
19.1.1 Autoflowing and Autowrapping ... 326
19.1.2 HTML Tag Syntax ... 326
19.1.3 Document Construction Guidelines ... 327
19.1.4 Sample HTML Document ... 327
19.1.5 Hyperlinks ... 330
19.1.6 Linking to Points Within Documents ... 331
19.1.7 URLs ... 331
19.1.8 Lists ... 334
19.1.9 Graphics ... 336
19.1.10 Server-Side Includes ... 339
19.1.11 For More Information About HTML ... 341
19.2 Information Design Issues ... 341
19.2.1 Document Modularity ... 341
19.2.2 Degrees of Hyperization ... 342
19.2.3 Automatic Versus Manual Hyperlinking ... 343
19.2.4 Style Guidelines ... 344
19.2.5 An Example of Information Design ... 344
19.3 HTML Authoring Tools ... 347
19.3.1 Emacs HTML Mode ... 348
19.3.2 FrameMaker ... 348
19.3.3 HoTMetaL ... 348
19.3.4 CyberLeaf ... 349
19.3.5 HTML Conversion Tools and Filters ... 349
19.4 Clickable Image Maps ... 350
19.4.1 Planning the Clickable Image Map ... 351
19.4.2 Mapping the Hotspots into a Map File ... 351
19.4.3 Connecting Your Map File to a URL ... 353
19.4.4 Referencing Your Clickable Image Map in HTML ... 354
19.4.5 Testing the Image Map ... 354
19.4.6 How It Really Works ... 355

20: Web: Gateways and Forms *357*

20.1 Gateways 358
20.1.1 The Common Gateway Interface 358
20.1.2 Prompting the User for Input 361
20.1.3 URLs in HTML Documents Returned by Gateways 366
20.1.4 Existing Gateways 366
20.1.5 Additional cgi-bin Directories 367
20.2 Forms Processing 368
20.2.1 HTML for Forms 368
20.2.2 Scripts to Handle Form Input 370
20.2.3 Adding Checkboxes to the Form 373
20.3 WAIS Access from the Web 376
20.3.1 Direct WAIS Access 376
20.3.2 Web-to-WAIS Gateways 377
20.3.3 Developing a Custom WAIS Gateway 377
20.3.4 WAISgate 378
20.3.5 Comparison of WAIS-to-Web Techniques 379

21: Web: Access Control and Security *381*

21.1 Access Control and User Authentication 381
21.1.1 Access Control Files 381
21.1.2 Domain-Level Access Control 382
21.1.3 User Authentication 384
21.2 Security 388
21.2.1 Links Outside the Document Tree 388
21.2.2 Access Control and User Authentication 389
21.2.3 Personal HTML Directories 389
21.2.4 Shell Metacharacters in Forms 390
21.2.5 Server-Side Includes 390

22: Introduction to Email Services *391*

22.1 A Simple File Server: canned_reply 393
22.2 Ways to Manage Mailing Lists 398
22.3 What's It Like to Use List Server Software? 399
22.3.1 From a Subscriber's Point of View 399
22.3.2 For a List Owner 401
22.3.3 Downside of List Servers 401

22.3.4 The Personal Touch 402
22.3.5 Mailing-List Security 402
22.4 Choosing a Mailing List System: A Feature Comparison 403
22.4.1 Simple Lists with Your MTA 403
22.4.2 Lists Served by Majordomo 404
22.4.3 Lists Served by ListProcessor 6.0c 404
22.5 Email Ethics 405
22.6 Email Services and Network Connections 406
22.7 The List-managers Mailing List 408
22.8 How Email Is Delivered 408

23: Simple Mailing Lists 413

23.1 Setting Up the List 413
23.2 Using a List Members File 415
23.3 Aliases and Your Local Network 416
23.4 Handling Bounces 417
23.5 Mail from Local Users 419
23.6 Envelope Sender in sendmail Version 8 419
23.7 Minimizing Bounced Mail 420
23.8 Changing the Message Header 421
23.9 Logging Messages 423
23.10 List Exploders 423

24: Automating Mailing Lists with Majordomo 427

24.1 An Overview of Majordomo 428
24.1.1 A User's View of Majordomo 428
24.1.2 Majordomo for List Owners 430
24.1.3 Majordomo for Administrators 431
24.2 Installing Majordomo 432
24.3 Setting Up Lists 440
24.3.1 Creating a New List 440
24.3.2 For MMDF Systems 444
24.3.3 Making a Digested List 444
24.3.4 Testing Your Installation 446
24.4 Day-to-day Administration 451
24.4.1 Setting Up a List Owner's Account 451
24.4.2 Editing Files with medit 451
24.4.3 Majordomo Logs 452

24.4.4 Managing the Archives 453
24.4.5 Disabling Majordomo Temporarily 453
24.5 The Majordomo Mailing List 454

25: The Majordomo List Owner and Moderator 455

25.1 List Owner Aliases 455
25.2 Majordomo Commands for List Owners 456
25.3 Changing a List's Configuration 457
25.3.1 Config File Variables 460
25.3.2 Regular Expressions for advertise and noadvertise 467
25.4 Making a Moderated List 469
25.5 Approving Subscriptions and Moderating 469
25.5.1 Approving Subscriptions and Moderating with approve 469
25.5.2 Approving Subscriptions Without approve 471
25.5.3 Moderating Lists Without approve 473
25.6 Returned Mail and the Bounces List 476

26: Ftpmail 479

26.1 Ftpmail for Users 480
26.1.1 A Sample Session 480
26.1.2 Using a Different Address 483
26.1.3 Overall Session Commands 483
26.1.4 File Transfer Commands 484
26.2 Installing Ftpmail 486
26.3 Testing Your Installation 490
26.4 Managing Ftpmail 492
26.4.1 Routine Checks 493
26.4.2 Restricting Ftpmail 493
26.4.3 Ignored Mail 494
26.5 The Ftpmail Developer's Mailing List 495

27: Firewalls and Information Services 497

27.1 What Is a Firewall? 498
27.2 Types of Firewalls 498
27.2.1 The Dual-Homed Gateway 499
27.2.2 The Screened Host Gateway 500
27.2.3 Other Firewall Topologies 501
27.3 Hurdles for Information Providers 501

27.4 Firewall Software 504
27.4.1 CERN Web Server Proxy Mode 504
27.4.2 SOCKS 505
27.4.3 The Firewall Toolkit 505
27.5 Locating Servers 506
27.5.1 Web Servers 506
27.5.2 Anonymous FTP 507
27.5.3 General Internal Location Concerns 509
27.6 Solutions for Various Clients 510
27.6.1 Telnet 510
27.6.2 Archie 510
27.6.3 FTP 511
27.6.4 Mosaic 512
27.6.5 Solutions for Various DOS/Windows/Mac Clients 512
27.7 For More Information 513

28: xinetd 515

28.1 What xinetd Does 516
28.1.1 Understanding inetd's Role in Security 516
28.2 How to Get xinetd 518
28.3 Building xinetd 518
28.4 Installing xinetd 519
28.5 Configuring xinetd with xinetd.conf 520
28.5.1 The Default Entry 521
28.5.2 Access Restrictions 522
28.5.3 Controlling Logging 523
28.5.4 Setting Environment Variables 524
28.6 Managing xinetd 524
28.6.1 Logging 524
28.6.2 Reconfiguration 526
28.6.3 Debugging 527
28.7 How to Spot Security Break-Ins or Attempts 527
28.7.1 Tracking Down a Culprit 528

29: Legal Issues *531*

29.1 What's Allowed on the Internet? 532
29.2 Intellectual Property Rights and Responsibilities 533
29.2.1 Types of Intellectual Property Protection 533
29.2.2 The Publishing Agreement 534
29.2.3 Copyrights 534
29.3 Other Publishing Pitfalls 537
29.3.1 Libel 537
29.3.2 Pornography 538
29.3.3 Bootlegged Commercial Software 538
29.3.4 Encryption Software 538

30: Protecting Intellectual Property *539*

30.1 Non-Cryptographic Approaches 539
30.2 Cryptographic Approaches 540
30.2.1 Some Background on Encryption 541
30.2.2 A Practical Example of Encryption Issues 543
30.2.3 Encryption in a Book Browser 544
30.3 Export Controls on Encryption 545

A: gopherd Options *547*

A.1 Defaults 547
A.2 The Options—an Overview 548
A.3 The Options—Explained 548
A.3.1 Disable chroot() (–c) 548
A.3.2 Disable Directory Caching (–C) 549
A.3.3 Enable Debugging Output (–D) 549
A.3.4 Running Under inetd (–I) 549
A.3.5 Log to a File (–l logfile) 549
A.3.6 Load Average (–L loadavg) 550
A.3.7 Alternate gopherd Configuration File (–o optionfile) 550
A.3.8 Run As a Specific Login-name (–u login-name) 550
A.3.9 Run Under Specific User ID (–U uid) 550
A.3.10 The Data Directory (data-directory) 551
A.3.11 port-number 551

B: Gopher: Client Compilation Options *553*

B.1 Setting an FTP gateway 553
B.2 Client Security Options 553
B.3 Setting Client Commands 554
B.4 Using Downloading in the Client 557

C: Gopher Tools and Gateways *559*

D: Web: More HTML Tags *567*

D.1 Common HTML Tags 567
D.2 HTML Tags for Forms 568
D.2.1 <FORM> 568
D.2.2 <INPUT> 569
D.2.3 <SELECT> 570
D.2.4 <TEXTAREA> 570

E: Web: httpd.conf Directives *573*

F: Web: srm.conf Directives *579*

G: Web: access.conf Directives *585*

H: Web: For More Information *591*

H.1 World Wide Web FAQ 591
H.2 Newsgroups 591
H.3 Mailing Lists 592
H.4 Examples of Web Servers 593
H.5 GNN's Best of the Net Servers 593
H.6 Online Conference Proceedings 595

Index: *597*

List of Figures

1–1 A typical full-time Internet connection 3
1–2 A user dialing up to a computer on the Internet 4
1–3 On-demand Internet link 5
1–4 How dotted-octet notation comes from a 32-bit IP address 9
2–1 Mosaic accessing a Gopher server 23
2–2 The xwais client 25
7–1 The WAIS indexer, server, and client 112
7–2 What a WAIS forwarder does 129
8–1 Mosaic accessing a WAIS database 143
14–1 How gindexd interacts with a Gopher server 246
17–1 California Virtual Tourist document display by Mosiac 282
17–2 A Web of Web servers 284
17–3 The world as seen from a Web browser 287
18–1 gwstat hourly traffic summary 318
18–2 A usage graph generated by wusage 319
18–3 Mosaic screen shot of an automatic directory index 322
19–1 Sample HTML document display by Mosaic 329
19–2 Nested bullet list rendered with Mosaic 335
19–3 Definition list rendered with Mosaic 336
19–4 Crocodile home page, displayed with Mosaic 346
19–5 Crocodile home page, displayed with Lynx 347
19–6 A digitized photo of my office 352
19–7 The virtual office clickable image map in Mosaic 355

20–1 Information flow through the Common Gateway Interface 359
20–2 Feedback form as displayed by NCSA Mosaic 369
20–3 Crocodile registration form displayed by NCSA Mosaic 375
22–1 Choosing a mailing list host 407
22–2 Envelope and contents of an email message 409
22–3 Basics of SMTP 410
23–1 Sending a message to the dim-sum list and its exploder 424
25–1 Approving subscriptions to closed Majordomo lists 473
25–2 A moderated Majordomo list 474
27–1 An Internet connection with firewall 497
27–2 The dual-homed gateway 499
27–3 The screened host gateway 500
27–4 Possible communication paths 502
27–5 Possible locations for service 503
27–6 Sample FTP session 508

List of Tables

6–1 File Formats and Corresponding Filename Extensions 95
11–1 Gopher 1.x Types 184
12–1 Gopher Default Recognized Extensions 216
13–1 Gopher Prefixes 226
13–2 Hardcoded FTP Types Under Gopher 1.x 231
25–1 Config File Variable Types 460
A–1 gopherd Default Options 547
F–1 AddIcon Values 580

Preface

Would you like to offer information or provide a service for the Internet's 24 million users? Or just for your own company with multiple offices? This book describes how to do it.

If you have access to an Internet-connected computer, you can run information servers and provide information to any or all of the other computers on the Internet. This book explains how to plan, set up, and manage a complete array of Internet services, including an FTP archive, a Gopher server, a WAIS (Wide Area Information Server), a World Wide Web (WWW) server, and electronic mailing lists. Each of these services provides a different method of information retrieval, appropriate for a different range of information or audience. You'll want to set up more than one of these services, to provide different kinds of access to the same set of information.

To demonstrate the setup and administration of these services, we'll show you examples from our prototype work with the Species Survival Commission (a part of the World Conservation Union). The Species Survival Commission (SSC) focuses on developing action plans for the conservation of endangered species around the world.* Because SSC is a worldwide network of conservation professionals, and because its projects and potential donors are worldwide, the Internet is an ideal medium for distributing SSC's information and its message.

We'll show you how we made one of those action plans available on the Internet, including text, images, and more; and how we linked together the various servers offering this information to present the data in a logical, compelling way. We'll also point out good design principles and nice features of other existing Internet services, and give you a "behind-the-scenes" peek into what makes them tick.

---

* O'Reilly & Associates has also been working with SSC to save the Victoria Crowned Pigeon that appears on the Nutshell Handbook *lex and yacc*. SSC needs your donations to complete that project. If you'd like to donate (and receive a beautiful tee-shirt or O'Reilly books), or you'd like more information on the project, please send email to *ssc-project-info@ora.com*. If you appreciate these book covers, please do your part to save the animals that made them possible.

If you already have a computer and Internet connection, offering a service is inexpensive. Most of the software described in this book is free. Although some incarnations of these services have been commercialized (WAIS, for example), and others require license fees for some uses (like Gopher), we'll concentrate on the freely available versions of the software, which will remain available. This enables you to set up your information services at little or no cost. If you decide later that you need features or support that only the commercial versions provide, then that's fine.[*] In most cases, basic administration is very similar in both the freeware and commercial versions of this software, so your effort won't be lost.

This book *won't* give you a tutorial on how to use the clients for these information services. For that, see *The Whole Internet User's Guide & Catalog*, also published by O'Reilly & Associates. You'll need a solid understanding of each client to understand how best to set up these services, so that book is a good starting point.

Audience

This book is mainly for UNIX system administrators, or those with fairly strong UNIX knowledge. Less technical people should have little trouble understanding the first two and last two chapters of the book, but the rest may be a challenge!

Setting up an Internet service requires two skills—UNIX system administration skill and skill in writing, organizing, or preparing the data. We believe most services will want to divide those tasks among two or more people, so this book is designed to help delegate the jobs. Some chapters and sections in the book, marked with this icon: 🕮 , are designed for someone we call the Data Librarian, who is responsible for the data presented by the service. This person doesn't need knowledge of software compilation and installation, and usually doesn't need the *root* password, but the chapters that describe the Data Librarian job are still pretty technical and require good UNIX knowledge. Enough of these chapters should be comprehensible to average UNIX users that they could contribute material for the Data Libarian to incorporate into the service.

The rest of the book assumes the reader has good UNIX system administration knowledge, but we don't assume you're a guru. In many cases these chapters describe tasks that require *root* permission, and involve the security of the system, not just the service. We describe all the procedures in detail, but we don't explain the UNIX background for all of them.

* Just so you know, none of us (the authors, editor, or publisher) are currently involved in any of these commercial enterprises, and none of us stand to profit by them.

Why We Wrote This Book

Although Internet publishing is going like gangbusters, the know-how necessary to publish still isn't disseminated widely enough: there are lots of folks who have useful information, but who don't have the time to learn how to set up the services needed to make that information available. If more people know how to create and run information services, then more information—and more diverse types of information—will be available.

And at this critical point in the paving of the Information Superhighway (or pick your nom du jour), it's important that we establish individual and small-scale publishing. If personal publishing is proven commercially viable on the Internet, provides compelling resources, and spurs entrepreneurship, perhaps the government and industry won't be able to ignore it. Otherwise we fear the future Internet may be like the worst of television—a few enormous conglomerates generating trash for the mass consumer.

So we hope you'll take the information in this book and create a terrific new information service with it—maybe a clearinghouse for information on your favorite nonprofit organization, or perhaps a cool, ground-breaking service for the Internet community that makes you money in the process. Either way, the Internet becomes a better place.

If it isn't a mass-market service, even better! One of the most interesting things about the Internet is its ability to sustain niches. If you have a connection and can run a service you think only 100 people in the world are interested in, do it anyway! You'll probably find that a lot more people than you think are interested. The Internet makes possible a kind of small-scale publishing that is impossible on paper.

Organization

This book is organized with one or more chapters on each service (except Chapter 3, *Finger-, Inetd-, and Telnet-based Services*, which covers three services). We progress from the services that are already a part of the standard software on most UNIX machines, to those that you have to get, build, and install. Also, the book generally progresses toward more sophisticated services, until it covers the World Wide Web. After that it continues with email services, which are non-interactive services, in an entirely different class than the other services described in the book.

Chapters intended for the Data Librarian are marked with 🕮 .

🕮 Chapter 1, *Internet Service Concepts*, describes how Internet services work and concepts necessary to understand the rest of the book.

🕮 Chapter 2, *Introduction to Information Services*, gives an overview of all the information services covered in the book, including some ideas for what you can do with them, and explains what human, computer, and networking resources you'll need to provide services.

Chapter 3, *Finger-, Inetd-, and Telnet-based Services*, explains how to set up these three services, which come standard on most UNIX systems, to perform useful, flexible Internet services.

Chapter 4, *Setting Up an FTP Archive*, describes how to set up the FTP server that comes with most UNIX systems.

Chapter 5, *The WU Archive FTP Daemon*, describes how to set up an enhanced FTP server developed at Washington University at St. Louis.

📖 Chapter 6, *Maintaining an FTP Archive*, explains how to prepare data for an FTP archive, organize the archive for easy access, limit access, and monitor usage.

Chapter 7, *Creating an Internet Database Server with WAIS*, tells you how to set up a Wide Area Information Server, based on the free version of WAIS. Later Gopher and World Wide Web chapters describe how to integrate WAIS into them.

📖 Chapter 8, *Creating WAIS Sources with waisindex*, describes how to index data for searching with a WAIS server.

📖 Chapter 9, *Gopher: Introduction*, begins the Gopher section by explaining Gopher's features and foibles, how it works, and the selection of server and client software.

Chapter 10, *Gopher: Compiling the Server*, describes the process of getting, compiling, and installing versions 1.x and 2.x of the University of Minnesota Gopher server and client.

Chapter 11, *Gopher: Managing the Server*, covers configuring, running, and monitoring the Gopher server.

📖 Chapter 12, *Gopher: Preparing Information*, explains how to set up the information within a Gopher server.

📖 Chapter 13, *Gopher: Linking Services Together*, explains how to set up links to other Internet services and local scripts.

Chapter 14, *Gopher: Incorporating Databases*, tells you how to include features for searching the data in your Gopher server.

Chapter 15, *Gopher: Veronica and Jughead*, explains how to include features for searching the menu items listed in your Gopher server, or in all Gopher servers worldwide.

Chapter 16, *Gopher+ Forms and Other New Features*, describes how to use the new features in the latest version of Gopher.

📖 Chapter 17, *Introduction to the World Wide Web*, describes World Wide Web concepts, the selection of servers and browsers, and what the Web can be used for.

Chapter 18, *Setting Up a Web Server*, describes getting, building, installing, and maintaining the NCSA Web server.

📖 Chapter 19, *Authoring for the Web*, covers writing HTML documents for the Web, including authoring tools, conversion scripts, and how to create clickable image maps.

Chapter 20, *Web: Gateways and Forms*, describes Web gateways to other services, how to create interactive forms and the scripts that handle the results, and how to interface with WAIS servers.

Chapter 21, *Web: Access Control and Security*, discusses controlling access to your Web server and keeping the machine on which your server runs secure.

Chapter 22, *Introduction to Email Services*, introduces email services and mailing lists: what they're good for and what software is used to set them up.

📖 Chapter 23, *Simple Mailing Lists*, explains how to set up mailing lists using *sendmail* or other system mail-transfer agents.

Chapter 24, *Automating Mailing Lists with Majordomo*, explains how to set up the Majordomo mailing-list management software.

📖 Chapter 25, *The Majordomo List Owner and Moderator*, explains how to run or moderate email lists managed by Majordomo.

Chapter 26, *Ftpmail*, tells you how to set up a service that allows email access to FTP archives, yours or the world's.

Chapter 27, *Firewalls and Information Services*, explains what a firewall is and how it affects Internet services. The chapter also gives an overview of approaches for dealing with firewalls between your Internet service and your customers.

Chapter 28, *xinetd*, covers a more secure version of the standard UNIX Internet services daemon.

📖 Chapter 29, *Legal Issues*, discusses the legal issues involved in providing Internet services.

📖 Chapter 30, *Protecting Intellectual Property*, discusses the various ways to prevent or discourage people from redistributing your data without your permission.

Appendix A, *gopherd Options*, lists all *gopherd* command-line options.

Appendix B, *Gopher: Client Compilation Options*, lists lots of useful tools that can be used to enhance or analyze a Gopher server.

Appendix C, *Gopher Tools and Gateways*, describes configuration options for the *gopher* text-based client that is compiled along with the Gopher server.

📖 Appendix D, *Web: More HTML Tags*, explains all the HTML tags that are not covered in Chapter 19, *Authoring for the Web*.

Appendix E, *Web: httpd.conf Directives*, is a helpful reference on the Web server's main configuration file.

Appendix F, *Web: srm.conf Directives*, describes all of the configuration directives for controlling the contents of a Web server.

Appendix G, *Web: access.conf Directives*, is a reference for the access control configuration file.

Appendix H, *Web: For More Information*, provides a list of additional information resources.

Versions

We have focused on UNIX versions of information servers. In some cases, there are also Macintosh, DOS, Windows, and other versions in existence, but we have not covered them in detail because they are not as mature as the UNIX versions right now, and because most of the machines with Internet connections suitable for running public services are UNIX machines.

Some of the servers covered in this book, namely *inetd*, *fingerd*, and *telnetd* are standard UNIX software and are stable. Here are the version numbers of the other server software we cover in this book. We will be making efforts to update the book when major new versions come out. You might want to use *archie* to help find the latest version of the software.

- GNU *fingerd* version 1.37
- Washington University *ftpd* version 2.4
- freeWAIS version 0.3
- University of Minnesota *gopherd* versions 1.13 (the last unlicensed version), 2.0.16, and some coverage of 2.1
- NCSA *httpd* version 1.3
- Majordomo version 1.92
- Ftpmail version 1.23

Obtaining the Example Programs

The example programs in this book are available electronically in a number of ways: by FTP, Ftpmail, BITFTP, and UUCP. The cheapest, fastest, and easiest ways are listed first. If you read from the top down, the first one that works for you is probably the best. Use FTP if you are directly on the Internet. Use Ftpmail if you are not on the Internet, but can send and receive electronic mail to Internet sites (this includes CompuServe users). Use BITFTP if you send electronic mail via BITNET. Use UUCP if none of the above works.

FTP

To use FTP, you need a machine with direct access to the Internet. A sample session is shown, with what you should type in **boldface**.

```
% ftp ftp.uu.net
Connected to ftp.uu.net.
220 FTP server (Version 6.21 Tue Mar 10 22:09:55 EST 1992) ready.
Name (ftp.uu.net:joe): anonymous
331 Guest login ok, send domain style e-mail address as password.
Password: joe@ora.com (use your user name and host here)
230 Guest login ok, access restrictions apply.
ftp> cd /published/oreilly/nutshell/miis
250 CWD command successful.
ftp> binary (Very important! You must specify binary transfer for compressed files.)
200 Type set to I.
ftp> get miis.9412.tar.Z
200 PORT command successful.
150 Opening BINARY mode data connection for miis.9412.tar.Z.
226 Transfer complete.
ftp> quit
221 Goodbye.
%
```

The file is a compressed *tar* archive; extract the files from the archive by typing:

```
% zcat miis.9412.tar.Z | tar xvf -
```

System V systems require the following *tar* command instead:

```
% zcat miis.9412.tar.Z | tar xof -
```

If *zcat* is not available on your system, use separate *uncompress* and *tar* or *shar* commands.

```
% uncompress miis.9412.tar.Z
% tar xvf miis.9412.tar.Z
```

Ftpmail

Ftpmail is a mail server available to anyone who can send electronic mail to, and receive it from, Internet sites. This includes any company or service provider that allows email connections to the Internet. Here's how you do it.

You send mail to *ftpmail@online.ora.com.* In the message body, give the FTP commands you want to run. The server will run anonymous FTP for you and mail the files back to you. To get a complete help file, send a message with no subject and the single word "help" in the body. The following is a sample mail session that should get you the examples. This command sends you a listing of the files in the selected directory and the requested example files. The listing is useful if there's a later version of the examples you're interested in.

```
% mail ftpmail@online.ora.com
Subject:
reply-to janetv@xyz.com        Where you want files mailed
open
cd /published/oreilly/nutshell/miis/
dir
mode binary
uuencode
get miis.9412.tar.Z
quit
.
```

A signature at the end of the message is acceptable as long as it appears after "quit."

BITFTP

BITFTP is a mail server for BITNET users. You send it electronic mail messages requesting files, and it sends you back the files by electronic mail. BITFTP currently serves only users who send it mail from nodes that are directly on BITNET, EARN, or NetNorth. BITFTP is a public service of Princeton University. Here's how it works.

To use BITFTP, send mail containing your ftp commands to *BITFTP@PUCC*. For a complete help file, send HELP as the message body.

The following is the message body you send to BITFTP:

```
FTP  ftp.uu.net  NETDATA
USER  anonymous
PASS  myname@podunk.edu  Put your Internet email address here (not your BITNET address)
CD  /published/oreilly/nutshell/miis
DIR
BINARY
GET  miis.9412.tar.Z
QUIT
```

Once you've got the desired file, follow the directions under FTP to extract the files from the archive. Since you are probably not on a UNIX system, you may need to get versions of *uudecode*, *uncompress*, *atob*, and *tar* for your system. VMS, DOS, and Mac versions are available. The VMS versions are on *gatekeeper.dec.com* in */pub/VMS*.

Questions about BITFTP can be directed to Melinda Varian, *MAINT@PUCC* on BITNET.

UUCP

UUCP is standard on virtually all UNIX systems and is available for IBM-compatible PCs and Apple Macintoshes. The examples are available by UUCP via modem from UUNET; UUNET's connect-time charges apply.

You can get the examples from UUNET whether you have an account there or not. If you or your company has an account with UUNET, you have a system somewhere with a direct UUCP connection to UUNET. Find that system, and type:

```
uucp uunet\!~/published/oreilly/nutshell/miis/miis.9412.tar.Z yourhost\!~/yourname/
```

The backslashes can be omitted if you use the Bourne shell (*sh*) instead of *csh*. The file should appear some time later (up to a day or more) in the directory */usr/spool/uucppublic/yourname*. If you don't have an account, but would like one so that you can get electronic mail, contact UUNET at 703-204-8000.

If you don't have a UUNET account, you can set up a UUCP connection to UUNET using the phone number 1-900-468-7727. As of this writing, the cost is 50 cents per minute. The charges will appear on your next telephone bill. The login name is *uucp*, with no password. For example, an *L.sys/Systems* entry might look like:

```
uunet Any ACU 19200 1-900-468-7727 ogin:--ogin: uucp
```

Your entry may vary depending on your UUCP configuration. If you have a PEP-capable modem, make sure `s50=255s111=30` is set before calling.

It's a good idea to get the file */published/oreilly/ls-lR.Z* as a short test file containing the filenames and sizes of all the files available.

Once you've got the desired file, follow the directions under FTP to extract the files from the archive.

Conventions Used in This Book

The following conventions are used in this book:

Bold is used to emphasize new terms and concepts when they are introduced.

Italic is used for options to commands, for file and directory names when they appear in the body of a paragraph, and for program and command names.

`Constant Width` is used in examples to show the contents of files or the output from commands; and to indicate environment variables, rules, entries, and targets.

`Constant Bold` is used in examples to show commands or other text that should be typed literally by the user. For example, **`rm foo`** means to type "rm foo" exactly as it appears in the text or example.

`Constant Italic` is used in code fragments and examples to show variables for which a context-specific substitution should be made. The variable *`filename`*, for example, would be replaced by an actual filename.

The symbol **+** is used in the Gopher chapters to indicate paragraphs that apply only to Gopher version 2.x.

Comments and Corrections

If you have comments on this book or suggestions for improvement, or if you find errors, please feel free to contact the editor by sending electronic mail to *adrian@ora.com*, or paper mail to:

```
Adrian Nye
O'Reilly & Associates, Inc.
90 Sherman St.
Cambridge, MA 02140
USA
```

Acknowledgments

The editor and all the authors wish to thank the reviewers for their careful attention. The reviewers were: Dan Gillmor, Dan Appelman, Randy Diffenderfer, Robert H'obbes' Zakon, Thomas Boutell, Bryan O'Connor, Robert Martin McCool, Brewster Kahle, Jim Fullton, Billy Barron, Neophytos Iacovou, John Labovitz, M. Strata Rose, Pei Y. Wei, Andy Oram, Rick Romkey, Dale Dougherty, Tim O'Reilly, Kevin Hughes, and Josh Blackman.

Each author would also like to thank the people who helped them individually:

Cricket Liu

Dale Dougherty and Rob Raisch helped me turn my early ideas about information services into a book. Josh Blackman provided much-needed legal advice, and Stephen Wolff helped me decypher the NSFNET Acceptable Use Policy. Bryan O'Connor reviewed the FTP chapters, and both Bryan and Chris Myers deserve recognition for writing the WU Archive FTP daemon itself. Thanks to Christopher Klaus for allowing me to use his FAQ on setting up anonymous FTP. Robert H'obbes' Zakon and Brewster Kahle helped with the WAIS material. And Allyn Fratkin was kind enough to let us use one of his scripts.

Special thanks are due the Denver Flyers, for giving me a much-needed break from writing twice a week; the managers I've had during this project, Rick, Kim, and Guy, who've all been supportive despite two changes of administration; and my wonderful wife, Paige, who put up with my writing another book much sooner than expected.

Jerry Peek

People who reviewed and helped with the chapters about email-based services include (in reverse alphabetical order, just to be different): Vincent Skahan, Richard Schultz, Daniel Rich, Gene Rackow, H. Milton Peek, Alan Millar, Jennifer Joy, Tim Irvin, Michael Grubb, Morna Findlay, Alex Deacon, David Barr, and Micah Anderson. Cricket Liu also read my chapters and helped in a lot of ways.

Special thanks to the people who developed the software I wrote about and reviewed my drafts: Brent Chapman and John P. Rouillard, for Majordomo; Lee McLoughlin, who wrote this version of Ftpmail; and Jeff Masters, who wrote The Weather Underground.

Russ Jones

I would like to thank the World Wide Web community and all of the contributors to the *comp.infosystems.www.providers* newsgroup. It was their give-and-take that defined the scope of the Web section.

I would also like to thank my reviewers, Thomas Boutell, Dale Dougherty, Kevin Hughes, John Labovitz, Rob McCool, Andy Oram, Rick Romkey, M. Strata Rose, Pei Y. Wei, and Robert H'obbes' Zakon. It was their criticism and suggestions that helped shape the final content.

I would also like to thank the folks at O'Reilly & Associates for the opportunity to do my first book. Credit goes particularly to my editor, Adrian Nye, who made sure it was done right. And finally, I would like to thank my wife Linda for her initial encouragement and patience over each of the six times I told her I was done.

Bryan Buus

First I would like to thank Neophytos Iacovou and Paul Lindner for their invaluable contributions to the Gopher section.

Thanks also to the following people for their technical comments or review of the Gopher section: Eric Pearce, Kaleigh Santos, Todd Miller, Brad Wherry, Robert Tarrall, Billy Barron, Robert H'obbes' Zakon, and Neophytos Iacovou (along with the rest of the Gopher Team).

I would also like to thank XOR Network Engineering for computing and printing facilities, Adrian Nye for his patience, and K. for putting up with too many months of late nights working on this "(ahem) book."

Adrian Nye

As editor I'd like to thank all the main authors for doing this book as their second full-time job. They remained in good humor despite being a little singed around the edges. It was a team effort, and everybody pulled hard to get it finished.

Many thanks also to Jeff LaCoursiere, Craig Strickland, Greg George, Paul Lindner, and Neophytos Iacovou, who all volunteered at the last minute to write needed chapters.

And as usual, thanks to Tim O'Reilly for slowly raising the bar and encouraging us to jump over.

Also thanks to Hiroshi Kawazoe and Tony Sanders, for helping to form our ideas about what the firewall and Web sections of the book should cover.

Michael Deutsch and Barry Herchenroder entered edits on the manuscript during the final push, saving my wrists from further abuse. Thanks!

I'd also like to thank my wife Andrea for bearing with me while I worked weekends to get this finished.

Ellen Siever copyedited the book and was the production manager, with the able assistance of Mary Anne Weeks Mayo, Nicole Gipson, Clairemarie Fisher O'Leary, and Stephen Spainhour. Chris Reilley created the figures, Jennifer Niederst did the design, Lenny Muellner and Norm Walsh provided tools support and implemented the design, and Susan Reisler created the index.

In this Chapter:
- *What Is the Internet?*
- *How Are Internet Services Structured?*
- *What Is TCP/IP?*
- *How Information Clients Talk to Information Servers*

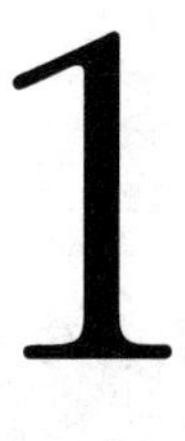

1 Internet Service Concepts

The services we describe in this book are built on complex layers of networking and software. You don't need to be an expert on internetworking or UNIX to set up the services, but you do have to understand the basic concepts. This chapter is a brief course on all the essential technical concepts you'll need to understand what we say later in the book. If things like UDP and *inetd* are old hat to you, feel free to skip this chapter.

This introduction sticks closely to what you need to know to set up an information service. If you want a more general introduction to the Internet, or more details on the underlying technology, see the O'Reilly & Associates books *The Whole Internet User's Guide & Catalog* and *TCP/IP Network Administration.*

1.1 What Is the Internet?

Though it gets lots of attention in the press these days, the Internet is also commonly misrepresented. Is it a technology, a bunch of people, or a dessert topping?

The Internet, simply put, is a federation of computer networks that speak the same protocols (particularly TCP/IP, which we'll tell you more about later in this chapter). The networks that make up the Internet are connected to each other with high-speed telephone circuits. The protocols spoken on the Internet are computer networking protocols, used to enable computers to communicate with each other, just as human protocols help humans communicate. Just as you say "hello" when you pick up the phone to indicate that you're there and listening, or say "uh-huh" periodically to let someone know you've heard what they've said, computers have to send certain sequences of binary data to introduce themselves and acknowledge each other.

There are three roles played on the Internet which we need to define. This book is about one of the roles, the *information provider.* The information provider makes information (like the weather) available for *users* (whom we sometimes refer to as *customers* of your information service), the second role. The third role is the *connection provider*, who provides the network connection for both information providers and for users. In other books and in the media, you sometimes see connection providers referred to as just "Internet providers," but we use the more specific term in this book.

1.1.1 What Does It Mean to Be on the Internet?

There are three major ways of accessing the Internet: modem access to a computer on the Internet, sometimes called "shell access,"* dial-up networking, and high-speed telephone circuits leased from the phone company. Most of the prospective users of your Internet service will have one of these flavors of Internet connectivity. Understanding what each enables them to do, and how it limits them, is important to making your service available and useful to the widest possible audience. You should also understand what caliber of connectivity you'll need to deliver your service.

When someone says he or his company is "on the Internet," what does that mean? Well, according to the strictest definition, computers that are "on the Internet" have a 24-hour-a-day connection to the Internet. This is the kind of connection that you, as an Internet information provider, need to have because it's the kind necessary to make almost any interesting service available on the Internet. Why should you be connected late at night? Since the Internet spans the globe, it's always daytime for some prospective Internet service customers.

Customers of your Internet service may have full-time connections, part-time connections, or dial in to a machine connected to the Internet. How they access the Internet affects how you should set up your services. The following sections describe each kind of Internet access.

1.1.1.1 Full-time IP connection

Computers that are "on the Internet" all the time may reside on a local area network that is connected to the Internet via a router, a specialized computer for linking together networks over long distances. Or they may connect to the Internet via a modem and a telephone line just like the one that comes into your house, except that their line is dedicated to carrying traffic to and from the Internet. What matters is that another computer on the Internet can talk to these computers at will, using the protocols that are common to all networks on the Internet (see Figure 1-1).

There are currently over three million computers on the Internet by this definition. Though this sounds like an awfully large number, it's still considered something of a luxury to have your own computer connected to the Internet full-time. There are a number of reasons this is so:

- Dedicated connections to the Internet are relatively expensive. The cheapest you're likely to find will cost several hundred dollars each month. That's fine if

* It's called shell access because command interpreters on UNIX computers are usually called **shells**. That's what you have access to with this type of an Internet connection.

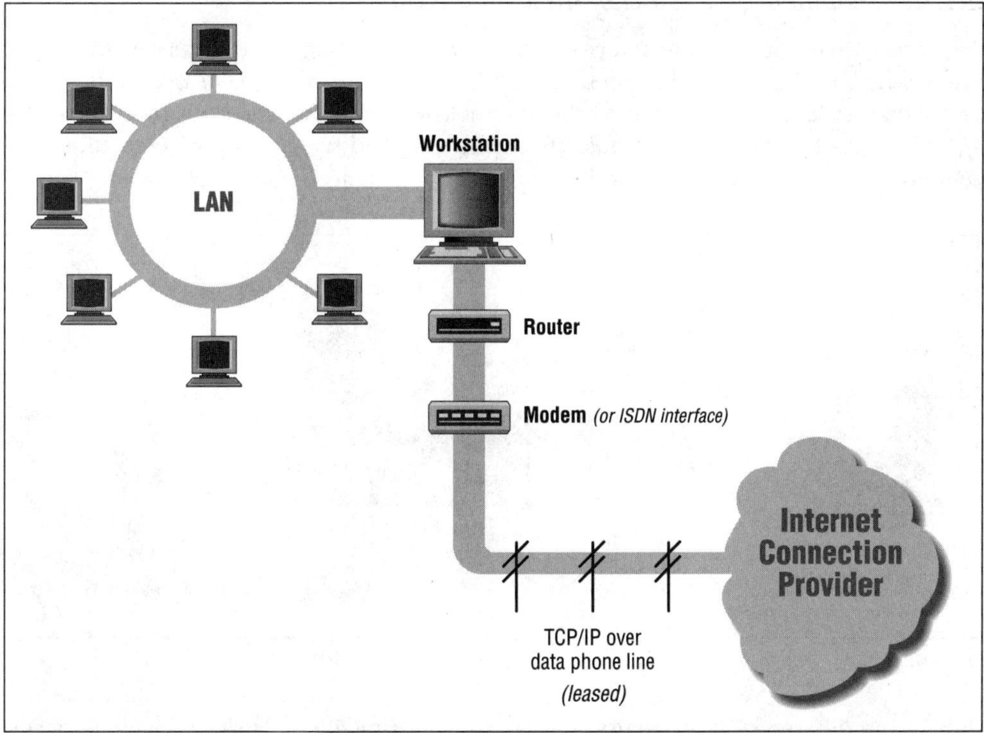

Figure 1-1. A typical full-time Internet connection

you're a university or a company, but if you're just looking for access from your PC at home, that's probably prohibitive.

- This kind of connectivity is fairly hard to set up. Experienced PC and Mac users all over the world have been toying with modems for years now. But dealing with dedicated, high-speed digital telephone lines leased from the phone company and the hardware that goes with them requires telephony expertise that not that many people have, and configuring networking software also requires skills that aren't common. Yet.

You will still find a large number of *people* with top-tier, high-speed Internet connectivity, though. Many people get their Internet connectivity through the company they work for or the university they attend. More and more public libraries are putting in high-speed Internet connections so that library users can access the Internet from public terminals or PCs.

But the state of the industry is changing rapidly. Telephone and cable companies are lining up to provide the infrastructure to connect more people to the Internet at lower cost, and developers are hard at work on software to make it easier to connect computers to the Internet and use it effectively.

1.1.1.2 Dial-up access to a computer on the Internet

In more casual use, "on the Internet" can mean something quite different. Individual users who say they're on the Internet may just mean that they have *access* to a computer that is directly connected to the Internet. Maybe they can use a modem to dial up this Internet-connected computer from their PC and use a terminal emulation program to run various programs on the computer (see Figure 1-2).

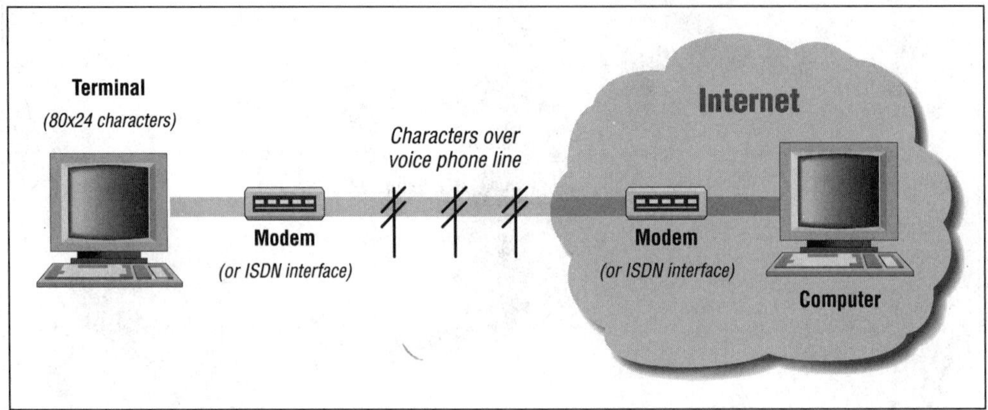

Figure 1–2. A user dialing up to a computer on the Internet

What's the difference? If your customer is using a terminal emulation package to access a remote computer, his computer isn't speaking TCP/IP, the common language of the Internet. That means he can't run programs on his PC that access the Internet directly. Instead, he runs programs on the Internet-connected computer that access the Internet, and the results are displayed via his terminal emulation software. That makes a big difference, because terminal emulation software emulates, well, a terminal, and terminals typically only support displaying characters on the screen. That means he can't run any software that uses graphics. And coincidentally, some of the most interesting software on the Internet, like Mosaic, uses lots of graphics, both for ease of use and to display image data.

Many people get their access to the Internet this way. Even though it's not the sexiest way to cruise the Internet, it's the cheapest. If you're designing services to provide on the Internet, keep these folks in mind. It's a good idea to provide character-based, terminal-oriented information in addition to any whiz-bang graphical stuff you may do, to reach the substantial proportion of the Internet populace not directly "on the Internet."

1.1.1.3 Running Internet protocols over dial-up

There's a hybrid type of access that gives users the benefits of being directly connected to the Internet at the cost of a little speed and the sacrifice of 24-hour connectivity. Users can run the Internet's standard protocols over a normal dial-up telephone connection, as opposed to running terminal emulation traffic over the same connection (see Figure 1-3). This lets them run graphical software that requires direct Internet connectivity, just more slowly than if they had a full-time connection to the Internet.

The same companies that sell access to Internet-connected computers often offer this service, too, usually at a somewhat higher cost. The low-level protocols used to carry Internet traffic over a dial-up connection are called SLIP, for Serial Line Internet Protocol, and PPP, for Point-to-Point Protocol.

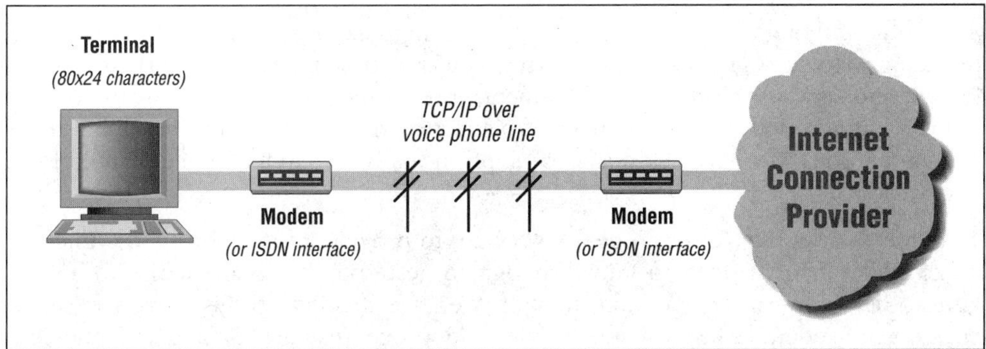

Figure 1-3. On-demand Internet link

Count on more and more people moving from the traditional terminal emulation camp into the dial-up internetworking camp over the next few years. Better off-the-shelf SLIP and PPP software packages will make it much easier for casual users to configure dial-up networking, and higher-speed modems will make access tolerably fast.

Also becoming more available is the ISDN (Integrated Services Digital Network), a special type of phone line that can be used for voice or data (or both at the same time). ISDN can be used for an on-demand network or a full-time network but it's as fast as some leased-line connections.

The perceived speed of all types of connections depends on how many people are using the connection. A slow personal connection may still be faster for its only user than the fastest connection with thousands of users.

1.1.2 What Is on the Internet?

So what's out there on the Internet that's so compelling that everyone thinks they need access to it? Lots of things. Three million computers, providing an enormous variety of information and services. An estimated 24 million people in dozens of countries, sending electronic mail, chatting with each other, discussing topics of little or global significance on one of 8,000 forums distributed throughout the Internet. And more important organizations and companies than you can shake a sharp stick at.

1.1.2.1 Computers

There's an amazing variety of computers connected to the Internet, from ancient PDPs to Crays and Connection Machines. Some of these act as pure computing resources, but most are valuable because of the information they provide or the people for whom they provide access. There are computers on the Internet that can give you a weather report or a traffic report, that can tell you about earthquake activity, and that can help you decide what breed of dog would be best for you.

An awful lot, though certainly not all, of these computers run some variety of the UNIX operating system. Right now, UNIX is the platform best-suited to providing Internet information services: most of the implementations of these services are on UNIX. Most services support delivery to a number of platforms, including PCs and Macs, but those computers don't yet have the speed or sophistication to handle hosting a full-blown information service.

That doesn't mean you need to be a UNIX guru to provide information on the Internet: it simply means you need to know enough to get around. Having access to a UNIX guru to help you out doesn't hurt, though. We have divided up this book so that the chapters not requiring UNIX system administration expertise are marked with the Data Librarian icon: 🕮 .

1.1.2.2 People

The current estimate (as of July 1994) of the number of people who have some type of Internet access is 24 million. That number has been increasing exponentially for the past five years. Whereas the Internet was once primarily a playground for research scientists and computer professionals (and university students), it's now home to educators, legislators, authors, lawyers, and a not-insignificant population of weirdos. That's a huge, diverse potential customer base.

1.1.2.3 Places

One of the most interesting developments on the Internet over the past few years is the increasing presence many organizations are maintaining on the network. Lots of companies that didn't take the Internet seriously for years are clamoring to get an Internet connection and become a part of the Internet community. Most companies want to make product information and other marketing material available, and a certain number simply want the cachet associated with being "on the Internet." Many non-profit organizations are connecting for less mercenary reasons.

Here's just a sample of the organizations currently connected to the Internet:

- Major science museums, like the Exploratorium in San Francisco
- U.S. government agencies, like the Peace Corps, the Federal Aviation Administration, the Federal Communications Commission, the Food and Drug Administration, and the Postal Service

- Most major universities, U.S. and international
- Non-profit organizations, like National Public Radio the Public Broadcasting System, the Sierra Club, Amnesty International, and the Freemasons
- International agencies like NATO and the World Bank
- Small companies, like Moe's Books in Berkeley, Mary and Michael's Wedding Photography in Palo Alto, and Grant's Florist and Greenhouse

1.2 How Are Internet Services Structured?

Another notable trait of the Internet is that many of the services that run over it are implemented using a client/server architecture. The term "client/server," unfortunately, is overused and not well understood.

In the classic client/server software architecture, there are two pieces (and guess what they're called):

- A client, responsible for interacting with the user; for example, by accepting keyboard input and displaying data to the user
- A server, responsible for performing tasks as directed by the client; for example, accessing data on the client's behalf, performing calculations, and so on, and then providing data or a simple response to the client

The client and the server can run on the same computer; more often, they'll run on different computers. The server may provide the client with resources or information the client doesn't have on its own host.

Information service clients typically accept queries or other keyboard (and mouse) input from users, send those queries or characters to the server, and then manage the display of the resulting data. The servers receive queries or other data from the clients, process it by reading files, conducting searches or executing commands, and send the results, or some indication of the status of the operation, to the clients.

There are many books about accessing information on the Internet using clients, such as *The Whole Internet User's Guide & Catalog.* This book is about setting up servers, but we do discuss clients a bit because it's sometimes relevant to setting up servers.

The client/server architecture of Internet information services is what makes it possible for any connected computer to provide services to any other. That's the biggest difference between the Internet and commercial networks like CompuServe, which provides all services from computers run by the network and doesn't allow users to supply information (except email) to other users.

1.3 What Is TCP/IP?

So what is this mysterious set of protocols that enables all of the networks of the Internet to communicate? The suite of protocols that makes it all happen is called TCP/IP. TCP/IP stands for Transmission Control Protocol/ Internet Protocol, which are actually the names of the two most commonly used protocols in the suite. Every computer on the Internet supports TCP/IP. If computer A in Sydney supports communication using the TCP/IP protocols, and so does computer B in St. Paul, and both are attached to interconnected networks that can carry TCP/IP, then they should be able to send data back and forth.

Computer networking protocols are made up of sequences of binary values collected into groups called packets, which are then transmitted over media like coax cable, fiber optic cable, or phone lines as electrical signals or pulses of light. Certain types of packets carry data, while others acknowledge data received.

The protocols in the TCP/IP suite are layered protocols. Layered protocol suites separate duties between individual protocols in the group. A "low-level" protocol may simply provide basic functionality, while a "higher-level" protocol makes more advanced functions available to Internet users. Think of this in the context of a telephone conversation: there is a low-level electrical protocol at work that enables you to carry on a higher-level conversation, in English or another human language.

1.3.1 Protocols

You don't need to understand all of the nuances of TCP/IP to create Internet information services,* but you should have a basic understanding of the services that each of the most important protocols in the TCP/IP suite provides. We'll cover the three major protocols that make up the TCP/IP suite: IP, the Internet Protocol; TCP, the Transmission Control Protocol; and UDP, the User Datagram Protocol.

1.3.1.1 The Internet protocol: IP

The Internet protocol is the foundation for the other major protocols in the TCP/IP family, TCP and UDP. TCP and UDP are "encapsulated" within IP in much the same way that letters are enclosed within envelopes. And just as envelopes provide the addressing information necessary to get the letter where it needs to go, the IP packet provides the address necessary to get the data to the right Internet computer.

Unlike the addresses on postal mail, though, the addresses on IP packets are simply large numbers. The address is a 32-bit number, ranging from zero to about 4.3 billion. So people don't have to remember a seemingly arbitrary ten-digit number, these IP addresses are usually written in a convenient shorthand, called **dotted-octet** notation. Dotted-octet notation groups the 32-bit address into four sets of eight bits (eight bits

* If you're interested, though, there are lots of good books available on the subject. Douglas Comer's *Internetworking with TCP/IP* series (Prentice Hall) is one of the best.

are an octet). Then each of those eight-bit sets is converted into a decimal number, and the four resulting decimal numbers are concatenated, separated by dots (hence the "dotted" part of dotted octet). Figure 1-4 illustrates how that works.

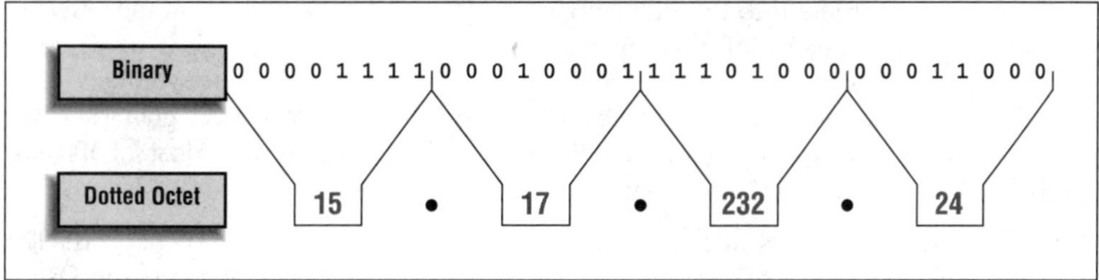

Figure 1-4. How dotted-octet notation comes from a 32-bit IP address

IP addresses are assigned to computers according to which Internet network the computer is on. For example, Hewlett-Packard runs a private network that is connected to the Internet. The computers on this network all have IP addresses that start with the octet 15 (that is, the first eight bits of the address are 00001111). HP further divides this network into subnetworks. Each subnetwork is identified by the first three octets of an IP address. Each local area network within the company is assigned a subnetwork (or "subnet," for short) address. For example, one of the LANs at HP's Corporate Offices is assigned the subnet 15.255.152. Each of the computers on this LAN has an IP address that starts with the octets 15.255.152.

There are a couple of reasons IP addresses are assigned this way. First, using a hierarchy of assignment (network, subnetwork and computer) allows people on the Internet to assign addresses relatively autonomously. When HP founded their network, the folks who ran the Internet assigned HP the first octet of their IP addresses,* guaranteeing that HP could assign IP addresses starting with 15 freely. Also, using hierarchical addressing simplifies the routing of IP packets between the sending and receiving computers. Since the Internet is a big place, with hundreds of thousands of links between networks, this is a decidedly non-trivial task. Imagine trying to navigate the complete U.S. highway system, including state highways and rural roads. There are probably a dozen reasonable ways to get from Boulder to Boston. The fastest route depends on traffic, weather, roadwork, and other factors. Routing takes into account similar Internet phenomena, like network congestion and failure of links. But routing's basic task is simply to get an IP packet to the correct address.

* Note that not everybody has the luxury of assigning 24-bits of IP address, like HP did. Smaller companies and organizations usually have the first two or even three octets dictated to them and only have 16 or 8 bits left to assign.

Because of hierarchical addressing, Internet routers only need to maintain a list of all the networks on the Internet and how to get to them.* Imagine if they had to know how to get to each individual computer—a table like that could have 4.3 billion entries in it! Once an IP packet has made it to the right network, the routers in that network can then route it to the right subnet, and finally to the right computer. Besides providing the addressing information that gets Internet data from place to place, IP doesn't do much. It does its best to deliver data, but doesn't guarantee delivery (a bit like the U.S. postal service?). It leaves that up to TCP. It also doesn't guarantee that packets sent in any particular order will arrive in the same order. Most of us have probably had that happen to our mail at one time or another.

Why not provide services like guaranteed delivery and serialization of packets? That makes it easy to route IP packets from place to place, simple to implement, and fast.

1.3.1.2 A connection-oriented protocol: TCP

TCP provides two major services that IP is missing: guaranteed delivery and serialization of data (making sure data sent in one order arrives in the same order). You can think of TCP as analogous to a long mail correspondence: the data is all carried in letters (IP packets), but there's information in the letters that allows you to determine the order in which they were sent and whether any letter is missing.

How does TCP accomplish this? TCP uses sequence numbers to indicate the order in which the data it's sending should appear. These sequence numbers increase by one each time TCP puts data into a new IP packet. The receiver of the IP packets can reorder the TCP data by the TCP sequence numbers if the IP packets are shuffled in transit. The receiver can also determine whether anything's missing. If the sequence numbers run 1, 2, 5 after reordering, two IP packets-worth of TCP data are missing. So TCP arranges for the missing packets to be resent.

Because TCP provides these two features, it can mimic a "stream" connection between two computers, like one that might run over a dedicated serial line, even though the underlying network doesn't really provide any kind of end-to-end continuity. Many information clients and servers use TCP to request and deliver data, because they require a guarantee that the requests and responses have arrived, and they need serialization of data for requests and responses that exceed the maximum size of an IP packet.

TCP provides another important feature: port numbers. Port numbers are like another layer of address below the IP address. IP addresses uniquely identify computers. Port numbers are used to identify services within a computer. Since you want to support more than one service running on an internetworked computer, you need to be able to supply an identifier telling the computer where you meant the TCP data to go: was it meant for the Telnet daemon, the FTP daemon or the Gopher server? The computer

* Actually, many don't even need to know this much. They know how to get to other subnetworks within their own network and how to get to a "smart" router that has more complete routing information.

receives the TCP data, looks at the destination port number, and uses that to determine which program to send the data to.

The port number is a 16-bit number (from zero to about 65,000). Many port numbers are "well known": used by the same server on most computers on the Internet. Port 25, for example, is reserved for use by a mailer speaking the Simple Mail Transfer Protocol (SMTP) on most computers. Similarly, port 23 is reserved for servers that understand the Telnet protocol. This makes it easy for other mailers and Telnet clients to find the appropriate server on an arbitrary destination computer: try the well-known port for your service. Port numbers below 1024 are called "privileged" ports in UNIX, since only *root* can start servers that listen to them. This is a security feature to prevent a random user from starting a server on a well-known port and listening to other people's mail or doing other such mischief.

1.3.1.3 A connectionless protocol: UDP

UDP is a pretty bare-bones protocol. It takes what IP provides and adds only two important features—and one of them is optional! The first is port numbers. UDP uses 16-bit port numbers, just like TCP. Their port numbers are distinct, though: sending mail to UDP port 25 won't get you anywhere, since SMTP mailers listen on *TCP* port 25. Some servers that speak both UDP and TCP use the same port number for both protocols, though. Like TCP ports, UDP ports identify services on a single computer.

The optional part of the UDP protocol is checksumming. This is a mechanism for determining whether part of the UDP data has been accidentally modified in transit. Quite often, however, checksumming is turned off to enhance performance.

So what is UDP good for? Short queries and responses, that can fit comfortably into an IP packet. If the whole information exchange can fit into a single packet, there's no reason to bother with TCP, which requires synchronization of sequence numbers at startup, plus other overhead to keep the conversation going. Because most of the servers we describe in this book send fairly long replies, though, UDP isn't used by them.

1.3.2 The inetd Superserver

This whole port notion works so well that it's possible to run literally dozens of servers on the same computer, all at once. Rather than having all of those servers waiting around for something to happen during idle periods, gobbling up valuable space in memory, many of them are started by *inetd*, the Internet superserver, as they are needed. *inetd* doesn't provide much useful functionality by itself, but it does serve as a kind of matchmaker. It listens simultaneously on a number of ports on behalf of other servers. When a client sends data to one of those ports, *inetd* looks to see which server's port the client is sending to. If it's sending to the Telnet port, *inetd* starts the Telnet server, *telnetd*, and lets it talk directly to the Telnet client (and the *telnetd* dies when the client disconnects). *inetd* determines which server to start by looking at the file *inetd.conf* at startup. For example, the entry to start the Telnet server looks something like this:

```
telnet      stream tcp nowait root /etc/telnetd  telnetd
```

The first field in the entry is the name of the service, which maps directly to a port number for *inetd* to listen to. Usually, this mapping is in the file */etc/services*. If you look for the string *telnet* in */etc/services*, here's what you'll find:

```
% grep telnet /etc/services
telnet        23/tcp                 # Virtual Terminal Protocol
```

This tells *inetd* to listen on TCP port 23 for Telnet requests.

The second and third fields in the *inetd.conf* entry tell *inetd* what kind of connection the service uses. `stream tcp` is a stream of serialized data provided by TCP. The alternative is `dgram udp`, which is a sequence of possibly unordered datagrams sent by UDP. The fourth field determines whether *inetd* starts a single server to service all clients that might need service (and `wait` until that server has died to start a new one) or starts a new server for each client (`nowait`).

The fifth field specifies the user ID used to run the server, and the next field specifies the pathname of the server's executable. The last field is called the argument vector and specifies any command-line options to pass along to the server.

When *inetd* receives a connection request from a remote client, it logs the transaction via *syslog* (assuming you have *inetd*'s logging option turned on):

```
Jul 25 22:53:33 ohbear inetd[349]: telnet/tcp: Connection from babs.nsr.hp.com
(15.17.232.24) at Mon Jul 25 22:53:33 1994
```

You can see the results of *inetd*'s mapping the port number to a server (`telnet/tcp`). *inetd* then starts *telnetd* and lets it take over communicating with the Telnet client on *babs.nsr.hp.com.*

1.3.3 Standalone Servers

inetd restarts servers whenever they are needed. That helps you set them up because you can change a server's configuration files and that change will take effect the next time *inetd* starts that server.

For a busy service, when you expect several connections from users each second, *inetd* starts to get inefficient. It takes time for *inetd* to start a server, and for the server to reread its configuration files each time it comes up. *inetd* may even start complaining about its workload with messages like "loop detected, shutting down."

The solution to that problem is to run the server standalone as a **daemon**. A server running as a daemon listens to its assigned port and spawns a copy of itself to handle each request that arrives. That's a fast process. The downside of standalone servers is that if they crash, it's likely that no one will notice, and the service will become unavailable. Also, you need to explicitly tell the server to reread its configuration files whenever you change them.

1.3.4 Naming

On the Internet, just as every computer has a unique address, every computer also has a unique name. In fact, it can have several names.* The names give us humans a convenient way to identify computers, since even dotted-octet IP addresses aren't that easy to remember. Most of the servers we discuss will accept these names on the command line or in configuration files, but they must map the name to an IP address. That's the job of the Internet's name service, called the Domain Name System. The Domain Name System, or DNS, uses hierarchical names. You've probably seen some of these: *ftp.uu.net*, *rs.internic.net*, *hp.com*, *ora.com*. These "domain names" are made up of text labels, separated by dots. The labels toward the beginning of the domain name are the most specific: the first one usually identifies a particular computer. The labels toward the end of the name are the least specific: at the very end, they often indicate the kind of organization that runs the computer. *com* means commercial, *net* names are networking organizations, *edu* is a school, *gov* is the government, and *mil* is the military. The last label may also be a two-letter country code taken from the International Standards Organization's document ISO 3166. In that case, it usually indicates the country the computer is in.

The servers that map names to addresses are called domain name servers. DNS clients, called resolvers, send queries to domain name servers for the IP address that corresponds to a particular domain name. The domain name server that receives a query may have to talk to other name servers to find the answer; it then replies to the resolver. To learn more than you ever wanted to know about domain name servers and the Domain Name System, see the O'Reilly & Associates Nutshell Handbook *DNS and BIND*.

Some domain names are actually aliases, pointers to other domain names. These aliases can be handy if you're providing an important service on a computer that already has a domain name, like *foo.bar.baz*. If you were running an anonymous FTP archive on *foo*, as well as a World Wide Web server, you could create the aliases *ftp.bar.baz* and *www.bar.baz* to point to *foo.bar.baz*. This would make it easier for people on the Internet to remember the name of the computer your servers run on, and easier for them to guess the name, if they don't already know it. For more information on creating aliases like these, see Section 4.2.4.

* Or several addresses, if it has multiple connections to the network.

1.4 How Information Clients Talk to Information Servers

Now let's move on to describing how a typical information service client talks to an information server. We'll use a Gopher client communicating with Gopher server as our example. Gopher protocol (not too surprisingly) is the language Gopher clients use to communicate with Gopher servers (and vice versa). Its basic purpose is to carry requests from the client to the server and documents (or information about what documents are available) from the server to the client. We'll go into exactly what the protocol looks like later in the book, since it's useful to know for testing your server. Here we'll just speak conceptually.

First, the user specifies that she'd like to see a resource on the Gopher server, like a particular document. Perhaps she does this by clicking on a menu item. The client accepts this input and translates it into an acceptable query to send to the Gopher server. The client looks in */etc/services* to find the proper port number at which to contact a Gopher server and finds this:

```
gopher          70/tcp
```

This line means that requests to connect to Gopher servers should connect to port 70 using the TCP protocol. The client then encapsulates the query within a TCP packet, or a series of TCP packets, if it's a long query, and sends it to the server at port 70 on the server's machine.

The Gopher server itself may be listening on port 70 on the destination computer, or *inetd* may be listening for it. If *inetd* receives the TCP packet, it checks the destination port number. It uses the same */etc/services* entry (on the server's system) to map the port number back to the name of the service, in this case, Gopher. Once it figures that out, it starts the Gopher server, *gopherd*, and turns the connection with the remote client over to *gopherd*.

The Gopher server processes the received TCP data and interprets the query. Since this is a request for a particular file on the server, the server opens and reads the file and then sends it back to the client over the network, as a stream of TCP packets. The client receives this information and caches it in memory or on disk. After the complete file has been sent to the client, the TCP connection is torn down using a special sequence of TCP packets. From the information in the serialized file, the client decides what to display to the user, including possibly starting a external image-viewer program. The cycle is complete. (Most clients today make the user wait for one transaction to be completed before allowing another, but that's only for convenience in programming.)

Note that the TCP connection is brought up and torn down again for every document request. There is no TCP connection while the user is reading documents.

Web servers are analogous to Gopher servers, in that each document creates a new TCP connection. However, the Web takes it one step further: each inline graphic in a Web document creates a separate TCP connection with the server that holds that graphic. So when the user requests one document, that might start multiple TCP requests with the same or different Web servers.

FTP is quite different from Gopher or the Web. It creates two connections between the server and the client, one for controlling the connection, and the other for sending data. The control connection stays up throughout the time the user is logged in. The data connection comes up when needed.

Hopefully you now have a good grasp of how Internet services work. In the next chapter, we'll introduce each service and discuss what to use them for, how to combine them, and so on.

In this Chapter:
- *An Overview of Internet Information Services*
- *What To Do with Internet Services*
- *System and Network Requirements*
- *Human Requirements*

Introduction to Information Services

Internet information services may be the primary way people access the publications and databases of tomorrow. You can already read your *Wall Street Journal* on the Internet, and soon you'll be able to read and search a hypertext version of the *Encyclopedia Britannica.* It's not a stretch to imagine checking an electronic book out of an Internet library, or purchasing a digital copy of your favorite musical artist's newest release from a virtual record store. Think of the waste that would reduce, in needless packaging and gasoline for trips to the store. Perhaps these services will even help us make good on the unfulfilled promise that computers would create a paperless society.

Internet information services based on these technologies are simple and cheap enough for individuals and small non-profit groups to set up. Unlike the centralized mass-media services of the past (and present), the architecture of the Internet allows almost anyone to become a specialized information provider for a world-wide audience.

Organizations on the Internet are deploying Internet services to provide customer service. Internet users now expect computer companies to provide at least an FTP server, supplying product and customer support information, and they often look for Gopher and World Wide Web servers. For companies in other industries, it's a way to be noticed by (and show an interest in) the millions of people who use the Internet regularly.

Internet information services are well on their way to making the progression from high-tech toys to serious business tools. The ultimate step on that path will be widespread availability of for-payment services, with secure financial transactions and confidence that only the purchaser gets the service. Not all of that infrastructure is in place today, but enough is so that online business is becoming possible.

For all of these reasons, Internet information services are exciting. Perhaps most interesting will be the decisions made about how to use these services. Internet services have just recently reached a critical mass, where the growing numbers of Internet users are attracting services and vice versa. You play a role in how it will change in the next few years.

Before we describe the nuts and bolts of building and maintaining Internet services starting in the next chapter, we'll introduce each of the services from the perspective of a service provider. We assume that you're already basically familiar with these services from a user perspective.

After the overview of the services (which you can skip if they're very familiar to you), we'll present some ideas on what to use these services for, and finally what it takes (in terms of hardware, network, and people) to start and maintain an information service. Overall, this chapter should help you decide which services will be appropriate for you, and get you ready for the task ahead.

2.1 An Overview of Internet Information Services

We cover email services, FTP, Gopher, WAIS, the World Wide Web, and a few other services in this book. This section introduces each service and is designed to help you decide which services might be appropriate for the information and audience you have in mind. Most likely, you will want to use some combination of these services, since each can present the same information to a somewhat different audience.

We've listed the services starting with those that have the widest potential audience, simply because they require the user to have less software and a less-sophisticated Internet connection, and ending with those that provide the most sophisticated capabilities.

2.1.1 Mail-based Services

If you want to make information available to the largest possible population of people, then email services are the ticket. Email from the Internet can reach not only people connected directly to the Internet and people who dial in to machines directly on it, but also users of commercial networks such as CompuServe, America Online, and Prodigy, and other worldwide computer networks like BITNET and Fidonet, totaling tens of millions of people. So it is important to provide email services in addition to the more interactive services like Gopher and the Web.

Since electronic mail is the predominant form of communications on the Internet, mailing lists are a good way to distribute "high-priority" information. Mail is more likely to grab attention because it is usually read soon after it arrives by active Internet citizens. (Clearly this varies from person to person, but take it from an admitted email junkie, you'll get an email reply from me faster than a returned phone call about 99 percent of the time.) Interactive communications, like Gopher or WWW, on the other hand, rely on the user's periodic checking of a server—possibly even firing up a special client to receive information.

We'll cover two types of mail-based services: mailing lists (and servers that manage mailing lists) and archive servers. A mailing list is basically a list of people's email addresses that can all be reached by sending email to a single address. An archive server sends out files by email in response to requests that users send in email messages. (A slight variation of an archive server can send information generated on the fly, such as the current time, not just static files.)

You can use mailing lists for any conceivable purpose, from the bizarre to the mundane. You might keep a mailing list of friends with an interest in information services and write a book together, using the list to keep each other abreast of developments, ask questions about writing style, and coordinate portions of the book.* A similar list can be made public to create a discussion group, where anyone can send messages to the list. An email mailing list can act as the electronic counterpart of the more conventional mailing list that an organization keeps for sending paper mail.† Managing a list of lots of people, or lots of lists, gets tedious quickly, so there are email list server programs like *Majordomo*, *listserv*, and *listproc* to automate parts of the task. Folks who are interested in joining a list can send mail to the list server and automatically be added to the list. This example shows the message a user would send to a *listproc* running on *online.ora.com*, to ask to be added to the mailing list for O'Reilly & Associates book news:

```
To: listproc@online.ora.com
--------
subscribe ora-news John Q. User of Some Organization
```

Archive servers, similarly, automatically handle users' requests to send files through electronic mail. You send electronic mail to the archive server, requesting an index of the information or files it has available, and it returns the index. You examine the index for the name of the file you want. Once you have the filename, you can send another message requesting that particular file or a number of files. The archive server encodes the files so that the mail transport system can carry them, splits large files into smaller pieces, and then sends them to you. You reassemble the files, decode them, and end up with the original files. This is a somewhat cumbersome process, because it can require several steps to get the file you want, but if you don't have direct Internet connectivity, you'll probably gladly put up with it to get files you need from the archive. Some archive servers, such as *ftpmail*, not only let you retrieve files from the host they're running on, but can also transfer a file from another Internet-connected host for you, and then deliver that to you via email. For this, you'd probably put up with twice as many steps, since otherwise you'd have no access at all.

* The authors of this book never met in person, in fact.

† Before you get too excited about a cheap alternative to paper direct mail, read Section 22.5 for information about restrictions on sending unsolicited commercial email.

2.1.2 FTP

FTP (the File Transfer Protocol) is the way most Internet users get files from other Internet machines, because it's the most widely available means to transfer files. It's similar to logging in to a machine, but it restricts users to a limited set of commands and, for anonymous FTP users, a limited set of files. The archives set up for public access are called **anonymous FTP** archives, because anyone can log in (the user's email address is requested as identification, but is verified only superficially). FTP clients are available for almost every flavor of computer, from palmtops to supercomputers. After email, FTP is the most commonly used Internet service. (If you've never used FTP, the Preface shows a sample session used to get the examples used in this book.)

FTP supports all file formats. Actually, it just doesn't care about file formats. You can make available ASCII text, PostScript or PCL documents, or software binaries for various platforms and operating system releases. With a little configuration and a special FTP server, you can define classes of users who are allowed privileged access to parts of your archive, log connections and transfers, and limit the number of users who are able to access the archive at once. In short, you can do a lot to control whether and how people access your archive.

What are FTP's weaknesses? Mainly, it's a slow process to browse through directories to find files, and FTP doesn't provide a description of the files. The traditional mechanism administrators use to help archive users locate files is to provide a recursive listing of the files in the archive (the *ls-lR* file), which isn't always very helpful. Some administrators also provide a README file in each directory that describes what each file and subdirectory contains, but these are often not kept up-to-date, and the standard UNIX FTP client (the *ftp* command) requires a trick most people don't know to read the README files while logged in (adding a hyphen to the get command, i.e., **`get README -`**).

2.1.3 Telnet and Finger

Telnet and *finger* are two services that come with most operating systems, so they are widely used even though they're fairly primitive.

Telnet basically allows you to log in to a system over a network just as though you were logging in from a terminal attached to the system. It's commonly used to provide an Internet service that is exactly the same as the one you'd get if you dialed into the system directly with a modem. In other words, if you already have a service available by modem, you can use Telnet to provide that same service over the Internet. See the box below for an example of a Telnet service.

Finger was designed to provide information on the users of remote systems (like the full name corresponding to a user's email address). But it can also be used to serve other short pieces of information, like stock quotes and weather reports.

DUATS—An Internet Service for Pilots

Commercial and private pilots are required to get a weather briefing and in some cases to file a flight plan before they fly. In the past, this meant calling (or visiting) a Federal Aviation Administration (FAA) Flight Service Station and talking to a briefer who has access to National Weather Service weather data. These calls are free to the pilot and cost the Federal government something like $9.00 each.

Some bright soul realized that the briefing and flight planning process would be much more efficient if the pilot could look at the weather data and enter flight plans directly. So the FAA contracted with the GTE Flight Service Division to provide this service by modem. The Direct User Access Terminal System (DUATS) provides a text-based interface to the same data that FAA briefers use. Once the Internet grew large enough, GTE realized they could provide the same DUATS service over the Internet with little effort, and at lower cost, because an Internet connection is cheaper than the banks of modems and phone lines needed to handle the same number of users.

Just *telnet* to *duats.gtefsd.com* if you're a student pilot, or *duat.gtefsd.com* if you're a licensed pilot. The service is impressive in the timeliness of the weather data (within the hour from all reporting airports in the U.S.). The flight planning feature contains a database of all U.S. airports (even tiny ones) and navigational facilities. It's neatest feature is that it takes into account the forecast winds and calculates the headings, time, and fuel required to reach each point on the route. Altogether, by getting the FAA weather briefer out of the loop, DUATS makes for safer and more convenient flying while saving money.

2.1.4 Gopher

Gopher, unlike FTP, does an admirable job of providing easy navigation of information resources. Gopher clients display a menu of text-labeled choices, and the user simply selects one, which may result in the display of another menu. The following example shows the text-based Gopher client:

```
                     Internet Gopher Information Client v2.0.16

                        Home Gopher server: wildlife.ora.com

 --> 1.  Introduction and Cover
     2.  Foreword
     3.  Country Accounts/
     4.  Search Country Data <?>
     5.  Wildlife FTP Site/


Press ? for Help, q to Quit                                        Page: 1/1
```

It's easy to backtrack to the previous menu. Included in the hierarchy of menus are documents, which can be displayed or saved, and searchable indexes, which allow the user to type keywords and perform a search. Some menu items may actually be links to other Gopher servers, or to another information server, like an FTP archive.

This simple architecture is surprisingly powerful when well-organized and maintained. It's also very easy to administer: structuring the information on your server is just a matter of organizing the directory in which the server runs. The subdirectories you create become menu items, and the files you put in the directories become available to Gopher clients. The challenge, really, is keeping the data current, providing sensible names for directories, and providing up-to-date links to other servers.

Gopher's limitations are in the types of data it supports and the variety of services it can reference. Gopher currently only displays ASCII text data, although you can transfer binary data and display it with other software. Other services, like WAIS and the World Wide Web, handle a richer set of data formats. Also, the Web can link from anywhere within a document, while Gopher can only link from menu items, and sometimes menu item text does not provide enough context to make finding things easy. Gopher can provide links to FTP archives, WAIS databases and Telnet services, but not to the same variety of resources that the World Wide Web can. Future Gopher development may address some of these concerns, of course.

Gopher browsers can be graphical or text-oriented, but the service is essentially text-oriented, so it performs well over slow links and can be used by people who only have dial-in access to a machine on the Internet.

2.1.5 *The World Wide Web*

The World Wide Web (WWW or Web) is the newest and most powerful information service on the Internet. WWW has great features of its own, plus it integrates most other information services in a way that is simple to use and understand. Whereas you once needed an FTP client to access FTP archives, a WAIS client to search WAIS servers, and a Gopher client to get to Gopher servers, a Web browser provides access to all of these services and more. Figure 2-1 shows Mosaic, the most popular World Wide Web browser, accessing a Gopher server.

WWW documents are written in a language called HTML, for HyperText Markup Language. In raw form, it looks like normal text interspersed with formatting commands. HTML also includes ways to specify networked links to FTP archives, Gopher servers, WAIS servers, and other Web servers. Web servers transfer HTML documents to each other through a protocol called HTTP, the HyperText Transfer Protocol.

A graphical Web browser takes the HTML provided by a Web server and beautifies it, performing the formatting specified by the HTML commands and indicating the presence of hypertext links with a visual cue like an underlined phrase. When a user follows a link (usually by clicking on it with a mouse), the browser brings up the target the link points to. If that's another HTML document, the browser displays it. If it's a

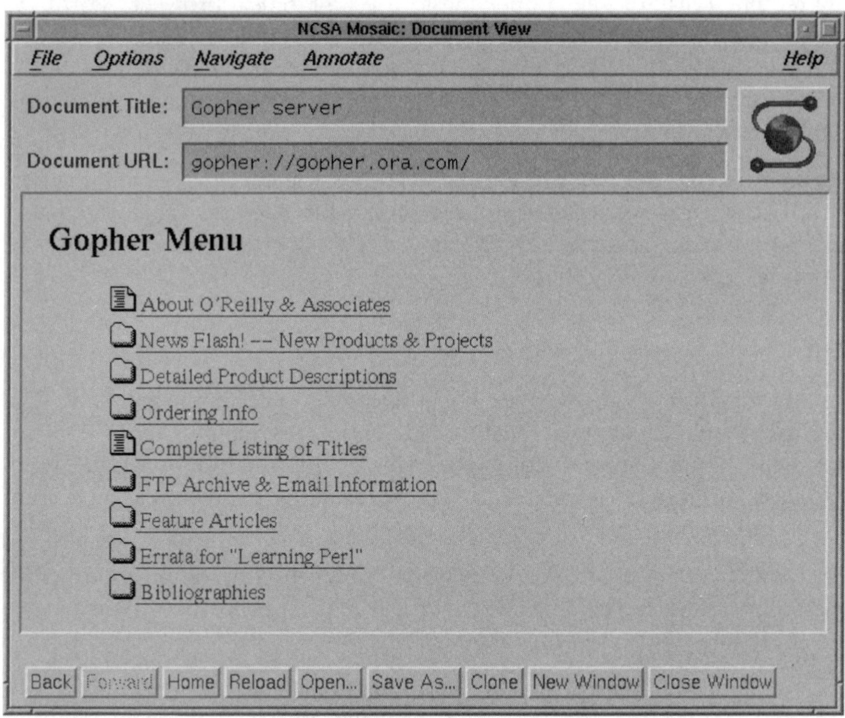

Figure 2-1. Mosaic accessing a Gopher server

directory in an FTP archive, the browser lists that directory and presents its contents to the user as a series of hypertext links named after the subdirectories and files in the listed directory. Following a subdirectory link changes directories to the subdirectory and lists it, while clicking on a file link retrieves the file and displays it, if possible. Or the user can transfer the file instead.

Similarly, following a link to a Gopher server displays a menu from that Gopher server—the link can specify the top-level menu, or any menu in the Gopher menu hierarchy. Each item in the menu acts as a hypertext link to the corresponding submenu. Newer Web browsers even support direct links to WAIS databases. These let you specify words to search for in the WAIS database.

The leading WWW browser, Mosaic, can display graphics intermingled with text and can automatically run separate programs to display high-resolution images, play audio, or show video clips when it receives data of the appropriate type. For example, on UNIX platforms, Mosaic can fire off a program called *xv* to view JPEG images. Likewise, Mac users can plug in their favorite JPEG viewer. (All these data types require users to have high-bandwidth Internet connections for good performance.)

To use a graphical browser, the user must have IP connectivity to the Internet, which today primarily means universities and businesses (and some home offices). Home users generally require a SLIP or PPP connection to use a graphical browser.* For users who dial in to an Internet-connected machine, or whose Internet connections simply can't support a bandwidth-hungry graphical browser, there are text-oriented WWW browsers, but they are not nearly as easy to use as graphical browsers, and of course, you can't see the pretty graphics.

The breadth of services that the World Wide Web can link together makes it the superglue of Internet information services. HTML documents can provide valuable context and navigation information, and then offer easy, single-click access to a myriad of other information servers.

2.1.6 WAIS

While Gopher and the World Wide Web are basically user interfaces for browsing data and have minimal search capabilities, WAIS (Wide Area Information Servers) is for searching data, with minimal support for browsing. Gopher and WWW assume users know where to look, while WAIS doesn't. In other words, a WAIS server is a good complement to a Web or Gopher server.

WAIS searches usually start at the Directory of Servers, which contains an index of all the other servers. Then the real search begins with the most appropriate servers.

WAIS searches the documents in a list of servers for one or more keywords and reports a score for each document (higher scores are more likely matches). In older WAIS software, you just look through the results to find what you want. Newer WAIS software supports further searches. If one or more of the resulting documents are similar to the desired data, but not sufficient, the user can add those *entire documents* to the keywords and perform the search again. The database engine uses the documents as additional search information and looks for documents that not only match the keywords, but are similar to the documents. This is called **relevance feedback**. Users will require some experience to be efficient at using iterative WAIS searches. Newer WAIS servers also accommodate boolean search expressions, wildcards, and other ways to specify searches (see Figure 2-2).

Using WAIS really requires a graphical browser and IP connectivity. While experienced users can use the text-based WAIS clients, it's pretty difficult.

WAIS works by indexing data beforehand so that it can be searched quickly when users send a query. The indexing software accommodates many different types of data, including ASCII text, LaTeX, PostScript, GIF and TIFF files, mail digests, and Internet NetNews archives. If the type of data you want to make available isn't already supported, it's relatively easy to add support for it. Together, the indexer and the WAIS database server let you create databases composed of many different types of docu-

* In the near future, it should also be possible to run X Window System graphical browsers with good performance over dial-up lines without IP using a technology called Low-Bandwidth X (LBX).

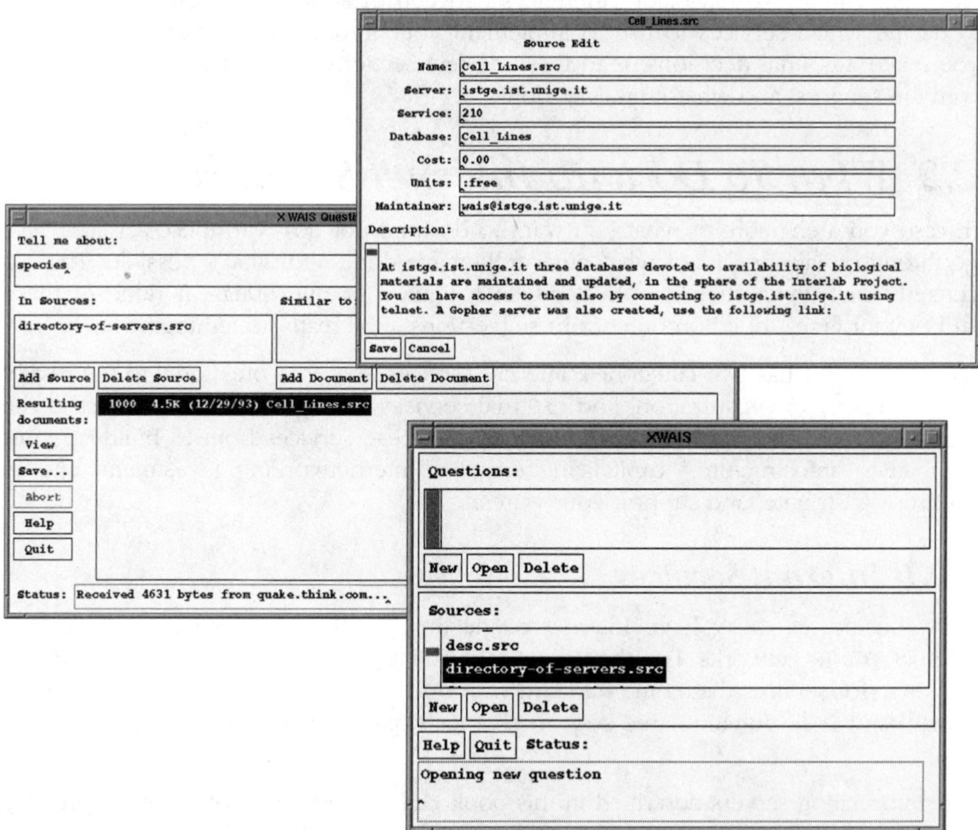

Figure 2-2. The xwais client

ments, images, and other files, and give Internet users access to the database through powerful, fairly easy-to-use clients.

Most WAIS clients provide viewers for a few basic WAIS document formats and allow users or administrators to specify external programs to process and present the more complicated types of data, an approach similar to Mosaic's. But even though WAIS handles many formats, WAIS searches work best with formats that contain a lot of words. If you index an image file, for example, WAIS has only the name of the file to work with. That makes searching databases of binary files clumsy. Administrators usually work around this problem by renaming their binary files to especially descriptive names, like *photo_of_a_rhino_charging_a_land_rover_and_its_surprised_occupants.gif*.

One problem with WAIS is that its database indexes are big. When WAIS has the luxury of working with text-based documents, the full-text indexes it builds can be as large or larger than the data itself! With large collections of text files, this can mean that you pay a premium in disk space to run WAIS. The developers of WAIS are well aware of this problem, though, and are working to trim down the size of the indexes.

Now that you know the major differences between these services, you may be ready to decide which services to use to implement your information resource. But before you make any final decisions, read the next few sections on what else you might do with the services, and what it takes to do it.

2.2 What To Do with Internet Services

In case you aren't sure of what you want to do (and not do) with these services, let's go through a laundry list of what other folks have done and what's possible. This list certainly isn't comprehensive, so don't let it limit your own ideas. If none of these strikes your fancy, build on one of our suggestions and create something better.

Our laundry list has two categories: internal services, that you offer only to the rest of your company or organization, and external services, that you offer to the rest of the world (or to particular customers). You can use these services both to build up your company's "infostructure," capitalizing on your internetworking investment, and to advertise, distribute, and support your wares.

2.2.1 Internal Services

Many businesses today have Internet connections, and even more have their own internal TCP/IP networks, but they don't take full advantage of them. They primarily use them for services that come standard with operating systems, like telnet, FTP, SMTP (email) and DNS (domain name system) protocols, plus a little Netnews and wide-area NFS.

The information servers described in this book can address some of the most pressing needs in business today: the need to make information readily available throughout an organization and the need to coordinate work between geographically separated workgroups.

Here are some ideas based on what folks around the Internet are doing, or are thinking of doing, with these technologies:

- You can make central corporate information available to all the outposts in your business empire, particularly with Gopher and WWW. This could include copies of your latest press releases, your current stock price (and maybe your competitors'), companywide documents like your standards of business conduct, and organization navigational aids like organization charts or Yellow Pages-style directories. Both Gopher and WWW have a notion of a default starting point that all users see at startup. That's a perfect place to put high-profile information that you want disseminated to your workforce.

- You can make catalogs of your organization's common logos, style sheets, and forms (e.g., for travel requests, travel expense reports, etc.) available via WAIS. WAIS allows users to conduct a keyword search for the relevant document and return the document in its native format for use with word processors.

- You can handle timecards (or anything similar) electronically by creating an electronic HTML timecard form for employees to fill out with a browser like Mosaic. Users can just click a button to submit the timecard. And no one needs to retype the information, since it's already in electronic form.
- You can make large archives of contributed and home-grown software available to your organization with FTP, or a combination of an archive server, FTP and WAIS. FTP can provide the basic archive, and a mail-based archive server can ensure that everybody—not just your Internet-connected sites—can pull files from it. With descriptive filenames or "multitype documents," you can use WAIS to allow users to search the database of titles or descriptions.
- You can create an employee directory with almost no effort. Wrangle a copy of your employee phone list from your human resources department (this is the hard part) and then index it with WAIS. Presto! Instant online employee phone book. (Same idea for an online job description database, so people can keep up with who does what.) Be careful what you do with personal information, though.
- You can use mailing-list servers to allow distributed workgroups to create their own mailing lists with almost no administrator intervention, and then index the archive of the messages using WAIS, so that list subscribers can search past messages without keeping all of them in their mailboxes.

2.2.2 External Services

External services are the kind you provide as a public service to the Internet community, or to your customers (free or maybe for payment). There's *lots* of great work being done around the Internet on this front, by both large and small organizations. For example:

- O'Reilly & Associates publishes an online electronic magazine, called the *Global Network Navigator* (or *GNN*), using the World Wide Web. *GNN* features sections on travel, science, and much more, with hypertext pointers to other, relevant Internet resources. *GNN* is beginning to support product ordering directly from advertisements.
- BSDI makes all of the manual pages for their BSD/386 product available via a World Wide Web server. If you're a BSDI customer with Internet access, you may be able to save disk space by using the WWW manual pages. At the very least, you should be able to see the latest, updated manual pages. BSDI also makes contact and ordering information available.
- DEC, HP, IBM, SGI, and Sun all have WWW home pages that lead to product and support information, price guides, and press releases. With WAIS, you too could make large databases of product information or long price guides searchable.

- A number of computer companies are investigating making their software patch catalogs available via WAIS. Using multitype documents, you could search a catalog of descriptions for the appropriate patch and then retrieve the patch you want.
- Some companies now accept bug reports via Mosaic's forms support. You simply find your way to the appropriate WWW server and fill out an HTML-based form describing the bug. No need to spend valuable time on hold waiting for the vendor's support organization.
- Many companies use mailing list servers like Majordomo to let you add yourself to their new-product mailing lists, or lists relevant to a particular product or service. Customers can add or delete themselves from the list, and the company doesn't need to dedicate a valuable person to maintaining the list.
- Some companies sponsor large archives of contributed, public-domain software that runs on their computer platform, or that helps maintain their routers, or that drives their printers, or whatever. This is great for public relations because it doesn't cost much for the company, and it makes their hardware more useful and their customers more productive. Most of these archives are FTP-based, but some also have mail-based archive servers for customers without Internet connectivity. With WAIS support, customers could search the archive for the type of software they were interested in.
- Non profits use Internet services to make information available worldwide that they can't afford to print and distribute.

The benefit to a company of running any one of these external services is fairly obvious: it helps your customers find information about your products and services easily, helps them use those products more effectively, and introduces them to new additions to your line.

2.2.3 Can You Charge Money?

What if you're interested in providing services for a fee? Good information costs money to collect and provide. Is there room for entrepreneurship on the information superhighway?

The good news is that it's not impossible to charge money. The bad news is that there are some challenges:

- Support for billing in the services themselves is immature. FreeWAIS, for example, lets you assign and advertise a cost for using a database, but then provides no real hooks for doing billing. All you can do is to record each query in a log file, then process that to determine who gets charged what. Most of the other services don't have any overt notion of billing, but, like WAIS, can maintain log files that tell you who's asked what of your information server.

- The authentication technologies employed so far are relatively crude and are too easily subverted to base real-money billing on. (We'll have more to say on this in Chapter 30, *Protecting Intellectual Property.*) FreeWAIS, for example, only logs queriers by their IP address or domain name. That's not very useful if the address or name belongs to a mainframe computer with thousands of users. (And even IP addresses and domain names can be forged.) FTP daemons also log the login name specified to access the archive, as well as the password the user gave at login. This password is by tradition the email address of the user accessing the archive, but there's no attempt to verify that.
- A potential bugaboo when billing for some kinds of service is the threat that many users will get the information from one paying user. To redistribute a file, for example, a user can just put it on one of the many FTP archives that allow anonymous users to upload files, then tell his friends. Or use a false name to post to a newsgroup. There's no real way to trace this. See Chapter 30, *Protecting Intellectual Property*, for more on using encryption to protect information.
- Even if you do trust your customer not to redistribute your priceless information, there's the possibility that some network brigand is monitoring the exchange of the information between your customer and the information server. Internet packets may pass through many unsecured networks on their way from hither to yon. There may well be someone peeking at the data as it passes.

Take heart, though: the designers and developers of these services are well aware of their weaknesses. The developers of Mosaic, for example, will include RSA authentication code with future releases, which information servers will be able to use to authenticate Mosaic users (but use in a server requires a license from RSA Data Security, Inc.). Likewise, the commercial (WAIS, Inc.) version of the WAIS server has much stronger billing support than the freeWAIS version.

Not all the problems will be solved by changes to the services, though. A major part of the problem is the lack of an appropriate authentication and security infrastructure on the Internet. This might take years to develop. For more on what infrastructure is required and why, see Section 30.2.1.

One last caveat to the would-be Internet information broker: remember that although most information server software is freely distributed, it's not always free for profit-making use. Also, some versions of one software package may be free, while later versions are not. If you do plan to use any of this code in a commercial enterprise, be sure to check with the developers first.

2.3 System and Network Requirements

If you're making information available to the Internet community via a server on one of your computers, this will obviously add to the network traffic your computer receives and sends, the load placed on its processor, and the disk space used. How much it adds depends not only on the type of services you offer, but also on their popularity. If you run a Gopher server that offers documents of interest only to Gambian philatelists, you probably won't see a surge in traffic. If you are masochist enough to run an Archie server,* you'd be wise to invest in an SMDS† connection.

As soon as you get some data on peak times and growth in demand, it's important that you plan ahead for future hardware needs.

2.3.1 Network Connection Type

To provide an Internet service, you'll require a full-time IP Internet connection. The only question is what speed. For a very limited service using Gopher, Telnet, Finger, or WAIS, you could start with a 28.8 Kbaud PPP connection, which requires only a standard modem and phone line. But for most services, a 56 Kbaud line is a minimum. For any serious service, you'll want a faster connection, like ISDN or even a T1 connection.

2.3.2 Network Load

There are two sources of network traffic from information servers: queries sent to the server and the responses it sends in reply. You need to measure both to determine the load your service is placing on your network.

In general, queries are usually small, while replies make up the bulk of the traffic unless you are serving tiny bits of information. Demand will, of course, have peaks at certain times.

2.3.2.1 Queries

Normal query sizes for mailing-list, mail archive, FTP, Gopher, WAIS, and WWW servers are fairly constant. Mailing-list servers almost always receive short messages requesting the modification of a mailing list. Of course, if the mailing list itself is hosted on the same computer as the mailing-list server, as it usually is, the mailing list may receive some fairly large email messages. Mail archive servers, similarly, almost always receive short messages requesting indexes or particular files—nothing lengthy. FTP clients, too, usually send short instructions to servers, possibly including one or more filename arguments. (The exception is when an FTP client is uploading a file to an archive, which can generate a substantial amount of network traffic—equal to the size of the file plus a little overhead.) Gopher queries are equally terse, usually specifying a menu item or a document to retrieve.‡ WAIS searches can be a little larger, since you can add documents to your search as relevance feedback (as described in the WAIS section earlier in this chapter), but what are actually sent to the server in the query packet are

* Archie servers are (heavily) used to search anonymous FTP archives for files. We don't describe Archie in this book.

† Switched Multimegabit Data Service, a telephone-company service that provides high-bandwidth data circuits.

‡ See Section 9.1 for details on selector strings, the short strings Gopher clients send to Gopher servers.

short document IDs unique to the documents, not the documents themselves. Consequently, WAIS queries aren't much longer, on average, than FTP or Gopher queries. Similarly, accessing HTTP (WWW) servers, WWW browsers pass back relatively short strings identifying the HTML document or resource they're accessing.*

2.3.2.2 Responses

If you run an information server, you can estimate the size of your server's average reply by looking at the size of the files the server offers and factoring in the likelihood they'll be retrieved. For example, a Gopher server that returns exclusively text files (and menus, of course) should send replies no larger than the largest document or the largest menu listing. The server will probably return the menus more often than the files, so if the menu listings are shorter than the documents—and they probably are—the average response size will be shorter still. This same line of reasoning holds for FTP servers, WAIS servers, and HTTP servers. With Web servers in particular, don't forget to factor inline images into the size of your documents—those can substantially increase the average size of a transfer.

If you know or have measured how often particular files are transferred, and how often a specific menu is listed,† you can compute an even better estimate of the average response size using a formula like this:

$$avg\_size = \frac{\sum_{i=1}^{n}(doc_n * pct\_chance\_this\_doc\_retrieved)}{n}$$

This formula simply multiplies the size of each document or menu by the probability that the document or menu will be retrieved, sums the result for all documents, and divides by the number of documents.

If you can estimate a rate at which you expect queries to arrive, or can measure that rate by examining log files, and you assume that each query generates an average-sized reply, then you can estimate the network utilization that you're likely to see from one of these services. This, in turn, may help you determine whether or not you need to consider upgrading your link to the Internet, and if you do, how much bandwidth you need.

More pragmatically-minded readers might want to dispense with this scientific method and just turn on network tracing on the server host for a certain amount of time and actually measure the amount of traffic sent to and from the server's port. Those well-equipped administrators with network monitoring devices like Network General Sniffers can do this independently of the host, for as many servers as there are on the

* WWW browsers with forms support, like Mosaic, can send large packets to Web servers if a user fills out a large form. We'll discuss forms support in Chapter 20, *Web: Gateways and Forms.*
† See the sections on logging in the chapters on each server for details on how they keep track of the documents transferred.

local network segment. Or you could simply estimate the network traffic by looking at the usage logs on your server.

Many of these servers operate on well-known ports,* which makes capturing and measuring their traffic very easy. Here's a table of the default ports the servers listen and talk on:

Protocol	Port
FTP (data connection)	20
FTP (control connection)	21
Gopher	70
Z39.50 (WAIS protocol)	210
HTTP (WWW protocol)	80

Mailing-list and mail archive servers are a little different from the rest of the information-server gang. First, a mailing-list server generates very little reply traffic (that is, replies to someone who posts a message)—just short mail messages indicating that the requested operation has been completed. But use of the mailing list itself can generate quite a bit of traffic: the actual numbers depend on the how many people are on the list, and how many different hosts they're on (since many mailers transfer only one copy of a message to a destination host with multiple recipients).

Mail archive servers, on the other hand, can generate huge amounts of reply traffic—there's no effective limit if your server will FTP files from other Internet sites for users, and there's no good way to predict an average response size. You can, of course, measure the responses with host-based tracing or network device-based monitoring.

Second, the job of monitoring is made a little harder because outgoing (reply) mail uses whichever source TCP port it wants to, typically an unreserved port number greater than 1023. That can make the traffic difficult to separate from other protocols. What's worse is that although the destination TCP port is always the SMTP port, 25, you still haven't separated your mailing-list server or mail archive server's traffic from normal user mail traffic on the host.

Probably the best way of determining how much traffic your mail-based server is generating is by dissecting your mailer's *syslog* output. *sendmail*, for example, can generate lots of useful *syslog* output, including source and destination email addresses (which can help you determine what messages your server sent) and the size of the message (which can help you figure out how much traffic your server is generating).

* If you're not familiar with TCP/IP's concept of well-known ports, see Section 1.3.1.2.

2.3.3 Computational Load

Figuring out how much computational power a given server will use is even more of a guessing game.

Mailing-list servers themselves are the least CPU-taxing of the servers we'll cover—they perform relatively simple operations on your *aliases* file and don't generate much network traffic. But use of the mailing lists that are maintained by the server can be very CPU-intensive, depending on the size of the mailing list and the size of the messages to be sent. *sendmail*, the program that delivers mail on most UNIX systems, is not designed for efficiently sending thousands of messages at the same time, as can occur when a message is sent to a huge list.

Mail-based archive servers can also chew up an enormous amount of CPU time performing file transfers for users, processing the files transferred, and then mailing those files. We describe techniques for giving priority to other processes and for shutting down the archive server entirely during busy times in Chapter 26, *Ftpmail*.

FTP, Gopher, and WWW servers consume CPU in proportion to the number of queries they receive and the size of the files they process. Popular FTP servers are notorious for bogging down processors. The Washington University FTP server software has special features that allow you to limit access to your FTP server to a set number of users during particular times of the day. We'll cover these features in Chapter 5, *The WU Archive FTP Daemon*.

Web servers are pretty demanding simply because the use of inline images makes the average document size large.

WAIS servers are computationally the most demanding of the servers. To handle a search request, a WAIS server must open index files, compute scores (how well a given document matches the search criteria), and perform other non-trivial tasks. Consequently, the per-query load a WAIS server places upon its host system is high. Since there are no mechanisms in WAIS for controlling access to your server based on system load, you'll need a fast processor to serve a large WAIS database.

It's important to monitor the trend in peak load average as your service grows in popularity, so you can predict the need for a faster machine before yours is on its knees!

2.3.4 Disk Space

Each of the information servers requires at least enough disk space to accommodate all of the files you'll be offering (e.g., the contents of your FTP archive, or the files in your WAIS database). How much extra overhead do they require, though? Are the ancillary files necessary to run the service tiny, or huge?

Of all of these services, only the mail servers and WAIS usually require a substantial amount of overhead disk space. As we mentioned early in the chapter, WAIS index files of textual databases can equal the size of the data, so you should plan on having a

WAIS server consume as much as twice the disk space of your data set. When mail is queued, both mailing lists and mail-based archive servers can consume a fair amount of space, since the headers and bodies of the mail messages will end up in your system's mail queue directory. This is more significant with mail-based archive servers, since they're more likely to transmit large mail messages, like *uuencoded* *split* binaries.

The other services typically need a few configuration files, *README* files, and maybe an index or two. Gopher, for example, needs index files in directories to tell it which menu choices to offer. FTP also requires a few programs set aside for anonymous users to list files and so on. But basically, these services won't often eat up more than a megabyte.

To run some of the services securely, though, may require that you have a separate copy of the data you'll be offering for each service, so that each server is restricted to its own copy. In other words, if you run Gopher, Web, and FTP servers, you may need three copies of the same data.

2.4 Human Requirements

Anyone with a connection to the Internet, a speedy workstation, and this book can run an information *server*. To successfully run an information *service*, however, requires an understanding of the material made available by the server, and a grasp of how to structure that material intuitively and effectively. It also demands the dedication to constantly update the information, to add new information, and to check the integrity of links from your server to other servers.

Many of the information services on the Internet today are run by the same people who compiled and installed the server. This isn't necessarily a bad thing: often, these people understand the information brokered as well as anyone. Sometimes, though, there's a real need to appoint a caretaker for the data in addition to (and separate from) someone to manage the server. This "data librarian" is responsible for the structure and content of the data served, but not the operation of the server itself. The librarian's duties can include:

- Authoring and formatting information to be served, especially meta-information like FTP *README* files, Gopher menus, and HTML "glue" documents that provide context and navigational help.
- Collecting information from other sources for distribution through the service and keeping this information up-to-date by periodically polling the source of the information.
- Providing and maintaining links to other valuable information resources, such as Gopher or WWW links to relevant FTP archives, WAIS databases, and Telnet-based services.
- Responding to users' requests for help, both in using the resource and in finding what they need.

So the attributes of the ideal data librarian are:

- Experience designing interfaces, or human factors training, or just an eye for aesthetics, since you want someone who can create a good-looking interface, and organize data sensibly and intuitively.
- Familiarity with the subject and audience of your service; that is, the information you're brokering and what people want to do with it. If you're managing a server that offers MPEG clips of movies, you don't want your librarian putting "Alien" in the light-comedy category, or branding "Looking for Mr. Goodbar" a "must-see for the entire family."
- The ability to navigate the Internet to find new information resources to point to, and to check the integrity of existing links. This helps keep your resource interesting and usable.
- A pleasant, patient demeanor if the librarian will be working directly with the public, like answering the phone or email. A lot of "techies" are too gruff and curt (we know who we are) to provide good customer service, or are simply too busy to respond as quickly as customers expect.

Internet Services and System Security

Putting a service on the Internet means taking a chance that someone will find a security hole. Firewall systems (see Chapter 27, *Firewalls and Information Services*) and other techniques can help to plug the leaks, but they aren't a guarantee.

For example, in June 1994, sites running Majordomo saw that crackers had found a hole. By using a clever address, crackers could make Perl execute any command. Most firewalls couldn't stop this kind of attack.

A warning and patches went out to the *majordomo* mailing lists (see Section 24.5)—and a new version of Majordomo was released.

This story doesn't mean that Majordomo is especially risky to run. *Any* service, commercial or freely-available, can have security holes. There are (at least) two morals to this story:

- Once you install any online service, keep an eye on it for suspicious activity.
- If there's a mailing list or Usenet newsgroup about your service or the software it uses, read it regularly.*

* The Computer Emergency Response Team posts security problems and fixes to the Usenet newsgroup *comp.security.announce.* You can also get the announcements by subscribing to their mailing list; send your request to *cert-advisory-request@cert.org*.

The data librarian's role, whether provided by the server administrator or someone else, is vitally important to the success of an information service. Even if your data is inherently valuable, poor organization and maintenance can quickly render your service difficult or even impossible to access or search. Internet users have low tolerance for services that don't work as advertised. If they follow too many stale links to extinct servers while using your service, they may quit using it altogether. If your support people are rude or never return email or calls, you'll lose customers faster than you can file Chapter 11. Internet services become a part of a company's public persona, so good services help the company image and poor services reflect badly. Don't take the quality of your services lightly.

In this Chapter:
- *Finger-based Information Services*
- *Inetd-based Information Services*
- *Telnet and Other Login-based Information Services*
- *Other Possibilities*

3 Finger-, Inetd-, and Telnet-based Services

Probably the simplest way to set up an Internet information service is to take advantage of servers already running or available on most UNIX hosts, such as *fingerd*, *inetd*, and *telnetd*. There's no source code to get, compile, or install, and configuration is easy. And you can be confident that all UNIX users already have the clients necessary to access these services (*finger* and *telnet*).

You can use *fingerd* or *inetd* to provide simple text announcements to Internet users. One good application is to give Internet users tips on how to use all the other information servers you've set up.

inetd can also start as a server any program (or script) that reads from standard input and writes to standard output, so it can handle the network part of the service for you, while you concentrate on what the service does.

telnet, together with custom, but straightforward, scripts, can provide interactive information services or provide a menu of your other network services. It's particularly good for providing services that you want to provide for direct dial-in (not over the Internet).

3.1 Finger-based Information Services

finger is a simple client originally designed to show who is logged in to a remote host and to retrieve basic information about a particular user on that host. It shows you how long a user has been logged in, where they're logged in from, and what their login name is. A user can create a *.plan* file in his home directory, which is displayed to users who *finger* his login. (If there's no *.plan* file, *finger* says "No Plan.") One of the great advantages of *finger* is that any user can make information available via *finger*, not just the system administrator.

The network server that provides this information and reads the *.plan* file is the *fingerd* daemon, which is started on demand by *inetd*.

There's a wide variety of information available on the Internet via *finger*. People use the *.plan* file to make weather reports, earthquake information, and the state of the local soda machine available to users all over the Internet. Here's what you'd see if you entered **finger pepsi@www.cc.columbia.edu**, for example:

```
% finger pepsi@www.cc.columbia.edu.
[www.cc.columbia.edu]
pepsi    Pepsi Machine      Never logged in
Project: All-night caffeine stop.
Mail forwarded to jte,dan,thor

    Location:  8th Floor, Watson Hall
    Last filled:  Probably within the last week or two.

    Inventory:
    ----------
    Pepsi                  [Full]        Lemon/Lime Seltzer   [Full]
    Diet Pepsi             [Full]        Lipton Iced Tea      [Full]
    7up                    [Full]        Apple Juice          [Full]
    Cream Soda             [Full]        Mountain Dew         [Full]

    Send mail to pepsi@columbia.edu if you have complaints, comments, or
    suggestions...

    URL--> http://www.cc.columbia.edu/~pepsi/
```

One great use for *finger* is to make introductory information about your other services available. Since so many different services are available, people need a place to start. Providing basic "getting started" information via *finger* can be invaluable to new users. Here's a list of what you might include:

- What servers are available, including a summary of their contents
- Which host names (or aliases) and which ports the servers run on
- The names of the databases they offer (for WAIS) or the paths to the home pages (for World Wide Web)
- How to access the login-based services: login names and passwords to specify

All you need to do to provide this type of navigational aid is create an obviously-named user (like *services*) and then write a *.plan* file in the home directory of user *services* that tells folks what to do. Then widely publicize the *finger* address, perhaps on the newsgroups and mailing lists that your users and prospective users frequent.

The data librarian who will maintain the *.plan* file can log in as the user *services* to maintain the file. Or the administrator can give the user *services* a login shell of */bin/true* and maintain the *.plan* file)

If you want to do something more sophisticated with *finger*, consider compiling and installing the GNU *finger* daemon. The GNU *fingerd* allows a user to set up a *.fingerrc* file in his home directory. This is a script that is executed when a remote user fingers the local user's account name. The standard output of the script is sent to the remote user. To help you customize the output, the normal *finger* output is sent to the *.fingerrc* script as the standard input, and three arguments are passed to the script:

- The domain name or IP address of the remote host
- The keyword *local* if the querier is on the local host, or *remote* if the querier is on another host
- The name of the user doing the fingering, or a null string if *fingerd* can't tell

For security's sake, the *.fingerrc* script

- Must be owned by the user who owns the home directory
- Must not be writable by anyone other than that user
- Must not be *setuid* or *setgid*
- Is run by the user *nobody*

The GNU *fingerd* is available via anonymous FTP from *ftp.gnu.ai.mit.edu* in the file */pub/gnu/finger-1.37.tar.gz.*

3.1.1 FIFOs for Smart Updating

What if you need to serve up-to-the-moment information with *finger*? A *cron* job could keep the *.plan* file up-to-date but would waste time updating it when it wasn't needed. What you want is a *.plan* file that is updated only when fingered.

Try this trick. On a UNIX system with FIFOs ("named pipes"), you can replace your *.plan* file with a FIFO named *.plan*, using a program that you can obtain from the *plan* directory in this book's archive (see the Preface). The program (by Tony Rems) makes the FIFO and waits; when a *finger* job opens *.plan* for reading, the *plan* program runs a child program and routes the child's output to the named pipe.

To prepare the *plan* program, edit *plan.c* to store the full pathname of your *.plan* file in the `FILENAME` macro. Pick a directory to hold the compiled *plan* program; put its pathname in the *Makefile* `DEST` macro. Run **`make`** and **`make install`**.

Finally, choose a program that *plan* will run for each *finger* job. Here's a sample shell script; we put it in an executable file named *planit*:

```
#! /bin/sh
log=/tmp/planit.log
echo `/bin/hostname` status: `/usr/ucb/uptime`
echo `/usr/ucb/wc -l < $log` other inquiries so far today.
/bin/date >> $log
```

Our demonstration *planit* script shows some system information and adds the current date and time to a log file. It also counts the number of "inquiries"—the number of lines in the log file. Of course, you can adapt *planit* to do whatever you want (probably something more useful than this!). You can also run any program that writes to its standard output; you don't need to write a special script like *planit*.

Although we installed *plan* on a special account named *status*, this setup can be run from a normal user's account. In the following example, we start the *plan* program by hand—but it could be started from a system */etc/rc** file. A *ps* command shows the *plan* process running, and an *ls -l* shows the FIFO in the home directory:

```
$ plan $HOME/bin/planit &
2383
$ ps 2383
  PID TT STAT  TIME COMMAND
 2383 Z3 S     0:00 plan /home/status/bin/planit
$ ls -l $HOME/.plan /tmp/planit.log
prw-r--r--  1 status      0 Aug 19 09:16 /home/status/.plan
-rw-r--r--  1 status     96 Aug 19 09:14 /tmp/planit.log
```

Now, to test the setup, we *finger* the account. It's best to specify the hostname, too (after an @); this makes sure that your *.plan* is accessible to all remote users:

```
$ finger status@ora.com
[ora.com]
Login name: status                      In real life: system status test
Directory: /home/status                 Shell: /bin/sh
On since Fri Aug 19 08:24 on ttyZ3
No mail.
Plan:
ora.com status: 9:17am up 13:20, 18 users, load average: 0.33, 0.37, 0.12
3 other inquiries so far today.
```

The last two lines came from the *.plan* FIFO.

Be sure that the *planit*-type script runs as quickly as possible. That's because only one *finger* job can read the *.plan* FIFO at a time, so only one *finger* at a time will see output from your *planit* script.

3.2 Inetd-based Information Services

The main function of *inetd*, as described in Section 1.3.2, is to start up other network service daemons when needed. It can also start normal UNIX programs or scripts as Internet servers.

For example, it's easy to set up *inetd* to display a given file when a user connects to a particular port. This works by using the *cat* command as a network server to display the file to the port.

Let's say we have a text file that is updated periodically to reflect the current share price of our company's stock (perhaps we get it over the Internet from another service). We store the file in */usr/local/stock/current.quote*. To let remote users see the file, you need an entry like this in your *inetd.conf* file: *

```
stock  stream  tcp  nowait  nobody  /bin/cat    cat /usr/local/stock/current.quote
```

The first field is the name of the service. The next three configure the networking for the service; on the Internet, they're usually `stream tcp nowait`. The service runs as user *nobody*. The last two fields are a bit less obvious. The second-to-last field is the path to the command (`/bin/cat`). The final field is the command to run and its arguments. Notice that `cat` appears twice.

You also need a `stock` entry in */etc/services* (or in the NIS *services* map, if you use that) to determine which port users will connect to in order to access the service. For example:

```
stock   2000/tcp            # stock quote service
```

has users connect to port 2000 to access the stock service.

Now both local and remote users can *telnet* to port 2000 on your host to receive stock information:

```
% telnet yourhost.foo.bar.com. 2000
Trying...
Connected to yourhost.foo.bar.com.
Escape character is '^]'.

Thursday, 30 September (273) 1993       16:23:27 PDT        (0930162393 27)

Stock Quote as of Sep 30 15:03 Pacific Time --

SYMBOL          VOL   HIGH/ASK  LOW/BID    LAST      CHG

HWP             6973    68.50    67.62    68.37     +0.50   (Hewlett-Packard)

                              9/30/93 - 5:02 p.m. CDT
     Dow Jones Industrial Avg  3555.12 off 11.20
     Dow Jones Transport Avg   1628.13 off  9.40
     Dow Jones Utility Avg      249.80 up   0.13
     Dow Jones Composite Avg   1324.54 off  4.50
```

You can even provide a short script to simplify this command for your users:

```
#! /bin/sh
#
# Simple script to retrieve stock quotes

telnet yourhost.foo.bar.com. 2000
exit $?
```

* We use the user *nobody* in this example, because it has very few privileges. You could also define a user *ourstock* in */etc/passwd* and use *ourstock* instead of *nobody*.

To be thorough, you might even create an alias for *yourhost* that reflects the service it offers. Using a service-specific, not host-specific, domain name for your service allows you to relocate the service more easily later. To create a hostname alias with the Domain Name System, just add a CNAME record to the primary master name server's zone data file:

```
stock    IN    CNAME    yourhost.foo.bar.com.
```

And if you're using NIS* or */etc/hosts*, add a new alias field to *yourhost*'s entry:

```
199.199.10.25 yourhost stock
```

Once you've updated the name service entry, your users can enter **telnet stock.foo.bar.com.2000** to get their stock quotes.

inetd is actually much more flexible than we've shown here: it can run any program that reads standard input and writes standard output. But before you charge off and configure *inetd* to start random programs as servers on your system, consider what the server gives users access to. Some programs and scripts give access to a shell that might allow users to do damage. Read the following section on Telnet services, because the programs used with *inetd* can be any of the same programs that can be used as the "login shell" of a Telnet service; the same security issues apply.

xinetd is an extended version of *inetd* that provides security and access control features. For more information, see Chapter 28, *xinetd*.

3.3 Telnet and Other Login-based Information Services

Using Telnet, you can offer simple or complicated interactive information services.

Telnet provides a remote character terminal over the Internet. It can be configured to look like a normal login, or use a customized login procedure, or no login at all.

Telnet can provide to remote users most of the services that can be provided on a local character terminal, such as a VT100, including those that use the curses screen-handling package or escape sequences to get graphical effects. Therefore, Telnet services are a good option if you already have a service available for direct dial-in, or you want to make your service available to people both on and off the Internet. It's usually easier to provide the same service on the Internet than by direct dial-in, since there's no need for a phone line and modem per simultaneous user, and no need for all that nasty modem configuration.

If you do nothing to configure *telnetd*, users see a normal login prompt when they connect using the *telnet* client. Once a user has logged in with *telnet*, the *telnetd*

* If you're using NIS, be sure to rebuild the *hosts* map and push it out to your slave NIS servers: **make hosts.time**.

daemon looks in */etc/passwd* for the "login shell" and runs it. This login shell is the program that implements the actual service.

The program you specify as the login shell can be any program that reads from standard input and writes to standard output, just like the programs that can be specified for *inetd* (and with the same security concerns). Usually this program or script works by supplying questions for the user to answer; sometimes the program provides a list of menu items and a request that the user select a number or letter.

The next five subsections describe options for what this login shell should be, beginning with what it shouldn't be.

3.3.1 Security for Telnet and Inetd Services

In all services, you want to provide access to information, but not to anything else on your system. In particular, you want to avoid giving access to the UNIX shells.

If you use a Telnet login to provide information services, you must not use a full-featured shell or command interpreter as the login shell. If you do, the user might be able to exploit security holes on your system to gain *root* privilege, and then all heck could break loose. Even without *root* privilege, a user with a real UNIX shell on a casually-run host can do damage.

Furthermore, with both *telnet* and *inetd* services, you need to make sure that whatever program you use as the service does not allow an escape to a full-featured shell. For example, the *more* and *less* pagers, although not shells, provide a way to escape to a shell (or to start any program). Many other programs, depending on how you compile them, incorporate these pagers.

With Telnet services, another security concern comes about when a user types the user name and password. The Telnet protocol uses clear text, so a user at any intermediate site that the packets traverse could intercept the user name and password. Therefore, it is important not to allow Telnet logins to access a shell even if you trust the people you give the passwords to.

3.3.2 Clients as Login Shells

The login shell can be an information service client, such as the *gopher* line-mode client (described in Chapter 10, *Gopher: Compiling the Server*). One advantage of using an information service client is that the user need not have that client installed on his own machine to use the service. For example, if you use the line-mode *gopher* client, the user needs the *telnet* client, but not the *gopher* client, to access the service. The other advantage is that information service clients tend to be more secure than the average program, since they are specifically designed for Internet use.

Some information service clients don't permit escape to a shell or use of general system commands. Other clients must be built in a way that disables the ability to escape to a shell, by setting the appropriate definitions before building the client.

For the World Wide Web, both the CERN line-mode browser and the Lynx browser can be used as login programs. The line-mode Gopher client also can serve as a login program, but you should run it with the *–s* (secure) option, which prevents users from saving files on your local system or escaping to a shell. Also, make sure it's compiled to use its internal pager, rather than *more* or *less*, since both those external pagers permit shell escapes.

3.3.3 Captured Shells as Login Shells

The more complicated way to offer an information service is to write a *captured*, or *no-break* shell. A captured shell permits a user to use only a limited number of commands, and no commands that might provide access to sensitive data or protected facilities on the host. For example, a simple captured shell might present a user with a menu that allowed him to access a source of information, examine a particular file (perhaps containing help information), or exit from the captured shell.

Here's a short Perl script to do just that. To use this script, make it the login shell in */etc/passwd* for the username to be used to access this service.

```
#!/usr/bin/perl

$stockcmd = '/usr/bin/telnet stock.foo.bar.com. 4444';

sub prompt {
    print
    "\n[P]rint stock quote\nGet [d]ate and time\n[H]elp\nE[x]it or [q]uit\n\n";
    print "Please enter your choice:  ";
    chop($response = <STDIN>);
    return($response);
}

print "Welcome to the Generic Information Server!\n";

while ($retval = &prompt) {
    if ($retval =~ /[Pp]/) {
        open(QUOTE, "$stockcmd |") || die "Couldn't access stock quote: $!\n";
        print STDOUT <QUOTE>;
         next;
    }
    if ($retval =~ /[Dd]/) {
        print STDOUT `date`;
         next;
    }
    if ($retval =~ /[Hh]/) {
        open(HELP, "helpfile") || warn "No help available: $!\n";
        print STDOUT <HELP>;
         next;
    }
    if ($retval =~ /[XxQq]/) {
        print STDOUT "Goodbye!\n";
        exit 0;
```

```
        }
        print STDOUT "Sorry, please choose one of [pdhxq]\n";
    }
```

This captured shell can be expanded to start network service clients like those described in the previous section, or to start X clients, as described in the next section, or both.

3.3.4 Starting X Clients in a Captured Shell

Another common way to deliver an information service is to use *telnet* as an interface for starting certain X clients to run on your host, but display on remote users' displays.

As an internal service for your company, X clients work fine. But they're probably not suitable as a service for the public. First, X clients generate a lot of network traffic, which is acceptable over Ethernet, but slow over all but the fastest Internet links. Also, some X clients might be a security concern. Mosaic, for example, can read and write local files.

Why not have the users start their own X clients on their own hosts? This may not be possible for a number of reasons. Maybe the client must be run on your host to have access to the information it displays. Maybe X clients aren't available for their operating system. Whatever the reason, the X protocol gives you the ability to display your client on anything from an Indigo to a Mac or PC running X server software, so it's a way of delivering the service to a wide variety of platforms.

Here's a Perl script to fire off an X client to a remote display. It's based on Larry Wall's sample server in *Programming Perl* (O'Reilly & Associates, Inc.). The server simply listens for incoming connections to a given port (specified at the command line, or 9999 by default). When a user connects to the port, the server determines the hostname or IP address the user is connecting from and prompts the user for the service to start. Once the user has selected a service, the server simply runs that X client, with the display redirected to the user's display.

```
#!/usr/bin/perl

require "syslog.pl";

($port) = @ARGV;
$port = 9999 unless $port;

$AF_INET = 2;
$SOCK_STREAM = 1;

$sockaddr = 'S n a4 x8';

($name, $aliases, $proto) = getprotobyname('tcp');
if ($port !~ /^\d+$/) {
    ($name, $aliases, $port) = getservbyport($port, 'tcp');
}
```

```
&syslog('info', "$0[$$]: Startup on port %d", $port);

$this = pack($sockaddr, $AF_INET, $port, "\0\0\0\0");

select(NS); $| = 1; select(stdout);

socket(S, $AF_INET, $SOCK_STREAM, $proto) ||
    &syslog('warning', "$0[$$]: socket: $!") && die "socket: $!\n";
bind(S,$this) || &syslog('warning', "$0[$$]: bind: $!") && die "bind: $!\n";
listen(S,5) || &syslog('warning', "$0[$$]: listen: $!") && die "listen: $!\n";

select(S); $| = 1; select(stdout);

$con = 0;
for(;;) {
    ($addr = accept(NS,S)) || &syslog('warning', "$0[$$]: accept: $!") &&
        die $!;

    $con++;
    if (($child[$con] = fork()) == 0) {

        ($af,$port,$inetaddr) = unpack($sockaddr,$addr);
        @inetaddr = unpack('C4',$inetaddr);
        (($host, $aliases, $addrtype, $length, @addrs) =
        gethostbyaddr($inetaddr, $AF_INET)) || ($host = join('.', @inetaddr));
        &syslog('info', "$0[$$]: connect from $host, port $port\n");

        $program = &askforsvc;
        print NS "\nStarting X client $program\n";
        exec("$program -display $host:0") ||
            printf(NS "Sorry, I can't start %s\n", $program) &&
            &syslog('warning', "$0[$$]: Can't start $program") &&
            die "Can't start $program: $!\n";

        close(NS);
        exit;

        } else {
    }
    close(NS);
}

sub askforsvc {
    print NS "Please choose one of the following services by number:\n\n";
    print NS "\t1) Archie (an Internet file locator)\n";
    print NS "\t2) Gopher (a distributed information service)\n";
    print NS "\t3) WAIS (the Wide Area Information Server)\n";
    print NS
        "\t4) World Wide Web (a distributed hypertext information service)\n";
    print NS "\nPlease enter your choice [1234]:  ";
    chop($service = <NS>);
    while ($service !~ /[1234]/) {
        printf NS "\nSorry, %s is an invalid choice.\n", $service;
```

```
        printf NS "Please enter a number between 1 and 4:  ";
        chop($service = <NS>);
    }
    return('xarchie') if ($service == 1);
    return('xgopher') if ($service == 2);
    return('xwais') if ($service == 3);
    return('Mosaic') if ($service == 4);
}
```

3.3.5 Customized Login and No Login Services

You can provide your own server to respond to the *telnet* client instead of using *telnetd*. You might want to replace *telnetd*'s usual login procedure with your own, to implement billing. Or you might want no login at all, so that users get to the service immediately instead of having to log in.

There are two ways to do this. The conservative method is to use a server that provides functionality like *telnetd*, but with your desired changes, and set it up to listen on a port other than the usual Telnet port. This way, *telnetd* still works as usual if anyone Telnets to your system without specifying the other port. You'd have to advertise this port to prospective users of your service, though. This is the tack taken by the implementors of the University of Michigan's Weather Underground service. For details on how the Weather Underground works, see Section 3.3.6.

The daring method is to replace *telnetd* entirely on a system, by using your own server to respond to the default Telnet port. This saves users from having to remember what port number to use.

Writing a server to replace *telnetd* isn't as hard as it sounds, especially if you don't want any login procedure. Three good starting points for servers like this are Larry Wall's sample server from *Programming Perl*, which you can grab from *ftp.uu.net* as part of the archive */published/oreilly/nutshell/perl/perl.tar.Z*; David Noble's *sock.pl* Perl library, posted to the newsgroup *comp.lang.perl*; and the FreeBSD *telnetd* source code, available through anonymous FTP from *freebsd.cdrom.com* in */FreeBSD/FreeBSD-current/src/libexec/telnetd*.

3.3.6 An Example: The Weather Underground

Want to see one of the most popular services on the Internet? Telnet to port 3000 on *downwind.sprl.umich.edu* or *madlab.sprl.umich.edu* and you'll see:

```
------------------------------------------------------------------------
*                       University of Michigan                        *
*                        WEATHER UNDERGROUND                          *
------------------------------------------------------------------------

Press Return for menu, or enter 3 letter forecast city code:

                      WEATHER UNDERGROUND MAIN MENU
```

```
******************************
 1) U.S. forecasts and climate data
 2) Canadian forecasts
 3) Current weather observations
 4) Ski conditions
 5) Long-range forecasts
 6) Latest earthquake reports
 7) Severe weather
 8) Hurricane advisories
 9) National Weather Summary
10) International data
11) Marine forecasts and observations
 X) Exit program
 C) Change scrolling to screen
 H) Help and information for new users
 ?) Answers to all your questions
   Selection:1
```

We selected the first item, U.S. forecasts. The next menu appeared:

```
          CITY FORECAST MENU
---------------------------------------------------
1) Print forecast for selected city
2) Print climatic data for selected city
3) Display 3-letter city codes for a selected state
4) Display all 2-letter state codes
M) Return to main menu
X) Exit program
?) Help
   Selection:bos
```

After we typed the airline city code for Boston, Massachusetts (bos), that shortcut bypassed the menu and took us straight to the forecast:

```
Weather Conditions at 1 AM EST on 14 MAR 94 for Boston, MA.
Temp(F)    Humidity(%)    Wind(mph)    Pressure(in)    Weather
====================================================================
  40          59%             SW at 9       30.03        Overcast

GREATER BOSTON METROPOLITAN AREA FORECAST
NATIONAL WEATHER SERVICE BOSTON MA
1000 PM EST SUN MAR 13 1994

 OVERNIGHT...OCCASIONAL LIGHT RAIN.  LOW 35 TO 40.  SOUTHWEST WIND
15 TO 25 MPH.  CHANCE OF RAIN 80 PERCENT.
   ...and so on...
```

As of March 1994, the Weather Underground was accessed 300,000 times a week. A lot of those accesses were from other sites that redistribute the data. You can use the service interactively by *telnet*, *gopher*, and more; there's also a batch interface for grabbing data non-interactively. If you want to see how it works (or even set up your own server), the source code is freely available. You can get the Weather Underground code and documentation by anonymous FTP from *madlab.sprl.umich.edu* from the directory *pub/underground.* The anonymous FTP area also has sample Bourne shell and Perl scripts for grabbing data non-interactively from the Telnet port. (There'll also be a new port, based on the Gopher protocol, that will make all the weather data available to automated scripts.)

Besides the weather forecast service we cover here, the Weather Underground has features for primary and secondary school teachers and students in Michigan. The state network, MichNet, hooks schools to the University's computer services. For instance, *blue-skies* is a unique Macintosh *gopher* client for weather and environmental images and animations. You can get *blue-skies* by anonymous FTP from *madlab.sprl.umich.edu* in the directory */pub/Blue_Skies.* For more information, send email to *blueskies@umich.edu.*

Here, we'll take a look at the Telnet-based UM-WEATHER service.* Jeff Masters, a graduate student, wrote the program as a class project from an idea by Professor Perry Samson in his Interactive Weather Computing class. The Weather Underground is a menu-driven, interactive C program that reads data files containing current weather information, and prints user-selected information to the screen. The program listens on a port of the host IBM RS/6000 computer. The original version of the Weather Underground had about 200 lines of C code, which displayed only one menu (forecasts for 240 cities across the U.S.), and it was accessed about 500 times per week in mid-1991. By June 1992, it had expanded to over 10 menus and 1700 lines of C code; there were over 100,000 accesses per week.

Data and forecasts come from a satellite data broadcast from Alden Electronics and captured using software provided by Unidata, a National Science Foundation–funded program. The data is piped to a Sun 4 computer and analyzed. Selected data is stored in standard ASCII files on the computer's hard disk and updated continuously as new forecasts and weather information come in. Data is selected with a special pattern file provided by Unidata and massaged by shell scripts.

The Weather Underground required about $20,000 in hardware. With current technology, you may be able to set up a similar service with as little as $4000 in hardware costs. The Weather Underground also pays a monthly fee for access to the satellite data. If you redistribute Weather Underground data to a large audience (100 users or more), please be sure to give credit where a first-time user of your redistributed data will see it. (This is important for the survival of the Weather Underground, according to the people who run it.) Here's a sample notice:

> *The National Weather Service data is made available courtesy of the National Science Foundation-funded UNIDATA Project and the University of Michigan.*

There's a mailing list that announces changes to the Weather Underground for users who automatically grab forecasts. To add your name to the list, send mail to *weather-users-request@zorch.sf-bay.org.*

* A lot of this information was adapted from Weather Underground help files. Thanks to Jeff Masters and Dr. Perry Samson for help with this section.

3.4 Other Possibilities

There are still other services that you can use to make information available. For example, you can use:

- Read-only network filesystems, like NFS or AFS, allowing remote hosts to mount the filesystems and users on those hosts to browse the information in them
- TXT records in your domain name server, to store small amounts of information and distribute them around the Internet. Users can then run small scripts that use *nslookup* or *dig* to retrieve the information.
- A simple X-based message service that pops windows up on users' displays, or a full-featured X messaging service, like Project Athena's Zephyr*

* For more information on Zephyr, see */pub/zephyr* on *athena-dist.mit.edu*.

In this Chapter:
- *What Is FTP Good For?*
- *The FTP Server*
- *The Filesystem*
- *Testing and Debugging Your Archive*

4

Setting Up an FTP Archive

If the Internet is today's information superhighway, then FTP (File Transfer Protocol) is its interstate trucking. FTP carries more freight by far than any other Internet service: a whopping 36 percent of the bytes transferred across the NSFNET T3 backbone are FTP traffic, according to the NSF's June 1994, statistics.* Like trucks, FTP goes just about anywhere: FTP servers are the most common type of information server, and almost every host on the Internet supports FTP as a client, server, or both. And it'll carry anything: FTP archives store everything from documentation in raw ASCII format, PostScript and SGML, to executable binaries, images, and sound files. For those of you unfamiliar with this Internet service, the File Transfer Protocol is spoken by FTP clients and FTP servers. It allows FTP clients to transfer files to FTP servers, sometimes referred to as "uploading," because it's roughly analogous to uploading files from a PC to a bulletin board. FTP clients can also request that FTP servers "download" files to them from the filesystem on the server's host.

There are two types of access that an FTP server can provide: user FTP and anonymous FTP. Anonymous FTP is the one that's an Internet service for the public, as we'll describe in a moment. User FTP is for people who have a user account on your host. They can transfer files from your system or to your system using an FTP client from anywhere on the Internet. They first have to log in by specifying their account name and password. This gives them free run of the your filesystem: they can download any file that they would be permitted to read if they logged in locally and upload to any directory they're allowed to write to. It doesn't give them the ability to execute arbitrary commands, though. The FTP server only provides certain functions, like listing and changing directories, and receiving and transmitting files, so it's not like having full shell access. User FTP creates a security problem, because when users log in to your system over the Internet by FTP, their passwords are sent as clear text. That means people with sniffer programs on any system along the way can sniff the username and password and then log in to your system using Telnet, since FTP uses the

* By comparison, Telnet is less than 5 percent of the backbone's volume, and SMTP, the standard mail protocol spoken over the Internet, is less than 6.5 percent of the volume.

same user accounts. With that Telnet access, miscreants can execute arbitrary commands. You don't want this!

Anonymous FTP access is of more interest to Internet publishers. An FTP server with anonymous FTP set up lets anyone access the server, whether they have an account on the host or not. A user who specifies the account *ftp* or *anonymous* is allowed to log in. Although the server doesn't check the password the user specifies, the password is usually logged. It has become a convention to ask users to specify their email address as the anonymous FTP password, so the server administrator can find out who is using the service.

Anonymous FTP users are restricted to seeing only the part of the filesystem that the FTP server has access to. This is sometimes called the "anonymous FTP area"; it lets the administrators of the FTP server control anonymous access. The "compartmentalization" of users and the limited functionality the FTP server provides make anonymous FTP a relatively safe service to provide on the Internet. And because it's fairly safe and can support any data format and most platforms, it's the most common way on the Internet to make large bodies of documentation and software available, in what's normally referred to as an FTP archive.

However, anonymous FTP archives are not entirely maintenance-free. Setting up the archive is non-trivial, especially if you're using an enhanced FTP server. There are also certain conventions that Internet FTP archives follow, and if you want users to find their way around your archive more easily, you need to follow these conventions. And there are maintenance duties to perform to keep your archive clean and tidy, and to ensure that users are getting the service they need but aren't abusing your hospitality.

This chapter covers setting up a basic FTP archive with the standard FTP daemon. Chapter 5, *The WU Archive FTP Daemon*, covers setting up the WU Archive daemon, which offers more control over access to your archive and its facilities. A system administrator setting up an FTP archive should read both of these chapters. Finally, Chapter 6, *Maintaining an FTP Archive*, offers instruction and hints for the maintainer of the archive, the Data Librarian.

4.1 What Is FTP Good For?

We've already explained a number of the reasons FTP is useful, but let's expand upon those reasons a little here, and contrast FTP with the other, sexier information servers we describe in this book.

We've mentioned that FTP will store data in any format. Why is that important? Although you may not have read that far yet, some of the other servers don't handle just any type of data. Most like to know the format of the data they're dealing with, so they can display or process it correctly. You may have to configure the server to do the right thing with binary data. With FTP, you simply put the file in the right directory, and you're ready.

Gopher and World Wide Web, in fact, support links to FTP servers, so your FTP server can do double duty. It can function as a standalone FTP archive and as an adjunct to your snazzier information services.

Supporting the largest base of potential customers is very desirable in an information service. Even though Mosaic is all the rage right now, some people either don't have access to Mosaic or another Web browser, and others don't have the type of access they need to run them (for example, they don't have a graphics display or don't have a fast enough Internet connection to run it). Almost anyone on the Internet can run FTP, and FTP transfers files fairly efficiently.

Unfortunately, the reasons FTP is popular are also the reasons FTP is abused. Internet bad guys often use FTP archives to stage pirated software, pornography, and other material of questionable taste and legality. As the administrator of an FTP archive, you have to be careful to avoid this kind of abuse, for the good of your archive, your social standing, and your criminal record.* We'll explain the mechanisms available to keep your archive from becoming a staging area for unauthorized files. For the latest news on how to prevent such problems, see */pub/tech_tips/anonymous_ftp*, available for anonymous FTP from *cert.org*, and CERT's *ftp* security FAQ on *rtfm.mit.edu* in */pub/usenet-by-group/computer-security_anonymous-ftp_FAQ*. The FTP chapters reflect the contents of those documents as of August 1994.

4.2 The FTP Server

An FTP archive really consists of two parts: a server, which responds to client requests by listing directories, returning files and such, and a filesystem, which the FTP server scans for directory listings and from which it reads the files. The standard UNIX implementation of the FTP server is called *ftpd* or *in.ftpd*, and usually lives in the */etc* or */usr/etc* directory. This server is just fine for small archives with no need for strong security. If you're going to be running a large or busy archive, or if you require special mechanisms to keep malicious users from abusing your archive, you should consider using the WU Archive FTP daemon (also called *ftpd*), which has special extensions to help in running a major archive. We discuss the WU Archive *ftpd* in Chapter 5, *The WU Archive FTP Daemon*. If you're interested in running it, read both this chapter and the next—we'll cover material relevant to both daemons in this chapter.

4.2.1 inetd Configuration

ftpd typically runs under *inetd*, the UNIX superserver. *inetd* listens for requests on a number of well-known ports, including the FTP control port, TCP port 21. When an FTP client first attempts to connect to an FTP server, it sends a TCP packet to port 21 on the destination host. *inetd* receives the packet, determines from the destination port number that the FTP service needs to be started, and `fork()`s and `exec()`s a new copy of

* Seriously, some of the legal issues surrounding liability for software and other material made available from FTP archives are still being hammered out. Don't be a test case.

ftpd. It's this *ftpd* that actually handles the client's requests. If other clients try to connect to the FTP server at the same time, *inetd* dispatches their own *ftpd*s to handle them.

The line in the *inetd* configuration file, *inetd.conf*, that controls how *ftpd* is started up, typically looks like this:

```
ftp      stream  tcp     nowait  root     /etc/ftpd        ftpd -l
```

Most UNIX vendors ship their *inetd.conf* files with an entry for *ftp* included, so you probably won't have to add your own. Still, understanding what each field means will help you modify the configuration later and configure new servers to run under *inetd*, so let's dissect that line field by field.

The first field (`ftp`) is the protocol field. This tells *inetd* which service this line pertains to. *inetd* can tell by looking in the */etc/services* file which port number `ftp` translates to (21). When *inetd* receives a packet for port 21, it uses this entry in *inetd.conf* to determine which server to start.

The second and third fields (`stream` and `tcp`) describe the type of communication this server expects to receive. In this case, the communication is being done over a TCP connection, which is essentially a serialized stream of data between two hosts, a little like a telephone call. FTP, the File Transfer Protocol, only works over TCP. Some other application protocols operate over UDP, the User Datagram Protocol, and communicate using UDP datagrams, which are individual, self-contained packets of data sent between Internet hosts, like sending postcards. The datagram packets may arrive in any order and may not even arrive at all if the network drops them.

The `nowait` entry in the next field tells *inetd* to start up a new server each time a client makes contact. Some UDP-based servers are written to handle a number of clients at once, rather than working one-to-one with a client, so *inetd* only starts a single server for those services. Such servers specify `wait` in this field, to tell *inetd* that it should wait until no server is running to start a new one, since a single running server can accommodate multiple clients.

The last two fields (`/etc/ftpd` and `ftpd -l`) specify the full pathname of the *ftpd* executable and the arguments (including the name of the program, *ftpd*) to be used when starting the server. Many vendors ship their *inetd.conf* files such that *ftpd* is started without any special command-line arguments. If you're running an FTP archive, you'll almost certainly want logging turned on (the `-l` option), so you may have to modify the last field. We'll talk about the few other command-line arguments standard *ftpd*s understand in a little while.

Check the copy of *inetd.conf* on your host. If it already includes a line for the *ftp* service, you don't need to do anything special to configure FTP. If it includes a sample, commented line for *ftp*, uncomment it and add a command-line option to turn logging on, if necessary. If the file doesn't even include a sample line, add one of your own. Everything but the sixth and seventh fields (the pathname of the executable and the arguments it takes) should be the same for nearly all hosts. To find the correct pathname for the *ftpd* executable, try **man ftpd**. You probably won't need to specify more than the *–l* (logging) option to *ftpd* to start with.

If you do change *inetd.conf*, either by uncommenting an entry or adding your own, *inetd* must be signalled to reread the configuration file and notice the changes you've made. Most *inetds* reread *inetd.conf* when you send them a hangup signal (SIGHUP) with the *kill* command: **kill -HUP** *pid* or **kill -1** *pid*. You can also run the FTP server under *xinetd*, an extended version of *inetd* that provides security and access control features. For more information, see Chapter 28, *xinetd*. (On HP-UX hosts, executing the command **inetd -c** is a simpler way of getting *inetd* to reread its configuration file.)

4.2.2 The ftp User

Once you've configured the FTP server to run under *inetd*, you need to add an *ftp* user to your host's */etc/passwd* file (assuming that you want to allow anonymous FTP access). *ftpd* will check for the existence of the *ftp* user before allowing an anonymous user to use the FTP service. If the *ftp* user doesn't appear in */etc/passwd*, *ftpd* denies users who specify an anonymous user (either *anonymous* or *ftp*) access to the FTP archive.

The *ftp* user's entry in */etc/passwd* should have a unique user ID and group ID and that user should *not* be allowed to log in through standard utilities like *telnet* and *rlogin*. To accomplish this, the password field of the *ftp* user's */etc/passwd* entry should contain `*`, which prevents any password from matching the encrypted password field, and the login shell should be set to */bin/false*, so that utilities that don't require a password don't permit login, either. This *shouldn't* affect *ftp*'s operation, but while the manual pages for most *ftpds* claim that the login shell field is ignored and can contain anything, a number of *ftpds* don't honor that claim and require that the field contain one of the values returned by `getusershell(3)`. Since `getusershell()` reads */etc/shells*, if it exists, you can work around this by adding */bin/false* to */etc/shells*.

The */etc/passwd* entry might look like this:

```
ftp:*:500:25:Anonymous FTP user:/users/ftp:/bin/false
```

The login directory field is also important. Anonymous FTP users are restricted to accessing files and directories below this directory. An anonymous FTP user accessing an FTP archive with the above */etc/passwd* entry wouldn't be able to *cd* to the root directory or *cat /etc/passwd*, but could list the */users/ftp/pub* directory, for example.

The restriction is accomplished by having *ftpd* call the `chroot()` ("change root") system call with the *ftp* user's login directory as an argument. This changes the FTP server's view of the filesystem so that the login directory (here */users/ftp*) becomes the server's root directory. The server's */etc* directory, then, is really the host's */users/ftp/etc* directory. *ftpd* only calls `chroot()` if the user specifies an anonymous login. Since *inetd* spawns a new *ftpd* process to serve each user, other users can access the FTP archive at the same time using non-anonymous logins and not be `chroot()`ed to the *ftp* user's login directory.

4.2.3 Other Standard ftpd Command-Line Options

We've already mentioned that *–l* is the only really interesting command-line option that the standard *ftpd* offers. The vanilla *ftpd* does support three other options, though, which you may have occasion to use at some point:

–t Sets *ftpd*'s inactivity timeout period. By default, *ftpd* disconnects any sessions that are inactive for 15 minutes. If you want to use a different timeout period, you can specify it, in seconds, as the argument to *–t*.

–T Sets *ftpd*'s maximum client-requested timeout period. An FTP client can request a higher timeout period than 15 minutes (or the one you specify with *–t*). By default, *ftpd* allows an FTP client a timeout of up to two hours if the client requests it. To cap that maximum timeout, you can use *–T* to specify a shorter timeout, in seconds.

–u (Available on some systems including HP–UX.) Sets the default *umask* that *ftpd* uses for files uploaded by an FTP user (both anonymous and other). The *umask* determines the permissions *ftpd* sets on files created by a user. By default, *ftpd* uses a *umask* of 027, which means that a file created by an FTP user is not writable by members of the file's group, and is not readable, writable or executable by others. To set the *umask* to something more liberal, specify a new default *umask* as an argument to the *–u* option. For more information on *umasks*, see the man page on the *umask* command.

Most *ftpds* let you specify the option arguments right after the option, like *–t50*, or separated from the option by whitespace, like *–t 50*. If you want to be safe, use whitespace.

4.2.4 Domain Naming

Many Internet sites have started using standard domain names for their FTP archives to make them easy to find, easy to remember, and convenient to relocate. The most common name is simply *ftp*; for example, *ftp.uu.net*. The name *ftp* is usually not the canonical, or official, name of the host; instead, it's an alias. Adding the alias is easy: if you edit your name server database files by hand, you'd just add a line like this to the database file for your zone:

```
ftp    IN    CNAME    official.domain.name.
```

Make sure you use your host's official, fully qualified domain name and make sure you terminate that domain name with a dot.

If there's only one FTP archive within the domain, creating an *ftp* alias for it has several advantages. (If there's more than one FTP archive within your domain, you might consider consolidating them.) First, if an Internet user is forced to guess which host your FTP archive is on, *ftp.domain* is an obvious guess. It's also an easy name for users to remember once they've discovered it.

From your standpoint as administrator, it also gives you flexibility in moving your archive. If *ftp.domain* is just an alias for a canonical host name, it's easy for you (or your domain administrator) to change that alias to point to another host. This could be necessary if your archive outgrows the computer it's currently running on, in terms of disk capacity or CPU cycles. Rather than needing to re-educate a user community that's come to know the archive by its canonical name, you simply clone the archive on another host and then change the alias to point to the new host's canonical name. No muss, no fuss.

If you do change the alias to refer to a new host, be sure to take into account the inherent latency in the Domain Name System. It takes a little while for the new alias to percolate out to all of the secondary master name servers for your zone. It also takes a certain amount of time—up to the time-to-live for data in your zone—for old alias records to time out of remote name servers' caches. (The time-to-live is the amount of time your name servers allow data about your zone to be cached by other name servers.) If you're especially responsible, you'll lower the time-to-live on the alias before the move, or ask your domain administrator to do it for you.*

4.2.5 Standard Aliases

It's also a good idea to set up a standard alias for the maintainer of your FTP archive, so that folks who have questions or problems can contact the right person easily. One common alias for FTP archive maintainers is *ftp-admin*. Setting up the alias itself is easy: you put an entry into your *aliases* file (usually */usr/lib/aliases* or */etc/aliases*) like this:

```
ftp-admin:    real-user-name@domain
```

then run *newaliases* or *sendmail -bi* to update the *dbm*-format database files *sendmail* really uses. If you're using NIS to distribute the aliases map, update the source for the map and **make aliases.time**.

If your archive maintainer would rather have the computer separate his *ftp-admin* email from his personal mail, you can set up a separate administrative user ID for him. The *ftp-admin* alias will then point to that user, and your archive maintainer will have to log in as that user to read mail. This can work out just fine; that separate user ID can also own the */pub* directory and take care of populating and administering the archive filesystem.

* For a more comprehensive treatment of domain naming issues, see Chapter 8 in O'Reilly & Associates' Nutshell Handbook, *DNS and BIND*, by Paul Albitz and Cricket Liu.

4.3 The Filesystem

The filesystem that the FTP server `chroot()`s to for anonymous logins must have a special structure and contain certain files and executables. Because the *ftp* user's login directory has become the FTP server's root directory, all references *ftpd* makes to system files and executables are remapped to filenames under that login directory. With the *passwd* entry shown above, a `chroot()`ed *ftpd*'s *exec* of the */bin/ls* executable (to list a directory for the anonymous FTP user, for example) would be mapped to */users/ftp/bin/ls*. Likewise, a *passwd* file lookup by *ftpd* reads */users/ftp/etc/passwd*, not */etc/passwd*.

4.3.1 Anonymous FTP Directory Structure

To accommodate `chroot()`ing, you have to populate the *ftp* user's login directory with all the subdirectories and executables *ftpd* might need. In particular, you need to create the *ftp* user's login directory and the following subdirectories:

bin
: This directory contains all of the executables that *ftpd* needs to service anonymous user's requests. Usually, all you need in this directory is the executable for the *ls* command.

etc
: This directory contains a *passwd* file (*not* the same one as the system *passwd* file—see the next section) that *ftpd* reads to determine access to privileged information. Also, executables in the *bin* subdirectory like *ls* use the *passwd* file and a *group* file in this directory to show file ownership and group membership (i.e., to map uids and gids back to names).

pub
: This directory contains the files you make available to the outside world.

Copy your host's *ls* program from */bin* into the *bin* subdirectory. *Don't* copy your host's *passwd* and *group* files into the *etc* subdirectory, though. This might allow anonymous FTP users to transfer a copy of these files onto their own hosts and crack your passwords offline.

4.3.2 passwd and group Files

The *passwd* and *group* files should only contain minimal information—as little as you can provide and still have your archive work. Since both files will be used by *ftpd*'s copy of *ls* to map user and group IDs of files back to names, you can include all the user and group IDs that appear in your archive's file and directory ownerships, but without the corresponding encrypted passwords. In fact, don't even give the user and group IDs the real login and group names that are in your system files. Use different names, so that someone who swipes your FTP *passwd* file won't know login names to try to break into.

If your archive contains files with owners like *ftp*, *bin*, and *root*, you can create a small *passwd* file with the following contents:

```
ftp:*:500:1:Anonymous FTP user:/users/ftp:/bin/false
bin:*:2:2::/:/bin/false
root:*:0:3::/:/bin/false
```

(Since these are all system accounts that are on all hosts, you probably don't need to worry about using the real login names.)

If all of your files and directories belong to groups *users*, *bin*, and *other*, you can create a stub *group* file that looks like this:

```
users:*:1:
bin:*:2:
other:*:3:
```

This gives *ftpd* the information it needs to map user and group IDs back to names, but omits dangerous encrypted password data.

4.3.3 File and Directory Permissions and Ownership

Since you don't want anonymous FTP users doing nasty things like overwriting your *ls* binary with some insidious Trojan horse, you should tighten up your file and directory permissions as much as possible. The *ftp* user's login directory and its subdirectories should have the following permissions and ownership:

login directory
: The login directory should be owned by *root* and should be readable and executable (searchable, really) by all users (mode 555).

bin
: The *bin* subdirectory should be owned by *root* and group *wheel* or *other*. The directory should be executable—but unreadable and unwritable—by all users (mode 111). This allows anonymous FTP users to execute *ls* to list the contents of your archive's directories.

etc
: The *etc* subdirectory should be owned by *root*, too, and should be executable, but unreadable and unwritable, by all users (mode 111). This allows anonymous FTP users to see file ownerships and group membership.

pub
: The *pub* subdirectory should be owned by *root* or the user who administers the FTP archive and should be readable and executable by all users (mode 555). If you want to allow anonymous users to upload files to your archive, you can make the *pub* subdirectory writable by all users (mode 777), but this also gives these users the ability to delete files and directories from *pub* and even allows them to replace existing files with their own. It's more prudent to set up an *incoming* subdirectory (described in Section 4.3.5), which doesn't have quite the same problems. Or you can use the WU Archive *ftpd*, which has finer-grained controls over uploading and directory creation and deletion.

Be careful not to use the *ftp* user as the owner of anything in your anonymous FTP hierarchy. The FTP daemon supports lots of functionality that would allow an anonymous user to manipulate files or directories owned by *ftp*.

A directory listing of the *ftp* user's finished login directory would look something like this:

```
# ls -l
total 18
dr-xr-xr-x   3 root      other        1024 Jun 12 13:11 .
dr-xr-xr-x   5 bin       bin          1024 Jun 11 10:45 ..
d--x--x--x   2 root      other        1024 Mar  3  1992 bin
d--x--x--x   2 root      other        1024 Mar  3  1992 etc
dr-xr-xr-x   2 root      other        1024 Jun 12 13:01 pub
```

The *ls* executable in the *bin* subdirectory should be owned by *root* and group *other* or *wheel*, and should be executable by all users (mode 111). This allows anonymous FTP users to list directories.

The *passwd* and *group* files in the *etc* subdirectory should be owned by *root* and group *wheel* or *other*, and should be readable by all users (mode 444). This allows anonymous FTP users to see file ownership.

The *bin* and *etc* directories should end up looking something like this:

```
# ls -l bin
total 260
d--x--x--x   2 root      other        1024 Mar  3  1992 ./
dr-xr-xr-x   8 root      other        1024 Jun 12 13:11 ../
---x--x--x   1 root      other      122880 Sep 11  1991 ls
# ls -l etc
total 10
d--x--x--x   2 root      other        1024 Mar  3  1992 ./
dr-xr-xr-x   8 root      other        1024 Jun 12 13:11 ../
-r--r--r--   2 root      other         126 Mar  3  1992 group
-r--r--r--   1 root      other         284 Mar  3  1992 passwd
```

4.3.4 A Note on SunOS and Solaris

If you're using a Sun as your FTP archive host, you have to do a little extra to create a working FTP archive. SunOS 4.X systems use dynamic linking, so you need to include both the runtime loader (*ld.so*) and the shared, standard C library (*libc.so*) in order to make *ls* work. SunOS binaries expect to find the loader and the standard C library in */usr/lib*, so you need to create a *usr* subdirectory under the *ftp* user's login directory, and a *lib* directory under that (remember that *ftpd* will `chroot()` there):

```
# cd /users/ftp    -or wherever your ftp user's login directory is
# mkdir usr
# mkdir usr/lib
```

Next, copy the runtime loader and the shared version of the standard C library into the newly created *usr/lib* subdirectory:

```
# cp /usr/lib/ld.so usr/lib
# cp /usr/lib/libc.so.* usr/lib
```

Then fix the permissions on the *usr* and *usr/lib* directories:

```
# chmod 555 usr/lib
# chmod 555 usr
```

SunOS also wants to find a */dev/zero* device file, but you can create that with a simple *mknod* command:

```
# cd /users/ftp          -or wherever your ftp user's login directory is
# mkdir dev              -create the dev subdirectory
# cd dev                 -change to the new dev subdirectory
# mknod zero c 3 12      -create the zero device file
# chmod 555 dev          -fix the dev directory's permissions
```

4.3.5 Optional Subdirectories

Besides the standard subdirectories we've mentioned so far (*bin*, *etc*, and *pub*, plus the two you need if you're running SunOS), there are two common, but optional, subdirectories used in many Internet FTP archives: *dist* and *incoming*.

dist subdirectories usually contain *ftp*able files made available by an archive in an official capacity. For example, if your archive were the One True Source for a suite of handy utility programs for the HP 95LX, you can keep them in your *dist* subdirectory. (Unless that's all you had in *dist*, though, you should probably create a separate *hp95lx* subdirectory under *dist* for them.) Other programs that your users make available via anonymous FTP, which were developed elsewhere, still belong under *pub*.

An excellent way to ensure that the files you're making available in *dist* aren't modified by a malicious intruder is to mount *dist* read-only as a separate filesystem. You can also do this with *pub*, or in fact with everything under the *ftp* user's login directory, if you don't need to let anyone upload anything to your archive. An even better alternative is to store *dist* or *pub* on write-protected media, like a magneto-optical cartridge with the write-protect tab flipped on. Now even someone gaining *root* privilege can't remount the filesystem as writable.

If you do intend to allow anonymous users to upload files to your archive, consider creating an *incoming* subdirectory and making sure none of your other FTP subdirectories are writable. Then create an *incoming* subdirectory owned by *root*, group *wheel* or *other*, with write and execute permissions set for group and other (i.e., mode 733). To protect files in the directory from being deleted or renamed by regular users of your host (as opposed to FTP users), set the sticky bit on the directory, too: **`chmod +t incoming`** or **`chmod 1733 incoming`**.

Now anonymous users can drop off files in the *incoming* subdirectory, but can't list what's in it. This helps discourage Bad Folks from using your archive as a staging area for their private manifestos or enormous images of a questionable nature. However, it won't prevent it: anonymous users who know the filenames of the files they want will still be able to download, since they don't need to list the directory and since downloading doesn't require read permission on the directory.

After legitimate users have uploaded files to *incoming*, they can write you a short email message to let you know, or you can periodically peruse the directory to see what gems people have left for you.

The CERT Coordination Center has received reports of people maliciously filling up incoming FTP sites, so it would be wise to put such an archive somewhere that can become full without causing serious problems.

4.3.6 Sublogins

An often-useful, but seldom-used, feature of FTP is the sublogin. Sublogins are password-protected identities that anonymous users can assume to gain access to restricted parts of the FTP archive. For example, say the administrator of a software company's FTP archive needs to allow another company's programmers access to source code that both companies are writing in collaboration. However, he doesn't want to give the other company's programmers free run of his host's filesystem by giving them FTP access via a regular user account. He also wants to make sure that other users of his company's FTP archive can't access the source code.

By using sublogins, he can require that the collaborator's programmers first use the anonymous login, thus restricting them to the `chroot()`ed view of the filesystem, then provide a sublogin name and password via the FTP *user* command to authenticate themselves. The source code they need can be placed in a directory readable only by the collaborator's sublogin name.

Setting up sublogins is very straightforward. Edit the *passwd* file in *~ftp*'s *etc* subdirectory (*not* the system *passwd* file!) and add entries for each sublogin. The format of each entry is the same as the format for entries in */etc/passwd*. To figure out what the encrypted password field should contain, you can temporarily set your password to the sublogin's password, cut the encrypted version out of */etc/passwd*, then change your password back. The uid should be unique—make sure it doesn't appear in the system */etc/passwd*. Otherwise, a non-anonymous user of your archive may unwittingly gain access to the files you're making available to the sublogin.

For the login shell field, use */bin/false* or something equally innocuous. Watch out for those *ftpd*s that require that the shell be one of those returned by `getusershell()`—see Section 4.2.2 earlier in this chapter for details.

The login directory field is interpreted relative to the root of the anonymous FTP filesystem. If you want people who use sublogins to automatically find themselves within their own private subdirectory, use that as the login directory. Otherwise, you can use */pub* or / and let the users change directories themselves.

Let's say we're setting up sublogin access for a group of people working on encryption software with us. We create a new entry for the *~ftp/etc/passwd* file that looks like this:

```
crypto:MBpEj1H3cQAw2:501:1:Encryption working group:/crypt:/bin/false
```

Now we create a subdirectory that only people using the sublogin can access:

```
# cd ~ftp
# mkdir crypt         -create the login directory
# chown 501 crypt     -change its owner to the crypto sublogin
# chgrp 1 crypt
# chmod 700 crypt     -make it readable, writable, and searchable
```

To use the sublogin, the folks working on the cryptographic software need the sublogin name and password. They access the FTP archive as normal, anonymous users, but then specify the *crypto* sublogin with the `user` FTP command:

```
# ftp ftp.crypto.com
Connected to ftp.crypto.com.
220 ftp.crypto.com FTP server (Version 1.7.109.2 Tue Jul 28 23:46:52 GMT 1992) ready.
Name (ftp.crypto.com:user): ftp            -same as anonymous but shorter!
331 Guest login ok, send ident as password.
Password:                                   -type user@domain as password
230 Guest login ok, access restrictions apply.
Remote system type is UNIX.
Using binary mode to transfer files.
ftp> cd crypt                               -try to cd to crypt
550 crypt: Permission denied.
ftp> user crypto                            -specify sublogin
331 Password required for crypto.
Password:                                   -type password for crypto sublogin
230 User crypto logged in.
ftp> pwd
257 "/crypt" is current directory.
```

A note on user IDs and sublogins: it may be confusing for you as the system administrator to have file ownerships in your anonymous FTP area that don't map back to usernames. If you want to be able to see the ownerships of the sublogin's files and directories, you can add stub entries to the system */etc/passwd* file, without login capability. For example, we might put this entry into our */etc/passwd* file to remind us of the significance of the *~ftp/crypt* directory:

```
ftpcrypt:*:501:1:Encryption working group:/users/ftp/crypt:/bin/false
```

Finally, a caveat: sublogins are not all that secure, especially since it's possible for someone to steal a copy of your *~ftp/etc/passwd* file and crack it offline, then assume the identity of the sublogin. Use a *really* good password on your sublogins, one that isn't easily cracked. If you want a more secure solution, check out the WU Archive FTP daemon.

4.4 Testing and Debugging Your Archive

Before you advertise your FTP archive to the rest of the world, it's a good idea to make sure everything's up and running correctly. You should try *ftp*ing to the archive yourself, change to and list some directories, download a few files, and upload a few if you intend to support that.

You should also make sure that you *can't* do things you don't want anonymous FTP users doing. For example, you want to make sure anonymous FTP users can't overwrite files they shouldn't.

Your best source of information when debugging problems with FTP is your host's *syslog* output. With logging turned on, *ftpd* emits lots of useful information via *syslog*. First, find the file your *ftpd* is logging to by checking *syslog.conf*. Vanilla *ftpd*s usually log using the *daemon* facility, so if your *daemon* output gets logged anyplace special, look there.* If you examine the *syslog* output assiduously when you have a problem, you may well find that *ftpd* has diagnosed its own problem for you. Before testing your archive, make sure you have logging turned on. Look for the *–l* option in *inetd.conf*:

```
% grep ftp /etc/inetd.conf
ftp          stream tcp nowait root /etc/ftpd     ftpd -l
tftp         dgram  udp wait   root /etc/tftpd    tftpd
```

The final field in the entry under `ftp` should show *ftpd* being started with the *–l* option (plus any other command-line options you want). If *–l* doesn't appear, add it and send *inetd* the hangup signal (with **`kill -HUP`**) to get *inetd* to reread *inetd.conf*.

Once you've gotten logging turned on, use your favorite FTP client to connect to your archive. Note that you don't have to connect from another host to do basic testing: **`ftp 0`** or **`ftp localhost`** should be adequate to make sure your configuration's okay. Be sure to check from a remote host before you're finished, to make sure remote hosts can connect. But *ftp*ing from the local host still exercises the FTP daemon and checks permissions.

While you're connecting to your archive, watch the *syslog* file with *tail –f* or your preferred file monitoring utility. In the following sections, we'll go over what you should see at each point in the connection process and during use of the archive, and we'll describe the error messages you'd see for common configuration mistakes.

---

* If you're testing or debugging the WU Archive *ftpd*, note that it may also log using the *local5* or *local7* facility by default. Check the *config* file in the *src/config* directory that you used when you built *ftpd* for the correct facility. The line will look like one of the following:

```
#define FACILITY LOG_LOCAL5
#define FACILITY LOG_LOCAL7
#define FACILITY LOG_DAEMON
```

4.4.1 Connecting to the Archive

The first command you'll execute is the one that starts the FTP client and connects it to the archive host. We'll use the plain vanilla UNIX FTP client, *ftp*:

```
% ftp 0        -use ftp to connect to the local host
```

If you've set everything up correctly, you should see a banner like this:

```
Connected to 0.
220 ohbear.home.hp.com FTP server (Version 1.7.109.2 Tue Jul 28 ▶▶▶
▶▶▶23:46:52 GMT 1992) ready.
Name (0:user):
```

and messages like this in your *syslog* output:

```
Aug 14 16:47:01 ohbear inetd[242]: ftp/tcp: Connection from ohbear ▶▶▶
▶▶▶(15.5.0.1) at Sat Aug 14 16:47:01 1993
Aug 14 16:47:01 ohbear ftpd[242]: connection from ohbear at Sat Aug ▶▶▶
▶▶▶14 16:47:01 1993
```

The first message was emitted by *inetd*: it's recording a connection from the host *ohbear* to the local host's FTP port. As configured in *inetd.conf*, *inetd* then started *ftpd*, which logged a similar connection message.

If FTP weren't configured to run on the host, we might have seen an error message like this after we typed our *ftp* command:

```
% ftp 0
ftp: connect: Connection refused
ftp>
```

Our connection to the FTP port on the host has been refused, because there's nothing listening on that port for connections. If you see a message like this, and you believe you've set up FTP correctly under *inetd*, kill *inetd* (assuming it won't disturb any users) and restart *inetd –l*. See what shows up in the *syslog* output. Many vendors' *inetd*s announce what services they're configured to run when they start up:

```
Aug 14 16:55:38 ohbear inetd[269]: Reading configuration
Aug 14 16:55:38 ohbear inetd[269]: ftp/tcp: Added service, server /etc/ftpd
Aug 14 16:55:38 ohbear inetd[269]: telnet/tcp: Added service, server /etc/telnetd
Aug 14 16:55:38 ohbear inetd[269]: tftp/udp: Added service, server /etc/tftpd
more of the same...
Aug 14 16:55:38 ohbear inetd[269]: discard/tcp: Added service, server internal
Aug 14 16:55:38 ohbear inetd[269]: discard/udp: Added service, server internal
Aug 14 16:55:38 ohbear inetd[269]: chargen/tcp: Added service, server internal
Aug 14 16:55:38 ohbear inetd[269]: chargen/udp: Added service, server internal
Aug 14 16:55:39 ohbear inetd[269]: Configuration complete
```

Make sure the pathname to the server is correct: if it's not, *inetd* won't be able to start it. Look for errors like:

```
Aug 14 16:59:14 ohbear inetd[273]: ftp/tcp: Unknown service
```

This means that *inetd* was unable to map the service name `ftp` to a port number to listen on. Check that the entry:

```
ftp    tcp/21
```

is in your */etc/services* file or, if you use NIS, is in your services map:

```
% ypmatch ftp services
ftp    tcp/21
```

If you can connect successfully, try logging in as the anonymous user:

```
Name (0:user): ftp            -ftp is synonymous for anonymous
```

If the *ftp* user has been set up correctly, you'll see a message like this:

```
331 Guest login ok, send ident as password.
Password:
```

If there's no *ftp* user, you'll see a cranky error message like this one:

```
530 Guest login not permitted.
Login failed.
Remote system type is UNIX.
Using binary mode to transfer files.
ftp>
```

Don't be fooled: although it looks like you're connected to the archive, you're not. Here's what you'd get if you tried to list the directory:

```
ftp> ls
200 PORT command successful.
530 Please login with USER and PASS.
ftp>
```

Recheck the */etc/passwd* entry for the *ftp* user if you see these messages.

If specifying the anonymous user works, type in your email address as the password and move on:

```
Password:                          -type your email address here
230 Guest login ok, access restrictions apply.
Remote system type is UNIX.
Using binary mode to transfer files.
ftp>
```

Make sure the password you typed was logged correctly in *syslog*:

```
Aug 14 17:11:43 ohbear ftpd[301]: ANONYMOUS FTP LOGIN FROM ohbear, cricket@hp.com
```

Make sure you don't type any of your real passwords at the password prompt: they'll end up in the *syslog* output!

4.4.2 Using the Archive

That's about all you'll get out of *syslog*: permission problems won't show up there, so you'll have to use the FTP daemon's error messages from now on.

List the top-level anonymous FTP directory. It should show you all of the subdirectories you laboriously created:

```
ftp> ls
200 PORT command successful.
150 Opening ASCII mode data connection for /bin/ls.
total 16
d--x--x--x   2 root     other        1024 Mar  3  1992 bin
drwx------   2 crypto   users          24 Aug 14 12:27 crypt
dr-xr-xr-x   2 root     other        1024 Jun 12 12:58 dist
d--x--x--x   2 root     other        1024 Mar  3  1992 etc
d-wx-wx-wx   2 root     other          24 Jun 12 12:57 incoming
dr-xr-xr-x   2 root     other        1024 Aug 14 12:34 pub
226 Transfer complete.
ftp>
```

If you see different output, make sure the permissions on the directory are set correctly. The directory should be owned by *root* and should be readable and executable (searchable) by *ftp*. If the directory isn't readable, you'll see an error like the following when you try to list it:

```
ftp> ls
200 PORT command successful.
150 Opening ASCII mode data connection for /bin/ls.
. unreadable
total 2
226 Transfer complete.
ftp>
```

If the directory isn't searchable, you'll see an error message like this:

```
ftp> ls
200 PORT command successful.
150 Opening ASCII mode data connection for /bin/ls.
. not found
226 Transfer complete.
ftp>
```

If listing the directory works, try to *cd* to the subdirectories. Make sure that the *pub* and *dist* subdirectories are listable by anonymous users:

```
ftp> cd pub
250 CWD command successful.
ftp> ls
200 PORT command successful.
150 Opening ASCII mode data connection for /bin/ls.
total 2
-r--r--r-- ftp      other        149 Jun 12 13:01 file
226 Transfer complete.
ftp> cd ../dist
```

```
250 CWD command successful.
ftp> ls
200 PORT command successful.
150 Opening ASCII mode data connection for /bin/ls.
total 2
-r--r--r--   1 ftp      other        99 Jun 12 12:58 otherfile
226 Transfer complete.
ftp>
```

If you can't list the directory, check that the *ftp* user has execute permission for the directory. If you see a `. unreadable` message, check that the *ftp* user has read permission.

Finally, try downloading a file or two. A successful transfer looks like this:

```
ftp> get otherfile /tmp/foo
200 PORT command successful.
150 Opening BINARY mode data connection for otherfile (99 bytes).
226 Transfer complete.
99 bytes received in 0.09 seconds (1.04 Kbytes/s)
ftp>
```

If the file isn't readable, you'll see the error:

```
ftp> get otherfile /tmp/foo
200 PORT command successful.
550 otherfile: Permission denied.
ftp>
```

If you've followed our advice, you'll need to *cd* to the *incoming* subdirectory to upload files. Try transferring one, then try to list the directory:

```
ftp> put /tmp/foo foo
200 PORT command successful.
150 Opening BINARY mode data connection for foo.
226 Transfer complete.
99 bytes sent in 0.00 seconds (34.28 Kbytes/s)
ftp> ls
200 PORT command successful.
150 Opening ASCII mode data connection for /bin/ls.
. unreadable
total 2
226 Transfer complete.
ftp>
```

If you can't *cd* to the subdirectory, make sure you have execute permission set for user *ftp*. If you can't upload to it, make sure you have write permission set. If you can't list it, good. You don't want to let people list it (see our rationale in Section 4.3.5). If you can list the *incoming* subdirectory, turn the read permissions off.

If your archive passes all of these tests, you're ready to let the rest of the world use it.

5

In this Chapter:
- *Compiling the WU Archive ftpd*
- *New ftpd Command-Line Options*
- *The ftpconversions File*
- *The ftpaccess File*
- *The ftphosts File*
- *Utility Programs*
- *For More Information*

The WU Archive FTP Daemon

If you'd like a commercial-grade (but free) FTP daemon to run on your archive, consider the Washington University (in St. Louis) version of *ftpd*. WU's *ftpd* has lots of nice features that make it more suitable for a heavy-use, uptime-critical situation. It's the version of *ftpd* used on *wuarchive.wustl.edu*, a major Internet FTP archive.

The WU Archive FTP daemon has a lot of additional functionality beyond that of the standard FTP that is either critical or very useful for large FTP archives:

- The server allows archive administrators to specify classes of archive users based on the account they access and the host they access the archive from. The administrator can limit the number of users within a particular class that may access the archive simultaneously. This limit can vary based on the time of day or the day of the week.
- Based on the assigned classes, the administrator can control access to certain archive functions. For example, the administrator can prevent anonymous users from deleting files or overwriting existing files.
- The server can automatically *uncompress*, *compress*, and *tar* files as it transfers them.
- The server can log uploads, downloads, or even every command sent to it by FTP clients. It also keeps track of the number of accesses by user class.
- The server lets you gracefully shut down your archive, by first disallowing any new users and warning current users of an impending shutdown, then by booting remaining users off the archive if they haven't disconnected.

The authors of the WU Archive FTP daemon have added a number of configuration files (and even a few new executables) to those present in the standard FTP daemon to handle this new functionality. It's important to understand which files control which aspects of the FTP daemon's configuration:

ftpaccess
: Defines user classes based on the account they access and the host from which they *ftp*. It also lets you deny access to particular classes of users or limit them to a certain number of connections during specific parts of the week. It contains most of the fine-grained access controls for classes and types of users: who gets to create subdirectories, where files can be uploaded, etc.

ftpconversions
: Determines how the automatic file conversions are done. The default *ftpconversions* file includes specifications of how to do on-the-fly *compress*ing, *uncompress*ing, and *tar*ing. Administrators can add entries to do custom automatic processing, like *gzip*ping and *gunzip*ping, to the *ftpconversions* file.

ftphosts
: Gives the administrator coarser control over remote access to the archive. The administrator can deny access to certain accounts to users from hosts listed in the *ftphosts* file, or can specify that only users on particular hosts may access a given account.

5.1 Compiling the WU Archive ftpd

Before you set any of this up, though, you need to build the WU Archive *ftpd* for your particular flavor of UNIX. You can get the source code from *wuarchive.wustl.edu* as */packages/wuarchive-ftpd/wu-ftpd-2.4.tar.Z.* Version 2.4 is the most recent as of this writing. If there's a newer version there that's not beta code, you might want to get it instead. Also, beware of version 2.2—because of a break-in on *wuarchive.wustl.edu*, some 2.2s had a Trojan horse in them. Get something newer.) Once you've *uncompress*ed and un*tar*ed the package, read the *NOTES* file, which contains advice about what to do and what not to do with the server. We'll cover most of it in the remainder of this chapter, but the server is a moving target, so it's best to read the file to get the most up-to-date information.

To build the server, follow the instructions in the *INSTALL* file, which tell you how to edit the *pathnames.h* file in the *src* subdirectory to fit in with your filesystem's layout. *pathnames.h* contains default values—if those look good for your host, leave them as-is.

The following is a long list of pathnames that need to be set. You don't need to read this in detail. We suggest you just scan for the defaults (in italics) and then read items that have defaults that don't seem to fit your file system:

_PATH_FTPUSERS This should be set to the full pathname of the *ftpusers* file, which lists those users who are not allowed to access FTP. The default path is */etc/ftpusers.*

_PATH_FTPACCESS This should be set to the full pathname of the *ftpaccess* file, which controls all special configurations of the WU Archive *ftpd*, including user classes. The default path is */usr/local/etc/ftpaccess.*

_PATH_EXECPATH This should be set to the pathname of the *directory* that will contain binaries that *ftpd* uses to list directories or handle on-the-fly conversions. The pathname is interpreted relative to the root of the anonymous FTP filesystem; that is, the pathname is interpreted after *ftpd* has `chroot()`ed to the *ftp* user's login directory. The default path is */bin/ftp-exec.*

_PATH_PIDNAMES This should be set to a pattern that generates the full pathnames of the PID files, files that store the process IDs of the *ftpd*s that are running. Since there is one PID file per user class, *ftpd* replaces occurrences of *%s* in the filename with the name of the class to generate a unique pathname.

The default path is */usr/local/daemon/ftpd/ftp.pids-%s.*

_PATH_CVT This should be set to the full pathname of the *ftpconversions* file, which specifies which commands the server should use to perform automatic compression, uncompression, etc. The default path is */usr/local/etc/ftpconversions.*

_PATH_XFERLOG This should be set to the full pathname of the file that will contain all logged transfer information. The default path is */usr/adm/xferlog.*

_PATH_PRIVATE This should be set to the full pathname of the group password file that *ftpd* will use. This will allow anonymous FTP users to change group membership. The default path is */etc/ftpgroups.*

_PATH_UTMP This should be set to the full pathname of the *utmp* file on your host. The default path is */etc/utmp.* If you're not sure where yours is, try executing **man utmp** (or **find utmp** on a Sun).

_PATH_WTMP This should be set to the full pathname of the *wtmp* file on your host. The default path is */etc/wtmp.* If you're not sure where yours is, try executing **man wtmp** (or **find wtmp** on a Sun).

_PATH_LASTLOG This should be set to the full pathname of the log file that the *last* command maintains on your host. The default path name is */usr/adm/lastlog.*

_PATH_BSHELL This should be set to the full pathname of the Bourne shell executable on your host. The default path is */bin/sh*.

_PATH_DEVNULL This should be set to the full pathname of the device file */dev/null* on your host. It's almost certainly just that, */dev/null*, which is also the default path.

Once you're satisfied with the pathname settings, you can build *ftpd*. WU thoughtfully includes a *build* script, which automates much of the build process. You simply need to execute **build** *platform*, where platform is one of the three-letter abbreviations for operating systems that *build* recognizes. Some of the most popular are:

- aix, for IBM's AIX
- bsd, for BSDI's BSD/386 or other pure BSD OSes, like 386BSD and 4.3BSD
- hpx, for HP's HP-UX
- sol, for Sun's Solaris 2.*x*
- s41, for Sun's SunOS 4.1.*x*
- ult, for DEC's Ultrix

If your operating system isn't in the list, you'll have to create an appropriate *config* file for it. Execute the following commands:

```
% cp src/config/config.gen src/config/config.platform
% cp src/makefiles/Makefile.gen src/makefiles/Makefile.platform
% cp support/makefiles/Makefile.gen support/makefiles/Makefile.platform
```

Now edit each of the target files to reflect the features of your operating system. The *config.platform* file will probably require the most work. It needs to reflect the support your platform has for various system and library calls. Try running *man* on the name of the system or library call in question to find out whether your system supports it, or *grep* for the names of the system and library calls in your include files if you're desperate.

The *Makefiles* may work pretty much as-is or with just a few defines set. Note that you'll need an ANSI C compiler like Sun's *acc* or the GNU compiler, *gcc*, to compile the WU Archive *ftpd*. You may also be able to get away with using an ANSI-to-K&R C* converter like *unprotoize*, available as part of the *gcc* package via anonymous FTP from *prep.ai.mit.edu* in */pub/gnu*, or *unproto*, available via anonymous FTP from *ftp.win.tue.nl* as */pub/unix/unproto5.shar*. If the build completes without any errors, type **build install** to install the server, a few other utility programs, and the man pages on your system.

* "K&R" C is the original version of C, developed by Brian Kernighan and Dennis Ritchie at AT&T.

5.2 New *ftpd* Command-Line Options

The WU Archive FTP daemon understands a few command-line options the stock *ftpd* doesn't. It groks the *–l*, *–t*, and *–T* options, like the stock *ftpd*, and also the following:

–d Sends debugging information to *syslog*.

–a Enables the use of the *ftpaccess* file. (This is the default.)

–A Disables the use of the *ftpaccess* file.

–L Causes *ftpd* to log all *USER* commands, which are used to specify or change username. (Note that if your users accidentally get out of sync and type their passwords where they should be typing their usernames, those passwords will end up in the *syslog* file.)

–i Causes *ftpd* to log all incoming (uploaded) files in the *xferlog* file (whose path was specified in *pathnames.h*).

–o Causes *ftpd* to log all outgoing (downloaded) files in the *xferlog* file.

5.3 The *ftpconversions* File

The WU Archive FTP daemon supports automatic processing of files according to common filename suffixes. For example, if the user lists a directory and finds a compressed file, but is using a DOS-based FTP client and doesn't have a DOS-based version of *uncompress* handy, she can have *ftpd uncompress* the file before transferring it:

```
ftp> ls
200 PORT command successful.
150 Opening ASCII mode data connection for /bin/ls.
total 4
-r--r--r--   1 ftp      other        99 Jun 12 12:58 .message
-rw-r--r--   1 root     sys         190 Aug 17 21:27 pullme.Z
-rw-r--r--   1 root     sys        2001 Aug 17 21:30 bigpullme
226 Transfer complete.
ftp> get pullme   --request the uncompressed file (no .Z suffix)
200 PORT command successful.
150 Opening BINARY mode data connection for /bin/compress.
226 Transfer complete.
ftp>
```

She now has an uncompressed copy of *pullme*. This doesn't save any network bandwidth, since *ftpd* uncompressed the file before sending it to the *ftp* client, but it *does* save the user the headache of trying to deal with a UNIX *compress*ed file on a different platform.

Conversely, if the user does have *uncompress* and wants a big file that isn't compressed on the FTP archive, she can compress the file as she downloads it:

```
ftp> get bigpullme.Z
200 PORT command successful.
150 Opening BINARY mode data connection for /bin/compress.
226 Transfer complete.
ftp>
```

The *bigpullme* file was compressed before it was sent, saving bandwidth and disk space on the client's end.

The *ftpconversions* file controls which file suffixes trigger which commands. Here's an excerpt from the file:

```
:.Z:  :  :/bin/compress -d -c %s:T_REG|T_ASCII:O_UNCOMPRESS:UNCOMPRESS
:  :  :.Z:/bin/compress -c %s:T_REG:O_COMPRESS:COMPRESS
```

The first field, which is blank in this case (it precedes the first colon), is a prefix to scan for at the beginning of a filename and strip off in conversions. The second field is a suffix to scan for at the end of a filename and strip off. The third and fourth fields, respectively, are prefixes and suffixes to add on to files that have been converted. (Actually, the prefix code doesn't work yet, but the suffix code does.)

The fifth field contains the command to run to process the file. The command is expected to write to standard output. `%s` is replaced in the command line with the name of the file being transferred. Also, the command's path is interpreted relative to the `chroot()`ed directory; if you specify */bin/compress*, that becomes *~ftp/bin/compress* for anonymous users and just plain */bin/compress* for regular users. Be sure the necessary binaries exist in both places, or use hard links if the directories are on the same filesystem, or symbolically link */usr/bin/compress* (i.e., your normal copy of compress) to *~ftp/bin/compress* (not the opposite—that won't work in a `chroot()`ed environment).

The sixth field describes the types of filesystem objects that the command works on. Possible values are:

`T_REG` For regular files

`T_DIR` For directories

`T_ASCII` For ASCII (text) files

The next-to-last field is the OPTIONS field, which is used in conjunction with the *compress* and *tar* commands in the *ftpaccess* file (see Section 5.4 for details) to determine whether or not a user has access to on-the-fly (un)compression and *tar*ing. The entries in *ftpaccess* for the *tar* and *compress* commands either allow or deny classes of users access to facilities that (un)compress or archive files. The options field tells the FTP daemon which family of operations a given conversion falls into, and hence which *ftpaccess* commands apply to it. For example, the GNU *gzip* command compresses files, albeit using a different algorithm than *compress*. Using *O_COMPRESS* in the

OPTIONS field describing *gzip* conversions places these in the same family as *compress*. Users denied access to *compress* with the *compress no* command are also denied access to on-the-fly *gzip*ping. Note that you can also use "|" (the logical OR operator) to indicate that a given conversion belongs to both the *tar* and *compress* families (e.g., *O_TAR* | *O_COMPRESS*).

The last field is used in error messages. For example, the daemon logs a "Cannot %s directories" message if the conversion is tried on an unsupported filesystem object, where %s is replaced by the text in the last field.

So this means that the first entry in our excerpt from *ftpconversions* instructs the FTP daemon to run */bin/compress –d** on a file to convert it from a *.Z* filename extension to no filename extension. The FTP daemon notices the discrepancy between the filename you're asking for and the filename that exists and *uncompresses* it before sending it to you. The second entry does just the opposite. It instructs the FTP daemon to run *compress –c* on a file when users add the *.Z* suffix to the file they want transferred. When users *get textfile.Z*, and only *textfile* exists, *textfile* is compressed before it's sent to the FTP client.

Adding a new entry is straightforward if there's a standard filename extension for the type of file you want to handle. Say you want to add an entry to automatically *gzip* and *gunzip* files.† Files compressed with *gzip* typically use the extension *.gz*. Entries to handle *gzip*ing and *gunzip*ing files might look like this:

```
: :  :.gz:/bin/gzip -c %s:T_REG|T_ASCII:O_COMPRESS:GZIP
:.gz: :  :/bin/gunzip -c %s:T_REG:O_UNCOMPRESS:GZIP
```

5.4 The *ftpaccess* File

Most of the custom configuration for the WU Archive FTP daemon is done in the *ftpaccess* file. *ftpaccess* defines classes of users and their access to the archive, controls which messages are displayed to users and when they are displayed, and controls various and sundry other intricacies of *ftpd*'s behavior.

5.4.1 Defining Classes of Users

The WU Archive FTP daemon allows administrators to define classes of users on the basis of the IP address or domain name of the host they're *ftp*ing from and the type of user account they're trying to access. The administrator can then restrict access to the

* *compress –d* is the same as *uncompress*. The *–c* option tells *compress* to write the compressed file to standard output, rather than overwriting the file it's compressing.

† *gzip* and *gunzip* are the GNUish siblings of the UNIX *compress* and *uncompress* utilities. They typically compress and uncompress files more efficiently (get better compression ratios) than *compress* and *uncompress* do. You can get copies from most major FTP archives, including the GNU archive, *prep.ai.mit.edu* (*gzip* is in */pub/gnu*).

archive or to certain capabilities on a class-by-class basis. There are three types of users, as *ftpd* sees it:

real
: Real users are those who access regular accounts on the FTP archive. These users, unless otherwise restricted, could just as easily *telnet* or *rlogin* to the machine and log in. Real user accounts aren't `chroot()`ed to a particular part of the archive's filesystem.

anonymous
: Anonymous users are any users accessing the FTP archive via the *anonymous* or *ftp* user. Their access to the archive is restricted by `chroot()`ing to a particular subtree of the overall filesystem.

guest
: Guest users are users who have unique identities and provide passwords, but are also limited to a particular part of the filesystem via `chroot()`. For more information on guest users, see Section 5.4.4.

To define a class based on IP addresses or domain names and categories of users (real, anonymous and guest, as defined above), use the *class* command in *ftpaccess*:

```
class classname type [,type...] address [address...]
```

The *classname* is a name you specify to identify the class of users, like *local* or *remote*, *authorized* or *suspicious*. The *type* field identifies the types of users (real, anonymous, or guest) associated with the class when they access the archive from an address matching the address specification. The address specification can be an IP address or a domain name and can include wildcards.

For example, the class definitions in the next example define three classes of users: local users, who use real accounts to access the archive; guest users, who access the archive via unique accounts from one of three domains; and anonymous users, who use anonymous FTP.

```
class local real *.ora.com
class guests guest *.hp.com *.bsdi.com *.xor.com
class anonymouses anonymous *
```

If an archive user matches more than one class, based on his source address and the type of user he specifies, he'll match the first class listed in *ftpaccess*. If an archive user doesn't match any class, he's denied access to the archive. That makes it important to set up your classes in such a way that you don't deny access to anyone you don't mean to shut out. The classes above, for example, deny *guest* users access from domains other than *hp.com*, *bsdi.com*, and *xor.com*, which may not be a bad thing. But they also deny real users access from outside of *ora.com*, which could be a nuisance.

5.4.2 Denying Access

Besides implicitly disallowing access to classes of users by not including them in *ftpaccess*, there are other ways of keeping certain people out. With the *deny* command, you can outright deny FTP access to people coming from certain IP addresses or domain names. In fact, you can even deny them access if their IP address doesn't map back to a legitimate domain name. Sound like any archives you know? (*ftp.uu.net*, one of the largest FTP archives in the free world, does this.)

deny also lets you display a message to the unlucky user explaining why you're denying him access. This is a good idea, since without an explanation, the user might report his lack of access to you as a problem.

To deny all users from Stanford hosts access to your archive, you could add the following line to *ftpaccess*:

```
deny     *.stanford.edu    /etc/ftpmsgs/msg.denied
```

When users on *stanford.edu* hosts try to log in, they are presented with the message in */etc/ftpmsgs/msg.denied*. Since the *deny* command is read before the server `chroot()`s, the pathname to the file is the same, regardless of the user. However, remember that for other *ftpaccess* commands, the path to the file containing the message may be interpreted differently depending on whether the user is accessing an anonymous or guest account (which is `chroot()`ed) or a real account (which isn't). You may have to copy or link the file containing the message to more than one place.

To disallow access from hosts that don't have a valid IP address-to-name mapping in the Domain Name System, use *!nameserved* in place of the domain name or address (replacing **.stanford.edu*). It's a good idea to create a custom message for these incidents, explaining a little about name service problems and how to deal with them. Something like this might suffice:

```
Sorry, you've been denied access to our archive because your IP address
doesn't map back to a legitimate domain name. Please ask your local
hostmaster (the person who runs your name servers) to fix this and try again.

See the O'Reilly & Associates Nutshell Handbook _DNS and BIND_ for details.

The Management
```

(Okay, that's a shameless plug—I coauthored that book.) One final note: *deny* doesn't seem to like more than one address or domain name per line, nor does it like it if you mix *!nameserved* with a domain name. If you want to deny access from multiple IP addresses or domain names, use separate *deny* commands.

5.4.3 Limiting Access

Unless you're running a multi-processor monster as your FTP archive server, there may be a time when you'd like to limit the number of anonymous FTP logins available. Every new connection requires a new *ftpd* process, after all. A hundred processes here, a hundred processes there, and pretty soon we're talking about real CPU load.

You can limit the number of users of a particular class who can access your archive at any one time using the *limit* command. *limit* even lets you specify which times of the week these limits apply. The format of the command is:

```
limit class number times message
```

The command

```
limit anonymouses 100 Any /etc/ftpmsgs/msg.toomany
```

limits anonymous users (users in class *anonymouses*) to 100 simultaneous connections at any time throughout the week. If you want to allow more connections on weekends, when your host isn't as busy doing other work, you can specify another limit:

```
limit anonymouses 200 SaSu
limit anonymouses 100 Any /etc/ftpmsgs/msg.toomany
```

The first matching *limit* command applies, so your archive would allow 200 connections on Saturday or Sunday, and 100 the rest of the week.

The format of the `times` field is the same as the format of the times in UUCP's *L.sys* or *Systems* file. The days of the week are represented as the first two letters of the day (*Su*, *Mo*, etc.), with *Any* representing the whole week. Time of day must be specified using military (24-hour) time. For example, `Sa900-1700` means Saturday, from 9 a.m. to 5 p.m. Multiple time specifications can be combined using the `|` (logical OR) operator: `Sa900-1700|Su1100-1500`.

As with *deny*, *limit* is read by *ftpd* before the server `chroot()`s, so you don't need multiple copies of the message file.

You may also want to limit the number of failed login attempts a user is allowed. Use the *loginfails* command in *ftpaccess* to do this; it takes a single argument: the number of failed login attempts allowed per user before the FTP daemon boots them off the archive by closing the connection. For example,

```
loginfails 2
```

limits users to two failed login attempts, down from the default of five.

The WU Archive FTP daemon even lets you restrict the use of on-the-fly conversions and certain commands by class or type of user. Use the *compress* and *tar* commands in *ftpaccess* to allow or disallow particular classes of users to *compress* and *uncompress* or *tar* files, respectively. Each command takes two arguments. The first is *yes* or *no*, which specifies whether you're allowing or denying access to the facility for the class of users, and the second is the class of user. So:

```
tar      no   anonymouses
compress no   anonymouses
```

disallows the use of automatic *tar*ing and *compress*ing by anonymous users.

The *chmod, delete, overwrite, rename,* and *umask* commands work very similarly to *tar* and *compress*: they determine whether particular users may change file modes, delete files, overwrite files, rename files, or change their umask, respectively. However, they operate on *types* of user (i.e., *real, guest,* and *anonymous*) rather than classes. The default is to allow all types of user to *chmod, delete,* etc., to their hearts desire (assuming, of course, that the relevant file permissions allow it). The command syntax is exactly the same as the syntax for *tar* and *compress*:

```
chmod     yes|no    type [type ...]
delete    yes|no    type [type ...]
overwrite yes|no    type [type ...]
rename    yes|no    type [type ...]
umask     yes|no    type [type ...]
```

Finally, you can even determine what kind of response anonymous FTP users can give at the password prompt. Most FTP daemons accept just about anything from an anonymous user and gratefully log it. The WU Archive FTP daemon demands that anonymous users' passwords adhere to at least some level of plausibility.

The *passwd-check* command lets you specify the level of checking, as well as what to do should the user's password fail the check:

```
passwd-check  none|trivial|rfc822  enforce|warn
```

passwd-check none gives you no password checking at all. *trivial* checks to see that the password at least contains an *@*. *rfc822* checks that the password is actually an RFC 822-compliant address (has a local part and a domain part, maybe an *!* or a *%* to spice it up). *enforce* actually boots the user off the archive if she specifies an unacceptable password, while *warn* simply gives her a stern message about her obligation as an archive user:

```
230-The response 'cricket' is not valid
230-Next time please use your email address as your password
230-        for example: joe@ohbear
```

One last note on passwords: some FTP clients truncate the password you type to eight characters, often resulting in passwords the FTP daemon complains about. Using the shorthand `user@` instead of your full email address usually works with these clients, since the daemon automatically appends the domain name of the host you're *ftp*ing from to the *@*.

5.4.4 Group Controls

Group membership can be used to give particular users greater access than anonymous users, but less than real users. Certain groups can be designated "guest" groups; users in those groups have their access limited to a `chroot()`ed portion of the filesystem, possibly a different portion than an anonymous user would see. Other groups may have access to the anonymous FTP filesystem, but users in those groups can gain greater access, because you configure *ftpaccess* to set their effective group ID to something besides the default once they have logged in as anonymous users.

To set up the first type of group—a group of guest users—create an entry in */etc/group*, the system's group file. We'll set up a group called guests:

```
guests:*:21:guest1,guest2,guest3
```

Then we create entries in */etc/passwd* for the guest users. These have the same format as other entries, but the login directory field is interpreted in a special way by *ftpd*. The login directory field is actually two pathnames, separated by `/./` (slash-dot-slash). The first pathname is the directory the guest user will be `chroot()`ed to, and the second is the pathname (relative to the `chroot()`ed directory) of the guest user's login directory. So the entry:

```
guest1:PCdGtGGP1Im4Y:202:21:Guest FTP user:/users/guests/./guest1:/bin/false
```

changes *guest1*'s view of the filesystem so that */users/guests* appears to be the root and logs her in to the new root's *guest1* subdirectory.

Finally, we have to configure *ftpd* to know which groups correspond to guest users. *ftpaccess*'s *guestgroup* command does that: it names one or more groups whose members are guest users:

```
guestgroup guests
```

Guest user access is particularly useful in situations where you'd like to make files available to a particular person or group of people, but don't want the whole world retrieving them. They're actually a lot like the sublogin feature of the standard FTP daemon, but better, since they allow you to keep the `chroot()`ed environments of these users completely separate.

To give certain classes of anonymous users special access, you can use the *autogroup* command. *autogroup* lets you set the effective group ID of anonymous users who belong to one or more of the classes you defined. For example, maybe you've defined a class of anonymous users coming from hosts within your company:

```
class   corp-anon   anonymous   *.hp.com
```

You'd like to grant these users access to a few subdirectories under your *~ftp* directory that you don't let garden-variety anonymous users see. To do that, you can create a new group for them (in */etc/group*):

```
hp::22:
```

Then you can instruct *ftpd* to put anonymous users who are part of the class *corp-anon* into the group *hp*. The syntax is simple:

```
autogroup   groupname class [class ...]
```

For *corp-anon*, that looks like:

```
autogroup   hp   corp-anon
```

Now make the directories readable by group *hp* (and not the *ftp* user or the *ftp* user's login group) and you're in business.

The last bit of group trickery that *ftpd* allows is the *site group* and *site gpass* commands. These are commands an FTP user can issue to change his effective group ID and possibly gain additional privileges. To enable this, you must set the *private* option to *yes* in *ftpaccess*:

```
private yes
```

This instructs the FTP daemon to allow *site group* and *site gpass* commands from FTP clients.

To set up additional group memberships, create the *ftpgroups* file in the directory you specified when you built *ftpd* (probably */etc*). Entries in this file contain the name of the group that FTP users will specify, an encrypted password for that group, and then the real group the FTP group maps to (i.e., the group name that appears in */etc/group*). If you use a group name that is not already in */etc/group*, you'll have to add it. You can use a * in the password field in */etc/group*, though: *ftpd* reads *ftpgroup* for the encrypted password.

For example, this entry in *ftpgroups* maps the FTP group field to the real system group hp-field, and sets the encrypted password:

```
field:rtQzw06RkUoOA:hp-field
```

Here's how a user actually sends the *site group* and *site gpass* commands that authenticate her as a member of the field group (assuming she's already logged in as *anonymous*):

```
ftp> site group field
200 Request for access to group field accepted.
ftp> site gpass password
200 Group access enabled.
```

Note that the password is echoed, so the user should be warned to make sure that no one's looking over her shoulder as she types! If she's using the X Window System, she can also use *xterm*'s Secure Keyboard mode to help ensure that her password isn't compromised.

5.4.5 Printing Information

In addition to providing the handy access control mechanisms, the WU Archive FTP daemon gives you the ability to keep users informed of where they are in the archive, what they should look at, and what's going on. The FTP daemon supports a powerful message facility that lets the administrator display important information to archive users.

The four commands you can use are *banner*, *message*, *readme*, and *shutdown*. *banner* is for displaying a file to the user at login. *message* displays a file when the user changes to a particular directory. *readme* lets you tell the user when a particular file has changed. *shutdown* lets you warn users that you are about to shut down the FTP server

5.4.5.1 The banner command

The *banner* command specifies the pathname of a file that is displayed to every archive user *before* the user logs in. This can be used to let people know what archive they're accessing, what the rules are, who to contact for problems, and so on. You can include macros in the file; the macros are replaced with current information before the file is displayed. The following macros are supported by both the banner and message commands:

%C Replaced by the name of the current working directory

%E Replaced by the email address of the archive maintainer. You set this in *ftpaccess* with *ftpaccess*'s *email* command, e.g., **`email ftpmanager@ora.com`**.

%F Replaced by the number of kilobytes free in the current working directory

%L Replaced by the name of the host the server is running on (i.e., the archive host). Compare this with %R, which is replaced by the name of the host that the FTP client is running on.

%M Replaced by the limit on the number of users in the current user's class

%N Replaced by the current number of users in the current user's class, including the user

%R Replaced by the name of the host the user is accessing the archive from, i.e., the client host

%T Replaced by the current local time, in the format *`Day Mon date hour:minute:second year`*, e.g., Tuesday Nov 8 10:04:23 1994

%U Replaced by the name the user specified at login

A simple banner message might look like this:

```
Welcome to the Endangered Species FTP Archive, running on %L!

Information about your login and any transfers you do are logged on this
host. If you don't like that, please disconnect now.

The Endangered Species FTP Archive is run pro bono by volunteers who are
concerned about the daily extinction of hundreds of species on our planet.

Please contact %E with any technical problems you may have accessing this
archive.

You are currently user %N out of a maximum %M users. It's %T in
Kalamazoo, MI.
```

If the banner message is in */usr/local/ftpd/msgs/banner*, you can display it with the command:

```
banner   /usr/local/ftpd/msgs/banner
```

in *ftpaccess*. Note that the pathname is relative to the system's root, not a `chroot()`ed root, so you don't have to worry about creating multiple copies.

5.4.5.2 The message command

The *message* command is a more general facility than *banner* for displaying files. *message* does all the macro substitutions that *banner* does, but also lets you specify when you want the user to see the message. You can have the message displayed at login, or when the user changes to a particular directory.

To display the message at login, use the following syntax:

```
message pathname  login
```

To display the message when the user *cd*s to a particular directory, use the syntax:

```
message pathname  cwd=dir
```

Note that *dir* can be `*`, in which case the message is displayed each time the user changes directories. You can use this to display short messages describing the contents of each directory, for example:

```
message .contents   cwd=*
```

The *.contents* file in the current working directory is displayed to a user changing to that directory.

To display the message only to users in a particular class, add the class to the end of the line, e.g.:

```
message /etc/msgs/msg.anonymous  login   anonymouses
```

You can specify multiple classes at the end of the line, separated by whitespace. However, watch out for the old `chroot()` gotcha: anonymous and guest users need another copy of the message file.

5.4.5.3 The readme command

The *readme* command lets the administrator tell the user when a particular file—especially a directory's *README* file—has changed. This warns the user that the information in the file has probably been updated. The *readme* command *does not* actually display the file; it's up to the user to do that.

The *readme* command's syntax is exactly the same as the *message* command's: you can specify when the user should be notified (using *cwd* or *login*) and which classes of user should be notified:

```
readme  pathname [login|cwd=dir]  [class] [class...]
```

As with *message*, *readme* lets you notify users of all changes to *README* files:

```
readme  README* cwd=*
```

When the user changes to a directory containing a file with a name that matches *README**, he sees a message like this:

```
ftp> cd tmp
250-Please read the file README.1ST
250-  it was last modified on Sun Oct  3 18:23:06 1993 - 0 days ago
250 CWD command successful.
```

And, as with *message*, remember that the `pathname` is relative to the anonymous FTP filesystem's root for anonymous users.

5.4.5.4 The shutdown command

The last informational facility is also partly a mechanism to control *ftpd*: it tells the daemon both when to shut down and what to tell users near the shutdown time.

The format of the command is simple:

```
shutdown pathname
```

ftpd checks periodically for the existence of `pathname`. If `pathname` exists, *ftpd* reads the information in the file that tells it when to start denying users access to the archive, when to disconnect live users, and when to shut down. *ftpd* reads the file before it calls `chroot()`, so you don't need to create any additional copies. The contents of the file are expected to be in the following format:

```
year month day hour minute deny disconnect
text of message
```

`hour` and `minute` are given in military time (`hour` is a number from 0 to 23 and `minute` from 0 to 59). `month` is in the range 0 to 11. `deny` and `disconnect` indicate how long before the shutdown time new users will be denied access and live users will be disconnected from the archive, respectively. Both are in the format HHMM, e.g., 0100 for one hour, 0015 for fifteen minutes. The message can contain any macro valid in the *message* command, plus these three particular to *shutdown*:

`%s` Replaced by the shutdown time

`%r` Replaced by the time new connections will be denied

`%d` Replaced by the time live connections will be dropped

Users who are denied access see a message like this:

```
500 ohbear.home.hp.com FTP server shut down -- please try again later.
```

Users who are on the system are warned of impending disconnection with the message you specified:

```
250-This FTP archive is coming down for maintenance at Sun Oct  3 18:25:00 1993.
250-Sessions will be denied starting at Sun Oct  3 18:23:00 1993, and all
250-sessions will be disconnected at Sun Oct  3 18:24:00 1993.
250-
250-ftpmanager@ora.com
```

The *ftpshut* command offers another way to handle shutdowns by automatically writing the *ftpshut* file. See Section 5.6.3 for a description of the *ftpshut* command.

5.4.6 Logging Information

The WU Archive FTP daemon provides logging capabilities over and above those the vanilla *ftpd* gives you. You can log individual user commands with the *log commands* command. *log commands* lets you specify a list of user types to log commands for (*real*, *guest*, or *anonymous*). The information is logged via *syslog*. If you have an active FTP archive, this naturally results in lots of information being logged. The full syntax of *log commands* is:

```
log commands type [type ...]
```

You must specify at least one type to turn command logging on.

If you turn on command logging, you'll automatically log downloads from your archive and uploads to it: they appear in the *syslog* output as `RETR` and `STOR` commands. If you want a bit more information, or you want your information in a more readable format, you can turn on transfer logging. Transfer logging, like command logging, can be done on a per-user type basis. You can also specify that you only want inbound or outbound transfers (uploads and downloads, respectively) logged.

To enable transfer logging, use the *log transfer* command:

```
log transfer type [type ...] direction [,direction]
```

where *type* is a valid user type and *direction* is either *inbound* or *outbound*. You must specify at least one direction in order to start transfer logging.

Transfer logging doesn't use *syslog*. You specified the pathname of the transfer log file way back when you built the FTP daemon—you probably don't remember, but you can check your *pathnames.h* file for the proper directory. Turning on transfer logging will log entries like this to *xferlog* (the default name of the transfer log file):

```
Mon Oct  4 20:07:24 1993 1 ohbear.home.hp.com 149 /pub/deposit ▶▶▶
▶▶▶b _ o a cricket@hp.com ftp 0 *
Mon Oct  4 20:12:58 1993 1 ohbear.home.hp.com 216 /pub/welcome.msg ▶▶▶
▶▶▶a _ o a cricket@hp.com ftp 0 *
Mon Oct  4 20:14:03 1993 23 ohbear.home.hp.com 4365 /users/cricket/xhpcalc ▶▶▶
▶▶▶b _ o r cricket ftp 0 *
```

So what is all that information? Well, some of it is pretty clear. `Mon Oct  4 20:07:24 1993` is the date and time the first transfer occurred. `ohbear.home.hp.com` is the name of the host running the *ftp* client that's accessing the archive. The next field—`149` for the first transfer—is the size of the transferred file in bytes, and the next field is the original name of the file.

The remaining fields are a little more cryptic. The field before the name of the client (`1` or `23`) is the number of seconds the transfer took. The field after the original pathname of the file (`a` or `b`) tells us whether the transfer was done in ASCII or BINARY mode.

The next field (_ in each of our log entries) tells us whether on-the-fly compression or tape archiving (*tar*ing) was used. The _ indicates that neither was used. If the file was compressed, we'll see a `C`; if it was uncompressed, we'll see a `U`. If it was *tar*ed, we'll see a `T`. If it was both compressed and *tar*ed, we'll see `CT`. Locally-defined conversions like *gzip*ping are categorized according to their entry in *ftpconversions*: if you used *O_COMPRESS* in *gzip*'s option field, on-the-fly *gzip*ping is logged with a `C`.

The field that's always `o` in our examples tells us whether the transfer was outgoing or incoming. Our transfers were all downloads: `o`utgoing. Uploads would show up as `i` for `i`ncoming.

The following field (`a` or `r` in our sample entries) logs whether the user was a real user or an anonymous user. If a user logs in as a guest user, the field is a `g`. If the user was real, the next field gives us his user name. If the user was anonymous, the following field tells us the password (presumably an email address) he used as a password. The field that's always `ftp` in our examples will probably always be `ftp` in your *xferlog*, too: it tells us the name of the service that was invoked.

The last two fields concern authentication. Two mechanisms are available for authenticating remote users: the very common but pretty-darn-insecure *none*, and RFC 931 authentication. RFC 931 authentication involves running an authentication server on the same host the user is *ftp*ing from. Not many places do this, so the FTP daemon mostly uses the *none* variety of authentication (i.e., trusting you are who you say you are). If the daemon uses *none*, the first of the two fields contains `0`, and the second, indicating the user ID of the authenticated user, contains `*`. If, perchance, the server's attempt to use RFC 931 authentication is successful, it logs a `1` in the first field and the authenticated user ID in the second.

You can use this data to compile all sorts of statistics: the top ten most-downloaded files, the total number of bytes transferred, the most active periods of the day. The *tar* package that the software comes in includes a Perl script called *xferstats*, which provides much of this functionality.

5.4.7 Easier Navigation

The WU Archive FTP daemon provides facilities to make navigating the FTP archive a little easier. The first of these is the support of simple aliasing with *ftpaccess*'s *alias* command. With *alias*, the administrator can define shorthand aliases for directories. The aliases only apply to *cd* commands issued by users. For example, if you want to give users an easy way of getting to your *source* directory, which is buried in your archive under */pub/local/sw/source*, you can define an alias for it like *source:*, as shown in this example:

```
alias     source:     /pub/local/sw/source
```

(Note that the alias ends in a colon.) Users can now type **`cd source:`** to change to the directory containing your source code. Since aliases aren't automatically visible to users, you might want to add a short note to the banner or login message describing the aliases available or telling them to execute **`quote site alias`** to see the available aliases.

You can also define a list of directories that will be searched when a user issues the *cd* command. Let's say you have a popular directory on your Network Information Center's FTP archive, */pub/netinfo*. Under */pub/netinfo* are directories containing lots of useful information: *dns*, *routing*, *email*, and so on. Unfortunately, some users have a hard time locating the information because it's so far down in the archive. If you make */pub/netinfo* part of the directory search path, they can simply *cd* to *dns*, *routing*, or *email* from anywhere in the archive.

To add a directory to the directory search path, use the *cdpath* command:

```
cdpath    /pub/netinfo
```

In case you're wondering, if you define both aliases and a directory search path, and a user tries to *cd* to *bin*, the following search algorithm is used:

1. The user's current working directory is searched for a *bin* subdirectory.
2. The aliases are checked for a *bin* alias.

3. The directories in the search path are searched, in the order they're listed in *ftpaccess*, for *bin* subdirectories.

5.4.8 Uploading Controls

The final *ftpaccess* configuration options control uploading: who can upload files, and what they can name those files. The first is the *upload* command. *upload* determines which directories anonymous users can upload files to, specifies the mode and ownership of any files uploaded to a directory, and determines whether or not anonymous users can create new subdirectories within the upload directory.

The *upload* command takes the syntax

```
upload hierarchy directory yes|no owner group mode [dirs|nodirs]
```

To disallow uploading to a particular directory, all you need is the first four fields:

```
upload /users/ftp * no
```

disallows uploads to all directories under */users/ftp* except those matched by more specific *upload* commands.

To allow uploading to a particular directory, specify *upload yes* and the hierarchy and directory names. The hierarchy name is simply the pathname to the root of the `chroot()`ed filesystem the directory is under. This lets you specify either the root of the anonymous FTP filesystem or the root of a guest user's filesystem. You can also specify the owner, group, and mode of all uploaded files. If you don't, uploaded files will have owner *ftp* and group ownership according to what group the user belonged to at the time of the upload (see the descriptions of *guestgroup* and *autogroup* in Section 5.4.4 to find out how an anonymous user can change groups). For example:

```
upload /users/ftp /incoming yes root other 0600
```

This allows uploads to the */incoming* directory (even if used with the *upload no* command above, since *incoming* is a more specific directory name than `*`). All files uploaded to */incoming* will be owned by user *root*, group *other*, and will be mode 0600. Changing the ownership of uploaded files from *ftp* and removing read and write access is a particularly good idea, since it means that after one anonymous user uploads a file, other anonymous users won't be able to download it or overwrite it. This effectively prevents evil-doers from using your archive as a staging area.

You can also add *dirs* as the last argument to specify that anonymous users should be allowed to create subdirectories under */incoming*, or *nodirs* if they should not. The default is to allow anonymous users to create subdirectories.

Administrators can also use the *path-filter* to limit the pathnames that users of particular classes can use as filename arguments when they upload. (Note that *path-filter* can apply to any class of users, while *upload* applies only to anonymous users.) For example, you might want to make sure anonymous FTP users can't upload files that begin with either `.` (period) or `-` (hyphen). *path-filter* lets you specify a regular expression that all filename arguments must match and, optionally, one or more regular expressions that all filenames *must not* match. If a filename argument doesn't match the "allowed" regular expression, or matches one or more of the disallowed regular expressions, the FTP server doesn't execute the command; instead it displays a message from the administrator.

Like the *upload* command, the *path-filter* syntax is fairly complicated:

```
path-filter types pathname allowed-regexp [disallowed-regexp ...]
```

The pathname is the name of the file that contains the message displayed to mischievous users who try to upload files with names that don't match (or do match) the allowed (or disallowed) regular expressions. The regular expressions allow most regular-expression constructs, including character classes (e.g., `[a-z]`), negated character classes (e.g., `[^0-9]`), and anchors (`^` and `$`). See the **regexp(5)** man page for details.

A good *path-filter* to use is one suggested in the WU Archive *ftpd* documentation:

```
path-filter anonymous /path/message ^[-A-Za-z0-9._]*$ ^. ^-
```

This allows anonymous uploads only to filenames consisting of alphanumeric characters plus `.`, `_`, and `-`. It also dictates that the files can't begin with either `.` or `-`.

5.5 The ftphosts File

There may be occasions when you have to deny some malicious person on a remote host access to your FTP archive. Perhaps someone's been abusing anonymous FTP from the host *ms.cree.net*. You can't very well shut down anonymous FTP for everyone by adding the *ftp* user to *ftpusers*. You *could* do some complicated work with classes, defining a special class of users consisting of all anonymous users logging in from *ms.cree.net*. Or you can use the *ftphosts* file. In any case, you are forced to cut off all users from that host, since you can't identify particular users.

ftphosts works very much like *ftpusers*, allowing you to deny users access to particular FTP accounts. However, *ftphosts* lets you specify which hosts are denied access to which accounts. For example, you can explicitly deny users on *ms.cree.net* access to anonymous FTP with the lines:

```
deny    anonymous    ms.cree.net
deny    ftp          ms.cree.net
```

Note that you currently need to deny access to both the *anonymous* and *ftp* accounts, even though *anonymous* and *ftp* are, well, synonymous. The FTP daemon sees them as different names. This minor annoyance will probably have been fixed in a new version of the WU Archive FTP daemon by the time you read this.

You can use wildcards and IP addresses in the host field to deny access to whole nets or whole domains. You can also list multiple patterns to check, separated by white-space:

```
deny    anonymous     *.cree.net 199.199.10.*
deny    ftp           *.cree.net 199.199.10.*
```

This denies anonymous FTP access to clients in the domain *cree.net* and clients on the network 199.199.10.

In addition to being less complex that specifying class definitions with *ftpusers*, *ftphosts* lets you specify individual accounts by name, whereas you have to use one of the three user types (*real*, *anonymous* and *guest*) in classes.

ftphosts also supports an *allow* command, which limits access to certain accounts to users coming from certain hosts. The brief description in the man page is a little confusing—it's easy to misinterpret it to mean that users *ftp*ing from the host specified would be forced to log in as the user named. Actually, it's almost the opposite: users *ftp*ing from the specified host (or hosts) can log in as *any* user; users from hosts that aren't listed in the *allow* command, however, can't access that account at all. For example:

```
allow    ftp          *.hp.com
allow    anonymous    *.hp.com
```

allows anonymous access from hosts in the domain *hp.com*, but from nowhere else. Be careful of the order in which you use *deny* and *allow*—the first domain name or IP address match is the one that applies to a given client, so:

```
deny     ftp     *.hp.com
allow    ftp     babs.nsr.hp.com
```

still denies *babs.nsr.hp.com* access to the *ftp* account.

5.6 Utility Programs

Three handy utility programs are included with the WU Archive FTP daemon: *ftpcount*, *ftpwho*, and *ftpshut*. We've already mentioned *ftpshut*; it gives you an easier way of shutting down the server than using *ftpaccess*'s *shutdown* command. *ftpcount* and *ftpwho* tell you who's using your archive (how many users of each class) and the resources they're using.

5.6.1 ftpcount

ftpcount simply shows you how many users of each class that you defined in *ftpaccess* are currently using your archive and the maximum number you defined for each class (with *ftpaccess*'s *limit* command). The output format is straightforward:

```
% ftpcount
Service class local                 -   2 users (  50 maximum)
Service class guest                 -   3 users (  20 maximum)
Service class corp-anon             -   1 users (  20 maximum)
Service class anonymouses           -   9 users (  10 maximum)
```

5.6.2 *ftpwho*

The *ftpwho* program is a lot like *ftpcount*, in that it tells you how many users of each class are currently using the archive and what the maximum for each class is. But *ftpwho* also gives you information about the *ftpd* process serving each user's session. You can use this, for example, to determine how much CPU time a given user is using.

The output format includes a one-line description of each *ftpd* process. The fields in the description come right out of a long *ps* listing:

```
Service class local:
  0 S     0   422     96  0 154 20 402ebd80   42 4034932c ?          0:00 ftpd
  -    1 users (  1 maximum)

Service class guest:
   -    0 users (  2 maximum)

Service class corp-anon:
  1 S     0   427     96  0 154 20 402eb940   43 40180c2c ?          0:00 ftpd
  -    1 users (  2 maximum)

Service class anonymouses:
   -    0 users (  1 maximum)
```

Since these fields vary on a system-by-system basis, check the man pages for your system's *ps* command to determine which are which.

5.6.3 *ftpshut*

ftpshut lets you warn users of impending downtime and then shut down the FTP archive. You can specify a time to shut down the FTP archive by killing all the *ftpd* processes, or you can simply specify *now*. The time can be in one of two formats: either +*n*, where *n* is the number of minutes to wait before shutdown, or *HHMM*, which specifies the absolute time to shut down the archive, in 24-hour time (e.g., *1315* for 1:15 P.M.).

By default, *ftpshut* disables new FTP connections ten minutes before shutdown, or immediately if shutdown is less than ten minutes away. Existing users get the boot five minutes before shutdown, or immediately if shutdown will occur in less than five minutes. *ftpshut* lets you specify different periods for these lead times: the *–l* option lets you specify how many minutes before shutdown new connections will be denied, and the *–d* option lets you determine how many minutes before shutdown current users will be dropped.

Finally, *ftpshut* takes an optional message to give current users as they are unceremoniously booted from the archive. The message can contain any of the macros valid in *ftpaccess*'s *shutdown* file; see the description of *shutdown* in Section 5.4.5.4 for a full list. (*ftpshut* understands all of the macros because it actually *writes* the file that the *ftpaccess shutdown* command reads. Note that you must already have a *shutdown* line in *ftpaccess* specifying where the *shutdown* file lives in order to run *ftpshut*.)

The full syntax for the *ftpshut* command is

```
ftpshut [-l min] [-d min] time [message]
```

5.7 For More Information

Bryan O'Connor, the current maintainer of the WU Archive FTP daemon, is still hard at work on the code. New versions come out periodically on *wuarchive.wustl.edu* in */packages/wuarchive-ftpd*, and Bryan updates the *CHANGES* file. There's even a mailing list to discuss the beastie: to subscribe, send an email message to *listserv@wunet.wustl.edu* with the text *SUBSCRIBE WU-FTPD*. The address you sent the mail from will be added to the list. One additional caveat: as of this writing, you could only send mail to the list from the same address you subscribed. This can be slightly annoying if you've got a number of email accounts.

In this Chapter:
- *Populating Your Archive*
- *Making Access Easier*
- *Denying and Limiting User Access*
- *Monitoring Log Files*
- *Reading Mail*

Maintaining an FTP Archive

The last two chapters have focused on how to set up and configure an FTP archive; they were targeted at a system administrator who has superuser access to the host the archive runs on. This chapter concentrates on the role of the "data librarian," the person chartered with populating the archive and making it useful to users. This is a person who understands the material being offered by the archive, who structures it so that it's easy to navigate, and who adds useful material describing what's available and what's relevant to what. It's also a person who doesn't necessarily have superuser access to the host, simply enough access to populate the *pub* subdirectory (and *dist*, if it exists) and to modify certain configuration files.

6.1 Populating Your Archive

Now that you have a working FTP archive, you need to populate it with all sorts of interesting stuff. You should take special care to make sure your archive is well-organized: disorganized FTP archives are exasperating to navigate. Whenever possible, divide your archived material into logical groups and separate those groups into directories. If your company has ten distinct products, create a separate subdirectory under *pub* or *dist* for each of them. If your organization has two major projects underway, separate them into subdirectories. For example, on the Endangered Species archive, we might have two separate directories, one for crocodiles and one for camelids:

```
/pub
    /camelids
    /crocodiles
```

If there are folks on the camelid and crocodile projects who can keep their information up-to-date better than the data librarian, the librarian can delegate each subdirectory to the appropriate maintainer simply by changing the directory's ownership (this assumes the librarian owns */pub* or asks the system administrator to change the ownership):

```
% cd ~ftp/pub
% chown lwall camelids
% chown jerry crocodiles
```

These representatives are then responsible for taking care of each subdirectory:

- Keeping the files in the directory up-to-date: removing old files and uploading and editing new ones
- Creating links to other parts of the archive (see Section 6.2.1)
- Creating subdirectories as necessary
- Maintaining a *README* file that describes what each file in the directory
- Maintaining the security of their section of the archive by ensuring that files and directories are not writable by anonymous FTP users

If you have a group of people responsible for administering the FTP archive, you (or your archive's system administrator) can create a group called *ftpadmin* or something similar and put all the administrators' user accounts in the group. Then change group ownership on the top-level directory and any subdirectories below that these administrators might need to do work in and *chmod* the directories to make them group writable. Now your entire group can add and delete files. If you want them to be able to modify files as well, you may have to change group ownership of files and make them group writable.

6.1.1 Standard Filename Extensions

To make it easier for anonymous FTP users to figure out the format of the files they're transferring, it's important to use standard filename extensions. For example, users expect PostScript files to have a *.ps* extension. Images typically have extensions like *.gif*, *.tif*, and *.jpg* for GIF, TIFF, and JPEG formats, respectively. Using standard filename extensions also helps users accessing your FTP archive with browsers like Mosaic, which have the ability to automatically display certain types of files.

Some software automatically adds the appropriate extension. For example, the UNIX *compress* program adds a *.Z* extension to files it has compressed. Likewise, the GNU *gzip* compression program adds a *.gz* extension to compressed files.

In many cases, however, there are no cues to tell the user the format of a file. The person making the files available should make sure to use a recognizable, standard filename extension to indicate the file format. If there is no standard filename extension for the file's type, the format should be noted in a *README* file in the same directory.

Table 6-1 lists common file formats, their corresponding filename extensions, and the utilities used to process them.

Table 6–1: File Formats and Corresponding Filename Extensions

Compression Program	Decompression Program	File Suffix	Typical Filename
compress	uncompress	*.Z*	*rfc1118.txt.Z*
gzip	gunzip	*.z or .gz*	*textfile.gz*
pack	unpack	*.z*	*textfile.z*
Stuffit	unsit	*.Sit*	*program.Sit*
PackIt	unpit	*.pit*	*report.pit*
PKZIP	unzip41	*.ZIP*	*package.ZIP*
zoo210	zoo210	*.zoo*	*picture.zoo*

6.2 Making Access Easier

Accessing an FTP archive is a lot like accessing a local filesystem, but without some of the most useful navigational tools. For example, the user probably can't run a recursive *find* on your FTP archive to search for a particular filename. This makes finding the way through an FTP archive difficult if the user doesn't know exactly where to look.

The keeper of the archive has a number of mechanisms available to help make the archive easier to navigate: symbolic links within the archive, aliases and special search paths,* *README* files, and *ls-lR* files.

6.2.1 Creating Links

Be liberal with symbolic links within your archive. If one of your software packages depends on a library available on your archive, create a sensibly named symbolic link to the directory containing the library from the directory containing the software. If you think people downloading one set of documents might be interested in another, provide a symbolic link from the directory holding one to the directory holding the other. Just remember that in a `chroot()`ed environment, the target of a symbolic link is interpreted relative to the new root. One way of dealing with this is to create symbolic links that only make sense in a `chroot()`ed environment, e.g.:

```
# ln -s /pub/incoming /incoming
```

where there's no */pub/incoming* directory in your regular filesystem, but there's a */users/ftp/pub/incoming* directory, and an anonymous user sees */users/ftp* as the root directory. If your local users or administrators are confused by these "dangling links," another way to handle this is to create symbolic links that use relative pathnames, like:

```
# ln -s ../dist official
```

* In the WU Archive *ftpd* only.

Be *very* careful with hard links, though: if you create hard links from your anonymous FTP file structure to files in the rest of your filesystem, `chroot()` won't save you. If you were to hard link a file in *pub* to your system *passwd* file, anonymous FTP users would be able to transfer it to their hosts, `chroot()` or no.

6.2.2 Aliases and Search Paths

The WU Archive FTP daemon gives administrators the ability to set up aliases for directories that users access often. The aliases are defined in the *ftpaccess* file and use the format:

```
alias   alias-name        real-dir-name
```

So, for example, you might set up a set of aliases for people who want shortcuts to your endangered species information:

```
alias   camelids    /pub/camelids
alias   camels      /pub/camelids
alias   crocodiles  /pub/crocodiles
alias   crocs       /pub/crocodiles
```

These aliases aren't immediately visible to users, so be sure to tell them to execute the command *quote site alias* from their FTP client to see what aliases are currently defined, or list the aliases in your archive's banner (for more information on *banner*, see Section 5.4.5). If your users need shortcut access to a number of directories, you might consider placing their parent directory into your FTP daemon's search path. Say your archive's structure looks like this:

```
/pub
   /endangered
      /camelids
      /condors
      /crocodiles
      /other-raptors
```

and you want an easy way to let folks change directories to any of the leaf directories. You can add */pub/endangered* to the search path by adding the line:

```
cdpath   /pub/endangered
```

to *ftpaccess*. Again, be sure and tell users that you've provided this shortcut, since it isn't immediately obvious to them.

For more information on both of these facilities, see Section 5.4.7.

The FTP archive on *ftp.ora.com:/pub/usenet/comp.mail.mime* has an unusual but useful setup. It's designed to help people get its contents, the archives of the USENET *comp.mail.mime* newsgroup, in several ways. The articles are archived in three subdirectories:

- The *month* subdirectory holds one archive for each month and year of the newsgroup. New articles are appended to the current file. After the end of a month, that month's archive is compressed.
- The *number* subdirectory holds articles filed by the article number.
- The *subject* subdirectory has subdirectories of its own, each named as the subject of an article or series of articles. This lets users find and read all articles with a certain subject.

  For instance, if article *number/23* has the subject *What's new in Metamail?* and *number/27* has the subject *Re: What's new in Metamail?* those two articles will be linked, respectively, into the pathnames:

  ```
  subject/What's new in Metamail?/23
  subject/What's new in Metamail?/27
  ```

  So, to find all articles on a certain subject, people can use commands like:

  ```
  ftp> cd subject
  ftp> ls
  Frequently asked questions about MIME
  What's new in Metamail?
  ftp> cd "What's new in Metamail?"
  ftp> ls
  23
  27
  ftp> mget *
  ```

  Because the directory names have spaces and other special characters in them, double quotes are required around the name in the *cd* commmand.

Files in the *number* and *subject* subdirectories are hard-linked to each other, so they don't take much more disk space than they would if they were filed only one way (by number or subject).

The script that builds this directory tree, *usenet.archive*, is in this book's online archive. See the Preface.

6.2.3 Printing Messages

The WU Archive *ftpd* also gives you the ability to display information on the user's screen when a user logs in, when a user changes directory, or when you've updated a *README* file. It's your responsibility to make sure the information provided is worthwhile.

If the system administrator makes the file containing the banner text writable to you, you can control the message displayed to users when they access the archive. The banner should provide all the information you want users to see before they start doing anything, including:

- Information on what your archive is all about: who runs it, why, where it is, what kind of stuff is available and where
- Any disclaimers
- Access information (how many users you allow and when, when you're unavailable, any sites you might not allow access from)
- Any restrictions you place upon access of your archive
- Notes on aliases, special search path entries, popular files directories, and
- Contact information, in case there's trouble (remember to use your *ftp-admin* alias if you have one!)

Try to keep the banner to a manageable length. The tops of banners longer than 24 lines will scroll off most users' screens.

There are a number of macros that you can include within the banner file that will be expanded when the daemon displays the file. For a list of them, see Section 5.4.5.

You can also use the *message* feature of the WU Archive FTP daemon to provide valuable information about the contents of each directory in your archive. If you or your system administrator puts the line:

```
message .contents    cwd=*
```

into the *ftpaccess* file, and makes sure that each directory contains a file called *.contents* that describes what's in it, the file will be displayed to each user changing to that directory. For example, here's a message displayed to users changing to the *incoming* directory:

```
ftp> cd incoming
250-This is the only directory on this archive that permits uploading.  All
250-files uploaded will be unreadable and unwritable--and unoverwritable--to
250-all archive users, including the uploader, for security reasons.
250-
250-If you've left us something important that you want us to look at
250-immediately, send email to ftp-admin@ftp.ora.com.
250-
```

```
250 CWD command successful.
ftp>
```

Remember to use the macros defined for banner messages in the message text wherever appropriate. For example, the email address at the end is actually defined in the source file as the macro %E.

The `message` directive also supports displaying a particular file when a user enters a named directory (*cwd=dir*) or after login (just substitute `login` for the *cwd=dir* field). The only difference between using the `banner` directive and *message /path login* is that the banner is displayed before login, while the message is displayed immediately after login. Finally, you can use the `readme` directive to specify that users should be asked to read certain files upon logging in or entering certain directories. Including:

```
readme  README*  cwd=*
readme  readme*  cwd=*
```

in the *ftpaccess* file tells the daemon to warn users to read the *README* file, if one exists, in the directory they change to if one exists. This differs from *message* in that the user receives a notification like this:

```
230-Please read the file README
230-  it was last modified on Sun Jul 17 18:38:04 1994 - 0 days ago
```

instead of seeing the text of the file. The user must transfer the file manually in order to see the contents. This still may be useful to you, however, as a reminder to archive users that the files are available. Some rookie users may not remember to look for a *README* file otherwise.

For more information on the `readme` directive, see Chapter 5, *The WU Archive FTP Daemon.*

6.2.4 *ls-lR Files and Archie Support*

Administrators can make maneuvering through an FTP archive easier by providing a few standard files to anonymous FTP users. The most common of these is an *ls-lR* file. As the name implies, an *ls-lR* file is simply a long-format, recursive listing of files on the FTP archive. Another way archive administrators can help users find files in their archive is to make their *ls-lR* files available to Archie, the Internet's FTP archive file location service. Archie lets users search all registered FTP archives for substrings or regular expressions matching file and directory names in the archives. Here's an example of just how powerful Archie is: let say we want to find out where to get a copy of the *traceroute* source code to compile on our host. We can use a command-line Archie client to search for the substring "traceroute":

```
% archie traceroute

Host alf.uib.no

    Location: /pub/Linux/PEOPLE/Linus
```

```
            FILE -rwxr-xr-x       5584  Mar 10 10:53  traceroute

Host ccsun.unicamp.br

    Location: /pub/aix/tools
            FILE -rw-r--r--      11394  Jan  7 20:52  traceroute

Host colonsay.dcs.ed.ac.uk

    Location: /export/netutils
      DIRECTORY drwxr-xr-x         512  Mar  1 1989  traceroute

Host dutiws.twi.tudelft.nl

    Location: /pub/other_sites/dutepp0/Unix/Linux/Kernel
            FILE -rwxrwxr-x       5584  Feb  2 07:44  traceroute
```

[*Lots more deleted*]

This information all comes from a compressed *ls-lR* file that the Archie server transfers off these archives periodically. An *ls-lR* file is a piece of cake to produce: just log in as the user who administers the FTP archive (i.e., the one who owns */pub*), *cd* to the top of your anonymous FTP file structure,* and run **ls -lR**:

```
# cd /users/ftp
# ls -lR > ls-lR    -recursively list FTP area into ls-lR
```

To keep the *ls-lR* file up-to-date, you can put an entry into your host's *crontab* file to generate the *ls-lR* file nightly. (*crontab* is a program that can run any program you want at a scheduled time. To edit its configuration file, use *crontab –e*.) If your host only supports a single *crontab* file, use *su –c* to run the *ls* as your *ftp* user, so you don't list directories and files hidden to everyone but *root*. The *crontab* entry might look like this:

```
0 0 * * *        cd /users/ftp && su ftp -c ls -lR > ls-lR
```

The *ls-lR* file should be readable, but not writable, by the *ftp* user. It's important that the *ftp* user not be able to write the *ls-lR* file you create, since that would allow anonymous users to modify it. Because only the *ls –lR* in this *crontab* entry is executed by *ftp*—the redirection of standard output is done by *root*—the output is written to *ls-lR*, even though it's not writable by *ftp*.

If your host supports a *crontab* file for each user, put the command into *ftp*'s *crontab* file:†

* Note that we said the top of the anonymous FTP file structure, not *pub* or *dist* or whatever. This is important if you're making your listing available to Archie. Archie wants to know the path to files from the *ftp* user's login directory, so *cd*ing to *pub* would throw it off.

† Before the *cron* job executes the first time, create the *ls-lR* file by hand. Otherwise, the first *chmod* will fail with a "file not found" error.

```
0 0 * * *    chmod u+w ls-lR && ls -lR > ls-lR && chmod a-w ls-lR
```

If you run a big archive, you might want to compress the *ls-lR* file:

```
0 0 * * *    chmod u+w ls-lR.Z && ls -lR | compress > ls-lR.Z && ▸▸▸
▸▸▸chmod a-w ls-lR.Z
```

The handy && construct allows you to execute the commands after the && only if the command before the && succeeds.

GNU *gzip* is often more efficient at compressing files, but many anonymous FTP users don't have access to *gzip*. In fact, some anonymous FTP users may not even have access to *compress*, so you may want to keep an uncompressed version of *ls-lR* around for those folks. You can provide *compress*ed and *gzip*ped files for those users who can digest them.

Here's a *crontab* entry that'll create both a *compress*ed and a *gzip*ped *ls-lR* file, and leave an uncompressed version:

```
0 0 * * *    chmod u+w ls-lR ls-lR.Z ls-lR.gz && ls -lR > ls-lR && ▸▸▸
▸▸▸compress < ls-lR > ls-lR.Z && gzip < ls-lR > ls-lR.gz && ▸▸▸
▸▸▸chmod a-w ls-lR ls-lR.Z ls-lR.gz
```

It's also fairly common to make an *ls-lRt* file (and compressed versions) available to users. The *–t* flag sorts files within a directory according to the time of their last modification, most recently modified files first. This helps users find the files that have been modified or added to your archive recently. You can create an *ls-lRt* file by adding a couple of t's to the command line and *crontab* entries above:

```
0 0 * * *    chmod u+w ls-lRt ls-lRt.Z ls-lRt.gz && ls -lRt > ls-lRt ▸▸▸
▸▸▸&& compress < ls-lRt > ls-lRt.Z && gzip < ls-lRt > ls-lRt.gz && ▸▸▸
▸▸▸chmod a-w ls-lRt ls-lRt.Z ls-lRt.gz
```

Another point you might want to consider: if there's any output at all from running your *crontab* entry, especially error output, you'll probably want to see it. By default, *cron* mails any output to the user executing the command. However, if you're running these commands as *root* or as another generic user, you may not get the mail. In that case, try wrapping the command in parentheses, to have it executed in a subshell, and redirect all the subshell's output to a mail command:

```
0 0 * * *    (ls -lR | compress > ls-lR.Z) 2>&1 | /usr/ucb/mail -s ▸▸▸
▸▸▸"ls -lR errors" ftp-admin
```

Once you've made an *ls-lR* file available, you're almost ready to add your archive's listing to Archie's database of *ftp*able files. The folks who run Archie ask that you check two things before you contact them:

1. Make sure all of your symbolic links resolve to something. Hanging symbolic links cause error messages that Archie's scripts can't digest to appear in the listings. Here's a short Perl script to check the integrity of your symbolic links. You run it

as *script pathname*, where *pathname* is the name of the directory you want to check for bad links and *script* is the name of the file you've saved the script in:

```
open(FIND, "find $ARGV[0] -type l -print |") || die "Can't run find: $!";

while (<FIND>) {
   chop;
   if ( ! -e $_ )
   {
      printf "target of link $_ (%s) doesn't exist\n", readlink;
   }
}
```

2. Make sure no "Permission denied" messages are generated by your *ls* command. Archie has a tough time parsing those, too. If you don't redirect your *ls* command's standard error into the *ls-lR* file, you won't have to worry about the messages. You might want to have standard error mailed to you so you can check out any errors, though.

Once you've checked both things, you can send a message to *archie-updates@bunyip.com*, letting them know your archive is up and available. Include your archive's domain name and IP address. They'll periodically pull a copy of your *ls-lR.Z* file and update their database with it.

6.3 Denying and Limiting User Access

There are a couple of reasons you might want to restrict access to your archive: you might want to deny access entirely to a user you know has been abusing your archive, or you might need to limit the number of simultaneous users to ensure adequate performance. Both of these are possible with the WU Archive FTP daemon.

The third technique in this section explains an unusual way to protect a directory. Only users who know the exact name can access the directory. This trick uses UNIX filesystem permissions, so it works with any FTP daemon on a UNIX-like system.

6.3.1 Denying Access

Denying users access is easiest with the *ftpaccess deny* directive. A line like

```
deny    dam.net    /etc/ftpmsgs/denied
```

denies users on the host *dam.net* access to your archive, printing the text in */etc/ftpmsgs/denied* before it shuts down the connection. Since it's relatively easy to spoof another user's identity, or to break into another account on a multiuser host, you may need to deny access to your archive to the whole host, rather than trying to punish just a single user.

If you only need to keep users on a particular host from accessing your anonymous FTP account, rather than denying them access to the entire archive, you can use *ftphosts*' `deny` directive. The entries

```
deny    anonymous    dam.net
deny    ftp          dam.net
```

deny users on the host *dam.net* access to your anonymous account. Note that you currently must specify both the *anonymous* and *ftp* accounts, though they're really the same, because the WU Archive *ftpd* does a simple string comparison.

For more information on the `deny` directive in *ftpaccess* and the related `deny` directive in *ftphosts*, see the appropriate sections of Chapter 5, *The WU Archive FTP Daemon*.

6.3.2 Limiting Access

If you run a popular FTP archive, or run your archive on an anemic little computer, you may find that your users' performance is suffering. Or you may want to run your archive on a host that's also used for other purposes, and you don't want FTP to eat up all of the CPU cycles on the host. The *ftpaccess* `limit` directive can help you keep the load down on your archive.

limit lets you determine how many users in a certain class* are allowed simultaneous access to your archive. You or your system administrator should probably create a class of remote anonymous archive users. Focus your limits on this class, since they're potentially the largest group of users of your archive. For example, let's say your local users are complaining of poor interactive response time, and you're sure the CPU is being hogged by all of the anonymous users accessing your archive. You can define a group called *anonymice*, anonymous users from outside your local domain, then limit them to ten simultaneous connections by adding the entry:

```
limit anonymice 10 Any /etc/ftpmsgs/msg.toomany
```

to the *ftpaccess* file. If you want to bump that limit up on weekends, when you don't have as many local users, you can specify that with another `limit` directive:

```
limit anonymice 20 SaSu /etc/ftpmsgs/msg.toomany
limit anonymice 10 Any /etc/ftpmsgs/msg.toomany
```

The date specification should follow the syntax accepted by the UUCP *L.sys* or *Systems* file. The first `limit` directive to match the current date (and time) applies. To specify a particular time of day, include a UUCP time specification, too. If your local users leave after 5 P.M., you can raise the limit on *anonymice* in the evenings like this:

```
limit anonymice 30 Any1700-800 /etc/ftpmsgs/msg.toomany
limit anonymice 20 SaSu /etc/ftpmsgs/msg.toomany
limit anonymice 10 Any /etc/ftpmsgs/msg.toomany
```

Because the first matching line applies, the limit on weekends after 5 (and any day after 5) is 30 users. If the `SaSu` line had come first, the limit would be 20 users on weekends, all day.

* For details on defining classes, see Section 5.4.1.

6.3.3 Hidden Directories

This section explains an unusual way to protect a directory or the files in a directory from prying eyes and fingers, while allowing access to people you tell the secret to. The method uses UNIX filesystem permissions, so it works with any FTP daemon on a UNIX-like system.

Here's how it works from the user's perspective. There is a directory in the FTP archive that is invisible to the *ls* and *dir* commands and is not in the *ls-lR.Z* file. But it does exist, and anyone who knows its name can *cd* to it and use it normally.

Here are two examples of when you might want to do this:

- You can serve hidden files to individual users from your anonymous FTP archive without setting up special access for them. Choose the filenames and tell authorized users the names of the hidden files. For example, a program or *cron* job could email the "hidden" filename to a user. A new filename could be created for each user, or *mv* could change an existing filename periodically. (Hard and symbolic links to files within the archive work, too.)
- A group of users may need to share files on an anonymous FTP server without using the sublogin feature (described in Section 4.3.6). This can be done with a hidden subdirectory. The directory can be fully writable or read-only.

The trick is to make a directory with execute permission, but not read permission. Files and subdirectories in it are "hidden." A person can use the "hidden" contents by typing the exact name, but *dir* and *ls* say the directory is "unreadable."

Here's an example. Your */pub* directory has `r-xr-xr-x` permissions (everyone can access and list files in it). Make a subdirectory named *private*.* Set its permissions so that everyone except you on the system has execute-only permission. Also make a subdirectory and a file with unusual names; set whatever permissions they need to have:

```
# pwd
/users/ftp/pub
# mkdir private private/SuBdIr
# cp /x/y/somefile private/aFILE1234
# chmod 711 private
# chmod 777 private/SuBdIr
# ls -ld private private/*
dr-x--x--x  3 root    other    1024 Jul 25 21:45 private
drwxrwxrwx  2 root    other    1024 Jul 25 21:45 private/SuBdIr
-r--r--r--  1 root    other    1641 Jul 25 21:45 private/aFILE1234
```

Now you tell users the exact name of the subdirectory (*SuBdIr*) or file (*aFILE1234*). Like everyone else on the system, they can access your *private* directory. They can't list it because they don't have read permission. (They may see an error message or no message at all.) They can get the file if they know its name (and, of course, if the file

* A less-secretive name might be better.

is readable by the *ftp* user). If they know the exact name of the subdirectory, they can *cd* to it, list it, and upload and download files, because the *SuBdIr* directory is writable, readable, and executable.

```
ftp> cd /pub/private
250 CWD command successful.
ftp> dir
200 PORT command successful.
150 Opening ASCII mode data connection for /bin/ls.
226 Transfer complete.        -Notice: no names are output
ftp> mget *
Bad directory components
can't find list of remote files, oops
ftp> get aFILE1234
200 PORT command successful.
150 Opening ASCII mode data connection for aFILE1234 (1641 bytes).
226 Transfer complete.
local: aFILE1234 remote: aFILE1234
1841 bytes received in 0.01 seconds (1.7e+02 Kbytes/s)
ftp> cd SuBdIr
250 CWD command successful.
ftp> dir
200 PORT command successful.
150 Opening ASCII mode data connection for /bin/ls.
total 85
-rw-r--r--    1 ftp    other    32407 Jul 25 21:47 secret.tar.Z
-rw-r--r--    1 ftp    other    54243 Jul 26 13:24 comments
226 Transfer complete.
143 bytes received in 0.0076 seconds (18 Kbytes/s)
ftp>
```

The *SuBdIr* subdirectory doesn't have to be world-writable (mode 777), which allows uploading. A mode like 755, which lets only the directory owner modify the contents, may be better. (In this case, the files are writable by the anonymous FTP user, but they wouldn't need to be.)

When you use a bizarre set of permissions like this, it's really important that you understand what you're doing. (The concepts actually aren't hard at all. They're just different than many people expect.) For example, some people think that if a file is unwritable, it's protected from deletion—but that's not true! *Write permission for a directory allows creation, renaming, or deletion of files within the directory.* Denying execute (search) permission for a directory denies access to all files in the directory. Write and read permissions for an individual file control access to that file's contents. For more information, see a reference book with thorough coverage of filesystem permissions—like the book *UNIX Power Tools* from O'Reilly & Associates/Bantam Books.

6.4 Monitoring Log Files

One of the least interesting duties of the archive maintainer can be monitoring log files, particularly *ftpd*'s *syslog* output and the WU Archive *ftpd*'s *xferlog* output, if you keep it. There's actually valuable information in there, believe it or not. A good log file summarizer can help make sense and significance of a long log file. A Perl script to summarize the *xferlog* file called *xferstats* is shipped with the WU Archive *ftpd* package in *util*. It produces nice output that looks like this:

```
TOTALS FOR SUMMARY PERIOD Tue Jul 19 1994 TO Tue Jul 19 1994

Files Transmitted During Summary Period            5
Bytes Transmitted During Summary Period       569048
Systems Using Archives                             0

Average Files Transmitted Daily                    5
Average Bytes Transmitted Daily               569048

Daily Transmission Statistics

                 Number Of   Number of    Average    Percent Of  Percent Of
     Date        Files Sent  Bytes  Sent  Xmit  Rate  Files Sent  Bytes
Sent
---------------  ----------  -----------  ----------  ----------  ----------
Tue Jul 19 1994           5       569048  51.7 KB/s     100.00      100.00

Total Transfers from each Archive Section (By bytes)

                                                 ---- Percent  Of ----
     Archive Section       Files Sent Bytes Sent  Files Sent Bytes Sent
------------------------- ---------- ----------- ---------- ----------
/incoming                          3      555080    60.00       97.55
/pub                               1       13906    20.00        2.44
Index/Informational Files          1          62    20.00        0.01

Hourly Transmission Statistics

                 Number Of   Number of    Average    Percent Of  Percent Of
     Time        Files Sent  Bytes  Sent  Xmit  Rate  Files Sent  Bytes Sent
---------------  ----------  -----------  ----------  ----------  ----------
00                        5       569048  51.7 KB/s     100.00      100.00
```

There's lots of useful information in here:

- Overall information on how busy your archive is (files and bytes transmitted, total and average daily)
- Weekly statistics so you can assess how usage varies day-to-day
- A breakdown of files sent and bytes sent by archive section, so you can see where in your archive filesystem most of the activity is

- Statistics on the transfer rate, so you can see how well your archive is keeping up with demand

You may also want to look through the raw *xferlog* output, or run your own custom summarizer on it, to get a feeling for which files folks are downloading most, or to see whether they're really reading your *README* files or not. You may also want to run a short Perl command like this to notify you of any new uploads:

```
% perl -ane 'print $F[8], "\n" if $F[11] eq "i"' /usr/adm/xferlog
```

This will print the pathnames of any uploaded files (presumably, they'll be under *incoming* if you've set everything up correctly). You can then go take a look at what the users have uploaded for you. You might want to run this from your *crontab* file nightly and have the output sent to you so you know what to go look for:

```
0 0 * * * /usr/bin/perl -ane 'print $F[8], "\n" if $F[11] eq "i"' ▶▶▶
▶▶▶/usr/adm/xferlog | /usr/ucb/mail -s 'Newly-uploaded files' ftp-admin
```

6.5 Reading Mail

If you're having all this mail directed to *ftp-admin*, you have to read that mail assiduously (for information on setting up the *ftp-admin* alias, see Section 4.2.5). You never know when someone's uploaded something nasty to your archive. Also, remember the other types of mail that may be directed to *ftp-admin*:

- Errors from trying to create your nightly *ls-lR* file
- Mail from users who were unable to access your archive but saw your banner or at least guessed your email address
- Mail from users who had problems using your archive or couldn't find what they wanted
- Mail from users requesting that you make something available or make something unavailable

In this Chapter:

- *What Is WAIS?*
- *Building WAIS*
- *Testing and Installing WAIS*
- *Configuring waisserver*

7

Creating an Internet Database Server with WAIS

If you've got a monstrous database of information you'd like to make available over the Internet, and you're looking for a way to give users the ability to efficiently search that entire database—and possibly other databases—for the one nugget of useful information they need, then WAIS may be your salvation. WAIS, the Wide Area Information Server, provides powerful database searching functionality over TCP/IP networks using a protocol called Z39.50, an ANSI standard. The latest public-domain WAIS software allows easy indexing of large databases of documents and other material. Some of this may be textual, while other parts may be binary. The server's search engine allows users to query databases looking for simple keywords or more complicated boolean expressions. And best of all, WAIS integrates nicely with Gopher and World Wide Web. Gopher or Web servers can act as front ends for WAIS databases, and the newest version of the Mosaic World Wide Web browser can talk directly to a WAIS server.

7.1 What Is WAIS?

WAIS was originally developed at Thinking Machines, the company that builds the Connection Machine, a massively parallel supercomputer. Thinking Machines developed WAIS as a prototype information service, working with Dow Jones, Apple Computer, and KPMG Peat Marwick, to prove that commercial-grade networked information services could be built using existing technologies like TCP/IP. They also wanted to show how well a Connection Machine worked as an information server, but we'll forgive them for that.

Thinking Machines made their UNIX implementation of the WAIS software, as well as a Macintosh client, freely available. The core of the software is an indexer, used to create full-text indexes of files fed to it, and a server that can use those indexes to search for keywords or whole English expressions among the files indexed. What's more, the server allows the user to specify that a particular document is similar to the one she wanted and uses the contents of the document to find more like it.

Besides the Macintosh client, Thinking Machines released UNIX text-based and X-based clients. These have been ported to most major UNIXish operating systems and are still in wide use today.

The software was such a hit on the Internet that Brewster Kahle, the leader of the WAIS project at Thinking Machines, founded WAIS Inc. to produce a commercial version of WAIS. Further development at Thinking Machines stopped, but CNIDR, the Clearinghouse for Networked Information Discovery and Retrieval, took over maintenance of the public-domain WAIS software. CNIDR merged functionality from several new strains of WAIS, including Don Gilbert's IUBio* enhancements, into the public-domain code to produce freeWAIS. So there are now two species of WAIS: one commercial, produced by WAIS, Inc., and the other public domain, maintained by CNIDR as freeWAIS. It's freeWAIS that we'll concentrate on in this chapter. For more information on the commercial WAIS, we suggest contacting WAIS, Inc. at *info@wais.com*.†

This chapter covers the role of the server administrator in compiling the WAIS software, setting up the server, and testing its operation. The next chapter discusses the part the data librarian plays: creating databases by indexing documents, registering those databases, and keeping them up-to-date. But before we jump into setting up the server, let's give everyone a short primer on how WAIS works.

7.1.1 Using a WAIS Database

Let's face it: databases can be boring. As we looked for a good WAIS example, one stood out. *jargon.src* (at *hal.gnu.ai.mit.edu*, port 8000) says it has "the latest version of the Jargon File, currently version 2.9.6, roughly what was printed in *The New Hacker's Dictionary* (by Eric S. Raymond, MIT Press, 1991)." We'd been having a hot argument about the difference between a "geek" and a "nerd" `:-)`, so this seemed like the perfect way to find out:

```
% waissearch -h hal.gnu.ai.mit.edu -d jargon -p 8000 nerd

 Search Response:
  NumberOfRecordsReturned: 9
   1: Score: 1000, lines:   2 'turbo nerd'
   2: Score:  333, lines:  11 'computer geek'
   3: Score:  333, lines:   6 'geek out'
   4: Score:  333, lines:  10 'J. Random'
   5: Score:  333, lines:   6 'J. Random Hacker'
   6: Score:  333, lines:   9 'JR[LN]'
   7: Score:  333, lines:   5 'YAUN'
   8: Score:  333, lines:  24 '-oid'
   9: Score:  333, lines: 348 'Appendix B: A Portrait of J. Random Hacker'
```

* The IUBio enhancements were written by Don at the University of Indiana's Biology Department, hence the name.

† The trademark WAIS is actually owned by WAIS, Inc.

```
View document number [type 0 or q to quit]: 1
Headline: turbo nerd

turbo nerd: n. See {computer geek}.

View document number [type 0 or q to quit]: 2
Headline: computer geek

computer geek: n. One who eats (computer) bugs for a living.  One
   who fulfills all the dreariest negative stereotypes about hackers:
   an asocial, malodorous, pasty-faced monomaniac with all the
   personality of a cheese grater.  Cannot be used by outsiders
   without implied insult to all hackers; compare black-on-black usage
   of `nigger'.  A computer geek may be either a fundamentally
   clueless individual or a proto-hacker in {larval stage}.  Also
   called `turbo nerd', `turbo geek'.  See also
   {clustergeeking}, {geek out}, {wannabee}, {terminal
   junkie}.

View document number [type 0 or q to quit]: q
Search for new words [type q to quit]: q
```

We both lost the argument: a nerd is the same as a geek. Who'd have thought! (There were no matches for "nurd.")

7.1.2 How Does WAIS Work?

Structurally, WAIS is divided into three main components: an indexer, a server, and a client. The indexer is responsible for taking documents of various formats in a database and digesting them into a number of different tables and indexes for efficient searching: a dictionary listing the words that occur in the documents, an index of where those occurrences are, etc. The server uses the indexes to determine whether the words a user is looking for occur in the database, and if so, which documents they occur in and where. The index contains the information the server needs to find a particular word in the database, but the server is responsible for disassembling a client's natural-language query into searches for multiple words, or for conducting the searches involved in a boolean expression and deciding which documents match the boolean criteria.

The clients simply build queries for the server in the appropriate Z39.50 format, display search results to users, and allow users to retrieve documents from the server. Sophisticated clients support many different document types, from plain ASCII text to graphical file formats like GIF and JPEG. In addition to the original Mac and UNIX clients, there are now clients available for graphical UNIX environments, like Motif and OpenLook, and for Microsoft Windows. The Mosaic browser, in particular, now has native WAIS support, meaning that the browser can communicate directly with a WAIS server. Together, Mosaic and WAIS can give you the ability to search large databases composed of all sorts of documents, including plain text and PostScript documents, image and audio files, and WWW's own HTML documents.

Figure 7-1 illustrates the relationship between the components.

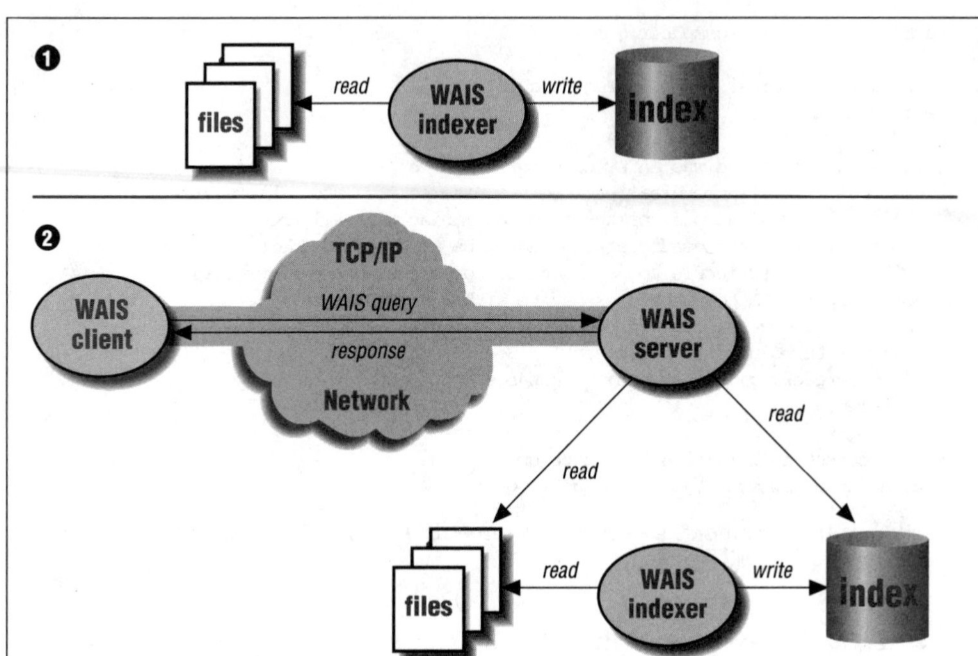

Figure 7-1. The WAIS indexer, server, and client

7.2 Building WAIS

The first step in setting up a WAIS server is getting the software. freeWAIS is available via anonymous FTP from *ftp.cnidr.org* as */pub/NIDR.tools/freeWAIS-0.3.tar.Z* (version 0.3 is the most recent as of this writing). *ftp.wais.com* serves as a repository for preported WAIS code, so you might want to check there also. If you see a newer version of freeWAIS in either place, you might consider using it. You could check the Internet newsgroup *comp.infosystems.wais* to see if there's any information about its stability. If it looks hardy enough, pull it instead.

Once you've *ftp*ed over the compressed tar file, you have to unpack it. To do that, issue the command:

```
% zcat freeWAIS-0.3.tar.Z | tar xvf -
```

in the directory you want the source code unpacked. This command creates a directory named *freeWAIS-0.3* (or whatever your version is called) and several subdirectories under that:

bin This directory contains scripts, some of which drive the executables you'll build, and is where most of the binaries you build will reside.

doc This directory contains documentation, both the original WAIS documentation (from Thinking Machines) and WAIS documentation from CNIDR (though that's currently just a Frequently Asked Questions file).

ir This directory includes the code for *waisindex* and *waisserver*, plus the search engine.

lib This directory contains library routines shared by various WAIS executables.

ui This directory contains the code for sample WAIS clients, including *waissearch* and *waisq*. The clients are built during the standard build process.

wais-sources
This directory contains the *.src* file for the Internet's directory of servers. This enables users to bootstrap their WAIS clients by searching the directory of servers source for other sources they may be interested in.

x This directory contains the code for an X11-based WAIS client.

The *ir*, *ui*, and *x* subdirectories include RCS subdirectories with copies of the original (Thinking Machines) WAIS code, for those interested in seeing what CNIDR did to update it.

The root of the *freeWAIS-0.3* directory also contains a number of files of documentation and instructions for building WAIS. The CNIDR-provided documents are currently pretty minimal; they refer you to URL* *http://cnidr.org/welcome.html*, but right now that's just a lot of CNIDR public relations material and HTML-formatted documents that come from the freeWAIS package, which you now have. Be sure to read the *INSTALLATION*, *Makefile*, *README*, and *RELEASE-NOTES* files, especially if you're using a version newer than 0.3 (the farther the version from 0.3, the more out-of-date our instructions may be!).

Now you'll need to customize the top-level *Makefile* (the one in the *freeWAIS-0.3* directory). Here's a list of the variables you're likely to need to set:

RANLIB Set this to the pathname to the *ranlib* command on your system. On SGIs and HPs, *ranlib* isn't necessary (the functionality is built into *ar*), so set *RANLIB* to */bin/true*.

CC If you have an ANSI C compiler, use it; otherwise, use *gcc* or your system's standard *cc*. freeWAIS was written to be portable, so any of these should work, though you may need to define *_NO_PROTO* (to turn off ANSI func-

* A URL is a Uniform Resource Locator, the type of ID used by World Wide Web browsers to uniquely identify a particular resource available over the network. To look at this URL, you could start the Mosaic WWW browser with the command line **Mosaic http://cnidr.org/welcome.html**. For more details, see Chapter 17, *Introduction to the World Wide Web*.

tion prototypes) as one of the CFLAGS in the *Makefile* for non-ANSI C compilers.

TOP Unless you use SunOS, you'll need to uncomment the line:

```
#TOP:sh = pwd
```

in the *Makefile* and set *TOP* to the full pathname of the directory under which the freeWAIS *tar* package was unpacked, e.g.:

```
TOP = /home/wais/freeWAIS-0.3
```

then, on all but Sun systems, comment the lines:

```
comment-me:
    @echo You must set "\$$(TOP)" to point to the freeWAIS src directory
```

so *make* doesn't complain.

You don't need to comment out the *echo* command for a SunOS host because SunOS's *make* understands the `\$$(TOP)` syntax and sets *TOP* correctly.

CFLAGS This is probably the most involved option to set: there are lots of flags you can use to customize freeWAIS's operation. First, set any flags specific to your architecture. Here's a list of possible architectures:

–DBSD Use this flag for old (pre-4.3) BSD operating systems.

–DBSD43 Use this flag for new (4.3 and 4.4) BSD operating systems.

–DSYSV Use this flag for System V (AT&T) UNIX.

–M3e –Zi Use these flags for XENIX.

–DUSG Use this flag if your version of UNIX includes the *dirent* routines in its C library.

–cckr Use this flag for SGI Irix 4.0.1 (it tells the compiler to expect Kernighan and Ritchie-style C).

The following flags affect the indexer's and the server's operation—you probably want to use most of them:

–DSECURE_SERVER
This flag lets the administrator use the *–u* option to reset the uid the server runs under. It's a very good idea to set this option.

–DRELEVANCE_FEEDBACK
This flag turns on relevance feedback, the WAIS feature that lets users refine their search by using documents found in an earlier

search. This is a standard feature of WAIS servers, so it's best to set this flag.

–DLITERAL
: With the *LITERAL* flag set, the server will support literal searches; i.e., searches for a particular string in a document, not just a word or set of words. The user conducting the search must enclose the string in single or double quotes. For example, a search for `'a duck and a drake'` matches only that phrase in a document. Double quotes must be escaped in a literal search, e.g., `\"a duck and a drake\"`.

waisserver's literal matching has a few limitations. First, the first word in the literal phrase must be indexed; i.e., it can't be a word in the stoplist (see Section 8.6.1). Also, literal indexing can interact a little oddly with stemming, described later in this section. Stemming attempts to find the "stem" of a word by removing endings like "s," "es," or "ing" from the end, so that "tables" becomes "tabl". With literal matches turned on, your users may find that they can no longer find the literal "tables".

–DBOOLEANS
: Compiling the server with this flag set lets users use the boolean AND and NOT operators in their searches. (You don't really need OR, since typing in "foo bar" as search words already gets you any files with either "foo" or "bar" in them.) This is a very handy feature, so it's worthwhile to set this flag.

If you do compile your server with boolean support, it's a good idea to mention it in your source description file, so users know boolean functionality is available. Users of conventional WAIS clients who use your server will save your source description in text form to their *~/wais-sources* subdirectory, and can usually examine it—and read the description you include—either with their client or by using a text editor to read the file itself.

–DPARTIALWORD
: Compiling the server with this flag set enables the wildcarding code within the server. If a user searches for "box*", for example, the search will match documents that contain "box", "boxes", and "boxcars".

–DBIO
: The *BIO* definition compiles in Don Gilbert's enhancements to the WAIS code, including the definable stoplist feature (discussed in Section 8.6.1) and configurable word delimiters. It

also compiles a whole swarm of new formats into *waisindex*, peculiar to biological databases.

–DUSE_SYSLOG
: Setting this flag tells the server to use *syslog* for logging instead of just *fprintf*ing to a log file.

–DNEED_VSYSLOG
: You should set this flag if you want to use *syslog* (i.e., you've set *USE_SYSLOG*) and your operating system doesn't have the `vsyslog()` call.

–DDUMP_CORE
: This flag tells *waisserver* to dump core when it aborts. Since those core dumps may contain valuable debugging information, this is a good flag to set while you're setting up and testing your server installation. Since those core dumps may be huge, though, you may want to rebuild the server without the flag set to put into production, if you're worried about large core files filling up your disk.

–DEND_MERGE
: This flag tells the indexer to merge its index files at the end, rather than as it runs. Jonathan Kamens' enhancement to merge the intermediate index files as *waisindex* runs saves disk space, so you probably don't want to set this.

–DSTEM_WORDS
: This flag turns on the Porter stemmer in the indexer and server. The stemmer tries to derive the stem of a word in a document or in a search so that the word "swimming" in a document will match the word "swims" in a search.

–DLIST_STEMS
: This flag instructs the indexer and server to log stemmed words.

That's the bulk of the customization.

Finally, go down in the top-level *Makefile* to the lines that begin:

```
x::
```

The two lines after `x::` control how *make* builds the X clients in the freeWAIS distribution. The first uses the X Consortium's *xmkmf* and *imake* programs.* The second uses

* If you have X, you probably have *imake* and *xmkmf*. The versions of *imake* and *xmkmf* on some releases of Sun OpenWindows don't work. If you want to set up working versions of *xmkmf* and *imake*, you can get *imake* via anonymous FTP from *ftp.uu.net* in */published/oreilly/nutshell/imake/imake.tar.Z*. The O'Reilly & Associates Nutshell Handbook *Software Portability with imake* has instructions on setting up both *xmkmf* and *imake*.

a standard *Makefile*, but is commented out in the distribution. If you want to build the X clients, and you have the *xmkmf* and *imake* programs, no changes to the *Makefile* should be necessary.

If you aren't interested in building the X clients at all, find the line in the *Makefile* that determines which targets *make* builds by default:

```
default: config.h lib ir ui bin x check
```

Remove `x` from this line and *make* will skip the X clients altogether.

If, for some reason, you don't want to use *imake*, uncomment the line that uses a standard *Makefile*, change the `./makex.sh` to `make -f My-Makefile`, and try to use the included, standard *Makefile*. If you do decide to use *My-Makefile*, be sure to edit it to reflect your installation of X. As shipped, it probably doesn't jive with where your X libraries and include files are. Here are some of the variables you may need to set or reset:

INSTALLDIR Set this to the directory in which you want the X binaries installed.

APPSDIR Set this to the directory in which your app-defaults files are stored.

LFLAGS Set this to the value of any flags that should be sent to the loader (*ld*), especially flags that tell the loader which directories contain the X libraries, if they're not in a standard place like */usr/lib* (e.g., *–L/usr/lib/X11R5*).

RESOLVER Set this to *–lresolv* if you need to explicitly link in the DNS name-resolution library. Not all operating systems require this: some include the resolver routines in the standard C library. If you're not sure, check the resolver man pages on your system.

LIBS Set this to the list of X libraries you want linked in. The list in *My-Makefile* is probably all you need, unless you're trying to build the Motif client. Note that the standard (non-Motif) X client requires the Xmu (miscellaneous utilities) library and the Athena widget set.

INCLUDES Set this to include any *–I* options for directories that include necessary header files (e.g., *–I/usr/include/X11R5*).

While the instructions claim you can build a Motif version by including the Motif library (usually *–lXm*) in *LIBS* and adding *–DMOTIF* to *CFLAGS*, we've had some problems with the Motif client and run-time X problems.

Once you're done with any modifications to *My-Makefile*, you should be ready to go for it! Change directories to the top-level directory and type **make**.

If you have any problems with the build, here are a couple of suggestions:

- Recent versions of freeWAIS haven't consistently used the *_NO_PROTO* define to select the correct function header for ANSI or K&R C compilers. Our copy of *ir/syslog.c* required some re-engineering, including rewriting the `strerror()` function header.

- Many OSes aren't able to pass environment variables in *Makefiles*, so you may have to modify *My-Makefile* to reset *CFLAGS*.

If you're totally stumped, you can turn to the Internet newsgroup *comp.infosystems.wais*. Be sure to scan the subject lines and check if anyone's already had your problem and asked your question. If not, ask for help. Lots of knowledgeable and helpful folks read the newsgroup.

7.3 Testing and Installing WAIS

Before installing the software in its permanent location on your system, it's a good idea to test it and make sure it works to your satisfaction. First, you should test the basic functionality of the indexer by indexing some files. Then you can use some of the *clients* you built to make sure they can use the indexes correctly. Finally, you should configure the server and use the clients to query it, to make sure the server works as advertised.

Create a directory to hold your WAIS index files and your server's log file. Depending on filesystem constraints, you may want this directly under the root, or under */usr/local*, or somewhere else. The location isn't really important, but it is a good idea to give the indexes their own directory. This makes them easier to find and manipulate. The server's log file doesn't have to be in this directory, though. That's up to you.

We usually use */wais* or */usr/local/wais*, depending on where we have more room:

```
# mkdir /usr/local/wais; cd /usr/local/wais
```

A WAIS **source** is an indexed database. As you'll see in the next chapter, where *waisindex* is covered in depth, a source contains a set of files, even if the database itself is only one file. *waissearch* uses this set of files to perform searches and prepare responses.

Now, to test your indexer, create a small source. One possibility is to index your */etc/hosts* file (if you still have one):

```
# waisindex -d ETCHOSTS -t one_line /etc/hosts
```

The *–d* option tells *waisindex* the name of the source you're creating. The *–t* option tells *waisindex* the format of the file you're indexing, and how you'd like it indexed. The *one_line* format creates a separate retrievable document for each line in the file. *waisindex*'s default format is *text*, which creates a full text index of the file, but makes the whole file a single document. In other words, with *one_line*, users can search for words in any line in the file and retrieve individual lines, while with *text*, they can search for words in any line in the file, but can only retrieve the whole file.

Of course, if you don't have an */etc/hosts* file handy, you can use any text file that's convenient. */etc/master* will do, or */etc/disktab*, or whatever.

Now you should check to make sure the index files were built correctly by searching for something in the source you just created. Randal Schwarz's *ws* front-end for *waissearch* is handy; it's a small Perl script included in the *bin* subdirectory of the freeWAIS package. If you don't have Perl on your host, you may have to use *waissearch* directly, or *waisq*.

Here's one way to test WAIS using *ws*:

```
$ WAISCOMMONSOURCEDIR=/usr/local/wais# or setenv for csh
$ export WAISCOMMONSOURCEDIR
$ ws ETCHOSTS babs# search the ETCHOSTS source for the word "babs"
waissearch -h  -d /usr/local/wais/ETCHOSTS -p babs

 Search Response:
   NumberOfRecordsReturned: 1
    1: Score: 1000, lines:   1 '15.17.232.24      babs'

View document number [type 0 or q to quit]: 1
Headline: 15.17.232.24  babs
15.17.232.24     babs

View document number [type 0 or q to quit]: q
Search for new words [type q to quit]: q
```

You have to set the environment variable `WAISCOMMONSOURCEDIR` before executing *ws* (or *waissearch*) to let the program know where to look for *.src* files. The client reads the *.src* file to find the information it needs to search the source.

Judging from the results, this source seems to be indexed just fine. The search returned a single hit, which we then retrieved. Here's the same example using *waissearch* directly:

```
$ WAISCOMMONSOURCEDIR=/usr/local/wais
$ export WAISCOMMONSOURCEDIR
$ waissearch -d ETCHOSTS babs
```

Note that if you try to include the *–h* and *–p* options to *waissearch*, as *ws* did when it *exec*ed *waissearch*, you've got to specify a null option argument for them, lest they gobble up the next argument on the line:

```
$ waissearch -h "" -d ETCHOSTS -p "" babs
```

It's hard to see the null arguments when *ws* spits out the *waissearch* command it's executing, but they are there.

If the index checks out, move on to setting up and testing the server.

7.3.1 Running waisserver Under inetd

You can run the server under *inetd*, the Internet superserver, or standalone. Running under *inetd* saves you the system overhead of always running a *waisserver* process listening on the Z39.50 port. We've heard folks argue against using *inetd* because it takes a little time to start servers when a request arrives. On a host fast enough to accommodate a WAIS server, though, starting up a new *waisserver* process won't take long, especially compared with the time it could take for *waisserver* to service the WAIS query. Besides, some operating systems (like HP-UX) have special security mechanisms for limiting access to services running under *inetd*, and you may want to take advantage of these.

To run *waisserver* under *inetd*, first make sure you have an entry for the Z39.50 protocol in */etc/services* (or in the *services* map, if you go for that NIS stuff):

```
z3950    210/tcp
```

Then add an entry in *inetd.conf* to tell *inetd* to listen to the Z39.50 port and to tell it which server to start and how:

```
z3950 stream tcp nowait root /usr/local/etc/waisserver waisserver.d \
-u wais -l 10 -e /usr/local/wais/server.log -d /usr/local/wais
```

Note that the *inetd.conf* entry may have to be on a single line if your system's *inetd* can't handle line-continuation characters. Check the *inetd.conf* man page if you're in doubt.

For information on what each of these fields means to *inetd*, check Section 4.2.1. It describes the meaning of each field, as does a good *inetd.conf* man page. The only field of real interest in this *inetd.conf* entry is the final field (`waisserver.d -u wais -l 10 -e /usr/local/wais/server.log -d /usr/local/wais`). This tells *inetd* the arguments to pass to the *waisserver* executable. There, we're actually starting *waisserver* with the name *waisserver.d*. This name tells *waisserver* to expect the streams of data from and to the client to be passed off to it as standard input and standard output, respectively. Since we don't want *waisserver* running as *root*, we specify the *–u* option, and tell it to run as the user *wais*. This assumes, of course, that there is a *wais* user in the password file. Our *wais* user is just a standard, unprivileged user who can't log in:

```
wais:*:200:20:WAIS:/usr/local/wais:/bin/sh
```

The *wais* user can, however, read all the document and index files and write all the logs files. Running *waisserver* as an unprivileged user helps ensure that any unknown bugs in *waisserver* don't result in someone gaining *root* access to our system.

The *–l* option tells *waisserver* its logging level, in this case `10`, the maximum. *–e* specifies the name of the log file, and *–d* specifies the default location of the indexes the server knows about. Beware—some versions of *inetd* limit the number of parameters you can pass in this last field, called the argument vector. If your *inetd* has a problem with this many fields, you can write a short shell script that will run the server for you.

You can then have *inetd* start the shell script. Though this adds a little extra overhead, it also lets you run *waisserver* with the options you want.

For example, you could use this shell script to start *waisserver* with the same options our *inetd.conf* entry above is starting it with:

```
#!/bin/sh

exec /usr/local/etc/waisserver -s -u wais -l 10 -e /wais/server.log -d /usr/local/wais
exit $?
```

We *exec waisserver* to save ourselves a process. This way, the shell process will *exec waisserver* and we'll only have *waisserver* running. Without *exec*, both the shell process and *waisserver* would run.

Also, note that we start *waisserver* with the *–s* option (to read from standard input and write to standard output), since we can't specify an alternate first argument (*waisserver.d*). If you call your script */usr/local/etc/waisserver.start*, your *inetd.conf* entry would read:

```
z3950 stream tcp nowait root /usr/local/etc/waisserver.start waisserver.start
```

Once you've added an entry for Z39.50 to *inetd.conf*, you need to signal *inetd* to reread *inetd.conf*. On most systems, you do this by sending the *inetd* process a HUP signal (as root):

```
# ps -ef | grep inetd
# kill -HUP <pid>
```

On HP-UX, the smarts to do this is built into *inetd*, so you can just run *inetd* with the *–c* (configure) option:

```
# inetd -c
```

Make sure *inetd* reconfigures correctly, and doesn't complain about any syntax errors on the line, or missing executables. Some versions of *inetd* log a message like this to *syslog* if the reconfiguration went smoothly:

```
Dec 29 15:00:02 babs inetd[111]: z3950/tcp: Added service, server ▶▶▶
▶▶▶ /usr/local/etc/waisserver
```

The WAIS server can also be run under *xinetd*, an extended version of *inetd* that provides security and access control features. For more information, see Chapter 28, *xinetd*.

7.3.2 Running waisserver Standalone

If you'd rather run *waisserver* as a standalone daemon, instead of under *inetd*, to save time in handling queries, you first need to start *waisserver* from the command line. You start *waisserver* with the same arguments that *inetd* would start it with, plus the *–p* (port number) option. By specifying the *–p* option, with or without a port number, you tell *waisserver* to listen for WAIS requests on that port, rather than from standard input, as it would running under *inetd*. If you don't specify a port number, *waisserver* listens on the Z39.50 port, which it finds by looking up *z3950* in */etc/services* or in your *services* NIS map. See the previous section for instructions on how to add Z39.50 to your */etc/services* file or NIS *services* map.

So to start *waisserver* standalone with the same options as in our *inetd* example, you'd run:

```
# waisserver -p -u wais -l 10 -e /usr/local/wais/server.log -d /usr/local/wais
```

Once you've tested your server and it's ready for public use, you'll probably want to start *waisserver* at system startup. Here's what we use in */etc/rc.local*:

```
if [ -x /usr/local/etc/waisserver ]
then
    /usr/local/etc/waisserver -p -u wais -l 10 -e /usr/local/wais/server.log \
    -d /usr/local/wais
fi
```

7.3.3 Testing waisserver

To test *waisserver*, first delete the old *.src* file and create a new one, with the source *exported*; that is, with *waisserver* host and port information included in the source. You must delete the old source description file manually because *waisindex* won't rewrite it unless it detects what it thinks are significant changes in the source. You create an exported source by running the same *waisindex* command shown earlier, but with the *–export* option added:

```
$ cd /usr/local/wais
$ rm ETCHOSTS.src
$ waisindex -d /etc/hosts -t one_line -export ETCHOSTS
```

.src files for exported sources contain the domain name and IP address of the host the server runs on, and the port number the server runs on. Without this information in the *.src* file, *ws* and *waissearch* will have a tough time finding the server.

But wait! Didn't *ws* and *waissearch* find the source even before we configured *waisserver*, when the source wasn't exported, and there wasn't even a server running? Yes, but that's because 1) we told them where to look for the *.src* files when we set `WAISCOMMONSOURCEDIR`, 2) they didn't need IP address and port information, because they've got the native intelligence to read local index files themselves, and 3) they could find out where the index files lived from the *.src* file.

Once you've created an exported source, run *ws* or *waissearch* to test the server. You still need to specify the `WAISCOMMONSOURCEDIR` for *ws*, so that the client can find the *.src* file and cull the host and port information from it:

```
$ WAISCOMMONSOURCEDIR=/usr/local/wais # in case you haven't set it already
$ export WAISCOMMONSOURCEDIR
$ ws ETCHOSTS babs
waissearch -h babs.nsr.hp.com -d ETCHOSTS -p 210 babs

 Search Response:
   NumberOfRecordsReturned: 1
     1: Score: 1000, lines:   1 '15.17.232.24     babs'

View document number [type 0 or q to quit]:
```

Or, with *waissearch*:

```
$ waissearch -p 210 -d ETCHOSTS babs

 Search Response:
   NumberOfRecordsReturned: 1
     1: Score: 1000, lines:   1 '15.17.232.24     babs'

View document number [type 0 or q to quit]:
```

Notice that *ws* now *execs waissearch* with *–h* (host) and *–p* (port) options, which it gleaned from the *ETCHOSTS.src* file in the WAISCOMMONSOURCEDIR. This time, the query went out over the network (well, to the loopback interface, anyway). Just to make sure the server answered the query, check your *syslog* output. If you're running *waisserver* under *inetd*, you should find a message like this:

```
Dec 29 16:40:14 babs inetd[6396]: z3950/tcp: Connection from ▶▶▶
▶▶▶ babs (15.17.232.24) at Wed Dec 29 16:40:14 1993
```

You can also check your *waisserver*'s log file to make sure the query was received:

```
7647: 0: Aug  7 11:05:35 1994: 1: Accepted connection from: ▶▶▶
▶▶▶ babs.nsr.hp.com [15.17.232.24], freeWAIS Release 0.3
7647: 1: Aug  7 11:05:39 1994: 100: Init message: waissearch freeWAIS ▶▶▶
▶▶▶ Release 0.3, from host: babs.nsr.hp.com
7647: 2: Aug  7 11:05:39 1994: 3: Search! Database: ETCHOSTS, Seed Words: babs
```

If your server didn't answer, re-check *inetd.conf*. With some *inetds*, you can kill and restart the server to see which services it knows about: it logs a list of them via syslog:

```
Jan  2 17:43:44 babs inetd[111]: Going down on signal 15
Jan  2 17:43:47 babs inetd[7241]: Connection logging enabled
Jan  2 17:43:47 babs inetd[7241]: Reading configuration
Jan  2 17:43:47 babs inetd[7241]: ftp/tcp: Added service, server /etc/ftpd
lots of lines deleted
Jan  2 17:43:47 babs inetd[7241]: rpc.walld/udp: Added service, server ▶▶▶
▶▶▶ /usr/etc/rpc.rwalld
Jan  2 17:43:47 babs inetd[7241]: rpc.rquotad/udp: Added service, server ▶▶▶
▶▶▶ /usr/etc/rpc.rquotad
Jan  2 17:43:47 babs inetd[7241]: rpc.sprayd/udp: Added service, server ▶▶▶
▶▶▶ /usr/etc/rpc.sprayd
Jan  2 17:43:47 babs inetd[7241]: spc/tcp: Added service, server ▶▶▶
▶▶▶ /usr/softbench/bin/softspcd
```

```
Jan  2 17:43:47 babs inetd[7241]: recserv/tcp: Added service, server ▶▶▶
▶▶▶ /usr/lib/X11/SharedX/recserv
Jan  2 17:43:47 babs inetd[7241]: z3950/tcp: Added service, server ▶▶▶
▶▶▶ /usr/local/etc/waisserver
Jan  2 17:43:47 babs inetd[7241]: Configuration complete
```

You can also try *telnet*ing to port 210 (the Z39.50 port) to see if the server is listening. If you don't get a connection, make sure the server is starting up. If the pathname to the server executable is wrong, or the arguments are wrong, the server won't start.

Again, if you have no idea why it isn't working, you can check the newsgroup *comp.infosystems.wais*. Scan the subject lines and check if anyone's already had a problem like yours. If not, ask for help.

Once you've verified that the server is installed and running correctly, you'll probably want to move the various binaries into their permanent homes. We use */usr/local/bin* for the standard clients, */usr/local/bin/X11* for X clients, and */usr/local/etc* for the indexer, server and support tools. If you move *waisserver*, be sure to update *inetd.conf* with the new pathname *and* signal *inetd* to reread its configuration.

7.4 Configuring waisserver

Although most of WAIS's configuration options belong to *waisindex*, there are a few interesting configuration wrinkles available with *waisserver*. Besides the basic command-line options we covered in Section 7.3, the *waisserver* in freeWAIS has security features that allow the administrator to restrict access to the server based on domain names.

7.4.1 waisserver Run-Time Configuration

We've already mentioned *waisserver*'s *–e* and *–l* options, which control logging. There are a few others that you may need if you want to run WAIS in a nonstandard way.

7.4.1.1 Changing the port waisserver listens to

By default, *waisserver* listens to the local host's *z3950* port, as defined in */etc/services* or the NIS *services* map. If you need to run the server on a different port, for testing purposes or perhaps to hide the sources it brokers, you can use the *–p* option. As an option argument, you specify a port number for *waisserver* to listen to.

Running *waisserver* on another port lets you run multiple *waisserver*s at once, which can be handy if you're testing one or more new sources. The production server can continue to run on the Z39.50 port, while the test server runs on a nonstandard, high-numbered port. Also, *waisserver* doesn't require *root* privileges to run on a port above 1023. You can have the developer or maintainer of a source bring up a server, test the sources, and get everything ready for production, all without *root* access, and then have the system administrator actually bring the new sources into production. WAIS clients will know to contact the server on the new port as long as the correct port number is listed in the source description file.

Some WAIS administrators also run their servers on non-standard ports in order to gain a modicum of security—"security through obscurity"—for their sources. While this is a poor alternative to real server security, it is a possibility; we'll discuss security in Section 7.4.2.

7.4.1.2 Running waisserver as a different user

No matter how you start *waisserver*—under *inetd* or standalone—if you run on the standard Z39.50 port you need to start it as *root*. The standard Z39.50 port, 210, is a UNIX reserved port, and as such can only be bound to by processes running as *root*. Since it's always possible that there are nasty ways of misusing the Z39.50 protocol to do dastardly things or clever means to exploit bugs in *waisserver*'s implementation to gain access to the host system, it's important to have *waisserver* switch over to running as another, non-*root* user as soon as it's bound to the Z39.50 port. The *–u* option, which we introduced in Section 7.3.1, lets you do this. It takes *–u*, the new user ID, as an option. We used *–u* in all the examples shown in this chapter.

7.4.2 Server Security

Francois Shiettecatte, who with Don Gilbert is responsible for many of the enhancements to the original WAIS, added two very useful security features to freeWAIS. The first is the ability to limit access to your server (and all sources offered by your server) to a particular set of hosts. The second is the ability to limit access to particular sources on your server to a particular set of hosts. Together, these features give administrators fine-grained control over who gets access to what using WAIS.

7.4.2.1 Server access control

Access to the server is controlled by entries in the server security file, defined in *server.h* by the variable `SERVSECURITYFILE`. By default, the filename is *SERV_SEC*. You should put *SERV_SEC* in the same directory as the index files. If the file doesn't exist, then the server grants access to any client. The file should be readable by the user *waisserver* runs as and writable only by authorized users. In fact, you probably only want to let *root* or your WAIS data librarian modify it.

Entries in *SERV_SEC* should have the format

```
domainname        [IP address]
```

The *domainname* field can contain the domain name of either a host or a DNS zone. This host, or hosts in this domain, are allowed access to the server and *potentially* to all of the sources brokered by the server. (The database security file, described in the next section, determines access to individual sources.) The IP address field is optional.

If the address field is filled in, then clients can match either the domainname field or the address field to gain access.

So, for example, the server security file

```
hp.com          15
ora.com         198.112.208
ohbear.boulder.co.us
```

allows users in the *hp.com* and *ora.com* domains, on networks with IP addresses 15 or 198.112.208, or on the host *ohbear.boulder.co.us*, access to the server running on the local host. Note that *hp.com* and *ora.com* are roughly equivalent to network 15 and network 198.112.208 in administrative terms. However, *waisserver* doesn't check whether the name and address you specify are the same. If you added:

```
foo.bar.baz     192.1.1.2
```

to *SERV_SEC*, where *foo.bar.baz*'s IP address isn't 192.1.1.2, your server would allow access to both the host named *foo.bar.baz* and the host with IP address 192.1.1.2 .

Hosts whose IP addresses don't map back to real domain names can cause problems with WAIS's server security, too. If a host's IP address doesn't map back to a domain name, the security check always fails. The same section of code in *waisserver.c* that tries to map the client's IP address back to a name doesn't convert the IP address into dotted-octet format if the reverse mapping fails, and unconverted IP addresses never match entries in *SERV_SEC*. Look for that to be fixed in an upcoming version of free-WAIS. Until then, you might want to consider fixing the code in *waisserver.c*. Delete the braces in the section that reads:

```
    if(peer != NULL) {
        sprintf(host_name, "%s", peer->h_name);

        sprintf(host_address, "%s",
#if defined(sparc) && defined(__GNUC__)
                inet_ntoa(&source.sin_addr)
#else
                inet_ntoa(source.sin_addr)
#endif                                      /* sparc */
               );
 }
```

so it looks like this:

```
    if(peer != NULL)
        sprintf(host_name, "%s", peer->h_name);

        sprintf(host_address, "%s",
#if defined(sparc) && defined(__GNUC__)
                inet_ntoa(&source.sin_addr)
#else
                inet_ntoa(source.sin_addr)
#endif                                      /* sparc */

              );
```

If you don't do that, the only way to allow access to folks without good name service is to open the source to everyone, with:

```
* *
```

in the *SERV_SEC* file. Of course, that defeats the purpose of *having* a security file.

Two other minor flaws in *SERV_SEC* implementation are worth pointing out: first, specifying an IP address like 15.59.16.1 in *SERV_SEC* inadvertently allows access to 15.59.16.10 through 15.59.16.19 because the security mechanism only checks that the prefix of the IP address matches what's in *SERV_SEC*. The solution is to use a trailing dot. For example, if you want to allow all of the network 128.11 access to your server, but not the networks 128.110 through 129.119, which start with the same prefix, use `128.11.` (that is, add a trailing dot) in *SERV_SEC*.

Also, you must use fully qualified domain names to identify hosts. While *hp.com* in *SERV_SEC* matches any host in *hp.com*, *ohbear* in *SERV_SEC* doesn't match the domain name *ohbear.boulder.co.us*, even if *boulder.co.us* is the server's local domain.

7.4.2.2 Database security

To control access to individual sources offered by the server, use the database security file. The pathname of the database security file is defined in *server.h* by the variable `DATASECURITYFILE`. The filename is *DATA_SEC* by default, and it is expected to live in the same directory as the index files.

Entries in the *DATA_SEC* file have the format:

```
source    domainname    [IP address]
```

source may appear on multiple lines. Each line grants access to the named source from the host or hosts specified by *domainname*. As with the server security file, the *IP address* field is optional. *DATA_SEC* currently misbehaves in much the same way as *SERV_SEC*: entries in the address field allow all IP addresses with the same prefix as that entry, so you should use fully-qualified domain names (with a trailing dot).

If the *DATA_SEC* file exists, all sources must be listed in it. Sources not listed in the file aren't accessible by anyone.

The *DATA_SEC* file also allows wildcards, so that it's convenient to allow access to everyone. The entry:

```
products    *    *
```

allows all hosts access to the *products* source.

If you're denied access via *DATA_SEC*, you'll probably see a message something like this:

```
$ ws ETCHOSTS babs
waissearch -h babs.nsr.hp.com -d ETCHOSTS -p 210 babs

  Search Response:
    NumberOfRecordsReturned: 1
    Code: T2, Unautorized access to database:
```

The spelling error is peculiar to *waisq* and *waissearch*, so you may be fortunate enough not to see it.

7.4.3 WAIS and Firewalls

If you're an administrator of a system with a group of users who run WAIS clients, you may well have to deal with a security firewall between you and the Internet. You may want to read part of Chapter 27, *Firewalls and Information Services*, for some background on what firewalls are and some ways to deal with them. If there's a firewall between your computers and the Internet, your computers can't send or receive IP datagrams—and therefore WAIS queries or responses—directly to the Internet. So your WAIS clients can't send queries to the Internet.

Fortunately, the WAIS code provides an easy way to deal with this. The server supports forwarding WAIS queries and responses, and the clients support using a forwarder if they can't talk directly to a WAIS server. You can set up a WAIS server with forwarding capabilities on a host with Internet connectivity (such as the firewall machine), then configure your WAIS clients inside the firewall to use that WAIS server to get to the Internet. When the clients need information from Internet WAIS servers, they send their queries to the forwarding WAIS server, which then passes those queries along to the real Internet WAIS servers. When the answers come back, the forwarding WAIS server sends them on to the clients. As far as the clients know, they're talking directly to the Internet WAIS servers.

Figure 7-2 shows what a WAIS forwarder looks like in graphical terms.

You can also recommend this solution to your users if you are setting up a WAIS database that the users can't access because they have a firewall between them and the Internet. But they need to convince the administrator of that firewall to follow these directions. There can be a forwarder on your firewall and one on theirs too, and it still works.

There are two changes you need to make to take advantage of this functionality:

- You need to modify the source code in the *source.c* file in the *ui* subdirectory. This enables the forwarding capability in your clients. The server already has the capability to handle forwarding WAIS queries and responses, but it must be installed on a host with Internet access.

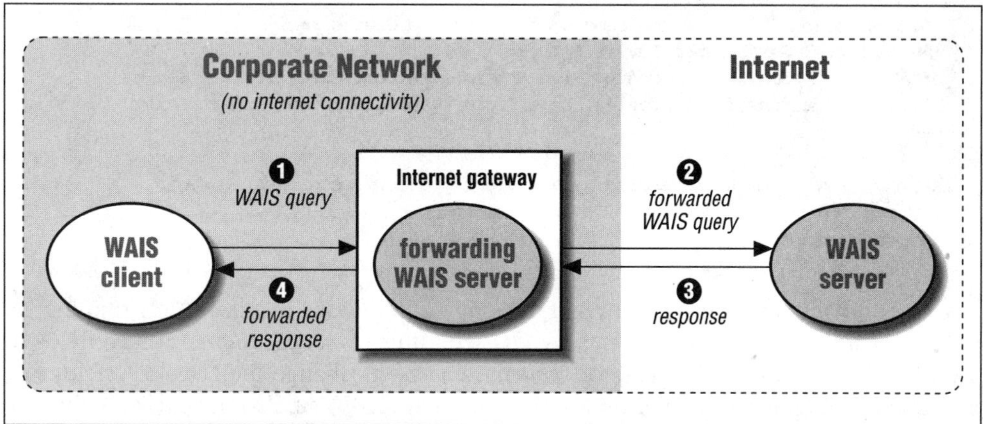

Figure 7-2. What a WAIS forwarder does

- You have to change the source descriptions of any Internet sources you'd like your internal (i.e., inside the firewall) users to access through the forwarding server.

First, find the file *ui/source.c*. In the freeWAIS 0.3 release, there's a commented line just before the `init_for_source()` routine that looks like this:

```
/* #define FORWARDER_SERVER "welchlab.welch.jhu.edu" */
```

This is where you define the domain name of the server you want WAIS requests passed off to if the client can't reach the server it wants. If your firewall host is called *relay.corp.com*, set the define to be:

```
#define FORWARDER_SERVER "relay.corp.com"
```

If you're running your forwarding server on a non-standard port, you also need to modify the line:

```
#define FORWARDER_SERVICE "210"
```

Change `210` to the port you're running your server on.

You now need to modify any Internet source description files your clients are using. In the spirit of reinventing government, let's modify (reinvent?) the source description file for the National Performance Review, which starts like this:

```
(:source
  :version  3
  :ip-address "152.2.22.81"
  :ip-name "sunsite.unc.edu"
  :tcp-port 210
  :database-name "National-Performance-Review"
  :cost 0.00
  :cost-unit :free
```

```
    :maintainer "jem@sunsite.unc.edu"
    :description " This is the report of the United States ▶▶▶
▶▶▶\"National Performance Review\" (NPR),
created by a committee headed by Vice-President Albert Gore. It is a series
of recommendations for improving the efficiency of government and reducing
waste.

keywords: government, bureacracy, management, review, economics, budget,
savings.
"
    )
```

You need to modify it just slightly, so that the source looks as though it's running on your own firewall host. You do this by changing the `ip-address` and `ip-name` fields to the IP address and domain name of your firewall host. Change the `tcp-port` field, too, if you're running the forwarder on a port other than 210. You also have to tack the real server's name onto the end of the `database-name` field, so that the firewall server knows where to go to contact the real server. The file ends up looking like this:

```
(:source
    :version  3
    :ip-address "192.1.2.3"
    :ip-name "relay.corp.com"
    :tcp-port 210
    :database-name "National-Performance-Review@sunsite.unc.edu"
    :cost 0.00
    :cost-unit :free
    :maintainer "jem@sunsite.unc.edu"
    :description " This is the report of the United States ▶▶▶
▶▶▶\"National Performance Review\" (NPR),
created by a committee headed by Vice-President Albert Gore. It is a series
of reccomendations for improving the efficiency of government and reducing
waste.

keywords: government, bureacracy, management, review, economics, budget,
savings.
"
    )
```

If the target server is running on a non-standard port, add `:`*port* to the `database-name` field (e.g., `National-Performance-Review@sunsite.unc.edu:9999`).

That's all it takes. Your clients will now either be spoofed into contacting your forwarding server for requests to the external Internet source or will use the defined `FORWARDER_SERVER` to get their information.

Just in case you're in the daunting—but increasingly common—situation of having to go through two firewalls to get to the source you need to reach, you can nest even more relays in the `database-name` field. For example, let's say you want to get through your company's firewall, across the Internet, through another company's firewall, and finally to the destination WAIS server. You could use a source file like this:

```
(:source
  :version  3
  :ip-address "192.1.2.3"
  :ip-name "relay.corp.com"
  :tcp-port 210
  :database-name "Private-Src@internal.othercorp.com@firewall.othercorp.com"
  :cost 0.00
  :cost-unit :free
  :maintainer "wais@internal.othercorp.com"
  :description ""
  )
```

When you query this source, your client sends the query to the WAIS forwarder on *relay.corp.com.* The forwarder then relays the query to the forwarder on *firewall.othercorp.com,* which passes the query to its final destination on *internal.othercorp.com.* Complicated, but possibly a lifesaver.

In this Chapter:
- *Index Files*
- *Relevance Ranking*
- *A Table for the Impatient*
- *Document Formats*
- *Other Command-Line Options*
- *Customizing waisindex Operation*
- *Updating Indexes*

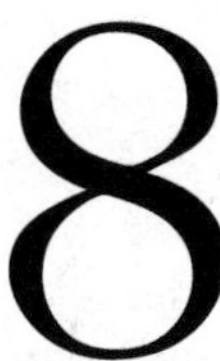

Creating WAIS Sources with waisindex

In WAIS, the data librarian's role is chiefly to build WAIS sources (databases) by indexing collections of documents. While that may sound dull, proper indexing of documents in WAIS is actually quite challenging. You've got to keep in mind who will be searching your database, what document formats they can handle, and what types of searches they'll be performing.

Most of the work the WAIS data librarian does is with the *waisindex* program. *waisindex* builds the WAIS index necessary for *waisserver* to conduct searches from a collection of files. At the beginning of Section 7.3, we created a small test source with *waisindex* from the */etc/hosts* file. Now it's time to move on to bigger and better sources, with more varied types of documents. *waisindex* supports a whole host of document formats besides the *one_line* format we used. We'll go over the major document formats *waisindex* supports and show how to index them. We'll also cover the other important command-line options. First, though, it might be helpful to describe what *waisindex* does and how it does it.

8.1 Index Files

waisindex actually does ahead of time most of the hard work necessary to service a query from a WAIS client. *waisindex* reads the files that contain the data for the source, parses them according to the format you indicate on the command line, and builds the index files. The format you specify tells *waisindex*:

- What delimits individual documents within the files you'd like it to parse (e.g., lines of dashes, file boundaries)
- Which part of the document to use as its "headline," the short description returned to a user when the document matched his search

- Which parts of the document to index. For example, you probably don't want *waisindex* to bother indexing the binary contents of a TIFF (graphics) file.

waisindex actually creates seven different index files for one database! Five of the index files are in a format intelligible only to *waisindex*, *waisserver*, and some clients (and administrators with the WAIS source code in front of them). The final two index files in our list are meant for human consumption. The original database files are also needed after indexing.

Dictionary (*.dct*) file
: The dictionary file contains a list of all the words that occurred in the files you fed *waisindex*, sorted alphabetically. Each word points to a position in the inverted (*.inv*) file. When *waisserver* searches the source for a word in a user's search, it looks in the dictionary file to see whether the word occurs. If the word does occur, the pointer to the inverted file tells it where it occurs.

Inverted (*.inv*) file
: The inverted file contains pointers from each word in the dictionary file to every document it appears in and where in each document the word appears. For each appearance of the word, the inverted file also includes a weight. The weight is based on factors like where in the document the word appears and how many times the word occurs in the document versus the document's size. (We'll discuss weight in more detail later in this chapter.) When *waisserver* performs a search, it uses the information in the inverted file to tell the user which documents contain the search words and to indicate how closely each document matched the search (using the weight).

Document (*.doc*) table
: The document table contains a list of the documents in the source and information on each of these documents, including:

  - A pointer into the filename table, to the name of the database file that contains the document.
  - The position of the document in the database file (remember that a single file can be parsed into multiple documents).
  - A pointer into the headline table, to the headline itself (which can be rather long).

Filename (*.fn*) table
: The filename table contains a list of all of the filenames used to create the source.

Headline (*.hl*) table — The headline table contains a list of all of the headlines in the documents in the source.

Catalog (*.cat*) — The catalog contains a list of all of the headlines that appear within the source and their corresponding document IDs. The catalog is usually returned when a user requests a search that produces no matches. The user can then retrieve the catalog and look through it to see how to craft a more productive search.

Source description (*.src*) — The source description, which we've already mentioned briefly, contains information on the WAIS source and its server, in a LISP-like format, including:

- Which host it runs on and the host's IP address
- Which port the server listens to
- The name of the source
- The cost of using the source*
- The email address of the maintainer of the source
- A description of the server

Only exported sources include host and port information. Only local clients can access non-exported sources.

Database files — These are the files originally indexed. They are needed even after they have been indexed, because *waissearch* extracts the information directly from them, using all the other files just to find things more quickly.

waisindex only creates a source description file if one doesn't already exist, or if the material you index looks sufficiently different from the last material you indexed. Relying on *waisindex*'s idea of "sufficiently different" is a little chancy. Consequently, if you change any of the important information in the source description file, you may have to update it manually or delete it and run *waisindex* again to update it. Also, some fields, like the description, are better written by the maintainer of the source and server than by *waisindex*. The maintainer can include valuable information like the features the server supports (stemming, boolean searches, etc.), while the server only injects a dull timestamp message into the field.

* This implies that there's support for billing in freeWAIS, but there really isn't much. About the best you can do is log queries and generate a bill from the log.

Here's a copy of the current source description file for the Internet's directory of servers, to give you an idea of what these puppies look like:

```
(:source
   :version  3
   :ip-address "192.31.181.1"
   :ip-name "quake.think.com"
   :tcp-port 210
   :database-name "directory-of-servers"
   :cost 0.00
   :cost-unit :free
   :maintainer "wais-directory-of-servers@quake.think.com"
   :subjects "general guide WAIS servers"
   :description
"Server created with WAIS-8 on Fri Mar  8 14:30:57 1991 by
 brewster@think.com
This is a White Pages listing of WAIS servers.  For more information on
WAIS, use the WAIS system on the wais-docs server, or add yourself to the
wais-discussion@think.com mailing list, or get the newest software from
think.com:/public/wais.

To server makers: Please make new servers of text, pictures, music
whatever.  We will try to list all servers in the directory that get sent
in to: directory-of-servers@quake.think.com (use the -register option on
the command waisindex), but I reserve the right to take servers out if they
are not consistently available.  I will send notice to the maintainer
before doing so.

To get a list of all available sources, search for 'source'.  This may be
limited by the maximum number of results allowed by a client.

Bugs and comments to bug-wais@think.com.
 -brewster@think.com
"
)
```

Note the extensive description added by the maintainers, and the email address. *waisindex* fills out the other fields, but these two, in particular, you should fill out yourself. The email address defaults to the address of the user who built the source with *waisindex*. You might want to create a *wais-admin* alias and substitute that for *root* or whoever actually ran *waisindex*.

8.2 Relevance Ranking

waisindex does most of the calculations necessary to determine which documents best match which search words as it builds the index files. It does this using a weighting algorithm that involves a number of different criteria:

Word weight
: A word occurring in a document has a weight assigned to it according to its position in the text. If the word appears in the portion of the document used

as the headline, it gets the highest weight. Capitalized words get the next-highest weight, and words that appear in the normal text of the document get the lowest weight.

Term weight

Term weight is based on the idea that a term that appears rarely in documents is probably important in the documents that it does appear in.

As *waisindex* parses the files you fed it, it keeps track of how often each word it encounters occurs. Words that occur frequently in the documents receive low term weights, while words that rarely occur receive high term weights. Consequently, if a user searches for "prices for Hewlett-Packard workstations" and "prices" occurs in every document in the source, while "Hewlett-Packard" appears in only one, the document which includes "Hewlett-Packard" receives a higher term weight for "Hewlett-Packard" than any document receives for "prices." (And since "Hewlett-Packard" is capitalized, its word weight should be higher, too.) The word "for," incidentally, is a **stopword**, a word so common in English that it's not even indexed. We'll talk more about stopwords later in this chapter.

Proximity

When a user searches for a number of words, and those words are found close together in a document, that document is assigned a higher weight than one in which the words appear scattered farther apart. In the document in which the words are found close together, it's more likely that they are being used in the same context as the user meant. For example, the query "What is love?" is more likely to be answered by a document including the phrase "what love is" or "love is what" than a document in which the three words appear widely separated.

waisindex must be invoked with the *–pos* option to enable the proximity feature. *waissearch*, though, actually calculates the proximity of the search words using the position information prepared in advance by *waisindex*.

Word density

Word density is simply the ratio of the number of times a word appears in a given document to the total size of the document, in words. This is an indication of how relevant the word is to the subject of the document. For example, a document that mentions "hovercraft" ten times in 1000 words is very probably about hovercraft, while one that mentions "hovercraft" only once in 1000 words could be only tangentially related.

Together, these factors are used to compute an overall relevance ranking for each document in a source given a particular search. The relevance ranking determines the order in which the resulting documents are presented to the user for retrieval.

8.3 A Table for the Impatient

Since not all of you are going to read straight through the rest of this chapter to find the information you need, here's a table to help you find your way. This table correlates *waisindex* command-line options to their function and then to the section they're described in:

Option	Function	Section
–a	Add to existing index	Section 8.5.4, Section 8.7.3
–d	Name of source	Section 8.5.1
–[no]contents	[Don't] index the contents of files	Section 8.5.7
–e	Log to file	Section 8.5.6
–export	Include network information in source description	Section 8.5.2
–l	Log level	Section 8.5.6
–mem	Limit memory use	Section 8.5.8
–nocat	Don't create a catalog file	Section 8.5.8
–[no]pairs	[Don't] index word pairs as phrases	Section 8.5.7
–[no]pos	[Don't] include word position information for proximity searches	Section 8.5.7
–r	Index subdirectories	Section 8.5.5
–register	Send source description to directory-of-servers	Section 8.5.3
–stdin	Get filenames from standard input	Section 8.5.7
–stop	Name of a file that contains a list of the stopwords	Section 8.6.1
–t	Document type for indexing	Section 8.4
–v	Print version	—
–M	Multitype document	Section 8.4.2
–T	Document type returned to client	Section 8.4.1

8.4 Document Formats

waisindex currently understands almost 30 different document formats specified with the *–t* option, and new formats are being added. Each of these formats uses a different combination of rules for determining which part of the file gets indexed and which part is used as the headline. The format chosen also determines what document type is returned to the WAIS client. For example, indexing files with the *gif* format causes the server to return the files to clients asserting they're type GIF. If the client can display a document of that type, great. If not, the best the server can do is to transfer a binary copy.

Here are the most common formats that *waisindex* can process:

text The *text* format is the default format and probably the most common. Each text file is parsed as its own document, and the entire file is indexed. The pathname of the file is used as the headline. Contrast this format with the *filename* format.

filename The *filename* format is identical to the *text* format, except that the filename, not the pathname, is used as the headline.

first_line The *first_line* format instructs *waisindex* to treat each indexed file as an individual document and the first nonblank line of the file as the headline. The rest of the file is indexed as text.

one_line *one_line* is the format we used to index the */etc/hosts* file: it treats each line in the input file(s) as both a separate document and as the headline for that document.

gif, tiff, and *pict*
These are graphical formats that tell *waisindex* not to index the contents of the files at all. Each file becomes a document, and the filename is used as the headline.

dash The *dash* format tells *waisindex* to look for a line of at least 20 dashes delimiting documents within each file. The line after the dashes is interpreted as the headline, and the remaining lines before the next set of dashes are indexed.

dvi and *ps* These are printer-output formats (device-independent TeX output and PostScript). Both are handled identically: each file is a separate document, the filename is used as the headline, and the contents of the file are indexed.

mail_or_rmail
This format parses standard UNIX mailbox (*mbox*) files into documents consisting of individual mail messages. The *Subject* field of each message becomes the corresponding document's headline, and the body of the message is indexed.

mail_digest
The *mail_digest* format parses standard Internet mail digests (as created by an MH *forw –digest* command, for example) into individual messages. Other than that, it's the same as the *mail_or_rmail* format: the *Subject* field becomes the headline, and the body of each message is indexed.

netnews The *netnews* format instructs *waisindex* to treat the input files as Internet standard News files. Each news posting becomes its own document, with the *Subject* field as its headline. The full text of the posting (not including the header) is indexed.

ftp The *ftp* format is used by special, modified WAIS clients. These clients have integrated FTP code, so that they can FTP files from a remote server. This code isn't common in WAIS clients yet, so this format isn't used often. Basically, you can use *waisindex* to index your *~ftp* directory, or those parts of it you want to make available with WAIS. This builds an index of all of the *README* and *INDEX* files in the hierarchy, which clients will search. They can select a filename from within those files and have the modified WAIS download it automatically using FTP.

URL With the URL format, you can induce the server to return headlines that are actually legal Uniform Resource Locators.* This enables a user with a World Wide Web browser that has native WAIS support to search your WAIS server. Since the server returns valid URLs as the result of the search, the user can choose one of the resulting URLs and have his browser access it directly. *waisindex* builds the URLs by stripping a prefix you specify from the names of the files you're indexing and then appending the remainder to another prefix you specify. So, for example, let's say you want to make your entire FTP area searchable by WAIS and retrievable by World Wide Web clients. You could run *waisindex* like this:

```
% /usr/local/etc/waisindex -d ohbear-ftp -t URL /users/ftp \
file://ohbear.nsr.hp.com -r /users/ftp/*
```

This indexes the entire filesystem under */users/ftp* as type URL. The contents of the files are indexed, and the URLs are built by taking the pathname of each file indexed, removing `/users/ftp` from the beginning, then adding `file://ohbear.nsr.hp.com` to the beginning. So if a user queries the source, and matches the contents of the file */users/ftp/pub/crocodiles/index*, the headline that the server returns to the user's browser is URL *file://ohbear.nsr.hp.com/pub/crocodiles/index*, which is presumably a valid URL for retrieving that file. If the user selects the headline, the browser transfers the file.

The only problem with using the URL format is that users with plain vanilla WAIS clients who search your source will get URLs back instead of the document headlines they're used to. Those familiar with URLs probably won't be too put off, but others may be mystified by the cryptic format of the URL.

server The *server* format is used to create a "source of sources": a database of *.src* files. The Internet's two *directory-of-servers.src* sources use this format. Each *.src* file is a separate document, with the filename as the headline. The contents of each file is indexed as text.

* Uniform Resource Locators tell World Wide Web clients what protocol to use to access an Internet resource, which host the resource is on, and how to identify it on that host. For more information, see Chapter 17, *Introduction to the World Wide Web*.

Even though there may be a number of different formats that specify the same rules for parsing documents from files, finding headlines, and indexing text, it's important to use the one that's correct for the type of data you're indexing. Some WAIS clients, including *xwais*, use the format to determine which viewer to execute to display a given document. If a user only has a GIF and TIFF viewer, and you index your GIF files in the *pict* format, he won't be able to view them.

8.4.1 Indexing Other File Types

Certain WAIS clients, Mosaic in particular, can handle lots and lots of document types, including quite a few that you can't specify with *–t*. To accommodate these clients, *waisindex* lets you use the *–T* option to specify a type it doesn't know anything about. The *–T* option takes the name of the type as an argument. The documents you index with *–T* are tagged and returned to clients identified as the type you specified. By default, the contents of the files aren't indexed, and the filename becomes the headline. To modify this default behavior and have the contents indexed, use the *–contents* command-line option to *waisindex*, described in Section 8.5.7

As long as the client understands the format, everything works fine; *waisserver* just sends the document to the client as a binary file. You can use the *–T* option to index any of the MIME* types that Mosaic understands, for example. The type you return should match the name of a filetype in the user's system's *mailcap* file, or an individual user's *.mailcap* file. For example, if the system's *mailcap* file includes the line:

```
video/mpeg; /usr/local/bin/X11/mpeg_play %s
```

to run *mpeg_play* to display files of type mpeg, you can index files with *–T MPEG*, and WWW browsers on your system that retrieve the file will display it with the *mpeg_play* program.

Let's index our local collection of HTML† documents, including their contents, so that users on our LAN can do keyword searches on them. To do this, we'll run *waisindex* like this:

```
# /usr/local/etc/waisindex -d WebDocs -T HTML -contents -export \
/usr/local/etc/httpd/htdocs/*.html
```

Mosaic users with native WAIS support available can now open the URL *wais://hostname:210/WebDocs?searchword* to search the source (replace *hostname* and

* MIME is the Multimedia Internet Mail Extensions, a specification for handling multipart and multitype mail messages. For more information on MIME, see RFCs 1521 and 1522. For more information on *mailcap* files, see Chapter 17, *Introduction to the World Wide Web* or the documentation contained in the *metamail* package, available via anonymous FTP from *ftp.uu.net* in */networking/mail/metamail*.

† For more information on HTML, World Wide Web, and the Mosaic browser, see Chapter 17, *Introduction to the World Wide Web*.

searchword with the local hostname and the word you'd like to search for). Documents the users retrieve are displayed by the Mosaic browser just like any other HTML document, and other HTML documents can include hypertext links to this WAIS server.

8.4.2 Associating One File with Another

Not only can the Mosaic browser talk directly to a WAIS server, it also includes a nice facility to show the user a set of files that are somehow related in the source being queried. So, for example, a user might search for a document about wolves, and Mosaic might find not only a text document about wolves, but also a related audio clip of a wolf's howl, a GIF picture of an arctic wolf, and a pretty PostScript version of the text document.

To provide links like these on a WAIS server, you must index your documents with a special command-line option, the *–M* option. This option controls the indexing of multitype documents, which is what WAIS administrators call related or associated documents of different types. *–M* takes as an argument a string of types that *waisindex* should look for in the set of files it's indexing. The files themselves must have filename extensions that tell *waisindex* their type—*waisindex* doesn't have the smarts to guess.

So, let's say you've got a set of text, PostScript, GIF, and audio files you'd like to index and associate with each other. Right now, they look like this:

```
$ ls
husky-howl.au   malamute-howl.au      wolf-howl.au
husky.gif       malamute.gif          wolf.gif
huskies.ps      malamutes.ps          wolf.ps
huskies.txt     malamutes.txt         wolf.txt
```

In order to use multitype indexing, all the files that you want associated with each other need to have the same base filename (the filename minus any file extension), and the file extension must match the format, in uppercase. So you need to rename the files so that they look something like this:

```
$ ls
husky.AU        malamute.AU     wolf.AU
husky.GIF       malamute.GIF    wolf.GIF
husky.PS        malamute.PS     wolf.PS
husky.TEXT      malamute.TEXT   wolf.TEXT
```

Note that the extension for a text file is `.TEXT`, not `.TXT`, since the format is called "text." To index these, use a *waisindex* command like this:

```
# /usr/local/etc/waisindex -d canids -M AU,GIF,PS,TEXT -export *
```

The format arguments to *–M* must be capitalized. This command indexes the text files and associates with them the other files with the same base name. When a Mosaic user searches for a word or phrase that results in a hit in *husky.TEXT*, the user will be offered all four files. Figure 8-1 is a screen shot of Mosaic showing just that.

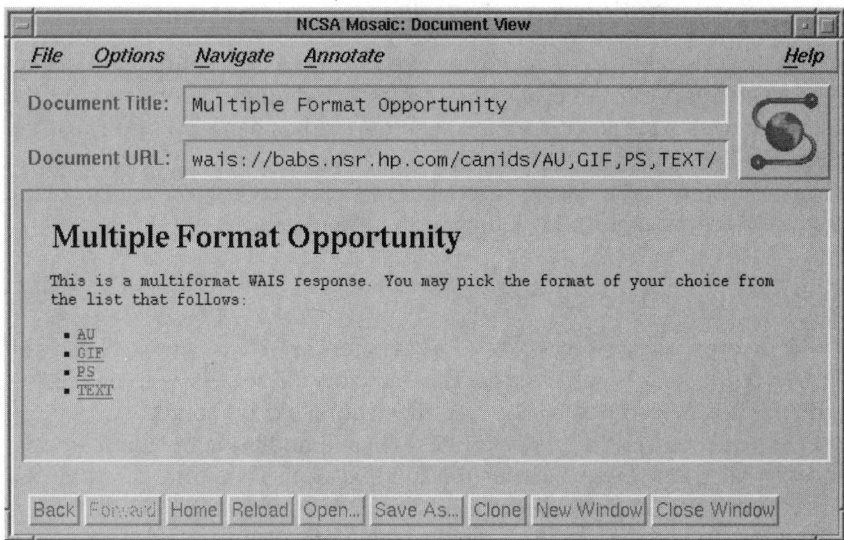

Figure 8–1. Mosaic accessing a WAIS database

Unfortunately, not all browsers currently support multitype documents, but others are sure to follow Mosaic's lead. Already, *xwais*, *MacWAIS*, and a few others support multitype documents. Since these are some of the most popular browsers available, don't hesitate to include multitype documents in your sources. Other browsers, incidentally, at least show users the text files.

8.5 Other Command-Line Options

waisindex gives the administrator the option to change the default behavior of various formats. For example, if you want to index the contents of a file, but the format you are using doesn't index the contents, you can tell *waisindex* explicitly to index the contents. Other options are available, too.

8.5.1 Naming Your Source

We've already shown several examples of building a source with *waisindex*. In each case, we specified the name of the source with the *–d* option. The string used as the name of the source dictates not only the base name for all of the index files, but the name that users will specify to contact the source. Therefore, it's a good idea to make it something memorable and recognizable.

8.5.2 Exporting Your Source

We've already covered this option—back when we created a test source and set up *waisserver*. We used *–export* to coerce *waisindex* into including the information in the *.src* file that remote clients need to contact the server—the hostname and port that the server is running on. Remember that we needed to delete our old *.src* file in order to update it, because *waisindex* won't always overwrite an existing *.src* file (it'll overwrite it only if it detects enough changes between versions of the source).

8.5.3 Registering Your Source

To find a new source on the Internet, WAIS users often search a source called the **directory of servers** (*directory-of-servers.src*). The directory of servers is a simple but powerful source. It's a collection of all the *.src* files submitted by source maintainers around the Internet, indexed in the *server* format. There's nothing particularly special about the *server* format—*waisindex* indexes the full text of the *.src* files. It's what the clients do with the files that's special: during a search, after a source description has been downloaded from the directory of servers, WAIS clients can use the description to contact the server that brokers that source. Since many of the *.src* files contain descriptive information about their sources, it's possible to search for keywords and discover sources that may be relevant.

If you want to register your source in the Internet's directory of servers, you should make sure you're going to put in the effort to keep your server and source up and available, and you should commit to keeping the directory of servers up-to-date should you make any changes (e.g., you move the server to another host or change the name of the source). Once you've made the commitment, run *waisindex* with the *–register* option. This invokes a section of code in *waisindex* that simply mails a copy of your source's *.src* file to both of the servers that export the directory-of-servers source.

8.5.4 Updating Existing Index Files

Once you've created a source by indexing a group of files, you'll have to update the index files periodically if the files change. For example, let's say you have a simple ASCII text database of names and phone numbers of people who work in your organization. You index it using the *one_line* format so that WAIS users can look up phone numbers given names, or vice-versa. What do you do when you get an updated file, though?

You could reindex the entire set of files, but that might take quite a while. If you have the changes to the database in their own file, you can tell WAIS to index just that file and add the index information to the existing index. That way, you save time.

The *–a* option instructs *waisindex* not to create a new index, but just to append the information to the existing index. Note that if you reindex, using *–a*, the same set of files that you created the index with, existing index information isn't updated—the new information is tacked onto the end. To keep the index accurate and remove index entries for old deleted data, you need to recreate the entire index.

8.5.5 Indexing an Entire Directory Tree

By default, *waisindex* won't descend into directories that you name on the command line. If you execute the command:

```
# waisindex -d TEMP /tmp
```

waisindex doesn't index the contents of your */tmp* directory. (To do that, you execute **waisindex -d TEMP /tmp/***.) If you want *waisindex* to recursively index directories, use the *–r* option. For example:

```
# waisindex -d FTP -r ~ftp
```

creates a source from the contents of all of the files under *~ftp*.

8.5.6 Configuring Logging

waisindex can log a lot of information as it builds an index. And like *waisserver*, *waisindex*'s *–e* and *–l* options control logging. *–e* takes as an argument the pathname of the log file, and *–l* specifies a logging level, between one and ten, with ten the most verbose.

Truth be told, only a few of the logging levels are meaningful. A logging level of zero means no logging at all. A logging level of one picks out only messages defined internally as priority *WLOG_HIGH*. A logging level of five adds in messages defined as *WLOG_MEDIUM*. Finally, a logging level of ten includes everything, even *WLOG_LOW* messages.

What kind of information is in these messages? *waisindex* issues various status messages, to say it's started indexing a particular file, or that it's detected enough differences between the words in the previous version of the source and the current version to rewrite the source description file.

8.5.7 Controlling Indexing

waisindex also lets you override the default indexing behavior in various ways. For example, if you want to allow proximity searches (searches that take into account how close together the words being searched for are in the document), you need to index with the *–pos* option. The opposite, *–nopos*, is the default, so proximity searching won't work unless you explicitly enable it.

By default, *waisindex* treats adjacent pairs of capitalized words as "word pairs" and adds them to the dictionary together, as a phrase. If you want to inhibit this behavior, use the *–nopairs* option. You're the best judge of whether adjacent word pairs in your data really form a unique phrase, or whether *waisindex* should simply index them as separate words.

Normally, *waisindex* indexes the contents of the files you're feeding it if the format you specify with *–t* tells it to. (See Section 8.4 for details.) If you're using a format that doesn't index file contents, but you want the contents indexed anyway, use the *–contents* option. *waisindex* will build a full-text index of the text in the file. Similarly, if the format indexes file contents, but you don't want them indexed, use the *–nocontents* option.

The *–stdin* command-line option gives administrators a useful way to index large sets of files that aren't easy to specify on the command line. *–stdin* tells *waisindex* to expect the pathnames of the files to index on its standard input, rather than specified as arguments. This lets you use powerful UNIX commands like *find* to pick out only those files that you want indexed.

For example, if you just want to add to your index the files in your */docs* directory that have been modified in the last day, you can use the command:

```
$ find /docs -mtime 1 -print | /usr/local/etc/waisindex \
-stdin -d ohbear-docs -export
```

If the files you need to select are beyond even the capabilities of *find* to pick out, you can write a shell script or Perl script that prints the filenames you need to standard output, then pipe that into *waisindex –stdin.*

8.5.8 Saving Space

If you're tight on disk space or memory, there are two *waisindex* options to help out: *–mem* and *–nocat. –mem* lets you specify the number of megabytes of memory *waisindex* can use for indexing. The smaller the limit, the slower the indexing goes. The actual memory allocated for the process won't be exactly the number of megabytes you specify, but there is a correlation between the number you specify and the real size.

The *–cat* option controls the creation of the catalog file, discussed in Section 8.1 earlier in this chapter. Since the catalog file is just a nicety—it lets users read through the headlines in the source and figure out what kinds of documents are available—you have the option of preventing its creation with *–nocat.* This probably only makes sense if you have a ton of documents in your source, or extremely long headlines, either of which would create a long catalog file.

8.6 Customizing waisindex Operation

Besides the many command-line options, there are a number of other ways to customize the way that *waisindex* indexes files. *waisindex* has a standard list of words that it'll ignore, called **stopwords**. Stopwords are words that occur so often in common English usage that there's usually not much sense in indexing them. You may, however, want to add new words that appear so frequently in your documents that you don't want them indexed. Or you may want to delete a few from the predefined list. *waisindex* also provides a mechanism for administrators to define synonyms for words that appear in their documents. Perhaps your documents contain lots of arcane or technical terms, and you'd like to help users find documents without necessarily knowing the right word.

8.6.1 Selecting Words for waisindex to Ignore

As of freeWAIS 0.3, there are 389 stopwords listed in *stoplist.c*. These range from "a," "an," and "the" to "hereafter" and "thereafter." To add new words permanently to the predefined stoplist, you can add the words to the *stoplist* array of strings in *ir/stoplist.c* and recompile *waisindex*. If you just want to redefine the stoplist for this run of *waisindex*, and you've compiled WAIS with the *–DBIO* flag defined, you can use the *–stop* flag with *waisindex* to name a file that contains a list of all stopwords. Note that this stoplist *replaces* the stoplist in *stoplist.c*, so if you want to add to the predefined stoplist, you need to copy all of the words from *stoplist.c* into a file. That's easy, though. A simple *awk* or Perl script will do that.

8.6.2 Setting Up Synonyms

A classic problem for users of searching systems like WAIS is that the user thinks of "hosts" while the documents in the source refer only to "machines," or the user searches for "LANs" and the documents call them "local area networks." Even neat features like stemming can't save users from that. What the administrator can do, manually, is define synonyms for certain words on a per-source basis. When a user searches for one of these synonyms, the server associates it with the word the administrator has defined. The server then looks that word up in the documents.

Defining synonyms for a source is easy. You create a file called *SOURCE.syn* in the directory that contains all the other *SOURCE* files (e.g., *SOURCE.dct*). Each line in *SOURCE.syn* is of the form:

```
word synonym [synonym...]
```

For example:

```
computer host machine CPU processor
```

Defines `host`, `machine`, `CPU`, and `processor` as synonyms of the word `computer` in the source's documents. If the user searches for "high speed processors," an article on "speedy computers" may turn up.

How do you decide which words your source's users need to have listed as synonyms? *waisserver*'s log files are the best place to start. With the logging level turned up to ten, you'll see the words or phrases your users are searching for. If they're not finding anything, *waisserver* logs the somewhat snide message:

```
Returned 0 results.  Aww.
```

Look and see if what they looked up is a synonym for another term in your source. If it is, add it to your list of synonyms. And if you change the synonym file, be sure to reindex the source.

8.7 Updating Indexes

How and when you update your sources depends a great deal upon the information you're making available. If your sources don't change much and your server is stable, you probably won't have to spend a lot of time on reindexing. If you constantly update your source, you may need to spend more time on keeping your index up-to-date. With a little up-front effort, though, you can minimize that additional effort.

Whenever you add to the set of files that comprises your data collection, you'll need to reindex them. There are two ways to reindex: create a new index from scratch, or add to the existing index using *waisindex*'s *–a* option.

8.7.1 Indexing from Scratch Without Downtime

There's no trick to reindexing from scratch: you run *waisindex* the same way you would if you were creating the index for the first time. If your *waisindex* command doesn't change from run to run, you can have *cron* do your work for you.

One potential problem to consider when you reindex your source from scratch: while *waisindex* is writing the new files, no one can access your source. That may not be a problem if your users are never on when *cron* reindexes your files, or if the reindexing operation takes just a minute or two. But if you're trying to run a production, Internet-connected WAIS server, or reindexing your source takes hours, you might want to keep the source available while reindexing is taking place.

A good way to keep the source available is to build your new index files in a directory separate from your production index files, and then move the new ones into place only after *waisindex* has finished running. This assumes, of course, that you've got enough room in this filesystem for two copies of your index files. For example, you might run a script like this nightly from *cron*:

```
#!/bin/sh
#
# Script to reindex our monster database offline and then overwrite the
# old index.

mkdir /tmp/mobysource
cd /tmp/mobysource
```

```
/usr/local/etc/waisindex -d News -t netnews -r /usr/spool/news
mv News.* /usr/local/wais
rm -r /tmp/mobysource
```

This minimizes the potential downtime. Another possibility is to reindex all of your sources in a new directory and then rename that directory once *waisindex* is done with it. For example:

```
#!/bin/sh
#
# Script to rebuild all indexes, then flash-cut them into production

cd /usr/local/wais.old
/usr/local/etc/waisindex -d News -t netnews -r /usr/spool/news
/usr/local/etc/waisindex -d Gifs -t gif -r ~ftp/pub/gif
/usr/local/etc/waisindex -d Docs -t text -r ~ftp/pub/doc
mv /usr/local/wais /usr/local/wais.tmp
mv /usr/local/wais.old /usr/local/wais
mv /usr/local/wais.tmp /usr/local/wais.old
```

This assumes that */usr/local/wais*, */usr/local/wais.old*, and */usr/local/wais.tmp* are all in the same filesystem. Since each of these moves only involves a simple inode modification, and only the first two have to complete before the server has a usable index again, your server should only be non-functional for a moment.

8.7.2 Adding to an Old Index

If you routinely add documents to a source but rarely remove old ones, you may want to use *waisindex*'s *–a* option to add to the index periodically rather than rebuilding it. *–a* is really only useful if you don't remove documents from the source, since it only adds new information to the index. If you replace half your documents with new ones and reindex with *–a*, the old documents still appear in the index, as do their replacements. The old documents won't be retrievable, of course.

To add to an existing index, you need to use *waisindex*'s *–d* option to specify the name of the source, *–t* for the format of the files to be parsed, and *–a* to append to the current index. Add any other options necessary. For example, to add indexing information for the new *~ftp/newproducts* directory to your existing FTP source, you might run this *waisindex* command:

```
# /usr/local/etc/waisindex -d FTP -t text -a -r ~ftp/newproducts
```

The indexing information for the new files will be added to the existing FTP source's index.

8.7.3 Indexes with Multiple Types

You may find another occasion for using *waisindex*'s *–a* option: if you want to create a source containing documents of different types. For example, maybe you'd like to create a source that contains both a master list of your GIF files, including a description of each, and the GIF files themselves. You'd certainly like the list's contents indexed, and you want the list displayed as text when folks retrieve it. But you don't want the GIF files' contents indexed, and you want them displayed as GIFs once they have been downloaded.

To accomplish this, create the source by indexing one type of file first, then add to the existing index with *–a*, specifying the correct format for the files added. To go back to our example:

```
# /usr/local/etc/waisindex -d GIF -t gif -r ~ftp/gif
# /usr/local/etc/waisindex -d GIF -t text -a ~ftp/gif.README
```

Now you're a WAIS expert, so go index some data! There are also some sections later in the book that discuss integrating WAIS with Gopher and the Web, that you may find useful.

In this Chapter:

- *How Gopher Works: the Gopher Protocol*
- *What Is Gopher+?*
- *Selection of Server Software*
- *Variety of Client Software*
- *The Gopher FAQ*
- *Overview of Gopher Chapters*

9 Gopher: Introduction

In computers, the most powerful tools are the most general. The word processor. The spreadsheet. They do one thing well, yet have many different applications. Gopher is one such tool. It looks like a trivial program for browsing through files and directories from across the Internet. But its usefulness and sophistication go well beyond its modest appearance.

At its simplest, Gopher allows users to browse through directories like this:

```
                    Internet Gopher Information Client v2.0.16

                       Home Gopher server: wildlife.ora.com

 --> 1.  Introduction and Cover
     2.  Foreword
     3.  Country Accounts/
     4.  Search Country Data <?>
     5.  Wildlife FTP Site/


Press ? for Help, q to Quit                                      Page: 1/1
```

When a user selects a file, the file is retrieved and displayed. If the file happens to be a compressed or a binary file, Gopher retrieves it in an appropriate way so that it can be used as intended (uncompressed if it's compressed text, viewed in an external viewer if it's an image, etc.). This ability to "automatically do the right thing" is a big improvement over FTP, for example, which requires the user to specify the correct download format (binary or ASCII), then manually uncompress the document or start a viewer.

A simple browser, right? Not quite. The power of Gopher is that those menu items can actually point to files or directories on other Gopher servers, to FTP archives, to Telnet services, and more. Gopher was the first service to offer this kind of transparency, where traversing different machines and different services on the Internet is as easy as browsing a local directory.

Finally, Gopher's user interface (even the most primitive-looking text client) is very simple. There are very few commands, and most of those are listed at all times at the bottom of the screen. The commands are all one or two characters—very concise. That network and interservice transparency, "do the right thing" ability, and simple user interface together make Gopher excellent for people not so adept at computers (and UNIX in particular). It's intuitive. (Even experts like something simple like Gopher once in a while.)

Gopher does have some limits to be aware of, though. One is that menu-item descriptions are brief, sometimes too brief. For users, finding what they want, even with Gopher's searching features, is a trial-and-error process.

A mixed blessing with Gopher is that it is not as graphical as the World Wide Web. There are GUI-based browsers for Gopher, but they do little more than the text client. On the one hand, this means all users see about the same thing, regardless of which of the many clients they use, so it is easier to cater to all of them. On the other hand, Gopher does not take full advantage of graphical presentation. It does not allow text and images to be mixed in one document and viewed together, and it does not allow links from or to certain positions within documents. (Both are weaknesses the Web overcomes.)

9.1 How Gopher Works: the Gopher Protocol

Like most Internet services, Gopher uses a client/server architecture (see Section 1.2 for a definition). To understand Gopher thoroughly requires knowing what it does and then figuring out which part, the server or the client, performs which role in the process. We've already sketched out what Gopher (the server and client together) can do, so we'll start with the protocol. How the server and client talk demonstrates how they divide responsibilities.

The Gopher protocol is surprisingly simple. The client connects to a server, sends the server a selector string—a string of characters that describes the location of a document on the server. The server responds by sending the requested file or directory. That's it!

Let's start with what happens when a client connects to the root directory of a server. In this case the selector string is a blank line, which tells the server to send the contents of its root directory. You can see the protocol by using *telnet* to connect to a Gopher server. After you connect, you type the *gopher* client side of the protocol, which is just a Return. All the rest of this is the server side of the protocol:

```
% telnet wildlife.ora.com 70
Trying 128.101.54.54 ...
Connected to bud.weiser.ora.com.
Escape character is '^]'.
```

```
<Return>
0Introduction and Cover 0/Introduction and Cover         wildlife.ora.com     70
0Foreword         0/Foreword       wildlife.ora.com     70
1Country Accounts         1/Country Accounts       wildlife.ora.com     70
7Search Country Data      7/Country Accounts/index/country   wildlife.ora.com   70
1Wildlife FTP Site        ftp:wildlife.ora.com@/   wildlife.ora.com     70
.
Connection closed by foreign host.
```

That's what the protocol containing the root directory of our sample server—the same directory we showed in the *gopher* client at the beginning of this chapter—looks like. Each line represents a menu item. Within each line are four **fields**, separated by tabs. Notice that the server sends a period on a line by itself after transmitting a text file or directory, to signify the end of data, then it closes the connection. (However, many clients actually wait for the connection to close before assuming that they've seen the end of the data.)

We'll go into the meaning of each field in a moment. First, let's see what the client sends to the server to get one of these documents:

```
% telnet wildlife.ora.com 70
Trying 128.101.54.54 ...
Connected to gopher.tc.umn.edu.
Escape character is '^]'.
0/Introduction and Cover
Crocodiles: An Action Plan for their Conservation

IUCN Species Survival Commission:  A Global Network for Species Survival

Habitats and their living natural resources are under increasing
pressures everywhere from humankind.  Species, the basic biotic units,
are consequently increasingly threatened with extinction.  To protect
and conserve biodiversity from species level to ecosystem requires
management based on understanding of not just biological sciences, but
also knowledge of local cultures, environmental economics, and
governmental structures and dynamics.

more output...
.
Connection closed by foreign host.
```

Notice that we sent the string that appeared in the second field of the directory protocol in the first example above. Now let's go back and look at that directory protocol in more detail. Our original example showed one directory in the protocol. Let's take a closer look at one line of the protocol, which describes one menu item:

```
1Country Accounts         1/Country Accounts       wildlife.ora.com     70
```

The first character on the line tells the client what type of data the line describes. In this example, we see type 1 (directory). (There are other types that we'll discuss later.) The type is used by the client software to tell the user what type of information this item contains (usually by displaying an icon or other notifier next to the menu-item text), and to do the right thing when the user selects an item. The number 1 indicates a directory, so the text client puts a slash after the menu-item text.

The characters between the type descriptor and the first TAB form the menu-item text that the client displays to the user.

The characters between the first tab and the next tab form the selector string that the client software sends to the server to retrieve the item. The selector string is most often a type descriptor followed by the pathname of the item. It may also be a "Cool Link" as seen in the last line, *ftp:wildlife.ora.com@/*. Cool Links will be introduced in Section 13.4.

The last two tab-separated items on the line are the host and port number that are used to retrieve that item.

Notice that the client finds out where to get the information from one Gopher server, but it actually gets the information directly from the (possibly different) Gopher server where the data is. In other words, the client talks directly to each Gopher server used, not through the previous Gopher servers that have been visited. The "tunnelling gopher" image, therefore, is a little off. You do not tunnel through each Gopher server to the next, you always tunnel directly from your client to each server.

Gateway services, like FTP and WAIS, go through the Gopher server. In other words, if a client requests an FTP transaction, the Gopher server handles that transaction with the FTP archive. The client only deals directly with the Gopher server. You can see evidence of this in the last line of the Gopher protocol we've been discussing. The selector string is `ftp:wildlife.ora.com@/`, which requests the root directory of an FTP archive. But notice that the port number is 70 (the Gopher port), so the client will be talking directly to the Gopher server, not to an FTP server running on the same machine.

The one extention to the protocol occurs when the client sends an index query. When the user selects an index to query, the client asks the user for a keyword. That keyword is passed to the server after the selector string. The selector string and the keyword are separated by a TAB character. For example, to search for "saltwater" in the index listed in the directory shown above, the selector string sent would look like `7/Country Accounts/index/country<TAB>saltwater`.

The beauty of this protocol is that the location of each item is totally transparent to the user. The protocol contains all of the relevant information required to retrieve the data. The data could be coming from the local machine, or it could be located on a machine on the other side of the globe; the user never needs to know where it's coming from.

We should also note that clients optimize their use of the protocol. For example, if you progress down through a series of menus, each new menu requires a protocol request to get the menu. But when you traverse back up through those same menus, the client remembers them instead of doing another protocol request to get them again.

9.2 What Is Gopher+?

Once people started using Gopher heavily, they quickly bumped up against its limits. These limits are due to the method of transferring data between the server and the client, the Gopher protocol. The simplicity of Gopher was also its limitation. There just wasn't much room to efficiently accommodate the enhancements many people wanted.

At the very first Gopher Conference in 1992, the University of Minnesota Gopher development team proposed a suite of extensions to Gopher called *Gopher+*. These enhancements include:

- An extensible method of fetching the *attributes* of a Gopher item. An attribute is specific information about the item, such as the file's size, administrator, and last modification date.
- The ability to have multiple formats of a document associated with a single menu item. For example, a single menu item could be available in plain text, PostScript, and Rich Text Format.
- A method of attaching a short description to a Gopher item (called an *abstract*)
- The ability to request that a client fill out a form before retrieving an item

To use these Gopher+ features, you need a Gopher+ server and a Gopher+ client. Gopher+ servers work with non-Gopher+ clients, but these clients cannot access the new features of Gopher+. Conversely, all Gopher+ clients support the old Gopher servers; you can upgrade either client or server at your convenience.

9.2.1 A Tour of Gopher+ Features

Unless you look closely, it's difficult to tell the difference between Gopher and Gopher+ clients. Both offer the same simple user interface. In fact, you might not notice anything different on this menu, other than the version number and the double question mark on item three:

```
                    Internet Gopher Information Client v2.0.16

                       Home Gopher server: wildlife.ora.com

 -->  1. Introduction and Cover
      2. Weather Forecasts/
      3. Macaw Parrot in the Rainforest <Image>
      4. TextBook Order Form <??>

Press ? for Help, q to Quit                                     Page: 1/1
```

There's a lot more to this Gopher+ menu than meets the eye. Press the equals (=) key to get information about an item (this works in both versions of Gopher), and you'll quickly notice some differences. Under a Gopher 1.x server, you'll see the following information, which we'll use later for making a link to this item:

```
Link Info (0k)                                                    100%
+-----------------------------------------------------------------------+
#
Type=1
Name=Introduction and Cover
Path=0/cover
Host=wildlife.ora.com
Port=70
URL: gopher://wildlife.ora.com:70/00/cover
```

Under a Gopher+ server, the information returned is much more extensive:

```
Link Info (0k)                                                    100%
+-----------------------------------------------------------------------+
#
Type=1+
Name=Introduction and Cover
Path=0/cover
Host=wildlife.ora.com
Port=70
Admin=Gopher Park Ranger <gopher@wildlife.ora.com>
ModDate=Wed Aug 10 20:51:13 1994 <19940810205113>
URL: gopher://wildlife.ora.com:70/00/cover

ABSTRACT
--------

The Introduction file is meant to be used as a quick guide to this
server.  Please read this file first, since it contains very useful
information.


Size       Language      Document Type
---------- ------------- ----------------------------
3k         English (USA) text/plain
18k        English (USA) application/rtf
14k        German        application/x-wordmasher

+-----------------------------------------------------------------------+
[Help: ?]  [Exit: u]
```

Now things are starting to look different. With the Gopher+ client we can find out the name and email address of the administrator of the document (Gopher Park Ranger, *gopher@wildlife.ora.com)*, the time it was last modified (August 10, 1994), and the World Wide Web URL (URL: *gopher://wildlife.ora.com:70/00/cover*), for use in World Wide Web documents. Placing this URL in a Web document creates a link to the associated Gopher document. We can also get an idea of what's in the document by reading the abstract. The bottom of the display shows the different formats of the document that are available. There are two versions in the English language and one in German.

The first item is an ASCII text version that's 3K in size. The next is in Rich Text Format (RTF), and the third is in a fictitious word-processor format called "WordMasher."

If you select this document, your client tries to figure out which format of the document you want. Different clients do this in different ways. The UNIX text client just asks you which one you want:

```
+----------------Introduction and Cover---------------------+
|                                                           |
|   -->    1. Text/plain English (USA) [3k] (default)        |
|          2. application/rtf English (USA) [18k]            |
|          3. application/x-wordmasher English (USA) [12k]   |
|                                                           |
|  Choose a document type (1-3):                            |
|  [Help: ?]  [Cancel: ^G]                                  |
+-----------------------------------------------------------+
```

If you choose item two, the rich text version of the document is transferred to your computer, and the appropriate display application is launched. Other clients, such as *WSGopher*, have a method of specifying the preferred document type and language. When you select a document with these clients you don't need to choose from a menu; it just selects your preference.

Next, lets go back to the main menu and select the item with the <??>, the TextBook Order Form. When you select this item, the client fetches a set of questions from the server and asks for your input:

```
+------------------------TextBook Order Form-------------------------+
|                                                                    |
|                          Wildlife University                       |
|                       Textbook Information Request                 |
|                                                                    |
|                         Instructor Information                     |
| Instructor:               ________________________________________ |
| Phone No:                 ________________________________________ |
| E-mail Address:           ________________________________________ |
|                                                                    |
|                           Course Information                       |
| Year:                     ________________________________________ |
| Quarter:                  Fall                                     |
| Campus:                   ________________________________________ |
| Dept:                     ________________________________________ |
| Course No:                ________________________________________ |
| Joint Day/Ext:            No                                       |
|                                                                    |
| [Help: ^-]  [Cancel: ^G]                                           |
+--------------------------------------------------------------------+
```

You need to fill out this form before retrieving the document associated with it.

9.2.2 The Gopher+ Protocol

By now, you may be asking yourself how the client can know all of this information about the Gopher items. To find out how this information is stored and interpreted, we need to discuss the Gopher+ protocol. How the server and client communicate will show us the format and location of the information about the item.

The Gopher+ protocol is a fairly simple extension to the original Gopher protocol. It's a superset of the original protocol, so a Gopher+ client can work with an old server. Likewise, old Gopher clients can be used with a new server.

Let's start by looking at what happens when a client connects to the root directory of a server. We'll use *telnet* to connect to a Gopher server and type Return:

```
% telnet wildlife.ora.com 70
Trying 128.101.54.54 ...
Connected to wildlife.ora.com.
Escape character is '^]'.
<Return>
0Introduction and Cover 0/cover wildlife.ora.com     70  +
1Weather Forecasts      1/Weather      wildlife.ora.com    70   +
1Macaw Parrot in the Rainforest 9/parrot         wildlife.ora.com     70  +
0TextBook Order Form     0/textbook      wildlife.ora.com   70    ?
.
Connection closed by foreign host.
```

This is the protocol that defines the root directory of our sample server—the same directory we showed in our tour of Gopher+ features. Note that the format looks almost exactly the same as the original Gopher protocol (see Section 9.1). The only difference is that there's an extra field at the end of each line that contains either a plus character (+) or a question mark (?). These special characters denote that the item supports the Gopher+ extensions.

When you select a Gopher+ item, the client attempts to find the attributes for the item by sending a request to the Gopher server. It appends a TAB character and an exclamation mark (!) to the selector string. This tells the Gopher+ server that the client wants the attributes for the item, not the item itself. The server responds with the item's attributes. Again, we'll enter the selector string, TAB, and exclamation point using *telnet*:

```
% telnet wildlife.ora.com 70
Trying 128.101.54.54 ...
Connected to bud.weiser.ora.com
Escape character is '^]'.
0/cover<TAB>!
+INFO: 0Introduction and Cover 0/cover wildlife.ora.com     70  +
+ADMIN:
 Admin: Gopher Park Ranger <gopher@wildlife.ora.com>
 ModDate: Wed Aug 10 20:51:13 1994 <19940810205113>
+URL:
 gopher://wildlife.ora.com:70/00/cover
```

```
+ABSTRACT:
 The Introduction file is meant to be used as a quick guide to this server.
 Please read this file first, since it contains very useful information.
+VIEWS:
 text/plain En_US: <3k>
 application/rtf En_US: <18k>
 application/x-wordmasher De_DE: <14k>
.
Connection closed by foreign host
```

Each attribute block begins with a plus sign (+) and is followed by the attribute name (*VIEWS*, *ADMIN*, etc.). Attribute-specific information is in the lines that follow. The example above illustrates a few of the common attributes of an item. The *ADMIN* block contains information about the administrator of an item, as well as the last time that the document was modified. The *ABSTRACT* block contains a short description of the item. Document types, sizes, and languages are stored in the *VIEWS* block. Other blocks, including an *ASK block* (a Gopher+ Form) can also be included here.

Once the client has this information, it can use it, displaying the abstract and the name of the administrator when the user asks for attribute information, and popping up a list of document types when the user selects an item to retrieve. This leads us to the next question: how does the client request a specific document type from the server? The client passes the specific document type to the server with another special request:

```
% telnet wildlife.ora.com 70
Trying 128.101.54.54 ...
Connected to wildlife.ora.com
Escape character is '^]'.
0/cover<TAB>+application/rtf En_US
+-1
{\rtf0\ansi{\fonttbl\f2\fnil Times-Roman;\f1\fmodern Helvetica;}
\paperw10860
\paperh11640
\margl880
more output...
.
```

In this example, we fetch the Rich Text Format version by sending the server an extra TAB, a plus sign, and the desired view's selector string. The string `application/rtf En_US` matches the line in the `VIEWS` block.

These two extensions, added item information and document format selection, are all that's needed to extend Gopher to a new dimension of functionality.

9.3 Selection of Server Software

Although Gopher server software is available for PCs, Macs, UNIX, and most other operating systems, we've chosen to cover only UNIX in this book because it's the most widely used operating system for Internet servers (and UNIX machines are more likely to have suitable Internet connections than PCs and Macs).

There are three major Gopher server software packages for UNIX:

- Gopher 1.13 from University of Minnesota. This was the last unlicensed version they did. It's still widely used and available, although development work stopped on it in mid-1993 (except for security-related fixes).
- Gopher 2.0.16 from the University of Minnesota. This is the current version under development. It requires licensing fees for commercial use (see below). This version is known as "Gopher+" because of its new features. Version 2.1 should be available by the time you read this.
- The *gn* server. This server is both a Gopher and a Web server rolled into one. It is distributed under the GNU Public License, which allows free use, including commercial use (but not sale of the server itself). It is compatible with the original Gopher (Gopher 1.x), but so far does not have Gopher+ features. Its main advantage over Gopher 1.x is that it supports per-directory access control. It can only run under *inetd* (it can't run standalone), which has a slight performance penalty.

We had to choose, so we selected the University of Minnesota servers to cover in this book. That does not imply there's anything wrong with *gn*. In fact, O'Reilly & Associates uses *gn*. But the University of Minnesota is the leader in Gopher development, and choosing their server made it easier to cover both Gopher 1.x and the Gopher+ features of Gopher 2.x.

For a list of other server software, Gopher to *gopher.tc.umn.edu*, and look in the directory "Information About Gopher" and then "Gopher Software Distribution."

9.3.1 Licensing of the Gopher 2.x Server

There was much hoopla on the Net when the University of Minnesota decided to start charging licensing fees for the Gopher 2.x server (the Gopher 2.x client is still free). But the reasoning is sound—that companies that profit from Gopher should be willing to help pay for its development. And the fees for most uses are reasonable. (On the other hand, competing services like the Web are still entirely free.)

The standard licensing terms describe three classes of organizations. The University of Minnesota says it is willing to individualize the agreement, to some extent, to fit the needs of an organization if one of these classes or the terms are not appropriate. The three classes are:

- Local, state, or federal government agencies or departments, or not-for-profit entities whose main activity is education. This group can use Gopher 2.x without licensing payments.
- Small businesses that have less than $3,500,000 in gross income per year. (Note: this says income not revenue, so some fairly big companies still qualify—even DEC does lately!) This group pays either $100 per year, $500 per year if the server lists products for sale, or 2.5% of the amount charged for access to the server (with $500 minimum).

- Everyone else (intended for bigger companies). This group pays either $100 per year, $2500 per year if the server lists products for sale, or 2.5% of the amount charged for access to the server (with $2500 minimum).

You'll have to decide for yourself whether these payments are worth the extra features of Gopher 2.x.

All Gopher 2.x licenses allow use only (you can't modify the code and resell it).

9.4 Variety of Client Software

As a service provider, you need to keep up to date on all the clients your customers might be using. They have a variety of features, and you might like to support the advanced features of some of them, without cutting off people with the more basic versions. Some probably have bugs to work around. This section gives you a brief overview of the selection. If you're serious about the service, it would make sense to get many of these clients and try them.

We have not tried all of these clients, and the order in the list does not imply preference or the number of users of each. Some of the following text was borrowed from descriptions in the release notes of the various clients. We have listed only free clients.

UNIX clients
: The main UNIX clients are *gopher* (the text client described in this book), *xgopher* (a simple X Window System version), *moog* (a simple X Window System version with a Motif user interface), and Emacs-client (a Gopher mode for the Emacs editor).

Macintosh clients
: TurboGopher is a text-based client for the Mac, by the Gopher development team at the University of Minnesota. Its neatest feature is that you can read the first part of a document or directory while the rest is being fetched. And you can cancel if you aren't interested in what you see. TurboGopher is available for anonymous FTP from *boombox.micro.umn.edu*; look in the */pub/gopher/Macintosh-TurboGopher* directory. Or you can fetch TurboGopher with Gopher by looking in the Information About Gopher folder on the University of Minnesota Gopher server.

: GopherApp provides a Finder-like interface to Gopher and was developed at Indiana University by Don Gilbert. It supports Gopher+ ASK forms and multiple view formats. It includes the ability to perform multithreaded operations, for handling several network connections at once. You may obtain GopherApp through anonymous FTP to *ftp.bio.indiana.edu*, in folder */util/gopher/gopherapp*, as *gopherapp++.hqx*.

: There are two other interesting Gopher clients for Macintosh. Blue-Skies is specifically for displaying information from the Weather Underground (see Section 3.3.6). It has interactive graphics capabilities that other current Macintosh *gopher* clients do not support. Gopher MOO is an experiment in combining collaboration with information retrieval. The collaboration part is a text-based virtual-reality environment. The idea is that the most useful form of information retrieval is: ask someone who knows. Gopher MOO was the Gopher application that won the "coolest use of Gopher" contest at the Gopher Conference in Minneapolis in the spring of 1993.

DOS and Windows Clients

Gophers for MS-DOS and Windows PCs include PC Gopher III from the University of Minnesota, PC Gopher for LAN Workplace for DOS, BCG (a Gopher from Boston College), and WSG, also called WinSock Gopher. The various commercial Gopher clients with DOS or Windows support include AIRGopher, Chameleon, GUIDE, and WinGopher.

9.5 The Gopher FAQ

The Gopher Frequently Asked Questions (FAQ) file contains some tips and pointers to information not included in this book. To get it, *gopher* to *gopher.tc.umn.edu*, and pick the "Information About Gopher" menu and then the "Frequently Asked Questions about Gopher" item.

9.6 Overview of Gopher Chapters

The following seven chapters describe different aspects of setting up a Gopher server. Chapter 10, *Gopher: Compiling the Server*, and Chapter 11, *Gopher: Managing the Server*, cover the administrator's roles: building, installing, and maintaining the server. Chapter 12, *Gopher: Preparing Information*, and Chapter 13, *Gopher: Linking Services Together*, describe the basic Data Librarian's role, setting up the information and links that will be offered. Chapter 14, *Gopher: Incorporating Databases*, explains how to integrate Gopher with WAIS and NeXT indexing. Chapter 15, *Gopher: Veronica and Jughead*, describes Veronica and Jughead, which are ways to index all Gopher servers or your Gopher server, respectively, so that users can find items more quickly. Chapter 16, *Gopher+ Forms and Other New Features*, describes the major features of Gopher+ (including Forms) and the new features in version 2.1.

In this Chapter:
- *Getting the Source Code*
- *Precompilation Configuration*
- *Compiling the Client and Server*
- *Installing the Client and Server*

10

Gopher: Compiling the Server

This chapter describes how to build and install the University of Minnesota Gopher server and client. (Elsewhere in this book we haven't covered building clients, but in this case, a client comes with the server and is compiled in the same process.)

Compiling the UNIX Gopher server and client is fairly simple. There are a few configuration files you'll need to modify, but there's nothing overly difficult.

10.1 Getting the Source Code

The two versions of Gopher described in this book are versions 1.13 (known as "Gopher0") and 2.016 (Gopher+). We also summarize version 2.1, which was in beta at press time. You can read Section 9.3.1 to determine which version to use.

These versions of the UNIX Gopher client and server can be found via anonymous FTP on *boombox.micro.umn.edu* in the */pub/gopher/Unix* directory. Their filenames are *gopher1.13.tar.Z* and *gopher2.016.tar.Z*. See the Preface for instructions about retrieving files from an anonymous FTP server.

10.1.1 Extracting the Files

Once you've retrieved the version of Gopher you want, change directories to where you like to keep source code. There's no need to make a new directory for this package; one is made for you when you un*tar* the sources. Now, *uncompress* and un*tar* the source file using the following command (substitute *gopher2.016.tar.Z* below for the Gopher 2.x version):

```
% pwd
/usr/local/src
% zcat gopher1.13.tar.Z | tar -xvf -
gopher1.13/object/DAarray.c
gopher1.13/object/DAarray.h
gopher1.13/object/Dirent.h
gopher1.13/object/GDgopherdir.c
```

.
.

If you'd rather not see every filename, you can leave out the *v* option to *tar*.

10.1.2 What's Here?

Now that you've extracted the sources, let's take a look at what's here:

```
% cd gopher1.13
% ls -F
MANIFEST                conf.h          make.com
Makefile                doc/            makefile.vms
Makefile.config         emacs/          misc/
Makefile.config.dist    examples/       object/
README                  gopher/
README.VMS              gopherd/
```

Here's an explanation of the files and directories that are located in the main directory of the Gopher source tree:

MANIFEST
: Contains a list of all the files in the distribution (the same list you saw when extracting the sources)

Makefile
: The main Makefile for the distribution. Nothing in this file should need to be changed, since all of the configurable options are contained in either the *Makefile.config* or *conf.h* files.

Makefile.config
: Specifies compile-time options, such as the location of your Gopher data directory and the directories where the compiled programs should be installed

Makefile.config.dist
: A duplicate copy of the *Makefile.config* file, so that you can later recall what you changed from the original

README
: Describes the contents of the Gopher source directories

README.VMS
: Information for people compiling Gopher on a VMS system

conf.h
: Where many Gopher server and client options are set, including the default host to connect to and the names of external programs that the client and server needs to use

doc/
: Documentation for the Gopher package. Included here are the manual pages for the programs you'll compile, files describing all of the changes made to the source code over the history of Gopher, and a file detailing the installation of Gopher.

emacs/ A Gopher client that runs inside the Emacs editor

examples/ A test Gopher data directory hierarchy. You'll use this directory to make sure that everything is working after you compile the Gopher source code.

gopher/ The source code files for the *gopher* text client

gopherd/ The source code files for *gopherd*, the Gopher server

make.com and *makefile.vms*
Used when compiling Gopher on a VMS machine

misc/ Various helpful utilities created outside the Gopher development group. None of these utilities are necessary for the base Gopher installation.

object/ Source code that is used in both the Gopher client and server

+ The Gopher 2.x version does not have the *misc*, *examples*, and *emacs* directories or the *makefile.vms* and *README.VMS* files. It does have a few files and directories that Gopher 1.x does not, however:

Copyright Copyright information for Gopher 2.x. This describes the licensing terms.

gophfilt/ Source code for a simple client, which can be used to retrieve individual Gopher documents

patchlevel.h Source code file containing the current revision level of Gopher 2.x

test/ A directory containing test Gopher data. This directory replaces Gopher 1.x's *examples* directory.

10.2 Precompilation Configuration

You need to configure Gopher to fit the environment at your site by editing the *Makefile.config* and *conf.h* files. If you're familiar with compiling source code and are anxious to just get it over with, you may opt to read the *Makefile.config* and *conf.h* files on your own. They contain helpful comments near the sections that may need editing.

The configuration that's described here is generally not machine (architecture or operating system) dependent. Here we'll walk through the configuration options that get compiled into the Gopher server and client. If you have problems compiling Gopher, read the *Makefile.config* file carefully. There are some compile-time options in it which are machine-specific.

10.2.1 Modifying Makefile.config

The *Makefile.config* file contains options that are used when compiling and installing Gopher. This file gets included in the main *Makefile* when you execute the *make* command. *Makefile.config* controls what server features are enabled, where things are installed, the domain name, and the default Gopher data directory and port number. (These last items can be overridden on the *gopherd* command line, but it's good to set them here if you plan to use *inetd* to run the server.)

10.2.1.1 Where should we install things?

A few pages into *Makefile.config*, you'll see a section that looks like this:

```
#-----------------------------------------------
# Where shall we install stuff?
#
PREFIX          = /usr/local
CLIENTDIR       = $(PREFIX)/bin
CLIENTLIB       = $(PREFIX)/lib
SERVERDIR       = $(PREFIX)/etc
MAN1DIR         = $(PREFIX)/man/man1
MAN5DIR         = $(PREFIX)/man/man5
MAN8DIR         = $(PREFIX)/man/man8
```

This section tells the *Makefile* where to install all of Gopher's files, once everything is compiled. The way it's currently configured is pretty standard. There's no reason to change this unless your site follows a different convention for installing "local" software. The following list shows you what files get placed in the directory specified by each symbol:

CLIENTDIR The *gopher* (client) executable resides here. With Gopher 2.x, the *gophfilt* program is also installed here.

CLIENTLIB The *gopher.hlp* (*gopher* client's help file) is placed in this directory.

+ In Gopher 2.x, the *Gopher* client configuration files, *gopher.rc* and *gopherremote.rc*, are also stored here.

SERVERDIR The *gopherd* (server) executable is placed here, along with the *gopherd.conf* configuration file. There are also two symbolic links made in this directory, *gindexd* and *gopherls*. They are links to the *gopherd* executable (*gopherd* behaves differently when it's called by the name *gindexd* or *gopherls*, as we'll see in Section 11.4). With Gopher 2.x, *gopherindex*, a program to help index files, is also installed here.

MAN1DIR The *gopher* manual page is placed in this directory. With Gopher 2.x, the *gophfilt* manual page is also placed here.

MAN5DIR The *gopherd.conf* manual page is placed in this directory.

MAN8DIR The *gopherd* manual page is placed in this directory. With Gopher 2.x, the *gopherindex* manual page is also placed here.

10.2.1.2 Setting server options

Skip down to the line that looks similar to this:

```
SERVEROPTS       = #-DBIO #-DDL # -DLOADRESTRICT
```

This line configures various options that can be compiled into the Gopher server. The # marks the beginning of a comment. Anything after the first # on a line is ignored when Gopher is compiled.

The -DBIO option should *only* be enabled if you're using the biology portion of Don Gilbert's modified WAIS code with your WAIS server (see Section 7.2). Unless you plan on serving data for a Biology department or firm, you probably won't be concerned with this.

The -DDL switch is used if you want to use "dl" databases. dl databases are generated by a package called Describe. It's used to create a database of file descriptions. Its most common use is to provide file descriptions for anonymous FTP users. On anonymous FTP sites which use Describe, the *ls* command is replaced with *dl*. This is one way to allow anonymous FTP users to see descriptions of files when they list a directory (the chapters on FTP in this book describe a different way). If you're currently using Describe, or if you decide to use it, you can use your Describe databases to name your Gopher files. You also need to modify the DLPATH line (right below the SERVEROPTS line) to point to the location of the compiled *dl* program and source code. Also, you need to uncomment the DLOBJS line below that (just take out the # at the beginning of the line).

You can set the server to restrict access to your Gopher service based on the current system load of your machine. In general, the Gopher server is not a system resource hog. However, if you're using a very slow machine or if you're using your machine for purposes other than serving Gopher data, you may want to consider using this feature. To restrict access based on your system's load, you need to uncomment the -DLOADRESTRICT option. If you use this option, you also need to uncomment the LOADLIBS line, found a few lines down, and you need to set the default machine load limit (the load at which you would like to stop serving Gopher data) in the *conf.h* file. Here's an example of the SERVEROPTS line with the load restriction option uncommented:

```
SERVEROPTS       = -DLOADRESTRICT #-DBIO #-DDL
```

Notice that the DLOADRESTRICT option was moved to the left of all # comment characters. Anything past the first # on a line is ignored.

+ Gopher 2.x has a few additional options that can be compiled into the server:

-DADD_DATE_AND_TIME
: This option tacks a date and file size onto every Gopher menu item that's a file. Although this is useful information for users, it tends to

make the Gopher menu look a bit crowded. The tags are formatted like this: `[14Apr94, 2kb]`.

`-DUMNDES` This option normally enables the "Admit1" authentication protocol. However, it has been disabled in this version, due to some problems inherent in its design. See Section 16.3.1 for more information.

`-DCAPFILES` This option enables Gopher 1.x *.cap* file processing. Since many of our examples in the book use *.cap* files, it's a good idea to enable this option, so you can try out the examples.

`-DSETPROCTITLE` This option changes the "process title" of the *gopherd* command. This changes the way the process is displayed by the *ps* command to the simple string *(gopherd)*, hiding any command-line options fed to *gopherd* at startup. This option is really only for neatness' sake.

+ With Gopher 2.x, there is also a section, just below the `SERVEROPTS`, for configuring client options:

`-DNOMAIL`.XET N This option stops the client from allowing users to mail files to themselves if the client is started in secure mode. This is useful if you want to make a client that is accessible to the public and want to restrict this feature.

`-DCLIENT_LOGGER`

This option enables logging of the client's actions to *syslog*, the system logger. The client's actions are reported to the *syslog* facility *daemon.info*.

`-DAUTOEXITONU` This option forces the client to exit without question when the user selects either "q" or "u" from the top-level menu (the user is *not* asked if he wants to exit the client). This feature is handy if the *gopher* client is being called from another application, making the transition more seamless.

There is one other option mentioned in this section of *Makefile.config*, `-DREMOTEUSER`, which is no longer used in the client and should be ignored.

10.2.1.3 Setting your domain name

A bit farther down the file, you'll see the line:

```
DOMAIN          = .micro.umn.edu
```

Before modifying this line, you need to determine if your machine knows its fully qualified domain name. To figure this out, try using the *hostname* command:

```
% hostname
wildlife
```

Here, *hostname* only returned the first part of the host's full name, so you need to tell Gopher what the rest of the fully qualified domain name is. If the fully qualified domain name of this host is *wildlife.ora.com*, you would use:

```
DOMAIN          = .ora.com
```

Note that you *must* include the leading . in this line.

However, if the *hostname* command returns a fully qualified domain name (e.g. *wildlife.ora.com*), then you need to leave this section empty (or comment out the line):

```
DOMAIN          =
```

10.2.1.4 Server data directory and port number

Right beneath the DOMAIN definition, you'll see the two lines:

```
SERVERDATA      = /home/mudhoney/gopher-data
SERVERPORT      = 70
```

These define the default location of the data on your Gopher server and the default port on which the server will listen for connections. 70 is Gopher's standard (designated) port number. Use this port if at all possible.

Most people hear about Gopher servers through word of mouth. Herb tells Trent "Yeah, I found all this cool stuff on *gopher.foobar.com*!" When Trent goes to find that information, he's going to issue the command *gopher gopher.foobar.com*. Gopher clients are configured to try the standard port, 70, when given a hostname to connect to. If your information isn't being served on port 70, then Trent is out of luck.

Both the SERVERDATA and the SERVERPORT options can be overridden on the *gopherd* command line, but it's a good idea to set them here to minimize the length of the *gopherd* startup command.

10.2.2 Modifying conf.h

The next file that you need to look at is *conf.h*. This file contains options that alter the behavior of the Gopher client and server. First, we suggest making a copy of the original, so that you can see later what you modified. Then, you'll need to make the file writable so that you can edit it:

```
% cp conf.h conf.h.dist
% chmod 644 conf.h
```

The server configuration is at the end of *conf.h*, but we'll cover that first.

10.2.2.1 Configuring the server

Near the bottom of the *conf.h* file are variables that are used to configure the server, *gopherd.*

If you're compiling Gopher 1.x, the first variable you'll see is `CACHE_TIME`. The *gopherd* server makes a cache file (called *.cache*) of a directory's contents when a user queries the directory. When another user queries the same directory, *gopherd* uses the contents of the file (instead of re-parsing the directory), unless the cache file is more than `CACHE_TIME` seconds old. The default `CACHE_TIME` is 180 seconds. So, each cache file is good for three minutes. You may want to set this threshold higher if you're not serving data that changes frequently. By setting the threshold higher, the data in the cache will be "valid" for a longer period of time. Thus, the server won't need to update the contents of the cache as frequently, which saves you some CPU cycles.

+ In Gopher 2.x, the cache timeout setting has been moved to the *gopherd.conf* file, discussed in Section 11.1. If you're compiling Gopher 2.x, the first variable you'll see is `WAISMAXHITS`. The `WAISMAXHITS` variable sets the maximum number of query matches that will be returned to the client from a single WAIS search. The default setting is 40 matches. You can leave this unchanged until experience dictates otherwise.

Next you'll see the `MAXLOAD` variable, which is initially set to 10.0. If you're going to compile the server with load restricting enabled (see Section 10.2.1.2 on `LOADRESTRICT`), then this number is the load at which the Gopher server stops serving data. Note that this number can be overridden on the *gopherd* command line.

The next variable, `SIGRETTYPE`, usually doesn't need to be modified. It indicates the data type that is returned by the `signal(3)` function. *signal* normally returns a *void.* If you're not sure about your system, read the manual page about `signal(3)` to figure out what it returns. For example, on SunOS systems, the man page says this:

```
NAME
     signal - simplified software signal facilities
SYNOPSIS
     #include <signal.h>
     void (*signal(sig, func))()
```

which indicates that `signal()` returns a *void* type.

The `READTIMEOUT` variable sets the amount of time *gopherd* waits before timing out for network reads. It's set to either five minutes (Gopher 1.x) or one minute (Gopher 2.x), which should be just fine.

The `LIST` variable (only in Gopher 1.x) specifies the prefix for temporary files generated when retrieving data from anonymous FTP sites. The default prefix is */tmp/gftp+*. If you'd like the temporary files stored elsewhere, change */tmp* to an appropriate temporary storage directory. This directory should have plenty of space, since any files that a Gopher client retrieves via an anonymous FTP link will be stored here temporarily. Note that the directory has to be writable by the user that *gopherd* runs as.

The ZCATCMD variable (only in Gopher 1.x) sets the command that is used to uncompress files to standard output before sending them to the client. The command used to do this is *zcat*, which is usually located in either */usr/ucb* or */usr/bin*. If your system doesn't have *zcat*, *uncompress –c* should work.

+ The CONF_FILE variable sets the location of the *gopherd.conf* configuration file. This file normally resides in the server's directory (for example, */usr/local/etc/gopherd.conf*).

10.2.2.2 Specifying the default Gopher server

The first lines that you'll want to modify in the *conf.h* file tell the Gopher client the default server and port number it should connect to when it's started. Here's what these lines look like when you first see them:

```
#define CLIENT1_HOST "gopher.tc.umn.edu"
#define CLIENT2_HOST "gopher2.tc.umn.edu"
#define CLIENT1_PORT 70
#define CLIENT2_PORT 70
```

The hostnames shown here are those of Gopher's "home" site at the University of Minnesota. From this Gopher site, you can connect to nearly every other Gopher server in the world. But as a Gopher server operator, you'd probably prefer the client to connect directly to your own server.

Notice that there are two hosts and two ports. When the Gopher client starts, it *randomly* chooses one of these two hosts to connect to. This feature exists so that if you have two separate machines with *duplicate* Gopher services, you can distribute the load of serving your Gopher data. Unfortunately, most people can only afford to have a single Gopher server. If you only have one server, simply set the second port (CLIENT2_PORT) to 0 (that's zero!). Alternatively, you can set both hosts and ports to be identical. Here's an example:

```
#define CLIENT1_HOST "gopher.ora.com"
#define CLIENT2_HOST ""
#define CLIENT1_PORT 70
#define CLIENT2_PORT 0
```

Here, the default *gopher* host has been set to *gopher.ora.com*. This default hostname and port number can be overridden on the *gopher* command line.

There is more client configuration in *conf.h*, and it's covered in Appendix B, *Gopher: Client Compilation Options*. You may want to read that if you intend to use the text client, but it's not necessary for running a server.

10.2.3 Optional Precompilation Setup

There are a few additional things to set up if you'd like to take advantage of the index capability of the server.

10.2.3.1 Compiling with WAIS indexing

If you plan on serving WAIS indexes, you need to retrieve and compile the WAIS sources (see Chapter 7, *Creating an Internet Database Server with WAIS*) *before* compiling the Gopher server.

In *freeWAIS-0.3*, there is a piece of debugging code left in the boolean-searching portion of the source code. This debugging information can really confuse the *gopher* client. This line of code needs to be commented out to make WAIS boolean searching possible with Gopher. The piece of code can be found on line 1025 in the file *ir/sersrch.c*:

```
if (gLastAnd) printf("search_word: boolean `and' scored\n");
```

You need to comment this out of the source code by adding **/* */** around the line:

```
/* if (gLastAnd) printf("search_word: boolean `and' scored\n"); */
```

WAIS then needs to be recompiled (if you had already compiled it before commenting out the line) by running a *make* in the main WAIS directory.

Once you have compiled WAIS, you need to make three symbolic links in your main Gopher source directory (where the *Makefile.config* and *conf.h* files are located) to WAIS's *bin*, *ir*, and *ui* directories. This allows the object libraries which search WAIS indexes to be linked into *gopherd*:

```
% pwd
/usr/local/src/gopher1.13
% ln -s /usr/local/src/freeWAIS-0.3/ui .
% ln -s /usr/local/src/freeWAIS-0.3/ir .
% ln -s /usr/local/src/freeWAIS-0.3/bin .
```

When you compile the Gopher server, it automatically looks for these links. If the links exist, a server with WAIS capability is built automatically.

10.2.3.2 Compiling with NeXT indexing

When compiling on a NeXT, the *Makefile* expects you to have a few extra files in place—the files necessary to enable the NeXT indexing capability.

Unfortunately, NeXT's indexing scheme has totally changed between NeXTstep 2.x and 3.x. The *ixBuild* command is now obsolete, being replaced by *ixbuild*, and the index format itself has changed. Gopher does not support the new indexing scheme. If you're using NeXTstep 3.x, your options are as follows:

- Don't use NeXT indexing at all. You may opt to use WAIS indexing instead.
- You can still use indexes built on a NeXTstep 2.x system—you can copy */usr/bin/ixBuild* and */usr/lib/indexing* from a NeXTstep 2.x machine and still get the same functionality on your 3.x system.

If you choose to follow the first plan, you need to modify the main Gopher *Makefile* so that it doesn't try to create a server with NeXT indexing capabilities. Edit the *Makefile* and look for the section:

```
gopherd/gopherd: objects
   @echo "Making server"
   @if [ -f /sdmach -a -d ./ir ]; then |
      (echo "Making server with NeXT and WAIS searching";\
      cd gopherd; $(MAKE) $(MFLAGS) "SEARCH=-DNEXTSEARCH -DWAISSEARCH" nextwais);\
   elif [ -f /sdmach ]; then \
      (echo "Making server with NeXT searching";\
      cd gopherd; $(MAKE) $(MFLAGS) "SEARCH=-DNEXTSEARCH" next);
   elif [ -d ./ir ]; then \
      (echo "Making server with WAIS searching";\
      cd gopherd; $(MAKE) $(MFLAGS) "SEARCH=-DWAISSEARCH" wais); \
   else (echo "Making data server"; cd gopherd; $(MAKE) $(MFLAGS) none) \
   fi
```

You need to cut out six lines, starting with the line that begins with `@if [ -f /sdmach`. The line that reads `elif [ -d ./ir ]; then` needs to be changed to read `@if [ -d ./ir ]; then`. Here's what this section should finally look like, with all of the references to NeXT indexing chopped out:

```
gopherd/gopherd: objects
   @echo "Making server"
   @if [ -d ./ir ]; then \
      (echo "Making server with WAIS searching";\
      cd gopherd; $(MAKE) $(MFLAGS) "SEARCH=-DWAISSEARCH" wais); \
   else (echo "Making data server"; cd gopherd; $(MAKE) $(MFLAGS) none) \
   fi
```

+ With Gopher 2.x, the lines that contain *./ir* will read *./ui* instead.

Now you should be able to execute `make` and have a server built without any NeXT indexing compiled in.

If you're running NeXTstep 2.x or choose to use 2.x indexing on a 3.x system, you need to grab a compressed *tar* file of the necessary indexing headers and libraries from *boombox.micro.umn.edu* in the *pub/gopher/Unix* directory. The file that you need to grab is called *NeXTtext.tar.Z*. Once you've retrieved this file, it needs to be un*tar*red in the main Gopher source directory:

```
% zcat NeXTtext.tar.Z | /bin/tar -xvf -
x btree/BTree.h, 6652 bytes, 13 tape blocks
x btree/BTreeCursor.h, 12875 bytes, 26 tape blocks
x btree/BTreeErrors.h, 755 bytes, 2 tape blocks
x btree/BTreeFile.h, 9851 bytes, 20 tape blocks
x text/wftable.h, 1321 bytes, 3 tape blocks
x text/ix.h, 11786 bytes, 24 tape blocks
x text/egrep.h, 165 bytes, 1 tape blocks
x text/fileutil.h, 715 bytes, 2 tape blocks
x text/pathutil.h, 1203 bytes, 3 tape blocks
x text/search.h, 1699 bytes, 4 tape blocks
```

```
x text/spell.h, 496 bytes, 1 tape blocks
x text/strutil.h, 458 bytes, 1 tape blocks
x text/text.h, 1041 bytes, 3 tape blocks
x text/webster.h, 6433 bytes, 13 tape blocks
x libtext.a, 1819832 bytes, 3555 tape blocks
x libbtree.a, 484438 bytes, 947 tape blocks
```

What's just been extracted are the header files and libraries necessary to use the NeXT indexing feature. Once you've extracted these files, you need to make the libraries, *libtext.a* and *libbtree.a*, visible to the compiler. You can do this in one of two ways—either put the libraries in a standard place (*/usr/lib*, for example), or modify the *Makefile* in the *gopherd* directory to tell the compiler explicitly where it can find the libraries.

If you choose to explicitly tell the compiler where to find the libraries, you need to change the line in *gopherd/Makefile* that reads:

```
NEXTLIBS        = -ltext -lbtree
```

to include an argument that instructs the compiler to look in an additional directory for libraries:

```
NEXTLIBS        = -L/usr/local/src/gopher1.13 -ltext -lbtree
```

Once you have the libraries where you'd like to keep them, you need to run *ranlib* on the libraries:

```
% ranlib libtext.a libbtree.a
```

Now, you should be ready to go. Just type **make** from the main Gopher source directory and watch it go.

10.3 Compiling the Client and Server

If you edited *Makefile.config* and *conf.h* according to the previous sections, you're ready to start the build. To compile the client and server, just type **make** in the main source directory. If you would like to compile only the server, type **make server**. Now, things should start to compile. You'll see each compilation command as the files are compiled.

Often, it's nice to keep a log file of the compilation, just in case anything goes awry. If you are using *csh* (or one of its derivatives), use the commands:

```
% make >& LOGFILE &
[1] 28017
% tail -f LOGFILE
```

If you're using *sh* (or one of its derivatives), use the commands:

```
$ make > LOGFILE 2>&1 &
[1] 28044
$ tail -f LOGFILE
```

The `tail -f` command lets you watch the compilation as it happens. The `tail -f` command doesn't exit when the Gopher package is done compiling; you need to do a CTRL-C to exit. The compilation log is now stored in the file named *LOGFILE*.

If you're compiling with WAIS and/or NeXT searching, you should see a message that reads "Making server with *search-type* searching" when the server begins compiling.

10.3.1 Compilation Problems

Here are some common problems that may occur when you compile the Gopher package.

10.3.1.1 Using pmake

If you're using *pmake* (a version of *make* found in the 4.4 and Net2 versions of the BSD operating system), you will get an error like the following:

```
% make
(cd gopher;     make)
"Makefile", line 30: Need an operator
Fatal errors encountered -- cannot continue
*** Error code 1
Stop.
```

This error is caused by the following line in the *Makefile*:

```
include Makefile.config
```

pmake doesn't understand this syntax. You have to change this line in the *Makefile* in the main source directory as well as those in the *gopher*, *gopherd*, *doc*, and *object* directories. You'll need to make the *Makefiles* writable before editing them:

```
% chmod 644 Makefile */Makefile
```

Now, edit each *Makefile*. You need to put a `.` before the `include` and place quotation marks around `Makefile.config`:

```
 .include "Makefile.config"
```

10.3.1.2 WAIS links incorrect

If, while you're trying to compile a Gopher server that has WAIS support built in, you see these compilation errors:

```
wais.h:68: source.h: No such file or directory
wais.h:69: document.h: No such file or directory
wais.h:71: question.h: No such file or directory
```

or this:

```
ld: No such file or directory for ../bin/inv.a
```

then the symbolic links to the WAIS *bin*, *ir*, or *ui* directories are incorrect. Make sure that you've made the links correctly, and that you were in the main Gopher source directory when the links were created.

10.3.1.3 Remaking a server with WAIS support

If you're trying to compile a Gopher server with WAIS support, and you come across lots of errors that look similar to:

```
source.c:73: Undefined symbol _fs_free referenced from text segment
```

then chances are good that you've already made a server without WAIS support, and you are now trying to add support in. The server needs to be remade completely—all previously compiled object files need to be removed first. Do a **make clean** in the source directory, and then remake the server. All object files will be recompiled with the WAIS ability built in.

10.4 Installing the Client and Server

To install the programs that you have just compiled, become the user *root* and type **make install**. You'll see the commands that are used to install the server, client, and manual pages:

```
# make install
(cd gopher; make  install);
mv /usr/local/bin/gopher /usr/local/bin/gopher.old
mv: rename /usr/local/bin/gopher to /usr/local/bin/gopher.old: No such ▶▶▶
▶▶▶ file or directory
*** Error code 1 (ignored)
install -c gopher /usr/local/bin
more output omitted
```

Don't worry about the errors from the *rm* and *mv* commands. The installation procedure is just making sure that it gets any old version of Gopher out of the way before it installs the new one. (One way to note real errors is to run `make install` twice—errors on the second pass are probably real.)

Even if no errors are reported, the installation won't work correctly if any of the destination directories haven't been created beforehand. For instance, if */usr/local* exists, but */usr/local/etc* doesn't, the files that should have been installed into the */usr/local/etc* directory (*gopherd* and *gopherd.conf*) are actually copied on top of each other to a file called */usr/local/etc* instead! If this happens, just delete that file, create the directory, and run `make install` again.

The installation procedure uses the `install` command. This is a standard command on most BSD UNIX systems, but it may not exist at all on other flavors of UNIX, or its command-line options may differ from the normal BSD `install`. If, when you try to do the installation, something looks like it's going amiss, you may need to change the `INSTALL` variable in *Makefile.config* to a BSD version of *install.* If your system does not have a BSD *install* command, you will need to install the package by hand—just execute the same commands that the installation procedure does, except substitute `cp` for `install -c`.

With Gopher 1.13, the automated installation procedure does not install the *gopherd.conf* manual page. You can install it manually by using the following commands:

```
# cd doc
# cp gopherd.conf.8 /usr/local/man/man8
```

If you're storing your manual pages in a different location, be sure to substitute that location for */usr/local/man.*

You're done; that's all there is to it!

In this Chapter:
- *Configuring the Server*
- *Running the Server*
- *Testing Your Server*
- *Running gopherd as gopherls and gindexd*
- *Making Sense of Gopher Logs*
- *How to Register Your Gopher Server*

11

Gopher: Managing the Server

While Chapter 10, *Gopher: Compiling the Server*, covered one-time compilation and installation, this chapter is about recurring tasks you'll do during the life of your server. It covers configuration, testing, public announcement, and maintenance.

11.1 Configuring the Server

Now that you've installed the server, you need to edit the configuration file (*gopherd.conf*) to control how the server works for the outside world (or whatever your purpose is). There are three things you need to do for all servers: name the server, specify what machines will have various levels of access, and customize the "access denied" message. Also, for Gopher 2.x, the global attributes must be customized.

There are a few other specialized things configured in *gopherd.conf*, and some tokens that do nothing at all, which we'll also cover.

You'll find *gopherd.conf* in */usr/local/etc*, unless you changed `SERVERDIR` before compiling. The *gopherd.conf* file consists of lines of the form "*Token*: *Value*", where *Value* defines the characteristics of the specified *Token*. Tokens are case-insensitive. Any line in the *gopherd.conf* that begins with a `#` is a comment.

11.1.1 Naming the Server: the Hostalias Token

The `hostalias` token defines the hostname of the Gopher server that the server returns to the client. This is useful if the server's real hostname is something like *zebra.ora.com* but you want people to see the machine as *gopher.ora.com*. In other words, *gopher.ora.com* is an alias of *zebra.ora.com*. The alias is simpler for users to remember, and if the Gopher server ever moves from one machine to another, you simply change the alias to point to the new machine, rather than having to notify users of the hostname change. You'll also have to configure DNS (the Domain Naming

System) to recognize the alias you want for your Gopher server, using a CNAME. For more information about hostname aliases and CNAMEs, see Section 3.2.

11.1.2 Controlling Access: the Access Token

The access token allows you to control what machines can request files, what machines can browse directories, and what machines can do searches. The format of the access token is:

```
access: hostname_or_ip-address access_control_string(s)
```

Here, *hostname_or_ip-address* can be either a full or partial hostname or an IP address. You can have multiple `access:` lines, each setting permissions for a different set of machines.

For instance, if the hostname *ora.com* is specified, anyone in the *ora.com* domain is affected by the access control. Hostnames are compared from right to left, so someone with the hostname *ora.com.yoyodyne.com* (however unlikely) is not affected.

You can also use partial IP addresses to control access. For example, *128.197* affects everyone with IP addresses starting with *128.197* (e.g., *128.197.22.3*). IP addresses are checked from left to right (opposite of hostnames), so someone with the IP address *192.108.128.197* is not affected.

You can specify the default access control (the access given to all hosts unless overriden by another `access:` line) by using the word *default* in the hostname field.

The *access_control_string(s)* control three types of access: the ability of clients to browse, read, and search your server. The three corresponding strings that the access token understands are *browse*, *read*, and *search*. Each of these keywords may have a `!` preceding it to negate the permission. For example, *read* means a client site can read files, while *!read* means a site cannot read files.

browse allows people to look, or prevents them from looking around your Gopher site, but does not directly control access to reading or searching. A *!browse* stops clients from querying the contents of directories on your Gopher site, but they can still access specific nondirectory items.

read controls a client's ability to actually view files. If read is turned off (*!read*), then clients trying to display items are prevented from displaying them, and the client sees the "BummerMsg" (described later).

search controls a client's ability to access items of the Gopher "index" type (Gopher type 7). Essentially, *!search* means that you're not allowing certain people to search indexes which you have made available via Gopher.

✚ Gopher 2.x also includes an *ftp* access token. *ftp* controls a client's ability to access items of the Gopher "ftp" type, essentially controlling the use of the server as a Gopher-FTP gateway.

+ With Gopher 2.x, you can also limit the number of concurrent sessions from a given host, where a "session" is the time during which a client is connected to the server (presumably retrieving file or directory data). The maximum number of concurrent sessions is specified by adding a number onto the end of the `access` token's line. Take a look at the example below for a better idea of how this looks. If you do not specify a maximum number of sessions for the *default* host, then only one person can access files on your server at a time. *gopherd* keeps track of concurrent session information in a directory specified by the `pids_directory` token described later in this chapter.*

Here's an example of default *access* settings that apply to all hosts:

```
access: default !read, browse, !search
```

+ For Gopher 2.x, you proably want to add on the default maximum number of concurrent sessions:

```
access: default !read, browse, !search 15
```

This `access` token allows everyone to browse the Gopher data directories, but denies access for reading files and doing searches. `access` tokens listed after the token containing the *default* hostname inherit the *default*'s access parameters. So, with the above default, the following `access` token allows anyone in the domain *yoyodyne.com* to read files, in addition to browsing directories:

```
access: yoyodyne.com read
```

However, they still won't be able to search, since this `access` line inherits the default's *!search* parameter. Here's another example using a partial IP address:

```
access: 197.12. read, search
```

This one allows anyone on the *197.12* network (any IP address beginning with *197.12.*) to read, browse, and search the Gopher tree. Notice that we included a "." (dot) after the *197.12.* If we hadn't, then anyone connecting from an address starting with *197.12* would be allowed access (e.g., *197.128.11.1*).

Unfortunately, only Gopher 2.1 or later supports per-directory access control. If you really must control access to a specific directory with earlier Gopher servers, you can run a separate Gopher server just to serve that directory. Then, use a link (see Chapter 13, *Gopher: Linking Services Together*) to include this separate server in your main Gopher tree. This method works, but is fairly inefficient, since you are running two *gopherd* processes to serve your data. If you have multiple directory structures that you need to control access to, you may need to look into using a different Gopher server (see Section 9.3), such as *gn*.

---

* Note that there may be some problems with concurrent server loading, in beta testing at this writing. One problem is that if the client interrupts its session while retrieving data, the session may never be removed from the `pids_directory`, causing an incorrect session count! It's best to set the concurrent session load fairly high until the bugs get worked out.

11.1.3 Global Attributes

Gopher 2.x assigns a number of attributes to each file and directory. The default attributes for all items are set in the *gopherd.conf* file. You can set the name of the organization by changing the `Org` token, the physical location of the server by setting the `Loc` and `Geog` tokens, and the default language by changing the `Language` token. The *gopherd.conf* file also contains the server administrator's name and email address, set by the `Admin` and the `AdminEmail` tokens, respectively. Here are some sample settings for a fictitious server called "The Wildlife Organization."

```
Admin: Gopher Park Ranger
AdminEmail: <gopher@wildlife.ora.com>
Org: The Wildlife Organization
Site: New York Wildlife Preserve
Loc: 100 Elephant Avenue, Buffalo NY, 55405
Geog: 44 58 48 N 93 15 49 W
Language: En_US
```

To view this information about a server, you can *telnet* to the Gopher 2.x server and enter a TAB character followed by an exclamation point:

```
% telnet wildlife.ora.com 70
Trying 128.101.54.54 ...
Connected to wildlife.ora.com.
Escape character is '^]'.
<TAB>!
+-1
+INFO 1New York Wildlife Preserve   wildlife.ora.com 70     +
+ADMIN:
 Admin: Gopher Park Ranger <gopher@wildlife.ora.com>
 Site: New York Wildlife Preserve
 Org: The Wildlife Organization
 Loc: 100 Elephant Avenue, Buffalo NY, 55405
 Geog: 44 58 48 N 93 15 49 W
 Version: U of Minnesota Unix 2.0 pl16
+VERONICA:
 treewalk: yes
+VIEWS:
 application/gopher-menu: <0k>
 application/gopher+-menu: <0k>
 text/html: <0k>
 Directory/recursive: <0k>
 Directory+/recursive: <0k>
.
Connection closed by foreign host.
```

Although these tokens also appear in the Gopher 1.x *gopherd.conf* file, they are not used in that version of the server.

11.1.4 Customizing the Access Denied Message: the BummerMsg Token

The string from the `BummerMsg:` token is displayed to a client that tries to access an item that it does not have permission to access. The default message is:

```
BummerMsg: Sorry Dude, we don't allow off-site access to this server.
```

This message was written for university environments, which often have Gopher access to local or commercial information that is available to the university community only.

Depending on how you set the `access:` token, you might want a message that explains how to get access, or the real reason access is not possible.

11.1.5 Recognizing a New Filename Extension

gopherd figures out a file's "type" by looking at a filename's extension. It maps a filename's extension to an actual file type (image, sound, etc.) by looking at the `ext` token (for Gopher 1.x) or the `viewext` token (for Gopher 2.x). If you are serving files with filename extensions that Gopher doesn't recognize, you may choose to add entries to make the server recognize these files. The following two sections talk about each of these tokens.

11.1.5.1 Gopher 1.x: the ext token

With Gopher 1.x, extension recognition is configured with the `ext` token. The general format for this token is:

```
ext: extension gopher-type path-prefix Gopher+-type
```

Here, the *`extension`* is a case-insensitive string that appears at the end of all files of this type. For example, if you want *gopherd* to recognize files that end with the string *.tif*, specify *.tif* as the *`extension`*.

The *gopher-type* tells the server the type of the files that end with the specified extension (for example, files that end with *.tif* are image files). The *gopher-type* must be one of the predefined Gopher types listed in Table 11-1, which shows the list of types and the default recognized extensions (as set by the default *gopherd.conf* file).

The *path-prefix* argument is a little odd; it's an additional file-type specifier that gets prepended to the item's Gopher directory name. This is a more general type specifier. It's usually either 0 (zero) or 9, specifying that the given extension identifies either a text or binary file type. The server uses this character to quickly parse client requests.

The *gopher+-type* field isn't used. What you use as the *gopher+type* doesn't make any difference—you can actually leave the *gopher+type* section empty and things work just fine. It's included in Gopher 1.x as part of the transition phase to the more flexible typing scheme used in Gopher 2.x.

Table 11-1: Gopher 1.x Types

Gopher Type	Description	Default Recognized Extensions
0	Text file	*.ps*
1	Directory	
2	CSO name server	
4	Mac HQX file	*.hqx*
5	PC binary	*.arc, .zip, .lzh, .exe, .zoo*
7	Full text index	*.src, .mindex*
8	Telnet session	
9	General binary file	*.tar.Z*
s	Sound	*.snd, .au*
I	Image	*.gif, .tiff, .jpg, .pict, .pcx*
h	HTML file	*.html*
M	MIME file	
T	TN3270 Telnet session	

Let's look at an example. Say that you'd like to let *gopherd* know that any files that end with a *.bmp* extension are picture files (bitmaps). Here's the line that you can insert into the *gopherd.conf* file to recognize files with this extension:

```
ext: .bmp I 9 image/bmp
```

The extension name is *.bmp*, the Gopher type is an image (I), the generic type is binary (9), and the Gopher 2.x type could be *image/bmp*. The Gopher 2.x type was just made up, as the field isn't in use.

11.1.5.2 Gopher 2.x: the viewext token

When a Gopher 2.x server reads a file that has a filename extension, it determines the file's type from the `viewext` tokens. Usually you use this token to add a type that isn't already defined. The following entry adds a new file extension mapping for TIFF graphic files:

```
viewext: .tiff I 9 image/tiff
```

The first argument for the *viewext:* item is the filename extension. The second is the one-character Gopher type. The types are the same as the types in Gopher 1.x, with one addition: the `;` character denotes movie files.

The next argument is the *path-prefix* for the server's selector string. This single character is used by the server to quickly parse client requests. Normally, you set this to one of two values: 0 for text files or 9 for binary files.

The fourth argument is the *Gopher+-type* for that kind of document. This naming convention is based on the official list of document types for the MIME electronic mail standard. This document type is used by the Gopher client to determine what application needs to be run to display the file. A list of currently defined types can be retrieved by anonymous FTP from *ftp.isi.edu* in the directory */in-notes/media-types/media-types.*

An optional fifth argument can contain the language for that type of document. The language tag is the ISO two-letter language code, an underscore (_), and the ISO two-letter country code concatenated. Some examples are: En_US (United States English), En_GB (British English), and De_DE (German). A longer list of language tags can be found in the *gopherd.conf* manual page. If most of your documents are going to be in one language, you should set the `Language` token in *gopherd.conf* to one of these language tags. The Gopher 2.x *gopherd.conf* defines all the extensions that Gopher 1.x did, plus a few more. Take a look at *gopherd.conf* to see the complete list.

You can also create your own document types if you like. The convention is to start non-standard MIME document types with *application/x-*. For instance, if you want to add support for a new word processor called "WordMasher 9000" you can add the following line to the *gopherd.conf* file:

```
viewext: .wm9 0 9 application/x-wordmasher
```

Once this new document format is added to the *gopherd.conf* file, you can add documents with this extension to the server (*document.wm9*, for example).

You may want to register your new document type so that others can properly interpret your document type. The procedure for registering a new document type is outlined in *RFC1590*, available at many FTP and gopher sites, including *ds.internic.net* in */rfc/rfc1590.*

There is another file-extension recognition token in Gopher+ called *blockext.* This token maps files that end with a certain extension into a specific Gopher+ attribute. The only place where the server uses this currently is to automatically tie ASK blocks and ABSTRACT blocks to the files that end with the appropriate extension (see Chapter 12, *Gopher: Preparing Information*). The default *gopherd.conf* file has these entries:

```
blockext: .ask ASK
blockext: .abstract ABSTRACT
```

People building extensions to the Gopher protocol might want to consider adding their own *blockext* tokens, but regular users can ignore them.

11.1.6 Excluding Files: the ignore Token

The values of *gopherd ignore* tokens specify case-insensitive filename extensions that you don't want shown to Gopher clients. Here's an example:

```
ignore: core
```

This example makes *gopherd* ignore any files or directories that end with the string "core". This includes files named *core* as well as those named *Apple Core.* Be careful with this token. You don't want to ignore valid files by accident!

The default *gopherd.conf* file currently ignores files and directories ending with these strings: *bin*, *lib*, *etc*, *usr*, *dev*, *tmp*, *lost+found*, ~ (tilde) and *core*. You need to change these if you plan on serving files that *end* with these strings. Most of these defaults are there to make *gopherd* ignore system-related directories or files that you may have in your Gopher data directories. *core* files are produced by programs which crash horrendously and files ending with a ~ are backup files generated by the *emacs* editor.

The only instance where *Gopher* does not pay attention to *ignore* tokens in within *ftp* links. The idea is that ftp sites are not always under your control so Gopher shouldn't make assumptions about which filenames are to be ignored.

+ In Gopher 2.x, there is another token that can also be used for ignoring files: *ignore_patt*. This token takes a regular expression as an argument. For example, the regular expression *^temp* ignores all files beginning with the string *temp*. The default Gopher 2.x *gopherd.conf* file uses this token to ignore files that *exactly* match the strings *tmp*, *usr*, and *core*.

11.1.7 Other Gopher 2.x Tokens

There are a few other tokens that are used only in Gopher 2.x. These include `cachetime`, `decoder`, and `pids_directory`.

The `cachetime` token controls how long a Gopher cache file is valid (in seconds). This token replaces the *CACHE_TIME* value that was compiled directly into *gopherd* in Gopher 1.x. Here's a sample setting:

```
Cachetime: 180
```

The `decoder` token is used to "decode" files *before* they are sent to the client. The two decoders which are specified by default are:

```
decoder: .Z /usr/ucb/zcat
decoder: .gz /usr/gnu/bin/zcat
```

The first argument specifies the filename extension of the encoded files, and the second argument specifies the program used to decode the files onto the standard output.

Lastly, the `pids_directory` token specifies the scratch directory that *gopherd* uses to keep track of the number of clients that are currently connected to the server. This information is used with the `access` token to determine if *gopherd* should stop serving data because there are too many clients currently connected. Note that if *gopherd* is running `chroot()`ed, this directory needs to be inside the Gopher data directory (for example, */usr/local/gopher-data/tmp*), and it needs to be writable by the user that *gopherd* runs as.

11.2 Running the Server

In deciding how to run *gopherd*, you have several important choices. First is the choice of command-line options, which control important things like security. The choice of options raises several interconnected issues. Instead of starting with a long-winded explanation of all the issues and options, we'll propose a recommended set of options and then explain why they make sense. An in-depth look at all of the options can be found in Appendix A, *gopherd Options.*

You'll also need to decide whether to run *gopherd* standalone or from within *inetd.* Running standalone is recommended for heavy use, but running under *inetd* is good for testing and light use. (You could also use *xinetd*, an extended version of *inetd*, if security or access control is critical. For more information on *xinetd*, see Chapter 28, *xinetd.*)

But before you start the server, you need to set up a Gopher data directory.

11.2.1 Preparing the Data Directory

Before you start *gopherd*, you have to create the Gopher data directory, and a few other directories within it. Because *gopherd* should be run `chroot()`ed, to limit access to the Gopher data directory, you'll need to provide some system files and directories there for various programs and scripts to use. For now, just create */tmp*, */bin*, and */usr/lib* directories in your data directory. The */tmp* directory (or whatever you specified as the `LIST` variable in *conf.h*) is needed for FTP downloads through the Gopher server under Gopher 1.x. If you're using Gopher 2.x, make sure that the directory specified by the `pids_directory` token in the *gopherd.conf* file exists in your Gopher data directory. Finally, the directories should be writable by the user that *gopherd* runs as, so that *gopherd* can create cache files (in our examples, the user is *nobody*). Here's an example of creating the data directory:

```
# mkdir /usr/local/gopher-data
# cd /usr/local/gopher-data
# mkdir tmp
# mkdir bin
# mkdir usr
# mkdir usr/lib
# chown -R nobody .
```

Section 13.4.2.2 describes the process of figuring out what files you might have to copy into the */bin* and */usr/lib* directories.

You may choose to create a new group (by editing the */etc/group* file), and put both the user that *gopherd* runs as and the data librarians in that group. Then, you can make all of the files and directories writable by that group, using a command like:

```
% chgrp -R newgroup /usr/local/gopher-data; chmod -R g+w /usr/local/gopher-data
```

This way, the librarians don't have to become another user to edit files.

11.2.2 Recommended Command-Line Options

We recommend you set the user (*–u*) and the logfile (*–l*) options as a minimum.

gopherd, because it's a daemon, is *started* by one user (UID) but should *run* as another. For example, since both ways of starting daemons (with and without *inetd*, as described in the next two sections) start *gopherd* as *root*, you should make sure that *gopherd* changes its UID to run as a less powerful user. Running the server as *root* isn't a good idea for security reasons, because it would give an intruder *root* access if there happens to be a security hole in *gopherd*. Use the *–u* option to set the user *gopherd* should run as. We use the user *nobody*, so the command would be *gopherd –u nobody*.

If you do not use *–u* because you cannot start *gopherd* as *root*, you should realize that by not doing so you are giving up important features. If *gopherd* is started as *root*, it uses the `chroot()` system call to restrict access to the Gopher data directory. The use of `chroot()` makes it totally impossible for a Gopher user to get access to other parts of your system, even if there is a security hole in *gopherd*. But if you do not start as *root*, *gopherd* cannot use `chroot()` and the entire system is potentially vulnerable. Furthermore, you can't use Gopher's normal port (70) unless you start *gopherd* as *root* (because ports under 1024 are privileged ports). The short version of the story is *always start gopherd as root*! The use of `chroot()` makes it a bit more difficult to set up your Gopher data directory, because all scripts, programs, and links you need to provide your service also are denied access to all other parts of the system. But it's worth dealing with this minor hassle for the security benefits.

You also should specify a logfile name with the *–l* option (that's lowercase L), since the log is useful and by default no log is written. So the complete recommended command is:

```
gopherd -l /var/log/gopher -u nobody
```

However, if you try to run this from your shell, you'll find it fails unless you are logged in as *root*. So the next step is to configure your system to start up *gopherd* using this command. The next two sections describe the two choices for starting *gopherd*.

11.2.3 Starting gopherd Standalone

One way to run *gopherd* is from a system startup file (a shell script that is run at boot time). On BSD-derived systems, this file is */etc/rc.local*. On System V variants, it'll be one of the files in the */etc/init.d* directory.

If you're starting the daemon from */etc/rc.local*, it should look something like this:

```
if [ -f /usr/local/etc/gopherd -a -f /usr/local/etc/gopherd.conf ]; then
   /usr/local/etc/gopherd -l /var/log/gopher -u nobody
   echo -n ' gopherd'
fi
```

The *if* statement checks to make sure that the *gopherd* executable and configuration file exist before attempting to start the daemon.

In the above example, *gopherd* is started with logging enabled to the file */var/log/gopher*, and the daemon is forced to run as the user *nobody*.

Here's another example:

```
if [ -f /usr/local/etc/gopherd -a -f /usr/local/etc/gopherd.conf ]; then
     echo -n ' gopherd'
    /usr/local/etc/gopherd -l /var/log/gopher -o /etc/gopherd.test.conf \
    -u nobody /online/gopher-data 70
fi
```

This example uses the *–o* option to specify an alternate *gopherd.conf* configuration file. Notice that we explicitly set the Gopher data directory (*/online/gopher-data*) and the port number (70), overriding any defaults that were compiled into *gopherd*.

You can reboot your machine to start the daemon the first time, or just start the daemon from the command line the first time.

When *gopherd* is started from the command line or from within a shell script, the Gopher daemon hangs out, waiting for a connection. When a client connects to the Gopher port, the *gopherd* process *forks*, creating another *gopherd* to deal with this specific connection. When this new process finishes feeding information to the client, it exits, leaving the single "listening" *gopherd*.

11.2.4 Using inetd

When *inetd* is used, the Gopher server isn't started until *inetd* determines that there has been a connection to the Gopher port. It then starts a *gopherd* process to deal with the connection. This saves you a bit of memory over running *gopherd* from the command line—instead of having a *gopherd* process running, listening on a port, *inetd* listens. Since *inetd* is already running (handing incoming *telnet*, *ftp*, and other services), you'll have one less daemon running. However, running under *inetd* is more CPU-intensive, as it starts a fresh instance of *gopherd* for each connection (and rereads *gopherd.conf*), as opposed to a standalone *gopherd*, which just `fork()`s a copy of itself.

11.2.4.1 Setting up inetd's configuration files

Configuring *gopherd* to work with *inetd* is a bit more involved than running it standalone. There are a few things you must do.

First, become the user *root*, and edit the */etc/services* file.* At the end of the file, stick in a line that looks like the following:

```
gopher          70/tcp          # gopher daemon
```

where 70 is the port on which *gopherd* is going to listen. If you're making *gopherd* listen on a port other than 70, replace 70 with that port number. Anything past the # is a comment. The spaces in this line are really TABs. Now, save this file and edit */etc/inetd.conf*, which is *inetd*'s configuration file. Go to the bottom of the file, and insert a line like the following:

```
gopher  stream  tcp     nowait  root  /usr/local/etc/gopherd  gopherd -I -u nobody
```

Again, make sure that each field is separated by TABs. Refer to Section 3.2 for a more in-depth discussion of the *inetd.conf* file.

The only fields that you should need to change in this example are the last two (the full pathname of the command and the command itself, with its options). If *gopherd* is located in a place other than */usr/local/etc*, substitute its full pathname in the second-to-last field. In the last field, you need to specify any options you'd like to use. The *–I* option *must* be used, since we're running the daemon under *inetd*. The *–I* option must also be the *first* option specified on the command line.

This example runs *gopherd* as the user *nobody*. Notice that we really start Gopher running as the user *root* (the fifth field). *gopherd* needs to start as *root* so that it can do the `chroot()` system call and open the log file. Once this is done, it then changes its user ID to the one you've specified using the *–u* option. If you do not specify an alternate user with the *–u* option, the server continues to run as the user *root*. For security reasons, you should always specify an alternate user for *gopherd* to run as.

WARNING

Most *inetd*'s can only accept *five* space-separated words in the last field. This is a (horrible) limitation of *inetd*. There are a few ways you can work around this limitation. You can combine flags which don't have arguments (for instance, *–I –c* can become *–Ic*), you can run *gopherd* (as described earlier), or you can run a shell script from *inetd* which calls *gopherd* with the necessary options.

Here's a sample *inetd* configuration running a shell script that calls *gopherd*:

```
gopher  stream  tcp     nowait  root  /usr/local/etc/gopherd-exec  gopherd-exec
```

Here's a sample *gopherd-exec* shell script. It must be located in */usr/local/etc*, as specified in the second to last field, and it must be executable.

* Note: If you're using Sun's NIS to distribute the *services* file, you'll have to modify the NIS master services map instead.

```
#!/bin/sh
exec /usr/local/etc/gopherd -I -l /var/log/gopher -u nobody /online/gopher-data 70
```

Here, we've used the shell script to start *gopherd* with seven options. Notice that we still have to use the *–I* flag, since this script is being called from *inetd.*

Note: If you use a shell script from within *inetd,* the shell script is executed *every time* a client connects to the Gopher port. This adds one extra (CPU- and memory-consuming) step to the process of starting each *gopherd.* If you run into this problem, we recommend that you start *gopherd* from a system startup file, rather than from *inetd,* to save valuable system resources.

11.2.4.2 Making inetd reread its configuration file

Now that you've configured *inetd,* you need to make *inetd* reread its configuration file. To do this, you need to send a HANGUP signal to the *inetd* process. First, find out *inetd*'s process ID (PID), and then, as the user *root,* send it a HANGUP signal using the *kill* command (substitute *–elf* for *–ax* below on System V–derived operating systems):

```
# ps -ax | grep inetd
   57 ??  Is      0:00.42 inetd
25179 p0  RV      0:00.02 grep inetd (tcsh)
# kill -HUP 57
```

On some systems, when adding a line to *inetd.conf, inetd* needs to be killed and restarted, instead of receiving a HUP signal. To do this, substitute a "9" (which kills *inetd* outright) for "HUP" in the above example and then restart *inetd.*

11.3 Testing Your Server

The easiest way to test your server is to use the test files in the *examples* directory (or the *test* directory for Gopher 2.x, which will give you different results than those shown below). To use the examples, copy this directory tree to your Gopher data directory and make the directories writable by the user that *gopherd* is running as (so that it can create cache files):

```
# pwd
/usr/local/src/gopher1.13
# mkdir /usr/local/gopher-data
# cp -R examples/* /usr/local/gopher-data
# chown -R nobody /usr/local/gopher-data
```

Now, you can test your server (assuming you've just started the daemon or have configured it to run from *inetd*). You should be able to *telnet* to the Gopher port, hit Return, and get a response from the server.

```
% telnet localhost 70
Trying 127.0.0.1...
Connected to localhost.ora.com.
Escape character is '^]'.
```

```
<Return>
1examples    1/examples    wildlife.ora.com    70
.
Connection closed by foreign host.
```

This shows you that there is one item in your Gopher data directory. You'll notice that the connection was closed after *gopherd* fed you the data. This is perfectly normal. *gopherd* only stays connected long enough to serve the single piece of data that was requested by the selector line sent to it (in this case, the selector was just a `Return` character).

Now, try this (for Gopher 2.x, substitute *data* for *examples* below):

```
% telnet localhost 70
Trying 127.0.0.1...
Connected to localhost.ora.com.
Escape character is '^]'.
1/examples
2Example CSO Link (Type 2) to UofMN phone book    uinfo.ais.umn.edu    105
1Example Directory Link (Type 1) to UofMN top level gopher ▶▶▶
▶▶▶gopher.micro.umn.edu   70
1Example FTP gateway link to wuarchive.wustl.edu ▶▶▶
▶▶▶ftp:wuarchive.wustl.edu@     wildlife.ora.com     70
8Example Telnet Link (Type 8) to UofMN public gopher   gopher ▶▶▶
▶▶▶consultant.micro.umn.edu   23
0README 0/examples/README  wildlife.ora.com    70
1Sample Directory   1/examples/Sample Directory    wildlife.ora.com   70
7Sample WAIS gateway search (lyrics.src) ▶▶▶
▶▶▶waissrc:/examples/lyrics.src    wildlife.ora.com 70
TTN3270 Link (Type T) to Pubinfo.ais.umn.edu    pubinfo.ais.umn.edu    0
.
Connection closed by foreign host.
```

If you see lines like these, then congratulations, you've got the server working! Now you should try using the *gopher* text-based client to connect to your server. A command like this should do the trick:

```
% gopher localhost
```

If you've compiled the *gopher* client to use your Gopher data directory and port by default, then you should just be able to type `gopher`. (You may need to type `rehash` if the shell can't find *gopher* yet, because you just installed it.)

11.3.1 Ack! My Server Isn't Working!

Ok, take a deep breath. It's not all that bad. There are a few things you can try if you don't get your server to respond the first time, depending on what happened when you tried to connect to the Gopher port using *telnet*.

11.3.1.1 "Connection refused"

If, when you try to test your server by *telnet*ing to the Gopher port, you see something like this:

```
% telnet localhost 70
Trying 127.0.0.1...
telnet: Unable to connect to remote host: Connection refused
```

then the daemon is not listening on the port. There are a few things you should check, depending on whether you're running *gopherd* from within *inetd*, or from the command line or shell script.

If you're using *inetd* and can't get the server to respond, try starting the Gopher daemon from the command line, without the *–I* flag. This will eliminate any problems that may have arisen from using *inetd*. If the server works from the command line, then check the following things.

- Examine *inetd*'s *syslog* output.
- Make sure that you're not using more than five words in the last field of your *inetd.conf* entry.
- Make sure that you typed in everything correctly in the */etc/services* and */etc/inetd.conf* files (use TABs, not spaces!).
- Make sure that *inetd* has reread its configuration files or has been restarted.

If you're running *gopherd* from the command line and you get a *Connection refused* message, chances are pretty good that the server isn't running. You can use your system's *ps* command to see if the server is running or not (for System V–derived systems, substitute *–elf* for *–axw*).

```
% ps -axw | grep gopherd
```

Pay close attention to the messages that the server shows you as it's starting. Often, you will see the cause of your problem in this battery of messages. Here's an example:

```
% gopherd -u nobody
Gopher Server, Copyright 1991,92 the Regents of the University of
Minnesota
See the file 'Copyright' for conditions of use
Data directory is /usr/local/gopher-data
Port is 70
Gopherd uses the privileged call chroot().  Please become root.
```

Here, *gopherd* was started from a normal user's account, instead of as the user *root*. *gopherd* couldn't execute the `chroot()` system call and reports the error (*gopherd* needs to be started as *root*, or a user authorized to execute `chroot()` on some systems, like HP-UX).

11.3.1.2 Errors in configuration or command line

Here are some other errors that you may encounter and what they mean:

`You should run without root perms`
: This warning is given under Gopher 1.x when you run *gopherd* as *root* and use the *–c* (no `chroot()`) option. If you use the *–u* or *–U* options on the command line along with *–c*, then you can ignore this warning, since you are actually running the server as a user other than *root*

`Warning! You really shouldn't run the server as root! . . .` *(Gopher 1.x)*

`Warning! You should run the server with the -u option!` *(Gopher 2.x)*
: This warning is given if you don't use either of the *–u* or *–U* options to make *gopherd* run as a user other than *root.* (It's OK to *start* it as root.)

`Cannot change to data directory!!` *`directory-name`*
: This error occurs when *gopherd* cannot *cd* into the Gopher data directory. Make sure that the data directory exists and that the user that *gopherd* is running as can access the directory (the directory must be both readable and executable by that user).

`Can't open the logfile:` *`logfile-name`*
: If *gopherd* cannot open the logfile, this error is reported. Make sure that the directory where the log file is going to be stored exists. The directory must also be writable by the user *gopherd* is first started as (normally the user *root*).

gopherd also logs some error messages via *syslog*, the system message logger. *gopherd* logs its errors to the *daemon.err* facility. Look in the */etc/syslog.conf* file to figure out what file the *daemon.err* logs are recorded in. The error you're most likely to see in a syslog file is one similar to this:

```
Jul 25 12:04:41 wildlife gopherd[29473]: server: can't bind local address
```

This error occurs when you try to start a Gopher server as a normal user (not *root*) and set the server to listen on a privileged port (any port number below 1024). If you want to run *gopherd* on a privileged port, then you must start the daemon as *root.*

11.3.1.3 "Can't set UID!" or "Could not find user in passwd file"

gopherd reports these errors for one of three reasons:

- If you specify a UID on the command line (via the *–U* option) that doesn't exist in the */etc/passwd* file. The UID needs to exist in order for *gopherd* to change users.
- If you specify a username on the command line (via the *–u* option) that doesn't exist in the */etc/passwd* file. The login needs to exist in order for *gopherd* to change users.

- If you start the Gopher daemon as a normal user and attempt to use either the *–u* or *–U* options to change the user that *gopherd* runs as. You can only use the *–u* or *–U* options if you start the server as *root.*

11.3.1.4 "System is too busy right now. Please try again later."

gopherd reports this error if the system load on your machine is above the maximum load limit allowed. *gopherd* gets this load maximum from the compiled-in variable MAXLOAD or from the *–L* option on the command line. Note that the load maximum only works if you compile *gopherd* with the load-limiting feature enabled.

+ With Gopher 2.x, you may also see a message "Sorry, too busy now...". This is returned when there are too many concurrent clients connected to the server, as set in the *gopherd.conf* file with the access token.

11.3.1.5 "Sorry Dude, we don't allow off-site access to this server" or "Bummer..."

If you see one of these messages when you try to connect to the server's port, then *gopherd* thinks that your machine is not allowed access to the server. Access is controlled via the *access* token in the *gopherd.conf* file.

11.3.1.6 If all else fails...

If you can't figure out what's going wrong, you may want to turn on the debugging flag (*–D*). This sends debugging output to standard output, so it only works when the server is started from the command line. There isn't a whole lot of useful information to be gathered by the *–D* flag, but it may give you some ideas. You can also look at the Gopher log file to see if you're getting connections or not.

If you're at your wit's end, try posting a message with detailed information about your problem to the *comp.infosystems.gopher* newsgroup. There's bound to be someone who will offer helpful advice! The Gopher development team can also be reached by sending email to *gopher@gopher.tc.umn.edu* .

11.4 Running gopherd as gopherls and gindexd

When the Gopher server was installed, two links to *gopherd* were made, *gopherls* and *gindexd.* The server runs differently when called by these names.

When called by the name *gopherls*, *gopherd* expects a pathname as an argument. What *gopherls* does is process the contents of the specified directory as if it were sending the directory to the Gopher client. It processes all *.cap* files and links it finds. It's output is the raw Gopher protocol that normally gets sent to the client. Here's an example:

```
% gopherls /usr/local/gopher-data
0Introduction and Cover 0/Introduction and Cover    wildlife.ora.com
70
0Foreword     0/Foreword     wildlife.ora.com     70
0Acknowledgments     0/Acknowledgments     wildlife.ora.com     70
```

Running *gopherd* in this manner is handy for seeing what your Gopher directories look like without having to run a Gopher client or *telnet* interactively.

With Gopher 1.x, running *gopherd* as *gindexd* is used for serving indexes. Take a look at Section 11.4 for an in-depth description of what *gindexd* is used for. The *gindexd* functionality has been removed from Gopher 2.x.

11.5 Making Sense of Gopher Logs

The next step is really to prepare your data, but that's the topic of the next chapter. Here we'll assume your service has been running for a few days.

Once you create a Gopher service, you'll be interested in who is using it and how many people per day/week/month are accessing your data. *gopherd* supplies a way to log incoming connections to the server via the *–l* `logfilename` option. `logfilename` is the full pathname to a file that contains a log of every connection to your server.

The log file ends up looking something like this:

```
Sat Sep 25 01:55:01 1993 13232 xor.com : Root Connection
Sat Sep 25 01:55:17 1993 13340 xor.com : retrieved directory /Help
Sat Sep 25 03:13:22 1993 15324 ora.com : retrieved binary /data.tar.Z
Sat Sep 25 03:13:51 1993 15609 ora.com : retrieved directory /Events & Entertainment
Sat Sep 25 03:14:01 1993 15701 teal.csn.org : retrieved file /About This Menu
Sat Sep 25 03:14:07 1993 15777 ora.com : retrieved directory /File Transfer (FTP)
Sat Sep 25 03:14:50 1993 16157 micro.umn.edu : retrieved directory /Libraries
Sat Sep 25 03:55:38 1993 17061 micro.umn.edu : search Doc/reports for phones
Sat Sep 25 07:56:42 1993 19175 teal.csn.org : retrieved ftp:ftp.xor.com@/
Sat Sep 25 07:59:28 1993 19232 192.108.21.11 : search Doc/reports for unix and delete
```

The first five columns tell us the date and time of the connection. The sixth column tells us the process ID of the Gopher server that answered the request (this PID is different every time, since a new *gopherd* handles each connection).

The column that contains hostnames tells us where each connection originated. If *gopherd* is unable to resolve the hostname, it'll list the IP address of the originator (as seen in the last line of the example log).

The information following the colon tells us what the person retrieved from the server. There are several messages that can appear in this column of the log:

`Root Connection`
Whenever someone connects to the "root" directory of your server (they make an initial connection to your main Gopher data directory) a `Root Connection` is reported.

`retrieved directory` *`directory-name`*
The person requested the contents of the named directory.

`retrieved file` *`filename`*
The person retrieved the named file.

`retrieved binary` *`filename`*
The person retrieved an image or other binary file (a file with the Gopher type of I or 9).

`search`*`database`* `for` *`keywords`*
The person searched the named *`database`* for *`keywords`*

`retrieved sound` *`filename`*
The person retrieved a sound file (a file of type s).

`retrieved maildir` *`spoolfilename`*
The person requested the contents of the named mail spool file.

`retrieved ftp:`*`ftphost@file_or_directory_name`*
The person retrieved the named file or requested the contents of the named directory via an *ftp* "Cool link".

`Executed` *`scriptname`*
+ The user selected an *exec* "Cool Link", running *`scriptname`* with *`arguments`*.

In addition to these logging notices, there are some errors that *gopherd* reports to its log. These are:

`Client went away`
The client disconnected while the server was trying to feed it data.

`System Load Too High`
Someone tried to access your server while your system load was too high (as set by the *MAXLOAD* variable in the *conf.h* configuration file or the *–L* command-line option).

`Malformed hostdata file`
An index's hostdata file is corrupt (see Section 14.3.2 "Create *hostdata* File" in the "Indexing" chapter for information about hostdata files).

`Couldn't open grep command`
: The server couldn't execute the *egrep* command it uses to search through files when doing a "grep index." You will probably never see this error, as the grep index type is broken in both Gopher 1.x and 2.x.

`Can't set UID!`
: The server could not change UIDs as set on the command line with either the *-U* or *-u* options. The server must be started as the user *root* in order to use these options.

`readline: Timed out!`
: The server's connection timed out while waiting for data from the client. The timeout value is set in the *conf.h* file by the *READTIMEOUT* variable.

`Possible Security Violation:` *'violation'*
: *gopherd* displays this message when it finds what might be a security violation in the arguments given to an *exec:* item, a shell script, or a *grep* index item.

`Denied access for` *host*
: + A host was denied access to data as configured by the access tokens in the *gopherd.conf* file.

11.5.1 Summarizing Log Data

Now that you have all of this information logged, what are you going to do with it?! Each line by itself really isn't very interesting. It's the "big picture" that we're interested in. Fortunately, there are tools available that summarize the mound of Gopher logs that have accumulated.

11.5.1.1 gla, the Gopher Log Analyzer

The best log analyzer that we've seen is a small public-domain Perl script called *gla*, which stands for "Gopher Log Analyzer." You can retrieve the analyzer via anonymous FTP from *boombox.micro.umn.edu* in the */pub/gopher/Unix/GopherTools* directory. Just grab the file *gla* from this directory.

You'll need *perl* to be able to use *gla*. The first line of *gla* reads:

```
#!/usr/bin/perl
```

However, many people keep their Perl program elsewhere. Change this line to correspond to the location of your Perl executable. You also have to make the file executable by using the command `chmod 755 gla`.

Now, you can generate your Gopher log analysis by feeding your log file into the *gla* program:

```
% gla < /var/log/gopher > log.analysis
```

Here, we've fed our Gopher log into the *gla* program and redirected the result of the analysis into the file *log.analysis*. *gla* compiles several types of summaries: It generates:

- Histograms showing the traffic on each day of the month, day of the week, and hour of the day
- Lists of the top 20 files and directories accessed, in order of popularity
- Separate lists of all hosts from which people connected, all files, all searches, and all menus requested

We make the *gla* output available internally through Gopher, so that anyone in the company can easily find it. Here's the menu we provide:

```
--> 1.  Jun 94 - Statistics
    2.  Jun 94 - Top twenty
    3.  Jun 94 - All hosts
    4.  Jun 94 - All files requested
    5.  Jun 94 - All searches requested
    6.  Jun 94 - All menus requested
```

Here's part of the first item from this menu, part of *gla*'s statistics output:

```
Date                 = Thu Jun 30
From  Jun 1   to  Jun 30
Total Transactions = 1556
Root menu accesses = 445
Sub-menu accesses  = 451
Text files fetched = 186
Searches requested =
Search ranges sent =
Access Denied      = 52

daily and hourly histograms omitted...

Histogram of activity by day of week:
Peak      = 353
Each '*' = 6 gopher transactions.
 Sun - ********
 Mon - ***********************************
 Tue - ***************************************************
 Wed - *************************************************
 Thu - ****************************************************
 Fri - ***********************************************************
 Sat - ********
```

gla gives you lots of interesting information and statistics, including:

Client Domains — A list of all the domains that contacted your server, the number of connections from each domain, and the percentage of total connections each domain was responsible for. This list is shown twice: once sorted alphabetically and once sorted by number of connections per domain.

Retrieved Items
: A list of the items on your server that were retrieved, the number of times each item was retrieved, and the percentage of total connections that this item was responsible for. This list is shown twice: once sorted alphabetically by item name and once sorted by number of times retrieved.

Short Summary
: A summary that includes the start date of the log, the end date of the log, the total number of connections, the average number of seconds between each connection, the number of different domains accessing your server, and the number of different files accessed.

Using *gla* certainly makes the data contained in the log much more readable and saves you the work of digging through it. It's really an indispensable tool.

11.5.1.2 glog, another Gopher log analyzer

glog is another log analyzer program that can be used. It actually comes packaged with the Gopher 1.x source distribution. It can be found in the *misc/Logging* directory in the source tree. If you're using Gopher 2.x, you can retrieve *glog* by anonymous FTP from *boombox.micro.umn.edu* in the *pub/gopher/Unix/GopherTools/glog* directory.

glog's output is similar to *gla*'s, but isn't formatted quite as nicely. It's written in C and can be compiled with your system's C compiler by executing the following command (substitute the name of your system's compiler for cc):

```
% cc -o glog glog.c
```

The executable will be named *glog*. You execute it in the same manner as *gla*:

```
% glog < /var/log/gopher > log.analysis
```

This log parser is a good alternative for *gla* if you don't have Perl installed on your system.

11.5.1.3 Locating search terms in the log

The only other thing you may find interesting from your log is the keywords people use when searching your databases. By grovelling through the log for the word "search," we can pick out these instances:

```
% grep search /var/log/gopher
Sat Sep 25 07:55:38 1993 11061 micro.umn.edu : search /reports for phones
Sat Sep 25 07:56:28 1993 12832 192.108.21.11 : search /reports for unix and delete
```

Here, we can see that users searched the *reports* database for the keywords *phones*, *unix*, and *delete*. Knowing what people are looking for can prompt you to add synonyms or to add data satisfying the most common search terms.

11.5.2 Rotating Logs

The log file can grow pretty fast—each connection takes about 70 characters. At a few hundred (or thousand!) connections a day, you'll probably want to rotate the log file at least monthly.

When you rotate a log file, there's no need to restart the *gopherd* program. *gopherd* reopens the log file every time it receives a connection (no matter whether you run the server standalone or under *inetd*). However, note that the log file must be writable by the user that *gopherd* is started as. Usually, this is the user *root*.

Here's a small shell script that rotates and compresses your log file for you. It'll keep the past seven log files. Once the script has been run seven times, the oldest log file is removed. You can run this as often as you'd like from *root*'s *cron* entry.

```
#!/bin/sh

# The name of your log file:
file='gopher'

# The directory the log file resides in:
directory='/var/log'

# Go to the log directory
cd "$directory" || exit 1

# We keep up to seven iterations of the file
j=7
for i in 6 5 4 3 2 1 0; do

  # Rotate each file if it exists
  if [ -f "$file.$i.Z" ]; then
    /bin/mv -f "$file.$i.Z" "$file.$j.Z"
  fi
  j=$i
done

# Move the current file
/bin/mv -f "$file" "$file.0"

# Create a new log file and make it writable only by the current user
> "$file"
/bin/chmod 644 "$file"

# Compress the latest file
/usr/ucb/compress "$file.0"
```

That's everything you should need to build, install, run, and maintain a Gopher archive (except for the data itself). The next chapter describes how to set up your server's content.

11.6 How to Register Your Gopher Server

This is a bit premature, since there's no real data in the server yet. But this is a task that the administrator should handle once the Data Librarians have done the work described in the next chapter.

Once your Gopher server is "stable" (not likely to change machines/hostnames or stop serving data unexpectedly), you should consider registering it with the central Gopher registry at the University of Minnesota. When you register your server, a pointer to your site will be placed in the "Master List of Gopher Servers." This is where most people look when browsing around for other interesting Gopher servers.

You can register your server in one of two ways: by sending mail to *gopher@boombox.micro.umn.edu* with the server's information, or by using a Gopher+ client to fill out a form. If you have a Gopher+ client, it's easier to fill out the form, which can be used by *gopher*ing to *gopher.tc.umn.edu* and selecting the "Other Gopher and Information Servers" directory and then the "Gopher Server Registration" form. You need the following information to register your server:

- The name by which you want your service to appear (what it will appear as in the list-of-servers). This is also known as the "GopherSpace Name."
- The fully qualified hostname of the server
- The port number at which the server process runs (by default, this is assumed to be 70)
- The Gopher administrator's name and email address
- The geographic location of the server (country, state)
- Wether or not you are running a Gopher+ server
- An optional Gopher "Path" selector. Giving a Gopher Path tells the registration that you want people to start at a place *other* than the root of your Gopher data directory. This is used primarily for sites that host more than one organization on a single Gopher server.

Before you send off this information, consider each of these items carefully. They determine how your Gopher server will appear in a list that thousands of people read and access every day. The following sections give an example and more detail on what each field should contain.

If you have a Gopher+ client installed, you can register your server using the ASK Form that's part of the `Other Gopher and Information Servers` directory on *gopher.tc.umn.edu*. This is also a good example of ASK Forms.

When you select `Gopher Server Registration` <??>, you should get a form like the one shown below. The simple text-editing commands are shown when you press CTRL– (control-dash); on some systems, use CTRL-/ or CTRL-7 instead to get the help message. Some of the editing commands are CTRL-P to move to the previous field and TAB or CTRL-N to move to the next field. To send the filled-in form, press RETURN; as in other Gopher menus, CTRL-G cancels the form.

```
+-------------------------Gopher Server Registration----------------+
|                                                                   |
| Administrator Name         Jerry Peek                             |
| Administrator E-Mail       gopher@foobar.com                      |
| GopherSpace Name           Foobar Inc. Product Information        |
| Hostname of Server         gopher.foobar.com                      |
| Port of Server             70                                     |
| Optional Selector                                                 |
| Geographic Location        New York, NY, USA
| Gopher+ Server (yes/no)?   no                                     |
|                                                                   |
| [Help: ^-]  [Cancel: ^G]                                          |
+-------------------------------------------------------------------+
```

The `Optional Selector` field is used when you want to register "part" of your Gopher server. A good example is an organization like Netcom, which "rents" Gopher space to individuals and groups. These groups want to have their own registration, but they're sharing space on a server with others. The selector field in the registration is the same as the path field in a link to that part of the Gopher server. For example, here's a link to an organization that uses part of a Gopher server:

```
Type=1
Name=Internet Society (includes IETF)
Path=1/isoc.and.ietf
Host=ietf.cnri.reston.va.us
Port=70
```

For this group, the `Optional Selector` would be `1/isoc.and.ietf`.

11.6.1 Example

When O'Reilly started their Gopher server, this is the information they sent in to register it:

```
Name: O'Reilly & Associates, Inc. (Book Publisher)
Hostname: gopher.ora.com
Port: 70
```

```
Gopher Administrator: gopher@gopher.ora.com
Geographic Location: USA, General
Gopher+: No
```

11.6.2 Server Name

You only get around 60 characters in which to describe your server, so use them wisely! Normally, you'd just use your company or institution name. If your institution runs more than one Gopher server, make sure that the names for each are unique and descriptive. If you're registering a company, you may want to tack on a descriptive phrase about the company.

11.6.3 Gopher Server Hostname

Use the alias, or CNAME, for your system, such as *gopher.company.com* instead of the actual hostname, *dino.company.com.* See Section 3.2 for more information about CNAMEs.

11.6.4 Gopher Port Number

Use the default Gopher port (70) if at all possible. Most people who use Gopher aren't familiar with the "port" concept. Using the default port allows anyone with a Gopher client to just aim the client at your Gopher hostname; they won't need to specify a port number too.

11.6.5 Administrator's Email Address

It's a good idea to make the Gopher administrator's email address something similar to *gopher@hostname* or *gopher-admin@hostname* by setting up an email alias to point from one or both of these addresses to the real Gopher administrator. This way, if the Gopher server administrator changes or if there are multiple people involved in administering the server, it's simple to change, add, or remove people from the administration list.

11.6.6 Geographic Location

If your institution is a university or provides a regional service, you should specify where you are located (by country, state). If you are a company or you don't fall into the regional status, you can specify your country and the fact that your service is "general." Sites that specify a geographic location will have their service placed in a menu under that country/state in the master list of Gopher servers. Sites that are "general" will be placed in the *General* category under their country.

In this Chapter:

- *The Easy Stuff—Text Files and Directories*
- *Menu Item Naming, Ordering, and Attributes*
- *Data Architecture*
- *File Types*
- *Chroot and Symbolic Links*
- *Converting an Existing FTP Structure*

12 Gopher: Preparing Information

Now we're on to the fun part! This is where the creativity comes in: organizing your information for easy Gopher accessibility.

As you know, Gopher uses a directory hierarchy that you set up. The challenge in setting up your information is to organize the directories, divide up the information into manageable pieces, name the pieces so people can find them, and make sure each piece still makes sense.

12.1 The Easy Stuff—Text Files and Directories

First off, you need to decide where to place your data. It's good to pick a directory on a disk that has enough room for you to expand your service. For these examples, we're going to use */usr/local/gopher-data* as our Gopher data directory.

The easiest way to begin once you've created your Gopher data directory is to copy a few of the files you'd like to serve into this directory. By default, the names of the menu items that the Gopher client displays are the names of the files that you've placed in the data directory. Likewise, when you make a directory, the Gopher client displays that directory's name in the menu.

Gopher clients understand which items are files and which are directories and signals the user appropriately. The UNIX text-based Gopher client (also called the "curses" client because of its use of the curses screen library) puts a `/` after entries that are directories, and either a `.` (Gopher 1.x) or nothing (Gopher 2.x) after entries that are text files.

For instance, if we place the files *Introduction* and *Calendar of Events** into our data directory:

```
% mv Introduction /usr/local/gopher-data
% mv 'Calendar of Events' /usr/local/gopher-data
```

and we make a subdirectory named *Wildlife Preserves*:

```
% cd /usr/local/gopher-data
% mkdir 'Wildlife Preserves'
```

the curses Gopher menu will look like this:

```
1. Calendar of Events.
2. Introduction.
3. Wildlife Preserves/
```

The Gopher server sorts the menu items alphabetically before sending them to the client. We'll talk more about setting the order of items on the menu in just a moment.

Notice that when we moved the file *Calendar of Events*, we used single quotes around the filename. If you're manipulating a file with a name that has spaces or other strange characters in it, use single quotes around the filename to ensure that all of the characters are interpreted as part of the actual filename. There are too many exceptions and details to tell the full story about filenames and shells, so if in doubt, just use the naming method described in the next section.†

12.2 Menu Item Naming, Ordering, and Attributes

Do long, verbose filenames annoy you? Would you like to order the menu yourself instead of letting *gopherd* alphabetize it for you? Would you like to set Gopher+ attributes such as item descriptions? Believe it or not, we're about to tell you how to do these amazing things.

With the *.cap* directory you can control the name and placement of each item, regardless of its filename. If you're using Gopher 2.x, you can use *.names* files to control menu-item naming and ordering, and to set Gopher+ attributes.

* Filenames longer that 14 characters won't work on some UNIX systems. The next section (on *.cap* directories) describes how to get this same effect (long menu item names) without long filenames.

† If you really want to know, the book *UNIX Power Tools* (O'Reilly & Associates, Inc./Bantam Books) has all the details.

12.2.1 So, what's a .cap directory?

When the Gopher server reads the filenames in each data directory, it looks for matching filenames in a directory named *.cap*. For each file in the data directory, the server uses the contents of the same filename in the *.cap* directory to determine the menu-item name and ordering.

Sound confusing? It's easier to understand from an example. Say we have the following files in one of our data directories:

```
% ls
calendar
intro
preserves/
```

Now, we need to tell the server what we'd like the menu items for these files to be named and how we'd like them ordered. To do so, we first make a directory called *.cap* in the current data directory.

```
% mkdir .cap
```

Inside this *.cap* directory, we make files with filenames corresponding to the files in the actual data directory. Inside these files, we place keywords that tell the Gopher server what we'd like to do:

```
% cd .cap
% cat > intro
Name=Introduction
Numb=1
^D
% cat > calendar
Name=Calendar of Events
Numb=2
^D
% cat > preserves
Name=Wildlife Preserves
Numb=3
^D
```

In this example, we used the *cat* command to create these files, but you can use any editor to create them.

Now, what have we done? We've used two *.cap* tokens, `Name` and `Numb`, to tell the Gopher server what we'd like to call these files and where we'd like them placed on the menu. `Name` tells the server what we'd like this file's menu item to look like, and `Numb` tells the server where we'd like the item placed on the menu. The resulting curses Gopher menu would look like this:

```
1. Introduction.
2. Calendar of Events.
3. Wildlife Preserves/
```

We've placed the *Introduction* file first, since we'd like people to read it before looking around our Gopher site. We actually could have left the `Numb` token out of the *calendar* and *preserves .cap* files. Read the box titled *"How Menu-Item Sorting Works"* to understand why this is so.

You might have noticed that we used the term "*.cap* file" in the previous paragraph. That's Gopher data librarian slang for "a file in the *.cap* directory."

NOTE

Tokens in the *.cap* file are both case- and space-sensitive. The first letter must be capitalized, and there can't be any space between the token and the = sign. Tokens that look like `name=Introduction` or `Name = Introduction` will *not* work.

Make sure that the *.cap* directory and files are readable by the user that *gopherd* runs as. If they aren't, the *.cap* entries won't have any effect (since the server won't be able to read the files!).

How Menu-Item Sorting Works

The Gopher server goes through the following steps to determine the order in which items are to be passed to the client (and thus the order in which the client displays them on its menu):

1. Determine if there's a *.cap* directory. If there is, then use any `Name` tokens in corresponding *.cap* files as the menu names for those files.
2. Items with a `Numb` token in their *.cap* files are sorted by their numbers and are *all* placed at the top of the menu. If you have one entry that has the token `Numb=3`, and none of your other entries have `Numb` tokens, the file with the `Numb=3` token will be first on the menu and *not* third. (That may seem silly, but that's the way it works!)
3. After all items with `Numb` entries have been ordered at the top of the menu, the entries without `Numb` tokens are sorted alphabetically by name. The alphabetic sorting is case-sensitive. Names starting with an upper-case letter come before names starting with a lower-case letter (`Zebra` comes before `apple`).

12.2.2 Gopher 2.x .names files

With Gopher 2.x, there is an alternative to using *.cap* directories. To control menu item names (and order), create any file that begins with a period, such as *.names*, in the same directory as the item you wish to rename or renumber. Although you can use any dot filename, these files are commonly called *.names* files. Next, create a line that begins with `Path=./` in this file. Append to this line the name of the file whose order you wish to modify. You can put any of the *.cap* file tokens after this line. You can customize multiple menu items in the same file; just separate the tokens for each menu item with a blank line or comment.

For instance, to do the same renaming/renumbering we did in the previous *.cap* example, we would execute the following commands to create a *.names* file and enter data into it:

```
% cd /usr/local/gopher-data
% cat >.names
# This is the Introduction to our Gopher site
Path=./intro
Name=Introduction
Numb=1

Path=./calendar
Name=Calendar of Events
Numb=2

Path=./preserves
Name=Wildlife Preserves
Numb=3
^D
```

There are a few other tokens that you can specify in *.names* to set Gopher+ attributes of an item. The `Admin` token forces an alternate administrator for the file (the default is specified in *gopherd.conf*). Gopher 2.x clients allow users to send mail to a file's administrator (which could be the data librarian). The `Abstract` token fills in the file's abstract block (see also Section 12.2.4). The `Domain` and `Domain_pat` tokens tell *gopherd* to check whether the requesting client is in the specified domain. If it is in the domain, *gopherd* renames the menu item accordingly. `Domain` expects a domain suffix, while `Domain_pat` expects a regular expression to match the domain on. These tokens allow you to customize menus based on the domain of the requesting client. Here's an example:

```
# The default Name
Path=./events
Name=Local Events at Wildlife University

# For people in the wildlife.ora.com domain, change the Name
Path=./events
Domain=wildlife.ora.com
Name=Local Events
```

In order for this feature to work, directory caching must be turned *off* by using *gopherd*'s *–C* option.

12.2.3 Gopher+ Multi-format Menu Items

If you have a couple of different formats or versions of a single document, Gopher 2.x allows you to have just one menu item for them. If the user selects that item, the client prompts her for the desired format.

To make a multi-format item, you make sure that each file has the same *base* name, but a different filename extension. For our example, we'll assume that we have the following files:

```
cover          A text file.
cover.rtf      A Rich Text Format document.
parrot.gif     A picture of a parrot in GIF format.
parrot.jpg     A picture of a parrot in JPEG format.
```

There are two base names here, *cover* and *parrot*. The extension is the text after the period (*.rtf*, *.gif*, etc.).

The Gopher+ server processes these files into two menu items called *parrot* and *cover*.

How do you control the text of a multi-format menu item? You create a line in *.names* that begins with `Path=./`, and append the name of the file whose menu item you wish to modify, *without any extension*.

For instance, to rename and renumber the *cover* and *parrot* files, you could execute the following command to create the *.names* file:

```
% cd /usr/local/gopher-data
% cat > .names
# This is the parrot file item
Path=./parrot
Name=Macaw Parrot in the Rainforest
Numb=3

Path=./cover
Name=Introduction and Cover
Numb=1
^D
```

12.2.4 Form and Abstract Attributes

As mentioned in Chapter 9, an abstract is a short description of a file or any short message that the data librarian wants the user to see with the = command. Forms will be described in Section 16.1. But to be complete about how attributes are set, we'll describe that aspect of the form and abstract attributes here.

The one line abstract can be specified in the .names file. For example, the abstract for the parrot file above might be:

```
Path=./parrot
Name=Macaw Parrot in the Rainforest
Abstract=photo taken 9/8/87 by E. Jennings, WWF
```

Longer abstracts, and all forms, are specified a different way.

Let's say you have a directory containing the following files:

cover.abstract	*A short text file describing the document.*
cover.ask	*A form definition.*
cover	*A text file.*
cover.rtf	*A Rich Text Format document.*

You have already seen in the last section that *cover.rtf* and *cover* are treated as two formats of one document and are represented by one menu item.

The other two suffixes, *.ask* and *.abstract*, are handled specially. Each adds the data in the file to a Gopher+ attribute. In our example, the contents of the *cover.abstract* file are automatically added to the *ABSTRACT* attribute of the *cover* file, and *cover.ask* is added to the ASK attribute.

You can also set the abstract for an item in the *.names* or *.Link* file. An abstract as defined in a *.Link* or *.names* file overrides an abstract in a *cover.abstract* file.

The UNIX curses Gopher client only shows the ABSTRACT attribute of a menu item to the user when the user presses the = key. Other clients, though, could show that information automatically when each item is highlighted (but before it is selected).

12.3 Data Architecture

Although making a Gopher data tree is pretty simple, there are a few things you should keep in mind as you develop your server. The overall goal of an information service is to provide a way to *efficiently* locate the information the users are after.

12.3.1 Menu Structure

The "root" of a major menu tree should almost always have an item at the very top of the menu that identifies what information is contained there. The name of this item could either state the topic of the menu (for instance, "Crocodile Species Accounts") or be something like "About this menu" or "Introduction." Inside this file should be a short description of the files accessible through this menu, to give the reader an overview of what's there.

These overviews are especially important if there are going to be links made to this menu from other Gopher servers. The reader may not have the benefit of seeing a good menu description before being shown the current menu. Overviews also provides a certain context for the reader. It's useful for them to know that they can just look at the first item in a directory to get a general overview of the information contained there, rather than spending time browsing through submenus, just to discover that this wasn't the information they were looking for.

As you design your service, keep in mind that the Gopher data is meant to be set up in a hierarchical, or tree, fashion, with one main menu as the root, and then submenus branching off of the main menu, and more menus off the submenus, and so on. Try to use this structure to your advantage, by splitting up your information into different topics and subtopics.

Try to keep each menu less than one page in length (a "page" in this context means between 15 and 18 menu items). It's hard to find information in long, multi-page "flat" menus. It's easier to browse multiple one-page menus to narrow down your information search. For users who utilize the curses client, menu items can be selected by typing the item's number—having menus of nine or fewer items makes this easier.

Sometimes you can't avoid having multi-page menus. However, you should try to keep your long menus at the "bottom" of your Gopher hierarchy. You shouldn't have any submenu items on a multi-page menu.

It's pretty easy to make a good "tree" structure if you just sit down and plan ahead before diving head-first into creating your Gopher data structure. Try to break down the information you'd like to serve into an outline form and then construct your data tree from that outline.

12.3.2 Menu Item Names

Menu item descriptions are brief by necessity, sometimes too brief. Because some Gopher clients do not allow cancelling the retrieval of a document, you need to make sure you warn people about entries that retrieve huge files. Gopher+ clients have a feature that allows users to find out the size of the file (the = command), but not all Gopher users know that command exists.

A classic bad example is a menu item such as "The blabla program," that, when selected, downloads a huge source-code archive. That menu-item name is misleading because it could just as well be a brief explanation of the program. You can help the user avoid getting stuck accidentally retrieving a huge document by, most importantly, writing accurate menu text. In addition, you can turn on the feature that automatically adds the file size and date to menu items (as described in Section 10.2.1.2). Unfortunately the size is not available separately so you get the date also, whether you need it or not. If you don't add the size, it's a good idea to put the word "big" on the end of menu items that result in long retrievals.

12.3.3 Document Length and Format

Scanning through long documents is just as tiresome as scanning through pages and pages of menu items. Try to keep your documents fairly short. Split up long documents by making an outline of the document and then dividing the document into parts, giving each part its own menu item.

Each document should have a title or heading at the top of it. This title could just be the menu item's name. This way, if the user decides to print, mail, or save the document, it'll be easy to remember what the document is about by just scanning its title.

12.3.4 Getting the Big Picture

Sometimes it's good to take a look at the overall structure of your Gopher data tree. There's no easy way to get the big picture by using a Gopher client, but there is a Perl script included in the Gopher 1.x distribution that lists the contents of a Gopher data tree. There are two files in the *misc/gophertree* directory that comes with the Gopher 1.x distribution: a *README* file that describes the command-line options, and *gophertree*, the actual program. If you're using Gopher 2.x, you can retrieve *gophertree* by anonymous FTP from *boombox.micro.umn.edu* in the *pub/gopher/Unix/GopherTools* directory.

Since this program is a Perl script, you may have to modify the first line of the program to point to the location of your Perl program. With that done, you can run the script on your Gopher server.

The syntax of the script is:

```
gophertree [-d -bn -ln -rn] host port [path]
```

The optional arguments make the script behave in the following manner:

-d Only list directories (not files) in the Gopher tree. The default is to list both files and directories.

-bn Limits the number of each non-directory item listed in every directory to *n*+1 (the +1 being a minor bug). So, if *n* is 3, only four files, four images, four sounds, etc. will be listed per directory scanned. The default is to list 16 of each item per directory.

-ln Sets the page length to *n* lines. The default is 55 lines per page.

-rn Limits the depth of the directories it traverses. The default maximum depth is 999 (making it go as deep as possible).

`Path` The Gopher path to start at. By default it starts at the root of your Gopher tree.

gophertree does not traverse off-host links and only delves into directory types—it won't look into *ftp* links. These are safety features to prevent diving into Gopherspace on someone else's host.

Here's an example:

```
% gophertree -b2 -r2 wildlife.ora.com 70

MSU Gopher Road Map                    Host: wildlife.ora.com
Last Update: 2/26/94                                      Page:   1
```

```
Lev Name                                       Type   Destination
--- ------------------------------------------ ------ -------------------------
  1 Introduction and Cover                     File   wildlife.ora.com
  1 Foreword                                   File   wildlife.ora.com
  1 Acknowledgments                            File   wildlife.ora.com
  1 Introduction and Conservation Priorities   Dir    wildlife.ora.com
  2   Human Exploitation of Crocodilians       File   wildlife.ora.com
  2   Crocodilian Conservation Programs        File   wildlife.ora.com
  2   Cropping Programs                        File   wildlife.ora.com
      . . .
  1 Country Accounts                           Dir    wildlife.ora.com
  2   Introduction                             File   wildlife.ora.com
  2   Africa                                   Dir    wildlife.ora.com
  2   Asia                                     Dir    wildlife.ora.com
  2   North and South America                  Dir    wildlife.ora.com
  2   Search                                   Index  wildlife.ora.com
  1 Species Accounts                           Dir    wildlife.ora.com
  2   Introduction                             File   wildlife.ora.com
  2   American Alligator (Alligator mississipp File   wildlife.ora.com
  2   American Crocodile (Crocodylus acutus)   File   wildlife.ora.com
      . . .
  1 Appendices                                 Dir    wildlife.ora.com
  2   List of Contacts                         File   wildlife.ora.com
  2   Summary of Species Data                  Dir    wildlife.ora.com
    . . .
```

This example listed out the first three items of each type in each directory and only went two directories deep into the Gopher tree. The ". . ." lines indicate that there was more to be shown, but the command-line options cut off the list at that point.

To only list directory items in the "Country Accounts" portion of the tree, we could use:

```
% gophertree -d wildlife.ora.com 70 'Country Accounts'

MSU Gopher Road Map                    Host: wildlife.ora.com
Last Update: 2/26/94                                               Page:   1

Lev Name                                       Type   Destination
--- ------------------------------------------ ------ -------------------------
  1 Africa                                     Dir    wildlife.ora.com
  1 Asia                                       Dir    wildlife.ora.com
  1 North and South America                    Dir    wildlife.ora.com
```

As you can see, this simple tool can help to give you the "big picture"—you may find that your server isn't organized as efficiently as you'd like on a large server; it may also point out misplaced files or files that are there accidentally.

This book is full of advice about what you *should* do. For a change of pace (with apologies to David Letterman), here are the . . .

Top Ten Ways to Make Your Gopher Server a Flop

10. Power your server with four gophers on a spinning wheel.*
9. Start your server "only when I feel like it."
8. Give your documents descriptive names like *xy12*, *moocow*, and *ff88ll.txt*.
7. Put all your files in a single directory.
6. Make your Gopher server look something like this:

```
1. A picture of me <GIF>
2. Some ingenious statement
     A list of my favorite Gopher Servers
3. gopher.tc.umn.edu
4. echonyc.com
```

5. Prefix everything with *Cyber* and end everything with *Space*:

```
1. CyberCampus Events and ActivitiesSpace
2. CyberEmployee InformationSpace
3. CyberStudent InformationSpace
```

4. Put lots of insults on your Gopher server:

```
1. Select Me you Idiot!!
```

3. Register a server as "The Junk Mail Mall."
2. Run your server on a Timex Sinclair 1000, connected to the Net with a 1200-baud modem.
1. Offer a database of recipes containing only lima beans and brussels sprouts.

—by Paul Lindner

12.4 File Types

A fundamental concept in the world of Gopher is that of a file *type*. As the Gopher server scans each data directory, it tries to assign a *type* to each file in the directory. With the examples that we've seen so far, only two different Gopher types have been used: text files and directories. However, Gopher supports quite a few other types as well. The Gopher server usually figures out a file's type by looking at the filename. For example, when *gopherd* sees a file that ends with *.gif* it knows that the file is of the *Image* type (and with Gopher 2.x, it knows that it is specifically the MIME type *image/gif*). The Gopher server's type determination from filename extensions is defined in the *gopherd.conf* file. See Section 11.1.5 for a complete explanation of this mapping.

* Try three Bobacs (see the Cover). They're much bigger. :-)

In a few cases *gopherd* looks inside the file to determine the type. These cases are described in Section 12.4.2, which also describes the special handling of compressed (.Z) files.

Gopher types are used to give the Gopher client and the user a better idea of what they're seeing in a Gopher directory. Clients often display a *tag* at the end of each menu item's title to show the user the item's type (Table 12-1 lists the tags displayed by the Gopher curses client). Clients also may react differently when retrieving files of different types. For example, when a user selects a file of the *Image* type, the curses client attempts to display the image graphically once it's been received (this only works if the curses client is operating in a terminal window on a graphics screen).

Table 12-1 shows the default list of different file types that *gopherd* supports and the extensions that it recognizes for each type (as defined by the default *gopherd.conf* file). Placing a file in one of your Gopher data directories with any of these extensions results in *gopherd* recognizing the file as the specified type. Text in italics relates only to Gopher 2.x.

Table 12-1: Gopher Default Recognized Extensions

Description	**Default Recognized Extensions**	**Curses client's tag**
Text file	Anything not listed below	. or blank with the Gopher 2.x client
Directory		/
CSO name server		<CSO>
Mac HQX file	*.hqx*	<HQX>
PC binary	*.arc, .zip, .lzh, .exe, .zoo, .dms*	<PC Bin>
Full-text index	*.src, .mindex*	<?>
Telnet session		<TEL>
General binary file	*.tar.Z, .tar, .dvi, .wri*	<Bin>
Sound	*.snd, .au, .wav*	<)>
Image	*.gif, .tiff, .jpg, .pict, .pcx*	<Picture>
Movie	*.mpeg, .mov*	<MOVIE> (Gopher 2.x only)
MIME file		Blank or <MIME> with the Gopher 2.x client
HTML file	*.html*	Blank or <HTML> with the Gopher 2.x client
TN3270 Telnet session		<3270>

You may notice that there was an attempt to build in support for HTML documents (the document scheme used in the World Wide Web), so that the Gopher client and server could use HTML documents. Unfortunately, the HTML code in most Gopher clients is either non-existent or does not work well. We do not recommend using Gopher to serve HTML documents.

12.4.1 Overriding the Default Type

You'll eventually want to serve a file that doesn't end in one of the recognized filename extensions. There are two ways to get the server to recognize the file as the desired type.

The first is to modify the *gopherd.conf* file to recognize a new filename extension. This is handy if you're going to be serving many files that have an extension that the server doesn't already recognize. For example, the server doesn't recognize files ending with *.com* as PC binaries. If you know you are going to be serving lots of PC *.com* files, you can put an entry in the *gopherd.conf* file to correctly recognize this extension. See Section 11.1.5 to see how this can be done.

The other way to recognize a file as a certain type is to use a *.cap* file (or a *.names* file with Gopher 2.x) to force the server to do so. This is handy if you've only got a file or two with unrecognized extensions. For instance, if you have a few *.com* PC binary files, you could use a *.cap* entry to force the server to recognize them as a general binary type.

The *.cap* keyword to force the Gopher-type is *Type.* For example, if you have a file called *phonebook.com*, and you'd like *gopherd* to recognize this as a General Binary File (type 9), you'd use a *.cap* file similar to this one:

```
% pwd
/usr/local/gopher-data
% cat > .cap/phonebook.com
Name=Phone Book Program
Type=9
^D
```

12.4.2 Special Files

There are some files that *gopherd* considers "special" and treats differently than other files. The recognition of these special file types is hardcoded in *gopherd.* The *ext* or *viewext* tokens in the *gopherd.conf* file have no effect on these special file types. Special files include compressed files, mail-spool files, shell scripts, μ-law sound files, and WAIS source files. The following sections discuss each of these in detail.

12.4.2.1 Compressed files

Files ending with a *.Z* extension are considered to be files compressed with the UNIX *compress* command. When *gopherd* encounters a file ending in *.Z* while scanning a data directory, it shows the filename without the *.Z* extension as the menu item (although a *.cap* `Name` entry can override this). When a compressed file is selected for viewing, the Gopher server uncompresses the file as it sends it to the client—the client receives the file uncompressed. With Gopher 1.x, the command used to uncompress the file on the fly is specified in the *conf.h* configuration file with the *ZCATCMD* variable (see Section 10.2.2.1) With Gopher 2.x, uncompressing or "decoding" files is configured with *decode* tokens in the *gopherd.conf* file (see Section 11.1.7).

There are two possible exceptions to this rule. When you're accessing an *ftp* link, *gopherd* assumes that since you're using FTP, you want to consider any files ending with *.Z* as binary files and not simply as compressed text files. Thus, it marks all files ending with *.Z* as general binary files (type 9). That means the server does not uncompress the file when it is selected for downloading.

The second exception occurs under Gopher 1.x when a file ends with *.tar.Z. gopherd* recognizes the fact that files ending with this extension are intended to be transferred compressed to save time and marks them as a general binary type (type 9). For some reason, Gopher 2.x does not behave in this manner.

If you're pressed for space, compressing your text files can save you lots of disk space—the *compress* command usually reduces the size of text files by around 50 percent. But it does increase the CPU load on your server because the files are *uncompressed* on demand.

Note that if you *compress* files which already have *.cap* files associated with them, the *.cap* files have to be renamed to include the new *.Z* extension. For example, if you have a file named *big_ol_file* with a *.cap* entry (*.cap/big_ol_file*), and you compress this large file to save space, the file is now called *big_ol_file.Z.* You have to rename the *.cap* file to *.cap/big_ol_file.Z* also.

+ However, this isn't true for *.names* files under Gopher 2.x. It's intelligent enough to chop off the filename extension before looking at the *Path* fields. So, using the previous example, a *.names* file would look like this:

```
% cat > .names
Path=./big_ol_file
Name=Big Old File
^D
```

If you're running in a `chroot()`ed environment and want to compress some files to save space, you'll need to put the uncompressing command into your `chroot()`ed Gopher data directory. For example, if the command you specify is */usr/bin/zcat* and your Gopher data directory is */usr/local/gopher-data*, you need to copy the *zcat* command into */usr/local/gopher-data/usr/bin* in order for *gopherd* to find the *zcat* command. If your *zcat* command uses dynamically linked libraries, you'll need to take a look at Section 13.4.2.3 for more information about configuring the `chroot()`ed server.

12.4.2.2 Mail spool files

When *gopherd* scans a directory, it tries to figure out what *type* each file is. *gopherd* peeks at the beginning of each file during this process. One of the things it tries to determine is if the file is a mail spool file. It scans the first line in the file, looking specifically to see if the line is formatted like this:

```
From Sender Day Mon dd hh:mm:ss Year
```

This is the standard format of the first line of a UNIX mail header. If the first line of a file matches this specification, it converts the file into a directory type. When users select this directory, they are shown a submenu with the subject of each mail message in this mail spool file. Selecting a subject entry displays the mail message.

This can be very useful for making mailing-list digests accessible. Simply copy the digest into a Gopher data directory and then let *gopherd* do the rest. Unfortunately, this neat feature does not work on a compressed mail spool file. If the spool file is compressed, *gopherd* treats it like a normal text file.

12.4.2.3 Shell Scripts

When a *text* file is selected, *gopherd* checks the first few bytes of the file to see if it's a shell script. If the first three characters in the file are "`#!/`", then it's considered to be a script. *gopherd* executes the script and sends the result to the client. This works identically to the `exec:` "Cool Link" type described in Section 13.4.2.

12.4.2.4 μ-law sound files

Another thing *gopherd* tries to determine while peeking at files is if the file is a μ-law sound file. If the first four bytes inside the file are `.snd`, then the file is treated as a sound file. Sound files are transferred to the client as binary files and are then fed into a sound-playing program.

12.4.2.5 WAIS source files

When *gopherd* encounters a file ending in *.src*, the file is considered to be a WAIS index source file (because the *.src* extension is mapped to type 7, index, in the *gopherd.conf* file by default). When this file is selected, it results in a WAIS query using the contents of the *.src* to figure out how to access the WAIS database. See Section 14.1.5 and Section 13.4.3 for more information about using *.src* files to point to WAIS databases.

12.5 Chroot and Symbolic Links

You may already have the data you want to serve on your system. Perhaps you are already providing access to it using a different service, such as FTP. If so, it is tempting to just put a symbolic link to it from your Gopher data directory. But that won't work in a securely run Gopher server, as described below. Even symbolic links inside the data directory need to be thought through carefully.

12.5.1 Symbolic Links to Outside the Gopher Data Directory

When using `chroot()` (as it should), the server can't access any data outside of the `chroot()`ed hierarchy. This means that a symbolic link to a directory outside of the Gopher data hierarchy will not work. For example, say that you have a data directory that has a symbolic link to some data outside of the tree:

```
/
 usr/
   local/
     lots-o-data/
     gopher-data/
       lots-o-data -> /usr/local/lots-o-data
       more-data/
       info-file
```

Now, when you run this server `chroot()`ed at the */usr/local/gopher-data* directory, this is what's left:

```
/
  lots-o-data -> /usr/local/lots-o-data
  more-data/
  info-file
```

In the Gopher server's view, */usr/local/lots-o-data* no longer exists. The only way to make *lots-o-data* visible to the `chroot()`ed server would be to copy the directory and its contents into the Gopher data hierarchy.

You may be tempted to move the data into *gopher-data* and then link to it from another service such as FTP, but *ftpd* also runs `chroot()`ed, and it would not be able to use a symbolic link into the Gopher directory. Therefore, if you have multiple services, some duplication of data is hard to avoid.

Even symbolic links within the Gopher directory require care, as described in the next section.

12.5.2 Symbolic Links to Within the Gopher Data Directory

If you use symbolic links to reference files within your Gopher data directory, you'll need to make sure that they're relative to the new `chroot()`ed root. For example, the following makes sense in the normal filesystem:

```
/
  usr/
    local/
      gopher-data/
        more-data/
```

```
          another-info-file -> /usr/local/gopher-data/info-file
        info-file
```

but would fail to work under a `chroot()`ed server. The link points to a "non-existent" file, and the server ignores the link since it's invalid. In order to make *another-info-file* reference *info-file* under a `chroot()`ed server, you'd need to make the symbolic link look like this:

```
/
  usr/
    local/
      gopher-data/
        more-data/
          another-info-file -> ../info-file
        info-file
```

With the above, when the Gopher data directory is `chroot()`ed, the symbolic link is valid, pointing to *info-file*. This link also works when using the normal filesystem.

Another way that works `chroot()`ed, but not un-`chroot()`ed, is the following:

```
/
  usr/
    local/
      gopher-data/
        more-data/
          another-info-file -> /info-file
        info-file
```

12.6 Converting an Existing FTP Structure

If your site runs an anonymous FTP server, it is very easy to convert your FTP directory structure into a usable Gopher hierarchy. The key is to use *.cap* files (or *.names* files under Gopher 2.x) to give your FTP site more explanatory menu-item names.

Most anonymous FTP sites have a directory called *~ftp/pub*, in which the public files reside for retrieval by anonymous FTP users. Simply tell your administrator to specify this directory as the *data-directory* option to *gopherd*. You may have anonymous FTP directories that you wish to "hide" from Gopher clients. You can use the *ignore* token in the *gopherd.conf* file to force *gopherd* to ignore those directories.

For each directory or file that could use a more verbose description (remember that, by default, only the filename is shown), make a *.cap* directory (or *.names* file) and create a descriptive `Name` entry.

If you're currently using a DL/Describe database to enhance your FTP area (not covered in this book), you can transparently use your DL database to name your Gopher files. Simply compile *gopherd* to include the code for handling DL databases (see Section 10.2.1.2 for instructions), and your DL descriptions show up as the names of your Gopher items. If you're using DL databases, the DL description overrides any `Name=` entry in a *.cap* file. However, other *.cap* keywords, such as `Numb=`, work as expected.

13.3 Links to CSO Phone Books and Telnet Sites

Now that you know the easy way to link to information on another Gopher server, we'll continue with a couple of more obscure link types. They follow the standard form, but warrant a more indepth look.

13.3.1 Linking to a CSO Phone Book Server

A CSO server is a "phone book" of computer residents. It can keep a small amount of information about a large number of people or things and provide fast access to that information over the Internet. Its most common use is to keep a "white pages" directory of people at an institution.

Unlike a printed directory, the information in a CSO database is dynamic. It can be updated at any time, from any computer on the Internet capable of running the client program, *ph*.

In order to create a link to a CSO phone-book server, you need to either set up a phone-book server or know the machine and port that a CSO server resides on. The following is a small blurb about CSO servers that was taken from the Gopher FAQ:

Q6: How can I set up a "CSO" phone-book server? Where is the software?

A6: CSO phone-book servers are also known as *qi* servers. The software implementation can be gotten via anonymous FTP from *vixen.cso.uiuc.edu* (128.174.5.50) as */pub/qi.tar.gz*. You may also see this referred to as *ph,* which is what most of the clients are called. A collected set of clients for Macs, PCs, VMS, VM, etc, are in the */pub/ph.tar.gz* file.

There is also an archive of the mailing list for qi/ph software on the same machine. It's in */pub/info-ph.archive*. You may join the list by sending email to *info-ph-request@uxc.cso.uiuc.edu.*

Once you have the CSO server running on a port (normally port 105), a CSO link like this one allows Gopher clients to query the CSO server:

```
Name=Boston University Phone Book
Type=2
Port=105
Path=
Host=ns.bu.edu
```

The curses client displays the tag <CSO> after this type, letting the user know that this is a CSO query.

13.3.2 The telnet Link Type (Including the TN3270 Type)

The *telnet* link type is used to start up a *telnet* session to a machine and port that you specify. Here's a simple example:

```
Name=Environmental Protection Agency Library
Type=8
Host=epaibm.rtpnc.epa.gov
Port=
Path=public
```

Here, we've created a *telnet* link to the Environmental Protection Agency's library. When a user sees this item in the Gopher curses client, it looks like this:

```
1.  Environmental Protection Agency Library <TEL>
```

The curses client automatically tacks the `<TEL>` tag onto the end of every *telnet* link. When the user selects this item, the client displays a screen explaining what is about to happen:

```
+-------Environmental Protection Agency Library--------+
|                                                      |
| Warning!!!!!, you are about to leave the Internet    |
| Gopher program and connect to another host. If       |
| you get stuck press the control key and the ] key,   |
| and then type quit                                   |
|                                                      |
| Connecting to epaibm.rtpnc.epa.gov using telnet.     |
|                                                      |
| Use the account name "public" to log in              |
|                                                      |
|                        [Cancel - ^G] [OK - Enter]    |
|                                                      |
+------------------------------------------------------+
```

When they hit the return key, a *telnet* session is started, connecting the user to *epaibm.rtpnc.epa.gov*.

The user usually needs a username to log into the remote site. Fortunately, Gopher provides a way for you to tell the user what username to use. You specify a login name after the `Path` token. In this example, we've used this feature to tell the user to use the login name *public* to log in. If nothing is given for the `Path` token, the "Use the account" line is not displayed.

Notice that the `Port` line was left blank in this example. Since it's blank, the Gopher client uses the *telnet* command's default port (23). If you'd like to specify an alternate *telnet* port, you can put the port number on the `Port` line. Here's an example with a specific port number:

```
Name=Geographic Name Server
Type=8
Host=martini.eecs.umich.edu
```

feature—you wouldn't want to accidentally ignore files or directories on an FTP site! The client receives a directory that looks like a normal Gopher menu. Selecting a directory retrieves the contents of that FTP directory as a submenu, and selecting a file retrieves that file.

4. If the item to retrieve is a file, the server determines if the file is a binary file by looking at its extension. Again, under Gopher 1.x, these extension-to-type conversions are hardcoded for the FTP links (see Table 13-2 for a list of recognized extensions). If it recognizes the file as a binary file, Gopher changes into binary mode. Otherwise, the file is transferred in *text mode* and is considered to be of the gopher type 0 (text file). The one exception to this rule is files that end in *.hqx*. They're text files, but the server recognizes that they're Macintosh BinHexed files (Gopher type 4). Under Gopher 1.x, the server then retrieves the file, temporarily placing it into the directory specified by the `LIST` variable in *conf.h* (see Section 10.2.2.1). Once the file has been retrieved from the FTP site, the server sends the file to the Gopher client and removes the temporary file. With Gopher 2.x, the code has been fixed to eliminate the temporary storage of the FTPed file on the Gopher server.

   As you can see, under Gopher 1.x, FTP transfer is really a two step process: FTP-site to Gopher-server and then Gopher-server to Gopher-client.

The following table lists the file extensions that are recognized under FTP when using Gopher 1.x. Files with any of these extensions (except for *.hqx*) are transferred in binary mode.

Table 13-2: Hardcoded FTP Types Under Gopher 1.x

Type	Description	Default Recognized Extensions
4	Mac HQX file	*.hqx*
5	PC binary	*.arc, .zip, .lzh, .exe, .zoo, .arj, .pak, .com, .ps, .hyp, .pct*
9	General binary file	*.tar, .Z*
s	Sound	*.snd, .au*
I	Image	*.gif, .tiff, .tif, .pict, .pcx*

One last thing to note: compressed files are *not* uncompressed prior to being sent to the client. Instead, they are sent as binary files (type 9).

13.4.1.2 What if an ftp link fails?

If you see the telltale "Nothing Available" box pop up in the Gopher curses client, there are a few things you should try to help you figure out what's going on.

If you're using Gopher 1.x, make absolutely sure the directory */tmp* exists and can be written in by the user that *gopherd* is running as. Without a writable */tmp* directory, all ftp-type transfers will fail. The */tmp* directory must also have enough space on it to store fairly large files temporarily.

If you're running the server `chroot()`ed, the */tmp* directory *must* exist in the root of the Gopher data directory. For example, if your Gopher data directory is */usr/local/gopher-data*, then the directory */usr/local/gopher-data/tmp* must exist and be writable in order for `ftp` types to work under a `chroot()`ed server.

Some FTP sites require that hosts connecting to the site be registered in the Domain Name System (DNS). If these FTP sites cannot do a "reverse lookup," matching your IP address to a valid domain name, they refuse FTP service. For a full explanation of DNS, see the O'Reilly & Associates Nutshell Handbook *DNS and BIND*.

If you're still stumped as to why an `ftp`-type link isn't working correctly, try to watch why it fails by using the *–D* (debug) flag when running *gopherd* from the command line. The *–D* flag forces *gopherd* to relay lots of debugging information, including login attempts to anonymous FTP sites.

13.4.2 Links That Execute Scripts

The Gopher server allows you to execute scripts to generate information dynamically using the `exec` link type. This is handy for generating or filtering data on the fly. The script can be any kind of script file (*perl*, *sh*, etc.) that's directly executable (the file starts with `#!/`). It cannot be a compiled program.

The syntax for this link is similar to that of the `ftp` link:

```
Name=Name of your choice
Path=exec:"args":scriptname
Type=Script's output type
Port=+
Host=+
```

The `Path` line contains all of the information about how to execute the script. *`args`* are any arguments you'd like passed to the script, and *`scriptname`* is the name of the shell script to execute. The *`scriptname`* must be a full pathname, relative to the root of the Gopher data directory.

The `Type` depends on the type of information that the script is going to return. Most often, it's the text type (0), but it could really be anything.

The `Port` and `Host` fields always contain just a `+`.

Let's take a look at a simple example. Say you'd like your users to be able to display the current month's or the current year's calendar. Here are two link entries with scripts that do just that:

```
Name=Display Calendar for this Month
Path=exec:"":/bin/displaycal
Type=0
```

```
Port=+
Host=+

Name=Display Calendar for this Year
Path=exec:"1994":/bin/displaycal
Type=0
Port=+
Host=+
```

The script *displaycal* looks like this:

```
#!/bin/sh
/usr/bin/cal $1
```

This script is located in the *bin* directory of the Gopher data directory (*/usr/local/gopher-data/bin/displaycal*).

We can't just call the *cal* program from an exec link explicitly because *cal* is not a script. *gopherd* only executes scripts.

13.4.2.1 When exec items fail

If, when you select an exec item, you see a message similar to:

```
sh: /usr/local/gopher-data/bin/displaycal: Permission denied
or
'/bin/displaycal' does not exist!!
```

then the server is having problems executing the script. Try checking these things:

- Make sure that the filename and pathname are correct and are relative to your Gopher data directory. The line `Path=exec:"":/bin/displaycal` refers to *gopher-data-dir/bin/displaycal* and *not* to */bin/displaycal.*
- Make sure that the path and script are both readable *and* executable by the user that *gopherd* runs as.

If, instead of seeing the output of the script, you see the script itself when you select the item, make sure that the first three characters on the first line of the script are `#!/`. If they're *anything* else, the server assumes that something's wrong and just displays the script instead of executing it. Also, make sure that the script is executable by the user that *gopherd* runs as. Note that some older versions of UNIX don't understand the `#!` syntax at all, in which case you're out of luck.

If you don't see anything when you select an exec item, it may be that your script is executing, but isn't giving the desired results. Make sure that when you run the script outside of *gopherd* that it works the way you'd like it to. If you're running the server `chroot()`ed, see the next section for additional things to check.

To see exactly what's going on when an exec item is selected, run *gopherd* with the *–D* (debug) option from the command line. This tells you what command gets executed and displays any error messages the script generates.

13.4.2.2 Executing scripts within a chroot()ed server

When running a `chroot()`ed server, everything that the server accesses while running *must* reside *within* the Gopher data hierarchy. This includes any programs or libraries that the script you execute (and any programs called by it) needs to run. Let's take a look at the calendar `exec` example. The script that we're executing looks like this:

```
#!/bin/sh
/usr/bin/cal $1
```

In order for this script to execute under a `chroot()`ed server, this script and both */bin/sh* and */usr/bin/cal* need to be contained in the Gopher data hierarchy. Here's what we need to do to accomplish this:

```
% pwd
/usr/local/gopher-data
% mkdir bin usr usr/bin
% cp /bin/sh bin
% cp /usr/bin/cal usr/bin
```

Now, we have both */bin/sh* and */usr/bin/cal* located in our Gopher data hierarchy. When the script executes, it'll be able to find these programs. However, it may still not have everything necessary to run these programs; read on.

13.4.2.3 Using dynamically linked programs

Unfortunately, it's not always this easy. Most systems these days use dynamically linked programs, including SunOS, Solaris, HP-UX version 8.0 or later, IRIX, NeXTstep, and FreeBSD (to name a few). This means that most programs need access to at least a general system library in order to run. In these cases, you also need to make the libraries, and whatever else the library uses, available in the Gopher data hierarchy. This can require a bit of trial and error, but you only have to do it once for each script.

To figure out what libraries and other files you need, run *gopherd* with the *–D* (debug) option. Then try to connect to the server and select the `exec` script item. The server should report any problems that occurred while executing the script.

An alternative to using *gopherd*'s debug option is to use the `chroot()` command to run the script in the `chroot()`ed environment.

Here's an example using SunOS 4.1.3 (continued from the above example—we already have */bin/sh* and */usr/bin/cal* in place):

```
# gopherd -D /usr/local/gopher-data 70
```

Now, either use another terminal or another window to connect to this server using a Gopher client and select the `exec` item.

If you choose to use the direct `chroot()`ing method (which is easier), execute the following command instead:

```
# chroot /usr/local/gopher-data bin/displaycal
```

When we select (or execute) the script, we see this:

```
crt0: no /usr/lib/ld.so
```

So, now we know that we need the file */usr/lib/ld.so*:

```
# pwd
/usr/local/gopher-data
# mkdir usr/lib
# cp /usr/lib/ld.so usr/lib
```

Now, we try selecting (or executing) the exec item again and see:

```
crt0: no /dev/zero
```

We need a */dev/zero* file—unfortunately, this isn't a "normal" file; it's a character device. We need to make a duplicate device. With SunOS 4.1.3, we need to become *root* and do the following:

```
# pwd
/usr/local/gopher-data
# mkdir dev
# cd dev
# ls -l /dev/zero
crw-rw-rw-  1 root        3,  12 May 22  1991 /dev/zero
# mknod zero c 3 12
# chmod 666 /dev/zero
```

The output from the `ls -l /dev/zero` command tells us that the device type (`c` for character) and the major and minor device numbers (`3` and `12` respectively) needed to create a new *zero* device using the *mknod* command.

We try our script once again and see:

```
ld.so: libc.so.1: not found
```

Here, the program is trying to locate the actual library. Looking in */usr/lib*, we see this:

```
% ls -l /usr/lib/libc.so.1*
-rwxr-xr-x  1 root       516096 Oct 11  1990 /usr/lib/libc.so.1.8*
-rwxr-xr-x  1 root       540672 Aug  3  1991 /usr/lib/libc.so.1.8.1*
```

We're going to want the "latest" library (the library with the highest version number), which, in this case, is */usr/lib/libc.so.1.8.1.*

```
# pwd
/usr/local/gopher-data
# cp /usr/lib/libc.so.1.8.1 usr/lib
```

Once more we execute the script, and it complains about needing the *libdl.so.1* library. We copy */usr/lib/libdl.so.1.0* into *usr/lib.*

Now, when we execute the exec item, it works! Phew! If the program needs more shared libraries, you may get more error messages, since only one is reported at a time. One way to find out all of the shared libraries a binary needs, in one pass, is to use the *ldd* command (in SunOS 4.1.3, anyway).

Unfortunately, the exact files that you're going to need to copy into your data directory vary depending on the operating system you're using. However, if you follow this method, you should be able to get a working `chroot()`ed server that allows you to run your script.

13.4.2.4 Compiling statically linked programs

The only way to get around this process on machines that use dynamic libraries is to make sure that all of your programs are *statically linked*. This means that they don't rely on the dynamic libraries—all of the functions that the program needs to run are contained in the executable. In order to make a statically linked executable, you need the source code to the program and a compiler to compile the code. When you compile the program, you need to tell the compiler to make the program static. This is usually done by using an option to the compiler that forces it to make the program statically linked. See your compiler manual for details.

The pitfall here is that most operating systems don't include the source code for their commands, so you're out of luck unless you can find a public-domain version of the program. Many common UNIX commands are freely available by anonymous FTP on *ftp.uu.net* in the *systems/unix/bsd-sources* and *systems/gnu* directories.

13.4.3 Links That Do WAIS Searches

The `waissrc` link type is one way to include a WAIS index (see Section 14.1 for the other ways). As you might expect, the syntax is similar to the other two "Cool Link" types:

```
Name=Name of your choosing
Path=waissrc:wais-source-file
Type=7
Port=+
Host=+
```

`wais-source-file` is the full pathname (relative to the Gopher data directory) of a WAIS source (*.src*) file. the *.src* file describes the location of a WAIS database, including the host and port the WAIS server is running on. This *.src* file is generated using the *–export* option to the *waisindex* program. This type of link is used in practically the same manner as a normal index (type 7) link. A link might look something like this:

```
Name=Query Database
Path=waissrc:/.wais-sources/big-db.src
Type=7
Port=+
Host=+
```

Now we've covered the syntax of all the link types.

In this Chapter:
- *Using WAIS Indexes*
- *Using NeXT Indexes*
- *Serving WAIS and NeXT Indexes with gindexd*
- *grep Indexes*
- *Script Queries*
- *Searching Multiple Indexes*

14

Gopher: Incorporating Databases

In this chapter, we'll discuss the different ways to incorporate database searching capability into your Gopher server. Included here is information about incorporating WAIS indexes, NeXT indexes, and custom script queries, which might search the same data as that presented by your Gopher server or a separate data set.

To allow searching of your Gopher menus, see Chapter 15, *Gopher: Veronica and Jughead*.

14.1 Using WAIS Indexes

In order to incorporate WAIS indexes into your Gopher server, you need to have compiled-in the WAIS portion of the *gopherd* source code. If you have not yet done this, look at Section 10.2.3.1. If you haven't already read the WAIS chapters, it may be best to do that now to get an understanding of WAIS indexing. This will help you considerably in understanding the following material. If you're using Gopher 2.x, you should also read about *gopherindex*, in Section 16.2.2. It automates many of the steps discussed in this section.

There are several ways to make the Gopher server recognize a WAIS index. The easiest is to make a link to a WAIS index *.src* file that's located in your Gopher tree as described in Section 12.4.2.5. There are a few alternate methods, including using a *.cap* entry instead of a link and pointing a link to a port that is configured to serve WAIS data.

Just pick out the scheme that sounds best to you (after reading what follows) and go with it.

14.1.1 Placement of WAIS Data

To make a WAIS index that's directly readable by the Gopher server, you'll need to make an index somewhere inside the Gopher data tree. It's a good idea to put indexes in subdirectories, separate from other data that you're serving.

The best place to put your WAIS data is into a *hidden* directory (a directory whose name starts with a dot). This often makes indexing a bit easier. Here's why: If the directory where you're storing your WAIS data resides in the same directory as the data you're indexing, you may end up "indexing the index." This is not desirable. It commonly happens when you use the * wildcard to pass the files-to-index to the *waisindex* program. Including the index directory in the files-to-index does three things that you probably want to avoid:

- It makes your index bigger.
- It takes approximately twice as long to index, since you're chewing on your data twice!
- When people query, they may get an extra hit—the *index.cat* file (a file which contains the filenames that were indexed).

Here's the correct way to generate the index with a hidden index directory:

```
% pwd
/usr/local/gopher-data/Country Accounts
% mkdir .index
% ls
Africa/  Introduction
Asia/    North and South America/
% waisindex -r -d .index/country *
11492: 0: Sep 13 19:40:07 1993: 6: Starting to build database country
  .
  .
  .
11492: 104: Sep 13 20:04:28 1993: 6: Flushing 7429 different words,
35986 total words to disk...
11492: 105: Sep 13 19:40:32 1993: 6: Done flushing version 0
11492: 106: Sep 13 19:40:33 1993: 6: Merging version 0 into master
version and generating dictionary.
11492: 107: Sep 13 19:40:36 1993: 100: Total word count for dictionary
is: 33439
0 out of 22
11492: 108: Sep 13 19:40:37 1993: 6: Finished build
```

Since the index directory started with a ., the * wildcard in the *waisindex* command didn't pick it up.

14.1.2 Creating an Index

We've just presented one example of creating an index. However, you should be aware of a few things when creating WAIS indexes for use by *gopherd*.

The *–T type* and *–t format* command-line options to *waisindex* can affect the menu item names that *gopherd* sends to the client. The default behavior, without using any WAIS typing, results in *gopherd* giving the name of the matching files and the files' full pathnames to the client. To avoid having the full pathname displayed to the client, the *–T text* option must be used when indexing.

The *–t format* option can change where the item names come from. For example, if you index the files with the WAIS format being *first_line*, then the server returns the first line of each document as the item's Gopher title. Here's an example:

```
% waisindex -t first_line -r -d .index/country *
```

Now, when this index is queried, the first line of each matching file is shown as the Gopher menu titles.

See Section 8.4 for more information about using the *–T* and *–t* typing flags. In Gopher 1.x, information in *.cap* files overrides the name information that *waisindex* generates. So, if you're using the *first_line* typing scheme and have an entry in *.cap* that assigns the name *Alternate Name* to a menu item, *Alternate Name* will show up on the Gopher menu generated by the WAIS query. However, for some reason Gopher 2.x *.names* files do *not* override the name information that *waisindex* generates.

You should also be aware that you cannot index and serve compressed files. Although *waisindex* indexes compressed files correctly, *gopherd* does not understand how to serve the files; *gopherd* looks for the filename without the *.Z* filename extension. One (very ugly) trick to get around this is to make links from each normal filename to the filename with the *.Z* extension. For example, if you have a compressed file named *big-data-file.Z*, which is indexed, you can create a symbolic link using the command **ln -s big-data-file.Z big-data-file** to make *gopherd* recognize the file correctly. This way, *gopherd* sees that the file exists and is able to serve it when requested.

14.1.3 Using a Link to Incorporate WAIS indexes

Now that you have created a WAIS index, you need to pick one of the three ways of making a link to let the Gopher server understand how to access the index. This section and the next two describe the three ways.

The link for the previous example would look like this:

```
% cat > .Links
Name=Search Country Data
Type=7
Path=7/Country Accounts/.index/country
Host=+
Port=+
^D
```

Here, we've told the server to call the item "Search Country Data," and we've forced the server to recognize the item as an index by putting in the `Type=7` line (7 is the index type). The `Path` line tells the server where to find the index. The `Path` should always start with 7, so that the server knows it's an index, and it should be followed by the full pathname of the index, relative to the Gopher data directory. So, even though the full pathname of this index is really */usr/local/gopher-data/Country Accounts/.index/country*, the `Path` is just */Country Accounts/.index/country*.

The Gopher server figures out that this item is a WAIS index (as opposed to another type of index) by looking for the file named *index-directory/index-name.src*. In this case that file would be *Country Accounts/.index/country.src*. This file is automatically generated when you make the index using the *waisindex* program.

The + in the `Host` and `Port` entries tell the server to look at the current host and current port number to retrieve the index data. If you are creating a link to an index on another Gopher server, the `Host` and `Port` should be the remote machine's hostname and Gopher port number.

14.1.4 WAIS Linking Using a .cap File

An alternate way to incorporate a WAIS index is to use a *.cap* file to force *gopherd* to treat a file or directory as a WAIS index item. For example, if the WAIS data directory is named *index*, you can use a *.cap* entry like the following:

```
% pwd
/usr/local/gopher-data/Country Accounts
% ls
Africa/                         North and South America/
Asia/                           index/
Introduction
% mkdir .cap
% cat > .cap/index
Name=Search Country Data
Type=7
Path=7/Country Accounts/index/country
^D
```

This looks very similar to the example using a link. We've forced *gopherd* to treat the directory named *index* as an indexing item by making its *Type* be 7 and its `Path` be the WAIS index. Notice that we have not included the `Host` or `Port` lines—they're not necessary in the *.cap* file.

14.1.5 Pointing to a WAIS server

The last way to incorporate WAIS indexes into your Gopher tree is to use a WAIS *source* file to point to a WAIS server. Copy a WAIS source file (the file ending in *.src*), which was generated using the *waisindex* with the *–export* option (see Section 8.5.2) into your Gopher data tree. The Gopher server automatically recognizes that it's a WAIS source file (since it has the *.src* extension) and uses the hostname and port information from the file to query the index. Here's an example of a *.src* file:

```
(:source
   :version  3
   :ip-address "140.186.65.25"
   :ip-name "wais.ora.com"
   :tcp-port 210
   :database-name "country"
```

```
    :cost 0.00
    :cost-unit :free
    :maintainer "wais@wais.ora.com"
    :keyword-list (
                  crocodile
                  species
                  wildlife
                  conservation
                  country
                  )
    :description "Server created with freeWAIS on May 2 13:12:17 1994
     by buus@wildlife.ora.com
 The files of type text used in the index were:
    /usr/local/gopher-data/croc/Country Accounts/Africa
    /usr/local/gopher-data/croc/Country Accounts/Asia
    /usr/local/gopher-data/croc/Country Accounts/North and South America
 "
 )
```

This file's name is *crocodile.src*. Without a corresponding *.cap* file, this source file shows up on the Gopher menu as *crocodile.src*. We can use a *.cap* file to rename it to something more appropriate:

```
% cat > .cap/crocodile.src
Name=Search Crocodile Data
^D
```

You would use this approach when your data and index are located on separate machines or if you've already got a WAIS server running with the data you'd like to make available through Gopher. In these cases, this method saves you the trouble of having to store and index duplicate data inside the Gopher data tree. This method also allows you to serve WAIS data within a `chroot()` ed server without having to make the changes described in the next section.

The only reason that you may *not* want to use this method is that it uses a bit of extra processor and data transfer time. A separate WAIS searching process is started once *gopherd* queries the WAIS server, and then any data returned travels from the WAIS server to the Gopher server to the Gopher client (one extra hop).

If you're going to use this approach, also take a look at Section 13.4.3, that describes the `waissrc:` Cool Link. It gives you the same functionality, with the added feature of being able to use a link file to point to the WAIS source file.

14.1.6 Using WAIS with a chrooted Server

When *waisindex* creates an index, it files away the full pathname of each file that it indexes. When the Gopher server queries a WAIS index with a keyword, it figures out what files contain the keyword and returns the list of appropriate filenames. The filenames returned are actually full pathnames. For example, if your data directory is

/usr/local/gopher-data, and you index a file called *crocodile*, the filename returned to *gopherd* from a WAIS query would be */usr/local/gopher-data/crocodile.*

If you're running the server in `chroot()` mode, requesting the file */usr/local/gopher-data/crocodile* won't work. With the Gopher data directory `chroot()`ed, the valid way to request this file is to ask for */crocodile.* Fortunately, there's a pretty easy way to fool the server into seeing */usr/local/gopher-data/crocodile* as a legal filename, even under a `chroot()`ed server. We trick the server by creating a few directories and a symbolic link:

```
% cd /usr/local/gopher-data
% mkdir usr
% mkdir usr/local
% cd usr/local
% ln -s / gopher-data
```

Now, we have a directory structure that looks like this:

```
/
  usr/
    local/
      gopher-data/
        crocodile
        usr/
          local/
            gopher-data -> /   (our symbolic link)
```

This may seem strange. However, when it's `chroot()`ed at the */usr/local/gopher-data* directory, you see that it then looks like:

```
/
  crocodile
  usr/
    local/
      gopher-data -> /   (our symbolic link)
```

While the directory is `chroot()`ed, a request for the file */usr/local/gopher-data/crocodile* works, since our symbolic link points the server back to the right place.

14.1.7 Avoiding Indexing Unwanted Files

When indexing Gopher data, you don't want to include *.cache* files or any files in *.cap* directories. It would be especially useful to be able to avoid including *.cap* and *.cache* files when using the *–r* (recursive) option to *waisindex.* Unfortunately, there's no direct way to tell *waisindex* to avoid adding these files to the index. The easiest way to avoid indexing these files is to use a combination of a *find* command and the *–stdin* option to *waisindex.*

The *–stdin* option to *waisindex* forces *waisindex* to read the list of files to index from the standard input. Using a carefully planned *find* command, we can feed the desired files to *waisindex.* Here's the general syntax to use:

```
% find directory-to-index -name name-to-avoid -prune -o -type f -print \
  | waisindex-command -stdin
```

Here's a real example:

```
% find archive -name .cap -prune -o -type f -print | waisindex \
  -d .index/index -T text -stdin
```

Let's break down this command a bit to see what's really going on:

`find archive` Recursively look for files in the *archive* directory.

–name .cap –prune
Throw out any files named *.cap* and do not recurse into any directories called *.cap*.

–o -type f –print Print out the names of all regular files (meaning that we're not printing out any directory names, symbolic links, special devices, etc.).

Here's another example, using *find* to exclude *all* files and directories begining with a dot. This excludes all link files, *.cap* files and *.cache* files.

```
% find archive -name '.*' -prune -o -type f -print | \
  waisindex -d .index/index -T text -stdin
```

And yet another that also excludes files and directories called *usr* and *tmp*:

```
% find archive -name '.*' -prune -o -name usr -prune -o -name tmp -prune \
-o -type f -print | waisindex -d .index/index -T text -stdin
```

14.1.8 If Things Don't Work

When trying to incorporate WAIS indexes, you may see the following errors when you try to access the data using the Gopher curses client:

`Unknown Index Type`
This can happen when you have mistyped the path information to the index file in the `Path` field of the link of *.cap* entry. Verify that the path is correct.

`Nothing Available`
In this case, make sure that your indexes have been generated correctly—see if you can access them using the *waissearch* client.

`Sorry, this isn't a WAIS`
`index...` *or*"

`This isn't a NeXT...is it?`
If you have not compiled in the indexing code into *gopherd*, you will get one of these error message when you try to access either a WAIS or NeXT index. See Section 10.2.3.1 for information on compiling the indexing code in.

`Cannot access directory`

This can happen for a few reasons. If the Gopher data directory name that you supply to *gopherd* is not a full pathname, then this error happens. It also happens if the Gopher data directory name that you supply to *gopherd* is a symbolic link to another directory. WAIS uses absolute pathnames when it stores its data and gets very confused when trying to retrieve data if either of these two conditions exists.

14.2 Using NeXT Indexes

If you're on a NeXT platform, have the necessary programs and libraries installed (see Section 10.2.3.1), and have compiled *gopherd* to include NeXT searching, you can generate and serve NeXT indexes from your Gopher server. The following sections outline how to create and serve NeXT indexes.

14.2.1 Building a NeXT Index

Creating a NeXT index of a directory or directories is quite simple. The command used to generate the index is called *ixBuild.* Inside your Gopher tree, go to the directory which you'd like to index. Now, issue the *ixBuild* command to index the current directory and all of its subdirectories. *ixBuild* creates a *.index* directory in the current directory to store its index file in.

```
% cd "/usr/local/gopher-data/Country Accounts"
% ixBuild
```

This generates the index file, *.index/index.ixif.* When using *ixBuild* without any arguments, nothing is displayed while the indexing is happening. If you'd like to watch it as it goes, try using *ixBuild –v.* Using the *–v* option causes *ixBuild* to display each file that it indexes, the description of that file, the file's type (e.g., ASCII, binary, etc.), and the names of any files that it excludes.

ixBuild only indexes text files, and it does not index files or directories beginning with a dot (.). It creates the "description" of the file (what gets shown on the Gopher menu) by concatenating the filename with the first 65 or so characters of the file. Here are some descriptions that it created from the above *ixBuild*:

```
Introduction: Country Accounts Introduction This section presents
Africa/Algeria: Algeria Nile crocodile Nile crocodile (Crocodylus
Asia/Papua New Guinea: Papua New Guinea New Guinea crocodile Salt
North and South America/Paraguay: Paraguay Broad-snouted caiman Y
```

14.2.1.1 Changing the description

ixBuild has two mechanisms that allow you to control the description of each file, but they can be somewhat painful to use. The *–D* command-line option forces *ixBuild* to *only* use the file's name as the description. Alternatively, you can use the *–d* option to feed each filename to a command that you must write, which outputs the correct description to the standard output. For example, the command *ixBuild -dchange_name* feeds each indexed filename to the program *change_name*. You write the *change_name* program to figure out what the real description of the file should be.

14.2.1.2 Excluding or including certain files

The *ixBuild* command has a facility to allow you to include or exclude files by using a wildcard. The *–n* and *–N* options allow you to consider only files matching a wildcard or to not consider files matching a wildcard, respectively. For example, the command **ixBuild -NA*** indexes all files *except* for those starting with the letter A. Likewise, the command **ixBuild -nA*** *only* indexes files starting with the letter A.

14.2.1.3 Storing an index in an alternate directory

If you'd like to store the index in a directory other than the directory where the *ixBuild* command is issued from, you can use *ixBuild*'s *–i* option to specify an alternate index location. However, if you use this option, the *.index* directory must be created before the *ixBuild* command is run. ere's an example:

```
% mkdir /usr/local/gopher-data/Alternate-directory/.index
% ixBuild -i /usr/local/gopher-data/Alternate-directory/.index/index.ixif
```

Unfortunately, you can not specify a file other than *.index/index.ixif. gopherd* locates NeXT indexes by specifically looking for a *.index* directory containing an *index.ixif* file.

14.2.2 Including a NeXT Index

To make a NeXT index accessible within a Gopher server, a link must be made which points to the directory in which the *.index* directory resides. Here's a link that works for our example:

```
% cat > .Links
Name=Search NeXT index of Country Accounts
Type=7
Path=7/Country Accounts
Host=+
Port=+
```

When *gopherd* accesses this link, it looks for the */Country Accounts/.index/index.ixif* file (relative to the Gopher data directory) that was generated by the *ixBuild* command.

If *gopherd* cannot find the *.index/index.ixif* file, it reports "Server error: Unknown index type." If this happens, make sure that the permissions on the *.index* directory and *index.ixif* file are set such that *gopherd* can access the directory and read the index file. Also make sure that the directory specified on the `Path` line is the directory in which the *.index* directory resides.

14.3 Serving WAIS and NeXT Indexes with gindexd

When you installed the Gopher server, a link to *gopherd* was made called *gindexd*. *gindexd* is meant to run as a separate server that processes queries on WAIS or NeXT indexes and sends the query results back to a Gopher client. *gindexd* only works in Gopher 1.x. The *gindexd* functionality was removed from Gopher 2.x, as it was deemed unnecessary.

The only good reason to use *gindexd* to serve indexes instead of using the normal scheme is if you'd like the processing of index queries to happen on a machine other than the one on which the Gopher server runs. You might want to do this in order to have a fast machine process index queries, but have a slower workhorse that actually feeds the files to a client. Figure 14-1 shows how this works:

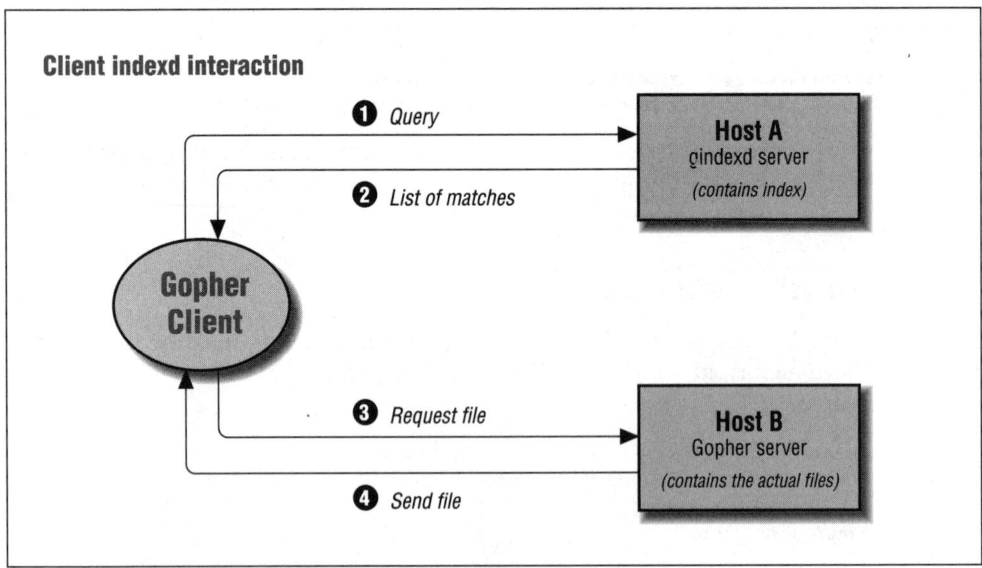

Figure 14-1. How gindexd interacts with a Gopher server

The client sends *gindexd* a query on a set of data. *gindexd* returns the list of files that match on the keyword(s). The Gopher links returned from *gindexd* to the client contain `Host` entries that point to the Gopher server on which the data itself is stored.

The following sections describe what needs to be done to make this happen correctly.

14.3.1 Creating and Placing Index Files

Once you've created your index files normally, they can be moved onto a different machine. For WAIS indexes, move all of the files that were created by the *waisindex* program:

```
% ls
country.cat      country.doc      country.hl      country.src
country.dct      country.fn       country.inv
% rcp * remote-machine:remote-directory
```

For NeXT indexes, you need to copy the *.index* directory and its contents:

```
% rcp .index/index.ixif remote-machine:remote-directory/.index
```

14.3.2 Creating a hostdata File

Now that the index is in the place where it's to be served from, you need to create a file named *hostdata* to tell *gindexd* which machine and port the actual data lives on. Also, if you're serving a WAIS index, you need to tell *gindexd* the pathname of your Gopher data directory, so that it can strip off that part of the pathname before sending the results to the client. For WAIS databases, place the *hostdata* file in the same directory as the index and name it *indexfile.hostdata*. For NeXT indexes, place the *hostdata* file in the directory in which the *.index* directory resides and call it *hostdata*. Here's an example for a WAIS index:

```
% pwd
/usr/local/WAISindexes
% ls
country.cat      country.doc      country.hl      country.src
country.dct      country.fn       country.inv
% cat > country.hostdata
wildlife.ora.com
70
/usr/local/gopher-data
^D
```

The first line of the *hostdata* file is the hostname of the Gopher server on which the data for the index resides. The second line contains the port number of the Gopher server. The third line contains the directory name of the Gopher data directory on the Gopher server (only necessary if you're serving a WAIS index).

14.3.3 Running gindexd

With the *hostdata* file in place, you're ready to run the *gindexd* daemon. Its syntax is:

```
gindexd [ gopherd-options ] index-directory/index-name port-number
```

Normal *gopherd* options can be used with *gindexd*. The ones that are the most important are *–u* or *–U* to make the server run as a user other than *root*, and *–l logfile* to log the queries made by clients. *gindexd* can also be started from *inetd* in the same manner as *gopherd*. See Section 11.2.4 for information about setting up a server under *inetd*.

For WAIS indexes, the *index-directory/index-name* is the full pathname of the index on this machine. For NeXT indexes, it's the full pathname of the directory in which the *.index* directory lives. The *port-number* is the port number on which the *gindexd* server should listen for queries. Here's how it would be executed for the previous WAIS example:

```
% gindexd -l /var/log/gindexd.log /usr/local/WAISindexes/country 5001
```

This tells *gindexd* to start serving the index */usr/local/indexes/country* on port number 5001. If we were to serve a NeXT index, we would specify the location of the directory containing the *.index* directory, like this:

```
% pwd
/usr/local/NeXTindex
% ls -a
.index/
% gindexd -l /var/log/gindexd.log /usr/local/NeXTindex 5001
```

As you may have noticed, you can only serve a single index from each *gindexd* process.

14.3.4 Testing the gindexd Server

To test *gindexd*, *telnet* to the machine and port number that the *gindexd* server is listening on. When you get connected, type in a keyword on which to query the index:

```
% telnet wais.ora.com 5001
Trying 192.112.208.27...
Connected to wais.ora.com.
smooth   (Lines are wrapped for readability)
0Suriname   /Country Accounts/North and South America/
  R0-2232-/croc/Country Accounts/North and South America/Suriname
  wildlife.ora.com 70
0Guyana   /Country Accounts/North and South America/
  R0-4664-/croc/Country Accounts/North and South America/Guyana
  wildlife.ora.com 70
.
```

This looks like it's working fine. If only a period is returned, then either you've entered a search string that doesn't have any matches, or something is set up incorrectly with the *gindexd* server.

14.3.5 Linking to the gindexd Server

To make the index server accessible from your Gopher server, you need to place a link on your Gopher server, pointing to the *gindexd* machine and port:

```
Name=Search Country Data
Host=wais.ora.com
Port=5001
Type=7
Path=
```

Notice that the `Path` has been left blank. You don't need to specify a `Path`, as the index server already knows what index needs to be searched, since it only handles a single index (the one specified in the *hostdata* file).

As you know, normal searches involve the user typing in a string to search for. But what if you want to have a menu item that searches for a predetermined string?

You can do this by manipulating the `Path` and `Type` of a link to a *gindexd* server. If the `Type` is changed to 1 (directory item), and the `Path` is changed to a search word, the index is searched for the keyword on the `Path` line. For instance, if you have a WAIS index of movies, you could have all of the movies starring Harrison Ford come up by using this link file:

```
Name=Harrison Ford Movies
Host=wais.ora.com
Port=5002
Type=1
Path=Harrison and Ford
```

Using the `Path` "Harrison and Ford" queries this index for files containing both of the words "Harrison" and "Ford." Setting the type to 1 tells the client to display this Gopher item as a directory instead of a query. This way, the user won't be asked for a keyword to search on. The client is returned a directory of items matching the keyword.

14.4 grep Indexes

Another type of built-in index is a *grep* index. If the `Path` that you specify isn't a path to a NeXT or WAIS index, the Gopher server looks to see if the `Path` is a directory. If it is, *gopherd* uses *egrep* to look through the files for the user-specified keyword. Unfortunately, because of a programming glitch, this useful feature is broken in both Gopher 1.x and Gopher 2.0. However, this type of "grep" index can be implemented by using a script query, as described in the next section.

The *grep* index feature will work in Gopher 2.1, according to the developers.

14.5 Script Queries

gopherd allows you to create your own "querying" type by letting you execute a script, with keywords specified by the Gopher client as arguments to the script. You make the Type of an item an index (7) and make the actual item a script (any file beginning with the string `#!/`).

Let's say that you'd like to have a custom index item that searches through a set of files, looking for a user-specified keyword. You can create a *.cap* file for your script query that looks something like this:

```
% cat > .cap/myscriptindex
Name=Search For Files Containing a Keyword
Type=7
^D
```

Since this *.cap* entry specifies an indexing item (Type=7), the Gopher server tries to figure out what kind of index you're trying to use. To let the server know that you'd like to use a script query, make the script the actual item:

```
% cat > myscriptindex
#!              script_language_of_choice code goes here
^D
% chmod 755 myscriptindex
```

The script programming language that you use doesn't need to be *sh*; it can be any script language: *perl*, *csh*, *sed*, *awk*, etc. Just pick the one that you're most comfortable with.

Now comes the tricky part. Your indexing program has to let the Gopher server know what the program found from its search. The server is expecting a list of items in the Gopher protocol format. See Section 9.1 and Section 9.2.2 for a description of this format.

+ In the 2.0x version of the server, *.cap* files unfortunately don't work for script queries. The script query code doesn't understand Gopher+ yet and returns unusable data to a querying Gopher+ client. This will be rectified in version 2.1 of the server. In any case, you can still create script queries that work correctly by using a *.Links* file to point to your script. The best way to do this is to put your scripts in a directory within the Gopher data hierarchy (say */usr/local/gopher-data/bin*) and make links to those scripts. So, in the example shown above, the script is */usr/local/gopher-data/bin/myscriptindex*, and the link file contains:

```
Name=Search For Files Containing a Keyword
Type=7
Path=7/bin/myscriptindex
Host=+
Port=+
```

The Path points to the location of the script.

Here's an example that acts as a simple *grep* tool. It searches all files in a given directory for the keyword specified by the user. Note that the script shown here *only* works under a `chroot()`ed server, as filenames are referenced using the Gopher data directory as the root directory. This script is named *grep.pl.*

```
#!/usr/local/bin/perl

# Get the keyword from the command line
$keyword = $ARGV[0];

# Directory to search, relative to the Gopher root
$directory = '/Country Accounts';

# This machine's fully qualified hostname
$hostname = 'wildlife.ora.com';

# The Gopher port
$port = 70;

# Get the contents of the directory to search
opendir(DIR, "$directory");
@contents = readdir(DIR);

# Look at each file in the specified directory
foreach $file (@contents) {

  # Skip this file unless it's a regular text file
  next unless -f "$directory/$file" && -T "$directory/$file";

  # Open the file or skip it if we can't
  open(FILE, "$directory/$file") || next;

  # Look at each line to see if we've got a keyword match
  while(<FILE>) {
    if (/$keyword/oi) {
      # We found a match - Print out Gopher protocol lines which
      # will allow the user to choose a file to view
      print "0$file\t0$directory/$file\t$hostname\t$port\n";

      # Look at the next file
      last;
    }
  }
}
```

To make this script usable, you need to make it executable and create a *.cap* file, so that the server and client treat the script as an index item:

```
% chmod 755 grep.pl
% cat > .cap/grep.pl
Name=Locate keyword in files
Type=7
^D
```

+ If you're using a Gopher 2.0x server, you need to use a link file (as described earlier) that looks similar to the following (assuming that you've relocated the script to the */usr/local/gopher-data/bin* directory):

```
Name=Locate keyword in files
Type=7
Path=7/bin/grep.pl
Host=+
Port=+
```

Note: Shell indexes *must* be executable by the user *gopherd* runs as! If you try to select a script query item and the script is not executable, the client reports "Nothing Available."

If you run into problems getting your script query to work, make sure that you're returning proper Gopher protocol to the server. If *gopherd* doesn't see standard Gopher protocol, it won't return *anything* to the client. While debugging, it's often easier to manually access the Gopher server using *telnet*, rather than to use a client. See Section 11.3 for instructions for manually testing Gopher entries.

The programs your script requires, and possibly also shared libraries, need to be copied into the Gopher tree if you're using a `chroot()`ed server (*/usr/local/bin/perl* needs to be located in the Gopher tree for the example shown above). See Section 13.4.2.

14.5.1 Combining Shell Indexes and exec: Links

One of the more creative and powerful uses for script queries is to use them to return a list of `exec:` links. For instance, you could use this type of query to link the *apropos* command with the manual page it finds. You do this with a script query that asks the user for a keyword and then uses the script to execute *apropos* on the keyword to find the relevant manual pages. Your script then parses the output of *apropos* and returns a list of `exec:` items that, when selected, bring up the desired manual page. Here's an example that was developed on a SunOS 4.1.3 system.

Make the script that parses the *apropos* output (this file is named *apropos.pl*):

```
#!/usr/local/bin/perl

# The thing we're looking for
$keyword = $ARGV[0];

# The apropos command to execute
$apropos = '/usr/ucb/apropos';

# The machine's fully qualified hostname
$hostname = 'wildlife.ora.com';

# The Gopher Port number
$port = 70;
```

```
# Make sure the manpath is correct
$ENV{'MANPATH'} = "/usr/man:/usr/local/man";

# Execute the apropos command, putting its output into the @response array
open(RESPONSE, "-|") || exec "$apropos", "$keyword";
@response = <RESPONSE>;

# Do NOT do this, for security reasons (see the next section)
# @response = `$apropos $keyword`;

# Now parse each line of apropos' output
foreach (@response) {

  # Chop off the Return at the end of the line
  chop;

  # Take out the tabs (and spaces) from the description.
  # We don't want any tabs because tabs are used in the Gopher protocol,
  # and would confuse the server.
  s/[ \t]*-[ \t]*/ - /;

  # Figure out the command apropos returned, putting the manual entry's
  # name into $1 and the manual entry's section number into $2
  /(\w+)[ \t,]+\((\d*)[\w]*\) - /;

  # Give the server the command to execute to bring up this manual page.
  # This returns lines that will look like:
  #0apropos-info<tab>exec:"manual-section manual-name":script<tab>host<tab>port
  #
  # Where script is the full pathname of the script, relative to the
  # Gopher directory.
  print "0$_\texec:\"$2 $1\":/.man-get\t$hostname\t$port\n";
}
```

Now, move this script into place, make it executable, and create a *.cap* entry for it:

```
% mv apropos.pl /usr/local/gopher-data
% cd /usr/local/gopher-data
% chmod 755 apropos.pl
% cat > .cap/apropos.pl
Name=Locate Manual Pages by Keyword Lookup
Type=7
^D
```

We've forced this entry to be an index type (7), so that when it's selected, the user can input a keyword to search for. Our script will then be executed with that keyword as an argument. ✚ If you're using a Gopher 2.0x server, you need to use a link file like the following (assuming that you've moved the script into the */usr/local/gopher-data/bin* directory):

```
Name=Locate Manual Pages by Keyword Lookup
Type=7
Path=7/bin/apropos.pl
```

```
Host=+
Port=+
```

Now, we need to create the *.man-get* script, which is executed when the user selects a manual page to view.

```
#!/usr/local/bin/perl

# The man command
$man = '/usr/ucb/man';

# The arguments are both in $ARGV[0], separated by a space
($section, $manpage) = split(/ /, $ARGV[0]);

$ENV{'MANPATH'} = "/usr/man:/usr/local/man";

# Execute the man command
open(MAN, "-|") || exec "$man", "$section", "$manpage";
print <MAN>;
```

Now, move this file into place and make it executable:

```
% mv .man-get /usr/local/gopher-data
% cd /usr/local/gopher-data
% chmod 755 .man-get
```

Try executing both scripts manually a few times to make sure that they're returning things that look correct before trying to use a Gopher client.

NOTE

In order to make this example work under a `chroot()`ed server, you need to copy all of the programs and data that these scripts use into the Gopher data hierarchy. The files to be copied include */bin/sh*, */usr/bin/perl*, */usr/ucb/man*, */usr/man/whatis.db*, and all of the manual pages found in */usr/man* and */usr/local/man*. This may seem like quite a bother, but, for security purposes, it is necessary.

14.5.2 Security Concerns with Shell Indexes and exec: Links

Whenever you allow direct user input to affect the data that is generated, security is a critical issue. In *gopherd*, you may expose a security hole when creating a script query or when combining a script query with `exec` links. The basic concern is that you should *never* let input from a user be interpreted by the shell. Think about what would happen if a user put in the string "`` `rm -rf *` ``" as the keyword search for a script query written in the Bourne shell that happened to execute the following command:

```
/bin/grep $keyword filetosearch
```

This would end up erasing your whole Gopher data hierarchy! Fortunately, the Gopher server tries to stop this type of abuse by not allowing the characters `;`, `"`, or `` ` `` as input to an index query.

Even though *gopherd* attempts to make searches secure, don't take it for granted that your scripts are safe. A smart cracker may be able to figure out how to exploit a friendly *apropos* script query into a potentially serious security hole.

The best thing to do to avoid security problems is to use a scripting language like *perl*, in which you can avoid having the shell interpret the user's input. The command above could be executed in a secure manner by using the *perl* commands:

```
open(GREP, "-|") || exec "/bin/grep", "$keyword", "filetosearch";
print <GREP>;
```

Using the `-|` lets the Perl script read the output of the *exec* command. Using the *exec* feeds the arguments directly to the command, avoiding the shell completely.

Security concerns like these are one primary reason that running a server `chroot()`ed and under a user ID other than *root* is so important. If your server is `chroot()`ed and a malicious user is able to exploit the server in any way, they will only be able to obtain access to the `chroot()`ed portion of the filesystem. By running the server as a user other than *root*, only files writable or readable by the user which *gopherd* is run as would be able to be modified or read.

14.6 Searching Multiple Indexes

At one point in the Gopher 1.x development, you could search multiple indexes from one Gopher index item. This feature used a separate daemon called *mindexd* to accomplish this. As of Gopher 1.13, *mindexd* was supposedly merged with *gopherd*. However, in release 1.13, it doesn't work at all. The final say: there isn't a way to search multiple indexes with Gopher 1.13.

With Gopher 2.x, the problem has been fixed. To create a single menu item that searches multiple indexes for the same keyword, create a file with the extension *.mindex*. Inside that file, place lines that have the following syntax:

```
remote-host gopher-port gopher-pathname
or
localhost gopher-port gopher-pathname
```

If you specify `localhost` as the hostname, the Gopher server does the search itself. Otherwise, the server contacts each *remote-host* on *gopher-port* and uses *gopher-pathname* to retrieve the results. Using `localhost` is very efficient, and it should be used when the indexes to be searched are on the local server. Here's an example of a *mindex* file:

```
% cat > multisearch.mindex
localhost 70 7/.index/country
zebra.ora.com 70 7/zebras/zebra-index
^D
```

You should also create a *.cap* file to change the name of this item (which is currently *multisearch.mindex*) to something more understandable.

In this Chapter:

- *Registering Your Gopher Server with Veronica*
- *Avoiding Veronica Registration*
- *Running a Veronica Server*
- *Local Links to Veronica Servers Using maltshop*
- *Making a Local Veronica Using Jughead*

15

Gopher: Veronica and Jughead

The *archie* Internet service lets users find out which FTP archives contain particular files. It works by connecting to all the FTP archives once a week and grabbing an index from each. When users request information, *archie* searches these indexes. Veronica is essentially an *archie* for Gopherspace (Veronica and Archie are both characters in the comic strip Archie). The people who developed Veronica claim that it actually stands for "Very easy rodent-oriented net-wide index to computerized archives."

Veronica is a service that provides a (very large) index of titles of Gopher items from most servers in Gopherspace. The result of a Veronica search is a set of Gopher items whose titles contain the keyword that the user was searching for. The user can then access the data items by selecting from a menu.

The Veronica index is accessed via a normal Gopher search item. Pointers to machines that provide Veronica searches can be found on the "mother" Gopher server (*gopher.tc.umn.edu*) under the "*Other Gopher and Information Servers/Search titles in Gopherspace using veronica/*" menu item, and on Veronica's home machine, *veronica.scs.unr.edu*, under the "*Search ALL of Gopherspace (4800 servers) using veronica*" menu item. The most common way to allow users to access Veronica is to put a link to one of these Gopher items into your Gopher tree:

```
Name=Search ALL of Gopherspace using Veronica
Type=1
Port=70
Path=1/veronica
Host=veronica.scs.unr.edu
```

15.1 Registering Your Gopher Server with Veronica

To have your Gopher menus in Veronica's massive database, you don't really have to do anything. Chances are that Veronica will find you! Veronica indexes all servers that are either registered in the "Master List of Gopher Servers" or are linked to from within a menu of another Gopher server that is registered. Note that the Veronica data-set builder can't include your server if you have restricted outside access to your site.

In order to index your site, Veronica "walks down" your Gopher data structure, accessing all possible menus on your server. This is done about once a month.

By the time you read this, there's a good chance that there will be some new Veronica-related software available which will allow you to create a prepared data-file for Veronica to fetch. This will save network bandwidth (since Veronica won't have to walk down your entire data tree), and decrease the time that it takes to create the main Veronica index. If at all possible, you should participate in this new scheme. Keep your eyes on the Veronica FTP site (*futique.scs.unr.edu*), the newsgroup *comp.infosystems.gopher*, and the Veronica Gopher menu for details. A newer version of Jughead (described later in this chapter), may also allow you to create a prepared data-file for Veronica. Take a look at Jughead's documentation for details.

15.2 Avoiding Veronica Registration

Veronica was developed under the assumption that any registered Gopher server or server accessible via the menu of a registered server is intended to be accessible to users at any Internet node. If, for some reason, you do not want your server included in the Veronica index, you can send mail to *veronica@veronica.scs.unr.edu* requesting that your site not be included. If there is only one portion of your site that you do not want indexed, take a look at the Veronica FAQ for ideas about index avoidance. The FAQ can be found in the Veronica Gopher directory shown in the link example at the beginning of this chapter.

+ If you're using Gopher 2.x, you can insert a *VeronicaIndex: no* token into your *gopherd.conf* file. This should keep Veronica from indexing your server.

15.3 Running a Veronica Server

If you're *really* ambitious and have the disk, CPU cycles, and bandwidth to spare, you can run a Veronica server locally. The Veronica server software can be obtained by anonymous FTP on *futique.scs.unr.edu* in the *veronica-code/Servers* directory. The server is a Perl script—it requires *Perl* version 4pl35 or later with *dbm* support. The data set the server uses can be obtained on the same anonymous FTP site, in the *veronica-data* directory. The data set is currently in the neighborhood of one gigabyte in size and growing. The master Veronica data set is updated approximately once a month. The *Perl* server script contains the necessary installation and configuration documentation.

15.4 Local Links to Veronica Servers Using maltshop

You can automatically create a menu on your own Gopher server which points to each individual Veronica server, by using a freely available Perl script called *maltshop.*

maltshop periodically polls a list of Veronica servers, determining which are available. Using this list, it builds a link file containing pointers to all of the currently active Veronica servers. Periodically, the script retrieves an updated list of Veronica servers from an authoritative site. The program needs no maintenance. Once it is set up, it runs out of *cron*, generating a new list as often as you like.

There are some good reasons for using this approach. Occasionally, public Veronica *links* (as opposed to servers) may be unavailable due to computer downtime, even though the actual Veronica servers are operating. Your users will have Veronica access even if the public Veronica links aren't available. The public Veronica access menus are also busy, sometimes causing substantial delays. Lastly, you have an up-to-date menu of Veronica servers. If a Veronica server is unavailable, or is too slow, it will not appear on your menu.

maltshop is currently undergoing some revisions to make it kinder on the Veronica servers. Hopefully, by the time you read this, *maltshop* will be available by anonymous FTP on *futique.scs.unr.edu* in the *veronica-software* directory.

15.5 Making a Local Veronica Using Jughead

Jughead is a tool for creating a Veronica-type search facility, but only for your local Gopher server. Jughead (another play on the Archie/Veronica joke) is said to stand for "Jonzy's Universal Gopher Hierarchy Excavation And Display." Using Jughead, you can create an index of some or all of your items and then create a Gopher menu item that allows users to search for menu titles containing keywords.

In the */pub/gopher/Unix/GopherTools/jughead* directory, Jughead can be retrieved from *boombox.micro.umn.edu.* The latest version as of this writing was contained in the file *jughead.0.9.tar.Z.* Building the *jughead* program is pretty straightforward. After extracting the source code, edit the *Makefile,* changing things as appropriate. The *Makefile* is documented pretty well, explaining things that may need changing. Once you've edited the *Makefile* to your satisfaction, do a *make* to generate the *jughead* binary.

This single binary is actually used in three very different ways. It is used to generate a hierarchy of menu titles, build a search table, and run as the search engine to query the tables.

15.5.1 Creating the Table

By default, *jughead* traverses the Gopher tree of the hostname that you give it, printing out menu items that it finds. You should start experimenting by using this default behavior, and then use *jughead*'s command-line options to help limit the included Gopher items if necessary. Here's an example of the default behavior:

```
% jughead wildlife.ora.com
Gopher root is [wildlife.ora.com] port = 70
    Introduction and Cover.
    Foreword.
    Acknowledgments.
    Executive Summary.
    Objectives and Organization of the Action Plan.
    Introduction and Conservation Priorities/
        Human Exploitation of Crocodilians.
        Crocodilian Conservation Programs.
    Country Accounts/
        Introduction.
        Africa/
            Algeria.
            Angola.
.
.
.
```

The command line switches *–s* and *–X* are the most handy in restricting the area that *jughead* searches. Both of these options take a Gopher `Path` string as an argument. The flag *–s* tells *jughead* where to start the traversal, and the *–X* flag tells *jughead* to exclude given parts of a Gopher tree. For example:

```
% jughead -s "1/Country Accounts" wildlife.ora.com
Gopher root is [wildlife.ora.com] port = 70
    Introduction.
    Africa/
        Algeria.
        Angola.
.
.
.
```

only goes through the "Country Accounts" portion of the Gopher tree. To avoid indexing the contents of the "Africa" directory, this command can be used:

```
% jughead -s "1/Country Accounts" -X "1/Country Accounts/Africa" wildlife.ora.com
Gopher root is [wildlife.ora.com] port = 70
    Introduction.
    Africa/
    Asia/
        Australia.
        Bangladesh.
.
.
.
```

Wildcards can also be used with either of these options. For instance, to avoid indexing all Gopher items that access FTP sites, you could use a command like **jughead -X "ftp:*" wildlife.ora.com**.

Just remember that the argument you specify with these options are Gopher `Path` items. See Section 9.2.1 for information about using the Gopher curses client's '=' command to get a menu item's `Path` entry.

15.5.2 Building the Table and Index

Once you have *jughead* printing out the Gopher tree that you'd like to have indexed, you need to use the *–B* and *–b* flags to create a table and index, which the server will use later to answer queries. First, use the *jughead* command that you used above, except include the option *–b datafile*, where *datafile* is the name of the file you would like to store *jughead*'s data in. In this example, we chose the file *.jughead/data*—we're storing this file in a *jughead* subdirectory of our Gopher data directory, so that the Gopher server doesn't display it to clients:

```
% pwd
/usr/local/gopher-data
% mkdir .jughead
% cd .jughead
% jughead -b data -s "1/Country Accounts" wildlife.ora.com
Gopher root is [wildlife.ora.com] port = 70
Removing any duplicates from [data].
[data] now contains the information with duplicates removed
and points to 99 different Gopher menu items
```

Once you have built the data file using the *–b* option, you need to generate the index of this data, which allows *jughead* to access the data efficiently. Simply run *jughead* like this:

```
% jughead -B data
Building the words tree...
words tree is now built.
Building the hash tables...
hash tables are completed.
```

This generates index files named *data.ix* and *data.ih*.

15.5.3 Running the Server

With the index built, you can start *jughead* to answer Gopher queries. Run *jughead* by using the command syntax:

```
jughead -S [ -l log ] [ -p port# ] [ -u username ] datafile
```

Here, *log* is an optional log filename, which stores the queries that people make. *port#* is the optional port on which *jughead* listens for queries. If you don't specify a port, the default from the *Makefile* is used (port 3000). *username* is the name of a user to run *jughead* as (we recommend *nobody* or *gopher*). This user must already exist in the password file for this option to work correctly. This option can only be used if *jughead* is started as the user *root*. Otherwise, *jughead* runs as the user it was started as. Here's an example:

```
% jughead -S -l /var/log/jughead -u gopher /usr/local/gopher-data/.jughead/data &
jughead, Copyright 1993, University of Utah Computer Center
Using index table /usr/local/gopher-data/.jughead/data
Using port 3000
Logging to /var/log/jughead
```

There are other command-line options that you might find useful, but we didn't review all of them here. *jughead* comes with pretty good documentation that you can look at for more information.

15.5.4 Rereading the Index File

Fortunately, if you regenerate an index, you don't need to stop and restart the server. Sending a HANGUP signal to the process forces it to reread its index file (substitute *–elf* for *–axw* on System V variants):

```
% ps -axw | grep jughead
14919 ?  IW    0:00 jughead -S -l /var/log/jughead -u gopher ▶▶▶
▶▶▶/usr/local/gopher-data/.jughead/data
% kill -HUP 14919
```

15.5.5 Linking to a Jughead Server

To make the *jughead* server accessible from your Gopher tree, you need to insert a link file similar to this:

```
Name=Search Country Account Titles
Type=7
Path=/
Host=wildlife.ora.com
Port=3000
```

This tells our Gopher server to ask the user for a search word (`Type=7`, the index type), and then to contact *wildlife.ora.com* on port 3000 to ask the query. The server returns a list of matches to the Gopher client. That's all there is to it!

In this Chapter:
- *Gopher+ Forms*
- *Other Features of Gopher 2.0.16*
- *New Features in Gopher 2.1*

16

Gopher+ Forms and Other New Features

We've described the minor differences between Gopher 1.x and 2.x throughout the Gopher chapters in this book. This chapter describes the major new features in the Gopher+ versions 2.0.16 and 2.1.

16.1 Gopher+ Forms

Gopher+ *Forms* (also commonly called *Ask Blocks*) are a means of querying the user for data. The questions to ask the user are retrieved from the server by looking at the item's *+ASK* attribute. The client presents the user with all of the questions appearing in the *+ASK* attribute block of an item, in the order that they appear. The user's response to the form is sent back to the server, where a script processes the response.

Gopher+ Forms are not dynamic, and therefore not truly interactive—the server cannot ask different questions depending on the response to a previous answer. Ask Blocks do not constitute a scripting language by any means.

16.1.1 Types of Form Input

Gopher+ Forms do more than present the user with simple yes-or-no questions. They can also present the user with dialog boxes, radio buttons, and other query mechanisms. The following list details the most common query types for Gopher+ Forms:

`Note:`
: Acts much like a comment to the user. It allows you to give information to the user, such as a form's title. `Note:` is also used to ask questions when another query type gets the response.

This chapter and other sections on Gopher 2.x features were written by Paul Lindner and Danny Iacovou.

`Ask:`
: Presents the user with a question, supplies an optional default answer, and allows the user to enter a one-line response

`Askp:`
: For passwords; `Askp:` presents the user with a question like the `Ask:` type, except that the user's response is not displayed.

`AskL:`
: Presents the user with a question and allows the user to enter several lines of response. Note that `Ask:` is for one-line input, but `AskL:` is for multiline input. (The L stands for Long, not Line.)

`Select:`
: Presents the user with a simple yes-or-no question. Most Gopher+ clients display this as a checkbox.

`Choose:`
: Presents the user with a few choices, only one of which may be selected at a time. Most Gopher+ clients display this as a set of radio buttons.

The following query types are not quite as widely supported. Use them at your own risk!

`ChooseF:`
: Asks the user to select an existing local file, presumably to send to the server. On some systems, the client or client administrator may restrict the selection of files to those in the current directory (thus preventing the client from sending things like password files, which reside in another directory).

`AskF:`
: Asks the user for a new local filename, presumably for storing the response to be returned by the server. `AskF:` may supply a default filename.

16.1.2 How to Use Ask Blocks

To use a form, you need to create two files. One file contains the Ask Block itself (named *filename.ask*), and the other file contains the script (named *filename*) that will be invoked in order to process the user's response. The two files must have the same base name, with the file containing the form definition having a *.ask* extension. Our example scripts are written in Perl, but you can use a shell (such as the Bourne shell) as well.

You should make sure that the permissions on the script allow the user that *gopherd* runs as to execute the script, and that the permissions on the *.ask* file allow that user to read the *.ask* file. Also, make sure that you have a directory named *tmp* in your root Gopher data directory.

16.1.3 A Simple Example Form

To demonstrate how to construct forms and their corresponding scripts, we'll look at an example, one piece at a time. At the end, we'll combine each piece together to create a "Textbook Order Form." This form is meant to allow professors at Wildlife University to electronically place their textbook requests for the upcoming quarter.

First, you need to create a form definition file. This file will contain your list of questions for the user. You can use any of the query types outlined in the previous section. In this first example, we'll use only one type, but later examples will demonstrate different types.

For this part of the example, put the following text in the file *textbook.ask* someplace within your Gopher data directory:

```
Note:                        Wildlife University
Note:                    Textbook Information Request
Note:
Note:                       Instructor Information
Ask: Instructor:<TAB>
Ask: Phone No:<TAB>
Ask: E-mail Address:<TAB>
```

The first four `Note:` lines are used to create a nice banner for our form. Notice that the third `Note:` is just a blank line. To create a blank line using `Note:` you must add one space after the `Note:` ("Note: ").

The three `Ask:` lines that follow prompt for the name of the instructor, her phone number, and her email address. The TAB character at the end of the line is not strictly necessary, but it allows older versions of the UNIX Gopher+ client to process the form correctly.

Next, create a script to process the form. This script processes the responses when the input from the completed form is sent to the server. For this example, create a form script called *textbook*:

```
#!/usr/local/bin/perl

##
# Get the values the user supplied via STDIN
##
$Instructor = <>;
$Phone = <>;
$Email = <>;

##
# Security precautions - only allow characters following the ^'s
##
$Instructor =~ s/[^A-Za-z0-9. ]//g;
$Phone =~ s/[^A-Za-z0-9.()- ]//g;
$Email =~ s/[^A-Za-z0-9.@ ]//g;
```

```
print <<"EOF"

Wildlife University
TextBook Information Request


Instructor:          $Instructor
Phone No:            $Phone
E-Mail Address:      $Email

EOF
;
```

The information that the user types is supplied to the standard input of the script, and the text printed on the standard output is sent back to the client. Your script should read the data one line at a time to process the information from the user. One nice consequence of this is that you can test your script by simply running it and typing information in one line at a time.

The Perl script above reads information from the standard input and loads the corresponding variables with the information (`$Instructor = <>`). The three "security precaution" lines strip any characters from the user's input that are not legal characters for the variable. This keeps curious users from possibly executing arbitrary (potentially harmful) commands (e.g., *cat /etc/passwd*). One thing to note is that there is a carriage return at the end of each input line. However, we have conveniently stripped it off by not specifying a carriage return (`\n`) as "legal" in our security precautions code. Finally, the `print` statement returns information to the client on the script's standard output.

To install this form, place the files *textbook* and *textbook.ask* in your Gopher data directory, and make *textbook* executable by the user that *gopherd* runs as. When the client selects the form, it looks like this:

```
+--------------------------textbook.ask-----------------------------+
|                                                                   |
|                       Wildlife University                         |
|                   Textbook Information Request                    |
|                                                                   |
|                     Instructor Information                        |
| Instructor:        _____________________________________________  |
| Phone No:          _____________________________________________  |
| E-mail Address:    _____________________________________________  |
|                                                                   |
| [Help: ^-]  [Cancel: ^G]                                          |
+-------------------------------------------------------------------+
```

The user can then fill in the information for the form. With the curses client, the user uses a TAB to move between fields and a Return to submit the form.

16.1.4 Adding Default Values and Radio Boxes (Choose)

We can add the following text to *textbook.ask* to continue our example:

```
Note:                                   Course Information
Ask: Year:<TAB>1994
Choose: Quarter:<TAB>Fall<TAB>Winter<TAB>Spring
Ask: Dept:<TAB>
Ask: Course No:<TAB>
```

In the first `Ask` line, we have supplied a default answer (`1994`), which the user may change. The default value must be separated from the `Ask` text by a TAB character.

The next line demonstrates the `Choose:` query type, which allows the user to choose one of a set of values. The choices should follow the question (in this case `Quarter:`), and be separated by TABs.

We append the following information to the *textbook* script:

```
##
# Get the values the user supplied via STDIN
##
$Year = <>;
$Quarter = <>;
$Dept = <>;
$Course = <>;

##
# Security precautions
##
$Year =~ s/[^A-Za-z0-9 ]//g;
$Quarter =~ s/[^A-Za-z0-9 ]//g;
$Dept =~ s/[^A-Za-z0-9 ]//g;
$Course =~ s/[^A-Za-z0-9 ]//g;

print <<"EOF"
Year:                   $Year
Quarter:                $Quarter
Department:             $Dept
Course:                 $Course
EOF
;
```

There are two things to notice in this example:

- Even though a default value has been provided for the year, we do not have to handle the input from the client in a special manner.
- Although the textbook may be used for any one of the three possible quarters, only one answer is sent back to the server. A `Choose:` token creates only one line of response from the user. Thus, we also don't have to do anything special in the script to handle this field.

16.1.5 Adding Multiline Input (AskL) and Checkboxes (Select)

The remaining common query types will finish off our form. We append the following information to the *textbook.ask*:

```
Note:                              TextBook Information
Note: Author:
AskL:
Note: Title:
AskL:
Note: Publisher:
AskL:
Note:
Ask: ISBN:<TAB>
Ask: Price:<TAB>
Note:
Note: Which Version Should be Purchased?
Select: Hard Cover?:1
Select: Latest Edition?:1
Select: With Supplement Notes?:0
```

`AskL:` and `Select:` queries are often a source of confusion.

The first thing to note is that the question posed by the `AskL:` does *not* reside on the same line as the `AskL:` token itself. Rather, it is placed in a `Note` on the previous line. On some Gopher clients, `AskL:` does not present the user with a question (which would normally be placed after the `AskL:` token), but instead just accepts input. By implementing `AskL:` items as a series of two commands, you can be assured your form will look right on all clients. The `AskL:` token should be followed by a space ("`AskL:` "). You should also keep in mind that the Gopher 2.x curses client supports a maximum of 10 lines of input from the user.

Each of the last three lines forms a checkbox. It is important to note the colon separating the question from the default setting; this colon is necessary. A `1` after the colon means the checkbox default is *on*. A `0` means the checkbox is turned *off*. It should also be noted that the 1s and 0s may be seen by the user as yes/no, true/false, or checked/unchecked. How this is presented to the user depends on the client software.

Finally, here's the rest of the script to complete our example:

```
##
# Get the values the user supplied via STDIN
##

# The number of lines in the first AskL block
$Numb_Lines = <>;

# Read lines until there aren't any more
while ($Numb_Lines-- != 0 )
{
```

```
    $entry = <>;                     # Read the line
    $entry =~ s/[^A-Za-z0-9.\n ]//g; # Take out any unwanted characters
    push(@Author, $entry);           # Add the line to the @Author array
}

# Do the same for the rest...
$Numb_Lines = <>;
while ($Numb_Lines-- != 0 )
{
    $entry = <>;
    $entry =~ s/[^A-Za-z0-9.\n ]//g;
    push(@Title, $entry);
}

$Numb_Lines = <>;
while ($Numb_Lines-- != 0 )
{
    $entry = <>;
    $entry=~ s/[^A-Za-z0-9.\n ]//g;
    push(@Publisher, $entry);
}

$ISBN = <>;
$Price = <>;

$Hard = <>;
$Latest = <>;
$Snotes = <>;

##
# Security precautions
##
$ISBN =~ s/[^A-Za-z0-9\- ]//g;
$Price =~ s/[^A-Za-z0-9\$\. ]//g;

$Hard =~ s/[^01]//g;
$Latest =~ s/[^01]//g;
$Snotes =~ s/[^01]//g;

##
# Convert some of the Select variables
##
if ($Hard eq "1") { $Hard = "Yes"; }
else { $Hard = "No"; }

if ($Latest eq "1") { $Latest = "Yes"; }
else { $Latest = "No"; }

if ($Snotes eq "1") { $Snotes = "Yes"; }
else { $Snotes = "No"; }

print <<"EOF"
Author:
```

```
@Author
Title:
@Title
Publisher:
@Publisher
ISBN:              $ISBN
Price:             $Price
Hard:              $Hard
Latest:            $Latest
Snotes:            $Snotes
EOF
;
```

Because of the AskL tokens in this form, the script gets a little bit more complicated. The first thing that AskL sends to the server is the number of lines the user entered, followed by each line of user input. We therefore need to have one variable acting as a counter (in the example above the counter variable was $Numb_Lines). We then proceed to read as many lines of input as the counter told us we should. As we read each line, we also strip out any characters we don't want to allow and then join the new line onto the end of the list of lines we have already read in. Notice that when stripping out unwanted characters, we allowed carriage returns (*\n*) in the response. Because we're putting the lines into an array, we want each line to end with a return for ease of printing the data later on.

16.1.6 Saving the Output

The final bit of code we're going to add to our script either saves the output to a file, or mails it to the bookstore, depending on which of the open lines are uncommented. Because we converted the values returned from Select: from 1 and 0 to "Yes" and "No", the output is more readable by humans.

```
# Write to a file - $$ is the process ID
open (OUTPUT, ">/tmp/textbook.$$") || die "Couldn't open /tmp/textbook.$$!\n";

# Uncomment to mail output to the bookstore
#open(OUTPUT, "|-") || exec "/bin/mail", "bookstore";
#print OUTPUT "To: bookstore\n";
#print OUTPUT "Subject: TextBook Information Request\n";

print <<"EOF"

TextBook Information Request


Instructor:          $Instructor
Phone No:            $Phone
E-Mail Address:      $Email

Year:                $Year
Quarter:             $Quarter
Dept:                $Dept
```

```
Course No:          $Course

Author:             @Author
Title               @Title
Publisher:          @Publisher

ISBN:               $ISBN
Price:              $Price

Hard Cover?         $Hard
Latest Edition?     $Latest
With Supplement?    $Snotes
EOF
;

close (OUTPUT);
```

Lastly, you will probably want to create a *.names* entry for this example, to change its menu item name to something understandable:

```
% cat > .names
Path=./textbook
Name=Enter Textbook Information
^D
```

Using this example as a starting point, you can create your own electronic bureaucracy!

16.1.7 Ask Forms That Return More Complicated Types

Typically, an Ask Form returns a text document. But what if you want it to return something else? An equally important question is: why would you want an Ask Form that returns another type?

Lets imagine that you have a database of books, and you want to allow users access to this database via Gopher. In order to allow users to easily access this database, you decide to create an Ask Form that queries the user for an author, a book title, and a subject. You then proceed to show the user all of the database hits that the query produced. One way of displaying the data to the user is to take all of the hits, concatenate them, and then give the user one large datafile. A better way of displaying the data would be to return a menu of items, each item corresponding to a database hit, and therefore to a book. The user can then select an item on the menu to learn more about a book. That menu of items is equivalent to a Gopher directory, so you'd want the search script to return a Gopher directory of items.

Our example will show how to create an Ask Form returning a directory (however, you can create Ask Forms that return any item type you'd like). To begin, we need to tell *gopherd* that the Ask Block will return a different type. We can do this by creating a *.Link* file and adding an entry like this:

```
Type=1?
Path=0/.bin/askdir
Name=Gopher Protocol Information
Host=+
Port=+
```

This tells *gopherd* that the Form will return a *Type 1?* item (an Ask item that returns a directory). The `Path` entry tells *gopherd* where the Ask Form is located and its type, *0* (textfile). We've told *gopherd* to find the form and its script in the directory *.bin*, hiding the underlying *askdir* files from view. The following is our Ask Form, *.bin/askdir.ask*:

```
Choose: Do you want to read about the Gopher protocol:<TAB>yes<TAB>no
```

This form asks the user if she wants to read about the Gopher protocol. If the user answers "yes," she will be shown the Gopher protocol papers. If she answers "no," she will be sent a polite message.

In our previous examples, we were able to simply print to the standard output and whatever we wrote was accepted by *gopherd* and displayed to the user. This was true because we were returning a text document. This is no longer the case. Now *gopherd* wants us to return information valid for a Gopher directory; this information is written in the Gopher protocol as a series of selector strings. Our script has to reflect this.

The *.bin/askdir* script follows.

```
#!/usr/local/bin/perl

##
# Get input from STDIN
##
$GetDir = <>;

##
# Security Precautions
##
$GetDir =~ s/[^A-Za-z]//g;

##
# Check to see if we are being told to return long or short directory listings.
# By default, assume short listings
##
$LongDir = 0;
$LongDir = 1 if ($ENV{"CONTENT_TYPE"} eq "application/gopher+-menu");

if ($GetDir eq "yes") {

  if ($LongDir == 1) {
    print "+INFO: 0Gopher Protocol\t0/gopher/gopher_protocol/protocol.txt▶▶▶
▶▶▶\tboombox.micro.umn.edu\t70\n";
    print "+INFO: 0Gopher+ Protocol\t0/gopher/gopher_protocol/Gopher+/Gopher+.txt▶▶▶
```

```
▶▶▶\tboombox.micro.umn.edu\t70\n";
    } else {
      print "0Gopher Protocol\t0/gopher/gopher_protocol/protocol.txt▶▶▶
▶▶▶\tboombox.micro.umn.edu\t70\n";
      print "0Gopher+ Protocol\t0/gopher/gopher_protocol/Gopher+/Gopher+.txt▶▶▶
▶▶▶\tboombox.micro.umn.edu\t70\n";
    }
  } else {
    if ($LongDir == 1) {
      print "+INFO: iSorry to hear that\tjunk\tboombox.micro.umn.edu\t70\n";
    } else {
      print "iSorry to hear that\tjunk\tboombox.micro.umn.edu\t70\n";
    }
  }
```

What is happening in this script is the following: The user inputs either a "yes" or a "no," as determined by the `Choose:` from the Ask Form (and now contained in the `$GetDir` variable). If the user says "no," then a message saying *Sorry to hear that* is displayed—this message is actually of the type *i* (information only, see Section 16.2.3). If the user says "yes," then two items, one pointing to a paper on the Gopher protocol and the other to a paper on the Gopher+ protocol, are offered.

So what is the variable `$LongDir` doing? There are two flavors of Gopher directories: ones presented in the long format and ones presented in the short format. Different clients expect to see different formats. As an example, the Gopher 2.x curses client expects the long listing, the University of Minnesota Macintosh client expects the short listing. Our script needs to take both into account.

As it stands, the script checks the `CONTENT_TYPE` environment variable. If it is set to *application/gopher+-menu*, then the variable `$LongDir` is flagged, telling the script to display the long format. The difference between the two formats is that the long format directory listing has a `+INFO:` prepended (in front of) each directory item in the protocol. If you do not check for the `CONTENT_TYPE`, and you just pass the information to the client to display, your Ask Form may not display anything. This is because you might not be passing the Gopher client anything it understands as valid data for the directory item type.

16.1.8 My Ask Block Doesn't Work!

Trying to debug Ask Blocks can be complicated ——there are many things that could be going wrong. Here is a checklist:

- If you're running `chroot()`ed, is your Gopher server set up to correctly run scripts? See Section 13.4.2.2.
- Do the permissions on the script allow the user *gopherd* is running as to execute it, and does the user have read permission on the *.ask* file?
- Does the script work? Since the script should have been written to take arguments from the standard input, it is fairly simple to test if it is working or not. From the

command line, execute your script. It should look as though it is hung—this is because it is waiting for input from you. Type in the input that your script expects. Here's an example using the first portion of our sample Ask Form.

```
% textbook
Professor Ranger<Return>
(303) 332-9922<Return>
jim@wildlife.ora.com<Return>

TextBook Information Request

Instructor:             Professor Ranger
Phone No:               (303) 332-9922
E-Mail Address:         jim@wildlife.ora.com
```

What happens when you test your script? If all goes well at this point, then you can be fairly certain that your script is not to blame.

- Check the form itself. What does it look like? To test this, you need to figure out the form's *selector string* (its *Path*). You can use the = function of the Gopher 2.x curses client to find it. Now, *telnet* to your Gopher server and type "*selector-string*<TAB>!<RETURN>" This gives you the Gopher+ information about the item you selected. For example:

```
% telnet wildlife.ora.com 70
Trying 128.101.54.54 ...
Connected to wildlife.ora.com.
Escape character is '^]'.
0/textbook<TAB>!
+-1
+INFO: 0Enter Textbook Information   0/textbook  wildlife.ora.com  70   ?
+ADMIN:
 Admin: The Bookstore <bookstore@wildlife.ora.com>
 Mod-Date: Fri Aug 19 23:56:15 1994 <19940819235615>
+VIEWS:
 Text/plain En_US: <3k>
+ASK:
 Note:                              Wildlife University
 Note:                         Textbook Information Request
 Note:
 Note:                            Instructor Information
 Ask: Instructor:
 Ask: Phone No:
 Ask: E-mail Address:
```

Part of this information should be the body of your Ask Block. Does the Ask Block shown here look correct? If it doesn't, then you have some errors in your Ask Form.

- If things are still not working, you can pretend to be a Gopher client by feeding data to *gopherd* and waiting to see the results. To do this, *telnet* back to your Gopher port, and type:

```
selector-string<TAB>+<TAB>1<RETURN>
+-1<RETURN>
data-your-script-expects-goes-here
.<RETURN>
```

For example:

```
# telnet wildlife.ora.com 70
Trying 134.84.132.7 ...
Connected to mudhoney.micro.umn.edu.
Escape character is '^]'.
0/textbook<TAB>+<TAB>1<Return>
+-1
Professor Ranger<Return>
(303) 332-9922<Return>
jim@wildlife.ora.com<Return>
.+-1

TextBook Information Request


Instructor:              Professor Ranger
Phone No:                (303) 332-9922
E-Mail Address:          jim@wildlife.ora.com
```

What does the output look like? If it is wrong, you may be running into a problem with how your script runs under Gopher. You might want to go back to the script and check things like paths to binaries and the permissions on files.

- If, when you use a Gopher+ client to fill out your form, the client hangs while waiting for a response, then chances are good that your script is still running for some reason—it may be erroneously waiting for input that it's never going to get.

16.2 Other Features of Gopher 2.0.16

Gopher 2.0.16 supports some other new features too. We detail them here.

16.2.1 The ADMIT1 Protocol

The Gopher 2.0.16 server was intended to be able to authenticate users with the University of Minnesota's ADMIT1 protocol (an addition to the Gopher protocol). However, support for this standard never took off because of problems inherent in its design.

A new authentication system based on Gopher+ forms is forthcoming in release 2.1 of the server. See Section 16.3.1.

16.2.2 New Indexing Script

A new command called *gopherindex* is installed with Gopher 2.x that automates the chores of indexing your Gopher server. The following example illustrates its use:

```
% /usr/local/bin/gopherindex -N "Text Index" -v /usr/local/gopher-data/text
```

This command indexes all of the files in */usr/local/gopher-data/text* and creates a searchable index link with the name "Text Index" in the same directory. The *-v* option tells the indexer to print out verbose messages. The *gopherindex* script works with either NeXT or WAIS indexing. (See Chapter 14, *Gopher: Incorporating Databases.*)

16.2.3 New Information-only Type

Under Gopher 2.x, there is a new Gopher type, *i*, which stands for *Information Only*. Items that have this type display their name, but do not display anything else when selected under Gopher 2.x clients. These items can be created by using a *.names* file:

```
% cat > .names
Type=i
Name=Big Long Informational Item
Path=
```

Notice that the `Path` is left blank—it doesn't matter what the path is set to, as it's ignored entirely. These informational-only items do not show up under non-Gopher+ clients.

16.3 New Features in Gopher 2.1

By the time this book is in print, the 2.1 release of the Gopher code should be available. This release contains many enhancements over the basic 1.x and 2.0.16 releases. The enhancements fall into two areas: user authentication and other server modifications.

Stay tuned to the Gopher anonymous FTP site (*boombox.micro.umn.edu*) and the Gopher newsgroup (*comp.infosystems.gopher*) for additional information.

16.3.1 User Authentication

The new Gopher 2.1 server can restrict access to directories or documents by username and password. Any item can be authenticated in this way.

Let's say you want to protect the directory *secretfiles* in your Gopher data directory. You could add username and password authentication to this item by adding the following item to your *gopherd.conf* file:

```
Authitem: unix /secretfiles
```

After adding this line, you need to restart your Gopher server if it's running standalone. Until you create a special link, if you try to access the *secretfiles* directory, you will receive an error message, *Sorry, no access to this item.*

To get access, you need to construct an authenticated item. You do this by adding a link to your Gopher server like this:

```
Type=1?
Path=validate 1/secretfiles
Name=Authenticated Access to Secret Files
Host=+
Port=+
```

Now, when you select this item, you are prompted for your username and password:

```
+-----------------------------------------------------------+
| The item /secretfiles is protected                        |
|                                                           |
| Your User Name:     ______________________________________ |
| Your Password:      ______________________________________ |
|                                                           |
| [Help: ^-]  [Cancel: ^G]                                  |
+-----------------------------------------------------------+
```

At this point you type your username and password as specified in the */etc/passwd* file. If you enter an incorrect username or password, you'll be denied access. If you enter a correct username and password, you will see the items within the */secretfiles* directory.

16.3.2 Updated FTP Gateway

Another new feature with release 2.1 is a full Gopher+ FTP gateway. Previous versions were unable to tell you the size or date of the items available via FTP. The new server removes this limitation.

16.3.3 Virtual Documents

Say you have a list of your favorite recipes in a single file, with each recipe separated by a row of dashes like this:

```
-------------------------------------------------------------
Cheese Puffs

 1 Cup Cheese
 1 Cup Puff
.
.
.
-------------------------------------------------------------
Salmon Spinach Cake

  1 Cup Salmon Loaf
```

```
    1 Cup finely minced spinach
  .
  .
  .
  -----------------------------------------------------------
  Caesar Salad

    Romaine Lettuce
    Anchovies
    Eggs
  .
  .
  .
```

If you want to make this easy to browse, you need to split the document into smaller pieces. This, of course, is time consuming.

However, the 2.1 server allows you to split a single document into a directory using a regular expression. To split the recipe file into multiple parts, add this line to the *gopherd.conf* file:

```
Filesep: ^-----------------------------------------------
```

This line tells the Gopher server to look for files that begin with a row of dashes. If the server finds such a file, it converts it into a directory, splitting the file into smaller documents, using each line that begins with dashes as a separator.

The Gopher server would see that the first line of every recipe in our recipe file had this line and would convert the file into the following directory:

```
1. Cheese Puffs
2. Salmon Spinach Cake
3. Caesar Salad
.
.
.
```

When the user selects one of these items, he only gets the specific portion of the document.

In this Chapter:

- *What Is the Web Good For?*
- *Basic Web Concepts*
- *World Wide Web Servers and Browsers*
- *Future Directions*
- *Overview of Web Chapters*

Introduction to the World Wide Web

The World Wide Web (known as the Web) is the most graphical Internet service, and it has the most powerful linking abilities. These features have made the Web the fastest growing Internet information service.

The Web allows highlighted words and pictures in a document to link, or point, to other media such as documents, phrases, movie clips, or sound files. The Web can link from any point in a document or image to any point in another document (not just from a menu item to the beginning of a document like Gopher).

With a browser that has a graphical user interface (GUI), the links are followed by simply pointing to the link with the mouse and clicking. These GUI-based versions are probably the easiest of all the Internet services to use and the most fun, because they can mix pictures with text.

The Web was initially developed at CERN, a particle physics laboratory in Geneva, Switzerland. The development work, led by Tim Berners-Lee, started in 1989. Most of the initial work focused on the definition of the HTTP client/server protocol, the development of a sample server, and a programming library called *wwwlib.* In 1992, CERN placed the sample *wwwlib* callable interface in the public domain. That spurred dozens of resourceful organizations and people around the Internet community to start innovating—developing their own Web browsers (programs used to view Web documents), supporting additional platforms, and developing new features. Web servers and Web browsers now support all major computer architectures and operating systems.

The most significant Web software development organization today is the National Center for Supercomputer Applications (NCSA) at the University of Illinois in Urbana-Champaign. Led by Marc Andreessen,* the Software Development Group created a

* Marc Andreessen is now at Mosaic Communications, Inc., a company developing a commercial version of Mosaic.

Web browser called Mosaic. It was built for UNIX, the X Window System, and OSF/Motif. Mosaic was later ported to Microsoft Windows and the Macintosh. Although many others have contributed Web browsers to the Web community, Mosaic remains the only Web browser to uniformly run on the three major desktop environments.

You are already part of the World Wide Web if you currently run an FTP server or a Gopher server. If you have compelling information that the online Web community values, they are probably already accessing your existing information server via the Web.

If you just want to have a personal Web business card (with your picture) and have a URL to include in your *.signature* file for newsgroup posting, you can do that without going to the trouble of setting up a Web server. You can develop your own HTML signature file and put it in your FTP archive. But if you want to set up a rich hypertext environment with extensive linking capability, then you probably should set up a Web server.

The NCSA Web server and related utilities are in the public domain. You can use this Web server with no licensing issues even if you are setting it up specifically as part of a money-making endeavor.

17.1 What Is the Web Good For?

The Web is being used for a wide range of purposes. Here are a few examples:

- Children's science museums are now on the Web, complete with special exhibit information, museum maps, course schedules, ongoing teacher support programs, and more.
- Newspapers are being electronically delivered prior to physical delivery into the community. Users can click to go to restaurant listings, quickly scan restaurants by category, click to look at a restaurant menu, and then click to go see the latest independent review. Readership, however, is global, instead of local. Letters to the editor now come from the other side of the world.
- Business has employed the World Wide Web to deliver product catalogs on demand to potential consumers' desktops. Users scroll through pages online, looking at product photos, clicking to enlarge photos for more detail, checking part numbers and prices—then using the Web to actually select the products and place an order.
- Electronic magazines such as the *Global Network Navigator* (*GNN*) have emerged. These new, innovative magazines are driven by advertising revenue and directly parallel traditional print magazines—they just happen to be electronic and global. But they are developing the capability to accept orders directly from ads, using Web order forms.

- Universities are online. Curious visitors from France can electronically visit a dinosaur exhibit at the Honolulu Community College. History buffs can tour the Vatican exhibit currently being hosted electronically at the University of Illinois.
- International organizations, such as the United Nations, the World Bank, and NATO, are using the Web to deliver information to their constituencies in every country of the world. Many United States agencies are online, as are many of the major proposals submitted to Congress by the Executive Branch—the full National Information Infrastructure (NII) proposal and National Health Care proposal among others. Not just the text of the proposals is available online; relevant photos and diagrams are included. Click on the audio icon, and the recording of the speech that launched the initiative is pulled back to your desktop and played if you have audio capability.
- Local community governments are going online. The City of Palo Alto, California, has a World Wide Web server that ties together the city government, the Chamber of Commerce, the local community historical association, community non-profits, and Palo Alto–based businesses. Many different city maps are online, as is an interactive commuter-train schedule. Users click on their destination and the World Wide Web displays the daily train schedule and the next train to catch.
- Many regions and communities use the World Wide Web as the basis for virtual tourism. Planning a trip to California? The World Wide Web tells you fun things to do and describes local establishments for food and lodging (see Figure 17-1).
- On a personal level, people are creating electronic business cards, with photos and hyperlinks they feel are important. These are the *.signature* files of the Web.

You are probably starting to get the idea that the main limit to what the World Wide Web can do is your imagination.

One downside of the Web is that using its full graphical capability requires the user to have both a GUI-based computer (not a character-based terminal) and an IP Internet connection (not dial-in to an Internet-connected computer). Not everyone has that capability. Also, graphics require a lot of data, so performance suffers over slow Internet links like those of home users.

In a way, the Web's capabilities and flexibility can be a disadvantage. In other services, like Gopher, you format things simply and forget them. The documents served by a Web server can be fine-tuned infinitely and consume more time on presentation (rather than substance) than they're worth. Anyone who has formatted a complicated document on paper probably has experienced this malady.

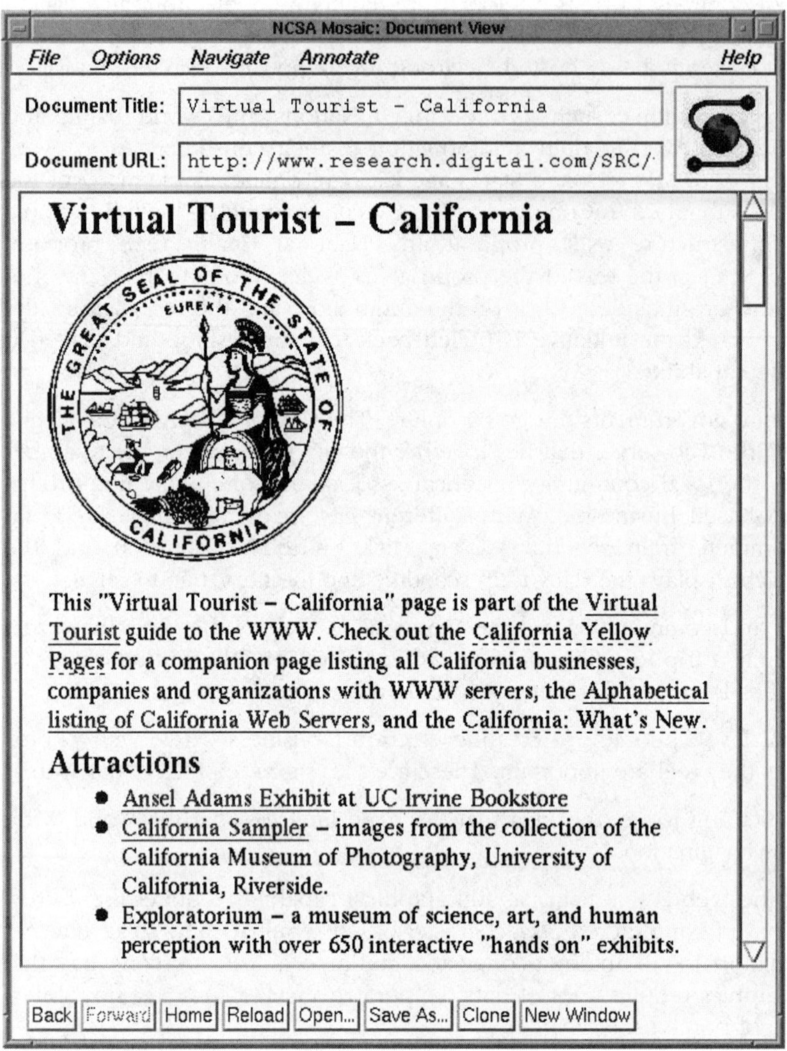

Figure 17-1. California Virtual Tourist document display by Mosiac

17.2 Basic Web Concepts

Here's a brief introduction to the basic concepts of the Web. If you've used the Web much, you might want to just skim this section.

17.2.1 Hyperlinking

To fully appreciate what the World Wide Web does, let's look at an example of hyperlinking in detail. Figure 17-1 showed a screen shot of the Mosaic Web browser displaying the California Virtual Tourist home page. (A home page is the central document on a Web server.) This page includes many embedded hyperlinks that are identified by underlining. The first hyperlink on this page appears as the words Virtual Tourist.

To navigate to the Virtual Tourist document, the user activates the hyperlink with a carriage return or a mouse click. After arriving at the Virtual Tourist document, the user can follow other hyperlinks to more documents or back up to the California Virtual Tourist page. The process of navigating, or following, hyperlinks from document to document is sometimes called surfing.* The power of the Web, and what differentiates it from other environments like Apple's Hypercard, is that hyperlinks can navigate to other documents in the same directory, anywhere on the same Web server, or anywhere on Web servers or other kinds of servers located anywhere in the world.

To illustrate this hyperlinking concept in more detail, Figure 17-2 shows an example of how hyperlinks are used to link documents found on four separate servers.

Server 1 is run by Digital Equipment Corporation, server 2 by State University of New York at Buffalo, server 3 by O'Reilly & Associates, and server 4 by The Exploratorium, a museum in San Francisco. Looking at each of these servers more closely we can put the documents and their hyperlinks into context:

Server 1:

- Document A is the California Virtual Tourist document shown in Figure 17-1. It has embedded hyperlinks from California Yellow Pages to document B on the same server, from Exploratorium to document F on server 4, and from Virtual Tourist to document C on server 2.
- Document B is the California Yellow Pages document. It is linked to from document A.

Server 2:

- Document C is the main Virtual Tourist guide. It is linked to from document A on server 1. It contains a map of the world, with hyperlinks embedded in the world map. It also contains an embedded hyperlink from *Global Network Navigator*'s Traveler's Center to document D on server 3.

Server 3:

- Document D is the *GNN* Traveler's Center. It is linked to from document C on server 2. It has hyperlinks to assorted travel logs and foreign correspondents. It has an embedded hyperlink to document E on the same server.

* Something like "crawling" would make a better metaphor for travelling on a Web. But that wouldn't give the right sense of speed and adventure!

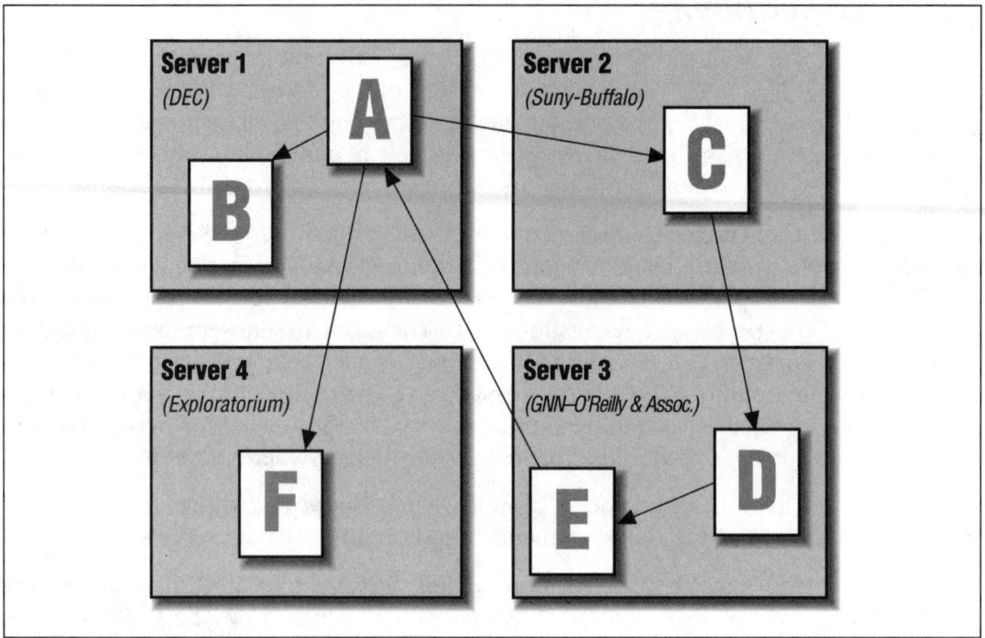

Figure 17-2. A Web of Web servers

- Document E is an index of travel resources by region, country, state, and city. It is linked to from document D. It also contains an embedded hyperlink to document A on server 1, the California Virtual Tourist document.

Server 4:

- Document F is the entry point to the Exploratorium, a hands-on science museum. It is linked to from document A on server 1. It has hyperlinks to local newsletters, an elementary-level science curriculum, and a vast library of photos.

Every document in this example can be further referenced, or pointed to, by other documents in the Web. Each document is a potential starting point for exploring the Web.

With this basic understanding of what the Web does, we can now discuss how it does it.

17.2.2 The HTML Tagging Language

Within the Web, ASCII text documents are marked up with a tagging language called the Hypertext Markup Language (HTML). Such documents are called HTML documents, and usually have a file extension of *.html.* HTML documents can be manually authored with your favorite ASCII text editor, can be converted by filters from other formats, or can be dynamically created at run-time by a Web server or script. The HTML tagging language is used to describe the structure of the document and hyperlinking information.

HTML describes the structure of a document, but not its exact formatting. Here's a little piece of HTML to give you the flavor (this has been edited and is not a complete HTML document):

```
<H1>NCSA Mosaic Demo Document</H1>
Welcome to NCSA Mosaic, an information browser developed at the National Center
for Supercomputing Applications at the University of Illinois,
Urbana-Champaign.
<P>
This document is an interactive hypermedia tour
of Mosaic's capabilities.
<H2>Introduction</H2>
<UL>
<LI> Mosaic is an Internet-based
<EM>global hypermedia</EM> browser that allows you to discover,
retrieve, and display documents and data from all over the Internet.
<LI> Mosaic is part of the World Wide Web project, a distributed
hypermedia environment originated at CERN and collaborated upon by a
large, informal, and international design and development team.
</UL>
```

We'll describe the complete syntax in Chapter 19, *Authoring for the Web*, but you can easily see headings (<H1> and <H2>), paragraphs (<P>), and a bulleted list (<UL>, <LI> and </UL>). Note that HTML does not specify exactly what size or style of fonts will be used. The browser determines those things. HTML does allow you to identify words to be emphasized (with <EM> in the example above), which might mean italics in a graphical browser but reverse video in a character browser.

HTML also includes tags that ask the user for input, either with simple questions or arbitrarily complex forms.

The current version of HTML is version 2.0. It is based on some of the concepts of SGML, the Standard Generalized Markup Language, which is an ISO standard used for marking up documents for both print and online publication. The next version of the HTML specification, HTML 3.0, will move HTML into full SGML–compliance. HTML 3.0 was previously called HTML+.

Chapter 19, *Authoring for the Web*, is about authoring with HTML.

17.2.3 The URL Concept

Each hyperlink in an HTML document is made up of two components—the anchor text or graphic that, when clicked on, triggers the hyperlink, and the Universal Resource Locator (URL) that describes what to do when the hyperlink is activated. From the user's perspective this means, "when this link is activated, jump to that resource for more information."

The URL describes the protocol used to reach the target server, the host system (or server name) on which the document resides, the directory path to the document, and the document filename. For example, here's an example of a URL to a remote resource. It points to the master list of all public World Wide Web servers throughout the world:

```
http://info.cern.ch/hypertext/DataSources/WWW/Geographical.html
```

This URL means that by using the HTTP (Web) protocol to reach a server called *info.cern.ch* (and using the default port), there is a directory */hypertext/DataSources/WWW* that contains a hypertext document named *Geographical.html*. Every file on the Internet is uniquely addressable by its URL. Besides the HTTP access method, the URL concept also supports other important Internet protocols such as Gopher, FTP, and Telnet. In addition, gateways or enhanced clients can allow the Web to access other types of servers such as Finger and WAIS.

The URLs described above are called absolute URLs, since they completely specify how to get a file. A simplified form of the URL, called a relative URL, is a shorter form for referencing other documents on the same server as the current document. Relative URLs also allow a Web browser to get direct access to files on the system it is running on, without using any server.

This uniform naming scheme for resources is what makes the World Wide Web such a rich information environment, and it's why many people consider World Wide Web browsers the universal Internet access tool.

17.2.4 What Is a World Wide Web Browser?

In the client/server environment of the Web, the control lies with the Web browser. The Web browser's job is to use the initial URL to retrieve a Web document from a Web server, interpret the HTML, and present the document to the user with as much embellishment as the user environment provides. A Web browser written explicitly for a bit-mapped graphic environment can embellish the HTML page to a greater extent than a Web browser written for a character-based environment. A good example of this is the hypertext link. On a graphics workstation, the text used as a hyperlink can be highlighted in a different color or underlined. On a character-based terminal, the same text is probably presented in reverse video.

When the user selects a hypertext link, the process starts all over again—the Web browser uses the URL associated with the hypertext link to request that document, waits for the document to be returned, and then processes and displays the new document.

Figure 17-3 shows the relationship between the Web browser and other Internet information servers discussed in this book.

When interacting with a Gopher server, the Web browser acts like a Gopher client and uses the Gopher protocol. When interacting with an FTP server, the Web browser acts like an FTP client and uses the FTP protocol. When interacting with a Web server, the

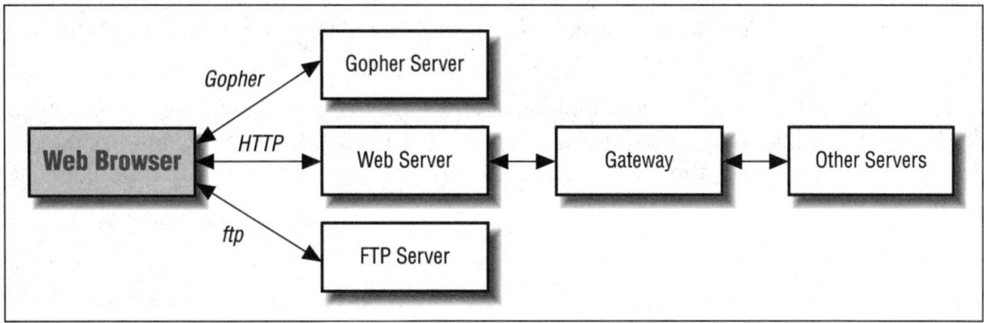

Figure 17-3. The world as seen from a Web browser

Web browser uses the HTTP protocol. Some (but not all) Web browsers can directly access WAIS servers, using the Z39.50 protocol.

Web browsers can also start up *telnet* sessions so that users can access remote Telnet resources and act like news readers to access local news servers.

Many Web browsers also let users do useful things with the current document, such as saving it to disk, sending it as an email message, directing it to the printer, searching through it locally for text strings, or even examining the document's HTML source.

17.2.5 What Is a World Wide Web Server?

The server software used with the World Wide Web is referred to as a Web server. It listens to port 80 (by default). When a client asks for a specific page, the server grabs the page and returns it to the client.

As shown in Figure 17-3, Web servers can execute special scripts that enable them to serve as gateways to other information resources on your system or on the Internet. Many of the most obvious gateway scripts are already available on the Web. You can install them as-is or customize them for your site. You can also develop gateways to access local information systems that might not be directly TCP/IP-accessible.

One kind of script handles input from forms. You can write custom scripts to do anything you want with the data that users enter into the forms.

17.2.6 HTTP

Web browsers and Web servers communicate using the HyperText Transfer Protocol (HTTP). HTTP is a lightweight protocol conceptually similar to the Gopher protocol. Every request for a document from a Web browser to a Web server is a new connection. When a Web browser requests an HTML document from a Web server, the connection is opened, the document is transferred, and the connection is closed.

You will currently see two flavors of HTTP mentioned around the Web, HTTP/0.9 and HTTP/1.0. HTTP/0.9 is being phased out. There is a large degree of compatibility between the two.

HTTP/1.0 supports the negotiation of data types between the Web server and Web browser, by adding MIME (Multimedia Internet Mail Extensions) header information to the protocol. HTML uses the MIME type name of "text" and the MIME subtype name of "html". This is written as:

```
text/html
```

There are many other types supported by Web servers and browsers, such as `image/gif`. With HTTP/1.0, every time a Web browser asks a Web server for a page, it passes along a list of the MIME types it can support. Using this information, the Web server tries to send only MIME types the client supports. The Web server responds first with the MIME type of the data file it is returning, a blank line, and then the actual data file.

The Web browser uses this MIME type information to interpret and display the data file if the type is "text/html" or "text/plain". Otherwise the MIME type information is used to direct the data file to the correct external viewing or playing mechanism. For example, under the X Window System, a Web browser that received a document with a MIME type of image/tiff might start up the program *xv* to display the image.

17.3 World Wide Web Servers and Browsers

Many of the concepts discussed in this chapter are best understood by simply playing with a Web browser to see how it works, how other people have set up their Web servers, and to get ideas about how you might set up your Web server. You will probably also use a browser for accessing documentation about the Web (the document itself is online as part of the World Wide Web), locating and retrieving your Web server kit, and testing the HTML documents you write. Moreover, part of running a Web server is making sure your server works with all of the different Web browsers that your user community uses.

17.3.1 Web Browsers

There are World Wide Web browsers for every conceivable platform, operating system, and graphical user interface (GUI). Web browsers fall into two categories—line-oriented and point-and-click graphical Web browsers. When authoring HTML documents, it helps to have several Web browsers on hand so you can test how your HTML looks with different browsers. Your HTML documents might even look different when displayed on a Macintosh version of Mosaic than it does on a Microsoft Windows version.

We will highlight the major released UNIX Web browsers here and mention some of the other Web browsers that are available or in development. For a complete list of all available browsers, see:

```
http://info.cern.ch/hypertext/WWW/Clients.html
```

17.3.1.1 Lynx

Lynx is a full-screen, character-based Web browser developed at the University of Kansas as a result of efforts to build a campus-wide information system. Figure 19-5 shows what Lynx looks like.

Lynx is a full-featured Web browser that is optimized for cursor-addressable, character-based display devices (such as VT100 terminals, VT100 emulators running on personal computers or Macintoshes, or any other "curses-oriented" display). It uses arrow keys to navigate among embedded HTML links, which are shown in reverse-video. It supports bookmarks to remember your favorite URLs. Lynx also supports forms.

Neat Feature: In interactive mode, the ability to post articles to newsgroups. In non-interactive mode, the ability to filter HTML to formatted ASCII text.

To get Lynx, point your Web browser at:

```
ftp://ftp2.cc.ukans.edu/pub/lynx/
```

This URL points to the FTP archive that contains all of the pre-built binaries for Lynx. There you will find binaries for IBM's RS/6000, DEC Alpha AXP (running OSF/1), SunOS, and DEC (ULTRIX).

Author: Lynx was designed by Lou Montulli, Charles Rezac, and Michael Grobe of Academic Computing Services at the University of Kansas. Lynx was implemented by Lou Montulli, *montulli@mcom.com.* You can send Lynx questions to *lynx-help@ukanaix.cc.ukans.edu* and bug reports to *lynx-bug@ ukanaix.cc.ukans.edu.*

17.3.1.2 MidasWWW

MidasWWW was written for the X Window System and has an OSF/Motif look and feel. It was developed at the Stanford Linear Accelerator Center (SLAC). MidasWWW is similar to Mosaic, with more extensive support for inline graphics. For example, it can display PostScript documents and GIF, JPEG, and TIFF files without using an external viewer. MidasWWW also has some navigation features such as a history tree showing all visited documents.

Neat Feature: MidasWWW blurs the visual presentation between PostScript and HTML.

For more information, see:

```
http://www-midas.slac.stanford.edu/midasv22/introduction.html
```

Author: Tony Johnson, *tony_johnson@slac.stanford.edu.* Questions on MidasWWW should be sent to *MidasWWW@slac.stanford.edu.*

17.3.1.3 Mosaic

Mosaic is the best known of the Web browsers. It was developed at the National Center for Supercomputer Applications at the University of Illinois and is available in prebuilt binary form for all major UNIX platforms, plus Apple Macintosh and Microsoft Windows. Figure 17-1 shows what the X Window System version of Mosaic looks like.

On UNIX, Mosaic was written for the X Window System and OSF/Motif. It supports inline graphics in either GIF or XBM format. File types that Mosaic cannot handle inline, such as MPEG movies, sound files, PostScript documents, and JPEG images, are automatically sent to external media players.

Neat Feature: NCSA Mosaic supports forms input as described in Section 20.2.

To get Mosaic, point your Web browser at:

```
ftp://ftp.ncsa.uiuc.edu/Mosaic/
```

This URL brings up an HTML page that takes you to all of the pre-built binaries. There you will find binaries for DEC (OSF/1 V1.3), DEC (MIPS/ULTRIX), HP-UX on Series 700 workstations, IBM's AIX, SGI IRIX, and SunOS. There are two versions for SunOS; which to use depends on how you've configured DNS and NIS.

Authors: NCSA Software Development Group in general, and Eric Bina, *ebina@mcom.com*, and Marc Andreessen, *marca@mcom.com*, in particular. You should direct Mosaic questions to *mosaic-x@ncsa.uiuc.edu.*

17.3.1.4 The Emacs World Wide Web browser

There is a World Wide Web browser mode for Emacs known as the w3-mode extension. This mode is extremely portable—any platform that supports an extensible Emacs supports the w3-mode extension. The w3-mode extension supports multiple fonts, bolding, italics, and the mouse if you are using Lemacs or Epoch with the X Window System. It also has forms support, as specified in the HTML 3.0 specification.

Neat Feature: Compatibility with Mosaic lets you use the same hotlist file, global history file, and personal annotation directory with both Emacs and Mosaic. This could be the best Web browser for people who use Mosaic at work, but still need consistent Web access when they dial in from home over slow lines.

To get the w3-mode extension, point your Web browser at:

```
ftp://moose.cs.indiana.edu/pub/elisp/w3/
```

There you will find source and the documentation for the w3-mode extension.

Author: William Perry, *wmperry@spry.com.*

17.3.1.5 NeXT

The NeXT Web browser was one of the original Web browsers developed at CERN to test concepts in use on the World Wide Web today.

The NeXT Web browser (frozen at V0.17) is available only for the NeXT 68000 workstations. A newer version that will support NeXTstep on other platforms is in development.

Neat Feature: The ability to author HTML and browse from the same Web browser.

To get the NeXT browser, point your Web browser at:

```
ftp://info.cern.ch/pub/www/bin/next/
```

This URL takes you to the FTP archive that contains assorted binaries and documentation for the NeXT Web browser.

Author: Tim Berners-Lee, *Tim.Berners-Lee@cern.ch*.

17.3.1.6 perlWWW

perlWWW is a character-based Web browser written in Perl. It relies on *termcap* for all screen manipulations. You can scroll the screen, select buttons, and press them, all with various keystrokes. It supports two sets of keystroke commands, consistent with Emacs and *vi*.

Neat Feature: It's pretty extensible because it's written in Perl.

To get perlWWW, point your Web browser at:

```
ftp://archive.cis.ohio-state.edu/pub/w3browser/
```

This URL takes you to the FTP archive where the perlWWW browser is kept.

Author: Thomas A. Fine, *fine@cis.ohio-state.edu* of Ohio State University.

17.3.1.7 ViolaWWW

ViolaWWW is an extensible, graphical World Wide Web browser for the X Window System.

Based on the Visual Interactive Object-oriented Language and Applications (Viola) scripting language and toolkit, ViolaWWW provides a way to build relatively complex hypertext applications that are beyond the abilities of the current HTML standard.

Neat Feature: HTML 3.0 support includes container paragraphs, nesting lists, input forms, and tables. Additional extensions include multiple columns, document insertion (client side), and dynamically collapsible/expandable lists.

To get ViolaWWW, point your Web browser at:

```
ftp://ftp.ora.com/pub/www/viola/
```

This URL takes you to the FTP archive containing the SPARCstation binary and the source code for other UNIX platforms.

Author: The initial work was done by the Experimental Computing Facility (XCF) at U.C. Berkeley. Pei Y. Wei, *wei@ora.com* of O'Reilly & Associates is currently driving the development of this Web browser. You can also send email to *viola@ora.com*.

17.3.1.8 Other Web browsers

A number of Web browsers are up and coming. You may want to keep an eye on them.

CERN Line Mode Browser: The Line Mode Browser is the original Web browser developed at CERN. It is a general-purpose information-retrieval tool for people with dumb terminals. In non-interactive mode, the browser is capable of fetching and converting documents and can be used as a filter. In interactive mode, it is similar to Lynx, but doesn't take advantage of the advanced video features found on most terminals. Hyperlinks are identified with a trailing numeric identifier in brackets. For more information, see:

```
http://info.cern.ch/hypertext/WWW/LineMode/Status.html
```

Chimera: Chimera is a Web browser with an X/Athena graphical interface. Chimera can access Web servers, FTP archives, and Gopher servers as well as local files. It also supports forms and inline images. Chimera is popular with users who do not want to use OSF/Motif. For more information, see:

```
ftp://ftp.cs.unlv.edu/pub/chimera/
```

TkWWW Browser/Editor for X11: The entire user interface of this browser is written in *tk*, the X toolkit built on *tcl*. TkWWW is the first browser for the X Window System with the ability to edit HTML. For more information, see:

```
http://info.cern.ch/hypertext/WWW/TkWWW/Status.html
```

In addition to these ten browsers, there are several more PC and Macintosh browsers, not to mention browsers for the more obscure systems. It is a lot to keep up with!

17.3.2 Web Servers

You have three public domain UNIX Web servers to choose from. Each has strengths and weaknesses. You will want to check out the latest versions of each to see which features and enhancements are in the latest revisions. There are also Web servers for other operating systems, but the UNIX Web servers are currently the most flexible and robust. This book describes how to set up the NCSA Web server, because it is the most commonly used.

17.3.2.1 NCSA

The NCSA Web server is a public-domain Web server written in C and designed to be small and fast. There are no licensing restrictions for any use.

The NCSA server is compatible with most HTTP/0.9 and HTTP/1.0 Web browsers. It supports directory aliasing so that documents can be served from any physical directory structure. You can customize your server to execute searches, handle HTML forms, provide clickable image maps, and control user access. The NCSA server also has support for including the output of commands or other files in your HTML documents.

Neat Feature: User-supported directories allow you to let your user community serve HTML documents from their home directories.

To get the NCSA Web server, point your Web browser at:

```
http://hoohoo.ncsa.uiuc.edu/docs/setup/PreCompiled.html
```

This URL takes you to a Web page that points to all of the precompiled *httpd* binaries for all major UNIX platforms.

Author: Rob McCool, *robm@mcom.com*. You can send questions or comments to the current developers of the NCSA Web server at *httpd@ncsa.uiuc.edu*.

17.3.2.2 CERN

The CERN Web server is a public-domain hypertext server written in C. There are no licensing restrictions for any use. The CERN server supports forms, clickable image maps, executable server-side scripts to synthesize documents on the fly, and the ability to plug in index search utilities (via CGI), and it provides access authorization. It also can provide document name-to-filename mapping for longer-lived document URLs.

Neat Feature: The main strength of the CERN server is its ability to provide proxy and caching support. A proxy Web server typically runs on a firewall machine, providing access to the outside world for people inside the firewall. It also can cache documents at the firewall, resulting in faster response times to your internal users.

For more information on the CERN Web server, point your Web browser at:

```
ftp://info.cern.ch/pub/www/bin/
```

This URL takes you to the FTP archive where all of the precompiled *httpd* binaries are stored.

Author: Tim Berners-Lee, *Tim.Berners-Lee@cern.ch* and Ari Luotonen, *luotonen@www.cern.ch*.

17.3.2.3 Plexus

Plexus is a public-domain Web server written in Perl. There are no licensing restrictions for any use. Plexus is designed to be extensible, easy to use, and have good performance. It currently supports both HTTP/0.9 and HTTP/1.0 protocols. To get the Plexus 2.2.1 Web server, point your Web browser at:

```
ftp://austin.bsdi.com/plexus/2.2.1/dist/Plexus-2.2.1.tar.Z
```

Neat Feature: It's written in Perl, so it is easy to modify. However, because Perl is not lightweight, it may not be the best choice for a heavily loaded server.

For the latest information on Plexus, point your Web browser at:

```
http://www.bsdi.com/server/doc/plexus.html
```

Author: Plexus is based on the Perl server developed at the University of Indiana by Marc VanHeyningen, *mvanheyn@cs.indiana.edu.* Plexus is maintained by Tony Sanders, *sanders@bsdi.com.* Tony is quick to point out that this project is not related to BSDI, his employer.

Just as with Web browsers, industrial-strength Web servers are under development at a number of different start-up companies. That is not to say there is anything wrong with these public-domain Web servers, but as always, there is a market for software that is supported, or more scalable and secure.

17.4 Future Directions

What does the future hold for the World Wide Web? The Web is evolving in three major technical directions: HTML enhancements, secure transactions, and uniform resource naming. The Web is also becoming more commercial.

You probably won't understand the significance of some of this without experience running a Web server (or authoring documents for one). You can come back to this after you've read some of the later Web chapters. The main point is that the Web is under rapid development. These future directions also hint at what the Web can't do very well today.

17.4.1 HTML Enhancements

On paper, HTML 2.0 has evolved into HTML 3.0, which is SGML-compliant. HTML 3.0 is described with an SGML Document Type Definition (DTD).

HTML 3.0 provides a rich environment for describing forms, tables, style sheets, and other tagging constructs missing in HTML 2.0. Support for mathematical equations will not make it into the specification until HTML 3.1.

The move towards HTML 3.0 will be extremely important for the part of the Web community that authors documents. Some of the major changes and additions found in HTML 3.0 includes:

New tags
: Allows authors to mark up text as *Footnote, Margin, Abstract, Note*, and *Role*.

Inline graphics
: Allows authors to identify figures (with optional captions above or below the figure) and have text wrapped around either side.

Tables
: Allows authors to identify multi-column, multi-row tables with the ability to mix inline graphics and text in the same table.

Forms
: Beyond what is described in this book, authors will be able to include multiple submit buttons per form.

Document toolbars
: Allows authors to create graphical navigation bars for long documents.

Validation
: Allows validation of HTML using SGML tools, so that you know it's correct without trying it in multiple browsers.

Clickable image maps have been redone to support the image map as part of the HTML document. This deliberately shifts the processing of the image map from the Web server out to the Web browser. It makes image-map processing more responsive to the user, as there is no round trip back to a Web server just to see if the user clicked on the right spot.

Graphical Web browsers will be able to optionally identify the hotspots to the user (a la HyperCard) and change the mouse cursor when moving over active hotspots on the inline graphic. Non-graphical Web browsers will be able to render an ordered list of options, even though they can't show the graphic.

For HTML authors, this means that clickable image maps can include relative URLs and can be easily moved around as part of an HTML document without having to go into elaborate server configuration details.

In layman's terms, HTML 3.0 provides the tagging features needed to fully implement more advanced real-world documents. However, in practice, until more than one Web browser implements the full HTML 3.0 processing definition, HTML 3.0 will not have the critical mass necessary for people to start authoring documents. For the latest information on HTML enhancements, point your Web browser at:

```
http://info.cern.ch/hypertext/WWW/MarkUp/MarkUp.html
```

17.4.2 Secure Transactions

The second major trend is towards providing higher levels of security at the transaction level. Although the current Web technology is adequate to deliver product catalogs to the user's desktop, security mechanisms are not built in to place orders over the Web with credit-card numbers, electronic signatures, and legally binding time stamps. Various efforts have made the first items possible in modified versions of current-generation tools (or with add-on components). But in the long run, these issues are being addressed with the development of a *Secure HTTP* specification.

Secure HTTP will ensure the authenticity of transactions and the confidentiality of information exchanged via HTTP. With a Secure HTTP–enabled application, a user could affix digital signatures that couldn't be repudiated, permitting digital contracts that are legally binding and auditable. In addition, sensitive information such as credit card numbers and bid amounts could be encrypted and securely exchanged. To see this specification, point your Web browser at:

```
http://www.commerce.net/information/standards/drafts/shttp.txt
```

For more general information about Secure HTTP, send an email message to *shttp-info@eit.com.*

Enterprise Integration Technologies (EIT), the National Center for Supercomputing Applications (NCSA) at the University of Illinois, and RSA Data Security have announced agreements to jointly develop and distribute secure versions of NCSA Mosaic and NCSA HTTP Web server based on RSA's public-key cryptography and EIT's Secure HTTP software. The enhancements are being made available to NCSA for public distribution for non-commercial use.

17.4.3 Uniform Naming

The third major trend is in the area of uniform resource naming. As important as the URL concept is to the Web, the URL does have limitations. Foremost is that the URL does not uniquely identify a document—it uniquely identifies an instance of a document. It does not account for mirrored documents and versions of information that are out-of-date.

The naming issue hasn't really been settled yet, but the general direction is to have another identifier called the *Universal Resource Name* (URN). The URN would be a unique document identifier much like the International Standard Book Number (ISBN). Every book published in the world has an ISBN that uniquely identifies its name, author, publisher, publication date, etc. It does not tell you which bookstore or libraries have the book, but it does contain the definitive metadata about the book. A URN would serve the same purpose for electronic documents. The general direction is to have URN servers that, given a URN, would return a list of all known URLs that identify instances of the document. Perhaps they could even return the URL of the instance that is electronically closest to your Web browser over the Internet.

The concept of URN's is not World Wide Web–specific, but does have obvious benefits to the Web. This is all based on the real-world observation that information on the Internet is not completely centralized but, in fact, is replicated and distributed all over the world for an assortment of valid reasons.

As we went to press, we heard that the trend seemed to be shifting toward calling the identifier a URC (Universal Resource Citation). The URC would be used with a URL and would include author, authoritative site, a digital signature or checksum, etc.

17.4.4 Commercialization

Taken as a whole, these technical trends are driving another major shift in the World Wide Web—the march towards commercialization:

- Many of the leading UNIX vendors are starting to bundle Web browsers into their base offerings. Santa Cruz Operation (SCO), Quarterdeck, and Digital Equipment Corporation have all struck licensing agreements with NCSA to bundle Mosaic with their products.
- Other firms, such as SPRY, InfoSeek Corp., Quadralay Corp., Spyglass, and California Software, Inc., are starting to license Web browsers and will be selling them as supported products in the commercial marketplace.
- NETCOM has announced NetCruiser, which is their own Web browser targeted at the home user. NETCOM is currently negotiating with modem manufacturers to bundle NetCruiser software with their products.

All of these marketing thrusts will accelerate the deployment of the Web onto more desktops. This will make the World Wide Web increasingly attractive for information providers and publishers.

The development of secure Web browsers and Web servers will provide a mechanism for electronic commerce. This move towards secure client/server transactions and the ability to exchange money electronically over the Web is laying the foundation for a number of initiatives:

Global Network Navigator (GNN)
: Sponsored by O'Reilly & Associates, *GNN* was the first online electronic magazine supported by advertising. Check the *GNN* MarketPlace to get an idea of the evolving commercial environment.

```
http://gnn.com/
```

CommerceNet

Sponsored by Smart Valley, Inc. in the San Francisco Bay Area, *CommerceNet* is intended to jump-start the Silicon Valley electronics industry onto the World Wide Web.

```
http://www.commerce.net/
```

NetWorth.XET N

Sponsored by Galt Technologies in Pittsburgh, *NetWorth* is intended to provide one-stop shopping for money market funds and financial services.

```
http://networth.galt.com/
```

MecklerWeb

Sponsored by Mecklermedia in Connecticut, *MecklerWeb* is intended to help the Fortune 1000 exploit the World Wide Web to establish an Internet presence.

```
http://www.mecklerweb.com/demo.html
```

Each of these has a slightly different focus, but all are intended to quickly ramp up the World Wide Web's use as a business tool. There are dozens of others.

17.5 Overview of Web Chapters

The next few chapters describe how to set up a World Wide Web server, how to author information for the Web, how to create gateways to information services that are not accessible directly from browsers, how to create forms and the scripts that handle form input, and how to control access to your Web server. If you are not a system administrator, you should concentrate on Chapter 19, *Authoring for the Web*.

In this Chapter:
- *Setting Up Basic Services*
- *Web Server Maintenance*
- *Enabling More Features*
- *Installation Summary*

18

Setting Up a Web Server

Setting up a Web server is not hard if you are familiar with UNIX system management. This chapter describes all the software installation, basic configuration, and maintenance. There are a lot of optional features that you can set up later once you've got the basic server working; they're described in Section 18.3. You should also be sure to read Chapter 21, *Web: Access Control and Security.*

18.1 Setting Up Basic Services

In these sections we describe how to get the NCSA Web server up and running in a basic configuration.

18.1.1 Installing a Precompiled Server

NCSA calls their Web server *httpd* (for HTTP daemon). The current version as of this writing is V1.3.

As of this writing, *httpd* binaries are available for the following platforms:

- IRIS Crimson VGXT running IRIX 4.0.5C
- SPARCserver 690MP running SunOS 4.1.3
- DECstation 5000 running Ultrix 4.2 Rev. 96
- DEC 3000 Model 500 running DEC OSF/1 V1.3
- IBM RS/6000 Model 550 running AIX 3.2.4
- HP 9000 model 730 running HP-UX 9.01

You should be fine with other platforms using the same architecture or an upwardly compatible version of the operating system. The easiest way to get the binaries is to point your Web browser at:

```
http://hoohoo.ncsa.uiuc.edu/docs/setup/PreCompiled.html
```

This URL contains a list of all the currently supported systems. Then you can use your Web browser to retrieve the appropiate kit. The kit contains a pre-built version of *httpd*, default configuration files, pre-built gateway scripts, assorted support scripts, and a collection of icons used for directory indexing.

If you are using the pre-built distribution kit, you can put the kit in */usr/local/src/* and call it *httpd.tar.Z*. Then at the command line you should unpack the distribution with:

```
% cd /usr/local/src
% zcat httpd.tar.Z | tar xvf -
```

When you uncompress and untar the kit using the above command, you will be creating a subdirectory called *httpd_1.3* that contains a *README file*, a pre-built NCSA Web server binary called *httpd*, and several subdirectories:

cgi-bin
This directory contains sample gateway scripts and precompiled gateway binaries. If you build your own gateways, this is usually where you will put them. The directory is called *cgi-bin* because gateways use a standard interface with the Web server called the Common Gateway Interface (CGI).

conf
This directory contains all the configuration files used to control the operations of your Web server.

icons
This directory contains an assortment of icons that are used for directory indexing.

logs
This directory is where the access log file and error log file are usually kept.

support
This directory contains programs that are used for global and per-directory access control.

If you can't use one of the precompiled packages, you need to grab the NCSA HTTP kit and build it from source. From the Web page listing all of the pre-built binaries, there is a hyperlink that takes you to a page from which you can download the source.

18.1.2 Compilation of NCSA HTTP

If you can use one of the pre-built binary kits mentioned above, you can skip this step completely and go ahead to Section 18.1.3. Otherwise, let's press ahead.

To get the source, point your Web browser at:

```
ftp://ftp.ncsa.uiuc.edu/Web/httpd/Unix/ncsa_httpd/current/httpd_source.tar.Z
```

You can use the following example as a guideline, but keep in mind that the command names and directory paths may be different on your system.

When you retrieve the NCSA HTTP source kit, you should put it in */usr/local/src* and call it *ncsa_source.tar.Z*. Then at the command line:

```
% cd /usr/local/src
% zcat ncsa_source.tar.Z | tar xvf -
```

This step uncompresses and un*tar*s the distribution source and puts it in a directory called *httpd_1.3*. The source distribution contains the same directories as the binary distribution described in the previous section, except for the additional *src* directory.

To build NCSA HTTP you must compile two things in separate steps: the *httpd* server and the gateways. First we'll build the *httpd* server. We *cd* to the source directory and make a backup copy of the *Makefile* using the following commands:

```
% cd http_1.3/src
% cp Makefile Makefile-dist
```

Now edit the original *Makefile* to make the following changes. Our general rule is: don't change any *Makefile* variables unless you know you have to. With your text editor:

- Change the CC variable to the name of the compiler you are using on your system.
- Change the CFLAGS variable if you want to use different compiler flags than the default. The default setting is probably OK.
- Add any extra libraries that are needed on your system with the EXTRA_LIBS variable.

If you are compiling for a SunOS 4.1.x environment (which is the default), you can save your changes and exit. Otherwise:

- Comment out the AUX_CFLAGS for SunOS 4.1.x.
- Uncomment the AUX_CFLAGS variable for your system.
- If you don't see your system, then the NCSA Web server probably hasn't been ported to your platform, and you should choose the system type you feel is closest to your actual system.
- Now save your changes and exit.

To build the *httpd* binary and move it into place, use the following commands:

```
% make
```

If this doesn't work, you must edit *src/httpd.h* and then try *make* again. If you have to do this, it is also important that you set the BSD flag correctly to either TRUE or FALSE according to your operating system. When the *make* works, move the Web server into the top-level directory:

```
% mv httpd ..
```

Let's move on to the CGI scripts. *cd* to the *cgi-src* directory:

```
% cd ../cgi-src
```

You can modify the *Makefile* like you just did the *httpd Makefile*. Then just *make* the scripts:

```
% make
```

This compiles and links all of the CGI scripts and moves them to *../cgi-bin*. Of particular importance is the imagemap CGI script. Keep this step in mind, because you need to change the *imagemap.c* source if you are not using the standard directories.

18.1.3 Site-Specific Configuration

Now that you have the binaries you need, you can configure the NCSA Web server to fit the environment at your site, by editing the three configuration files.* The configuration files are:

httpd.conf Main server configuration file

srm.con Server resource configuration file

access.conf Global access control file (ACF)

The *httpd.conf* and *srm.conf* configuration files are the main ones you'll adjust. You also have to edit the *access.conf* configuration file to match what you specify in *httpd.conf*.

There is also a minor configuration file called *mime.types* that is used to control the mapping of file extensions to MIME data types. It doesn't need to be modified unless you are trying to set up non-standard file-type-to-application correlations. For now, you can ignore the *mime.types* configuration file.

All three of the main configuration files are unloaded into a directory called *conf* and are initially found with a *.conf-dist* file extension. These you can leave alone as a reference and make site-specific copies with just a *.conf* file extension:

```
% cp httpd.conf-dist httpd.conf
% cp srm.conf-dist srm.conf
% cp access.conf-dist access.conf
```

When you modify any of these *.conf* files remember that:

* If you built the *httpd* binary from source, you can controthe HTTP server configuration by editing the *src/httpd.h* file and recompiling. However, it is more convenient to control your NCSA Web server with the configuration files.

- Everything is case-insensitive except pathnames and URLs.
- All comment lines begin with #.
- You can have only one directive per line.
- Extra whitespace is ignored.

The first thing we'll do with these configuration files is show what is needed to quickly get your NCSA Web server up and running for unrestricted public access. We'll also assume at this point that this is your Web server and only you have control of its operation. We will highlight the defaults that matter and describe the absolutely minimal changes needed to bring up your NCSA Web server. Later we'll cover how to customize your configuration.

18.1.3.1 Basic httpd.conf setup

httpd.conf controls how your server actually runs, but not details relating to the files it serves (which are handled in *srm.conf*).

To bring up your NCSA Web server as a standalone daemon for general, unrestricted public access, you should:

- Modify `User` and `Group` to whatever name you want. These define the user id (UID) and group id (GID) that the standalone server uses when it runs. We recommend:

  ```
  User http
  Group WWW
  ```

- Make sure the names exist in */etc/passwd* and */etc/group*, respectively. (The default UID is *nobody* and the default Group is *–1*.)
- Modify `ServerAdmin` to be *webmaster@your.domain* (and make sure you set up that email alias so that mail sent to it gets to you). This email address is given to users so they can report run-time problems with your Web server.
- Change `ServerRoot` to the absolute path to the directory where you plan to put the *httpd* binary. This also determines where other related files will go, so it should not be a directory that already contains files. The default is */usr/local/etc/httpd.*
- Specify `ServerName` to be *www.your.domain.* You will later set up a CNAME alias record to define this hostname.
- Change `ServerType` if you want to run the server under *inetd* instead of standalone. The default is standalone.

We will discuss some of these *httpd.conf* directives more later with the discussion of the feature each controls. For a reference on each *httpd.conf* directive, see Appendix F, *Web: srm.conf Directives.*

18.1.3.2 Basic srm.conf setup

The *srm.conf* configuration file controls where your *httpd* server finds your documents and scripts. To initially bring up your NCSA Web server for unrestricted public access, you should:

- Modify the `DocumentRoot` directive to point to the directory you want to be the top of your document tree. This is the main directory from which *httpd* will serve files. The default is */usr/local/etc/httpd/htdocs.*
- Modify the `UserDir` directive to DISABLED while you set up the server. This prevents users from serving files to the public from their home directories (a potential security risk). The default is *public_html.*
- Modify the `Alias` or `ScriptAlias` directives if you plan to put your *icon* subdirectory or *cgi-bin* subdirectory in a non-default location. The default locations are */usr/local/etc/httpd/icons/* and */usr/local/etc/httpd/cgi-bin/.* Additional `Alias` and `ScriptAlias` directives allow you to make some documents or scripts appear to the user to be in one directory, while you actually keep them in another. These are also known as virtual directories.

Many of the directives found in the *srm.conf* configuration file only make sense in the context of implementing advanced features in your Web server. Those directives will be discussed later with the feature each controls. For a reference on each *srm.conf* directive, see Appendix F, *Web: srm.conf Directives.* See Section 18.2.3 for information about the `Alias` directive.

18.1.3.3 Basic access.conf setup

The global Access Control File (ACF) is called *access.conf.* This configuration controls what type of access Web browsers have to your whole Web server or to certain directories.

The default *access.conf* file is:

```
<Directory /usr/local/etc/httpd/cgi-bin>
     Options Indexes FollowSymLinks
</Directory>

<Directory /usr/local/etc/httpd/htdocs>
      Options Indexes FollowSymLinks
      AllowOverride All
      <Limit GET>
              order allow,deny
              allow from all
      </Limit>
</Directory>
```

These defaults enable all features to all Web browsers without any security precautions. There's a whole chapter (Chapter 21, *Web: Access Control and Security*) about access control, so we won't try to explain all this here. For now, to initially bring up your NCSA Web server for unrestricted public access, you should:

- Modify the first `Directory` directive if your *cgi-bin* directory is in a different location.
- Modify the `Options` directive associated with the *cgi-bin* directory to remove the `Indexes` option. It is not a good idea to let users on the Web randomly look through your *httpd* script directory.
- Modify the second `Directory` directive if necessary so that it matches the path defined with the `DocumentRoot` directive in the *srm.conf* configuration file.
- Modify `AllowOverride` from `All` to `None`. You don't want others on your system or in your HTML authoring community to be overriding your global ACF without regard to security.

18.1.4 Installing the Server

You are now ready to move the *httpd* server and its associated files and directories to the `ServerRoot` prior to starting the Web server. Assuming that you didn't modify the `ServerRootx` location and unpacked the server kit in the same directory that we did, use the following commands to move your *httpd* server into place:

```
% cd /usr/local/src/httpd_1.3
% mkdir /usr/local/etc/httpd
% cp -r httpd conf logs icons cgi-bin /usr/local/etc/httpd
```

Remember, the *logs* directory should be writable by the user your server will run under (as defined by the User directive in the *httpd.conf* configuration file). The easiest way to arrange that is:

```
% cd /usr/local/etc/httpd
% chown http logs
```

18.1.5 Starting the Server

You start your Web server differently depending on whether you want to run it standalone or under *inetd*. Basically, running under *inetd* is a good idea while testing and prototyping, whereas running standalone is better for heavy use.

But before we start it up, here's a summary of the three NCSA *httpd* command-line options. Unlike most other services described in this book, *httpd* has very few options, because almost everything is controlled in configuration files. When executing *httpd*, three command-line flags are available:

–d directory If you changed `ServerRoot` in *httpd.conf*, you must also specify the same directory here with *–d*. This controls where *httpd* looks for its configuration files.

–f file This specifies an alternative *httpd.conf* configuration file for *httpd* to read.

–v This just displays the current *httpd* server version. You can execute this while your *httpd* server is running.

18.1.5.1 Standalone startup

If you have used all of the defaults in the configuration files, to start the server, simply execute the binary as *root*:

```
% httpd &
```

httpd should be started from *root* so that it can bind to port 80 (which is a reserved port) and open the three log files. Then it changes UID to the group/user specified by the `Group` directive and `User` directive in the *httpd.conf* configuration file, for security reasons.

If you are using a `ServerRoot` other than */usr/local/etc/httpd*, you need to start the daemon with:

```
% httpd -d /your/server/root &
```

where */your/server/root* is the setting of your `ServerRoot` directive. You will want to automatically start *httpd* when the system comes up. This is done through modifications to a file in */etc/rc** depending on your system. There's an example in Section 7.3.2.

18.1.5.2 Restarting the standalone httpd

You'll probably change the configuration files, especially while setting up your data and scripts. To reboot the *httpd* server after you have changed any configuration file, use the following command:*

```
% kill -HUP `cat logs/httpd.pid`
```

Alternatively, you could use the *ps* command and *grep* for the process id of the *httpd* server. To make sure you are killing the parent *httpd* process, you should look for the *httpd* with the lowest process id and a parent process id of 1.

* Where *logs/httpd.pid* is the default path and filename specified as `PidFile` in the *httpd.conf* configuration file. It is relative to the `ServerRoot` directory.

To test that the *httpd* server restarted successfully, you should check the last line of the *httpd* server's error log (*logs/error_log* by default—see Section 18.2.2). It should say:

```
httpd: successful restart.
```

18.1.6 Startup Under inetd

If you modified your ServerType directive in the *httpd.conf* configuration file, you need to set up *inetd* to run your Web server:

- Edit */etc/services* to add a line which resembles the following:

  ```
  http port-number/tcp
  ```

  `port-number` must match the `Port` directive you specified in the *httpd.conf* configuration file. Normally, it should be 80.

- Edit */etc/inetd.conf* to add a line that resembles the following:

  ```
  http stream tcp nowait nobody /usr/local/etc/httpd/httpd httpd
  ```

  Replace */usr/local/etc/httpd/httpd* with the path to the server binary, and `nobody` with the username you want requests fulfilled as (we suggest *http*). The final reference to *httpd* (only) needs `-d ServerRoot` arguments if you changed `ServerRoot` in the *httpd.conf* configuration file.

- Restart *inetd* by finding the *inetd* process using *ps* and using *kill –HUP* to restart it.

Using this method, you will never need to restart the *httpd* server, as it is restarted when needed by the *inetd* process. Of course, the downside is the performance penalty you will pay on every request to your Web server, because *httpd* has to read all the configuration files at startup.

To take down your service, you need to comment out the line you put in *inetd.conf* and restart *inetd*. You might also want to consider using *xinetd*, an extended version of *inetd* that provides security and access control features. For more information on *xinetd*, see Chapter 28, *xinetd*.

18.1.7 Mapping URLs to Documents

To open an HTML document on your Web server, you need to understand how URLs are mapped against your document tree. The first thing to look at is the minimal URL that reaches your Web server:

```
http://server-name
```

When a URL does not include a directory path or a filename, the Web server either returns the contents of a file called *index.html* in the `ServerRoot` directory or, if the file is nonexistent, automatically generates a directory index similar to *ls -1* (that's the number one, not lowercase L).*

If you are running your *httpd* server on something other than the default port, you need to include the non-standard port number in the minimal URL. For example, if you run *httpd* on port 8001, the minimal URL to reach your Web server is:

```
http://server-name:8001
```

To retrieve anything other than the root-directory index, you also need to append the virtual name of the document to the URL. The virtual name identifies the path to the document according to the Web server. It is not the absolute pathname of the document on your system. Actually, a virtual name is a virtual directory plus a real filename.

The *httpd* server translates URLs to real directories as follows:

- It looks at the beginning of the URL path for any virtual directories defined by `Alias` or `ScriptAlias` directives in *srm.conf*. If it finds one, it replaces the virtual directory with the real directory and processes the request. Virtual directories let you have separate trees for different kinds of information.
- It looks for a prefix of */~user-name* (slash tilde followed by a valid system user name) in the URL and, if it is found, looks in the specified user's public HTML subdirectory (*public_html*) for the file. If the public HTML subdirectory for the specified user doesn't exist, it returns an error. This step is skipped if `UserDir` is set to DISABLED in *srm.conf*.
- Otherwise, it inserts `DocumentRoot` at the beginning of the path and processes the request.

`Alias`, `ScriptAlias`, and `UserDir` directives are all found in the *srm.conf* configuration file. Each `Alias` or `ScriptAlias` line in *srm.conf* defines a virtual directory. For example, the following default `Alias` line:

```
Alias          /icons/      /usr/local/etc/httpd/icons/
```

defines a virtual directory of */icons/*, which, when it appears in URLs, is mapped by the Web server to */usr/local/etc/httpd/icons/*. For example, the URL:

```
http://server-name/icons/mybitmap.xbm
```

is fulfilled with the file */usr/local/etc/httpd/icons/mybitmap.xbm*.

* *index.html* is the default filename. The actual name can be controlled by the DirectoryIndex directive in the *httpd.conf* configuration file.

18.1.8 Testing Your HTTP Server

The next step is to make sure your Web server is running properly. Use your Web browser to open the minimal URL for your Web server and see what happens. If you have an *index.html* file (one that matches the file identified by the `DirectoryIndex` directive), it should be returned. If not, you should see an index of the filenames at the top of your document tree. If you see either, it means your Web server is up and running.

You can also test your Web server directly by *telnet*ing to the port that *httpd* is listening to and then acting like a Web browser by typing HTTP protocol:

```
% telnet www.ora.com 80
Trying 198.112.208.13 ...
Connected to amber.ora.com.
Escape character is '^]'.
HEAD / HTTP/1.0<CR><CR>

HTTP/1.0 200 OK
Date: Saturday, 20-Aug-94 20:33:28 GMT
Server: NCSA/1.1
MIME-version: 1.0
Content-type: text/html
Last-modified: Tuesday, 02-Aug-94 15:32:19 GMT

Connection closed by foreign host.
```

This shows that the Web server is up and running and its version number. Using *telnet* is also useful when you are trying to debug MIME typing problems.

If you can't get your Web server to respond from your Web browser and a direct *telnet* to your server doesn't produce the results shown above, you should take a look at the access log and the error log to see what they say (see Section 18.2.2).

If you are testing from the same system as your *httpd* server is running on, also try it from another system. If this isn't convenient, you might ask a friend who has access to a different system to test your server for you.

18.1.9 Setting Up Home Pages

Although every document on your Web server is potentially the first thing on your server that someone will see, most often the entry point is the home page. By convention this file is named *home.html*. You can have a single *home.html* document or several (in different directories), depending on whether your Web server serves one purpose or is used by multiple unrelated people or organizations. The next chapter describes how to create HTML documents in general. Here, we'll just mention the conventions for home pages.

When constructing a home page you should:

- Sign your work. This is usually done by placing a hyperlink to your HTML signature page at the bottom of your home-page document. We will do this in our sample HTML document in Chapter 19, *Authoring for the Web*, and usually do it on every HTML document. This allows people to report bugs and updates.
- Date your home page with a creation or modification date. We generally like to do this on every HTML document, not just the home page.
- Give the status of the Web server. Indicate whether it is under construction or is stable. Users will use the server's status to decide whether or not to send you email when they find a broken hyperlink. It is fine to start out with a Web server that is "under construction."

You should place a single home page at the top of your document tree in order to have your home page URL as short as possible. For example, the URL for Digital Equipment Corporation's home page could be:

```
http://www.digital.com/home.html
```

To shorten this even further, so that *home.html* does not need to be specified, you can either copy *home.html* into *index.html*, or set your `DirectoryIndex` to be *home.html*.

If your Web server has multiple uses, you will probably have multiple home pages located in different parts of the document tree. In this case, individual home-page URLs are based on where they are located in the document tree. You may want to manually write the *index.html* file in the root directory as an HTML document that gives a structured description of all the home pages hosted by your system.

18.1.10 Delegating Document Tree Management

So far, we have assumed that you have exclusive control of the document tree and its contents. Let's look at how you can release content maintenance to your HTML authoring community, either by project or by individual.

If your Web server supports different organizations or functions, you may want to give each a subdirectory in the document tree that they can manage themselves. You don't have to modify any of the directives in the configuration files to do this. You can control which users on your local system can write and modify different sections of the document tree by using standard UNIX file and directory permissions.

If any of the organizations want to use image maps, gateways, or access control, they need to coordinate it with you. You can also activate specific server features on an organization-by-organization basis.

If your Web server needs to present documents authored by the general user population on your system, you can let individuals serve HTML documents out of a special directory in their personal home directories. This is controlled by the `UserDir` directive in the *srm.conf* configuration file. If `UserDir` is set to *public_html*, that tells *httpd* to service requests of the form:

```
http://server-name/~user-name/blah.html
```

by remapping it to the file:

```
~user-name/public_html/blah.html
```

where *user-name* is a user in the */etc/passwd* file. If *~user-name/public_html* does not exist, the person requesting this URL gets an error.

If you specify DISABLE for the `UserDir` directive, the remapping of *~user-name* doesn't occur. The URL above only works if there is a directory called *~user-name* (with the ~) in the `DocumentRoot`.

You should read Chapter 21, *Web: Access Control and Security*, before you enable this Web server feature. You need to understand and minimize potential security risks that your user community might unknowingly create.

18.1.11 Conventions for Public Access

There are several conventions that you should follow as you set up your World Wide Web server for public access. One involves the server name that you have already set up. Although the server name is by default the same as your system name, this is not recommended. The Web convention is that your server name should start with *www*. If your host is *zeus.fredonia.edu*, you might want your server name to be *www.fredonia.edu*. It pays to have a CNAME alias record that maps the Web server name to an actual system name. This give you the flexibility to move your Web server around from system to system as your computing resources change or your system load increases. For more information on how to establish a CNAME alias record, see Section 3.2.

Prior to bringing your Web server online for the public, you should establish an email alias that people can use to send comments, tips on broken pointers, or requests for links. By convention, this alias is called the webmaster alias. This is similar in concept to the postmaster or newsmaster. It is generally a good idea to include a reference to *webmaster@domain-name* on the server home page. Usually the webmaster is the person who looks after the server installation, configuration, and maintenance. This may or may not be the same as the person or people providing the HTML content. For content issues, users usually send email to the person identified as the document owner by his or her signature on the bottom of each HTML page.

18.1.12 Announcing Your Server

Once your Web server is online (and it has some valuable content) you may want to announce your server to the Web community. There is no formal registration process, but there are well-established norms. Your announcement should state what organization, person, or entity owns the Web server, what type of content it contains, whether it is "ready for use" or "under construction," and the URL of the home page. You can:

- Send the announcement message to the *www-announce@www0.cern.ch* mailing list.
- Post the announcement message to a moderated newsgroup called *comp.infosystems.announce.*
- Send the announcement message to *www-request@info.cern.ch.* This gets your announcement on the CERN World Wide Web Servers list. This is how you get your Web server listed alphabetically by continent, country, and state.
- Send the announcement message to *whats-new@ncsa.uiuc.edu* in HTML format and written in the third person. This is how you get your announcement on the NCSA Mosaic "What's New" page.

In the first three cases, you should make sure that your URL stands out visually from the rest of the message. Most people place it on a line by itself with a blank line before and after. Do not embed it in the announcement text with punctuation. The trailing period (.) in a sentence changes your URL when people with cut-and-paste capabilities grab it and try to visit your new Web server.

Prior to hitting the send key, double-check that you have included the URL of your home page in your announcement. Then check three times that it is correct. It's not convenient to change your announcement once it has escaped onto the Internet.

18.2 Web Server Maintenance

Once your Web server is up and running reliably, it requires very little maintenance. The two most common things you will do periodically is update the HTML and rotate the log files. You will also occasionally have to restructure the underlying disk and directory structure without breaking existing hyperlinks that point into your Web server.

18.2.1 Updating HTML Documents

There is no need to stop or reboot your *httpd* server when you update the HTML documents in the document tree. You simply lay the new or modified HTML documents right on top of the existing online document tree. Some people edit their HTML documents in place while the Web server is online for Internet access. Depending on the availability of disk space, others like to keep two parallel environments, one for offline development and one for online Internet access.

We like to keep an offline copy, with relative URLs (described in the next chapter), that we can work on at our own pace. The relative URLs let us preview and verify from a local disk (without involving a Web server). When we're ready to roll it into public use, we *tar* up the offline copy and then just lay it back down on top of the online version. Another way to do that, assuming both versions are in the same filesystem, is to just move the directories:

```
% cd /usr/local/etc/httpd
% mv htdocs htdocs.old && mv htdocs.new htdocs
```

The directory name *htdocs* is defined as the default DocumentRoot.

18.2.2 Managing the Log Files

On a daily or weekly basis you should move or archive the log files to keep them from growing too big and to facilitate HTTP log analysis. It's a good idea to automate this process.

If you are running *httpd* under *inetd*, this is very easy. You just move the log files, using *mv*, with no effect on the server. The next client request opens up a new `TransferLog`.

If you are using *httpd* standalone, the *httpd* daemon opens the log files once when it starts up and does not close them until *httpd* is killed. To relocate one of the log files, the following steps are required:

1. Move the log file to a new name with the *mv* command. The *httpd* server will continue to write to the same log file, even though it has a new name.
2. Restart the standalone *httpd* server, as described in Section 18.1.5.2.

Step 2 causes all new *httpd* processes to log to the new log file. You may then do what you wish with the old log file.

18.2.3 Moving Directory Structures

Occasionally you will have to move sections of your document tree to deal with disk space constraints or a changing systems environment. This is where the `Alias` directive can be helpful.

Let's look at an example in which you want to spread your document tree over two disk drives. If your original document tree used the default path, and you have three organizations on your Web server, your physical directory hierarchy might look like this:

```
% ls /usr/local/etc/httpd/htdocs
chemistry/
physics/
biology/
```

To move the Biology department to a new drive mounted as */archive/1*, you would take the following steps:

1. Create a *biology* directory on */archive/1*.
2. Copy the current *biology/* directory tree to */archive/1/biology*.
3. Add an `Alias` directive to your *srm.conf* configuration file:

   ```
   Alias /biology/ /archive/1/biology/
   ```

   Reboot your *httpd* server if it is running standalone so that the new Alias directive takes effect.
4. Delete the current */biology* directory.

Using this technique, URLs of the form *http://www.fredonia.edu/biology/* continue to work transparently, even though the underlying directory structure has been changed.

18.2.4 Mirroring Documents and Servers

The *htget* Perl script gets HTML non-interactively from a Web server. You can use it to get a single document, or to mirror (duplicate) part or all of another host's directory tree. Why would you want to do that?

- Are you making heavy use of a remote server, with lots of graphics or over a slow line? Pre-fetching the HTML document and the graphics in it—in the background, or overnight when the network is faster—will speed up your server.
- If you have a heavily used server, other servers can mirror your server's HTML documents and spread out the load.
- You want a quick and easy way to grab an HTML document from the UNIX command line or from a non-interactive program like a shell script or a *cron* job. *htget* can write the document to a file or to its standard output.

Oscar Nierstrasz wrote *htget*. You can get it from this book's archive (see the Preface). The version at *http://cui_www.unige.ch/ftp/PUBLIC/oscar/scripts/README.html* may have been updated since we grabbed it.

htget has several options. These make big changes in what it does, so it's important to decide which one you need:

- With no option, *htget* copies the HTML file you specify to your current directory:

  ```
  % htget http://nearnet.gnn.com/mkt/travel/center.html
  htget: created center.html (2203 bytes)
  ```

- The *–s* option writes the file to standard output. For example, you could search an HTML document by typing:

```
% htget -s http://nearnet.gnn.com/mkt/travel/center.html | grep Thailand
```

- The *–abs* option converts all relative URLs to absolute URLs. If you're retrieving a single file that has relative links in it, this option makes sure that you can access all the links from your local copy.

  The following are two examples of the same HTML document, *http://tbl.com/tbl/TBLhome.html*. These lines were copied with no *htget* options:

  ```
  <IMG ALT="TBL" SRC="graphics/DIRECTORY.gif">
  <A HREF="/tbl/tbl.html">
    <IMG SRC="/tbl/graphics/whatsup.gif" ALT="[What's Up at TBL]"></A>
  ```

  Here are the same lines with *–abs*:

  ```
  <IMG ALT="TBL" SRC="http://tbl.com:80/tbl/graphics/DIRECTORY.gif">
  <A HREF="http://tbl.com:80/tbl/tbl.html">
    <IMG SRC="http://tbl.com:80/tbl/graphics/whatsup.gif"
    ALT="[What's Up at TBL]"></A>
  ```

- Finally, the *–r* option copies recursively. *htget –r* creates subdirectories under your current directory, and also retrieves graphics and other files. This re-creates the remote tree in a way that lets you use it locally (either directly within a Web browser or in a server document tree). The script uses some interesting tricks to make your local copy of the tree correct:
  - It gets the file and all files that are reachable from that URL, but only when the files are in the same directory hierarchy on the same host. This avoids copying a much larger tree than you expected.
  - When *htget* retrieves a file, any absolute URLs in other retrieved documents that point to that file are converted to relative URLs. This makes sure that you use your local copy of a file whenever possible.
  - When *htget* doesn't retrieve a file (because it's from another tree), any relative URLs in other retrieved documents that point to that file are converted to absolute URLs (including the remote host name and port number). This makes sure that you can always access files that weren't copied.

htget is only good for getting `http:` URLs. There are "hooks" in the code for `ftp:` and `gopher:` URLs, but the functionality isn't there.

Before you start grabbing and using all the HTML files you can find `:-)`, remember the copyright implications of copying other people's work. You shouldn't grab people's stuff without asking, even if they are giving it away.

18.2.5 HTTP Logs and Log Analysis

There are two Web server log files, the `Error` log and the `Transfer` log. By default they are in *logs/error_log* and *logs/access_log* in the `ServerRoot` directory. You can change the location or filename with the `ErrorLog` and `TransferLog` directives in *httpd.conf* (see Appendix E, *Web: httpd.conf Directives*.

After you have announced your Web server, you will want to know who is using it and what for. There are several readily available tools to help you analyze activity on your Web server. Every time someone grabs a file using your Web server, *httpd* logs the host name, the date and time, and the URL request. A typical log file looks like:

```
topcat.ug.eds.com - - [29/Jul/1994:04:07:11 -0700] "GET /Update/940620.html ▶▶▶
▶▶▶HTTP/1.0" 200 4327
cathy.ijs.si - - [29/Jul/1994:04:07:19 -0700] "GET/info.home.html ▶▶▶
▶▶▶HTTP/1.0" 200 2241
cathy.ijs.si - - [29/Jul/1994:04:07:45 -0700] "GET/master-subject.html ▶▶▶
▶▶▶HTTP/1.0" 200 9348
topcat.ug.eds.com - - [29/Jul/1994:04:07:47 -0700] "GET/whats-new.html ▶▶▶
▶▶▶HTTP/1.0" 200 28123
144.122.171.70 - - [29/Jul/1994:04:08:36 -0700] "GET / HTTP/1.0" 200 2153
cathy.ijs.si - - [29/Jul/1994:04:08:40 -0700] "GET /key-vax-index.html ▶▶▶
▶▶▶HTTP/1.0" 200 77847
ceng.metu.edu.tr - - [29/Jul/1994:04:08:55 -0700] "GET/pics/dec-logo.gif ▶▶▶
▶▶▶HTTP/1.0" 200 15 36
silver.fe.msk.ru - - [29/Jul/1994:04:10:06 -0700] "GET /demo.html HTTP/1.0" 200 786
```

This log file is in what is called the common log format because most Web servers generate it. Formally, the format of your access log is:

```
host rfc931 authuser date-time request status bytes
```

Where each item means:

host
: `Hostname`

RFC931
: The RFC 931 username if active, a dash (–) if not. It is normally (–) if *httpd* is configured with `IdentityCheck` off, which is the default. If `IdentityCheck` is turned on, *httpd* attempts to use the RFC 931 protocol to talk to an RFC 931-compliant daemon on the system running the Web browser to determine the name of the user running the Web browser. This whole thing hinges on whether users' systems are configured with an Identity daemon. Most are not.

`authuser`
: HTTP/1.0 authenticated user, a dash (–) if none. It is normally (–) unless the directory containing the file being accessed is protected with user authentication. If so, `authuser` is the authorized username that was used to access the file.

`date-time`
: Local time of the request, with time zone offset from GMT at the end

`request`
: The request as sent by the client

`status`
: The HTTP/1.0 status code from this transaction

`bytes`
: The number of bytes sent in this transaction, not including the header. If not applicable, this is a dash (–).

The common log format is supported by the latest CERN and Plexus Web servers. Many Gopher servers also support it. This helps in the development of log analysis tools like *getstats*, *wwwstat*, and *wusage*. These tools are not included as part of the NCSA HTTP kit, so you will have to go grab one yourself. Here is a summary of some of these tools:

18.2.5.1 getstats

getstats is a C program that produces Web server statistics on everything from a monthly basis down to an hourly basis. You can cut the logs by domain, page request, or directory tree. It works with any Web server supporting the common log format. There is even an HTML forms interface for *getstats*.

Just point your Web browser at:

```
http://www.eit.com/software/getstats/getstats.html
```

Author: *getstats* was developed by Kevin Hughes, *kevinh@eit.com* at Enterprise Information Technology.

18.2.5.2 wwwstat

Author: *wwwstat* is written in Perl. *wwwstat* does not make any changes to or write any files in the server directories. This means that you can assign the log analysis to someone without root privileges.

Just point your Web browser at:

```
http://www.ics.uci.edu/WebSoft/wwwstat/
```

wwwstat was developed by Roy Fielding, *fielding@ics.uci.edu* at the University of California, Irvine, Department of Information and Computer Science. To see an example of what *wwwstat* can do, point your Web browser at:

```
http://www.ics.uci.edu/Admin/wwwstats.html
```

wwwstat includes a companion tool called *gwstat* that can translate *wwwstat* summary data into graphical charts. Figure 18-1 shows the results of *wwwstat* and *gwstat* used together to summarize the hourly traffic on a Web server. Because the graphical summaries are in GIF format, they can be included with HTML.

18.2.5.3 wusage

Author: *wusage* is a C program that produces Web server statistics on a weekly basis and produces graphs of the results in GIF format. Pie charts by domain show the geographic distribution of users. A graph of accesses over time shows server usage growth; a smaller version this graph is provided for use as a home-page icon, linked to the statistics page. Textual versions of the above information, in addition to the top ten sites and top ten URLs requested, are output for each week in HTML format.

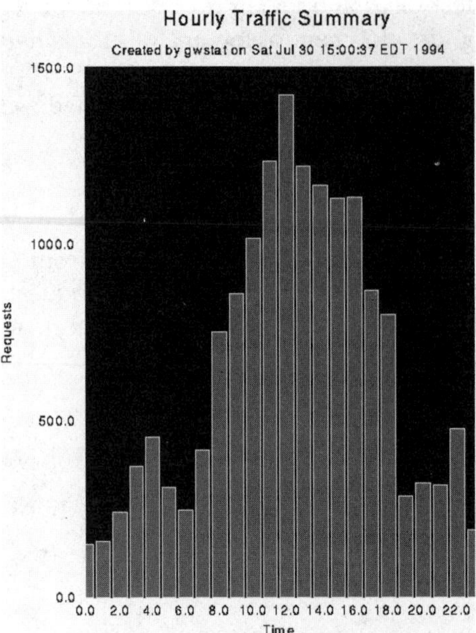

Figure 18-1. gwstat hourly traffic summary

Just point your Web browser at:

```
http://siva.cshl.org/wusage.html
```

wusage was developed by Thomas Boutell, *boutell@netcom.com* at Cold Spring Harbor Labs, Cold Spring Harbor, New York. Figure 18-2 shows an example of what *wusage* can do.

18.3 Enabling More Features

Once you've got your basic Web server operating, there are a few useful features you can enable if you want to. You can add support for new MIME types or expand how the Web server recognizes existing types. You can enable server-side includes, which allow the Web server to automatically fill in the last-modified date or read a file into an HTML file before sending it to the user. Or you can customize how the Web server displays directories.

18.3.1 Adding MIME Types

As your server matures, you may find file types that aren't supported. As described earlier, Web browsers and Web servers using HTTP/1.0 pass MIME types back and forth.

You can add support for new MIME types in your server (or new ways for the server to recognize existing types).

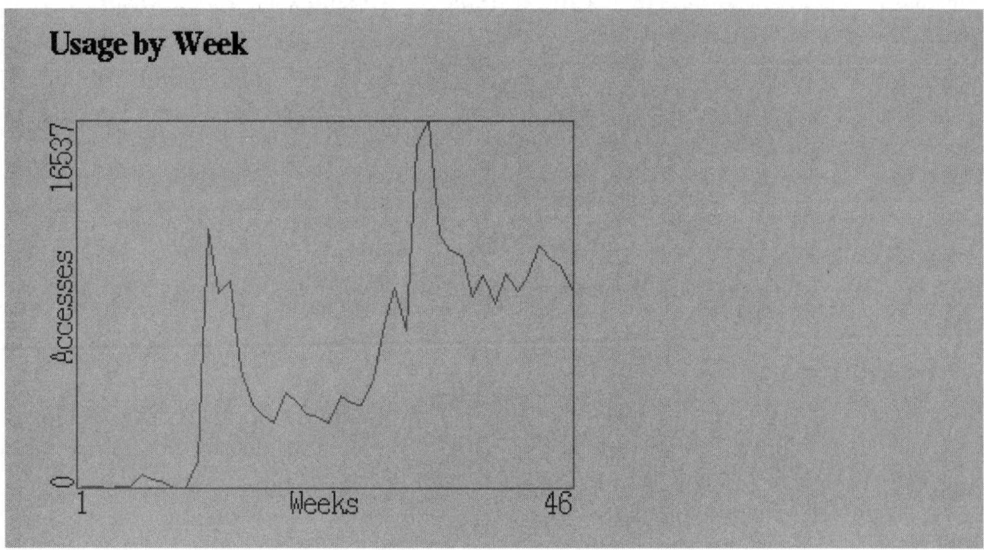

Figure 18-2. A usage graph generated by wusage

You should be aware that adding new types may also require users to add support on their end. On the client side, Web browsers that are HTTP V1.0-compliant know how to use the MIME type that comes back from the Web server. They use the *.mailcap* configuration file to decide which external players and viewers to invoke for each incoming data type.

In typical use, if a user retrieves a file that ends with the *.ps* file extension, the Web server passes the file back to the Web browser and tells the Web browser using MIME that it is a PostScript file. The Web browser caches the PostScript file to a local temporary directory, then looks up the PostScript viewer command from the *.mailcap* file. It then invokes the PostScript viewer and hands the viewer the local copy of the PostScript file. This same technique is used with motion picture files, audio files, and some types of images.

On the server side, the Web server knows how to map file types and file extensions to standard MIME data types. This is controlled in the *mime.types* configuration file. This configuration file is very complete for most people. However, there are directives that you can add to the *srm.conf* configuration file to add special MIME extensions to your Web server:

`AddType`
: Allows you to override MIME-type definitions found in the *mime.types* configuration file

`AddEncoding`
: Adds unique MIME encoding directives for the client/server handshake

`DefaultType`
: Used to establish a default MIME-type to be returned to the Web browser

Full definitions of these directives can be found in Appendix F, *Web: srm.conf Directives.*

A good example of the use of the `AddType` directives is to extend *httpd*'s ability to identify HTML documents. *httpd* determines that a file contains HTML by checking to see if it meets one of these two conditions:

- The first line of the file contains an <HTML> tag
- The filename ends with a *.html* file extension

The *.html* file extension is used because the default *mime.types* configuration file identifies:

```
text/html html
```

If you were serving HTML documents that had been authored on an MS-DOS personal computer, they would typically end with a *.htm* file extension, due to the 8.3 filename size restriction. You can tell *httpd* that all files ending with a *.htm* file extension should be typed as HTML by adding another MIME type definition:

```
AddType text/html htm
```

You can also use MIME type information to extend the list of document types that Web browsers know how to process. For example, by adding MIME type information for WordPerfect documents, you could serve WordPerfect documents (in their proprietary format) off your Web server and configure Windows-based Web browsers to invoke WordPerfect when WordPerfect documents are retrieved via URL.

18.3.2 Enabling Server-Side Includes

Server-side includes are similar to include files in any programming language; however, they can include not only files, but also the values of environment variables. They are an easy way to consistently include dates, document size, author names, or any HTML in a number of HTML documents. For an example of a server-side include, and to see how it is used in HTML, see Section 19.1.10. See Section 21.2.5 for more information about the security implications of server-side includes.

Server-side includes are not enabled by default in the NCSA *httpd* server. Server-side includes can be enabled server-wide or on a per-directory basis by specifying the `Includes` or `IncludesNoExec` clause on the `Options` directive in *access.conf* or *.htaccess* (see Chapter 21, *Web: Access Control and Security*, for more on these files):

```
Options IncludesNoExec
```

The `IncludesNoExec` option is more secure than Includes (for reasons described in Section 21.2.5).

You also need to specify which files get the includes inserted. How you do that depends on how many files you want processed. If you plan to use server-side includes in almost every file, add a single directive to the *srm.conf* configuration file:

```
AddType text/x-server-parsed-html .html
```

Using server-side includes does take CPU cycles and you might not want to do that on every file. If you plan to use server-side includes sparingly, you should (instead of the above) define a new file extension to identify the files that need processing. Modify the *srm.conf* configuration file to add:

```
AddType text/html shtml
AddType text/x-server-parsed-html .shtml
```

The convention is to use *.shtml* as the file extension for files that need server-side include processing. The first directive tells *httpd* that files with the *.shtml* extension are to be treated as HTML documents. The second directive tells *httpd* that only files that have the *.shtml* file extension are processed for possible server-side includes. You'll have to remember which files are *.shtml* files instead of *.html* files when creating links to these files.

18.3.3 Automatic Directory Indexing

When a URL points to a directory instead of a file, the Web server first tries to return the file *index.html* in the specified directory.* If *index.html* doesn't exist, then the Web server can automatically generate HTML text describing the contents of the directory. This is called automatic directory indexing. Figure 18-3 shows an automatically generated directory index displayed with Mosaic.

You can enable or disable automatic directory indexing in the global ACF (*access.conf*) (or the per-directory ACFs) using the `Options` directive. By default, it is enabled server-wide. When it is disabled for a directory, and there is no *index.html* in that directory, the Web server returns an error whenever a user tries to use that URL.

There are two types of automatically generated directory index, plain or fancy. The type that's used can be controlled on a server-wide or per-directory basis in *srm.conf*. The initial *srm.conf* configuration file has `FancyIndexing` enabled server-wide.

With plain indexing, the filenames are listed in a single column, similar to the *ls -1* (that's the number one, not lowercase L) shell command. The user can click on the filename to retrieve the file.

With fancy indexing, an associated icon, the file size, and an optional file type description are displayed next to each filename.

You can control the icon associated with each file type. For example, sound files (identified by their MIME type of audio/) by default have a sound icon. You probably wouldn't want to change it, but you could define a different sound icon, or an icon for some type that has no default icon.

When an icon is associated with a filename, a reference to that icon is included as an inline graphic in the HTML that the Web server automatically generates. The icons are

* Or the filename identified by the *DirectoryIndex* directive in the *srm.conf* configuration file.

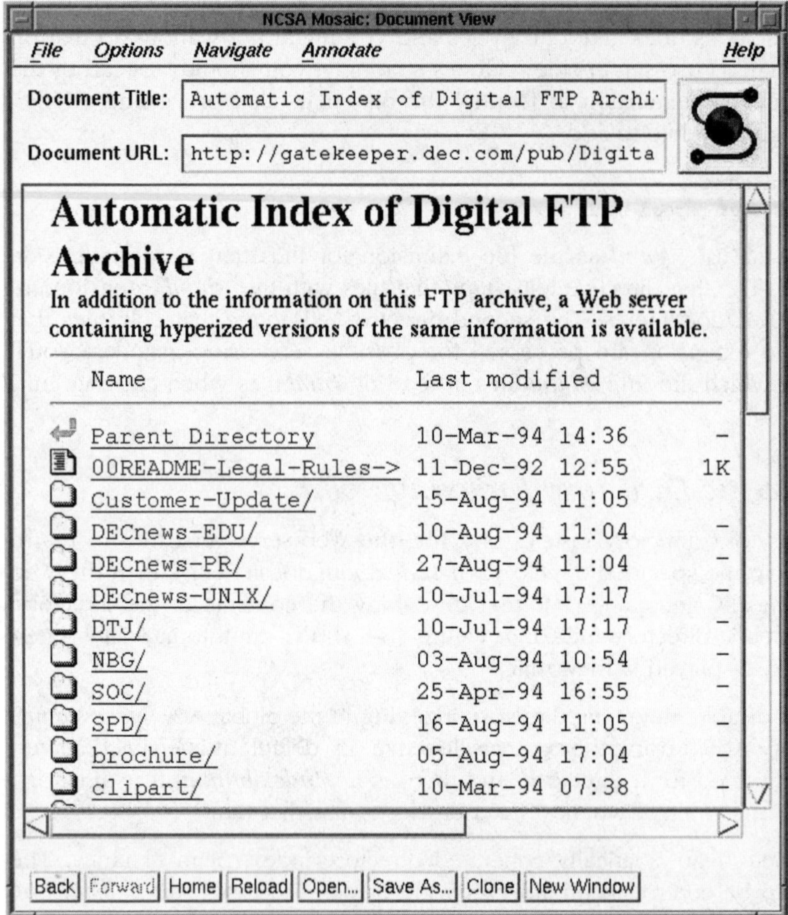

Figure 18-3. Mosaic screen shot of an automatic directory index

neither part of nor embedded in Web browsers. Instead, they are just like any other image that you can serve from your Web server.

The optional file type description of fancy directory indexing is useful in non-graphical Web browsers.

Fancy indexing also allows you to control header and trailer information displayed before and after a directory index. The header information, by default the *HEADER* file, is displayed prior to the actual directory index. The trailer information, by default the *README* file, is displayed after the directory index. This header and trailer information can be plain text or HTML. You can also tell the Web server (using the `IndexIgnore` directive) to ignore certain filenames when generating an automatic directory index. By default *HEADER* and *README* are ignored, so they don't appear in automatic directory listings.

Automatic directory indexing is useful if your Web document tree is the same as your FTP archive directory hierarchy. Web browsers can navigate the directory hierarchy of your FTP archive and retrieve files by *ftp*. With fancy indexing turned on, you can visually enrich the information on your FTP archive even though there are no HTML documents contained in that FTP archive. But this enrichment only works when the FTP archive is viewed through your Web server—not if a Web client uses FTP to go directly to the FTP archive.

Automatic directory indexing is controlled with directives in the *srm.conf* configuration file. Here's a quick summary of the relevant directives:

`AddIconType`
: Defines which icons are associated with documents according to MIME-type mapping

`AddIcon`
: Defines which icons are associated with documents according to file types and names

`DefaultIcon`
: Defines which icon to use when no icon can be automatically associated with a given file

`AddDescription`
: Defines the descriptive phrase associated with a particular type of file

`IndexOptions`
: Defines whether icons are treated as hyperlinks, whether HTML documents are scanned for document titles to be used as descriptive text phrases, and the degree to which file characteristics are suppressed

For a reference to each *srm.conf* directive, see Appendix F, *Web: srm.conf Directives.*

The defaults for automatic directory indexing are:

```
AddIconByType (TXT,/icons/text.xbm) text/*
AddIconByType (IMG,/icons/image.xbm) image/*
AddIconByType (SND,/icons/sound.xbm) audio/*
AddIcon /icons/movie.xbm .mpg .qt
AddIcon /icons/binary.xbm .bin
AddIcon /icons/back.xbm ..
AddIcon /icons/menu.xbm ^^DIRECTORY^^
AddIcon /icons/blank.xbm ^^BLANKICON^^
DefaultIcon /icons/unknown.xbm
ReadmeName README
HeaderName HEADER
IndexIgnore */.??* *~ *# */HEADER* */README*
```

The `AddIcon` line that uses `^^DIRECTORY^^` defines the icon used to indicate directories in a directory listing. The `^^BLANKICON^^` icon is used just to fill in space in the directory listing output, so that everything else lines up like a table when the browser processes the HTML.

18.4 Installation Summary

At this point you have a working Web server online. You have pulled the NCSA Web server kit, configured it for your site, moved it into place, started it up, and tested it. You have a home page and, with enough content to justify it, have announced it to the online Web community. People are accessing it, and you are generating logs and analyzing the log files to determine usage and trends.

Congratulations—you are now a *webmaster*!

In this Chapter:
- *HTML Overview*
- *Information Design Issues*
- *HTML Authoring Tools*
- *Clickable Image Maps*

Authoring for the Web

Anyone can create documents for the Web. You don't need to know anything about server administration. It is common for the people developing, or authoring, Web documents to be different from the person installing and running the Web server.

Web documents are written in HTML, the HyperText Markup Language. Most Web browsers can read HTML directly from a file, without the involvement of a server. That means that you can write your HTML and test it without making the document available to the public during the development and without setting up a separate server.

This chapter describes the HTML language, including how to create links to other documents and services. Near the end of the chapter, we describe some of the tools available to make HTML authoring easier. This chapter also describes how to create clickable image maps, which allow you to create links from certain areas in an image instead of from certain words in a document.

19.1 HTML Overview

An HTML document is an ASCII text file that contains embedded HTML tags. On a UNIX server, it typically has a filename extension of *.html*. In general, the HTML tags are used to identify the structure of the document and to identify hyperlinks (to be highlighted) and their associated URLs.

HTML identifies the structure of the document and it suggests the layout of the document. The display capabilities of the Web browser determine the appearance of the HTML document on the screeen.

Using HTML you can identify:

- The title of the document
- The hierarchical structure of the document with header levels and section names
- Bulleted, numbered, and nested lists

- Insertion points for graphics
- Special emphasis for key words or phrases
- Preformatted areas of the document
- Hyperlinks and associated URLs

HTML cannot control the:

- Typeface used for any document component
- Point size of any specific font
- Width or height of the screen
- Centering, spacing, or line breaks of information, except in preformatted text
- Background, foreground, or highlight colors

These things all depend on the browser, which may allow the user to control them.

19.1.1 Autoflowing and Autowrapping

The most basic element in the HTML document is the paragraph. The Web browser flows all the contents of the paragraph together from left to right and from top to bottom given the current window or display size. This is called *autoflowing*. How you break lines in that paragraph in the HTML is irrelevant when that page is displayed by a Web browser.

The Web browser wraps anything that doesn't fit on the current line, putting it on the next line. For example, a paragraph that displays six lines long on an 8-inch wide window rewraps to be about 12 lines long if the user resizes the Web browser window to be half as wide. This is called **autowrapping**.

Your document will be read by both graphical and character-based Web browsers. Furthermore, there will be display differences with graphical Web browsers given different screen resolutions. So just because one browser breaks a line at one place, that doesn't mean others will do so at the same place. Just remember that on the Web, you live in a world that is left-justified and flows from top to bottom.

19.1.2 HTML Tag Syntax

HTML tags are encapsulated within less-than (<) and greater-than (>) brackets. Some of the tags are single-element tags that can stand by themselves. These are referred to as standalone tags. The syntax is simple:

```
<tag>
```

The most common standalone tag is <P>, which ends a paragraph.

Other tags are used in pairs. The beginning tag tells the Web browser to start the tag function and the ending tag tells the Web browser to stop. The ending tag is created by adding a forward slash (/) to the beginning tag. The syntax is:

```
<tag>object</tag>
```

The tag identifies the function that is being applied to the object. For example, if you wanted to add special emphasis to a phrase, you would encapsulate the phrase with the <EM> tagging pair as illustrated:

```
<EM>text to emphasize</EM>
```

Many of the standalone tags and the beginning tag of tagging pairs can have options included. So to be complete the syntax is:

```
<tag option1 option2 option3>
```

A mistake you will make when manually authoring HTML with a text editor is to forget the ending tag or leave out the slash (/) in the ending tag. Don't worry—it will be obvious when this happens, and it's simple to correct.

19.1.3 Document Construction Guidelines

Now let's look at the three tagging pairs used to create the highest level of structure in an HTML document:

```
<HTML> entire HTML document </HTML>
<HEAD> document header information </HEAD>
<BODY> body of the HTML document </BODY>
```

The following is a skeletal HTML document that shows the required nesting of these three tagging pairs:

```
<HTML>
        <HEAD>
                Head elements
        </HEAD>
        <BODY>
                Body elements and content
        </BODY>
</HTML>
```

Remember that physical layout in an HTML document, like indentation and line breaks, is meaningless to Web browsers. So you can format your HTML according to your own preferences.

19.1.4 Sample HTML Document

The following is an example of the HTML template that I keep in my home directory. I pull it into a text editor as a starting point for creating a new HTML document.

Although you could have a slightly more bare-bones HTML template, it's easier to delete than add. Here is the sample HTML document:

```
<HTML>
<HEAD>
<TITLE>Sample HTML Document</TITLE>
<LINK REV="OWNER" HREF="mailto:rjones@ix.netcom.com">
</HEAD>
<BODY>
<IMG SRC="my-logo.gif" ALT="logo">
<H1>Sample HTML Document</H1>
<EM>To demonstrate HTML style</EM>
<P>
<HR>
<P>
Hello World.
<P>
<HR>
<P>
Creation Date: <EM>Sat Apr 9, 1994</EM>
<P>
<ADDRESS><A HREF="rjones.html">DRJ</A></ADDRESS>
</BODY>
</HTML>
```

Figure 19-1 shows how this sample HTML document looks when displayed with Mosaic.

Let's go through it and look at the new tags it uses:

`<TITLE>` *`text-phrase`* `</TITLE>`

: The <TITLE> tag pair is used once per document and identifies the document title. It should appear at the top of the document within the <HEAD> section. Many Web browsers display the document title in a special area. This is also the document name that is used when a user adds the document to her hotlist or list of bookmarks for later reference. Although not absolutely required, it is a good idea to have a document title in each HTML document.

`<LINK REV="OWNER" HREF="`*`internet-address`*`">`

: The <LINK> standalone tag is used in a special way here to identify the email address of the document owner. This information is not displayed by a Web browser, but is used by some browsers when sending an email message on behalf of the user to the document owner. Other uses of the LINK tag will be described later.

`<IMG SRC="`*`URL`*`">`

: The <IMG> standalone HTML tag inserts an image into the current autoflow stream. Note that you specify the image with its URL. See Section 19.1.7 for more on URLs, and Section 19.1.9 for more on image insertion.

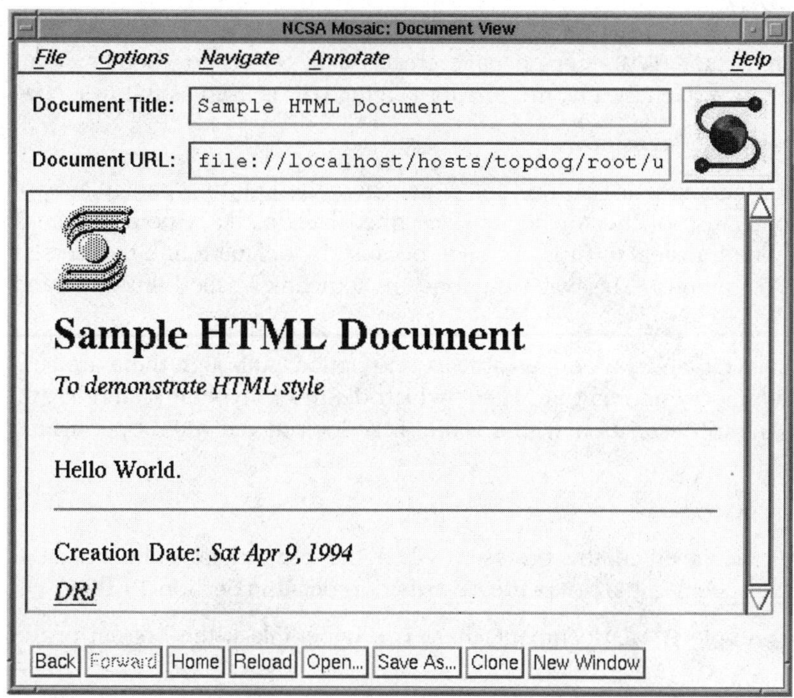

Figure 19-1. Sample HTML document display by Mosaic

<H1>*text-phrase*</H1>
: The <H1> header-level tag pair indicates a level of structure in your document. There are six levels of headers, H1 through H6. Headers, like paragraphs, autowrap if the phrase cannot fit on a single line. Header tags also force paragraph breaks before and after the header.

<EM>*text*</EM>
: The <EM> tagging pair marks a phrase to be rendered with generic emphasis. On a graphical display, the phrase could be italicized, while on a character-mode display it might be underlined.

<P>
: The <P> tag ends a paragraph and places a blank line after the paragraph on the display. Two paragraph break tags result in a single blank line.

<HR>
: The <HR> (horizontal rule) tag forces the Browser to generate a horizontal rule, or line, across the display. It breaks pages into logical sections and is useful when creating forms. There is no equivalent vertical rule.

<ADDRESS>*text*</ADDRESS>
: The <ADDRESS> tagging pair is used to identify addresses. Depending on the Web browser, the text is rendered in a special point size, typeface, or font.

19.1.5 Hyperlinks

One of the most important HTML tagging pairs creates a hyperlink to another document or Internet resource. Generically, the Anchor tagging pair is used as follows:

```
<A option1 optionN>anchor-text</A>
```

It's called an Anchor tagging pair because this tag anchors the link to a particular spot in your HTML. Another use of the Anchor tag described later marks a point within a document where a link transfers to (it is optional, because by default a link transfers to the beginning of a document). The two variations are sometimes called **link-from** and **link-to** tags.

The beginning Anchor tag always requires at least one option. Although there are several options, the two most important are HREF, which defines a hyperlink, and NAME, which identifies a link-to destination within a file. Let's look at the HREF option first. Here's the syntax:

```
<A HREF="URL">anchor-text</A>
```

The *anchor-text* is displayed in the browser. When the user triggers the link, the browser retrieves the specified URL. URLs are described in detail in Section 19.1.7.

Going back to our sample HTML document, there is a hyperlink at the bottom of the document:

```
<A HREF="rjones.html">DRJ</A>
```

I use this hyperlink to sign each of my pages. My initials, DRJ, become the anchor text for a hyperlink to another HTML document called *rjones.html* in the same directory.

My signature hyperlink is actually enclosed within an <ADDRESS> tagging pair:

```
<ADDRESS><A HREF="rjones.html">DRJ</A></ADDRESS>
```

This demonstrates how hyperlinks can be embedded in other tagging constructs. Anywhere you have text within the body of the HTML document, you can create a hyperlink. The text could be in a paragraph, a header, a quote, or as part of an address. However, the reverse is not always true. You can put an anchor tagging pair inside a header, but you should not embed headers inside an anchor pair.

Instead of using text as the hyperlink anchor, you can use an image. This is done by enclosing the <IMG> tag with the anchor tagging pair:

```
<A HREF="org-overview.html"><IMG SRC="my-logo.gif"></A>
```

When the inline image is displayed, it becomes sensitive. If the user triggers it, the browser retrieves the document identified by the associated URL, in this case a file called *org-overview.html*.

19.1.6 Linking to Points Within Documents

By default, links point to the top of a document. You can also create hyperlinks that jump to other points in an HTML document. First, you must identify and name the link-to point. This is done with the NAME option of the Anchor tag.

```
<A NAME="anchor-name">anchor-text</A>
```

This tagging pair identifies a link-to point in the HTML document and names that point. The tagging pair provides an alternative entry point into an HTML document. The anchor-text cannot be omitted.

This link-to point is then referenced by using `#anchor-name`. For example, say you have a document with an appendix in the same file, and you want to link to the appendix. The header that starts the appendix should be turned into a link-to point. The HTML that indentifies the beginning of your appendix might look like:

```
<H2><A NAME="Appendix-A">Appendix A</A></H2>
```

You can then create hyperlinks to the appendix from within the same document like this:

```
Details are in <A HREF="#Appendix-A">Appendix A</A>.
```

You could also link directly to the appendix from an external document. From another HTML document you would reference it as:

```
<A HREF="URL#Appendix-A">Appendix A</A>
```

The URL can be a fully qualified URL or a relative URL.

If the syntax of the anchor is incorrect, most Web browsers are forgiving and display the anchor-text or inserted image, but not make it sensitive as a hyperlink. This can be done intentionally to temporarily disable links without removing all the HTML that defines the link.

19.1.7 URLs

A URL points to a file or directory.* There are three distinct types of URLs: absolute, relative, and local. There are also a couple of special-case URLs supported by some browsers.

Absolute URLs completely describe how to get a file on the Internet. Relative URLs and local URLs are both ways to specify a file on the same server as the document they appear in. The following sections describe each type of URL in more detail.

---

* The file may be a script or a program, rather than a document. That's described in Chapter 20, *Web: Gateways and Forms*.

19.1.7.1 Absolute URLs

Absolute URLs can be used to reference any resource on the Internet, including local resources. However, it's better to use relative URLs for local resources for reasons described in the next section. The full syntax for an absolute URL is:

```
access-method://server-name[:port]/directory/file
```

If no port is specified, the default port associated with the given access method is used. The URL of a document that is on a Web server has an access method of *http:*. For example, the master list of all public World Wide Web servers throughout the world can be accessed using the following URL:

```
http://info.cern.ch/hypertext/DataSources/WWW/Geographical.html
```

This means that by using the HTTP protocol to reach a server called *info.cern.ch* (using the default port), there is a directory */hypertext/DataSources/WWW* that contains a hypertext document named *Geographical.html*. Every file on the Internet is uniquely addressable by its URL, regardless of the type of file or the type of server it is provided by.

Besides the *http:* access method, the URL concept also supports other important Internet protocol access methods such as Gopher, FTP, and Telnet.

The URL to access a file on a Gopher server follows the standard remote URL specification. Here's the URL to the campus Gopher server at the University of Minnesota:

```
gopher://gopher.micro.umn.edu/
```

To look at the FTP archive run by O'Reilly & Associates, you could open the following URL:

```
ftp://ftp.ora.com/pub/
```

You might sometimes see references to both the *ftp:* and the *file:* access methods. The *ftp:* nomenclature has replaced the earlier *file:* nomenclature, as it more accurately reflects the protocol being used. When using the *ftp:* access method to reference the contents of a directory you should make sure you close the URL with a trailing slash (/). When referencing a file in a directory, this is not necessary.

The URL to a Telnet resource is no surprise:

```
telnet://info.cern.ch/
```

When any URL appears in one of your documents, the Web browser uses the URL to go directly to that resource; it doesn't go through your Web server. That means that users who cannot *telnet* directly to a host from the shell command line (because they are blocked by a security firewall or because they do not have the password) will not be able to access the host via a Web browser either, even if you can access it from the machine where your HTML resides.

If any server is running on an unusual port, you need to include the port number as part of the URL. The standard ports are:

Port	Service
21	FTP
23	Telnet
70	Gopher
80	HTTP

The following URL shows how to specify a Gopher server running on port 1250:

```
gopher://garnet.berkeley.edu:1250/
```

Many sites around the Web have created public-access gateways to other common Internet services. The URLs for these gateways are based on file URLs, but can have various special syntaxes. Section 20.3 describes several WAIS gateways.

19.1.7.2 Absolute versus relative URLs

A relative URL assumes the same access-method, server-name, and directory-path as the document the URL appears in. It indicates the relative position of the target URL from the current URL. For example, here's a URL to a file in the same directory as the document the URL appears in.

```
<A HREF="page-7.html">Next Page</A>
```

Relative URLs are also sometimes called partial URLs. They are used to point to information resources in the same directory or on the same server. Absolute URLs, on the other hand, are usually used to point to information resources on other servers. In practical terms, this means that you can use relative URLs to direct navigation between documents that you author and use absolute URLs to direct navigation to resources elsewhere on the Internet.

The distinction between absolute and relative URLs is totally hidden from the Web server. When a user selects a relative hyperlink, the Web browser uses the current URL to determine the access-method, server-name, port-number, and directory-path, and sends only absolute URLs to the server.

Relative URLs allow you to author your HTML with total disregard for where your final HTML directory structure will be placed on the Web server or even what system the server will run on. You can direct the relative navigation between HTML documents using the same directory path navigation constructs that you use on UNIX to move up and down a directory tree. For example, to have a hyperlink that jumps up two levels in the directory structure to your home page, the following HTML could be used:

```
<A HREF="../../home.html">Return To Home Page</A>
```

Relative URLs also give you the flexibility to move your HTML directory structure anywhere on the Web. Your administrator may want another site to have a local copy of your HTML directory structure for various reasons.

Relative URLs also work when files are read directly from the file system by a Web browser, without the intervention of a Web server. This is very useful for Web authoring.

Don't use symbolic links in your document tree, because they defeat the purpose of relative URLs, and make the document tree unportable. If you are tempted to use a symbolic link, use the Alias directive in *srm.conf* instead. (This is described in more detail in Section 18.2.3.)

A relative URL can be relative to the document root instead of the directory of the current document. This kind of relative URL starts with a slash. In other words, it looks like an absolute URL, but without the access method and server name.

19.1.7.3 Oddball URLs

There are a couple of other URLs supported by certain browsers. They access articles from the local news server or send an email message to a document's owner.

For example, to read the *comp.infosystems.www.providers* newsgroup with your Web browser instead of a news reader, you would open the following URL:

```
news:comp.infosystems.www.providers
```

Some Web browsers, such as Lynx, support sending email back to the owner of a page. To identify ownership of a page, you can use the following local URL, as shown in the sample HTML document in Section 19.1.4:

```
mailto:internet-address
```

However, `mailto:` is not widely supported yet.

19.1.8 Lists

Another key HTML construct is the list. There are three types of lists:

- Unordered (bulleted) List: <UL>list</UL>
- Ordered (numbered) List: <OL>list</OL>
- Definition List: <DL>list</DL>

In the first two types of lists, the elements of the list are designated with the <LI> list-item tag. For example, a simple bulleted list with three items would be tagged like this:

```
<UL>
<LI>First bullet
<LI>Second bullet
```

```
<LI>Third bullet
</UL>
```

As you might expect, if a list-item phrase is wider than the display width, the Web browser autowraps the phrase and aligns the next line to indent under the previous line. Lists can also be nested:

```
<UL><LI>First bullet
        <UL><LI>First sub-bullet
        <LI>Second sub-bullet
        <LI>Third sub-bullet</UL>
<LI>Second bullet
<LI>Third bullet</UL>
```

Figure 19-2 shows how these nested lists would be rendered by Mosaic.

- First bullet
    - First sub-bullet
    - Second sub-bullet
    - Third sub-bullet
- Second bullet
- Third bullet

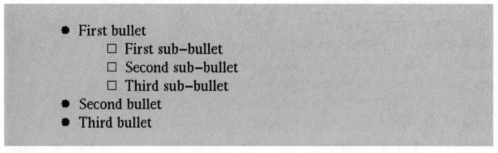

Figure 19-2. Nested bullet list rendered with Mosaic

The third type of list, the definition list, is used when the list items do not need to be bulleted or numbered and can stand on their own. A good example might be a glossary, which lists terms and their definitions. Definitions do not use the <LI> tag to mark a new list entry. Instead they use the <DT> and <DD> tagging pairs. The <DT> tagging pair identifies the primary text and the <DD> tagging pair identifies the text associated with and indented below the <DT> tagging phrase.

For example, a definition list of three publications looks like:

```
<DL>
<DT>Action Plan for African Primate Conservation</DT>
<DD>Compiled by J.F. Oates and the IUCN/SSC Primate Specialist Group,
1986, 41 pp.</DD><P>
<DT>Dolphins, Porpoises and Whales. An Action Plan for the
Conservation of Biological Diversity</DT>
<DD>Second Edition. Compiled by W.F. Perrin and the IUCN/SSC
Cetacean Specialist Group, 1989, 27 pp.</DD><P>
<DT>Otters. An Action Plan for their Conservation</DT>
<DD>Compiled by P. Foster-Turley, S. Macdonald, C. Mason and the
IUCN/SSC Otter Specialist Group, 1990, 126 pp.</DD>
</DL>
```

Figure 19-3 shows how this definition list would be rendered by Mosaic.

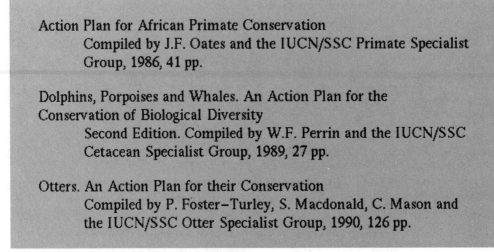

Action Plan for African Primate Conservation
: Compiled by J.F. Oates and the IUCN/SSC Primate Specialist Group, 1986, 41 pp.

Dolphins, Porpoises and Whales. An Action Plan for the Conservation of Biological Diversity
: Second Edition. Compiled by W.F. Perrin and the IUCN/SSC Cetacean Specialist Group, 1989, 27 pp.

Otters. An Action Plan for their Conservation
: Compiled by P. Foster-Turley, S. Macdonald, C. Mason and the IUCN/SSC Otter Specialist Group, 1990, 126 pp.

Figure 19-3. Definition list rendered with Mosaic

19.1.9 Graphics

Graphics were briefly mentioned earlier when the <IMG> HTML tag was introduced. Fundamentally, there are two different ways to present graphics—inline images and external images. Inline images are displayed by the Web browser as part of your document and are automatically retrieved along with the document. External images are displayed by a separate viewer program (started by the Web browser when needed) and must be specifically requested by triggering a hyperlink.

Inline graphics involve the transfer of a lot of data and so retrieving them can be slow. Fortunately, many Web browsers let users optionally delay downloading of the inline images. With delayed downloading, inline images must be triggered by a hyperlink before they will be downloaded. When triggered, they still appear inline, not in an external viewer.

When contemplating the use of graphics within your HTML, you should consider the user community that will be accessing your Web server. Will they be using graphics-capable Web browsers, such as Mosaic, or will they be using line-oriented Web browsers, such as Lynx? The decision is easier if one class of Web browser dominates, but is more complicated if you expect people with both types of browsers to be using your Web server.

19.1.9.1 Inline images

The inline image is just one more piece of information that is included in the autoflow and autowrap of your HTML on the Web browser screen. In other words, an image is treated just like a word. So an image can appear in the middle of a paragraph. If you want the inline image to stand alone you need to make sure you place <P> or
 HTML tags around it in your HTML document.

For inline images, the two supported graphics types are the Graphics Image Format (GIF) and the X Bitmap (XBM) format. GIF images support 256 colors and are the more common of the two image types. X Bitmaps are black and white.

When inline images are autoflowing as part of a paragraph, you can explicitly control the alignment of the image with the text line by using the optional ALIGN option of the <IMG> tag. The three values for ALIGN are:

```
<IMG ALIGN=TOP SRC="filename.GIF">

<IMG ALIGN=MIDDLE SRC="filename.GIF">

<IMG ALIGN=BOTTOM SRC="filename.GIF">
```

TOP alignment places the top of the image even with the top of the current line of text, and so on. If ALIGN is omitted, bottom alignment is the default.

In terms of image placement and autoflow, both image formats normally provide square outlines. It is possible to develop images in either format that have translucent (or clear) backgrounds to eliminate the square outline. With a translucent image background, the background color of the main window display can show through the translucent areas of the image. You see this technique used particularly with cursive signatures at the bottom of HTML documents, or to make a circular university seal appear circular, instead of circular in a square image. Here's the URL of a document that explains how to do translucent backgrounds:

```
http://melmac.corp.harris.com/transparent_images.html
```

In browsers running on color graphics systems, your images might be sharing the color map with other applications. Mosaic, in particular, only allocates a colormap table with 50 entries. If an inline image has more colors than can be displayed, it still is displayed with the available colors, but it won't look as good as the full-color image. With these colormap issues in mind, you should probably reduce the number of colors used in your GIF files to under 50. If you are going to include multiple GIF images in a single HTML document, you should use the *ppmquantall* utility from the pbmplus package to force all of the images to share a common colormap.* These colormap issues also influence whether you enrich your HTML documents with photographs

* The pbmplus package and its utilities are described in the books *UNIX Power Tools* (O'Reilly & Associates/Bantam Books) and *Encyclopedia of Graphics File Formats* (O'Reilly & Associates, Inc.).

(which require many colors) or with clip-art, which has a more well-defined and limited color palette.

Also think about performance. It takes a lot longer for a Web browser to retrieve an HTML document that has inline images than to retrieve one that does not (unless the user specifies delayed downloading). The larger the inline image, the longer it takes. In fact, the time is proportional to the square of the dimension (a four-inch-square image takes almost twice as long as a three-inch-square one). One thing working in your favor is that many graphically-based Web browsers cache inline images. So if the inline image has been used in previous HTML documents in the user's navigation chain, that image might still be cached. Caching also happens when the same inline image appears multiple times in the same HTML document. It is retrieved only once.

One trick that's used to solve the performance problem of big images is to use "thumbnails". A **thumbnail** is a small version of a figure displayed inline, which is a link to the full-sized image displayed externally. With image manipulation tools such as the pbmplus utilities, it is easy to create a smaller version of an image. The HTML to do this looks like:

```
<A HREF="file-full.gif"><IMG SRC="file-thumb.gif"></A>
```

This HTML uses the syntax for external images, which we'll describe in the next section.

Don't let these issues discourage you from enriching your HTML document with graphics. Use of graphics can add meaning and clarity to the information in your HTML document and can increase the overall usability of the information. You will also see in Section 19.4 that specific areas in inline graphics can become link anchors (clicking on different parts of an image can trigger different links).

19.1.9.2 External images

External images are images that are not displayed inline as part of your document, but in a separate window, by an external viewer program. This is the technique to use if you have TIFF, JPEG, RGB, or HDF images and don't want to convert them to GIF. This technique is also useful for displaying very large GIF images. Instead of using the <IMG> HTML tag described earlier, you simply include the URL of your external image file as part of the hyperlink. For example, to display a JPEG image in an external window, you can include the following in your HTML document:

```
<A HREF="filename.jpg">anchor-text</A>
```

The *filename*.jpeg in this example can be replaced by any URL; it doesn't have to be a local file. See Section 18.3.1 to better understand the handshake between Web server and browser that makes this work. Suffice it to say for now that the user needs an external viewer installed that knows how to deal with the incoming external image file and the Web browser needs to know how to recognize the type of data that's arriving and how to start the appropriate viewer.

Using external images with your HTML document further limits the usability of your HTML document. Just as there are users who can't display inline graphics, there are more who have not configured their environment to support the display of external images.

19.1.9.3 Inline images with character-based Web browsers

Inline images can't be displayed on character-based terminals. Character-based Web browsers indicate that an image is in the autoflow stream by displaying:

```
[IMAGE]
```

However, you can override this default and make your inline images more meaningful in character-based Web browsers by using the ALT option:

```
<IMG SRC="filename.GIF" ALT="image-description">
```

The ALT option makes character-based Web browsers display the image-description instead of [IMAGE]. You can also make the browser ignore an image using a null ALT option:

```
<IMG SRC="filename.GIF" ALT="">
```

When a character-based Web browser sees the null ALT option, it ignores the image-insertion tag. The HTML authoring convention is that if you are going to insert inline images in your document, you should at least describe the image with a word or phrase for users with character-based Web browsers.

19.1.10 Server-Side Includes

The NCSA Web server can include information from files and environment variables into an HTML file just before the file is sent to the user. It also can automatically include the last-modified date, current date, document size, and a few other useful pieces of information. This capability is collectively called **server-side includes**.

Let's look at a quick example. We modify the bottom of our sample HTML template to look like:

```
Creation Date: <EM><!--#echo var="LAST_MODIFIED"--></EM>
<P>
<!--#include file="owner.txt"-->
</BODY>
</HTML>
```

We also create a file called *owner.txt*, which contains a single line:

```
<ADDRESS><A HREF="rjones.html">DRJ</A></ADDRESS>
```

Now all our HTML documents that are based on the sample HTML template will automatically have their last modification date (from the filesystem) and the owner of the file included by the Web server whenever a user requests that file. This guarantees that the document's modification date is correct—no need to enter it manually. It also gives us the ability to change the owner of every HTML document with a simple edit to *owner.txt*.

Depending on how your Web server is set up, you may have to rename the HTML files that you want processed for server-side includes (usually to use the suffix *.shtml*). Ask your Web server administrator or read Section 18.3.2. It's also possible that the server-side includes feature might not be set up. Or it might have been disabled for security reasons (see Section 21.2.5).

You might have noticed that the ASCII text file *owner.txt* actually contains HTML. *owner.txt* is not called *owner.html*, because it doesn't contain fully structured, legal HTML and because it isn't intended for standalone viewing. (You may want to tell the Web server to ignore included files like *owner.txt* when it does automatic directory indexing, since included files are not intended to be viewed alone. See Section 18.3.3.)

Generically, the format of the include statement is usually:

```
<!--#command tag="value"-->
```

The two commands demonstrated in the HTML above were `#echo` and `#include`. Two others are `#fsize` and `#flastmod`, which include a file's size and last-modified date. The `file=` tag of the `#include` command is used to reference a document in the same physical directory as the HTML document (or a directory relative to that directory). The `var=` tag of the `#echo` command reads and displays the value of an environment variable, which can include any of those defined by the CGI (described in Section 20.1.1), plus the six listed below.

Another `#include` tag (not shown) is `virtual=`, which specifies a file relative to the document root. You would use the `virtual=` tag instead of the `file=` tag if you wanted to have standard boilerplate such as a copyright notice used with every document on your Web server, independent of the document tree structure.

All the tags valid with `#include` are also valid with `#fsize` and `#flastmod`.

The six environment variables (not counting all the CGI variables) you can use with `#echo` are the last modification date (`LAST_MODIFIED`), and:

`DOCUMENT_NAME`
: The current filename

`DOCUMENT_URI`
: The virtual path to this document

`DATE_LOCAL`
: The current date and local time

`DATE_GMT`
: Same as `DATE_LOCAL` but in Greenwich mean time

`QUERY_STRING_UNESCAPED`
: The search query the client sent, if any

There are two more commands not covered here: `#exec`, which runs a script and includes its output, and `#config`, which controls the format of the size and date commands. For complete information, see the URL:

```
http://hoohoo.ncsa.uiuc.edu/docs/tutorials/includes.html
```

19.1.11 For More Information About HTML

How to write forms in HTML (and handle the input that comes from them) is described in Section 20.2.

Appendix A, *gopherd Options*, describes all the tags and options we haven't discussed in this chapter, but doesn't provide any examples.

Not surprisingly, the definitive guide to HTML, *A Beginner's Guide to HTML,* is available on the Web. Point your Web browser at URL:

```
http://www.ncsa.uiuc.edu/General/Internet/WWW/HTMLPrimer.html
```

You should take a look at this document, because it describes all the other HTML tags that are available. It also describes some additional options to the HTML tags that we have outlined here.

Remember also that many Web browsers give you the ability to view the HTML source of the document being displayed, or even to store it locally on your own system. If you see a neat trick that someone else has done with their HTML, just look at the HTML source to see how they did it. In graphical Web browsers, you can also cut and paste from the HTML of existing documents to avoid retyping the tags.

19.2 Information Design Issues

Now that you understand the basics of HTML, you should look at some other issues involved in structuring HTML. This includes how you chop up big documents, how many links you include, how you make those links, and overall style conventions.

19.2.1 Document Modularity

For every document you intend to place on your Web server, you need to think through an assortment of document modularity issues. Should you take documents as they are and convert them directly to HTML? Well, that depends on the length of your documents—three pages (sure), nine pages (maybe), eighteen pages (probably not). Long documents can be slow to download, especially if they include inline graphics.

Do you envision a document broken into a logical hierarchy? Five levels of hierarchy inside your original document does not necessarily have to be broken into five levels of modules with hyperlinks between them. Keep in mind that every time you ask the user to activate a hyperlink, a certain percentage of them will not do it. It is another thing to click on, another couple of seconds to wait (or longer depending on the bandwidth between your Web server and their Web browser), and there is always the slight possibility that the connection won't go through.

On the other hand, if your document is logically structured into major chapters, it is certainly reasonable to break it into multiple HTML documents (one per chapter or one per major section). If you have sidebars, they too might be broken out from the main flow of the chapters.

You should ask yourself if each HTML document can stand alone or if it is a dangling document that depends on another document for context. Remember that any document on your server might be the first one from your server to be seen. As soon as you place an HTML document on the Web, its URL is available for others to embed in their hyperlinks. On the other hand, people who reference your documents in their HTML have some responsibility for not creating hyperlinks to any dangling documents that might remain.

Many people use a compromise between the single document and multiple document approaches. They have a single HTML document, but provide a table of contents at the start of the document that hyperlinks to other anchors further into the same document. This gives you the best of both worlds. Users can quickly hyperlink to sections if they know what they are looking for or can casually browse the document as a whole. This also establishes alternative entry points into your HTML document, which could be valuable to others who want to reference specific information in your document, but do not want their users to have to wade through the full document.

19.2.2 Degrees of Hyperization

How much time and effort do you direct towards tagging and hyperlinking HTML documents?

On the one hand, you don't have to spend any time at all. You can place ASCII text documents directly on your HTTP directory structure and Web browsers can directly display them. But you lose many of the benefits of the World Wide Web—no autowrapping and autoflowing, no inline graphics, and no hyperlinking to other relevant documents. If you have 2000 ASCII text documents that are preformatted with lots of tables, though, this might not be a bad way to start. At least users can get to your information. It also helps to learn *sed* and/or *awk* to automate the tagging of large numbers of documents.

At the other end of the scale, there is full HTML authoring. Each document is painstakingly crafted with hyperlinks, content is embellished with diagrams and pictures, audio is added where it makes sense, key points of emphasis are highlighted. The reader can more easily grasp the information content and meaning when this is done with care. But it takes time and effort. This level of hyperization also requires maintenance, because links tend to go out of date as Web servers are reorganized and Webmasters come and go. Full authoring is probably worthwhile if you are doing only a single paper or a couple of Web pages. You might also want to take this approach with the pages that get the most attention in your Web server—your home page, your signature page, and master index pages.

There is also a compromise between these two extremes. The compromise involves the use of the <PRE> tagging pair. Each document to be converted can be divided into two components—the component that is easily converted to HTML and the component that might be too detailed or complicated. The second component can be encapsulated within the <PRE> tagging pair and left alone. The worst scenario in this case is that the entire ASCII text document is encapsulated. This might seem like a waste of time, but the advantage with this approach is that your document is no longer an ASCII text document: it is an HTML document. So the preformatted information in the document can contain hyperlinks.

Documents that never change, such as papers submitted to a conference, have a high payback on the hyperization effort because, once completed, they are never modified and never need to be reconverted. You simply place them online in your Web server and others will read them, enjoy them, and create their own links to them.

19.2.3 Automatic Versus Manual Hyperlinking

Given the primitive state of authoring tools for the creation of HTML documents, most hyperlinks that you embed will be done manually (using a text editor). For frequently accessed documents and major entrypoints into your Web server, that works fine. However, manual hyperlinking becomes tedious when you are dealing with hundreds or thousands of HTML documents.

There are filters and conversion tools for changing other formats to HTML, but there are very few tools that automatically generate hyperlinks in HTML documents. This is primarily because the opportunity to do so tends to be specific to the content found on each Web server. However, if you have a very well-defined information environment you may be able to develop scripts that look for specific instances of phrases—part numbers, people's names, document names, acronyms, etc.—that you might be able to automatically identify, determine the appropriate URL and embed the hyperlink in the HTML document. This technique is also useful if you have preformatted information where each field has well-defined semantics.

HTML conversion tools and filters are discussed further in Section 19.3.5. Often there are cross-references embedded in many of the proprietary document formats. FrameMaker documents and Microsoft Word documents are good examples of this. Usually the HTML conversion filters are able to convert cross-references to hyperlinks when generating HTML.

Embedding absolute URLs (to information resources found outside of your information set) is even more certainly a manual process.

19.2.4 Style Guidelines

You should develop some HTML style guidelines for your site. Consistent HTML style increases the usability of your server—which directly affects how long people spend using your Web server and how often they come back.

Some of the issues are the same as in any authoring environment, but there is a slight twist for the Web. The rules about mixing and matching typefaces go out the window because control of the typeface is not in your hands—it is a Web-browser attribute. However, you still need to consistently use bolding, italics, and other emphasis techniques and to guard against their overuse.

Fortunately, you don't have to start from scratch. People have gone down this path before and have placed their style guidelines on the Web. One of the best is *Style Guide for Online Hypertext* by Tim Berners-Lee of CERN:

```
http://info.cern.ch/hypertext/WWW/Provider/Style/Overview.html
```

Let's go back to our sample HTML document and look at it from a style point of view. Having a standard template will help keep your HTML consistent. We like to have the <TITLE> document title and the <H1> document title match and reinforce one another. The <TITLE> document title is what is placed on a user's hotlist or in their list of bookmarks, while the <H1> document title is the first thing a user sees when the HTML document is displayed.

As we add content, we use <H2> tags to identify major section headings. We also like to frame our documents with a horizontal rule (<HR>) at the top and bottom of the page. This visually separates the document content from title information on the top, and from version control and author signature on the bottom.

Your overriding concern should not be what your style guidelines are, but that you have some and use them! If you are consistent, it is not too difficult to make global changes.

19.2.5 An Example of Information Design

To illustrate these HTML concepts we will now show a more complicated HTML file: the HTML we set up for presenting an Action Plan developed by the Species Survival Commission.

We decided to focus the most important components of the document on the home page. We did not try for a one-to-one mapping between the cover of the paper document and the top-level HTML document. In addition to capturing the document title, cover photo, and author/editor information, we also opted to include the copyright information (found on the inside cover) and the main section titles from the table of contents.

To capture the photo, the document was taken to the local desktop publishing center and the crocodile picture was scanned in as it appears (6″ × 4″) and returned in GIF format at 200 dpi. *xv* was used to try several scaling factors. We settled on 20 percent of full scale as the best size for the home page. By scaling the crocodile photo to that size and saving it in GIF format, we were able to include it as an inline graphic.

The home page HTML contents look like this:

```
<HTML>
<HEAD>
<TITLE>Crocodiles: An Action Plan for their Conservation</TITLE>
</HEAD>
<BODY>
<H1>Crocodiles</H1>
<H2>An Action Plan for their Conservation</H2>
<IMG SRC="crocodile.gif" ALT="Picture of a Crocodile">
<H2>Table Of Contents</H2>
<DL>
<DT><A HREF="foreword.html">Foreword & Acknowledgements</A></DT>
<DT><A HREF="executive.html">Executive Summary</A></DT>
<DT><A HREF="objectives.html">Objectives and Organization</A></DT>
<DT><A HREF="intro.html">Introduction and Conservation Priorities</A></DT>
<DT><A HREF="countries.html">Country Accounts</A></DT>
</DL>
<P>
<HR>
<P>
<EM>&#169 1992 International Union for Conservation
of Nature and Natural  Resources<EM>
<P>
Compiled by <A HREF="jthor.html">John Thorbjarnarson</A><BR>
Edited by <A HREF="hmessel.html">Harry Messel</A>,
<A HREF="wking.html">Wayne King</A>, and
<A HREF="jross.html">James Perran Ross</A>
</BODY>
</HTML>
```

We started with the HTML document template shown earlier. We decided not to use two horizontal rules, as it just seemed too complicated-looking for the home page. Relative URLs were used to create the hyperlinks from the table of contents to the subordinate documents. We used the ALT option with the <IMG> image insertion tag for the benefit of line-mode Web browsers. If the Web browser can't display the inline image, it inserts the phrase "Picture of a Crocodile" instead.

Figure 19-4 shows how this HTML document looks when displayed with Mosaic. To reinforce the differences in look and feel between Web browsers, we've also shown in Figure 19-5 how this same document looks when displayed in a terminal window with Lynx.

You probably also spotted a new HTML technique used in this example. We used a special insertion code (©) to produce the copyright symbol, shown at the bottom of Figure 19-4. For more information and examples of all the ISO 8859 insertion codes, point your Web browser at:

```
http://www.uni-passau.de/~ramsch/iso8859-1.html
```

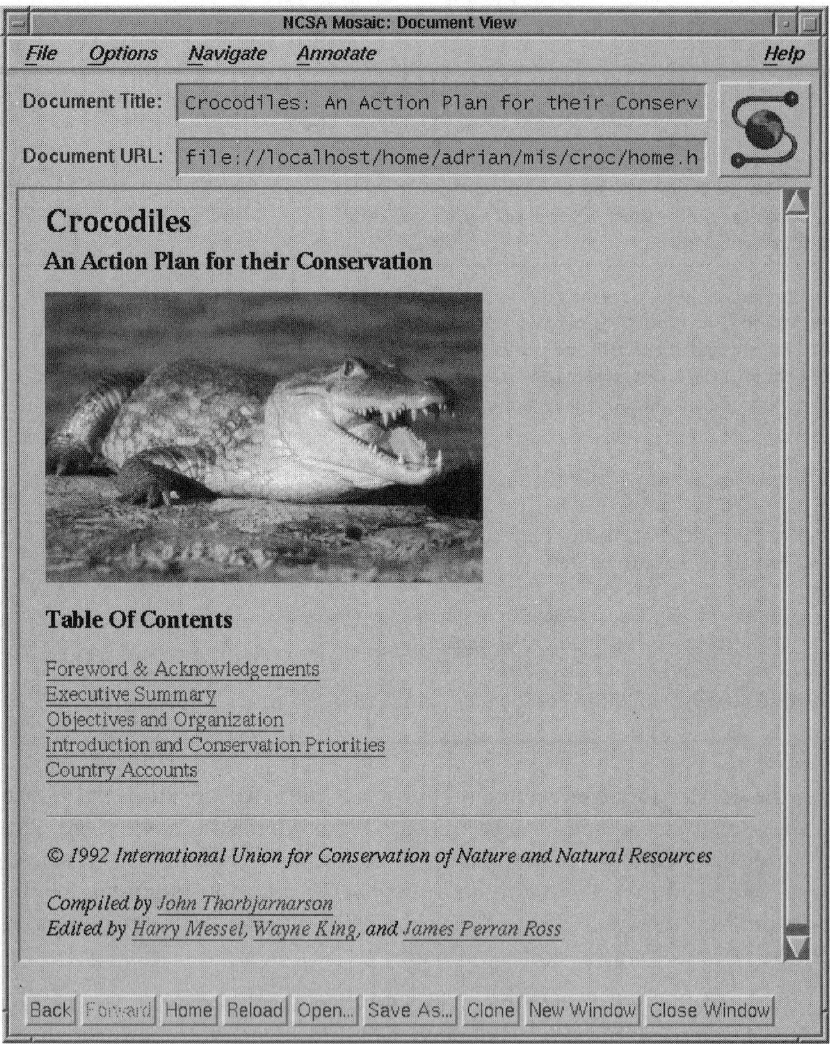

Figure 19-4. Crocodile home page, displayed with Mosaic

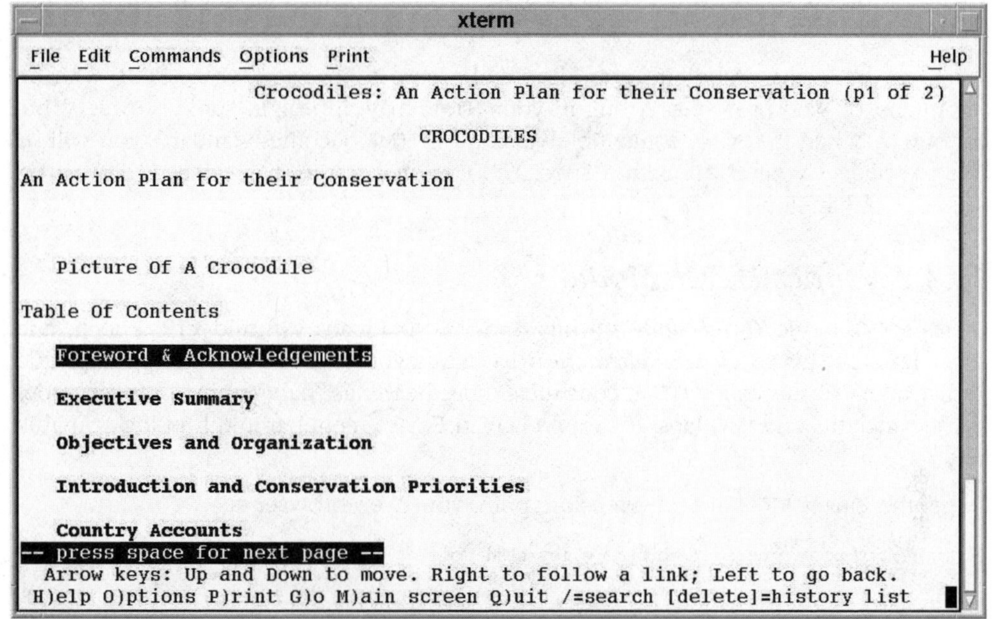

Figure 19-5. Crocodile home page, displayed with Lynx

19.3 HTML Authoring Tools

The subject of HTML authoring tools is the most undeveloped area of the World Wide Web. HTML authoring tools differ from HTML conversion tools (listed in the next section) in that the documents are built from the ground up and have some notion of global hyperlinking with URLs. There are four ways to author HTML documents:

- You can directly embed HTML tags with your favorite text editor or perhaps you can get some assistance from the HTML mode available for Emacs.
- You can use one of the free HTML editors available for the X Window System. One called *htmltext* supports WYSIWYG HTML editing. For more information, point your Web browser at:

  ```
  http://web.cs.city.ac.uk/homes/njw/htmltext/htmltext.html
  ```

  Don't forget that TkWWW (mentioned in Section 17.3.1.8) is an HTML editor. However, because it's also a Web browser, you can try out links immediately after creating them.
- You can use a traditional commercial publishing package such as FrameMaker and then convert your documents to HTML format.
- You can use one of the emerging commercial HTML authoring tools for the Web such as HoTMetaL from SoftQuad or CyberLeaf from Interleaf.

The NeXT-based Web browser developed at CERN has HTML authoring features. Unfortunately, you have to have the orphaned NeXT workstation to use it.

Whatever authoring technique you choose, be sure to preview your HTML with an assortment of Web browsers. A bug in your HTML may appear in some browsers, but not others. When the SGML-compatible version of HTML becomes standard, you will be able to validate your HTML with a special tool to make sure it is syntactically correct without using multiple browsers.

19.3.1 Emacs HTML Mode

Emacs HTML mode *(html-mode.el)* runs under GNU Emacs v18 and v19, Epoch, and Lucid Emacs. This extension allows you to use keyboard commands to prompt and format many of the major HTML constructs: title, headings, paragraphs, different types of lists, anchors, and IMG tags. It supports Lucid Emacs menubar and font-lock capabilities.

To get the Emacs HTML-mode extension, point your Web browser at:*

```
ftp://ftp.ncsa.uiuc.edu/Web/html/elisp/html-mode.el
```

19.3.2 FrameMaker

If you already have FrameMaker, it might be easier to author with an HTML document style template, save the document in Maker Interchange Format (MIF), and then convert to HTML. The following URLs identify various filters and templates that are available for FrameMaker authoring:

```
http://info.cern.ch/hypertext/WWW/Frame/fminit2.0/www_and_frame.html

http://www1.cern.ch/WebMaker/WEBMAKER.html

ftp://bang.nta.no/pub/

ftp://ftp.alumni.caltech.edu/pub/mcbeath/web/miftran/
```

19.3.3 HoTMetaL

SoftQuad HoTMetaL is a WYSIWYG HTML editor that is available for Sun/Motif and Microsoft Windows. SoftQuad has established a collaborative relationship with NCSA, and the two organizations are integrating HoTMetaL and Mosaic for better interoperation. Because it is context-sensitive, HoTMetaL guides authors in creating new HTML documents and cleaning up old ones.

* Note: all the URLs in this book are included in a file in the book's code archive. If you get this file, it can save you from retyping the URLs and also lets us update the ones that change.

HoTMetaL comes in two flavors, an unsupported free version and an enhanced commercial version. The free version can be retrieved by pointing your Web browser at:

```
ftp://ftp.ncsa.uiuc.edu/Web/html/hotmetal
```

SoftQuad HoTMetaL Pro is a fully-supported commercial version of HoTMetaL that handles more complex document structures, such as tables and forms. It is currently available for UNIX; support for additional platforms is forthcoming. For more information, send email to *hotmetal@sq.com*.

Simultaneously with the announcement of SoftQuad HoTMetaL, Avalanche Development announced companion conversion tools that convert WordPerfect and Microsoft Word documents to HTML.

19.3.4 CyberLeaf

Interleaf's CyberLeaf product is billed as a commercial-grade tool for HTML document creation, assembly, and conversion. Interactive resolution of URLs provides live integration of the CyberLeaf authoring environment with the Web. CyberLeaf features point-and-click hyperlinking within and between documents.

CyberLeaf also provides interactive or batch-mode conversion of existing Interleaf documents to HTML. It supports an extensive collection of bidirectional and compound filters for Microsoft Word and WordPerfect documents. For more information, send email to *pwerner@ileaf.com*.

19.3.5 HTML Conversion Tools and Filters

HTML conversion tools and filters are much more numerous than native HTML authoring packages. To learn more about some of the more popular tools, point your Web browser at the URLs listed below to either retrieve the tool (and look at the *README* file) or learn more about the tool via its online description.

In many cases, there are multiple versions of some conversion tools. An original version was created and then others used that as a starting point to add different features. You can also find out the author of each tool and correspond with them on bug fixes and suggestions for additional functionality.

ASCII Text to HTML:

```
http://www.seas.upenn.edu/~mengwong/txt2html.html
```

BibTeX to HTML:

```
ftp://gaia.cs.umass.edu/pub/hgschulz/windex-1.2.tar.Z
http://www.research.att.com/biblio.html
```

Interleaf to HTML:

```
http://info.cern.ch/hypertext/WWW/Tools/il2html.html
http://info.cern.ch/hypertext/WWW/Tools/interleaf.html
```

LaTex to HTML:

```
http://cbl.leeds.ac.uk/nikos/tex2html/doc/latex2html/latex2html.h tml
ftp://skye.aiai.ed.ac.uk/pub/tex2rtf/
```

Mail to HTML:

```
ftp://ftp.uci.edu/pub/dtd2html/
```

Look in the directory for the latest *perlWWW tar* file.

Mosaic Hotlist to HTML:

```
ftp://ftp.uci.edu/pub/dtd2html/
```

Look in the directory for the latest *perlWWW tar* file.

PostScript to HTML:

```
http://stasi.bradley.edu/ftp/pub/ps2html/ps2html-v2.html
```

Texinfo to HTML:

```
http://asis01.cern.ch/infohtml/texi2html.html
```

Troff to HTML:

```
http://cui_www.unige.ch/ftp/PUBLIC/oscar/scripts/ms2html
```

To check the latest information on conversion tools and filters, point your Web browser at:

```
http://info.cern.ch/hypertext/WWW/Tools/Filters.html
```

19.4 Clickable Image Maps

Let's say you want people to be able to get their local weather from your Web server. What would be better than to show them a map of the country (inline), and allow them to click on any location to get that location's weather? That's what a clickable image map does. It has many other uses, for example:

- To help users better understand a picture or diagram by allowing them to click on a component represented in the graphic to see an explanation
- To let users move down to finer levels of detail on a map of a campus or building

Clickable image maps only work with graphically-oriented Web browsers. You should always try to provide alternate text-based methods of accessing the same information.

There are several well-defined steps you need to take when creating a clickable image map. The steps are:

1. Get an image and figure out where to put the **hotspots** (the areas that trigger links)
2. Develop an image-map file that describes where each hotspot is located and specifies the URL associated with each hotspot
3. Tell your Web server how to reach the image-map file
4. Reference the image map in an HTML document
5. Test the clickable image map

Let's take a look at each of these steps in detail.

19.4.1 Planning the Clickable Image Map

First select the inline image you will use. As with any inline image, the graphic needs to be in GIF format for maximum portability. Most graphics service bureaus can scan photographs to create GIF files, or you can draw the graphic with a paint program.

Then rough out mentally where you will place the hotspots. Let's take a look at an example. Figure 19-6 shows a photo of my office. I'm going to use this as the basis for creating a virtual office. With the blurring between the physical world we live in and the virtual online world found on the Web, I should be able to have some fun with this photo.

Arbitrary rectangles, polygons, and circles can be used to identify the hotspots. Figure 19-6 shows how the hotspots in this image are conceptualized. I can directly hyperlink from some of the physical things found in the photo to their virtual equivalents found out on the Web. For example, I placed a copy of *Wired* magazine on my table. I established a hyperlink from the magazine in the photo to *Wired* magazine's Web server. Where virtual equivalents don't exist, I can create them.

Which shapes should be used depends on what your graphic represents:

- A map of an office floor plan might represent each office as a rectangle.
- A map of a class photo might represent each person's head as a circle.
- A map of an airplane might represent the jagged outlines of the wing or a tail section as a series of polygons.

19.4.2 Mapping the Hotspots into a Map File

The second step is to develop an image-map file. You need to create a separate image-map file for each clickable image map on your Web server.

Each of the bordered greyed areas indicate a hotspot.

Figure 19-6. A digitized photo of my office

Each line in an image-map file defines a hotspot, by defining an area within the graphic and the corresponding URL to be returned if someone clicks on that area. You can include comment lines by beginning the line with the pound (#) sign.

Hotspots are formatted as:

```
shape URL coordinate-1,coordinate-2 ... coordinate-n
```

where shape is one of the following:

circle A circle (with two coordinate pairs: center and any edgepoint)

poly A polygon (with at most 100 vertices; each coordinate is a vertex)

rect A rectangle (with two coordinate pairs: upper-left and lower-right)

Coordinates are x,y pairs counting in pixels from the upper lefthand corner of the image.

The URL can be either an actual URL pointing to any resource on the World Wide Web or a URL on your server, but without the *http://hostname*.

Let's look at the image map that I put in the file *office.map*:

```
default /map/none.html
poly /map/upper-right-drawer.html 423,319 423,352, 499,359, 499,326
poly /map/lower-right-drawer.html 423,352 422,416 498,425 499,359
poly /map/home-page.html 425,220 419,226 442,271 447,222
poly /map/workstation.html 519,364 517,460 633,478 638,376
rect /map/bookshelf.html 0,60 139,143
```

```
poly http://www.wired.com/ 51,357 77,393 144,385 115,365
poly http://nearnet.gnn.com/gnn/gnn.html 55,413 46,429 120,425 126,410
poly /map/books-on-table.html 0,375 0,436 45,413 46,380
poly /map/t.html 0,395 0,467 155,458 230,436 273,401 225,371 153,364 67,372
rect /map/stereo-speaker.html 221,90 268,140
poly /map/wall-picture.html 167,0 171,89 226,96 263,0
```

The server takes the coordinates from a user's mouse click and steps through the map file to determine if the click is within any hotspots. As soon as the first match is found, its corresponding URL is used to redirect a document to the user's Web browser. If no matches are found, a default URL (that you specify in the image-map file) is returned. There can be only one default per map file.

It is normal to mix and match circles, multiple polygons, and assorted rectangles in the same map file. Although you should try to minimize overlapping hotspots in the image map, if there are any, the first match is the one used. Just make sure they are ordered the way you want them.

How do you determine the x,y pixel coordinates to go into each entry? One way is to use *xv* to view the image and then just click on the graphic to get the coordinates needed according to the shape you want to use for each hotspot.

Note that all the URLs given in the map file point to HTML files, not graphic files, even though some of them actually display pictures. I could have had the URL for the photo on the wall point directly to a GIF file of that photo, but I didn't. That would have made the assumption that the user has an external viewer capable of handling GIF files (because only graphics invoked from within HTML documents are shown inline). Instead, I have each hotspot point to a *.html* file. Then each *.html* file handles the graphic as an inline image.

For default URLs (for when someone clicks on a spot that isn't hot), the virtual office returns an error message along with a smaller version of the same photo of the office with the hotspots marked. Actually, it's a lot like Figure 19-6. Don't return a complicated graphic that only says "sorry; try again." On a slow link, the error message/graphic can take quite a while to retrieve, and it can be frustrating when the user sees that the graphic it took 30 seconds to retrieve wasn't what he wanted. Or use a simple text error message if the default is an error message.

19.4.3 Connecting Your Map File to a URL

The next step ties your map file to the map name that you will use in your HTML. The *imagemap.conf* configuration file contains a list of all your server's map-file locations and their corresponding names. It is usually found in the */conf* directory in your Web server root directory. In *imagemap.conf*, lines beginning with a pound sign are comments. Every other nonblank line is an entry that consists of:

```
name: path
```

Where *name* is the map name and *path* is the absolute path to an image-map file, or a relative path from the Web server root directory. In the example we have used so far, you would include the following map entry in the *imagemap.conf* file:

```
office: /map/office.map
```

The *imagemap.conf* file is not loaded when you start your *httpd* server. It gets loaded every time someone clicks on a clickable image map.

You can place map files anywhere you want to on your server. You may want to keep the map files for one server all logically together in the same */map* directory or you may want to encourage individuals to keep their image maps together with the images and any supporting HTML documents in the same directory structure.

19.4.4 Referencing Your Clickable Image Map in HTML

We discussed earlier how to include inline graphics in your HTML document using the image insertion HTML tag:

```
<IMG SRC="URL">
```

The final step in creating an image map is to tell the Web browser accessing the HTML document that the inline image it will display is a clickable image map. This is done by adding the optional ISMAP qualifier to the <IMG> tag:

```
<IMG SRC="URL" ISMAP>
```

In practice, what you do is create a link where this image is the link trigger and the URL invokes the imagemap script and passes it the map name:

```
<A HREF="/cgi-bin/imagemap/map-name"><IMG SRC="URL" ISMAP></A>
```

We'll explain how this actually works in a moment. But all you really need to know is to use exactly this HTML, substituting your map name (from before the colon in *imagemap.conf*) and your URL. In our example, we would reference the virtual office image map with the following HTML:

```
<A HREF="/cgi-bin/imagemap/office">
<IMG SRC="/map/office.gif" ISMAP></A>
```

19.4.5 Testing the Image Map

Now, if the magic works, the image map should be working. First we open the URL of the document containing the HTML just shown. An inline image should appear in the browser (see the left side of Figure 19-7).

Clicking on the bookshelf on the left wall of the office brings up a bibliography of the books on the shelf, as shown on the right in Figure 19-7.

Clicking on one of the books retrieves information about the book from the publisher's Web servers.

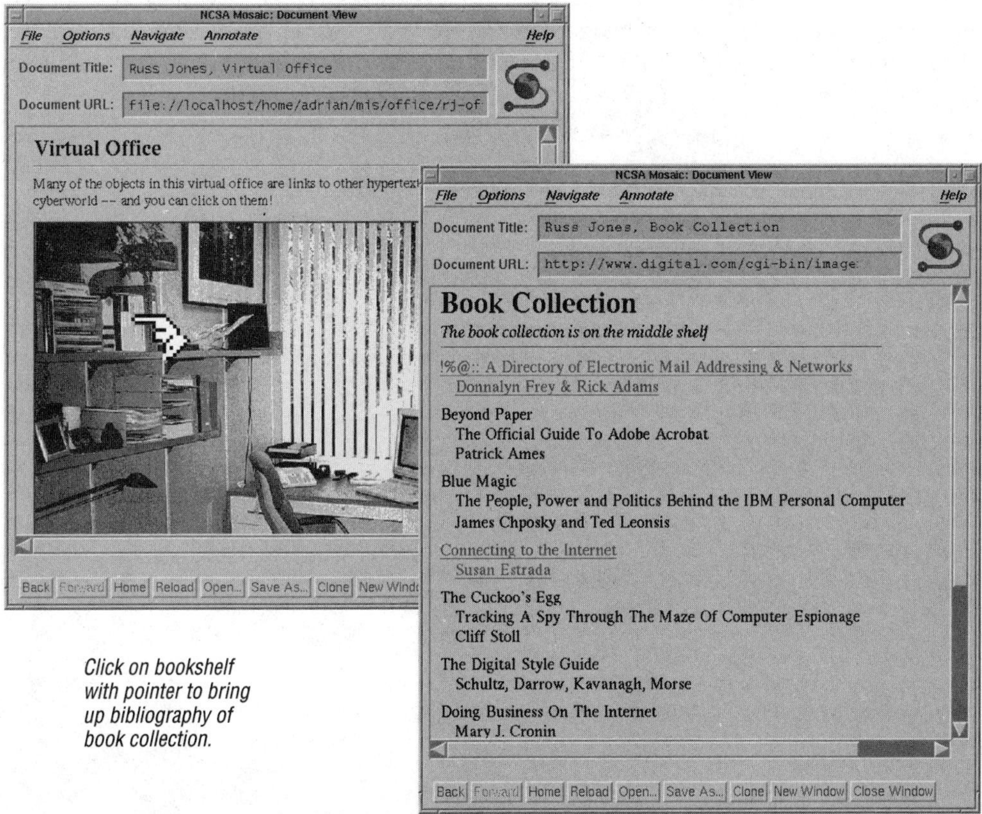

Figure 19-7. The virtual office clickable image map in Mosaic

19.4.6 How It Really Works

imagemap is a precompiled gateway that is included in the *cgi-bin* directory with the Web server distribution.*

Here's how an image map actually works. When the user clicks on the image, it triggers the link, which makes the Web server invoke the *imagemap* program, passing it the map name. The *imagemap* program opens *imagemap.conf* and uses the map name to get the right map file. Then it opens the map file and searches for the first hotspot that matches the button click. When it finds one, it returns the matching URL.

* If you have changed the default directory where the *imagemap.conf* configuration file is kept to anything other than */usr/local/etc/httpd/conf*, then you need to change the *imagemap.c* source and recompile it to reflect the actual location of the *imagemap.conf* file.

One revelation you get by understanding how it works is that two files are opened and read for every click on an image map. There is also some processing to determine which hotspot matches the click. So image maps are not free, and you should take care to keep *imagemap.conf* and your map files as short as possible.

In this Chapter:
- *Gateways*
- *Forms Processing*
- *WAIS Access from the Web*

20

Web: Gateways and Forms

Web browsers can directly access several types of Internet information services, but not every type. For example, Archie and Finger are not supported. Furthermore, not all local information sources fit the Web authoring mold in which you create static files and place them in directories. Perhaps the information is dynamically generated, or comes from an ORACLE database.

Gateways solve these problems by providing an extension mechanism for the Web server. A gateway takes an information source that doesn't fit the mold and makes it look to the browser like a file on the Web server. In practice, a gateway is just a script or program invoked by your Web server, that can accept user input through the Web server and can output HTML, a URL, or some other data back to the user through the Web server.

A form provides a nice familiar way to collect data from the user. The Web server passes the form input to a script or program on your system, which can do whatever you want with the input. Form scripts are closely related to gateways, because the scripts or programs in both cases pass data to and from the Web server in the same way.

The input provided by a form can be used by a gateway to get information, or the input can just be filed or emailed to someone. For example, O'Reilly & Associates uses a form to allow people to subscribe to its *GNN* online magazine on the Web.

While some Web browsers provide direct access to WAIS databases, most don't. So you may want to provide a gateway to your WAIS server. This chapter describes the four ways of accessing WAIS servers and explains how to pick one.

20.1 Gateways

You can use gateways running on the Internet, install gateways that have been developed by others, or develop your own. You don't always have to set up your own. But if you want better performance or you want to control the formatting of the information that is displayed to a user, you need to run the gateway and control the HTML it automatically generates.

20.1.1 The Common Gateway Interface

The *Common Gateway Interface* (CGI) is the mechanism for communicating between your gateway and your Web server.

Figure 20-1 illustrates the basic information flow through the CGI, the Web server, and the client. When the user enters text on a form or in response to <ISINDEX> query and hits the return key, the Web browser sends keystrokes captured from the user to the *httpd* server. The *httpd* server accepts the input, starts up the gateway and hands the input to the gateway via the CGI. The user's keystrokes are passed to the gateway either via environment variables (called the GET method) or using standard input (called the POST method.) The gateway then parses the input and processes it. It may generate HTML output, which is returned to the *httpd* server to pass to the client, or it may save data in a file or database or send email to someone.

The gateway can be a script or programs, written in C/C++, Perl, tcl, the C Shell, or the Bourne Shell. Each language has its own strengths as a gateway language.

CGI gateways that generate HTML output are required to preface the HTML output to *stdout* with the following line:

```
Content-type: text/html
```

This line must be followed by a blank line before the first <HTML> tag is sent.

The gateway does not have to generate HTML. It could return the URL of another file, indicating to the browser that it should get that file. This is called *URL redirection.* CGI gateways using URL redirection write the following line to *stdout*:

```
Location: URL
```

This line, too, must be followed by a blank line before the *stdout* data stream terminates.

20.1.1.1 Sample gateways

The NCSA Web server kit is distributed with a set of sample gateways. Some are directly useful, while others should help you understand CGI scripts and help you create custom gateways. The following CGI test scripts are located in *cgi-bin* (the language they are written in is shown in parentheses):

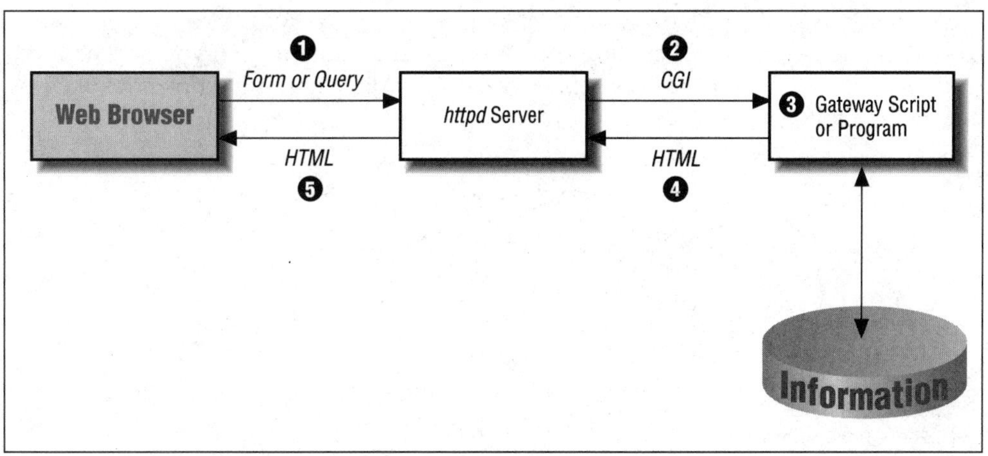

Figure 20-1. Information flow through the Common Gateway Interface

- *test-cgi* (sh)
- *nph-test-cgi* (sh)
- *test-cgi.tcl* (tcl)

There are also a number of simple gateways in *cgi-bin*:

archie (sh)	A very simple gateway to Archie
calendar (sh)	An interface to the UNIX *cal* command
date (sh)	Prints the current date
finger (sh)	A simple gateway to Finger
fortune (sh)	Random fortune teller

In the *cgi-src* directory are source files that show how to implement a custom gateway as a program:

uptime (sh)	Prints the server's load average
jj (C)	A sample HTML form to order a submarine sandwich
phf (C)	An HTML form interface to CSO phone book servers
query (C)	A general-purpose form response script
imagemap (C)	Handles clickable image-map queries
wais.pl (Perl)	One type of WAIS gateway

Section 14.1 and Section 19.4 describe how to use the *wais.pl* script and the *imagemap* gateway, respectively.

20.1.1.2 How scripts work

Let's try the *test-cgi* script. Assuming your Web server is running, and you haven't modified the *ScriptAlias* directive that defines the *cgi-bin* directory, the script is invoked by opening the following URL:

```
http://hostname/cgi-bin/test-cgi
```

When invoked, it should produce HTML output that describes how your *httpd* server is configured and what information is being passed generically to all CGI scripts. The output should look like this in a browser:

```
CGI/1.0 test script report:

argc is 0. argv is .

SERVER_SOFTWARE = NCSA/1.3
SERVER_NAME = hostname
GATEWAY_INTERFACE = CGI/1.1
SERVER_PROTOCOL = HTTP/1.0
SERVER_PORT = 80
REQUEST_METHOD = GET
HTTP_ACCEPT = text/plain, application/x-html, application/html,
text/x-html, text/html, image/*, application/postscript, video/mpeg,
audio/basic, audio/x-aiff, image/gif, image/jpeg, image/tiff,
image/x-portable-anymap, image/x-portable-bitmap, image/x-portable-graymap,
image/x-portable-pixmap, image/x-rgb, image/rgb, image/x-xbitmap,
image/x-xpixmap, image/xwd, image/x-xwd, image/x-xwindowdump, video/mpeg,
application/postscript, application/x-dvi, message/rfc822, application/x-latex,
application/x-tex, application/x-texinfo, application/x-troff,
application/x-troff-man, application/x- troff-me, application/x-troff-ms,
text/richtext, text/tab- separated-values, text/x-setext, */*
PATH_INFO =
PATH_TRANSLATED =
SCRIPT_NAME = /cgi-bin/test-cgi
QUERY_STRING =
REMOTE_HOST = xxx.xxx.xxx
REMOTE_ADDR = xxx.xxx.xxx.xxx
REMOTE_USER =
AUTH_TYPE =
CONTENT_TYPE =
CONTENT_LENGTH =
```

All of the capitalized variable names (like SERVER_NAME) are environment variables that are set by the CGI. These are available to be used by your gateway.

test-cgi is an example of a gateway that requires no input, but it does print out any input you give it. In this case, `argc is 0. argv is .` means we didn't give it any. However, parameters can be passed to a gateway by appending them to the URL using the following scheme:

```
URL?first+second+third
```

For example, to pass your name (*John Q. Public*) to the *test-cgi* gateway, you would open the following URL:

```
http://hostname/cgi-bin/test-cgi?John+Q.+Public
```

The incoming parameter is appended to the base URL after the `?` character, with blanks replace by the `+` character. The parameter is set as an environment variable called QUERY_STRING, but is not passed to *test-cgi* as a command-line option, or in standard input. The HTML output returned from this URL would be exactly as shown previously, except for:

```
argc is 3. argv is John Q. Public.

QUERY_STRING = John+Q.+Public
```

Passing parameters to CGI scripts by appending them to the URL is referred to as the GET method. CGI scripts written to use the GET method must explicitly read the QUERY_STRING variable to get and then parse the query. The GET method is usually used to invoke a simple CGI script with a single parameter.

Alternatively, parameters can be passed to CGI scripts using standard input. This is called the POST method. It is used when there is a large amount of information that would be awkward to append to the end of the URL (as with the GET method) or when the parameters need to be encoded. Most of the advanced work on secure transactions is focused on secure encoding techniques for the POST method. The POST method is generally used with forms processing. See Section 20.2 for more information.

When using the POST method, two parameters, for a user's name and email address, might look like:

```
NAME=John+Q.+Public&EMAIL=jpublic@netcom.com
```

The CGI script would then parse the two parameters as:

```
NAME    John Q. Public
EMAIL   jpublic@netcom.com
```

The `&` character separates the parameter pairs and the `=` character separates each parameter name from its value. The `+` character is used again as a substitute for blanks. The Perl CGI library contains code to parse standard input to load an associative array for processing.

20.1.2 Prompting the User for Input

For most CGI scripts that search or return selected data, you will prompt the user for input to pass to the script. This is accomplished by using the <ISINDEX> HTML tag. When an HTML document contains an <ISINDEX> tag, the browser displays an input box with the phrase:

This is a searchable index. Enter search keywords: <type-input-here>

This does not mean your HTML document is automatically a searchable index. The <ISINDEX> tag just captures user keystrokes and sends those keystrokes to a gateway using the GET method. The gateway performs the actual search.

If the gateway doesn't exist, placing the <ISINDEX> tag in the HTML document will not make it exist, although it will look to the user as though it exists. The user can certainly key in a search string. But when the Return key is hit, no search will occur. To have your Web server perform search functions you must develop or set up a gateway to perform the search.

20.1.2.1 Simple search gateways

The trick to developing your own simple search gateway is to use a dual-purpose CGI script. It is dual-purpose because when invoked with no argument, the script asks for the search string. When invoked with arguments (appended to the URL), the arguments are taken as the search string, and the script executes the search.

For example, the following URL might be used to prompt for a search phrase:

```
http://www.fredonia.edu/cgi-bin/simple-search
```

This URL invokes a script called *simple-search*. The following HTML shows you how to reference the simple search script as part of a hyperlink:

```
Or you can <A HREF="/cgi-bin/simple-search">search</A> to
locate the latest information.
```

The following HTML shows you how to reference the simple search script with a predefined search phrase:

```
Or you can search the database for a list of
<A HREF="/cgi-bin/simple-search?crocodile">crocodiles</A> that are
endangered.
```

Notice that the search phrase is appended to the URL after a question mark. Let's look at the two functions of the simple search script more closely. The logic of the simple search is:

- Was the CGI script invoked with the search string appended to the URL?
- If not, then:
    1. Generate the initial query request using the <ISINDEX> HTML tag.
    2. Write the query request to *stdout*.
- If so, then:
    1. Get the search phrase from the QUERY_STRING environment variable.
    2. Parse the query string to convert the search phrase back to English.

3. Invoke the search.
4. Write the results to *stdout*.

Before we show a script that does this, we need to say a few words about security so you'll be better able to understand the script.

20.1.2.2 Scripts, programs, and security

As mentioned earlier, you can develop gateways using almost any scripting language or programming language.

You need to be aware of security holes that you could introduce in your Web server if you are not careful in writing your CGI script. Anytime you capture user keystrokes, those keystrokes could be malicious. Someone attacking your Web server can embed shell metacharacters in their input that could result in shell syntax errors or the execution of arbitrary commands on the system that runs your gateway. The danger is particularly common with CGI gateways written in the Bourne or C Shell, in Perl, or in any language where an interpreter can execute commands external to your gateway.

This doesn't mean that you shouldn't write a CGI gateway in these languages, just that you should be careful. Fortunately, people have developed callable libraries that make sure keystroke input is clean of malicious metacharacters. The CGI library for Perl is available from:

```
ftp://ftp.ncsa.uiuc.edu/Web/httpd/Unix/ncsa_httpd/cgi/cgi-lib.pl.Z
```

When we write CGI scripts, rather than trapping "problem" metacharacters, we simply use the following regular expression to check for legal keystrokes:

```
[a-zA-Z0-9_\-+ \t\/@%]
```

It's hard to tell, but there is a blank space after the plus (+) sign. Blanks are certainly safe! If you are developing CGI scripts in Perl, the code fragment to validate input might look like:

```
if ($variable-name !~ /^[a-zA-Z0-9_\-+ \t\/@%]+$/) {
        &report_evil_characters;
        exit;
}
```

variable_name is the name of the variable that holds the typed-in characters. *report_evil_characters* is a subroutine that formats an error message in HTML to be sent to the user. You do not have validate every value—just the ones you are going to pass directly to interpreters outside of your CGI script.

20.1.2.3 Search gateway example

Now we'll show you the search gateway that implements the logic described in Section 20.1.2.1 and accounts for the security concerns described in Section 20.1.2.2. This gateway is called *alias-search* and shows how a CGI script can be used to search the system *aliases* file for email aliases. The following example shows the Perl code used to implement the gateway.

You can easily modify this example to search data files other than */etc/aliases.* If the data you are searching has a predetermined format or syntax, you can refine this example by getting rid of the <PRE> tagging pair and using other HTML tags to format and add emphasis to the search results. This same general search model can also be used for forms processing, which will be discussed in Section 20.2.

```
#!/usr/local/bin/perl

$data_file = "/etc/aliases";

# make sure arguments are passed using the GET method
if ($ENV{'REQUEST_METHOD'} eq 'GET') {
        # Get the query in phrase1+phrase2 format from the QUERY_STRING
        # environment variable.

        $query = $ENV{'QUERY_STRING'};

        # If the query string is null, then there is no search
        # phrase appended to the URL
        if ($query !~ /\w/) {

                # No argument, so prompt the user for the search string
                # using the <ISINDEX> HTML Tag.
                &html_header("Alias Search Query");
                print "<ISINDEX>";
                &html_trailer;
        }
        else {
                # The search string is appended to the URL.  Massage it
                # back into a useable form.

                $query =~ tr/+/ /;
                $query =~ s/%([a-fA-F0-9][a-fA-F0-9])/pack("C", hex($1))/eg;
                # Check for illegal metacharacters

                if ($query !~ /^[a-zA-Z0-9_\-+ \t\/@%]+$/) {
                            &html_header("Illegal Characters");
                            print "The search phrase contains illegal \n";
                            print "characters. Please back up and resubmit \n";
                            print "the query.\n";
                            &html_trailer;
                }
                else {
                            # Start the HTML stream back to the Web server.
```

```
            &html_header("Alias Search Results");
            print "<PRE>\n";

            # Open the datafile and search through it.
            # Write out any matches to stdout.

            open(DATAFILE,"$data_file");
            while (<DATAFILE>) {
                if (/$query/i) {print;}
            }
            close(DATAFILE);
            # terminate the HTML stream back to the the Web server.

            print "</PRE>\n";
            &html_trailer;
        }
    }
}

# ======================================================
# This subroutine take a single input parameter and uses
# it as the <TITLE> and the first level header.
# ======================================================
sub html_header {
    $document_title = $_[0];
    print "Content-type: text/html\n\n";
    print "<HTML>\n";
    print "<HEAD>\n";
    print "<TITLE>$document_title</TITLE>\n";
    print "</HEAD>\n";
    print "<BODY>\n";
    print "<H1>$document_title</H1>\n";
    print "<P>\n";
}
# ======================================================
# This subroutine finishes off the HTML stream.
# ======================================================

sub html_trailer{
    print "</BODY>\n";
    print "</HTML>\n";
}
```

The line:

```
if ($ENV{'REQUEST_METHOD'} eq 'GET') {
```

verifies that the CGI script was invoked using the GET method (not the POST method). Well-written CGI scripts handle invocation using either CGI method (GET or POST). Less well-written CGI scripts handle one or the other, but at least verify the method at run-time. Poorly written scripts do not check the CGI method and bomb at run-time.

20.1.3 URLs in HTML Documents Returned by Gateways

HTML documents returned by CGI gateways can contain absolute URLs for all hyperlinks. Relative URLs won't work by themselves, because there is no "current document" from which to fill in the access method and server name.

If you want to use relative URLs, the <BASE> HTML tag explicitly states the base URL of the HTML document containing the relative URLs. Here's the syntax of <BASE>:

```
<BASE HREF="URL">
```

The <BASE> tag specifies the URL of the document itself, to be used when the document is read out of context, such as by a gateway. Relative URLs within the document will be resolved relative to this base URL, as opposed to the URL used to reach the document. There can only be one <BASE> tag per HTML document, and it is included in the <HEAD> section.

The use of the <BASE> tag negates the portability of the HTML, but you still have the simplicity advantage of specifying URLs relative to your document tree. However, the <BASE> tag is not consistently implemented across all Web browsers yet, so you may want to use this with caution. (Mosaic for UNIX supports it. Mosaic for the Macintosh and Windows does not, nor does Lynx. However, it's part of the HTML standard.)

20.1.4 Existing Gateways

People contributing to the World Wide Web have created many of the obvious gateways to common resources found on the Internet. The following gateways are freely available and can be installed on your Web server as needed. For information on the WAIS gateway, see Section 20.3.

Hytelnet Gateway

Hytelnet provides menu-driven access to Internet-accessible *telnet* sites. *Hytelnet* lists libraries, Campus-Wide Information Systems, and Freenets around the world. This gateway provides run-time conversion of the *Hytelnet* database to HTML.

```
http://info.cern.ch/hypertext/WWW/HytelnetGate/Overview.html
```

Author: Earl Fogel <*earl.fogel@usask.ca*> at Computing Services, University of Saskatchewan.

man2html Gateway

man2html takes *man* pages in formatted *nroff* and outputs HTML. The *nroff* output is surrounded with <PRE> tags, with the exception of section heads and overstruck words, which are marked up with the appropriate header level and emphasis.

man2html can be used as either a conversion filter or installed as a gateway. By installing it as a gateway, you never have to worry about HTML versions of *man* pages growing stale as you upgrade your operating system. On the other hand, it uses CPU cycles to do the HTML conversion each time someone accesses a *man* page through the gateway. The *man2html* kit is available at:

```
ftp://ftp.uci.edu/pub/dtd2html/
```

Look in the directory for the latest *perlWWW tar* file.

Author: Earl Hood <*ehood@convex.com*> at CONVEX Computer Corporation.

ORACLE Gateway

The ORACLE gateway takes a URL query, translates it to an SQL SELECT statement, and returns the results formatted as a table surrounded by <PRE> tags. Although not very polished, this is a a good starting point for providing a hypertext view of an ORACLE database. This gateway requires the ORACLE Pro*C preprocessor. For more information, point your Web browser at:

```
http://info.cern.ch/hypertext/WWW/RDBGate/Implementation.html
```

Author: Arthur Secret.

Genera Gateway

Genera is a gateway used to integrate Sybase databases into the World Wide Web. It can be used to retrofit a Web front end to an existing Sybase database, or to create a new database. *Genera* is more flexible than most gateways because it allows you to develop a custom schema notation that controls the mapping of the Sybase database to the resultant HTML. *Genera* also supports form-based relational querying and whole-database formatting into text and HTML formats. For more information, point your Web browser at:

```
http://cgsc.biology.yale.edu/genera.html
```

Author: Stanley Letovsky <*letovsky@cs.jhu.edu*> at Johns Hopkins Medical School.

20.1.5 Additional cgi-bin Directories

Gateway scripts are usually kept in *cgi-bin*, the CGI binary directory in your ServerRoot directory. If you plan on having dozens of custom gateways developed by different people, you might want to give each person their own *cgi-bin* directory off in their own area of the document tree. If you do this, modify the *srm.conf* configuration file to add the *ScriptAlias* directive for each new *cgi-bin* directory you add to your Web server. For example, to support three cgi-bin directories on your Web server, the Alias directives in the *srm.conf* configuration file might looks like:

```
ScriptAlias /cgi-bin/      /usr/local/etc/httpd/cgi-bin/
ScriptAlias /cs-cgi-bin/   /cs/http/cgi-bin/
ScriptAlias /ee-cgi-bin/   /ee/web/scripts/
```

The ScriptAlias directive is fully described in Appendix G, *Web: access.conf Directives.*

20.2 Forms Processing

Forms are a natural progression from simple queries. If we can collect a search string from the user, why can't we collect a whole form's worth of information?

Forms are officially part of HTML V3.0, but the NCSA Web server provides support for forms. NCSA Mosaic, Lynx, and ViolaWWW support a general-purpose subset of this functionality. Enough functionality is supported to make forms practical and useful.

Let's start with an example. We'll first show you what the final form looks like, then describe the HTML used to generate the form, and finally the CGI script we used to process the results of the form. Figure 20-2 shows a form used to capture user feedback displayed with Mosaic. The users are asked for their name and email address and are given the ability to type an arbitrary amount of feedback text. When done, they can click on Send Comments to terminate the form-entry process. At any point, they can click on Clear Form to reinitialize the form and start over.

When the user terminates the form, the input is sent to the Web server and is passed to a CGI script that formats the input and sends it as a mail message to the Webmaster.

The HTML part of a form is known as the **front end**, while the script that handles the input is known as the **back end**.

20.2.1 HTML for Forms

The form definition is described using HTML and is included as part of the HTML document. The HTML document that displayed the form in Figure 20-2 is:

```
<HTML>
<HEAD>
<TITLE>Crocodile Action Plan Feedback Form</TITLE>
</HEAD>
<BODY>
<IMG SRC="crocodile-thumb.gif">
<H1>Crocodile Action Plan Feedback Form</H1>
<EM>Please send us your comments!</EM>
<P>
<HR>
<P>
<FORM METHOD="POST" ACTION="/cgi-bin/comments">
Name: <INPUT TEXT NAME="feed_name" size=36><BR>
Email: <INPUT TEXT NAME="feed_email" size=36>
<P>
<TEXTAREA NAME="feed_comments" ROWS=8 COLS=40>
</TEXTAREA>
<P>
<INPUT TYPE="submit" VALUE="Send Comments">
<INPUT TYPE="reset" VALUE="Clear Form">
</FORM>
<P>
```

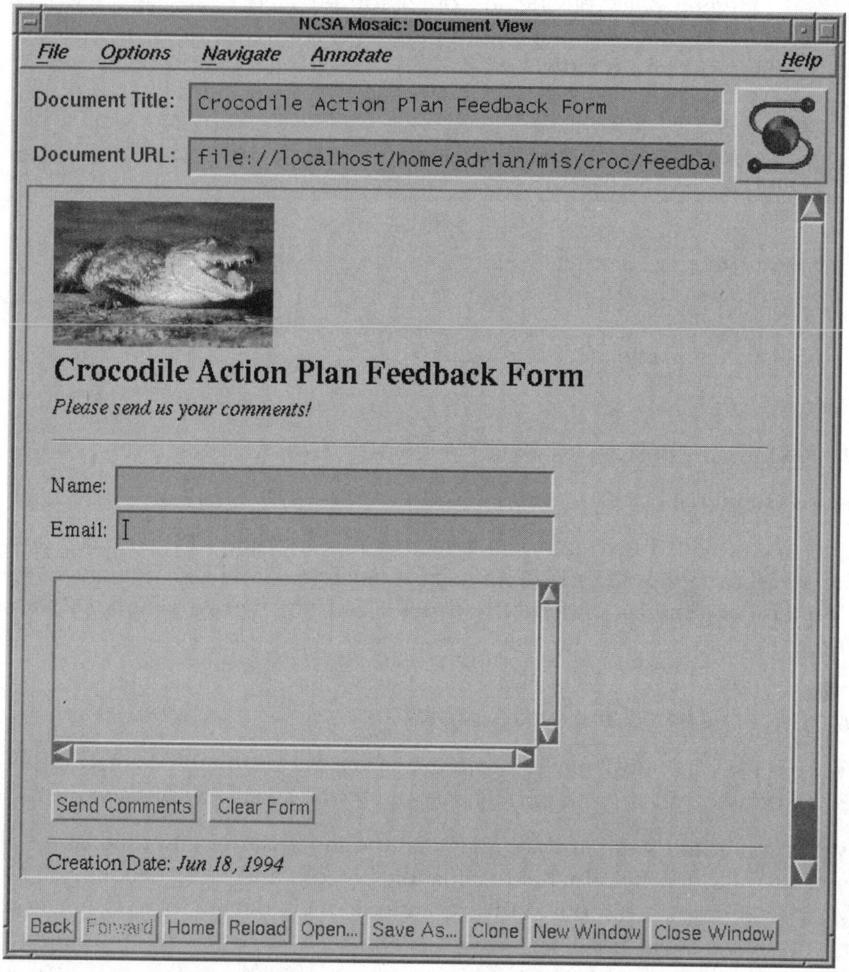

Figure 20-2. Feedback form as displayed by NCSA Mosaic

```
<HR>
<P>
Creation Date: <EM>Jun 18, 1994</EM>
<P>
<ADDRESS><A HREF="rjones.html">DRJ</A></ADDRESS>
</BODY>
</HTML>
```

This HTML is based on the template described in Chapter 19, *Authoring for the Web*. The major new HTML tag introduced in this example is the <FORM> tag. The <FORM> tagging pair is used to enclose the contents of your form and to identify the URL of the CGI script that will process the form input.

Inside the <FORM> tagging pair you include other form-related HTML tags and any other HTML construct. You can have multiple forms in a single HTML document. However, you cannot nest forms inside forms.

Constructs that can be in the form include:

- Text entry fields
- Password fields
- Scrollable text areas
- Checkboxes (on/off toggle)
- Radio buttons (one-of-many checkbox toggles)
- Pop-up menus
- Scrollable lists
- Push buttons (submit and reset)

In this example, we provided text entry fields to the user with the <INPUT> tag, and scrollable text areas with the <TEXTAREA> tags. Checkboxes will be demonstrated later in this chapter. For a full list of the form-related HTML tags, see Appendix D, *Web: More HTML Tags.*

20.2.2 Scripts to Handle Form Input

The feedback form uses the POST method to transmit the various fields defined in the form and their associated values back through the CGI to the script */cgi-bin/comments.*

There is no validation at the Web browser level that the input is logically valid or even present. This means that the field-by-field validation process and error handling must happen in your CGI script. This obviously requires a high degree of coordination between the form definition in HTML and the CGI script that processes the form input.*

The next example is the comments CGI script, written in Perl, that we use to process the feedback form. Its function is to take all of the variable input through the CGI, format it, and then send the form contents to the webmaster as an email message.

```
#!/usr/local/bin/perl

$webmaster = "rjones@ix.netcom.com";

#check that POST method is used
if ($ENV{'REQUEST_METHOD'} eq 'POST') {
     # POST method dictates that we get the form
     # input from standard input
```

* However, in-browser validation is on the horizon in HTML 3.0, and some Web browsers, like ViolaWWW, can do it today (although it is difficult to use.)

```
read(STDIN, $buffer, $ENV{'CONTENT_LENGTH'});

# Split the name-value pairs on '&'
@pairs = split(/&/, $buffer);

# Go through the pairs and determine the name
# and value for each form variable.

foreach $pair (@pairs) {
        ($name, $value) = split(/=/, $pair);
        $value =~ tr/+/ /;
        $value =~ s/%([a-fA-F0-9][a-fA-F0-9])/pack("C", hex($1))/eg;
        $FORM{$name} = $value;
}
# Now all the form variables are in the $FORM
# associative array.

# Before proceeding, validate the keyed in email
# for address for evil characters

if ($FORM{EMAIL} !~ /^[a-zA-Z0-9_\-+ \t\/@%]+$/) {
        &html_header("Illegal Email Address");
        print "<HR><P>\n";
        print "The Email address you entered contains illegal";
        print "characters. Please back up, correct, then resubmit.\n"
        &html_trailer;
        exit;
}
# The users email address is clean, so open up
# the email message to send the feedback to the
# webmaster and copy the user.
open (MESSAGE,"| mail $webmaster $FORM{feed_email}");

# Format email header information.

print MESSAGE "To: $webmaster\n";
if ($FORM{feed_email} ne "") {
        print MESSAGE "Reply-To: $FORM{feed_email}\n";

}
# Write the actual email message

print MESSAGE "Subject: Comments from $ENV{'REMOTE_HOST'}\n\n";
print MESSAGE "Name: $FORM{feed_name}\n\n";
print MESSAGE "$FORM{feed_comments}\n";
close (MESSAGE);

# Thank the user and acknowledge the feedback

&html_header("Thank You");
print "<HR><P>\n";
print "Your comments have been emailed to the webmaster.\n";
print "You have been copied on the message.\n";
```

```
    &html_trailer;
}
else {
    # Format an error message for the user

    &html_header("Comment Form Error");
    print "<HR><P>\n";
    print "Form input was not proccessed.  Please mail your ";
    print "remarks to $webmaster\n";
    &html_trailer;
}

# ======================================================
# This subroutine take a single input parameter and uses
# it as the <TITLE> and the first level header.
# ======================================================
sub html_header {
    $document_title = $_[0];
    print "Content-type: text/html\n\n";
    print "<HTML>\n";
    print "<HEAD>\n";
    print "<TITLE>$document_title</TITLE>\n";
    print "</HEAD>\n";
    print "<BODY>\n";
    print "<H1>$document_title</H1>\n";
    print "<P>\n";
}
# ======================================================
# This subroutine finishes off the HTML stream.
# ======================================================

sub html_trailer{
    print "</BODY>\n";
    print "</HTML>\n";
}
```

The Perl script checks only the email address for possible illegal metacharacters. Although it's not the only variable in the form, it is the only one that is piped directly out to the shell level (in this case with the *mail* command). Note that this script does not accept UUCP-style email addresses, because they include the ! character, which is too dangerous to allow in a Perl script.

The step that formats the mail header does not control to whom the mail message is sent (that is done when the output stream to the *mail* command is opened). However, the mail header is useful so that the Webmaster can reply directly to the email message.

Note especially how the *thank_you* subroutine is used to generate HTML to be sent back and displayed in the user's Web browser. It writes the HTML to *stdout*. When generating HTML from a CGI script, it is absolutely critical that the first line written to *stdout* identify *text/html* MIME-type information. This must be followed by a blank line.

Debugging CGI scripts can be a little tricky. First, make sure your script executes cleanly by itself without syntax errors before you place it in the *cgi-bin* directory and try to execute it by submitting a form. We always check this from the *csh* prior to placing the script or script modification into the *cgi-bin* directory. Otherwise, when we execute the script with the form front end, it may hang and never return control back to the Web browser.

When you run a CGI script from a shell, any run-time errors are reported. You have to emulate the CGI environment by setting up the appropriate environment variables. Otherwise, even if the script is clean, it will fail when it tests whether the REQUEST_METHOD is POST (because that environment variable isn't set) so it will just generate the error HTML back to *stdout*.

20.2.3 Adding Checkboxes to the Form

Our second forms-processing example illustrates how you can use checkboxes with a form. The form registers users who are interested in becoming more involved with crocodile conservation. This example is an extension of both the feedback form and CGI script shown earlier. Figure 20-3 shows what this form looks like when it is displayed using Mosaic.

The HTML used to generate this form started with the HTML from the previous example. Here it is now:

```
<HTML>
<HEAD>
<TITLE>Crocodile Action Plan Registration
Form</TITLE>
</HEAD>
<BODY>
<IMG SRC="crocodile-thumb.gif">
<P>
<EM>I want to be involved in saving endangered crocodiles!</EM>
<P>
<HR>
<P>
<FORM METHOD="POST" ACTION="/cgi-bin/registration">
<INPUT TEXT NAME="reg_name" size=36> Name<BR>
<INPUT TEXT NAME="reg_email" size=36> Email<BR>
<INPUT TEXT NAME="reg_phone" size=36> Phone<BR>
<TEXTAREA NAME="reg_address" ROWS=4 COLS=36></TEXTAREA> Postal
<P>
<DL>
<DT>I would like:</DT>
<DD><INPUT TYPE="checkbox" NAME="reg_catalog"
VALUE="yes">Volunteer work</DD>
<DD><INPUT TYPE="checkbox" NAME="reg_info"
VALUE="yes">
More information on the Species Survival
Commission</DD>
```

```
<P>
<DT>Please contact me about:</DT>
<DD><INPUT TYPE="checkbox" NAME="reg_volunteer"
VALUE="yes">
Volunteer work</DD>
<DD><INPUT TYPE="checkbox" NAME="reg_cash"
VALUE="yes">
Making a monetary contribution to save
endangered crocodiles</DD>
</DL>
<P>
<INPUT TYPE="submit" VALUE="Send Comments">
<INPUT TYPE="reset" VALUE=" Clear Form">
</FORM>
<P>
<HR>
<P>
Creation Date: <EM>Jun 18, 1994</EM>
<P>
<ADDRESS><A HREF="rjones.html">DRJ</A></ADDRESS>
</BODY>
</HTML>
```

To process this form, we copied the */cgi-bin/comments* script used in the first form example to */cgi-bin/registration* and then modified the Perl code that writes the actual email message. The following example shows the modified Perl code:

```
# Write the actual message
print MESSAGE "Subject: Involvement Request \n";
print MESSAGE "Name: $FORM{reg_name}\n\n";

print MESSAGE "Email: $FORM{reg_email}\n\n";
print MESSAGE "Phone: $FORM{reg_phone}\n\n";
print MESSAGE "Address:\n$FORM{reg_address}\n\n";
print MESSAGE "Involvement or Request:\n";
if ($FORM{reg_catalog} eq "yes") {
    print MESSAGE "- I would like a catalog.\n";
}
if ($FORM{reg_info} eq "yes") {
    print MESSAGE "- I would like more information on ";
    print MESSAGE "the Species Survival Commission.\n";
}
if ($FORM{reg_volunteer} eq "yes") {
    print MESSAGE "- I would like to volunteer.\n";
}
if ($FORM{reg_cash} eq "yes") {
    print MESSAGE "- I would like to make a donation.\n";
}
close (MESSAGE);
```

We also modified the "Thank You" message to thank the user appropriately.

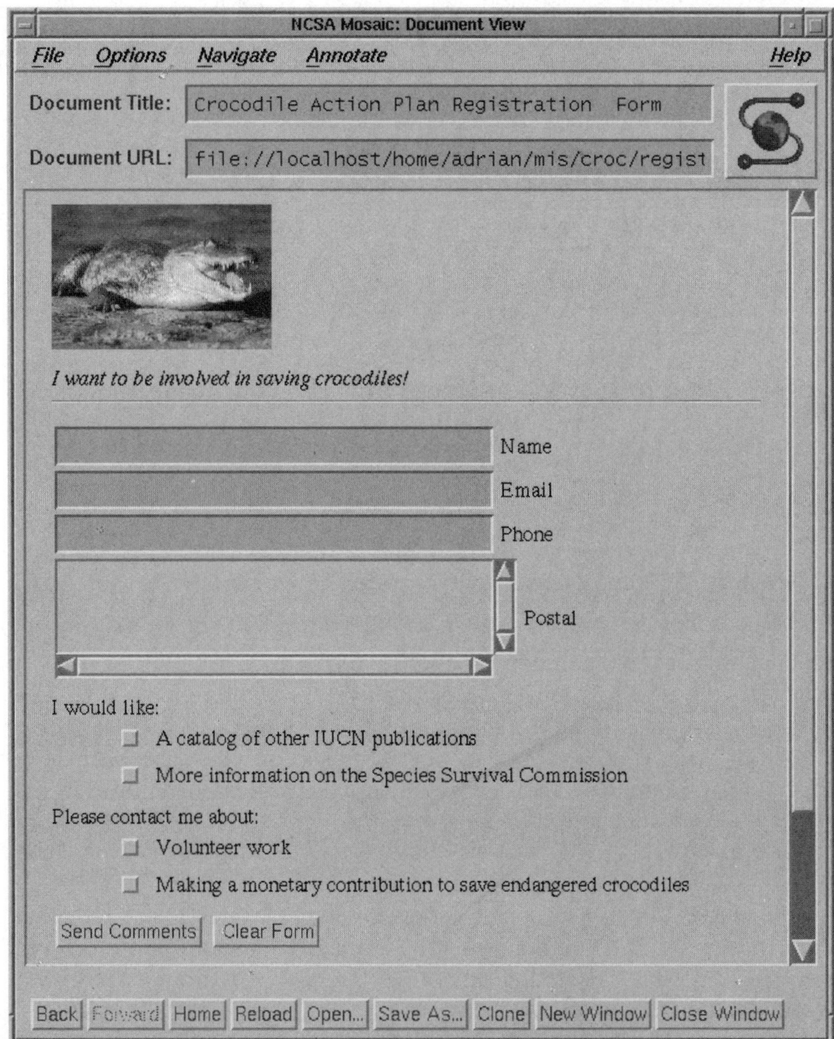

Figure 20-3. Crocodile registration form displayed by NCSA Mosaic

The client/server model used by Web browsers and Web servers is *stateless*. For example, say you wanted to develop a series of three different HTML forms to walk a user through the class registration processing. This seems an obvious use for forms input, but the input captured in the first form is not automatically associated with the input captured in the second form. If a user completes the second form, after having completed the first form, the Web server itself would not know whether the first form had been properly completed or what information was in it. In fact the Web server would have no recollection of handling that first form at all (the server adds a line in a log file, but never looks at it later).

Maintaining state between forms can be done, but your CGI script itself must maintain state information between form transactions. It is not as simple as setting a flag that says "Form 1 has been completed" because you need to keep a record of who completed it. More than one person may be in the process of registering at the same time.

20.3 WAIS Access from the Web

There are four different ways (excuse the pun) that users can access WAIS from the World Wide Web:

- Direct Web browser-to-WAIS-server access. In this method, which doesn't involve your Web server at all, browsers like Mosaic can access WAIS servers directly.
- A public-access Web gateway on the Internet. This is a Web server running on someone else's machine that interacts with WAIS servers and converts the results to HTML.
- A custom WAIS gateway. This is a script or program that is part of your Web server and that interacts with your own WAIS server (or maybe other WAIS servers).
- WAISgate, a commercial Web gateway that provides a forms-based user interface to WAIS queries

All four are viable techniques. Which one you choose depends on whether or not you want to sink time into developing a custom WAIS gateway, how accessible you want your interface to be to the general Web community, or how integrated you want your Web server to be with your WAIS server. The next four sections describe each technique, and Section 20.3.5 summarizes the strengths and weaknesses of each technique.

20.3.1 Direct WAIS Access

Mosaic version 2.0 includes direct WAIS server access. Mosaic operates as a WAIS client, but it displays the results in the HTML window. This approach has nothing to do with your Web server, as all of this prompting and WAIS interaction is done in the Web browser. For example, the following URL directly interacts with a WAIS server from Mosaic:

```
wais://cnidr.org/directory-of-servers
```

When this URL is opened directly, or by hyperlink, the user is prompted for a search query and then the WAIS server at *cnidr.org* processes the query against the *directory-of-servers* WAIS database. Alternatively, the user can specify the search string in the URL using the GET method. For example, in the following URL, the WAIS server running on port 210 at *ds.internic.net* processes the query phrase *MIME* against the *rfcs* WAIS database:

```
wais://ds.internic.net:210/rfcs?MIME
```

To make this direct WAIS access work for searching your data, you must set up a WAIS server and use *waisindex* with the special URL datatype. This directs *waisindex* to build headline files that are formatted as legal URLs. Chapter 8, *Creating WAIS Sources with waisindex*, describes how to use *waisindex*.

As helpful as this direct access is to Mosaic users, using this approach limits your readership to just the Mosaic subset of the Web community. This technique also forces your descriptive headline to be the document URL. This could be confusing to users accessing your WAIS index from dedicated WAIS clients.

20.3.2 Web-to-WAIS Gateways

The oldest technique used to access WAIS servers is to use one of a number of public Web-to-WAIS gateways that are available on the Internet. The two publicly accessible gateways can be accessed with the following URLs:

```
http://info.cern.ch:8001/wais-server-name:port-number/database-name?
http://www.ncsa.uiuc.edu:8001/wais-server-name:port-number/database-name?
```

In practice, both of these appear to be somewhat flaky.

These gateways are actually Web servers that also function as WAIS clients. The Web-to-WAIS gateway interacts with the Web browser to determine the query phrase. Then the gateways execute the query on behalf of the user and take the results of the WAIS search and convert it into HTML on the fly. This is a good way to jump start WAIS/Web interaction. A Web-to-WAIS gateway can be used to access any WAIS database. This technique uses the GET access method described in Section 20.1.1.

20.3.3 Developing a Custom WAIS Gateway

With the advent of the Common Gateway Interface (CGI), it has become much easier to develop your own WAIS gateway. In addition to being able to control the searching function yourself (and generate the resulting HTML yourself), this approach is also desirable because it can be used with any Web browser.

Let's use the same Perl script we used for the *alias-search* example as a starting point. We'll leave the bulk of the structure the same. The user prompting and CGI interaction is the same. The only thing we have to change is the actual search engine, which we will change from an inline regular-expression search to *waisq*. This is the code fragment we will change:

```
# Open the datafile and search through it.
# Write out any matches to stdout.

open(DATAFILE,"$data_file");
while (<DATAFILE>) {
        if (/$query/i) {print;}
}
close(DATAFILE);
```

waisq is the command line interface to WAIS. To invoke the search with the validated search phrase in *$query* we replace the above with:

```
$wais_source = "database-name.src";
$wais_path = "/wais/wais-sources/";
$waisq = "/usr/local/waisq";
$hit_limit = "40";

open(HITS, "-|") || exec ($waisq,"-f","-","-s","$wais_path",
            "-S","$wais_source","-m",$hit_limit,"-g",
            $query);
```

This tells *waisq* that:

–f
: There is no pre-built question file, so use the source identified by the –S switch and the query identified by the –g switch.

–s $wais_path
: The directory where the *.src* file is located

–S $wais_source
: The name of the *.src* file

–m $hit_limit
: The maximum number of document hits to return

–g $query
: The search phrase is in the $query variable

You can play around with these options to use a pre-built WAIS question file. This technique is used to search across multiple WAIS databases with a single query. Using that approach, search results are relevance-ranked within the scope of their respective databases. A search across three different WAIS databases could potentially have three documents all ranked as 1000 (the highest ranking).

In this particular example, after executing the code fragment above, the results of the search are open as an input stream that we can read from HITS. We then loop through that input stream and parse it looking for *:headline*, *:rank*, and *:number-of-lines.*

We then use the associated data to build our own HTML output stream that gets sent back through the Web server to the Web browser that initiated the search. We could leave the search hits enclosed in the preformatted <PRE> HTML tags, or we could use another type of tagging. We could structure it as a list of bullets, where each entry is the document name. To see an example of how this is done, look at the *wais.pl* code in the *cgi-bin* directory.

20.3.4 WAISgate

WAISgate is a commercial gateway between the World Wide Web and WAIS. WAISgate allows WAIS database providers to customize entry points into their WAIS database, input forms, search results, and generate HTML documents on the fly. WAISgate requires a Web browser that handles forms, so it can't be used with all Web browsers. Forms support is required so that WAISgate can generate structured boolean queries. Other features include:

- Access to local and remote WAIS databases
- Single-step processing: search of directory-of-servers, search of a database, and document retrieval
- Multitype documents with associated icons for each document format
- Search by fields in commercial WAIS databases
- Table-lookup conversion from WAIS types to MIME types

WAISgate is available from WAIS, Inc. You can get an online version for general use from:

```
http://www.wais.com/directory-of-servers.html
```

You can't copy or customize this resource, but you can see how WAISgate can be used to reach and search the WAIS directory-of-servers.

20.3.5 Comparison of WAIS-to-Web Techniques

Direct WAIS Access:

- Strength—No development required. Super-clean interface to a local WAIS database.
- Weakness—Only available in Mosaic and then only with direct WAIS patches. Not a general-purpose solution for an extended user community. No customization of search results.

Web-to-WAIS Gateway:

- Strength—No development required. Some degree of integration with your WAIS database and Web server. Public-access Web-to-WAIS gateways already on the Web.
- Weakness—Extensive overhead. WAIS database is often Web-specific and doesn't work with general-purpose WAIS clients. Users typically run into firewall issues. No customization of search results.

Custom WAIS Gateway:

- Strength—You totally control the gateway. Close integration between your WAIS database and Web server. You can customize the search results.
- Weakness—Custom development. When you complain about the gateway, you have to fix it.

WAISgate:

- Strength—Best functional interface to WAIS databases. No development required. Public-access WAISgate interface already on the Web. No firewall issues.
- Weakness—No integration between your WAIS database and your Web server. No customization of search results.

In this Chapter:
- *Access Control and User Authentication*
- *Security*

21

Web: Access Control and Security

You may be happy to give the world unrestricted access to the documentation on your server. If so, the setup described in Chapter 18, *Setting Up a Web Server*, is fine and there is no need for you to read Section 21.1. But you should definitely read Section 21.2, which describes issues involving the security of the system on which your Web server is running.

21.1 Access Control and User Authentication

Access can be controlled using two independent methods:

- Domain-level access control, where rejection or acceptance of connections is based on the Internet address of the system running the Web browser
- User authentication, where rejection or acceptance of connections is based on username and password access authorization. Only a few browsers, like Mosaic, support user authentication.

Access can also be controlled using a combination of these two methods.

21.1.1 Access Control Files

Access control and user authentication can be set up on a server-wide basis or on a directory-by-directory basis:

- Server-wide access and per-directory access is controlled by a global ACF (Access Control File). This ACF is called *access.conf*. The NCSA *httpd* requires that you always set up and administer a global ACF.
- If you choose, per-directory access can also be controlled by per-directory ACFs called *.htaccess* by default.* Per-directory ACFs can be restricted or completely forbidden by the global ACF. You should only use per-directory ACFs if there is a

* The per-directory ACF filename can be changed using the `AccessFileName` directive in the *srm.conf* configuration file.

good reason to decentralize access control (e.g., your server handles multiple independent projects, and each project team needs to handle its own access control).

Per-file access control is not available. If you need to protect an individual file, you should put the file into a directory by itself.

Let's look at how you could control access to two subdirectories in your document tree. With the first approach, subdirectory-1 and subdirectory-2 each has its own <Directory> directive in the global ACF:

```
<Directory /usr/local/etc/httpd/htdocs/subdirectory-1>
        <Limit GET>
        order, deny, allow, & require directives
        </Limit>
</Directory>

<Directory /usr/local/etc/httpd/htdocs/subdirectory-2>
        <Limit GET>
        order, deny, allow, & require directives
        </Limit>
</Directory>
```

If access to each directory needs to be controlled by a different person, both *.htaccess* in subdirectory-1 and *.htaccess* in subdirectory-2 can contain:

```
<Limit GET>
  order, deny, allow, & require directives
</Limit>
```

Outside of the <Limit> section, but within the <Directory> section, in the global ACF, the `Options` directive controls which advanced features you allow on your Web server, and `AllowOverride` defines whether you allow per-directory ACFs to override the global ACF. For more information on these *srm.conf* directives, see Chapter 20, *Web: Gateways and Forms.*

21.1.2 Domain-Level Access Control

You can allow or deny users access to your Web server based on their Internet domain address. This mechanism allows you to control access across an organization or department without regard to specific user names. Domain-level access control is done totally by your Web server, so it works with all Web browsers, unlike authentication.

First, we'll explain a bit about the various directives that control access and then give some examples of various access configurations.

21.1.2.1 Domain control directives

Access control files are sectioned by directory with the <Directory> directive. Within a directory section, the access-control directives are placed within a <Limit> section.

The directives that control access are:

`order` Defines the order in which `deny` and `allow` directives are evaluated within a Limit section

`allow` Defines which hosts can access the directory

`deny` Defines which hosts are denied access to the directory

Let's look at examples of how you alter access control files to satisfy different scenarios.

21.1.2.2 General unrestricted access

The initial Web server configuration described in Chapter 18, *Setting Up a Web Server*, brought your *httpd* server up for general unrestricted access. All users were allowed access to all information. Whether or not this unrestricted access was truly public depends on whether your Web server is running exposed on the Internet, is running behind a firewall, or is on a private TCP/IP network. But your Web server does nothing to restrict access.

21.1.2.3 Local-domain access only

You may be on the Internet or on a private TCP/IP network, but want to restrict access to your local campus or local organization. Assuming you are using the default `DocumentRoot`, just modify your *access.conf* configuration file to look like the following and reboot *httpd*.

```
<Directory /usr/local/etc/httpd/htdocs>
      Options Indexes FollowSymlinks
      AllowOverride None
      <Limit GET>
              order deny,allow
              deny from all
              allow from fredonia.edu
      </Limit>
</Directory>
```

If you compare this against the general unrestricted access configuration you will see that:

- The `order` directive was changed from `allow,deny` to `deny,allow`. This tells `httpd` to evaluate the `deny` directive first and then grant exceptions based on the *allow* directive.
- The `deny from all` directive was added.

- The `allow` directive was changed from `all` to just the local domain (in this case *fredonia.edu*).

You could use the same approach to further restrict access to a subdomain, such as *cs.fredonia.edu.*

You could also extend this approach down to the directory level by including the <Limit> section shown above in an *.htaccess* file in a subdirectory:

```
<Limit GET>
     order deny,allow
     deny from all
     allow from fredonia.edu
</Limit>
```

By putting this directive sequence in an *.htaccess* file in a specific subdirectory, you can have general unrestricted access to your overall Web server, but limit one area to local-domain access only. This technique also works to protect your personal HTML directory, if you place the *.htaccess* file in your personal *public_html* subdirectory.

21.1.2.4 Multi-organization access only

In this scenario, we are creating a private Web on the Internet. This might be for three organizations that are collaborating on a community Web server and want to fully develop the server before opening it up to public access.

If the three organizations are *fredonia.edu*, *non.profit.org*, and *acme.net*, each modifies its respective *access.conf* configuration files to have the same general access control as the previous example, except each would include the following `allow` directive:

```
allow fredonia.edu non.profit.org acme.net
```

This allows anyone from these three domain names to look at the Web server, but denies access to everyone else.

21.1.3 User Authentication

With user authentication, you can allow or deny individuals access to your Web server or document tree directories on a username and password basis. There is no correspondence between your system-level usernames/passwords (in */etc/passwd*) and the Web server's username/password file.

When users access pages that are protected with this mechanism, they are given two prompts (username and password) to which they must respond correctly before access is allowed. Once authenticated, they can navigate from page to page without repeated authentication prompts. This works because the Web browser remembers the hostname, directory path, and name/password for subsequent retrievals. The same name/password pair is reused anytime the Web browser accesses a URL with the same hostname and directory path.

User authentication requires cooperation between a Web browser and your Web server, so unless the Web browser supports user authentication, users cannot be authenticated. Mosaic and Lynx currently support user authentication.

To use user authentication, you have to maintain a private hypertext username/password file. By convention, this file is called *.htpasswd*. User authentication is designed so that a user doesn't need an account on your system in order to be authenticated for access to files on your Web server.

21.1.3.1 Managing the htpasswd file

To manipulate the *.htpasswd* file, you need a program called *htpasswd*. This program is not included with the pre-built binary kit, so you need to get the full source kit and compile it from source. The source is called *htpasswd.c* and is found in the *support/* subdirectory. See Section 18.1.2 for information on how to compile NCSA HTTP (but only follow the directions in the *support/* subdirectory). *htpasswd* is invoked as follows:

```
% htpasswd [-c] .htpasswdusername
```

username is the name of the user you wish to add or edit. The *–c* flag, if present, tells *htpasswd* to create a new hypertext password file instead of editing an existing one.

If *htpasswd* finds the user you specified, it asks you to change the user's password. Type the new password twice. *httpd* then updates the file. If *htpasswd* doesn't find the specified user, it asks you to give the user an initial password.

You can have multiple *.htpasswd* files, or you can use a different filename. The key is that the file must be in a different directory than the one you are protecting and must be located outside the document tree structure.

21.1.3.2 Individual authentication

Individual authentication is accomplished using a combination of access control directives and a private *.htpasswd* file. Let's look at an example of how to restrict access to only individuals knowing the password.

Assuming you are using the default `DocumentRoot`, just modify your *access.conf* configuration file to look like the following.

```
<Directory /usr/local/etc/httpd/htdocs>
      Options Indexes FollowSymlinks
      AllowOverride None
      AuthUserFile /usr/local/etc/httpd/conf/.htpasswd
      AuthGroupFile /dev/null
      AuthName By Secret Password Only!
      AuthType Basic
      <Limit GET>
              require user username
      </Limit>
</Directory>
```

If you compare this to the general unrestricted access configuration you will see that:

- The `AuthUserFile` directive is added to specify the absolute pathname to the hypertext password file.
- The `AuthGroupFile` directive has been added, but set to */dev/null*, which by UNIX standards indicates that the file doesn't exist.
- The `AuthName` directive is added to specify the prompt to be given to the user for the username (in this case `By Secret Password Only!`).
- The `AuthType` directive is added and set to `Basic`. You currently don't have a choice about this, as `Basic` is the only authorization type available.
- All four `Auth` directives go outside the Limit sectioning directive.
- The `order` and `allow` directives were removed from the <Limit> sectioning directive and replaced with the `require` directive. This tells *httpd* to prompt for a username and password and that the username has to be *username*. Using the `require` directive dictates the need to include the `AuthUserFile`, `AuthGroupFile`, `AuthName`, and `AuthType` directives.

Next, create a hypertext password file for the username specified in your *access.conf* configuration file:

```
% htpasswd -c /usr/local/etc/httpd/conf/.htpasswd username
```

htpasswd prompts you for the password. Remember that for any changes to the configuration files (including *.htpasswd*) to take effect, you must reboot *httpd* as described in Section 18.1.5.2 (unless you are running the server under *inetd*). After your Web server restarts, access is restricted to only those individuals that know the user name and the accompanying password.

If you want to use individual authentication on a directory-level basis to protect the */usr/local/etc/httpd/htdocs/subdirectory-3* directory, you need to place the following directives in a *.htaccess* file in that directory:

```
AuthUserFile /usr/local/etc/httpd/conf/.htpasswd
AuthGroupFile /dev/null
AuthName By Secret Password Only!
AuthType Basic
<Limit GET>
    require user username
</Limit>
```

21.1.3.3 Group authentication

In addition to authenticating users individually, you can also place them into groups and then treat each group as a whole. There are three steps to this process:

- Modify the global ACF (*access.conf*) file.

- Create a hypertext group file (*.htgroup*) with multiple users as members.
- Double-check that all the users in the hypertext group file are also in the hypertext password file.

Let's look at a specific example. Using the previous global ACF we used for individual authentication as a starting point, you would modify it to look like this:

```
<Directory /usr/local/etc/httpd/htdocs>
     Options Indexes FollowSymlinks
     AllowOverride None
     AuthUserFile /usr/local/etc/httpd/conf/.htpasswd
     AuthGroupFile /usr/local/etc/httpd/conf/.htgroup
     AuthName By Secret Password Only!
     AuthType Basic
     <Limit GET>
          require group groupname
     </Limit>
</Directory>
```

If you compare this against the starting point, you will see that:

- The `AuthGroupFile` directive was modified from */dev/null* to point to a group password file called *.htgroup*. It's a good idea to place this file in the same directory as the hypertext password file.
- The `require` directive was modified from `user` to `group` and the *`username`* was changed to *`groupname`*.

Then, in the second step, you create the */usr/local/etc/httpd/conf/.htgroup* file with a text editor and place the following group definition in it:

```
groupname: username1 username2 username3 usernameN
```

Usernames are separated by spaces. Multiple groups could be identified in the hypertext group file, one per line.

If you have already defined the usernames you associated with the group name, then you just need to reboot *httpd* to have these changes take effect.

If you added usernames to the group file that are not entered into the hypertext password file, then you use the *htpasswd* program to add usernames and associated passwords to the existing *.htpasswd* file. For example,

```
% htpasswd /usr/local/etc/httpd/conf/.htpasswd username2
% htpasswd /usr/local/etc/httpd/conf/.htpasswd username3
```

Note that *htpasswd* is invoked without the *–c* flag, since the hypertext password file already exists and these new usernames are just being added to it.

21.1.3.4 Simultaneous access control and user authentication

User authentication can be used in conjunction with domain-level access control. For example, in either of the two preceding examples, you could have specified that only users from the *fredonia.edu* domain could get to the user authentication prompts. To do this, you would modify the <Limit> section to look like:

```
<Limit GET>
        order deny,allow
        deny from all
        allow from fredonia.edu
        require group groupname
</Limit>
```

Using the two together adds another level of security to your Web server.

21.2 Security

When configuring access control for your Web server, you want to make sure you do not give unauthorized access to anyone who may deliberately try to harm your system. Your Web server is secure if you set it up as described in Chapter 18, *Setting Up a Web Server*, for unrestricted access. However, as you incorporate advanced features into your Web server such as gateways, you should also incorporate a heightened sense of caution.

All of the following security concerns should be tempered by how your system is connected to the Internet. If your system is protected behind a firewall, your security concerns are different than if you are directly attached to the Internet.

21.2.1 Links Outside the Document Tree

FTP and Gopher both have the `chroot()` feature, wherein access is absolutely restricted to files within the data tree. Web servers don't have this feature. However, Web browsers can't randomly walk across the directory structure on the system. All access is relative to the top of the document tree (as defined by the DocumentRoot directive). Even when looking through a directory with automatically generated indexes, *httpd* does not let users change directories up past the top of the document tree.

However, unlike FTP and Gopher (when set up properly), links from within the document tree to outside the tree do work. The biggest danger for a webmaster is a system with users who might create a symbolic link to a directory outside the document tree. This could happen either in the document tree itself or in a user's private HTML directory. To safeguard against this, the webmaster should either disable the *followsymlink* option in *access.conf* or at least change it to *SymLinksIfOwnerMatch*.

21.2.2 Access Control and User Authentication

Access control and user authentication make your Web server relatively safe, but not bulletproof:

- With domain-based access control, your Web server is only as safe as DNS, the Domain Name Server. If you trust DNS, you should trust domain-based access control.
- With user authentication, the password is passed over the network in *uuencoded* format (simple ASCII encoding not to be confused with encryption). This method is similar to Telnet-style username and password security. So if you trust your machine to be on the Internet (open to Telnet attempts by anyone), then you have no reason not to trust this method as well.

The bottom line is that if you absolutely cannot have information be seen by outside people, you probably should not use the NCSA Web server (or any other current Web server).

21.2.3 Personal HTML Directories

When configuring your Web server, if you do nothing with the `UserDir` directive in the *srm.conf* configuration file, your Web server provides public access to a *public_html* directory under each user's home directory. Some users on your system will not even be aware of this, in which case there is no problem. Others will want to serve HTML documents from this directory. These are the users that need protection and, sometimes, the ones you need to protect against.

If all of your users have their home directories in one physical location (such as */home*), protection is easy. You include the following directives in your *access.conf* configuration file:

```
<Directory /home>
    AllowOverride None
    Options Indexes
</Directory>
```

If they are not all in one location, then you should use a wildcard pattern matching the name of the `UserDir` directive to protect the directories:

```
<Directory /*/public_html*>
    AllowOverride None
    Options Indexes
</Directory>
```

Setting the `AllowOverride` directive to `None` and the `Options` directive to `Indexes` prevents users from accidentally executing CGI scripts with potential security problems, purposely including executable CGI scripts in the HTML stream, or establishing symbolic links that lead out of the document tree.

If you want to give your users the ability to create symbolic links, at least add the `SymLinksIfOwnerMatch` clause to the `Options` directive to assure that they can only establish symbolic links to files and directories they own.

21.2.4 Shell Metacharacters in Forms

The addition of interactive forms gives users the ability to key in shell metacharacters in form input fields in an attempt to create shell syntax errors or execute arbitrary commands on your system. These must be trapped in the CGI scripts associated with each form. This problem and how to protect against it are described in detail in Section 20.1.2.2.

CGI scripts can be placed in three locations, the main *cgi-bin* subdirectory, alternative *cgi-bin* subdirectories (that you establish with the `ScriptAlias directive`), and in users' personal HTML subdirectories. You will have to either police all of these areas or else have confidence in your user community to not expose security holes in their personal CGI scripts. If you can't trust them to do this, you simply make sure that the Options directive used to protect users' personal HTML directories is not set to `All` or `ExecCGI`. The best way to handle users who can't be trusted is to specify the Options directive in *access.conf* to be used server-wide and then use `AllowOverride None`.

21.2.5 Server-Side Includes

Server-side includes have not been discussed in detail, but can be a potentially dangerous security issue. Similar to an untrusted CGI script, server-side includes can be used to write anything into the HTML stream going back to a Web browser. It is generally a good idea to completely disable server-side includes wherever possible. Not only will you be plugging a potential security hole, but you will also be getting a big performance gain on your Web server.

Server-side includes are enabled, server-wide or per-directory, by setting the `Options` directive to either `All` or `Includes`. If you do allow includes, particularly in user's personal HTML directories, at least make sure you set the `Options` directive to `IncludesNoExec`, which does not allow executable CGI scripts to be included for execution in the HTML stream.

In this Chapter:
- *A Simple File Server: canned_reply*
- *Ways to Manage Mailing Lists*
- *What's It Like to Use List Server Software?*
- *Choosing a Mailing List System: A Feature Comparison*
- *Email Ethics*
- *Email Services and Network Connections*
- *The List-managers Mailing List*
- *How Email Is Delivered*

22

Introduction to Email Services

Why would you want to provide email services instead of (or in addition to) one of the newer and sexier services in this book, like Gopher and World Wide Web? One important reason is that email can reach many more people than any other service in this book. As reviewer Randy Diffenderfer said, it's the only way to reach the far corners of your "electronic empire." Email reaches people with any kind of Internet connection or UUCP link, plus all the people who dial in to other networks such as CompuServe, Prodigy, America Online, and MCImail that have gateways to and from the Internet.

Email has several other advantages:

- It uses only the software that the customer is most likely to have and use most often—the email reader. Email services tend to fit into the daily work flow better than services that use special browsing tools.
- It's flexible enough to provide a wide range of services.
- Because of security concerns on the Internet, many companies set up firewall machines, which prevent some Internet services from getting in or out. Email is the one service that is almost universally permitted.
- The security infrastructure for email is better than for any other service if you use Privacy Enhanced Mail (PEM). However, PEM does require licensing for some commercial purposes.

- Email can spread out the load on busy systems and network links because it handles messages sequentially. In comparison, an interactive service may overload a system or deny access if too many people are using it at once. In general, email services require the least network bandwidth, hardware, and software from the information service provider (although it can still add up).

The non-interactive nature of email can be both a plus and a minus. The downside is that email users may have to wait longer for a reply (or an explanation of what went wrong). The upside is that email isn't expected to be instant, so delays can be less annoying than waiting for a slow interactive service.

This chapter introduces two types of email services: email information servers and mailing lists.

An *email information server* is a program that accepts emailed requests for information and sends the information back by email. One example is an email file server: a user sends an email message to request the desired files, and the file server reads the message and mails the files back. This chapter explains a simple email file server named *canned_reply*, which sends back a single file. It can be modified to send any kind of information. Chapter 26, *Ftpmail*, covers Ftpmail, which is a type of email file server; it lets sites that aren't directly on the Internet get FTP'ed files through email.

A *mailing list* is a group of email addresses that can all be reached by sending a message to one address: the *list address*. Mail sent to that address is redistributed to all *subscribers* (to all addressees on the list). Subscribers can have a discussion by sending messages to the list address (often called "posting to the list"); each message will be distributed to all the list's subscribers. The list of addressees can be maintained by hand or with an automated *list server* system like Majordomo or ListProcessor. The Majordomo list server, described in Chapter 24, *Automating Mailing Lists with Majordomo*, and Chapter 25, *The Majordomo List Owner and Moderator*, manages mailing lists and also includes an email file server.

Mailing lists are good for many things, including:

- Distributing information from a central source to lots of people (like the O'Reilly *ora-news* mailing list of people who want to be notified about new products)
- Discussing a project among several participants (like the authors of this book)
- Exchanging questions and answers with other users of a product or service, or perhaps company technical-support personnel

First we'll describe how to set up an email information server (*canned_reply*). Then we'll introduce mailing lists. Finally, we'll discuss some important issues raised by email services.

22.1 A Simple File Server: canned_reply

Email file servers are programs that send files by email in response to email requests. To get a file, a user sends an email message to the file server's email address. Standard UNIX mail (without MIME extensions) can deliver only text files. But file servers can encode non-text files (pictures, sound, executable programs, and so on) into plain ASCII text with a program like *uuencode*. The recipient uses a program like *uudecode* to extract the original file from the *uuencode*d message.

Our simple file server is a Perl script named *canned_reply*. It's in this book's sample file archive; see the Preface. *canned_reply* can mail a file or send an automatic reply to a mail message. At O'Reilly & Associates, we use it to answer special email addresses we've set up for common requests. For example, *canned_reply* answers messages sent to *info@gnn.com* by sending a subscription form for the online magazine *Global Network Navigator*. It also answers the address *listserv@ora.com* by sending an introduction to our *listproc* mailing-list server. (*canned_reply* does not allow the user to specify a filename; it is limited to serving one file for each incoming email address. Because the same script can answer multiple addresses, though, you can distribute many different files by creating one email alias per file.)

To install *canned_reply*, just put the script somewhere on your system and set up an email alias for each address you want the script to reply to. You may need to modify the `$replies` or `$mailer` variables for your system—the script gets the rest of its information from arguments specified in the email alias. Here's an example of a *sendmail* alias that answers our *listserv* address:

```
listserv: "|/usr/local/etc/canned_reply listserv@online.ora.com
      listserv-gone listmaster"
```

When someone sends mail to *listserv*, *sendmail* runs *canned_reply* with the three arguments shown. The first argument (`listserv@online.ora.com`) is the full email address of the alias being answered by *canned_reply* this is used in error messages to the postmaster. The second argument (`listserv-gone`) is the relative pathname of a file in the directory of canned reply files (specified in the script as */usr/local/lib/canned_replies*); if you use a full pathname (starting with a `/` character), *canned_reply* won't look in the default directory. The third argument (`listmaster`) is the address you want error messages to go to (this address becomes the envelope sender, as described in the box in Section 23.4).

Here's the complete *canned_reply* script. It's a bit long but all it really does is extract the appropriate email address from the user's message.

```
#! /usr/local/bin/perl
##
##  canned_reply - send an automatic reply to mail
##
##  Usage (in /etc/aliases):
##      owner-alias: bounceaddr
```

```
##      alias: "|progpath alias replypath bounceaddr"
##  or
##      alias: "|progpath alias replypath bounceaddr", /archive
##  where:
##
##  - progpath = full pathname of this script
##
##  - alias = name of alias @ actual host,
##      like: book-info-request@online.ora.com
##
##  - replypath = pathname of file we send as the canned reply.
##      If no leading /, reads file from $replies directory (defined below).
##      File should start with NO BLANK LINE, then From:, Subject:
##      and any other header except To: (which this program fills in).
##      Then, before message in file, put a single blank line.
##
##  - bounceaddr = address (envelope sender) to send bounces to
##
##  - /archive = full pathname of archive file to save all incoming messages
##      (usually needs to be mode 666 unless no messages come from local host)
##
##      by Jerry Peek, 8/17/93


# TABSTOPS IN THIS SCRIPT SET AT 4 (IN vi, USE :se ts=4 sw=4)

# Modify $replies and $mailer for your system if necessary:
$replies = "/usr/local/lib/canned_replies"; # Default directory for reply files
$mailer = "/usr/lib/sendmail -f$ARGV[2] -oi";
$* = 1;

#
# Tack path onto reply file if it doesn't start with a slash:
#
$replypath = (($ARGV[1] =~ m@^/@) ? "" : "$replies/") . $ARGV[1];

#
# If wrong number of args or unreadable canned reply file,
# send error and sender's mail message to postmaster:
#
if (scalar(@ARGV) != 3) {
    $complaint = "need 3 arguments, got:\n\t@ARGV";
}
elsif (! -r $replypath) {
    $complaint = "can't read reply file '$replypath'.";
}
if ($complaint) {
    open(MAIL, "|$mailer postmaster") || die;
    print MAIL "$0 aborting from '$ARGV[0]' alias:\n\t$complaint\n\n";
    # End string with > to prefix the From line in the message:
    print MAIL "This message needs a reply:\n\n>";
    print MAIL <STDIN>;
    close(MAIL);
```

```
        exit(0);     # We don't want sender to know that something went wrong
}

#
# Read (only) header into the variables $from (for envelope sender)
# and $header (for the rest of the header)
#
while (<STDIN>) {
    last if /^$/;
    # Make key lower-case:
    if (/^From /) {
        # listproc system is case-sensitive on first line;
        # if it's "from" instead of "From", it's a syntax error.
        # So, save From line separately.
        @from = (split(/^([-\w]+)[  ]*/));
    }
    elsif (/^\S/) {
        @part = (split(/^([-\w]+:?)[    ]*/));
        $part[1] =~ tr/A-Z/a-z/;
        $header .= "$part[1] $part[2]";
    }
    else {
        $header .= $_;
    }
}

#
# Put headers into array.  Note: values (but not keys) end with newlines.
# (Adapted from "Programming Perl" chapter 4.)
# Note: loses multiple lines with same key (like Received:):
#
$header =~ s/\n\s+/ /g;      # Merge continuation lines.
%head = ('FRONTSTUFF', split(/^([-\w]+:?)[  ]*/, $header));

# Here you can read body from <STDIN> if you need to...
# (But we don't need to.)

#
# Get address to use:
#
if (defined($head{'reply-to:'})) {
    $useaddr = $head{'reply-to:'};
}
elsif (defined($head{'from:'})) {
    $useaddr = $head{'from:'};
}
elsif (defined($head{'apparently-from:'})) {
    $useaddr = $head{'apparently-from:'};
}

#
# If we got an address, use it.  Else, bounce to bounceaddr:
#
```

```
if (defined($useaddr)) {
    chop $useaddr;
    open(REPLY, $replypath) || die;
    open(MAIL, "|$mailer -t") || die;
    print MAIL "To: $useaddr\n";
    # REPLY file may start with From:, Subject:; MUST then have blank line:
    print MAIL <REPLY>;
    print MAIL "\n\n ---------- Your original message is below ----------\n\n";
    print MAIL <STDIN>;
    close(MAIL);
    close(REPLY);
}
else {
    # BOUNCE TO bounceaddr
    open(MAIL, "|$mailer $ARGV[2]") || die;
    print MAIL "$0 aborting: can't find address to reply to.\n\n";
    # End string with > to prefix the From line in the message:
    print MAIL "This message needs a reply:\n\n>";
    print MAIL <STDIN>;
    close(MAIL);
}
exit(0);     # We don't want sender to know if something went wrong
```

The default directory for reply files is set to */usr/local/lib/canned_replies*; you can change it by editing the script. If *canned_reply* will be answering mail sent to several addresses, you can put all the reply files in the default directory and use the filenames (instead of the full pathnames) in the aliases.

Let's take a look at a sample session. Jerry sends mail to *listserv@ora.com*:

```
Reply-to: Jerry Peek <jerry@ora.com>
From: jerry@somehost.ora.com (Jerry Peek)
To: listserv@ora.com

help
```

canned_reply reads his message header, sees the "Reply-to:" address, and uses that. If there's no "Reply-to:" address, *canned_reply* chooses the "From:" address. Finally, it defaults to the "Apparently-From:" address set by some mail transport agents. The contents of the message, in this case "help", is irrelevant to *canned_reply* (but you might want to have scripts you write look at it). Here's the reply it mails:

```
From listmaster@online.ora.com  Sun Sep  4 07:06:50 PDT 1994
Date: Sun, 4 Sep 1994 10:05:27 -0400
Message-Id: <199409041405.AA20398@online.ora.com>
To: Jerry Peek <jerry@ora.com>
From: O'Reilly & Associates Mailing List Manager <listmaster@online.ora.com>
Subject: Your message to listserv at ORA

(This is an automatic reply.)

We received your message to "listserv".  We don't run listserv here...
   ...explain listproc help facility, give other info...
```

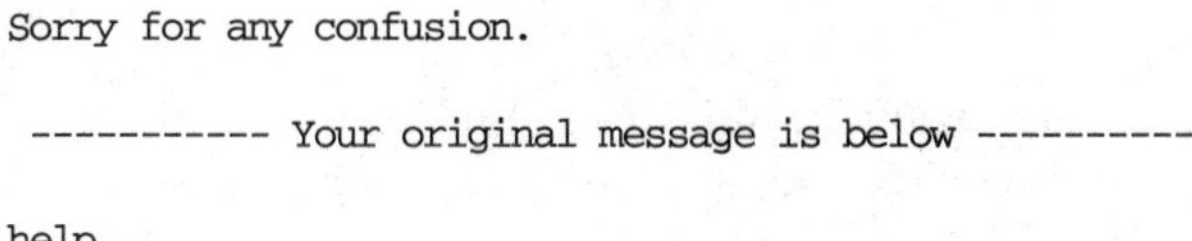

```
Sorry for any confusion.

 ---------- Your original message is below ----------

help
```

The reply file is shown below. When *canned_reply* sends a reply, it adds the "To:" header field; the reply file should start with any other valid fields you want to add (usually at least "From:" and "Subject:"). For instance, if you want blind copies of all the replies *canned_reply* sends, include your address in a "bcc:" field. Whether you add header fields or not, put a blank line before the first line of the body:

```
From: O'Reilly & Associates Mailing List Manager <listmaster@online.ora.com>
Subject: Your message to listserv at ORA

(This is an automatic reply.)

We received your message to "listserv". We don't run listserv here
at O'Reilly & Associates. We run a similar program, ListProcessor 6.0.
The ListProcessor requests aren't quite the same as listserv requests.
So, we're returning your message unprocessed.

The address for our ListProcessor is: listproc@online.ora.com
You can send a HELP request (in the body of your message) for a
summary of valid listproc requests.

If you have questions about our mailing lists, please mail the
list manager: listmaster@online.ora.com

If you didn't want information about mailing lists, please send
your mail message to our general email address:  info@ora.com

Sorry for any confusion.
```

canned_reply adds a copy of the original message at the end. This makes it easy for the sender to reconstruct their new message if they didn't save a copy of the original.

You can elaborate on the *canned_reply* script to provide more advanced email services. Instead of having the script just dump the contents of a file, you can have it generate some information on the fly, possibly based on text in the incoming message. For example, if you have a database of stock prices, you can search incoming mail for stock-ticker symbols, look up the current quotes for those stocks, and reply with mail containing those prices. To get even more elaborate, you can log information about each request (for billing purposes), or check another file to see if a certain user has paid for the privilege of receiving the quotes. All of these additional features can be inserted into *canned_reply* near the middle, at the comment that says "Here you can read body from standard input if you need to."

But if you just want to serve small files, *canned_reply* is fine as it is. Or you can use the file servers built into the Majordomo and ListProcessor mailing-list servers, which have the advantage that they can deal with changing numbers of files and changing filenames (unlike *canned_reply*, which serves only one file per alias). The *ftpmail* program (see Chapter 26, *Ftpmail*) is also an email file server, but it gets its files by FTP from the Internet, and it's smart enough to chop up huge files into smaller pieces before mailing.

22.2 Ways to Manage Mailing Lists

There are basically three ways to set up a mailing list: using only an MTA (Mail Transport Agent—such as *sendmail* or MMDF), using Majordomo, or using ListProcessor.* This section introduces the three ways, including the unique features of each. Section 22.4 is a feature comparison to help you pick the best method for the lists you want to set up. Finally, Section 22.3.3 discusses the downside of automated list-manager programs; they aren't a perfect solution.

The next three chapters cover *sendmail*-only lists and Majordomo lists in complete detail. ListProcessor is too complex to be covered completely in this book, so we'll do no more than introduce it and use it in a few examples.

Small mailing lists can be set up using nothing but *sendmail*. Other MTAs, such as MMDF, can be set up to do the same thing. The list of subscribers is stored as a *mail alias*, a single address that the MTA expands into the complete list when a user sends mail to it. For these small mailing lists, someone maintains the subscription addresses by hand. People who want to subscribe to a list or cancel their subscription send mail to the person in charge of subscriptions. When anyone mails a message to the list address, it's redistributed right away—there usually aren't restrictions on who can post, how or when the messages are distributed, and so on. Chapter 23, *Simple Mailing Lists*, describes how to set up these lists.

More-complex lists are easier to maintain if they're implemented with list-server software such as Majordomo or ListProcessor. Here is a basic list of features that either package provides:

- Handles subscriptions mostly without help from a human
- Allows a human (a *moderator*) to control what messages appear on the list
- Can distribute messages as *digests* to users who want frequent messages to arrive grouped in a single message instead of one by one. A message digest is one file containing several complete messages—it is not a condensed version of the messages (like the condensed articles in *Reader's Digest* magazine). A digest may include a summary of the subjects covered.
- *Archives* previous postings to a list and makes them available. Archives can hold files related to email lists or unrelated files: programs, graphics, or anything else that people might want to receive at their option.

* You can find other freely available list-management software on the net, but these are the major packages. A good place to read about other list servers is the archive of the mailing list about mailing lists. See Section 22.7.

- Provides some help in handling bounced messages. A *bounced message* is one that was sent to a subscriber, but gets returned as undeliverable. (Messages bounce for many reasons. A network may be down, the email address may have changed, etc.)

22.3 What's It Like to Use List Server Software?

List servers use a special email address (usually *majordomo@host.x.y* for Majordomo) that accepts all commands for all lists on that host. The list-server program reads the messages sent to that address and, if the message has valid commands, the program executes them. The message must be in a certain format, with one command per line. The user's mail can include commands to subscribe to a list, unsubscribe, find out which mailing lists are available, get help for the system, and so on.

Most list-server software has one person (or more) who is the *list owner.* A list's owner can control the list: add or delete users, approve each message before it's sent to the list, and change the list configuration. The list owner may be located at a remote computer—and may control the list by email.

The following sections describe how a user sees a list server, a brief summary of the list owner's job (details are in Chapter 25, *The Majordomo List Owner and Moderator*), some disadvantages of automated list servers, and ways to work around those problems.

22.3.1 From a Subscriber's Point of View

Let's take a look at a series of messages between a person named Andrea and the List-Processor at O'Reilly & Associates. We've used ListProcessor here, even though it's not covered in detail in this book, because you can actually try these examples. The example also illustrates a security problem with mailing lists, how ListProcessor attempts to solve it, and the problems that causes.

Andrea (a bookworm) knows that ORA has a mailing list with general announcements about new books and products—and she's heard that the email address for the server is *listproc@online.ora.com.* She sends a message containing two commands: *help* and *lists.* Although command names vary from system to system, those two are fairly standard. The first command asks for general help; the second asks for a description of the mailing lists available:

```
From andrea@mac23.mogo.edu  Sat Sep  3 13:51:03 1994
Date: Sat, 3 Sep 1994 11:51:03 -0600 (MDT)
From: Andrea_Thompson@mogo.edu
To: listproc@online.ora.com

help
lists
```

The server reads her message and sends either one or two messages in return. ListProcessor sends one message per command; here's the first one:

```
From listproc@online.ora.com  Sat Sep  3 11:52:37 1994
Date: Sat, 3 Sep 1994 13:52:37 -0400
From: listproc@online.ora.com
To: andrea@mac23.mogo.edu
Subject: HELP
X-Listprocessor-Version: 6.0c -- ListProcessor by Anastasios Kotsikonas
X-Comment: O'Reilly & Associates List Processor

                              ListProcessor 6.0

Here is a brief description of the set of requests recognized by
ListProcessor.
    ...
information <list>
------------------
Get information about the specified list.
    ...
```

Here's the reply to Andrea's second command:

```
From listproc@online.ora.com  Sat Sep  3 11:52:39 1994
Date: Sat, 3 Sep 1994 13:52:39 -0400
From: listproc@online.ora.com
To: andrea@mac23.mogo.edu
Subject: LISTS
X-Listprocessor-Version: 6.0c -- ListProcessor by Anastasios Kotsikonas
X-Comment: O'Reilly & Associates List Processor

Here is the current active list of the 7 mailing lists
served by this server:

consort@online.ora.com    Consortium of Small Internet Service Providers
    ...
ora-news@online.ora.com   Announcements from O'Reilly & Associates, Inc.
```

The *help* output tells her about a command named *information* that gives more information about a list. The *lists* output mentions a list named *ora-news*.

Andrea sends another message to *listproc* that has the commands *help subscribe* and *information ora-news*. Back comes detailed information about the *subscribe* command and a few paragraphs of information about the *ora-news* list.

She's decided to subscribe, so she sends a third message to *listproc* with this line in the body:*

```
subscribe ora-news Andrea Thompson of Mogollon University
```

* Different list servers use different syntax for subscription commands. For instance, Majordomo would be confused by Andrea's name and organization; it expects an optional email address after the list name.

If *ora-news* is a list that's open to the public (it is), and if other (optional) conditions are met, Andrea's email address, name, and organization will be added to the *ora-news* mailing list. The list server will send her a confirmation—or a rejection, if something's wrong.

The next time someone sends an announcement to the *ora-news* list, Andrea will automatically get a copy. She'll get copies of new messages until she sends an *unsubscribe* request to *listproc.*

Now that Andrea is on the list (subscribed), the server may have other commands she can use to control her subscription. For example, she can ask for copies of old digests or other archive files related to the list.

22.3.2 For a List Owner

This section is a short description of a list owner's job. Chapter 25, *The Majordomo List Owner and Moderator*, has a more detailed explanation for list owners whose lists are run by Majordomo.

The person who *owns* a list is often (but not always) the person who had the idea for the list in the first place. The list owner doesn't have to be a software expert. The list owner usually controls the list by email, by sending commands in mail messages to the list server.

The owner can make a list *private*, controlling who is allowed to subscribe. The owner can *moderate* a list, controlling the articles posted to it. Under Majordomo, a list owner can change almost all of the list configuration options by email. (The system administrator does the first-time list setup for the owner.)

The server forwards some messages to the list owner for action or approval. The owner mails commands to the server in response. Bounced (undeliverable) messages also come to the list owner; the owner can change subscribers' addresses or "unsubscribe" them (cancel their subscriptions).

22.3.3 Downside of List Servers

Our goal in this section is to lower your expectations. :-) If you expect to start up a list server and have it manage a list of 10,000 people* all by itself, think again!

Running such a big list with a list server is certainly easier than doing without one, especially if you want all those nice features beyond automatic subscription management. But a list server can be complicated to install and maintain. There may be lots of configuration files to keep track of, log files to check, bugs and software features you don't like, cryptic error messages sent to subscribers, grumpy subscribers who have trouble making the software do what they need, outdated bouncing subscriptions that you need to cancel, and more. All of this takes time for the people who run the lists.

* Or just a few hundred people.

The moral is that list servers need substantial human oversight. Fortunately, they do at least take care of most routine list maintenance.

22.3.4 The Personal Touch

O'Reilly & Associates' mailing lists have thousands of members. The addresses are advertised worldwide. Novice users don't know the conventions. We send instructions, but some people don't read them or don't understand. More than a few people send a chatty message to our *listproc* address, like "Hi—please subscribe me," and get an automated rejection.

Some day, list-server software may be friendlier to people who don't know how to use it. For now, though, if customer relations are important to you, do a careful evaluation of automated systems. You may be more technically-inclined than many of your list's users, so you might not see obvious problems in instructions; the best evaluator might be a non-technical novice.

Our compromise has been to:

- Change server error messages that aren't clear to novices. Add specific instructions, information about our main mailing lists, and explain how to reach a human for more help.
- Read the server's log file often. Look for mail from people who tried to subscribe or unsubscribe, got an error, and didn't try again. Process the person's request by hand and send them a personal message to tell them that we've done it.

22.3.5 Mailing-List Security

This isn't a huge issue, but it should be mentioned. A user's address (especially the "From:" header field) can be forged. That means that someone could send the email list server (or even a person managing a list) a message pretending to be someone else. A malicious person could unsubscribe that other person, or post a message to the list pretending to be that other person. The upshot is that mailing lists should be used very carefully if there will be any sensitive information.

It is sometimes possible to detect these forged messages by comparing the "From:" (with colon) header field to the "Received:", "Return-Path:", and "From" (with no colon) fields. If there isn't a reasonable similarity, something may be wrong. (See the sidebar in Section 23.4 for details.) But only the ListProcessor 6.0c (and earlier) mailing list server does this checking for you—and it does so in a way that creates other hassles, caused by the fact that "From:" and the envelope sender are often different in a valid message. For instance, look at the sample messages in Section 22.3; compare the address of the envelope sender (*andrea@mac23.mogo.edu*) with the "From:" address (*Andrea_Thompson@mogo.edu*).*

Another slight security issue involves how the list server recognizes mail from a list owner—a person with special privileges to control a list. List owners include a password with their commands. The password is sent as clear text in a mail message to the list server, so it's far from completely secure. Still, the password system stops most troublemakers.

We've been talking only about the security of the list, not the security of the entire system. In general, mailing list servers are not known to be a threat in terms of allowing access to the system on which they run, at least not more than other network services. But any public service you provide just naturally opens the door a little wider to undesirable people: with all of the benefits, there are a few risks. For example, in June 1994, crackers found and exploited a long-standing security hole in Majordomo versions 1.90 and before. Monitor your system, keep in touch by reading the mailing lists that discuss your server and other software, and be sure to watch for CERT advisories.

22.4 Choosing a Mailing List System: A Feature Comparison

This section compares simple mailing lists handled by MTA aliases and *sendmail* (covered in Chapter 23, *Simple Mailing Lists*), with lists served by Majordomo (in Chapter 24, *Automating Mailing Lists with Majordomo*, and Chapter 25, *The Majordomo List Owner and Moderator*) and ListProcessor version 6.0c. Although this book doesn't cover ListProcessor, we've used it as an example of a list server with more features.

This list includes only the major differences.

22.4.1 Simple Lists with Your MTA

Advantages:

- No new programs needed
- Simple maintenance
- "Personal touch" for subscribers

Disadvantages:

- All subscription adds/deletes are done by hand.
- Subscribers have to wait for help when the list maintainer isn't at work.
- Little or no control over messages sent to a list unless you add extra software

* If Andrea reads any mail at an address other than the one *listproc* chose (*andrea@mac23.mogo.edu*), she won't see ListProcessor's messages. ListProcessor has special alias files to deal with this problem, but the list owner has to maintain them by hand.

22.4.2 Lists Served by Majordomo

Advantages over simple MTA lists:

- Handles most subscriptions automatically
- Handles moderated and private mailing lists
- List owners can be at a remote site and handle list by email
- Less work if you administer a lot of lists

Advantages over ListProcessor:

- Easier setup and maintenance
- Flexible handling of email addresses (subscribers can subscribe or unsubscribe themselves from any address; can be configured for list owner to approve non-routine changes)

Disadvantages versus ListProcessor:

- Majordomo rewrites outgoing message header for better delivery and error handling, but still depends on the system MTA to deliver messages
- Unsophisticated archive management
- Only basic control of bounces and messages sent to the wrong address (messages sent to a list instead of to *majordomo*)
- Can't batch user's commands for later processing

22.4.3 Lists Served by ListProcessor 6.0c

Advantages over Majordomo:

- Manages processing of messages according to system load
- Resumes delivery after many kinds of errors
- Automated handling of many bounced mail messages
- Good control of mail loops and messages sent to the wrong address
- Subscribers can control subscription and retrieve archived files interactively, over the Internet.
- You can split one list across several listprocs; each maintains part of the list. These are called peer lists.
- If the list server is shut down, messages are queued and processed when the server is started again.
- Requests can be "batched," and results sent late at night, when the computer is less busy.

Disadvantages versus Majordomo:

- Uses envelope sender address for security, but many envelope sender addresses are bogus or not optimal. See Section 23.4 for more on the envelope sender.
- Complex system takes an administrator days or weeks to learn thoroughly
- Documentation is fairly complete, but scattered in different manual pages, in program source code, etc.

ListProcessor version 7.0, a licensed software package available for a fee, is fairly different than the freely available version 6.0c described here.

22.5 Email Ethics

There is a culture of consideration on the Internet, which is part of what makes the Internet such a useful tool. For new users coming to the Internet, it is not always obvious what the rules are.

A good rule of thumb for creating mailing lists is never to send email to someone unless they have specifically asked for that type of message. In other words, you should create a mailing list by announcing that it exists and asking that people request to be on the list. Even though it's easy to do, you must not gather a list of thousands of Internet users without their consent, make a mailing list, and send anything (particularly advertisements) to them. People who do that are widely despised. Another no-no is sending a message to random mailing lists where it doesn't belong. If someone subscribes to a list about chemistry, they aren't asking for mail about a great land deal in Florida.

Why do people mind getting electronic "junk mail"? Several reasons. Most important, they resent spending time handling the messages (particularly those disguised with misleading subject lines). Many users depend on email for their livelihood, so making email less productive is a serious matter. Second, many people have to pay for their email access, so it's highly inconsiderate to make them pay for your advertising. Finally, junk mail is just not culturally acceptable.

If you're a list owner, we recommend making your "no junk email" policy clear to your subscribers. There are lots of "newbies" (new users) joining the Internet every day; a little education about netiquette does everyone some good. If someone abuses your list, remind them of the policy (and, possibly, send a copy to the person's postmaster). The last resort is making the list moderated and private—and making the subscriber file accessible only to list members (or to no one at all). But let's hope that we don't have to put up big fences all over the Internet: cooperation makes everyone's life easier!

22.6 Email Services and Network Connections

When a message goes out to a mailing list of 1,000 subscribers, one of several things happens—depending on how you've configured the list and the MTA. One possibility is that your MTA will attempt to start 1,000 simultaneous SMTP network transactions to deliver all the messages at once. That will drag almost any system to its knees.

Instead, you can configure the list server or MTA to queue outgoing messages (handle them one at a time) to soften the impact on the system and network connection. That helps considerably— there will be a smaller number of SMTP transactions at a time, but for a longer time. That can still be a drag on the system and network in the middle of a busy work day. (For *sendmail* the *–odq* option invokes mail queueing, as described in Section 23.4.)

Another way to soften the load is by configuring a server to put many subscribers' addresses in each message envelope. There will be fewer messages to deliver, but each message will take longer. *listproc* can deliver messages this way.

Unfortunately, there's no way to tell any list server we know of to delay sending messages out to the list until late at night, when computers and the network are least busy. That wouldn't be appropriate in discussion-oriented lists anyway.* Otherwise, for the largest lists (which, like *ora-news*, are usually customer lists where only postings from a few company employees are allowed), it's wise to tell those employees to post only at night!

There's a conundrum involving your Internet connection and mailing lists. On the one hand, you want a fast connection so that your mailing list traffic doesn't bog it down too much for other uses. But on the other hand, a fast connection speeds up the avalanche of errors caused by a mail loop.

You'll get a **mail loop** if some computer sends a message to your list, your list mails it back to that computer, that computer sends it back to yours, and so on. With a high-speed network connection, these messages can swamp your computer, the network, and all other computers that your list sends mail to. Unless your computer has a full-time administrator, mail loops can be a serious (although probably infrequent) problem. ListProcessor makes several kinds of checks for mail loops, and Majordomo has a simple system too. Still, if one message gets through and starts a loop, you can be glad for a slow network that gives you time to get things under control. A periodic network connection, like UUCP, is great at slowing down loops, because there can be at most one loop per UUCP transaction. (Remember that UUCP can be used over a TCP/IP network as well as via a direct phone call.) On-demand PPP/SLIP connections also might help, because they are fairly slow and can be easily disconnected as soon as a loop is detected (but while the PPP/SLIP link is connected, any number of loops can occur).

* That kind of thing can be done with some custom hacking of your server and MTA. For example, with *sendmail*, make a separate queue directory for the list and process the queue late at night with a separate *sendmail* process. Experienced list administrators have a lot of tricks like these; for more information, see the Nutshell Handbook *sendmail* from O'Reilly & Associates.

But assuming you are willing to be vigilant to catch any loops quickly, a fast network is better. Take a look at your network configuration to find bottlenecks. For instance, as Figure 22-1 shows, O'Reilly & Associates' main Internet connection is in its Massachusetts office. There's a full-time (but fairly slow) network connection from the California office to Massachusetts. It makes much more sense for our servers to run in the Massachusetts office—where there's fast access to the Internet—than to bog down our interoffice network with hundreds or thousands of mail messages each time something is sent to a list. (Of course, depending on your configuration, the load on your computer can also limit the speed of your network connection. Busy computers can't always handle much network traffic.)

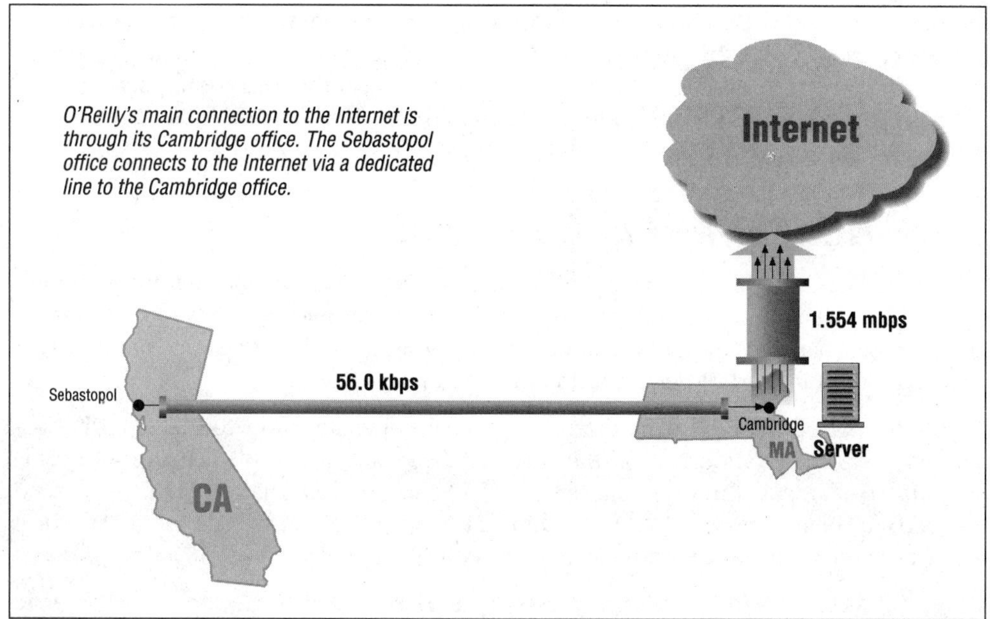

Figure 22-1. Choosing a mailing list host

If you want to serve *files* by email to large numbers of people, you'll need a good network connection. You might even want a dedicated connection, just for that machine, to keep from bogging down other users of your network connection. Or you might use a list-server system like ListProcessor that can *batch* file requests, handling them sometime when the network isn't busy (like overnight). Note that this feature only works for file requests—not for postings to the list.

Another good thing, if you can afford it, is a separate computer that's dedicated to mail handling. Sending a message to O'Reilly's big lists takes our mail server (a small Sun) several hours.

22.7 The List-managers Mailing List

There's at least one mailing list for people who manage mailing lists. It's named *list-managers*. The list is for discussions of issues related to managing Internet mailing lists, including (but not limited to) software, methods, mechanisms, techniques, and policies. (To discuss a particular list server, though, use its specific mailing list. For example, the *majordomo-users* mailing list—Section 24.5—is about Majordomo itself.)

The *list-managers* list is served by Majordomo, but it's for users of all kinds of mailing lists. Send your subscription request to *majordomo@GreatCircle.com* (see instructions for the Majordomo server in Chapter 24, *Automating Mailing Lists with Majordomo*).

All messages sent to *list-managers* are stored in compressed archive files. You can get files from the archive by anonymous FTP from *ftp.greatcircle.com* in the directory *pub/archive*. You can also get the archives by email from the Majordomo server; send *index* and *get* commands. (Chapter 24, *Automating Mailing Lists with Majordomo*, explains *index* and *get*.)

22.8 How Email Is Delivered

The background in this section on how email is delivered will be helpful in understanding the chapters that follow. It's helpful, for example, when you're trying to understand what caused messages you sent (or a mail list sents) to bounce (get returned to you instead of getting to the intended recipient).

There are lots of email systems these days. We'll concentrate on the "standard" two-part UNIX system in wide use on the Internet. One part is the MUA (**mail user agent**) program. The MUA is the program, like */usr/ucb/mail* or *elm*, that a user uses to send (or read) an email message. You can think of a mailing-list server as an MUA, too; it prepares an email message automatically, instead of manually.

When the MUA is ready to send a message, it passes the message to the MTA (**mail transport agent**)—for example, *sendmail*. Although a mail message can cross different kinds of networks on its way from the sender to the receiver, we'll concentrate on messages sent over the Internet.

Before the local MTA can send a message, it needs to know what address the message is from and what address(es) the message is going to. This is called the **envelope data**. The two important parts for mailing lists are the **envelope sender** and the **envelope recipient**. (RFC 821 calls these the **reverse-path** and **forward-path**, respectively.) An email envelope is a lot like the return address and delivery address on a (paper) postal envelope. The envelope is separate from the contents, which is the message you're sending.

By default, for the *sendmail* MTA, the envelope sender is the user who's executing *sendmail*. (For instance, if you send a message with your computer's MUA, and your UNIX username is *jerry*, the envelope sender is also *jerry*.)

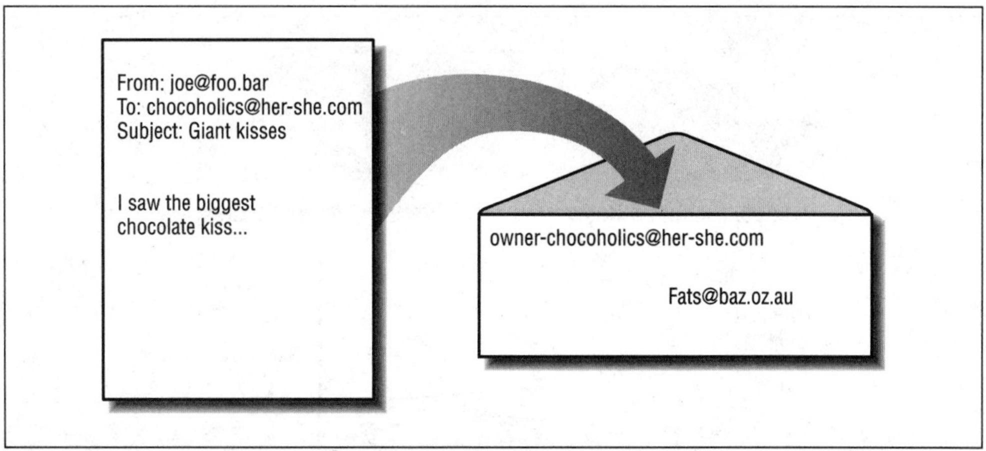

Figure 22-2. Envelope and contents of an email message

The MUA can specify the envelope recipients by listing them on the *sendmail* command line. For example, here's a sample message to the mailing list *chocoholics*:

```
From: joe@foo.bar
To: chocoholics@her-she.com
Subject: Giant kisses

I saw the biggest chocolate kisses...
```

If the mailing list has three subscribers, *sendmail* might be invoked this way:

```
# sendmail ann fats@baz.oz.au joe@foo.bar < msgfile
```

The three envelope recipients are *ann*, *fats@baz.oz.au*, and *joe@foo.bar*. *ann* is a local user—*ann* is simply the name of her account on the local computer. *fats@baz.oz.au* and *joe@foo.bar* are remote addresses. *joe@foo.bar* is probably the user with the account named *joe* on the computer with the domain name *foo.bar*. *fats@baz.oz.au* could be a whole list of people on the computer *baz.oz.au*.

The MTA looks at the recipients. Then one of two things happens:

- If the message will be delivered locally (in this example, to *ann*), the MTA handles that.
- Otherwise, the MTA on the sender's computer connects to a remote MTA. The remote MTA may be on a network gateway, a mail exchanger, or it may be on the computer that holds the destination user's mailbox.

When MTAs talk across the Internet, they generally connect to port 25 on the remote host and use SMTP (the Simple Mail Transfer Protocol). The basics of SMTP are shown in Figure 22-3.

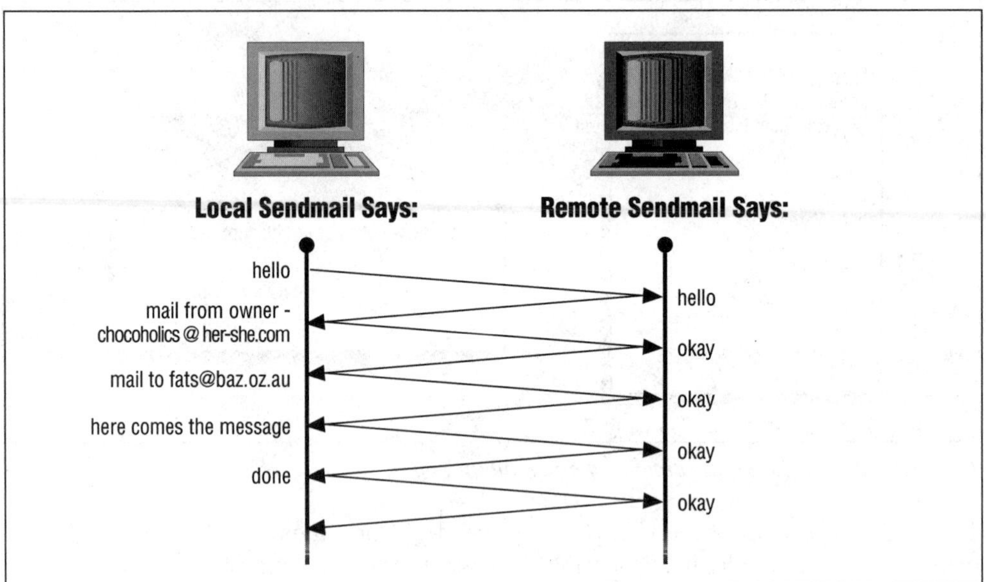

Figure 22-3. Basics of SMTP

You can watch that transaction happen if you use the *–v* switch when starting *sendmail.* Try it yourself, if you'd like. The */usr/ucb/mail* MUA, and others too, accept a *–v* switch on their command line—and pass the *–v* on to sendmail.

In the example below, lines starting with >>> are what the local MTA is saying to the remote MTA. The return messages start with a reply code; this number tells the local MTA whether the remote MTA is accepting the command. More details after the example:

```
# who am i
her-she!root  ttys6  Jul 8 22:43
# sendmail ann fats@baz.oz.au joe@foo.bar < msgfile
ann... Connecting to via local...
ann... Sent

fats@baz.oz.au... Connecting to baz.oz.au via ether...
Trying 198.112.208.25...  connected.
220-baz.oz.au Bazcom Sendmail 8.6.8 ready at Sat, 9 Jul 1994 17:35:13 -0400
220 ESMTP spoken here
>>> HELO her-she.com
250 baz.oz.au Hello her-she.com [127.0.0.1], pleased to meet you
>>> MAIL From:<you@her-she.com>
250 <you@her-she.com>... Sender ok
>>> RCPT To:<fats@baz.oz.au>
250 <fats@baz.oz.au>... Recipient ok
>>> DATA
354 Enter mail, end with "." on a line by itself
```

```
>>> .
250 RAA23127 Message accepted for delivery
>>> QUIT
221 baz.oz.au closing connection
fats@baz.oz.au... Sent

joe@foo.bar... Connecting to relay.foo.bar via ether...
Trying 192.22.33.44...  connected.
220-relay.foo.bar Foo's Bar and Chocolate Shop Sendmail 8.6.8.1 ready ...
   ...omitted...
```

If the local MTA hadn't been able to connect to all the recipients' hosts, it would *queue* the message for those hosts and try later. After trying for a while (typically three to five days), the local MTA bounces the message back by sending a copy of it to the envelope sender address. The bounced mail often starts with a "Transcript of Session" that shows the failed SMTP transaction.

A message might be bounced by the remote MTA, or by some other MTA that the remote MTA relays your message to. In both cases, the bounce should be sent to the original envelope sender address.*

* Badly behaved MTAs don't follow this rule; they use an address in the message header. This causes lots of problems for mailing-list managers.

In this Chapter:
- *Setting Up the List*
- *Using a List Members File*
- *Aliases and Your Local Network*
- *Handling Bounces*
- *Mail from Local Users*
- *Envelope Sender in sendmail Version 8*
- *Minimizing Bounced Mail*
- *Changing the Message Header*
- *Logging Messages*
- *List Exploders*

23

Simple Mailing Lists

Chapter 22, *Introduction to Email Services*, introduced email mailing lists and summarized several approaches for managing them. This chapter goes into detail about the simplest way to run a mailing list, using the system MTA (mail transport agent) directly (without a list server program). This chapter uses *sendmail* as the MTA in the examples. Other MTAs can do the same things with similar syntax.

This chapter also describes some general issues in managing mailing lists and some details about how *sendmail* affects mailing lists. Both of these topics are useful even if you plan to use Majordomo, because Majordomo uses the system MTA to receive mail from and send mail to subscribers.

23.1 Setting Up the List

Let's imagine a group of 15 people who want to cheat, uh, save money on their tax bills. One of the group, Janet, offers to set up a mailing list on her computer at the address *tax-savers@giantbank.sf.ca.us.* When one of the group sends mail to that address, it's distributed to the 15 people at computers (in this case) all over the U.S.A.

Simple mailing lists like *tax-savers*, with a small group of members that doesn't change often, can be handled by one person with hand maintenance and your system's *sendmail* MTA (mail transport agent). Your MTA is the program that manages electronic mail on your computer. The MTA receives and distributes messages from local users and users of other computers. It also sends messages.

A *sendmail* mailing list, like *tax-savers*, should have two other addresses associated with it:

- *listname-request* is by convention the address for sending subscription requests and occasional correspondence about the list. Messages to this address aren't distributed to the list members: they go to a person who modifies the list itself, the owner/maintainer. So list members don't have to see (as many) requests like "subscribe me."

  For example, an Internal Revenue Service agent might send a message to *tax-savers-request@giantbank.sf.ca.us* (from his personal account, *joe@innocent-corp.com*, of course) and ask to be added to the list. The list maintainer (in this case, it's probably Janet) would get that message and decide whether to add Joe.

  You should remind your subscribers to use the *–request* address for any correspondence about the list. One way to do so is to add a comment in the mail header, as described in Section 23.8. Even with reminders, you'll still get some "subscribe me" messages going to the wrong address and therefore to the whole list, but fewer than if you don't publicize the *–request* address.

- *owner-listname* is the address used by the local *sendmail* (on the machine where the mailing list runs) to return error messages. On most lists, it's just a configuration detail that you don't need to tell subscribers about. For our typical small list, mail to *owner-tax-savers* might go to the same person who reads *tax-savers-request*.

To set up this mailing list, the computer's system administrator or postmaster needs to make entries in the system's *sendmail* alias file. Its name is usually */usr/lib/aliases* or */etc/aliases*. (Note: this is not the same alias file as each user's individual mail alias file—such as *.mailrc*.) The basic syntax of each entry is:

```
alias-name: addresses
```

For example, Janet, the list owner and maintainer, would have lines like these in her system's *sendmail* alias file:

```
tax-savers: janet, wimv@frst-bnk.com, ... ,
    ...,
    joe@innocent-corp.com
tax-savers-request: janet
owner-tax-savers: tax-savers-request
```

If the list of addresses is too long to fit on one line, you can continue it by ending one line with a comma (,) and indenting the next line with a tab character.

Remember to run the command *newaliases* or *sendmail –bi* after you edit the *aliases* file.

The setup in this example is as simple as you can get. The result has quite a few problems, though. The next sections explain the problems and present some solutions.

23.2 Using a List Members File

If your list has lots of members or the members change often, editing the *aliases* file can be a pain—especially if you have to ask the system administrator to do the editing for you. In that case, it's better to put a list of addresses in a file somewhere on your filesystem and tell *sendmail* to read the file with its `:include:` command.

NOTE

> Some earlier versions of *sendmail*—for instance, the version shipped with ULTRIX before 4.3—don't support the include file feature. To be sure, check your system *aliases(5)* or *sendmail(8)* manual pages, or ask your system postmaster.

The next example shows a replacement for the list alias from the previous example. This new version reads in the latest contents of Janet's *tax-savers/members* file each time a message is sent:

```
tax-savers: :include:/home/janet/tax-savers/members
owner-tax-savers: tax-savers-request
tax-savers-request: janet
```

In the *members* file, you store one address per line. If more than one address is on the same host, you may need to put those addresses on adjacent lines so that *sendmail* can send the message to that group with a single transaction. To find out whether your *sendmail* sorts the addresses for you, send mail to an unsorted list and watch the *sendmail* log file: If all messages to a host aren't sent in one transaction, you need to sort your list.* An easy way to sort the file by hostname is the command below. It sorts uppercase and lowercase letters together, uses the `@` sign as a field separator, and sorts on the first field that follows the `@`.

```
% sort -o filename -f -t@ +1 filename
```

Janet could store the list of *tax-savers* members in a file named */home/janet/tax-savers/members*. Here's part of Janet's *members* file:

```
janet (Janet Fernandez)
wimv@frst-bnk.com (Willem Verlag)
ethelm@frst-bnk.com (Ethel Murmad)
joe@innocent-corp.com (Joe Doe)
```

You can put comments in parentheses—real names, organizations, and so on—to help you remember who's who.

* You don't need to organize addresses listed on lines specified directly in your *aliases* file because *sendmail* sorts those automatically as it delivers.

CAUTION

It's important that no one but the list owner can modify the file of members. Set the file permissions to 644 (use **`chmod 644 members`**) and the directory permissions to 755 or 711. That lets all users read the file (important so that *sendmail* can read it), but lets only you edit it. Otherwise, a malicious user can add lines to make *sendmail* do bad things any time a message comes into the list.

23.3 Aliases and Your Local Network

If your local computer shares its *sendmail* alias file with other computers—via NFS, NIS, or just by copying the file between hosts—you need to be sure that the changes you make on one machine work on all machines.* (The same thing is true for other MTAs, of course.)

If you use the *sendmail* `:include:` command as part of a list alias, every machine that has the alias must be able to read the included file through the same pathname. Some workarounds (with the best listed first) are:

- If you have a mail hub with its own *sendmail.cf* file, define the list alias there. Make all other hosts' aliases point to that central site. For instance, if the *tax-savers* alias is defined on the machine *mailhub.yourcorp*, all hosts in your network should have this alias:

  ```
  tax-savers: tax-savers_@mailhub.yourcorp
  ```

  Notice the underscore after the name. On the mail-hub machine, put the actual alias:

  ```
  tax-savers: tax-savers_
  tax-savers_: :include:/home/janet/tax-savers/members
  ```

  Now, if the network connection to *mailhub* (or *mailhub* itself) is down, the local *sendmail* queues messages for the list and waits until they can be delivered.

- If you're using NIS, and your system reads the local *sendmail* alias file before it reads NIS aliases, you can add this entry to the NIS maps:

  ```
  tax-savers: tax-savers@mailhub.yourcorp
  ```

  And add this entry to the *sendmail* aliases file on *mailhub*:

  ```
  tax-savers: :include:/home/janet/tax-savers/members
  ```

  Every host except *mailhub* will get the *tax-savers* alias from NIS. But on *mailhub*, the *sendmail* alias file overrides the NIS map.

- An obvious approach, that doesn't work well, is to put the included alias file on a filesystem that's mounted from all hosts. For instance, let's say that the

* Jennifer Joy contributed a lot of good ideas for this section.

/usr/share/local filesystem from a central server is mounted on all the hosts. You might think that the list-members file could be stored on the central file server, and the list alias could be:

```
tax-savers: :include:/usr/share/local/mail-aliases/tax-savers --wrong
```

But, with this setup, if the network to the central server is down and someone mails to the *tax-savers* list, the mail may fail with an ugly "can't open file" error. Instead, use the approach in the first bullet.

Here's something else to think about. If there are local users' addresses in the alias, be sure those users can get mail at those addresses when the mail is sent from any of the hosts. As an example, *penguin.ca.yourcorp.com* is the name of the workstation on which Linda reads her mail. But her address in the *tax-savers* alias list (*members*) only says *linda@penguin.* Hosts that have the *tax-savers* alias, but aren't part of the *ca.yourcorp.com* domain, may not be able to send mail to just *linda@penguin.* To fix that, Linda's address in the *members* file should be *linda@penguin.ca.yourcorp.com.*

We can't cover all possible network setups in this book, so here's the bottom line: If your *sendmail* alias file or NIS aliases are shared by more than one computer, take a close look and do some tests. Be sure that everyone on every computer can send and receive mail from the list.

23.4 Handling Bounces

The simple setup in the last example is fine for a small list with a few members. As your list gets larger, though, you'll have problems with bounced messages. There might be mailer errors returned for some messages (because a computer is down, a user's account has been closed, and so on). Those errors will be delivered to the person who sent the message, instead of to the person who can fix the problem (the list owner).

You can help solve the problem by changing your list alias to start a new *sendmail* process for each message sent to the list. The next example shows how. (If your host uses *sendmail* version 8, see Section 23.6 instead.) You add a new alias to contain the addresses on the list; in this example, we called it *dist-tax-savers*:

```
tax-savers: "|/usr/lib/sendmail -ftax-savers-request -oi dist-tax-savers"
dist-tax-savers: :include:/home/janet/tax-savers/members
owner-tax-savers: tax-savers-request
tax-savers-request: janet
```

Now, mail sent to *tax-savers* is resent in a new "envelope." The **envelope sender** address (also called the "Return-Path:" or "out-of-band sender" or "SMTP From") is set to *tax-savers-request.* (See the following box.) Errors are often returned to that address.*

From versus From:

On many UNIX systems, an email message has two header lines that start with the word "From". One ends with a colon character (`From:`); the other doesn't (`From`):

```
From jerry@ora.com Thu Sep 1 12:15:24 PDT 1994
  ...
Return-Path: <jerry@ora.com>
  ...
From: Jerry Peek <jerry@ora.com>
  ...
```

The first "From", without the colon, shows the **envelope sender** (or SMTP FROM) address. The MTA sets this address when the message is sent. Trusted users can change the envelope sender with the *sendmail –f* option (described in the alias example above). The envelope sender may also be shown in the "Return-Path:" field. The second "From:", with the colon, is often set by the user's mail program.

At sites with many computers, a user may have the same "From:" address on all hosts, but a different envelope sender on each host.

The *–oi* option tells *sendmail* not to quit reading a message at a line with a single dot (.). *sendmail* should stop at a single dot only when it's reading an original message—and the user signals the end of the message that way. When it distributes mail for a list, *sendmail* should stop only at the end of the message.

If your list is large, you should consider adding the *–odq* option to force *sendmail* to queue the message for individual handling. You can also add the *–om* option if you want to be sure that local users get a copy of messages they send to the list—without it, *sendmail* may deliver the message to everyone except the local originator of the message.

MTAs may also send errors to the addresses in the "Errors-To:" or "Sender:" header fields. Majordomo sets those fields for you; if you're using a simple *sendmail* list, the *fix_hdrs.sed* script can set them, too—see Section 23.8.

* Here's another good reason to set the envelope sender to the list's *–request* address. The *vacation(1)* program, for sending automatic replies to mail when a person is out of the office, won't send automatic replies to mail with an envelope-sender address ending in *–request.* This means that your mail won't generate 100 "vacation" replies when you send it to *huge-dist-list* on December 24.

23.5 Mail from Local Users

The *sendmail –f* option for setting the envelope sender (described in Section 23.4) may only be used by "trusted users." (Trusted users are listed at the `T` entry in your computer's *sendmail.cf* file.) When mail arrives for your list from a remote user (from another computer), your list's *sendmail* job is usually run by the user *daemon* or *uucp*. Because *daemon* and *uucp* are typically trusted users, the *–f* option does take effect.

But users who send mail from your local machine cause *sendmail* to run with their privileges. Most users aren't trusted (in *sendmail*'s view), so the *–f* option on your list won't take effect for them. Users on your local host may need to send their mail to the *dist–* address (*dist-tax-savers* in the example in Section 23.4) to have their message go out at all.

One easy work-around is to move the list to another computer where none of the list members have accounts; then all messages should run with *daemon* or *uucp* privileges. Or, you can use a program like *resend* (with *wrapper*) from the Majordomo distribution. (See Chapter 24, *Automating Mailing Lists with Majordomo*.) The system administrator can set *resend* to run SUID to a trusted user; this allows *resend* to change the envelope-sender address.

23.6 Envelope Sender in sendmail Version 8

If an alias has a corresponding "owner-" alias, *sendmail* version 8 automatically sets the envelope sender to that "owner-" address. For example, a mailing-list setup like this:

```
tax-savers: :include:/home/janet/tax-savers/members
owner-tax-savers: janet
```

sets the envelope sender to *janet*. That may confuse list subscribers if they forget who "janet" is. A better solution is to point the "owner-" alias to the "-request" alias. For example, the following aliases set the envelope sender to *tax-savers-request*:

```
tax-savers: :include:/home/janet/tax-savers/members
owner-tax-savers: tax-savers-request
tax-savers-request: janet
```

This routes errors to (and shows users the address) *tax-savers-request*, which in turn goes to *janet*.

With the Majordomo mailing-list manager under *sendmail* version 8, the first example shown above is still bad for the reasons given. But the second example also doesn't work. Because Majordomo automatically processes mail to its *–request* addresses, you don't want errors to go there. You want them to go to a person.

Under *sendmail* version 8, adding another address to the *–request* alias makes sure that the envelope sender is the alias name itself (in the next example, *owner-tax-savers*) instead of a person (*janet*). Because the envelope sender can't be multiple addresses, *sendmail* uses the alias name instead.

If your system has a mail alias named *nobody* that points to */dev/null* (the UNIX "black hole"), you can add *nobody* to the alias:

```
# Adding "nobody" prevents expansion to "janet" under sendmail v8:
owner-tax-savers: janet, nobody
```

If your system doesn't have the *nobody* alias and can't create it, make another mail alias, named, for example, *trashcan*, pointing to the "file" */dev/null*; use the *trashcan* alias instead of *nobody* in the setup below.

```
# Adding "trashcan" prevents expansion to "janet" under sendmail v8:
owner-tax-savers: janet, trashcan
```

23.7 Minimizing Bounced Mail

Mailing lists can have trouble when a, subscriber's address changes or becomes invalid—or when a network goes down. The subscriber's MTA will probably—but not always—try to send an error message to your server. This is called "bouncing" the message. You almost never want bounces to be sent to your list's subscribers, but some MTAs do that. Taking the precautions explained here reduces (but doesn't necessarily eliminate) the problem.

You can control where many errors are sent by *rewriting* (editing) the headers of messages to your list—and also by setting the envelope sender address to the list owner's address. Section 23.8 shows ways to manipulate message headers. But first, what should your headers contain?

The "Precedence:" message header field is poorly documented but important. A lot of administrators add the following field:

```
Precedence: bulk
```

Not all MTAs read the "Precedence:" field. The exact meaning depends on the remote mailer that receives the message. (If the remote mailer is *sendmail*, for example, the effect depends on how that system's *sendmail.cf* file was written.) The effects might be one or more of the following:

- MTAs deliver other messages with higher Precedence values (like "first-class") sooner.
- If there's a problem delivering the message, only the message header is returned to you; the body isn't.
- If there's a problem delivering the message, you aren't notified.

- Nothing at all (the "Precedence:" is ignored).

Without knowing how every system's MTA is set up, there's really no way to tell what will happen. Most medium- to large-sized mailing lists use "Precedence: bulk" in the headers of messages sent to their lists (but not for replies to specific requests, like sending an index of the available lists). File servers should use that header field for *all* requests, though, to help prevent huge files from being returned to you.

Of course, if you never receive error messages from some mailers (about bad addresses, users who've moved, and so on) your subscription list can slowly accumulate more and more bad addresses. A good compromise is to send a message to your lists, every month or two, without a "Precedence: bulk" field. You'll get a flood of new "bounced" mail that had previously been suppressed, and you can spend some fun hours cleaning up your subscriber list.

One other benefit of adding that field is that many *vacation(1)* auto-reply programs won't reply to messages with "Precedence: bulk".

Another header field that may help with bounces is "Errors-to:". If the remote mailer understands, it sends error reports to that address. For example, to ask mailers to send errors to *listmaster@online.ora.com*:

```
Errors-to: listmaster@online.ora.com
```

Some administrators tell you not to use "Errors-to:" because it's old technology (designed for systems that don't handle the envelope sender) and not a standard. Depending on the mailers your list subscribers use, adding "Errors-to:" to a message can cause multiple copies of bounced messages. But it's better to get multiple bounces from some hosts than get none at all from other hosts.

23.8 Changing the Message Header

As just explained, you may want your list messages to have header fields like these:

```
Precedence: bulk
Errors-to: listname-request@hostname
```

One way to edit the message header automatically is with a "front-end" message processing script. When a message arrives for the list, the system MTA runs the front-end program. The message is passed to the program's standard input. The front-end program reads the message, does whatever it needs to, then writes the message to its standard output. That standard output is piped to *sendmail*, which delivers the message to the list.

To run a front-end program, use a line like the one in this example:

```
listname: "| /bin/sed -f /script | /usr/lib/sendmail options"
```

The `/script` should be an absolute pathname (starting with a /) for the script file.

This book's online archive (see the Preface) has a *sed* filter script named *fix_hdrs.sed*. Here it is (the line numbers like *5>* are for reference; they aren't part of the script):

```
1> #!/bin/sed -f
2> 1,/^$/ {
3>       /^[Rr]eply-[Tt]o:/s/^/X-/
4>       /^[Pp]recedence:/d
5>       /^$/i\
6> Reply-to: listname@x.y.z \
7> Errors-to: listname-request@x.y.z \
8> Precedence: bulk \
9> Comment: This message comes from the listname mailing list. \
10> Comment: To subscribe or unsubscribe, mail to listname-request@x.y.z.
11> }
```

This script can cause some serious problems if it doesn't work right; be sure that you understand it and test any changes before you install it. For example, if you want to edit any header fields that typically have more than one line ("To:" or "cc:" often have several), you'll need to add a test for continuation lines (they start with whitespace) and use a loop with multiline *sed* commands like *H*. We can't give a *sed* tutorial (try the Nutshell Handbook *sed & awk* instead), but here's a quick explanation of the script.

- Line 1 isn't a *sed* command (in fact, the # makes *sed* ignore the line). If your UNIX system can directly execute files that start with `#!`, use the command *chmod +x fix_hdrs.sed* to make your script file executable—in that case, you don't need to use `/bin/sed -f` in the alias that executes the script. You can use an alias like this:

  ```
  listname: "| /path/fix-hdrs.sed | /usr/lib/sendmail options"
  ```

- Lines 3 through 10 are bracketed by `1,/^$/ {` and `}`, which makes them edit only the message header (the first line up to the first empty line). Line 5 adds more fields to the end of the header (inserts them before the empty line at the end of the header). Lines 6 through 10 are inserted; there's a backslash (\) for continuation at the end of every line except the last one.
- Line 3 changes any "Reply-to:" field to "X-Reply-to:" and line 6 adds a new "Reply-to:" field that requests replies be sent to the list instead of to the original sender.*
- If the message had a "Precedence:" field, line 4 deletes it. Line 8 adds a new "Precedence: bulk" field.
- Lines 9 and 10 add a comment that helps subscribers remember where to send subscription requests.

This script is just an example. Edit it to do what you need. For instance, you might not want to fiddle with the "Reply-to:" field or add "Comment:" fields. Or you might want

* A header field that starts with "X-" is "user-defined." We use it to keep the original "Reply-to:" address in the header for people to see, but make mailers ignore it.

to add new lines to the end of the script that write a subscription reminder at the end of every message body:

```
$a------------NOTE: This message comes from the listname mailing list.
  To subscribe or unsubscribe, mail to listname-request@x.y.z
```

23.9 Logging Messages

There's an easy way to keep a copy of all messages sent to a list. Just give the full pathname of a file along with the list of other addresses in the *listname* alias. *sendmail* will append each new message to the end of the file:

```
listname: :include:/address-file-path, /archive-pathname
```

The log file's permissions may be a problem. The file is written by *sendmail*, which runs with a different UID and GID in different situations. The exact rules for your system depend on settings in your *sendmail.cf* file, your version of *sendmail*, whether the mail is coming from a local or remote user, and more.

So, in general, a log file like this needs to be world-writable. That makes it a target for any troublemakers on your system. If that's likely to be a problem, read Chapter 30, *Options*, in the Nutshell Handbook *sendmail*—or check your system's *sendmail* documentation.

23.10 List Exploders

There may be several users at your site who want to join a mailing list that's distributed by another host. If the list host is far away, and if your local users are spread across several computers at your site, the list host may send more than one copy of the message to your site. That's a waste of network bandwidth (especially over international network links) and can be expensive if you pay for each of your incoming email messages.

In cases like that, you can make a *list exploder* on one of your local computers. Technically, an exploder is set up just like a *sendmail* mailing list. There are two differences:

- It's meant for redistributing messages that come from a remote computer.
- Messages for the list go to the main list address. The list host (at the remote computer) redistributes the message to your local exploder.

For example, let's say that your company in the U.S. has a branch office in Hong Kong. The Hong Kong employees have a mailing list named *dim-sum* to discuss those wonderful Cantonese goodies. Some people in your U.S. offices want to join the *dim-sum* list too.

To set up the exploder at your site, pick a central host for the exploder, like *mailserv.yourcorp.com.* Figure 23-1 shows how messages will be distributed on both sides of the ocean after the exploder has been set up.

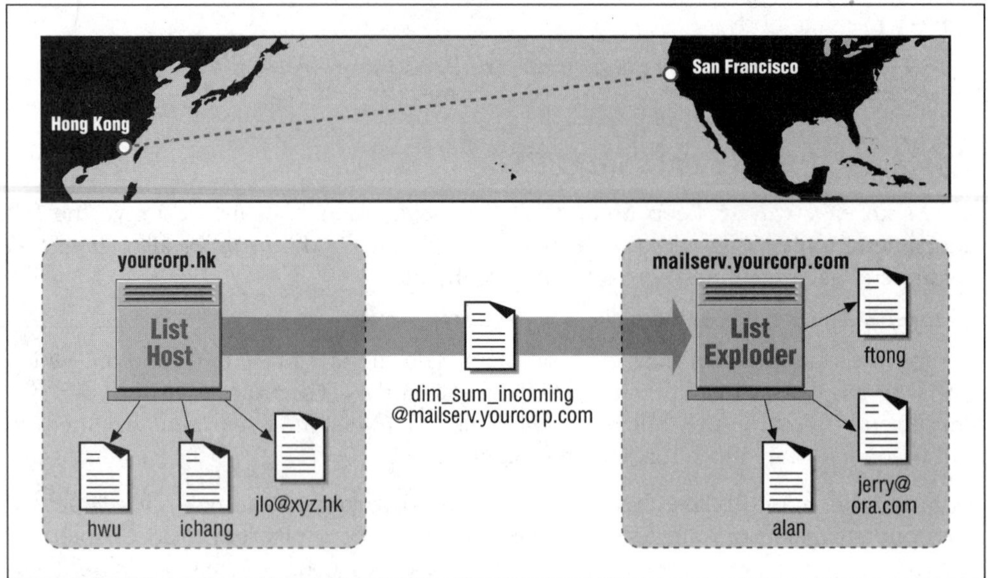

Figure 23-1. Sending a message to the dim-sum list and its exploder

To set up the exploder:

1. Create a file on *mailserv* to hold the local (U.S.) subscribers' addresses, one per line. The local exploder maintainer (for example, *carol*), can have the file in her directory—writable by her, readable by all users. Her file could be */home/carol/dim-sum-members*.

2. Add these aliases to the *sendmail* aliases file on *mailserv*:

```
dim-sum: dim-sum@yourcorp.hk
dim-sum-incoming: "| /usr/lib/sendmail -oi -fdim-sum-request dim-sum-local"
dim-sum-local: :include:/home/carol/dim-sum-members
dim-sum-request: carol
owner-dim-sum: dim-sum-request
```

   You might also add a front-end script like *fix_hdrs.sed* (see Section 23.8) to the *dim-sum-incoming* alias. It should redirect errors to the local exploder maintainer instead of to the central site in Hong Kong. The front-end script could also add comments to each message to remind people that they're subscribed through the exploder, remind them how to mail submissions to the central list address, and give them the local address for subscription changes. Both of these changes avoid puzzling messages for the central list maintainer from users at your local site.

3. People in the U.S. who want to join the exploder can send mail to *dim-sum-request@mailserv.yourcorp.com*. Carol will add their addresses to her *dim-sum-members* file.

U.S. subscribers can post to the list at *dim-sum@yourcorp.hk*. Or, if they mail to *dim-sum@mailserv.yourcorp.com*, the alias on *mailserv* routes the message to the master list *dim-sum@yourcorp.hk*.

4. Carol sends mail to the list owner in the Hong Kong office. She asks them to add her exploder *dim-sum-incoming@mailserv.yourcorp.com* to the main list of *dim-sum* subscribers.

Now, when mail goes to the *dim-sum* members in Hong Kong, a single copy also comes to the U.S. office. The exploder reroutes it to the *dim-sum-local* members.

In this Chapter:
- *An Overview of Majordomo*
- *Installing Majordomo*
- *Setting Up Lists*
- *Day-to-day Administration*
- *The Majordomo Mailing List*

24

Automating Mailing Lists with Majordomo

Majordomo is a set of Perl* programs that automate the operation of multiple mailing lists. Majordomo automatically handles routine requests to subscribe or unsubscribe; it also handles **closed lists** that route all subscription requests to a **list owner** for approval. It supports **moderated lists** that send all messages to a **moderator** for approval before they're sent to subscribers. The system can also maintain archives and deliver files from the archive via email.

Once the list is set up, it can be controlled completely by electronic mail, so the list owner need not be on the machine where Majordomo is running. The list owner's job is described in Chapter 25, *The Majordomo List Owner and Moderator*. If you'll only be a list owner and will leave administration to someone else, just read Section 24.1 and then proceed to Chapter 25, *The Majordomo List Owner and Moderator*.

Although you don't need to know Perl to run Majordomo, the Perl interpreter must be installed on the computer where you run Majordomo. Perl's source code is freely available from archives around the Internet, such as *ftp.uu.net*. You can also get ready-to-run versions of Perl from the CD-ROM that comes with the book *UNIX Power Tools* by O'Reilly & Associates/Bantam Books.

Majordomo's developer, Brent Chapman, wrote Majordomo for his own purposes (managing the mailing lists for SAGE, the System Administrators Guild). It was a simple and straightforward system: Brent didn't try to make the software do everything a list server could possibly do. Since then, John P. Rouillard has taken over development of Majordomo and added more features. This chapter covers Majordomo version 1.92, which is available free via FTP.

* For more information about Perl, see the Nutshell Handbooks *Learning Perl* by Randal Schwartz and *Programming Perl* by Larry Wall and Randal Schwartz.

CAUTION

The Bad Guys know about a security hole in versions of Majordomo before 1.92. We recommend version 1.92 or later.

One of Majordomo's strengths is its relative simplicity. You can figure it out in a few hours. ListProcessor, another major mailing-list management system—requires much more time—so much so that we couldn't cover it effectively in a book of this size. We've left it for another book. But if you intend to manage huge lists, ListProcessor provides useful features that can make it well worth the effort. O'Reilly & Associates uses ListProcessor for its company mailing lists. Chapter 22, *Introduction to Email Services*, has a short comparison of Majordomo and ListProcessor.

Majordomo is actually a suite of Perl scripts, not just one. In this chapter, the name Majordomo (with an uppercase M) refers to the whole package of programs and files. *majordomo* (in italics, with a lowercase m) means the individual program and the email address with that name.

The first section of this chapter gives an overview of Majordomo as it is seen by users, list owners, and administrators. Then comes installation, creation of lists, and testing. Finally there are descriptions of how to run and maintain a list.

24.1 An Overview of Majordomo

Before we dip into the intricacies of setting up and running Majordomo mailing lists, it will be helpful to know how the system works from the user's perspective, how the list owner manages a list, and how the various programs that make up the Majordomo package work together.

24.1.1 A User's View of Majordomo

First, here's a user's guide to the Majordomo package. It explains subscription, unsubscription, and all the other Majordomo commands available to users. (Section 22.3.1 shows how users interact with a list server, so we won't repeat that here.)

The commands below subscribe you to a list, or give you information about your subscription or those of other users. Use them in email to the *majordomo* server. Where you see `listname` below, replace it with the name of the list you're interested in. Put the commands in the body of the mail message (not on the "Subject:" header field). If a command is too long for a single line, you can continue (with Majordomo version 1.90 and above) by ending the first line with a backslash (\). Other than whitespace, the commands must be the first text in the message body; in other words, don't begin with "Dear Majordomo."

The commands below are meant for the email address *majordomo@hostname*. Majordomo version 1.90 and later can also be configured to read mail sent to the address *listname-request@hostname.* When sending mail to the *listname-request* address, you can omit the `listname` parameter in the commands below.

In the commands below, items in brackets (`[]`) are optional. If you include the optional item, don't type the brackets.

`help`
: Send one-line summaries of *majordomo* commands. The first line of output tells which version of Majordomo the server is running.

`info` *`listname`*
: Send an introduction to the list *listname*

`lists`
: Show the lists available from this Majordomo server

`subscribe` *`listname`* [*address*]
: This command subscribes you to the named *listname*. Unless you include the optional *address*, Majordomo uses the email address in the mail message header (the "Reply-to:" field, if any, otherwise "From:") to send you mail.

  List names may come in pairs: *listname* and *listname-digest*. In that case, subscribe to the *listname* if you want to get each list message as soon as possible; subscribe to *listname-digest* to get a periodic digest.

`unsubscribe` *`listname`* [*address*]
: This unsubscribes you (or *address*) from *listname*.

`which` [*address*]
: Tell which lists you (or *address*) are subscribed to. This command may be restricted to subscribers only.

`who` *`listname`*
: List the subscribers of *listname*. This command may be restricted to *listname* subscribers only.

`index` *`listname`*
: Give a listing of files in the *listname* archive. This command may be restricted to *listname* subscribers only. Only for Majordomo versions 1.54 and later.

`get` *`listname filename`*
: Mail a file named *filename* from the *listname* archive. This command may be restricted to *listname* subscribers only. Only for Majordomo versions 1.54 and later.

`end`
: Stop reading the message. This is useful if your mailer adds text (like a signature) to the end of a message.

  A line that starts with a dash (-) is also treated as an "end" command by newer versions of Majordomo. Because many mail message signatures start with some dashes, this avoids error messages.*

---

* Also, when Majordomo mails a reply to a command, the first line of the reply starts with a dash. That way, if the reply is returned to *majordomo* (as undeliverable, etc.), the dash stops a mail loop from forming. Clever, eh?

24.1.2 Majordomo for List Owners

The list owner is the person (or persons) who runs day-to-day operations of a mailing list by responding to mail messages from Majordomo. Each mailing list can have a different list owner.

Majordomo has "open" and "closed" lists. Subscribers to an open list are approved automatically, unless they specify an *address* different from the one in their email header. All subscriptions to closed lists are sent to the list owner for approval.

If you'd like a list with the absolute minimum of maintenance (but also a minimum of security), you could create an "auto" list, where all subscription or unsubscription requests are honored without any input from the list owner. For example, anyone could unsubscribe anyone else.

The owner can potentially receive four types of messages through several mail aliases:

- Requests to approve subscriptions (or unsubscriptions), sent to the address *listname-approval*
- Notifications of successful subscriptions or unsubscriptions, sent to the address *listname-approval*
- "Bounced" messages: requests to approve messages to the list. This includes messages to a moderated list, messages that are too large, and messages that fail "administrivia" tests (Section 25.3.1).

  This term can be confusing to experienced email users. In other mailing list systems, a bounced message is one that was returned because it couldn't be delivered to a subscriber. To be consistent with Majordomo's usage, though, we call this undeliverable mail "returned messages"; see the next bullet.

  Majordomo sends bounced messages to the address *owner-listname*.*
- Returned messages: messages sent to the list that weren't delivered to a subscriber because of a network problem, because the subscriber has left her job, and so on. If the remote MTA is set up correctly, it sends these messages to the envelope sender address *owner-listname*.

All the list aliases can send mail to the same person, or duties can be split up by assigning each of the list aliases to a different person.

Majordomo provides the *approve* script to help handle approval of subscriptions and "bounced" messages, and *bounce* to help handle returned messages. (Note to experienced list owners: the *bounce* script is for handling returned messages, which are called bounced messages by everyone except Majordomo.) Section 25.5.1 and Section 25.6 describe these scripts in detail.

---

* In a future version of Majordomo, bounced messages that need approval will be sent to the new address *listname-moderator*.

24.1.3 Majordomo for Administrators

The administrator in this context is the person who installs Majordomo, creates new lists, and watches the system for technical problems. Unlike a list owner, the administrator needs to have direct access to the system where Majordomo is running. In many cases, the list owner and the administrator are the same person, but they don't need to be.

Here is an outline of what each program and file in the Majordomo package does:

- *majordomo* (the program itself) is run each time a message arrives for the address *majordomo@hostname* (also, in some configurations, the address *listname-request@hostname*). It decides whether approval is needed. If so, *majordomo* sends mail to the list owner. Otherwise, it performs the requested commands.
- *resend* checks messages that arrive for a list (at *listname@hostname*) according to its configuration file settings. If the message must be approved or if there are other problems, the message is forwarded to the list owner. Otherwise, *resend* edits the header, then passes the message to the computer's MTA for distribution to the list.
- *archive2.pl* is one of a set of scripts for making archives of a list. Of the set, we've chosen *archive2.pl* because it will eventually be integrated into Majordomo.
- *digest* builds and sends digests of messages to a list.
- The *wrapper* program allows other Majordomo programs to run as "trusted users" so they can set the correct envelope sender address. *wrapper* also improves file security, because files will always be accessed by the same user. *wrapper* is the only part of the Majordomo package that's written in the C language.
- The *bounce* script helps owners handle subscribers whose mail is being returned. The *bounce-remind* script tries to notify those subscribers about the problem.
- The *approve* script is also for owners. It simplifies approval of subscriptions or moderated messages.
- *new-list* answers mail sent to a new list. It asks people to wait to send messages until the list owner opens the list for business.
- *request-answer* can be used to automatically answer mail to the address *listname-request* (see Chapter 23, *Simple Mailing Lists*). It tells people to mail to *majordomo*—and how to find out more about the server.

  Beginning with version 1.90, Majordomo can be configured to read the *–request* address and execute commands in those messages. If you use that configuration, you won't need *request-answer*.
- *medit* lets you edit a file, locking the file so that Majordomo won't try to modify it.

- *majordomo.cf* sets the overall configuration of the Majordomo system. The list owner (or anyone with a list's administrative password) can control whether a list is open, public, moderated, and several other aspects of a list by changing the settings in the individual list's *config* (configuration) file.
- *config_parse.pl* reads and updates list *config* files. *shlock.pl* locks files to prevent simultaneous edits. *majordomo.pl* has miscellaneous subroutines.

By default, the owner is notified of all successful subscribe and unsubscribe actions. If you don't want the owner to be notified, you can edit two subroutines in the *majordomo* Perl script: *welcome* sends subscription notices; *do_unsubscribe* sends unsubscription notices.

Unlike a lot of Internet services, the Majordomo programs don't run constantly (as a daemon), nor are they started by *inetd*. They're started by your system MTA when each message comes in to *majordomo* or one of its lists. The disadvantage is that you can't slow down or postpone Majordomo operations on a busy system. The advantage is that there's no daemon process to crash.

24.2 Installing Majordomo

To set up Majordomo, you'll need to edit the *majordomo.cf* file, and maybe tweak a couple of the scripts. You'll also need a C compiler for the *wrapper* program (although you can work around that by copying a compiled version of *wrapper* from someone else who has Majordomo installed in the same filesystem location on the same type of computer and operating system). Because Majordomo is simple and the code is straightforward, it isn't hard to solve problems (especially if you've joined the *majordomo-users* mailing list—see Section 24.5).

In the directions below, a name like `$whoami` is a Perl variable. Most variables are defined in the *majordomo.cf* file (see below).

Here are the installation steps:*

1. Be sure that your system has Perl version 4.035 (or later) and its libraries.
2. Some sites give *majordomo* another name (*listmgr*, *lists*, etc.). We don't recommend doing that unless you have a good reason: especially as more documentation about Majordomo becomes available, users may get confused if you give the system other names. Also, after Majordomo upgrades, you'll have to patch the system again.

   If you decide to change the name, edit all of the code references to Majordomo that are visible to users. For example, change the subject of mail messages that

* Although we show a step-by-step procedure here, we can't promise that the following steps are exactly what you need for your computer. Your system might be different, or you may have a different version of Majordomo than the one we installed. Please use these steps as a *guide* only.

say "Majordomo Results." You don't need to change filenames like *majordomo.cf.* You definitely should not change the help file line that says "This is Brent Chapman's Majordomo mailing list manager."

3. Pick a username, group name, and home directory for Majordomo. A good name for both user and group is *majordom* (but not *majordomo*; it's over the eight-character limit). We made the home directory */usr/local/majordomo.*

   As superuser, add that user and group to */etc/passwd* and */etc/group* (or your NIS password and group files). Make the home directory, set its owner and group to *majordom*, and set its mode to 775.

   If the person who manages Majordomo doesn't want to *su* to *majordom*, you should add the manager's account to the *majordom* group. (We think it's not a good idea to maintain Majordomo as the superuser; it's too easy to set the wrong permissions and ownerships.) If there are list owners on the system, and if they should be doing routine maintenance, add them to the *majordom* group, too.*

4. Now you can *su* to the new *majordom* account and *cd* to the home directory. (Most of the rest of the installation doesn't need to be done as the superuser.)

5. Get a Majordomo distribution file from *ftp.greatcircle.com* in the */pub/majordomo* directory.

   In the directory */pub/majordomo/archive* are monthly archive files of all the articles posted to the *majordomo-** mailing lists. They're worth browsing through someday in your copious free time. There's lots of information that we don't have the room to cover in this book.

6. Extract the Majordomo distribution file into the *majordom* home directory.

   ```
   % zcat majordomo-1.92.tar.Z | tar xvf -
   ```

   (On System V systems, use **tar xovf** instead.) *tar* will create a subdirectory named *majordomo-1.92*; *cd* into it.

NOTE

Unless you plan carefully ahead of time, don't try to extract the archive into the home directory itself (without using the *majordomo-1.92* subdirectory). The Majordomo *Makefile* is designed to build the system in the *majordomo-1.92* subdirectory and install it into the home directory.

7. Glance through the documentation:

   - The *Description* file gives an overview of the Majordomo package.
   - *README* has an overview, installation instructions, and other tips. Read or skim it.

* Note that if a host has more than one list owner, and some of the lists are "private," one list owner will be able to read another owner's private list.

- *Ignore* the *resend.README* file. It explains how to use the *resend* program in standalone mode; for a normal Majordomo installation, you don't want to do this!

Now *cd* to the *Doc* subdirectory.

- The file *majordomo.lisa6.ps* is Brent's paper about Majordomo, in PostScript format. It's titled *Majordomo: How I Manage 17 Mailing Lists Without Answering "-request" Mail.* The paper has an interesting overview of how and why he wrote Majordomo, as well as an introduction to Majordomo for users and administrators. The Majordomo version it covers is out of date now.
- *list-owner-info* is a Majordomo overview designed for people who run mailing lists.
- The *FAQ* file has frequently asked questions about Majordomo. This book doesn't cover a lot of the good tips in that file; it's worth skimming.

8. *cd* up one level. It's time to build the system.

   First, install the *wrapper* program. It lets Majordomo scripts run as a "trusted user." On non-POSIX systems, that's normally the user *daemon*; on POSIX systems, it's *root.*

   (Some day the *wrapper* program may be eliminated. If you're using a Majordomo version newer than 1.92 and *wrapper* is missing, see the *Changes* file.)

   Read and edit the *Makefile*:

   - Set the *make* macros `W_BIN` and `W_MAJORDOMO_CF` for the *wrapper* program, as follows. `W_BIN` should point to the home directory (for example, */usr/local/majordomo*). Give `W_MAJORDOMO_CF` the absolute pathname to the *majordomo.cf* file like */usr/local/majordomo/majordomo.cf.*
   - Check `W_PATH`, `W_HOME`, and `W_SHELL`. They set the environment variables `PATH`, `HOME`, and `SHELL`, respectively, when *wrapper* runs.
   - If you're using a POSIX system, remove the comment characters (#) from the front of the POSIX section and add them to the non-POSIX section.
   - Check the user and group: `W_USER` and `W_GROUP` on non-POSIX systems; or `W_UID`, `W_GID`, and `W_CHOWN` on POSIX systems.

   Type **`make wrapper`** to build the *wrapper* program.

9. Next, install other Majordomo programs into the home directory and into subdirectories of the home directory by typing **`make install`**. This creates two new subdirectories of the home directory, *Tools* and *bin*, and installs programs there. If the distribution directory has a *majordomo.cf* file, it is copied to the home directory; otherwise, the *sample.cf* file is copied to become the *majordomo.cf* file.

   The *bin* directory contains maintenance scripts. Add its pathname to the shell search path of the *majordom* account and other accounts (including list owners' accounts) that will need the scripts.

10. If any of your lists will be archived, the *Makefile* lets you choose one of three scripts for building the archives. The examples in this book assume that you've installed *archive2.pl*. To install it, type **make install-archive2**.

11. Go back to the superuser account.* To install *wrapper* as a setuid program, type **make install-wrapper**.

12. *Majordomo* looks for its configuration file in */etc/majordomo.cf* unless you set the `W_MAJORDOMO_CF` variable for *wrapper* that makes it look somewhere else. (The `W_MAJORDOMO_CF` variable is passed through *wrapper* as the `MAJORDOMO_CF` environment variable.) Jerry's personal preference is to keep master copies of his local files off of */etc*. In case a script doesn't have the `MAJORDOMO_CF` environment variable set—and searches */etc* for the *majordomo.cf* file—you can make a symbolic link from */etc/majordomo.cf* to */usr/local/majordomo/majordomo.cf*.

13. Go back to the *majordom* account. Set up the directory structure for Majordomo lists.

    Although we like to keep all of Majordomo and its list files under Majordomo's home directory, you don't have to. The structure is flexible; you can separate the programs and the lists if you want to (see the sample *majordomo.cf* file a few steps ahead). Here's the structure we're using.

    Our home directory holds the `$log` file, the "system" Majordomo scripts, and the *majordomo.cf* configuration file. The subdirectories are:

    - *archives* has subdirectories that hold list archive files.
    - *digests* is a work area for the *digest* program. If any of your lists will have digests, you'll need this directory.
    - *lists* has the files for the lists: config files, subscribers, passwords, and so on.

    Create those directories now, check their ownership and set their mode to 775. Create an empty `$log` file with owner and group *majordom* and mode 664.

14. Each Perl script in the home directory and the *bin* subdirectory starts with a line that contains the pathname of the Perl interpreter. If that pathname isn't right for your Perl, you'll need to edit all the script files that start with `#!` and fix that line. For instance, if your Perl executable is */stuff/bin/perl*, change the first lines to look like:

    ```
    #!/stuff/bin/perl
    ```

    Note that the version of *resend* with Majordomo 1.92 (and probably others) has a *–U* option at the end of the `#!` line. If you change the line, don't forget the *–U*.

* If your shell has job control and the *suspend* command, that's an easy way to drop back to *root*. (That's assuming you originally typed **su majordom** from the *root* account.) When you're ready to be *majordom* again, just use *fg*.

15. You might want to look through each program for an idea of how it works.

    The *request-answer* program from Majordomo 1.92 (and before) has a bug that can cause a mail loop. To fix it, edit line 40, which looks like this:

    ```
    exec("/usr/lib/sendmail", "-f$list-request", "-t") ||
    ```

    Change *–f$list-request* to *–f$list-approval.*

16. Configure Majordomo. Edit *majordomo.cf* to set the locations of directories and files as well as configuration variables. This is Perl code, so each line (except comments) must end with a semicolon (;):

    ```
    # $whereami -- Hostname to advertise for machine I'm running on:
    $whereami = "ora.com";

    # $whoami -- Address for users to send my requests:
    $whoami = "majordomo@$whereami";

    # $whoami_owner -- owner of the above, in case of problems:
    $whoami_owner = "owner-majordomo@$whereami";

    # $homedir -- Directory with my extra .pl files, like
    # majordomo.pl, shlock.pl, and majordomo_version.pl:
    $homedir = "/usr/local/majordomo";

    # $listdir -- Directory with files for mailing lists:
    $listdir = "/usr/local/majordomo/lists";

    # $digest_work_dir -- the parent directory for digest's queue area
    # Each list must have a subdirectory under this directory in order for
    # digest to work. E.G. The bblisa list would use:
    #     /usr/local/majordomo/digests/bblisa
    # as its directory.
    $digest_work_dir = "/usr/local/majordomo/digests";

    # $log -- Full pathname of the log file I write:
    $log = "/usr/local/majordomo/Log";

    # $mailer -- Program and arguments I use to send mail:
    # The variable $to can be interpolated into this command line,
    # however the $to variable is provided by the person sending mail,
    # and much mischief can be had by playing with this variable.
    # Use $to with care.
    $mailer = "/usr/lib/sendmail -f\e$sender -t";

    # Majordomo will look for "get" and "index" files related to $list
    # in directory "$filedir/$list$filedir_suffix":
    $filedir = "/usr/local/majordomo/archives";
    $filedir_suffix = "";

    # $index_command -- Command for processing an "index" request.
    # Majordomo does chdir("$filedir/$list$filedir_suffix") first.
    # Don't define if you use ftpmail: $index_command isn't used.
    ```

```
# This one makes a little heading without permissions, links,
# or owner name. This won't work if you use ls -lRL instead:
$index_command = "/bin/ls -lL | \e\e
  /bin/sed -e 's/^......................//' \\
  -e '1s/.*/   SIZE  DATE   NAME/'"

# If you want to use FTPMAIL, rather than local access, for
# file transfer and access, define the following:
#  $ftpmail_address = "ftpmail@decwrl.dec.com";
#  $ftpmail_location = "FTP.$whereami";

# if you want the subject of the request to be included as part of the
# subject of the reply (useful when automatically testing, or submitting
# multiple command sets), set $return_subject to 1.
$return_subject = 1;

# if you are using majordomo at the -request address, set the
# following variable to 1. This affects the help message and the
# welcome message that is sent to a new subscriber.
$majordomo_request = 0;

# set the umask for the process. Used to set default file status for
# config file.
umask(007);

# For Perl "require" function:
1;
```

The `sendmail -f\$sender` (near the middle of this *majordomo.cf* file) sets the message's envelope sender address (see the box in Section 23.4). The backslash (\) makes sure the Perl variable `$sender`, which is set by *resend*, isn't interpreted until the mail is sent. You might add a *–oi* option so *sendmail* won't treat a line with just a dot (.) as the end of a message. If you have big lists or a busy system, you might also add *–odq* to queue all messages for sending one at a time instead of trying to deliver them all immediately.

Of course, if you don't have *sendmail*, use a command for sending mail with your system's MTA.

We've hacked the `$index_command` in *majordomo.cf* to make a simpler archive index than the default `ls -lRL` command does. This makes the output more user-friendly for users who don't know UNIX, but it won't work if a list's archive has subarchives (subdirectories).

Don't delete the cryptic-looking `1;` at the end of the file. It keeps the Perl *require* function happy.

17. As the superuser, edit the MTA alias file to add aliases like these for *sendmail*:

```
owner-owner: postmaster
#
# Majordomo
```

```
#
owner-majordomo: jerry
majordomo: "|/usr/local/majordomo/wrapper majordomo"


majordom: owner-majordomo
# Needed "just in case" for Majordomo version 1.9x:
Majordomo-Owner: owner-majordomo
```

(There's a sample MMDF aliases file in Section 24.3.2.) Here's information about the aliases:

- If your *aliases* file doesn't have an *owner-owner* alias, we recommend it (actually, the Nutshell Handbook *sendmail* does). Using this special alias helps to find any problems with the zillions of other *owner-xxx* aliases that you'll be adding as you configure Majordomo lists. The *owner-owner* alias sends errors in any other *owner-* alias to the system postmaster.

- The *owner-majordomo* alias is for the Majordomo administrator. This address is listed as `$whoami_owner` in *majordomo.cf.* It gets returned mail from commands sent to *majordomo. sendmail* also mails error reports from the *majordomo* alias to *owner-majordomo.*

  There's a problem with the *owner-xxx* aliases under *sendmail* version 8. The setup above makes a person's address (here, *jerry*) the envelope sender of messages. This is probably not what you want. It's better to use an address associated with the system, like *owner-majordomo.* If you use *sendmail* version 8, we suggest adding a "dummy" address to the end of the alias:

  ```
  # Adding "nobody" prevents expansion to "jerry" under sendmail v8:
  owner-majordomo: jerry, nobody
  ```

  See Section 23.6 for details.

- Notice that the *majordomo* alias doesn't have the absolute pathname of the *majordomo* program. For security, the absolute pathname is hardcoded into the *wrapper* binary. If you move the *majordomo* program, the alias won't work until you edit and recompile *wrapper.*

- Be sure that mail sent to the *majordom* user (or whatever name you gave Majordomo's account) is routed somewhere. An alias could route it to *majordomo* (a good choice if you'll be getting much mail from systems that truncate mail addresses to an 8-character length). The alias above routes *majordom* mail to the person in charge of Majordomo. You could also use a program like *canned_reply* (see Chapter 22, *Introduction to Email Services*).

- The address *Majordomo-Owner* (capitalized that way) is buried inside one of the Majordomo routines as a default; it will probably never be used. Many sites running Majordomo have used the address *Majordomo-Owner* instead of *owner-majordomo,* so some people who've used Majordomo at other sites might expect you to have the address, too. For safety, therefore, it's a good idea to define a *Majordomo-Owner* alias pointing to *owner-majordomo.*

If this *sendmail* alias file is shared by more than one host, and they won't all be running the same Majordomo setup (which isn't likely), you've got some configuring to do. Section 23.3 has some tips. If your system needs it, run *newaliases* to rebuild the alias database.

18. You or the list owners may want to have a *bounces* mailing list set up. If you do, this is a good time to add the aliases and make the list files. (See Section 24.3 and Section 25.6.)

   To set up the *bounces* list:

   - Make sure that the *nobody* user exists on your system. There should also be a mail alias for *nobody* pointing to */dev/null*:

     ```
     nobody: /dev/null
     ```

     If your system doesn't have that alias or you can't create it, try this. Make a mail alias that has an obvious name (*trashcan*, *dustbin*, *nothing*, etc.) pointing to */dev/null*; use it in the setup below.

   - Follow the steps in Section 24.3.1 to make the *bounces* list.

   - In the previous step, you created a config file. Set `precedence` to *bulk*; this helps to stop returned mail messages from invalid addresses (see Section 23.7). Set `reply_to` and `sender` to *nobody*. Do *not* set `strip`; the comments in the subscriber list hold the name of the list and the date the person was subscribed. It's a good idea to set `noadvertise` to `/./` (slash dot slash); that regular expression matches all addresses, so the list won't appear when anyone except list members uses the *lists* command.

   - Check the *bounce-remind* script to be sure that the path to the Perl interpreter on the first line is correct. Take a quick look through the script. Notice the default location of the *majordomo.cf* file.

   - Make a *crontab* entry to run *bounce-remind* once a night.

     The `MAJORDOMO_CF` environment variable might not be set during *cron* jobs. So, if the *bounce-remind* script has the wrong location for your *majordomo.cf* file, you'll either need to edit the script or set `MAJORDOMO_CF` on the *crontab* line that runs *bounce-remind.*

   - Help list owners set up their accounts with the *bounce* script. Remember that the owners' *.majordomo* files need an entry for the *bounces* list as well as the other lists.

Before you turn users and list owners loose on the system, set up at least one list and test your system. The section below explains how to do that.

24.3 Setting Up Lists

Once you've got Majordomo installed, you'll want to create one or more mailing lists. The following sections provide a step-by-step procedure for creating a mailing list and a digested version, and testing the list to be sure it's working.

24.3.1 Creating a New List

New lists are created by:

- Adding files and subdirectories under the directories specified in *majordomo.cf*
- Making entries in your MTA aliases file
- Mailing a *config* command to *majordomo*, editing the configuration file it sends you, and mailing back the file

In the steps below, replace *listname* with the name of the list. A name like `$listdir` is a Perl variable from the *majordomo.cf* file. Here are the steps:

1. Pick a name for the list: lowercase letters, digits, underscores (`_`), or dashes (`-`) only. Because Majordomo already uses dashes in addresses, using underscores in your system's listnames can confuse users. Names with both underscores and dashes, like *foo_bar -digest*, are easy to get wrong.

2. Make a file in the `$listdir` directory to hold the list's subscribers. The filename is the *listname*.

3. The owner should pick the administrative password. Store it in the *listname.passwd* file in the `$listdir` directory. Use *chmod* to set the file mode to 660. As for all other Majordomo files, be sure that the group owner is *majordom*.

   (Later, the list owner can set the `admin_passwd` password—in the list's config file—by using the *newconfig* command. But this *listname.passwd* file is a good fallback if there are ever problems with the config file.)

4. The owner should write a description of the list to be mailed out in response to *info* requests and new subscriptions. (Hint: a good description in the *info* file will save the list owner's time by avoiding questions later.)

   If this is the first list you've created, store the description in the *listname.info* file in the `$listdir` directory and set the file mode to 664. After that, when you're sure your Majordomo setup is working, the owner can create *listname.info* by mail with a *newinfo* command. Using *newinfo* also makes sure that a date stamp is added if the `date_info` config variable has been set to *yes*.

5. If you want the list to be archived, create a directory in the archive area specified by the *majordomo.cf* file. (`$filedir/`*`listname`*`$filedir_suffix` will be the directory pathname.) If you're using the *archive* program, it creates the archive files; you only need to create the directory. If the archive is being written directly from

a mail alias (without the *archive* program), create the archive file, too. Set the directory mode to 775—and the mode of the file, if any, to 666.

6. If the list will also be available as a digest, follow the instructions in Section 24.3.3.

7. Add list aliases to the *sendmail* (or other MTA) aliases file. Here is an example for an archived list named *sample* on the host *foo.com.au*:

```
#
# Sample mailing list
#
owner-sample: jerry
sample: "|/usr/local/majordomo/wrapper resend -l sample
  -h foo.com.au sample-outgoing"
sample-approval: owner-sample
sample-outgoing:
  :include:/usr/local/majordomo/lists/sample, sample-archive
owner-sample-outgoing: owner-sample
sample-archive: "|/usr/local/majordomo/wrapper archive
  -f /usr/local/majordomo/archives/sample/sample -m -a"
owner-sample-archive: owner-sample
sample-request:
  "|/usr/local/majordomo/wrapper request-answer sample"
owner-sample-request: owner-sample
```

(There's a sample MMDF aliases file in Section 24.3.2.) Most of the alias names starting with `owner-` tell *sendmail* where to send errors caused by the corresponding alias. For example, if there's a problem with the `sample-archive` alias, *sendmail* complains to `owner-sample-archive`. These `owner-` aliases are usually easier to maintain if you point them to an overall alias (like `owner-sample` or `postmaster`) instead of a particular user (like `jerry`).

The other aliases are:

- `owner-listname` is the list owner, the person (or people) in charge of the list. A lot of the other aliases can point to this one.

  As Chapter 23, *Simple Mailing Lists*, explains, *sendmail* uses the *owner-xxx* aliases for errors. Under *sendmail* version 8, adding a "dummy" address to the end of the alias makes sure that the envelope sender of all messages is *owner-listname* instead of a person (here, *jerry*). So, for *sendmail* version 8, use an alias like this:

  ```
  # Adding "nobody" prevents expansion to "jerry" under sendmail v8:
  owner-sample: jerry, nobody
  ```

- `listname` runs the *wrapper* program to set the correct UID and GID. Then *wrapper* starts *resend* to send the message to the list.

The *resend* script receives and distributes mail for each list. (Strictly speaking, you don't need *resend* for a simple list. You can let *majordomo* manage the subscriber list—and use an `:include:` directive in a simple *sendmail* alias to distribute messages. But unless you have a problem with *resend*, its features are usually a help.) The only *resend* options you should use are *-l* (the list name) and *-h* (the host name). The rest of *resend*'s features are set in the *config* file. The alias ends with the distribution address (here, `sample-outgoing`).

- *listname–approval* is the person (or people) who approves subscriptions to closed lists, "non-routine" subscriptions or unsubscriptions (for an address other than the sender's), and mailings to moderated lists. This can usually point to `owner-`*listname*.
- *listname–outgoing* is the actual list of people subscribed to the list. The *sendmail* `:include:` directive reads the subscribers list from a file at the time a message is sent.

  If the list is to be archived, add an entry that calls *wrapper* to run the archive script you've chosen. We've made a separate *listname–archive* alias, but you can add the archive command to the *listname–outgoing* alias if you'd rather. We've chosen the *archive2.pl* script, which will eventually be integrated into *majordomo*. (Note: Whatever script you chose when you installed Majordomo, the *Makefile* installed it with the name *archive*.) Here's the usage information from the top of the program:

  ```
  archive -f archive {-u|-a} [-d|-m|-y] [file ...]
     -f archive REQUIRED; specifies base file name for archive
     -u  Input is a UNIX archive (separated by "From " lines) to split
     -a  Input is a message to append to archive
     -d  Archive file is archive.YYMMDD
     -m  Archive file is archive.YYMM
     -y  Archive file is archive.YY
  Exactly one of "-u" or "-a" must be specified.
  At most one of "-d", "-m", or "-y" may be specified; if none is
  specified, archive name is simply archive
  ```

  To use *archive* (*archive2.pl*) on a list alias, decide how often you want a new archive to be started: daily (the *–d* option), monthly (*–m*), yearly (*–y*), or never (no option). For automatic archiving from a mail alias, you'll need the *–a* option. The base archive filename is usually the same as the list name. So, the `sample-archive` alias above makes a new archive file each month: *sample.9501* in January 1995; *sample.9502* in February; and so on.
- Optional (but recommended): By convention, many Internet mailing lists have a subscription address of *listname–request*. Although our *sample* list doesn't use that address (it uses *majordomo*), the *request-answer* program could answer mail sent to that address. By default, *request-answer* sends a generic reply that gives the *majordomo* subscription address and some

overall information. You may want to edit the *request-answer* script to send a different message—for example, to give information about places to get help and information (local addresses, phone numbers, etc.) at your company.

Majordomo 1.90 and above can also be set to read the alias `listname–request` for commands. If you want that, change the alias to:

```
sample-request: "|/usr/local/majordomo/wrapper majordomo -l sample"
```

The option `-l` (lowercase letter L) gives the list name.

- Optional: The *new-list* script can answer mail sent to the list for the first few days. The message asks people to wait to post messages for a few days until most subscribers have joined the list. *new-list* also returns the sender's message.

  To install *new-list*, "comment out" the `listname` alias and put *new-list* in its place temporarily:

  ```
  # sample: "|/usr/local/majordomo/wrapper resend -l sample
  #    -h foo.com.au sample-outgoing"
  sample: "|/usr/local/majordomo/wrapper new-list sample"
  ```

  After a few days, the system administrator should install the permanent list alias. The owner should send an announcement that the list is "open for business."

As before, if this *sendmail* alias file is shared by more than one host, and they won't all be running the same Majordomo setup, there are tips in Section 23.3.

8. The most common cause of Majordomo problems is inadequate file and directory permissions. When *sendmail* reports an "Unknown mailer error," it's often caused by a directory that can't be written or a program that can't be executed.

   Make sure everything is owned by group *majordom*, and writable by both owner and group (mode 664 for files, 775 for directories). Scripts (programs) should be executable (mode 755); *wrapper* is also SUID (and SGID, on non-POSIX systems). In a lot of cases, files and directories don't need world access; you can use modes 660 and 770. But check and test; it's better to leave everything world-readable unless you're sure things work okay without it.

   If you need to be careful about security, think about how each file will be read and written. Many files are accessed by programs invoked from *wrapper*; those files only need permission for access by *wrapper*'s UID and GID. Files that will be written by users logged on interactively (like the list administrator) may need write permission for the *majordom* group. Files written directly from a *sendmail* alias, without *wrapper*, probably need world write permission because of the variety of UIDs and GIDs that *sendmail* may run as.

The list owner (or you) should send commands to create and set the *config* file options. See Section 25.3.

24.3.2 For MMDF Systems

The examples in the steps above are for systems with the *sendmail* MTA. Here are examples for systems that use the MMDF MTA.* The leading name `majordom|` means the *majordomo* and *sample* aliases will run as the user *majordom*. This is from the MMDF *aliases* file:

```
majordomo: "majordom|/usr/local/majordomo/wrapper majordomo"
owner-majordomo: jerry
```

Here are entries from the MMDF *lists* file for the sample mailing list. In MMDF, mailing lists have their own channel:

```
sample:            sample-outbound@list-channel
sample-outbound:   :include:/usr/local/majordomo/lists/sample
sample-request:    "majordom|/usr/local/majordomo/wrapper request-answer sample"
sample-approval:   jerry
owner-sample:      jerry
```

24.3.3 Making a Digested List

Lists can come in pairs: *listname* and *listname-digest*. To add a list digest, first set up the normal version of the list. Then, add another set of MTA aliases that run the *digest* program, and do the other steps for creating a new list. (Instructions are below.) Subscribers to the *listname* list get each list message as soon as it is posted; subscribers to *listname-digest* get a periodic digest of the messages from *listname*.

For example, to add a digest for our *sample* list:

1. Change the *`listname`*`-outgoing` alias to include a call to *digest*. Use the *digest* options shown below: *–r* tells *digest* to read a message from its standard input, *–C* reads the digest list's config file, and *–l* (lowercase L) gives the list name. The last *digest* argument is the address for outgoing messages. (See the *digest* script if you want more information.) Also add aliases like the others shown here:

```
sample-outgoing:
    :include:/usr/local/majordomo/lists/sample, sample-archive,
    "|/usr/local/majordomo/wrapper digest -r -C -l sample-digest
    sample-digest-outgoing"

sample-digest: sample
sample-digest-outgoing: :include:/usr/local/majordomo/lists/sample-digest
sample-digest-request:
    "|/usr/local/majordomo/wrapper request-answer sample-digest"
owner-sample-digest: owner-sample
owner-sample-digest-outgoing: owner-sample
owner-sample-digest-request: owner-sample
sample-digest-approval: sample-approval
```

* Thanks to Morna Findlay for these examples.

The alias names for the digested list *must* end in *–digest* and *–digest-outgoing*. The programs that process digests expect those suffixes.

2. Add *listname-digest.passwd* and *listname-digest* files. Add a *listname-digest* directory in `$digest_work_dir`.

   Also, because of a bug in Majordomo 1.92, you need to create a directory named `$filedir/digest-name$filedir_suffix`, where `digest-name` is the name provided to the *–l* option of *digest* in all-lowercase letters. (In our sample *majordomo.cf*, the `$filedir_suffix` is empty. So, the directory we need to create is */usr/local/majordomo/archives/sample-digest*.) This bug will be fixed in later versions. If you don't want to keep the list digests, you'll need to set up a *cron* job to remove old files from the directory periodically—like:

   ```
   cd /usr/local/majordomo && find *-digest/. -type f -mtime +1 -exec rm {} \;
   ```

   Set the permissions on all files and directories as you would for any list.

3. Add a config file for the new *listname-digest* list. The easiest way to do this is to get a copy of your existing *listname* config file (send the command `config listname password` to *majordomo*), edit it for the digest, then send it back (`newconfig listname-digest password`). This preserves your password, description, and other variables from the *listname* list. You'll want to change the following variables:

   - Change `digest_name` from *listname* to *listname-digest*.
   - Set `maxlength` to the digest size you want to be sent automatically.
   - Set `reply-to` to *listname* (not *listname-digest*) so that replies come to the main list address.
   - Change `sender` from *owner-listname* to *owner-listname-digest*.
   - If you've set `message_headers`, check it. You may want to change `message_fronter` (add the `_SUBJECTS_` expansion token and remove other tokens). Remember that you can't use expansion tokens within `message_footer` in a digest.

4. Use the command `newinfo listname-digest` to make a *listname-digest.info* file. (If the info file for the original *listname* is very long, it might be easier to adapt its file for the digest. Get the file with an `info listname` command.)

Digests are sent to digest subscribers whenever the digest has more than `maxlength` characters (set in the *listname-digest* config file). They're also sent when the list owner (or anyone who knows the password) mails a *mkdigest listname* command to *majordomo*. To automate this, the list owner can set up a *cron* job to mail a *mkdigest* command periodically.* If there are no digest messages to send, Majordomo mails the owner a message full of ugly errors.

* If the list password changes, the *cron* job will have to be changed too.

24.3.4 Testing Your Installation

You should have set up at least one list by now. A nice way to test Majordomo is with the */usr/ucb/mail -v* (verbose) switch; it shows you what's happening. If your version doesn't support *–v*, try the *–v* options of */usr/bin/mail*, */bin/mail*, or */usr/lib/sendmail*.

In case something is set up wrong, it's a good idea to have a superuser shell ready to do some fast cleanup.

1. If you want to watch the `$log` file and you have a spare window, type a command like this:

   ```
   % tail -f Log
   ```

   Another useful file to watch, if you have permission, is your MTA's log file.

2. Send a test "help" message to *majordomo*. We found a permission problem right away:

   ```
   % echo help | /usr/ucb/mail -v majordomo
   majordomo... aliased to "|/usr/local/majordomo/wrapper majordomo"
   "|/usr/local/majordomo/wrapper majordomo"... Connecting to  via prog...
   shlock: open(">/usr/local/majordomo/shlock4344"): Permission denied
      at /usr/local/majordomo/shlock.pl line 131, <> line 1.
   shlock: open(">/usr/local/majordomo/shlock4344"): Permission denied
      at /usr/local/majordomo/shlock.pl line 131, <> line 1.
      ...error message repeated every second or so...
   ```

   Even though we started this command as a normal user, we couldn't kill the *perl* process because *wrapper* changes the UID. You should have a superuser shell ready. We deleted the queued message from the */usr/spool/mqueue* directory, fixed the permission problem (the home directory wasn't group-writable), and tried again. (One of this book's reviewers told us that his system required all files be owned by *daemon*. He also had to set `W_UID` in his *Makefile* to *daemon*'s UID. We don't see why, but there are a lot of systems out there; this tip might help you too.)

   After we fixed the problem, and tried again, *majordomo* sent a help message:

   ```
   From owner-majordomo@ora.com Mon May 16 11:36:15 1994
   Return-Path: <owner-majordomo@ora.com>
   Date: Mon, 16 May 1994 11:36:13 PDT
   To: jerry
   From: majordomo@ora.com
   Subject: Majordomo results
   Reply-To: majordomo@ora.com

   >>>> help
           ...omitted...
   Commands should be sent in the body of an email message to
   "majordomo@ora.com".
   ```

```
Commands in the "Subject:" line NOT processed.

If you have any questions or problems, please contact
"owner-majordomo@ora.com".
```

Check the addresses in that message to be sure they're right. Especially, check the envelope sender address (on the "From " or "Return-Path:" lines). If the address isn't what you set in *majordomo.cf*, check the permissions on the *wrapper* script. (Compare them to what was set by the *Makefile*.) If *wrapper* can't run the mailer as a "trusted user," the mailer can't change the envelope sender address.

3. If you use the *request-answer* program, test it by mailing to *listname-request* (my test list was named *sample*):

   ```
   % echo help | /usr/ucb/mail -v sample-request
           ...
   ```

   Again, we checked the addresses in the returned message. In this message and the one before, the envelope sender (shown in the "From " or "Return-Path:" lines) should be one of the Majordomo aliases:

   ```
   From sample-approval Mon May 16 11:41:26 1994
   Return-Path: <sample-approval>
   ```

   The address is correct because the *wrapper* program runs as *daemon* (or, on POSIX systems, as *root*)—and those users are on the trusted-user list in the *sendmail* configuration file (such as */etc/sendmail.cf*):

   ```
   T root daemon uucp
   ```

   The trusted user settings aren't something to experiment with. If you're having trouble getting the right envelope sender address, check a reference for your MTA. (The Nutshell Handbook *sendmail* should be a help if you use that MTA.)

4. Next, be sure that your system's MTA is configured correctly to send mail across a network. Go to another account on another computer, send mail to *majordomo*, then check the return addresses in the message headers. You might ask a friend at another company to do the same thing.

5. Subscribe to the sample list. (We did it from another computer.)

   - If the list isn't closed, you should get a welcome message:

     ```
     From owner-majordomo@ora.com Mon May 16 15:22:28 1994
     Date: Mon, 16 May 1994 12:24:42 PDT
     To: jerry@foobar.ora.com
     From: majordomo@ora.com
     Subject: Welcome to sample
     Reply-To: majordomo@ora.com

     Welcome to the sample mailing list!
     ```

```
If you ever want to remove yourself from this mailing list, send the
following command in email to "majordomo@ora.com":

    unsubscribe sample jerry@foobar.ora.com (Jerry Peek)

Here's the general information for the list you've subscribed to, in
case you don't already have it:
```

–you should get a copy of the sample.info file here–

You should also get a "Majordomo results" message:

```
From owner-majordomo@ora.com Mon May 16 15:22:30 1994
Date: Mon, 16 May 1994 12:24:41 PDT
To: jerry@foobar.ora.com
From: majordomo@ora.com
Subject: Majordomo results
Reply-To: majordomo@ora.com

>>>> subscribe sample
Succeeded.
```

The list owner should get a confirmation:

```
From owner-majordomo@ora.com Mon May 16 15:22:29 1994
Date: Mon, 16 May 1994 12:24:40 PDT
To: sample-approval@ora.com
From: majordomo@ora.com
Subject: SUBSCRIBE sample
Reply-To: majordomo@ora.com

--

jerry@foobar.ora.com (Jerry Peek) has been added to sample.
No action is required on your part.
```

- If the list is closed, you should get a notice that your request has been forwarded to the owner, and the list owner should get a request for approval. (If you'd like to see examples, look ahead to the Section 25.5.2.) The list owner should approve the subscription.

6. If you've configured *majordomo* to read the list's *–request* alias, test it. Send *info*, *which*, and *who* commands (you can send them all in the same message); whether those commands have been made private or not, you should get results because you're subscribed to the list:

```
% /usr/ucb/mail -v sample-request
Subject:
info
which
who
^D
   ...
```

If you aren't using *listname-request*, use the *majordomo* address.

The results all come in one message:

```
From owner-majordomo@ora.com Mon May 16 15:23:34 1994
Date: Mon, 16 May 1994 12:25:45 PDT
To: jerry@foobar.ora.com (Jerry Peek)
From: majordomo@ora.com
Subject: SUBSCRIBE sample
Reply-To: majordomo@ora.com

--

>>>> info
[Last updated on: Mon May 16  9:39:13 1994]

This is the sample list.
>>>> which
The string 'jerry@foobar.ora.com' appears in the following
entries in lists served by majordomo@ora.com:

List                    Address
====                    =======
sample                  jerry@foobar.ora.com

>>>> who
Members of list 'sample':

jerry@foobar.ora.com
```

7. Send a message to the sample list:

```
% /usr/ucb/mail -v sample@ora.com
Subject: test message to sample list; will this make an archive?

Hi, folks.
^D
        ...watch the transaction...
```

If the list is moderated, the list owner should get the message and approve it. (See Section 25.5.3.) Look at the message sent to the list:

```
From owner-sample@ora.com Mon May 16 15:27:12 1994
From: Jerry Peek <jerry@foobar.ora.com>
Date: Mon, 16 May 1994 12:26:58 EDT
To: sample@ora.com
Subject: test message to sample list; will this make an archive?
Sender: owner-sample@ora.com
Precedence: bulk

Hi, folks.
```

Be sure that the message is going into the list archive file, if any.

If you're planning to set up the *new-list* script, comment out the list's current *resend* alias (add a # before it) and set up *new-list*. Test it to be sure you get a reply.

8. If your list has digests, test them. Subscribe to the *listname-digest* list. Send two messages to *listname*; make their total length more than the `maxlength` variable setting in the digest's config file. You should get a digest.

9. Try sending a message from another account to unsubscribe you. Your request should be forwarded to the list owner unless you've set the `subscribe_policy` variable (in the list's configuration file) to *auto*.

10. Try the *passwd* command from the list-owner account. (See Section 25.2.) Be sure that the backup password file *listname.passwd* in the list directory is updated.

11. If you've made a list archive, there should be a file in it by now. Get a listing of the archive and a copy of the file. If you've set `$return_subject` to *1* in *majordomo.cf*, try adding a subject; it should be echoed in the "Majordomo results" reply you get:

```
% /usr/ucb/mail -v majordomo
Subject: Checking index stuff
index sample
get sample sample.9405
^D
majordomo... aliased to  "|/usr/local/majordomo/wrapper majordomo"
"|/usr/local/majordomo/wrapper majordomo"... Connecting to via prog...
"|/usr/local/majordomo/wrapper majordomo"... sent.
```

If you didn't see any errors, you should get two mail messages. One is a copy of the file; the other holds the results of the Majordomo session:

```
Return-Path: <owner-majordomo@ora.com>
To: jerry
From: majordomo@ora.com
Subject: Majordomo file: list 'sample' file 'sample.9405'
Reply-To: majordomo@ora.com

--

From owner-sample Mon May 16 12:37:46 1994
Received: by ora.com (5.65c/Spike-2.1)
        id AA05037; Mon, 16 May 1994 12:35:17 -0700

  ...copy of messages from the list...

Return-Path: <owner-majordomo@ora.com>
To: jerry
From: majordomo@ora.com
Subject: Majordomo results: Checking index stuff
Reply-To: majordomo@ora.com
```

```
--

>>>> index sample
     SIZE    DATE        NAME
     5383 May 16 01:58 sample.9405
>>>> get sample sample.9405
List 'sample' file 'sample.9405'
is being sent as a separate message.
```

24.4 Day-to-day Administration

The Majordomo administrator is often the computer's system administrator too. Day-to-day administration means watching the system log and other files for errors, setting up new lists, and managing archives. Sometimes you'll need to reconfigure the system. This section explains how to do those things.

Administrators also help new list owners get started. So, besides knowing how to administer a system, the administrator needs to understand the list owner's job. The next chapter is for list owners and moderators; administrators should read it, too.

24.4.1 Setting Up a List Owner's Account

A list owner only needs to be able to send and receive email. The owner doesn't need to have login access to the system where the list server runs.

The list owner doesn't even need to be on a UNIX system, although Majordomo comes with some UNIX scripts (*approve* and *bounce*) that make life easier for the list owner. Add the *bin* directory from the Majordomo account (such as */usr/local/majordomo/bin*) to the list owner's shell search path—or copy the scripts to the owner's computer.

24.4.2 Editing Files with medit

The *medit* script locks a file, then starts your favorite text editor. When you exit the editor, *medit* removes the lock. The lock keeps Majordomo from editing the file while you do.

The script uses the editor given in your `EDITOR` environment variable; the default is *vi*. It reads the *majordomo.cf* file specified in the `MAJORDOMO_CF` environment variable, if any, or */etc/majordomo.cf* by default. So, people who use *medit* often should set those variables on their accounts.

Edit and quit as quickly as you can! If a file stays locked too long while Majordomo also needs to make changes, Majordomo gives up and aborts.

24.4.3 Majordomo Logs

Majordomo keeps a log file. The file's pathname is set in the `$log` variable in your *majordomo.cf* file. It's a good idea to read the file every day or two and clean it out periodically. A handy script in the *contrib* directory, *logsummary.pl*, makes a summary of the log.

When Majordomo is busy (such as after you've added a new list), you may want to run *tail -f* to watch messages as they're being added to the log. We've found it useful to keep compressed copies of old log files for reference.

The log file won't give you much help with security problems. (As Brent has made clear, security wasn't one of Majordomo's main goals.) Transactions are logged with the "Reply-to:" or "From:" address in the mail message header. For example, you can send a message like this:

```
Reply-to: John Doe <johndoe@nowhere.org>
From: Your-real-name <your-real-address>
To: majordomo@bakers.org

passwd donut-makers oldpassword newpassword
```

The following is logged (and it will be "FAILED" only if the old password was incorrect):

```
May 15 21:06:31 bakers majordomo[27604] {johndoe@nowhere.org}
        FAILED passwd donut-makers OLD NEW
```

There's no trace of the original sender or any way to see the OLD password he tried. One way to track messages like these is by reading your system MTA log file. Another is by making duplicates of all mail sent to *majordomo*. For instance, the following alias would send a copy of all *majordomo* requests to *owner-majordomo*:

```
majordomo: owner-majordomo, "|/usr/local/majordomo/wrapper majordomo"
```

Of course, on a busy system, the person who is *owner-majordomo* will get a lot of mail; a mail filter program like *procmail** can store that mail and help to sort out the messages you might really want to see.

Instead of a mailbox address, you can make an alias that uses one of the archive scripts to log all incoming *majordomo* mail:

```
majordomo-archive: "|/usr/local/majordomo/wrapper archive
   -f /usr/local/majordomo/logs.mail/incoming -a -m"
```

A *cron* job can compress and/or remove old messages periodically.

* You can get *procmail*, by Stephen R. van den Berg, from many anonymous FTP sites including *ftp.informatik.rwth-aachen.de*. Another popular tool is *deliver* by Chip Salzenberg; an up-to-date copy is harder to find, but we found one (version 2.1.12, as of this printing) on *ftp.cs.uni-sb.de*.

24.4.4 Managing the Archives

An archive is a file containing messages that previously appeared on the mailing list. You can create an archive simply by running the *archive2.pl* script as described in Section 24.3.1.

You can also put any ASCII file in the archive and set up a directory hierarchy. But you need to do that by hand. For example, if you want *majordomo* to mail files that contain nontext characters, you'll need to preprocess the files with a utility like *uuencode* or *btoa*.

If your site has an anonymous FTP area, you can set *majordomo* to store your archives there. You can also configure the *majordomo.cf* file to handle *get* commands by forwarding requests to an *ftpmail* server, described in Chapter 26, *Ftpmail*. To do that, define the variables `$ftpmail_address` (and optionally `$ftpmail_location`—the default is the local host) in the *majordomo.cf* file. If you use *ftpmail*, don't bother defining `$index_command` in the *majordomo.cf* file (*majordomo* handles an *index* request by mailing a *dir* command to *ftpmail*). The *ftpmail* setup assumes that the FTP archive is structured the same way as your local archive directory. It uses the pathname `$filedir/`*`listname`*`$filedir_suffix` for the archive directory, then issues an FTP *get* command for the file specified.

24.4.5 Disabling Majordomo Temporarily

Once Majordomo is set up on your system, how do you do maintenance? Majordomo always active, because incoming mail can start the programs anytime. If you make a mistake in your maintenance, incoming mail can be returned as undeliverable. One way to disable Majordomo is to shut off your system's *sendmail* daemon, but that affects all mail on your system.

An easier way is to make a small "stub" shell script named *majordomo.hold*:

```
#!/bin/sh
exit 75
```

Make that file executable with **`chmod 755 majordomo.hold`**. Then quickly (so there's less chance of causing incoming mail to be returned) swap the *majordomo* Perl script and your *majordomo.hold* script:

```
% mv majordomo majordomo.tmp && mv majordomo.hold majordomo
```

(The shell's && operator lets you type both command lines before executing either of them. It does the second *mv* command only if the first one succeeds.) When mail comes in, *sendmail* runs your little script, which returns an exit status of 75. This special status makes *sendmail* defer (queue) the incoming message and try to deliver it to "majordomo:" again later. When you're done with your maintenance, swap the script with the real *majordomo* script and mail will be processed again. (Special exit statuses like 75 are listed in the file */usr/include/sysexits.h*.)

The same thing works with *resend*; disabling it disables all of the lists.

Note that your *sendmail* may convert pathnames of commands run by deferred messages to all lowercase letters. This problem may only bite you after you defer messages. For example, if your *archive* alias looks like this:

```
sample-archive: "|/usr/local/majordomo/wrapper archive
   -f /usr/local/majordomo/Archives/sample/sample -m -a"
```

The A in that pathname may be changed to lowercase (a) when the message is deferred. If it is, the *archive* script won't be able to find the archives directory. The fix for this problem is to either change your *sendmail.cf* file (so it doesn't change case), add a symbolic link to the directory using the lowercase name (for example, link *archives* to *Archives*), or only use lowercase letters in your file and directory names.

24.5 The Majordomo Mailing List

A good way to learn more about Majordomo is by subscribing to the *majordomo-users* mailing list. Send a subscription request to *majordomo@GreatCircle.com*. Another list on the same host, *majordomo-announce*, announces new versions of Majordomo as well as bug fixes. The *majordomo-workers* list is for people who develop and test Majordomo; it's a good place to send bug reports and ideas for new features.

In this Chapter:

- *List Owner Aliases*
- *Majordomo Commands for List Owners*
- *Changing a List's Configuration*
- *Making a Moderated List*
- *Approving Subscriptions and Moderating*
- *Returned Mail and the Bounces List*

The Majordomo List Owner and Moderator

As described in Chapter 22, *Introduction to Email Services*, you don't need to be a system administrator or even know much about UNIX to be a Majordomo mailing list owner or moderator. The list owner and moderator communicate with Majordomo by email, and so don't even need to be on a UNIX computer (although it helps).

The potential list owner or moderator should read Section 24.1 before reading this chapter, so that you know what list features you'd like the system administrator to set up. The rest of Chapter 24, *Automating Mailing Lists with Majordomo*, which covers Majordomo administration, is not necessary for understanding this chapter or for being a list owner or moderator.

25.1 List Owner Aliases

Majordomo makes day-to-day operation of a mailing list easier, but there are still things to do. This chapter's introductory Section 25.2 lists the commands necessary to do the list owner's job.

Each list has the following aliases that can get mail related to the list:

- *owner-listname* receives messages that were returned as undeliverable. (Most email users call these "bounced" messages. But Majordomo uses that term for something else. So, in this book's Majordomo chapters, we use the term "returned messages" for messages that were undeliverable.)
- *listname-approval* receives requests to approve subscriptions (or unsubscriptions). It also gets notifications of successful subscriptions or unsubscriptions.

  In Majordomo 1.92 and before, this address also receives what Majordomo calls "bounced" messages. These are requests to approve messages for posting to the list. (In a future version of Majordomo, a new *listname-moderator* address will get these requests for approval.)

If you point those aliases to more than one person, keep that in mind as you read the sections below. We've assumed that all list messages needing action go to a single "list owner."

25.2 Majordomo Commands for List Owners

The commands for users (described in Section 24.1.1) can also be used by list owners. But there are seven more commands (all password-protected) for list owners. These aren't mentioned in Majordomo's help file. If the owner doesn't have an account on the machine where Majordomo runs, these commands allow routine housekeeping via email:

`approve` *`password`* `subscribe/unsubscribe` *`listname address`*
: Subscribe or unsubscribe someone from the list *listname*. When you add a subscription, it's useful to keep the subscriber's name (and possibly other information) with the address; use a legal RFC 822 syntax. If the `strip` variable is set in the list's config file, though (see Section 25.3.1), only subscribers' email addresses (*user@host*) are stored; in that case, don't bother sending anything other than the address. To unsubscribe someone, enter that person's address as it's listed in the subscribers file. For example:

```
approve !BooM! subscribe donut-makers Bob Baker <rpbaker@sandia.gov>
approve !BooM! unsubscribe donut-makers john.dough@bakers.org
```

`passwd` *`listname old-password new-password`*
: The *passwd* command changes the "backup" administrative password that's used when the config file is missing or corrupted. The usual way to change a list's passwords is by editing the list's config file (see `config` and `newconfig`).

  This command changes the administrative password for *listname* (stored in the *listname.passwd* file) from *old-password* to *new-password*. Remember that this password is stored, unencrypted, on the computer running Majordomo. Don't use your login password!

  When you change a list password, you may want to change the digest password (if any) too.

`newinfo`*`listname password`*...*info file contents here*...`EOF`
: Change the text in the *listname.info* file (the text users receive when they mail an *info* command or subscribe to the list). The text is taken from the rest of the mail message until a line that begins with the three uppercase letters `EOF`.

  If the `date_info` config file variable is set to *yes*, a date line is added above the text you send. In that case, you may want to start your text with a blank line to separate it from the date line.

An easy way to change the existing info file is to get the old file first (with an *info listname* command). But remember to delete the date line from the file before you send back the edited version.

`config` *`listname password`*
: Emails a copy of the configuration file for *listname* to the owner. You can edit the configuration file and send it back with *newconfig*. See also Section 25.3.

`newconfig` *`listname password`...config file contents here...*`EOF`
: The *newconfig* command installs a new configuration file for *listname*. After you type the *newconfig* command, follow it with a copy of the new configuration file—and end with the string `EOF` on a line by itself.

`writeconfig` *`listname password`*
: Rewrites an existing configuration file into a standard form which includes all documentation.

`mkdigest` *`listname password`*
: Force a digest to be generated for *listname*, using all the messages since the last digest was created.

25.3 Changing a List's Configuration

Each list has its own configuration file in the `$listdir` directory. The config file sets all kinds of list parameters; see Section 25.3.1. The filename is *listname.config*—for instance, for the list named *sample*, the filename is *sample.config*. A list digest has its own config file; the name is *listname-digest.config* (for example, *sample-digest.config*).

Although it's tempting to edit the config file directly (if you have an account on the host running Majordomo), it's safer to use the *config* and *newconfig* Majordomo commands to get the config file and send back an edited version. The *newconfig* command validates the new config file and also makes sure that permissions are right.

When a list is first created, the list owner (or anyone who knows the password stored in the *listname.passwd* file) should send a *config* command to *majordomo*. Majordomo will create the config file from the system defaults and mail you a copy of the file. Here's part of the mail message with the default file. We've omitted the block of instructions at the top of the file and most of the configuration settings:

```
From owner-majordomo@bakers.org Sun May 15 08:56:09 1994
To: postmaster@yummybake.com
From: majordomo@bakers.org
Subject: Majordomo results
Reply-To: majordomo@bakers.org

--

>>>> config donut-makers PASSWORD
# The configuration file for a majordomo mailing list.
```

```
# Comments start with the first # on a line, and continue to the end
          ...omitted...

          # admin_passwd     [word] (donut-makers.admin) <majordomo>
          # (Default is specified in the file <listname>.passwd) The password
          # for handling administrative tasks on the list.
admin_passwd    =   donut-makers.admin

          # administrivia     [bool] (yes) <resend>
          # Look for administrative requests (e.g. subscribe/unsubscribe) and
          # forward them to the list maintainer instead of the list.
administrivia    =   yes

          # advertise     [regexp_array] (undef) <majordomo>
          # If the requestor email address matches one of these regexps, then
          # the list will be listed in the output of a lists command. Failure to
          # match any regexp excludes the list from the output. The regexps
          # under noadvertise override these regexps.
advertise       << END
END

          # approve_passwd     [word] (donut-makers.pass) <resend>
          # Password to be used in the approved header to allow posting to
          # moderated list, or to bypass resend checks.
approve_passwd  =   donut-makers.pass

          # archive_dir     [absolute_dir] (undef) <majordomo>
          # The directory where the mailing list archive is kept. This item does
          # not currently work. Leave it blank.
archive_dir     =

          ...omitted...
#[Last updated Fri May 6 17:04:03 1994]
```

You should save the mail message in a file, or read it into a reply message. Then remove everything from the top of the message up to and including the line `>>>> config` *`listname password`*. If your email program adds characters at the start of each line, remove those extra characters.

There are two kinds of lines in a config file:

- Comments; these start with a hash mark (#).
- Lines that set *variables*. These start with the name of the variable. Next comes either:
  - An equal sign (=) for storing a single word, number, or string in the variable.
  - Or, the characters `<< END`, which start a **here document**. A here document stores an *array* (a series of values) in the variable. The values start on the following line, one value per line. The word `END` on a line by itself ends the here document (and the array).

Don't leave empty lines in a here document (except the line just before the END). To store an empty line, or a line that starts with whitespace, put a dash (-) in the left margin. To store a line that starts with a dash, use two dashes. For example, the here document below has three lines. The first is completely blank, the second is indented, and the third starts with two dashes:

```
message_footer << END
-
-   Thanks for subscribing to mud-wrestlers. Have a nice day.
---Bertha, the moderator
END
```

Within a here document, the character # does *not* start a comment.

In the config file shown above, the admin_passwd, administrivia, approve_passwd, and archive_dir variables are set with an equals sign. The advertise variable is set with a here document—in this case, it's empty.

To unset a variable, leave its value empty. In the config file above, the advertise and archive_dir variables are empty.

The comments above each variable explain how to set it and what it's for. Let's look at the admin_passwd variable again:

```
# admin_passwd     [word] (donut-makers.admin) <majordomo>
# (Default is specified in the file <listname>.passwd) The password
# for handling administrative tasks on the list.
admin_passwd    =  donut-makers.admin
```

The first line of the comments shows:

- The name of the variable (admin_passwd).
- The type of value in the variable, shown in square brackets ([word]). Table 25-1 lists the choices.

  If a variable type ends in _array, the variable can hold more than one value; set it with a here document. For instance, in the example config file above, the advertise variable has the type regexp_array; it's a list of regular expressions (see Section 25.3) set with a here document.
- The default value of the variable is shown in parentheses. For example, the default admin_passwd is *donut-makers.admin.* (undef) means that, by default, the variable is undefined or not used in this version of Majordomo; the comments explain.
- Next is the name of the program that uses this variable, shown inside angle brackets (<majordomo>). The three program names are:

  1. *majordomo* handles administrative requests (subscriptions, indexes, archives, etc.)

2. *resend* handles messages sent to the lists.

3. *digest* handles digests of list messages.

The last lines of the comments describe what the variable is used for.

So, if you wanted to change the administrative password to *HaHaHa*, you'd change that part of the config file to:

```
# admin_passwd     [word] (donut-makers.admin) <majordomo>
# (Default is specified in the file <listname>.passwd) The password
# for handling administrative tasks on the list.
admin_passwd     =  HaHaHa
```

After you make changes, you must mail the whole config file to *majordomo* with a *newconfig* command. (Future versions of Majordomo may let you change only the parts you need to.)

Table 25-1: Config File Variable Types

Type	Explanation
`absolute_dir`	An absolute directory pathname (pathname that starts with /)
`absolute_file`	An absolute file pathname (pathname that starts with /)
`bool`	Choose from `yes, no, y, n.`
`enum`	Choose one of a list of possible values shown between slashes. For example, `/open;closed;auto/` means you can choose open or closed or auto.
`integer`	An integer
`float`	A floating-point number with decimal point
`regexp`	A Perl-style regular expression with leading and trailing slash (/) characters. See Section 25.3.2 for more information.
`restrict_post`	A series of filenames, separated by spaces or colons (:). See the explanation of the `restrict_post` variable, below.
`string`	A single line of text with zero or more words. Whitespace (spaces and tabs) at the start and end of the line are removed.
`word`	A single word. (More exactly, text with no embedded whitespace.)

25.3.1 Config File Variables

This section describes the config file variables in more detail than the comments in the config file.*

You don't need to read all this on a first pass. Skim it now to get an idea of the available settings, then use it as a reference. This section omits variables that don't work in version 1.92 or that shouldn't be changed.

* Parts of this section were adapted from comments in the config file.

`admin_passwd` (type=*word*, default=*listname.admin*, used by *majordomo*)
The password for list administration commands. (The default password is stored in the *listname.passwd* file.) If you change a list password, you also may want to change the digest password (if any).

`administrivia` (type=*bool*, default=*yes*, used by *resend*)
Search incoming list messages for Majordomo commands and forward the messages to the list maintainer. With this option, *resend* does two checks of each message. If the message's subject contains an uppercase or lowercase word that ends in "subscribe" or "unsubscribe", starts with "help" or "RCPT:", contains "change... address" or "request... addition", the message is bounced to the list owner. Also, if the first five lines of the message body have the words "change... address", "add me", "delete me", "subscribe", "sub", "unsubscribe", or "unsub", in uppercase or lowercase, anywhere in those lines, the message is bounced to the list owner.

The list owner can bypass the administrivia checks by adding a valid "Approved:" line and resending the message to the list.

`advertise` (type=*regexp_array*, default=*undef*, used by *majordomo*)
This is an array of regular expressions (see Section 25.3.2). It tells *majordomo* who should be able to find out about this list from the *lists* command. When someone sends a *lists* command, that person's email address is compared to the regular expressions in the `advertise` array. If the address doesn't match, this list won't be included in the *lists* output.

The `noadvertise` regular expressions override these. (But list subscribers will always see their lists in the *lists* output; `noadvertise` doesn't affect that.)

If both `advertise` and `noadvertise` are empty, the list will be advertised to everyone.

`approve_passwd` (type=*word*, default=*listname.pass*, used by *resend*)
This is the password that list owners should use in the "Approved:" line to allow posting to a moderated list or to bypass *resend* checks. (See Section 25.5.1 about approving messages, below.) If you change a list password, you also may want to change the digest password (if any).

`comments` (type=*string_array*, default=*undef*, used by *config*)
This variable holds arbitrary comment text for the (human) administrator. You don't have to define it. It can be defined only once in each config file.

When you use *writeconfig*, all comments are replaced with standard comments; any comments you've added (with a # before them) are lost. If you want to add comments that will be preserved, add them to this special "dummy" variable.

`date_info` (type=*bool*, default=*yes*, used by *majordomo*)
If `date_info` is set to *no*, *majordomo* changes the output of the *info* command by adding a date line that tells when the list's *info* file was last modified.

If date_info is set to *yes*, Majordomo adds a date line at the top of the text that you send with a *newinfo* command. This is useful if the file is also sent out by some means other than Majordomo (such as *finger* or FTP).

debug (type=*bool*, default=*no*, used by *resend*)

Don't actually forward the message, just output a list of the actions that would be performed and the text of the message. You can see this text by mailing from the local Majordomo host with a command that shows the session, such as */usr/ucb/mail –v*. For example:

```
% /usr/ucb/mail -v sample
Subject: Just playing around
Hi there.
^D
sample... aliased to "|/usr/local/majordomo/wrapper resend -l Sample
  -h ora.com    sample-outgoing"
"|/usr/local/majordomo/wrapper resend -l Sample -h ora.com
  sample-outgoing"... Connecting to via prog...
Command: /usr/lib/sendmail -fowner-sample sample-outgoing
Date: Mon, 16 May 1994 15:37:40 PDT
From: jerry (Jerry Peek)
Message-Id: <9405161237.AA02279@ora.com>
To: sample
Subject: Just playing around
Sender: owner-sample@ora.com
Precedence: bulk

Hi there.

This is the sample list message footer from the message_footer
variable.
"|/usr/local/majordomo/wrapper resend -l Sample -h ora.com
  sample-outgoing"... Sent
```

description (type=*string*, default=*undef*, used by *majordomo*)

If description is undefined, the *lists* command output gives only the list name. If you store a description of the list (50 characters or less) in description, it is shown after the list name.

digest_issue (type=*integer*, default=*1*, used by *digest*)

The issue number of the next digest. The *digest* program changes this when it sends a digest.

digest_name (type=*string*, default=*listname*, used by *digest*)

The subject line for the digest. This string has the volume and issue appended to it automatically.

digest_volume (type=*integer*, default=*1*, used by *digest*)

The current volume number

`maxlength` (type=*integer*, default=*40000*, used by *resend, digest*)

When used with *resend* (for incoming messages): the maximum size of an unapproved message in characters.

When used with *digest*: a new digest is automatically generated if the size of the digest exceeds this number of characters. Otherwise, the list owner can send a digest by hand with the *mkdigest* command.

`message_footer` (type=*string_array*, default=*undef*, used by *resend, digest*)

Text to be added to the end of all messages posted to the list. The text is expanded before being used. The following expansion tokens are defined, but *only for original messages (not for digests)*:

`$LIST`	The name of the current list. Example: `sample`.
`$SENDER`	The sender, taken from the "From:" header field. Example: `fred@bar.edu (Fred Wilmot)`.
`$VERSION`	The version of Majordomo. Example: `1.92`.

For example, to add a reminder about list policy to the end of every message sent from a list, use these lines (that use a here document) in the config file:

```
message_footer  << END
-
The $LIST list is run automatically by Majordomo version $VERSION.
Please mail questions to owner-$LIST@foo.com.au
END
```

To separate the footer from the message, you'll probably want to put a blank line at the start. To preserve whitespace inside a here document, put a dash (-) at the start of the line. (The introduction to this section has more information about dashes in here documents.)

`message_fronter` (type=*string_array*, default=*undef*, used by *resend, digest*)

Text to be prepended to the beginning of all messages posted to the list. The text is expanded before being used. In a nondigest message, the same expansion tokens are defined as for the `message_footer` variable, above. If used in a digest, though, *only* the expansion token `_SUBJECTS_` is available; it expands to the list of message subjects in the digest.

For example, to start a digest with a list of the subjects in it, add this entry to the config file:

```
message_fronter  << END
Today's topics:
-
-  _SUBJECTS_
END
```

All the subjects have the same indentation as the `_SUBJECTS__` token.

Here's the start of the digest you get:

```
sample-digest     Monday, 9 May 1994   Volume 01 : Number 004

Today's topics:

  Just a sample message
  Another sample message
  Are we having fun yet???

----------------------------------------------------------------------

From: fred@bar.edu (Fred Wilmot)
Date: Mon, 9 May 94 11:29:16 PDT
Subject: Just a sample message
  ...
```

`message_headers` (type=*string_array*, default=*undef*, used by *resend, digest*)

These fields are appended to the header of the posted message. The text is expanded before being used. The same expansion tokens are defined as for the `message_footer` variable, above.

For example, to add two "Comment:" fields to each outgoing message header:

```
message_headers  << END
Comment: To get off of this list, mail an "unsubscribe" command to
Comment: $LIST-request@foo.bar.au
END
```

`moderate` (type=*bool*, default=*no*, used by *resend*)

If *yes*, all postings to the list must be approved by the moderator.

`mungedomain` (type=*bool*, default=*no*, used by *majordomo*)

When set to *yes*, addresses of the form *user@x.y.z* are considered equivalent to addresses of the form *user@y.z*. This allows a user to subscribe to a list using the domain address rather than the address assigned to a particular machine in the domain.

For example, a user who has the three accounts *jan@foo.abc.com*, *jan@bar.abc.com*, and *jan@baz.abc.com* could subscribe as *jan@abc.com*. List messages will be sent to *jan@abc.com*, but Jan can control her subscription from any of her accounts. (Hint: add a note about this to the list's *info* file.)

`noadvertise` (type=*regexp_array*, default=*undef*, used by *majordomo*)

If the requestor's email address matches one of the regular expressions in the array, the list won't appear in the output of a *lists* command. (But list subscribers always see their lists in the *lists* output; `noadvertise` doesn't affect that.) Addresses in `noadvertise` override the ones in `advertise`.

`precedence` (type=*word*, default=*bulk*, used by *resend, digest*)
Add a "Precedence:" field with the given value to the outgoing message header (see Section 23.7).

`private_get` (type=*bool*, default=*yes*, used by *majordomo*)
When set to *yes*, only subscribers can *get* files from the list archive.

`private_index` (type=*bool*, default=*no*, used by *majordomo*)
When set to *yes*, only subscribers can use the *index* command on a list's archive files.

`private_info` (type=*bool*, default=*no*, used by *majordomo*)
When set to *yes*, only subscribers can use *info* to get information about the list.

`private_which` (type=*bool*, default=*no*, used by *majordomo*)
When set to *yes*, only subscribers can use *which* to search the addresses of list subscribers.

`private_who` (type=*bool*, default=*no*, used by *majordomo*)
When set to *yes*, only subscribers can use *who* to get the addresses of list subscribers.

`purge_received` (type=*bool*, default=*no*, used by *resend*)
Remove all "Received:" fields from the message header before resending the message.

`reply_to` (type=*word*, default=, used by *resend, digest*)
Add a "Reply-to:" field with the given value to the outgoing message header. If the value is the token `$SENDER`, the sender's address is used. This is the value of the "Reply-to:" header field for digest lists.

`resend_host` (type=*word*, default=*undef*, used by *resend*)
The host name that is appended to all address strings specified for *resend*. See the `sender` variable.

`restrict_post` (type=*restrict_post*, default=*undef*, used by *resend*)
This variable is used to restrict who can post to a list. The ***`filenames`*** argument is a list of one or more files, separated by colons (`:`), in the `$listdir` directory. The files contain addresses that are allowed to send messages to the list. If the message doesn't have a valid "Approved:" line and the sender's "From:" address isn't on this list, the message is bounced to the list owner.

For example, a company might want a general announcements list that only a few employees should send messages to. Instead of making the list moderated (which would add overhead) they can use the name of a file with the addresses of people who are approved to send mail to the list. This isn't very secure, because any user can forge a "From:" address easily. Still, it is an easy way to stop messages (replies, for example) from being sent to the list accidentally. It also doesn't require all the people who post to know the article approval password.

This mechanism will be replaced in a future version of Majordomo.

`sender` (type=*word*, default=*owner-listname*, used by *majordomo, resend, digest*)
The envelope sender and "Sender:" addresses for the resent mail are made from the value of `sender`, an `@`, and the value of the `resend_host` variable. The value of `sender` is also used as the "Sender:" address for the welcome message mailed to new subscribers.

`strip` (type=*bool*, default=*yes*, used by *majordomo*)
Normally, *majordomo* stores the complete address it gets for each subscriber. That includes comments like `"Jerry Peek"` or `(Phone 123-4567, FAX 234-5678)`. These can help you (and other people) find subscribers when the email address isn't enough. If you set the `strip` variable, though, comments aren't stored with addresses.*

`subject_prefix` (type=*word*, default=*undef*, used by *resend*)
This word is be prefixed to the message "Subject:" if it isn't already in the subject. The text is expanded before being used. The following expansion tokens are defined:

`$LIST`	The name of the current list
`$SENDER`	The sender (taken from the "From:" header field)
`$VERSION`	The version of Majordomo

`subscribe_policy` (type=*enum*, default=*open*, used by *majordomo*)
This variable can have one of three possible values:†

- *auto* means all subscription requests are approved automatically, including requests by any user to subscribe or unsubscribe any other user. The list owner is notified when people subscribe or unsubscribe, but doesn't have to approve them.
- *open* means that nonroutine subscriptions (requests by any user to subscribe or unsubscribe any other user) are sent to the list owner. Routine subscriptions are approved automatically.
- *closed* requires the list owner to approve all subscriptions.

* If the file *listname.strip* exists in the `$listdir` directory, it is the same as setting `strip` to *yes*. This can be overridden by setting `strip` to *no*.

† If you leave the variable undefined, and there's a file named *listname.closed* in the `$listdir` directory on the machine running Majordomo, it is the same as setting the variable to *closed*. Similarly, the presence of a file named *listname.auto* is the same as setting the variable to *auto*. Setting the variable overrides either of those files, though.

25.3.2 Regular Expressions for advertise and noadvertise

The config file variables `advertise` and `noadvertise` let you control the output of the *lists* command. If those variables aren't defined in a list's config file, then the list is completely "public": everyone can find out about the list. But you might not want everyone to know about a list. For instance, your Majordomo server might run some lists that are only for employees of your company. You would want to restrict who can see those lists in the output of the *lists* command.

majordomo can check the email address of a person who sends a *lists* command and compare it to the `advertise` and `noadvertise` variables. Those variables are arrays of *regular expressions—regexps* for short. To tell *majordomo* which lists should be advertised, you need to write regexps that match certain addresses.

A regular expression is a pattern that matches a string of characters (for example, an email address). If you haven't studied regular expressions before, check a good introductory UNIX book. Lots of UNIX programs use regular expressions: *grep*, *awk*, *sed*, the shell (for filename wildcards), Perl, and (probably) your text editor. Each of those programs accepts a different kind of regular expression.

majordomo accepts a limited set of regexps designed to match email addresses. The metacharacters it understands are all Perl-like:

- Word characters (`\s`, etc.) and `.` (dot)
- For disabling special meaning, `\`
- Repetition metacharacters `*`, `?`, and `+`
- Anchor characters `^` and `$`

Majordomo regexps start and end with a slash (/).

For example, a regexp that matches an email address with "ora" in it looks like this:

```
/ora/
```

We might try that regexp to prevent advertising the ORA (O'Reilly & Associates) in-house mailing lists to non-ORA users. It matches email addresses like *jer@ora.com*, *adam@ruby.ora.com*, *ora!jennifer*, and so on—because those all contain the string *ora*. But it would also match *flora@boz.baz.za*.

Because `advertise` and `noadvertise` are arrays of regexps, you can store a series of expressions that get progressively more specific. For example, in a config file:

```
advertise  << END
/ora.com/
/ora!/
END
```

That's almost good enough. But the first regexp would also match *oralcomps@mti.edu* because the dot (.) matches any single character. And the second regexp would match an email address like *snora!zzzs* because it contains *ora!*.

Here's a new version that handles those problems:

```
advertise  << END
/ora\.com$/
/^ora!/
END
```

Like other UNIX regular expressions, $ "anchors" a regexp to match only at the end of a string. The ^ (caret) forces the regexp to match only at the start of a string. And adding a backslash (\) before a special character like a dot disables the special meaning of that character—so \. only matches a literal dot instead of any single character.

There's another problem with those regexps: they don't match local addresses. When someone sends mail from the same host where Majordomo is running, their address may not have a hostname (like *@ora.com* or *ora!*) added to it. You can usually match local addresses with a regexp like /^\w+$/. That regular expression matches an address that contains only letters, digits, and underscores (_)—thanks to Perl's \w operator.

The noadvertise regexp array sets addresses that a list is not to be advertised to. It overrides the advertise array. Let's say you own mailing lists at a university. One list has announcements of graduate seminars. Undergraduates work on the computers *uga.mti.edu.au*, *ugb.mti.edu.au*, *ugc.mti.edu.au*, and so on. To restrict advertisement of the mailing lists to graduate students at your university, you'd set advertise to show the lists only to addresses at your university, and noadvertise to keep undergraduates from seeing the lists. That is:

```
advertise  << END
/^\w+$/
/@.*\.mti\.edu\.au$/
END
noadvertise << END
/@ug.\.mti\.edu\.au$/
END
```

If you have to be very careful who sees a list in the *lists* output, you should do more checking. For example, some email addresses contain *source routing* like this:

```
@mail.uunet.ca:dudley@mountie.ca
@mail.uunet.ca:mountie!dudley
```

With addresses like those, you can't assume that the first @ comes before the user's hostname. If a list is that private, you probably shouldn't depend on hiding the list from everyone who shouldn't find it. You should also approve every subscription by setting subscribe_policy to *closed*.

25.4 Making a Moderated List

A list owner may want to approve each message before it goes to the list. The list might distribute official company statements, or a discussion list might begin to carry lots of inappropriate messages and "noise" that subscribers don't want to see. One common reason is that people accidentally send subscription requests to the list itself instead of to the *majordomo* address. Having one person filter these out can potentially save thousands of people from wasting time on them. (Also see the `administrivia` and `restrict_post` config file variables.)

To make a list moderated, set the config file `moderated` variable to *yes*. Also be sure that `approve_passwd` is defined; its value will be the password that the list owner adds to a message to approve an article, as in:

```
Approved: PaSsWoRd
```

To find out how to approve a message, read on!

25.5 Approving Subscriptions and Moderating

You'll use the same tools and techniques for approving subscriptions and for moderating a list, so we'll cover both in this section. There are two approaches; the first applies if you are on a UNIX system that has the *approve* script, while the second applies if you don't have *approve*, or if you're on another kind of system. If you can, you'll want to get the *approve* script (from the Majordomo distribution), since it makes these tasks easier.

25.5.1 Approving Subscriptions and Moderating with approve

The *listname-approval* alias (and, in later versions of Majordomo, the *listname-moderator* alias) receive three types of mail messages from Majordomo:

- For subscriptions that need approval, you get a message with APPROVE in the subject line. For closed lists, all subscriptions need approval. For open lists, approval is necessary only for subscriptions where the subscriber specifies an email address other than their own.
- For messages to be posted to moderated lists, or for other messages that *resend* rejects (for example, messages that are too long or that fail administrivia checks), you'll get a message with BOUNCE in the subject line. The subject tells you the reason for the "bounce," and the body contains the whole bounced message. You decide whether this message is appropriate to be sent to all the subscribers.

NOTE

The messages that say "BOUNCE" are really requests for the moderator to approve the message. They are not bounces in the "returned message" sense. Real bounces go to a different alias: *owner-listname.**

- Reports of successful subscriptions and unsubscriptions. (These require no action.)

Majordomo includes *approve*, a Perl script for making these chores easier. For subscription requests, *approve* sends an email message back to *majordomo* indicating that the subscription should be accepted. For messages submitted to moderated lists, *approve* adds an "Approved:" header field and resends the message to the list. Section 25.5.2 and Section 25.5.3 show how to do these things manually in case the list owner is on a system where *approve* (or Perl) can't run. They also show the email messages that fly back and forth.

approve can be run either on the machine where Majordomo is running or on a remote machine where the list owner is managing the list by email. The *approve* script assumes that the Perl interpreter is in */usr/local/bin/perl*. If Perl is somewhere else, the first line of the *approve* script should be edited to the path for that system:

```
#! /usr/local/bin/perl
```

approve uses a file named *.majordomo* (the name starts with a dot) in the owner's home directory. The file has an entry for each of the owner's lists: the list name, list password and email address of its Majordomo server. There's a tab character (*not* space characters) between the three fields in each line. For example, this is the *.majordomo* file for the owner of the *donut-makers* and *mud-wrestlers* mailing lists:

```
donut-makers	!BooM! majordomo@bakers.org
mud-wrestlers	GoJoan majordomo@foo.bar.com
```

For security, it's a good idea to protect the file from other users. Use a command like **chmod 600 .majordomo**.

To approve a request, feed the original approval-request message from Majordomo to the *approve* script. Messages can be saved in separate files, one per message, and named on the command line:

```
% approve file1 file2 etc.
```

Messages can also be fed to the standard input of *approve*, which is usually more convenient because it can be done from within most UNIX mail readers. Here's how to do it in the Berkeley *mail* program (and the *mailx* look-alike):

```
        ...
> 32 majordomo@bakers.org Mon May 16 07:10 29/804 APPROVE donut-makers
        ...
```

* In future versions of Majordomo, the *listname-moderator* aliases will get these messages.

```
& | approve
Pipe to: "approve"
"approve" 29/804
```

The next example uses the MH mail handler, where the *show* command displays a message. Add -noheader (or -noh) to suppress the "(Message folder:number)" line. If you use *mhl* formatting or any other kind of *showproc*, you may want to add -noshowproc (or -nos) to cancel the formatting.

```
% scan 32
 32+ 05/16 majordomo@bakers.o APPROVE donut-makers<<-- postmaster@yu
% show -noh | approve
```

For other mailers, check your documentation or help screen.

25.5.2 Approving Subscriptions Without approve

It's possible that a list owner may be using a PC or another system where the *approve* script won't run. In that case, everything that *approve* does can be done manually. This section and the next may also be useful for those who want to know what *approve* does in more detail.

If someone sends a nonroutine subscription to *majordomo*, the server sends a message to the list owner. There are two kinds of nonroutine subscriptions. One is when the person sends a subscribe/unsubscribe command with a different email address than the one in their email header. The other is if the list is closed—that is, when the owner must approve all new subscriptions.

For example, the system postmaster at a bakery might want to set up a list exploder (see Section 23.10) for the *donut-makers* mailing list. She adds an exploder named *donut-makers-dist@yummybake.com* and sends this mail to the *majordomo* server:

```
From: postmaster@yummybake.com
To: majordomo@bakers.org

subscribe donut-makers donut-makers-dist@yummybake.com
```

When *majordomo* gets the message, it sees that the subscription address isn't the same as the sender's address. So it sends the following mail message to the list owner:

```
From owner-majordomo@bakers.org Sun May 15 08:56:09 1994
To: donut-makers-approval
From: majordomo@bakers.org
Subject: APPROVE donut-makers
Reply-To: majordomo@bakers.org

--
postmaster@yummybake.com requests that you approve the following:

  subscribe donut-makers donut-makers-dist@yummybake.com
```

```
If you approve, please send a message such as the following back to
majordomo@bakers.org (with the appropriate PASSWORD filled in, of course):

  approve PASSWORD subscribe donut-makers donut-makers-dist@yummybake.com

If you disapprove, do nothing. Thanks!

majordomo@bakers.org
```

If an owner doesn't want to approve the subscription request, we suggest that he do something, despite the fact that *majordomo* said to "do nothing." If a subscription is rejected, it's a good idea to reply and explain why. Otherwise, the subscriber will probably write to ask because she already got a message like this:

```
From owner-majordomo@bakers.org Sun May 15 08:56:09 1994
To: postmaster@yummybake.com
From: majordomo@bakers.org
Subject: Majordomo results
Reply-To: majordomo@bakers.org

--
>>>> subscribe donut-makers donut-makers-dist@yummybake.com
Your request to majordomo@bakers.org:

    subscribe donut-makers donut-makers-dist@yummybake.com

has been forwarded to the owner of the "donut-makers" list for approval.
This could be for any of several reasons:
  You might have asked to subscribe to a "closed" list, where all new
    additions must be approved by the list owner.
  You might have asked to subscribe or unsubscribe an address other than
    the one that appears in the headers of your mail message.
When the list owner approves your request, you will be notified.

If you have any questions about the policy of the list owner, please
contact "donut-makers-approval@bakers.org". Thanks!

majordomo@bakers.org
```

As the message to the list owner explained, the owner can approve the subscription; he does this by mailing an *approve* command to the *majordomo* server:

```
From: owner-name@owner-address
To: majordomo@bakers.org

approve !BooM! subscribe donut-makers donut-makers-dist@yummybake.com
```

(where "!BooM!" is the list password).

The process for approving a subscription to a closed list is similar. Figure 25-1 shows the four steps.

First, the subscriber mails a subscription request to *majordomo*. Second, Majordomo sends a request to the list owner. Third, if the owner approves the subscription, she

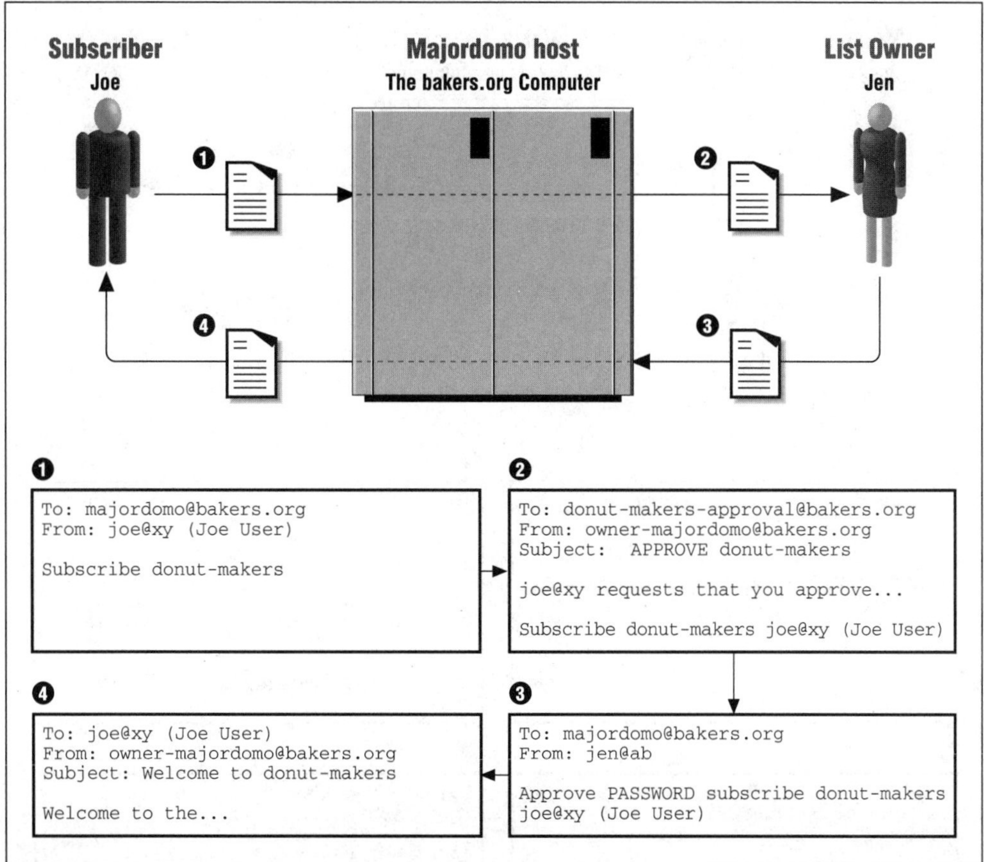
Subscriber
Joe
Majordomo host
The bakers.org Computer
List Owner
Jen
1
2
3
4
To: majordomo@bakers.org
From: joe@xy (Joe User)
Subscribe donut-makers
To: donut-makers-approval@bakers.org
From: owner-majordomo@bakers.org
Subject: APPROVE donut-makers
joe@xy requests that you approve...
Subscribe donut-makers joe@xy (Joe User)
To: joe@xy (Joe User)
From: owner-majordomo@bakers.org
Subject: Welcome to donut-makers
Welcome to the...
To: majordomo@bakers.org
From: jen@ab
Approve PASSWORD subscribe donut-makers
joe@xy (Joe User)

Figure 25-1. Approving subscriptions to closed Majordomo lists

mails an *approve* command to *majordomo*. Fourth, Majordomo adds the subscriber to the list and mails him a welcome message.

25.5.3 Moderating Lists Without approve

This section describes how to moderate messages manually if you can't use *approve*. It also shows the messages that are passed between the list owner and Majordomo.

Figure 25-2 shows the four steps in sending and delivering a message to a moderated list.

First, the user sends mail to the list address. Second, because the list is moderated, the message is "bounced" to the list owner. Third, if the list owner approves, she sends the message with an "Approved:" line to the list address. Fourth, Majordomo distributes the message to the list subscribers.

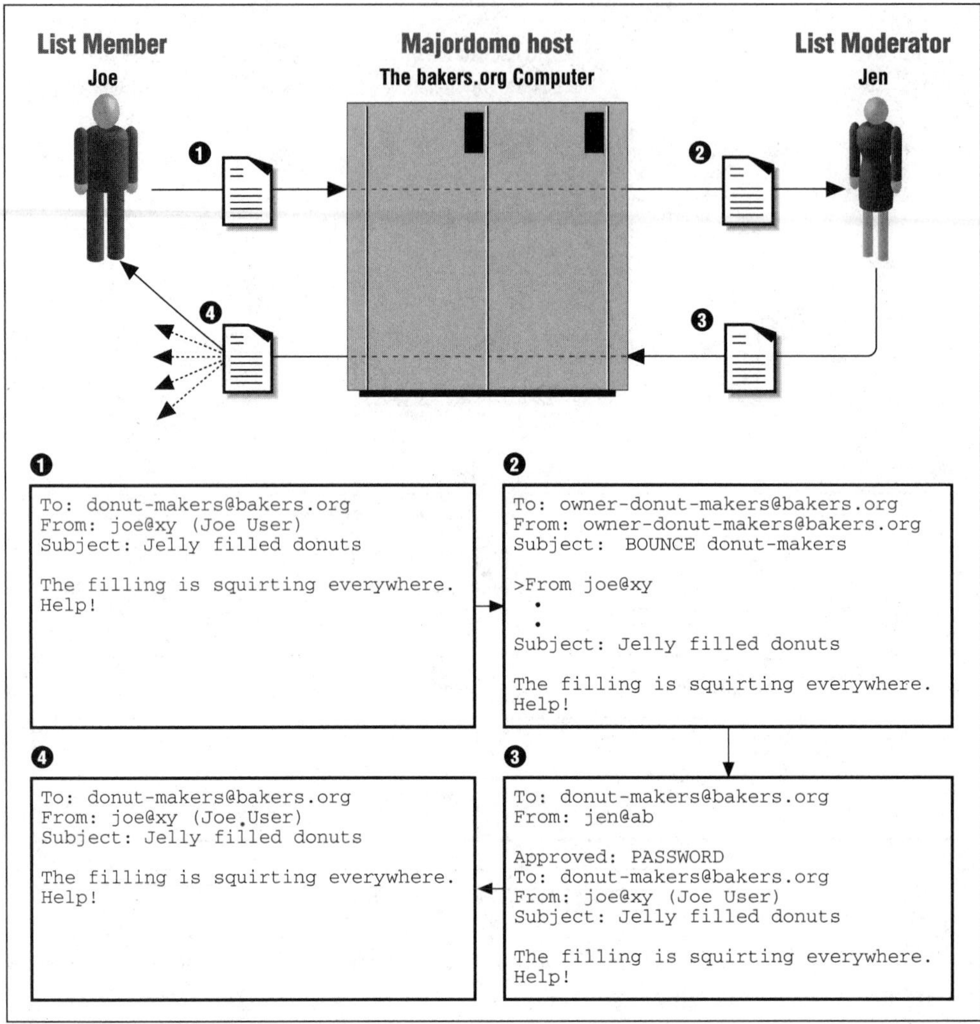

Figure 25-2. A moderated Majordomo list

Let's look at this process in more detail. Here's a message that the *donut-makers* list owner just received:

```
Date: Sun, 15 May 1994 22:17:34 PDT
To: owner-donut-makers@bakers.org
From: owner-donut-makers@bakers.org
Subject: BOUNCE donut-makers@bakers.org: Approval required
```

```
From elliek@hearthbake.com Sun May 15 22:17:29 1994
Date: Sun, 15 May 1994 22:17:29 PDT
From: elliek@hearthbake.com (Ellie Katella)
To: donut-makers@bakers.org
Subject: jelly donuts

What's your favorite recipe for jelly donuts? Thanks.
```

If the owner doesn't want to approve the message, it's courteous to mail a note to the original sender and explain why. (Maybe Ellie should read the *donut-makers* "Frequently Asked Questions" list.)

There are a few ways to tell Majordomo (actually, the *resend* script) to send an approved message. The easiest is the *approve* script. Otherwise, the owner should send mail to the list address (in this case, to *donut-makers@bakers.org*). The owner adds a line like this to the message header of the approved message—or on the first line of the body of the message:

```
Approved: password
```

There are two ways to do that:

- On a mail system like MH that lets people modify the mail message header, send the approved message to the list address as a new message. Add the "Approved:" header field at the top. Delete fields like "Date:"; leave "From:", "To:", and "Subject:". For example:

  ```
  Approved: PaSsWoRd
  From: elliek@hearthbake.com (Ellie Katella)
  To: donut-makers@bakers.org
  Subject: jelly donuts

  What's your favorite recipe for jelly donuts? Thanks.
  ```

  Or, create a file like the one above and give it to *sendmail* directly:

  ```
  % /usr/lib/sendmail -oi -t < msgfile
  ```

  If the "Approved:" line appears with the message header, these header fields are used when the message is sent to the list. Compare that to the next method:

- Here's another way to approve messages. It's handy for owners who can't modify their mail headers.

  Send a new mail message to the list address. Start the message body with the "Approved:" line. (The "Approved:" line *must* be the *first* line in the message body. Some mail programs and gateways add an extra blank line or other junk to the top of the message body; if yours does this, you'll have problems.) Next, read in a copy of the approved message. Delete any useless header fields and send it.

For example, in the Berkeley *mail* command:

```
  ...
 N 17 owner-donut-makers Sun May 15 22:17 23/733 BOUNCE donut-makers
  ...
& mail donut-makers@bakers.org
Subject:
Approved: PaSsWoRd
~f 17
Interpolating: 17
(continue)
~v    ...editor starts...edit the header of the forwarded message...
(continue)
~p    ...shows message you've edited...
-------
Message contains:
To: donut-makers@bakers.org
Approved: PaSsWoRd
Date: Sun, 15 May 1994 22:17:29 PDT
From: elliek@hearthbake.com (Ellie Katella)
To: donut-makers@bakers.org
Subject: jelly donuts

What's your favorite recipe for jelly donuts? Thanks.
(continue)
^D    ...sends message...
&
```

In this second method, the message sent to the list contains the header fields below the "Approved:" line. Lines above the "Approved:" aren't used.

Either way, Ellie's message goes to the list with no trace of the password:

```
From owner-donut-makers@bakers.org Sun May 15 23:40:22 1994
Date: Sun, 15 May 1994 22:17:29 PDT
From: elliek@hearthbake.com (Ellie Katella)
To: donut-makers@bakers.org
Subject: jelly donuts
Sender: owner-donut-makers@bakers.org
Precedence: bulk

What's your favorite recipe for jelly donuts? Thanks.
```

25.6 Returned Mail and the Bounces List

The person who receives mail to the *owner-listname* alias gets very familiar with messages like these:

```
Return-Path: <MAILER-DAEMON@mukluk.ice.ca>
Date: Sun, 10 Oct 93 13:24:11 EDT
From: MAILER-DAEMON@mukluk.ice.ca (Mail Delivery Subsystem)
Subject: Returned mail: Cannot send message for 3 days
Message-Id: <9310101724.AA20948@mukluk.ice.ca>
```

```
To: listown@online.ora.com

  ----- Transcript of session follows -----
421 tuna.ice.ca: Host tuna.ice.ca is down

  ----- Unsent message follows -----
Received: from online.ora.com by mukluk.ice.ca (4.1/4.7)
    id <AA13653> for shh@tuna.ice.ca; Thu, 7 Oct 93 13:05:22 EDT
Received: by online.ora.com (5.65c/Spike-2.1)
    id AA13466; Thu, 7 Oct 1993 10:13:03 -0400
Date: Thu, 7 Oct 1993 10:13:03 -0400
  ...
```

If your lists will be busy, you'll probably want to set up a special list named *bounces*. It's a list for subscribers of any of your lists whose mail is returned as undeliverable. The address of the subscriber is removed from the list they belong to and added to the *bounces* list. The system (actually *cron*) runs the *bounce-remind* script every night to send mail to all the people with bad addresses. The administrator of your Majordomo host needs to do some special setup to eliminate returned mail from the *bounces* list; there are instructions in Section 24.2.

Each night (or less often, if the adminstrator sets a different interval), a message like the one below is sent to every subscriber:

```
To: Bounces@bakers.org
From: nobody@bakers.org
Subject: Bouncing email from mailing lists at bakers.org
Reply-To: majordomo@bakers.org

Your address has been moved to Bounces@bakers.org
from some other mailing list at bakers.org
because email to you was bouncing.

Here are the addresses currently on Bounces@bakers.org (...omitted)
so that you can see which of your addresses is among them.
The comment for each address shows the date it was moved,
and the first list it was removed from. If you were on
multiple lists here, you may have been removed from them
as well, but only the first list you were removed from
will show up in the comment below.

If the problem has been fixed, you can get off of
Bounces and back on to the other list by sending the
following to majordomo@bakers.org:

  subscribe your_list
  unsubscribe bounces

To subscribe or unsubscribe an address other than where you're
sending the command from, append the other address to the end
of the "subscribe" or "unsubscribe" command (for example,
"subscribe your_list foo@bar.com").
```

```
You'll need to access the mailing list archives if you want to catch
up on whatever you missed while you were off the main list.

If you don't want to keep getting these reminders every day, but
don't want to resubscribe to the list, send just the "unsubscribe"
command shown above.

If you need to contact a human being regarding this, send a message
to owner-majordomo@bakers.org.
```

If the mail gets through to a subscriber, the subscriber will find out what has happened and how to fix it. If the problem isn't fixed after a while (usually, a month or so), the list owner can review the *bounces* subscriber list and remove the hopeless cases.

Bounced messages come in so many different formats that it's hard to completely automate subscriptions to the *bounces* list. (In fact, in some cases, the addressee of the bounced mail won't even be shown in the message!) If the list owner's system can run a Perl script, the *bounce* script makes the job easy; it works differently than *approve*. The script doesn't read a message from a file or standard input. Instead, it reads its command line arguments:

```
% bounce listname user@xyz.com
```

This command unsubscribes the address *user@xyz.com* from the *listname* list and adds it to the *bounces* list. An owner who can't run the *bounce* script can send mail to Majordomo with two commands like these:

```
approve passwdA unsubscribe listname user@xyz.com
approve passwdB subscribe bounces user@xyz.com (940805 listname)
```

The first command unsubscribes the user from the current list. The second one subscribes the user to the *bounces* list, with a comment that shows the date in the format YYMMDD (here, 940805—that's August 5, 1994) and the name of the list they were on.

Make yourself a note to check the *bounces* subscribers once a month or so. (Send *who bounces*. You could set up a *cron* job to do it automatically.) Unsubscribe anyone who's been on the list for more than a month.

In this Chapter:

- *Ftpmail for Users*
- *Installing Ftpmail*
- *Testing Your Installation*
- *Managing Ftpmail*
- *The Ftpmail Developer's Mailing List*

26

Ftpmail

An Ftpmail server is an email file server that gets the files by FTP from the Internet. It reads email messages that contain FTP commands, connects to an FTP site, runs the commands, and mails the results to the person who asked for them. Ftpmail is the only way that people who have email-only Internet access can get the wealth of software and data that's kept in FTP archives.

To run an Ftpmail server, your computer must be connected to the Internet. (In other words, email access isn't enough.)

There's a well-known public Ftpmail server at *ftpmail@decwrl.dec.com.** Why would you want to set up one of your own? One reason is that, because *decwrl*'s server is well-known, it's busy; there can be long waits until users get their files. By setting up Ftpmail, you can provide your customers quicker access to your FTP archive. It's easy to set up, and can be limited to accessing your own archive, so you won't get tremendous traffic like *decwrl* does. Or you might want an Ftpmail server for people at your company who want to have FTP access to the whole Internet—but their computers aren't on the Internet for security or other reasons.

Ftpmail is a set of Perl scripts written by Lee McLoughlin, *lmjm@doc.ic.ac.uk*, with contributions from a lot of other people. Although you don't need to know Perl to install or run Ftpmail, the computer where you run Ftpmail will need the Perl interpreter installed. (For more information about Perl, see the Nutshell Handbooks *Learning Perl* by Randal Schwartz and *Programming Perl* by Larry Wall and Randal Schwartz.) This chapter covers Ftpmail version 1.23.

This chapter has two parts. The first part explains what Ftpmail does from a user's perspective (how to use it). The rest of the chapter explains how to install and run the Ftpmail server.

* The user interface to *decwrl*'s server is fairly similar to the server covered in this book, but it's a different program.

26.1 Ftpmail for Users

If you haven't used a UNIX-like FTP command before, please read an introduction such as Chapter 6, *Moving Files: FTP* in *The Whole Internet User's Guide & Catalog*. This section is an introduction to Ftpmail, not FTP.

To use the Ftpmail server, send mail to *ftpmail@hostname*, where *hostname* is the name of the host running the Ftpmail server. Ftpmail commands must be the first text in the message body. (You can indent lines or leave empty lines if you want to; Ftpmail ignores leading whitespace.) There can't be other text at the start of the message (no "Dear Ftpmail"!). If your mailer adds a signature at the end of the message and you can't prevent that, the Ftpmail command *quit* can be used to make Ftpmail ignore the signature.

Ftpmail accepts two sets of commands. One set controls what Ftpmail does. The other set controls the FTP session that Ftpmail handles for you.

First we'll show a sample session: this will demonstrate the email messages you might send and receive when first using Ftpmail. The rest of the sections describe all the Ftpmail commands.

26.1.1 A Sample Session

When using an Ftpmail server for the first time, it's a good idea to get the help message, which describes how to use the particular Ftpmail server and any defaults or limits it might have. We'll send it to the Ftpmail server we set up later in this chapter, which happens to be on our local system:

```
% Mail ftpmail@ora.com
Subject:
help
^D
%
```

Here's part of the help message that we receive in return:

```
Date: Wed, 7 Sep 1994 00:41:42 PDT
From: ftpmail (ftpmail server)
To: jerry
Subject: <FTP EMAIL> response

<FTP EMAIL> response
ftpmail@ora.com - ftp's files and sends them back via electronic mail.

If you have problems please email ftp-manager@ora.com
and quote the following line:
$Revision: 1.16 $

            ...omitted...
open [site [user [pass]]]    Site to ftp to. Defaults are
```

```
                ftp.ora.com anonymous reply-to-address.
```

...omitted...

```
Example scripts are:

open
dir
quit
    Connect to ftp.ora.com and send back the contents of the top level
    directory
```

...omitted...

Receiving this indicates that the Ftpmail server is working and that the server's default FTP archive is *ftp.ora.com.* Let's get an index for that archive:

```
% Mail ftpmail@ora.com
Subject:
open
cd pub
get Index
^D
%
```

Since our open command does not specify an FTP archive (like *ftp.uu.net*), Ftpmail connects to *ftp.ora.com.* You'll get at least three messages back. The first one shows the job submitted:

```
Date: Wed, 7 Sep 1994 00:44:02 PDT
From: ftpmail (ftpmail server)
To: jerry
Subject: <FTP EMAIL> response

<FTP EMAIL> response
Ftpmail has received the following job from you:
   reply-to jerry
   open ftp.ora.com anonymous ftpmail/jerry@ora.com
   cd pub
   get Index

Ftpmail has queued your job as: 097091.474
Your priority is 0 (0 = highest, 9 = lowest)
Requests to ftp.ora.com will be done before other jobs.
There are no jobs ahead of this one in the queue.

To remove send a message to ftpmail@ora.com containing just:
delete 097091.474

Your original input was>>
Date: Wed, 7 Sep 1994 00:43:52 PDT
From: jerry
To: ftpmail
Cc: jerry

open
```

```
cd pub
get Index
<<End of your input
```

The next message has the file we asked Ftpmail to get:

```
Date: Wed, 7 Sep 1994 00:44:39 PDT
From: ftpmail (ftpmail server)
To: jerry
Subject: ftp.ora.com:/pub/Index (get Index)

These files are for publications from:

    O'Reilly & Associates, Inc.
    103 Morris Street, Suite A
    Sebastopol, CA 95472 USA
    email: nuts@ora.com or uunet!ora.com!nuts
    phone: (800)998-9938 toll-free in US and Canada
         +1 707 829-0515 everywhere else
    fax: +1 707 829-0104

The subdirectories and files in them are listed below.
The directory names end with a slash (/):

Index        This file
book.catalog   Listing and descriptions of books from
         O'Reilly & Associates
         ...
```

Finally, you'll get a mail message showing the FTP transaction:

```
Date: Wed, 7 Sep 1994 00:44:41 PDT
From: ftpmail (ftpmail server)
To: jerry
Subject: ftpmail job completed

<FTP EMAIL> response

Your job was (lines beginning DONE show completed transfers):
   reply-to jerry
   open ftp.ora.com anonymous ftpmail/jerry@ora.com
   cd pub
 DONE get Index

The ftp log contains:
Connecting to ftp.ora.com
 220 ruby FTP server (Version wu-2.4(1) Fri Apr 15 14:14:30 EDT 1994) ready.
 ---> USER anonymous
 331 Guest login ok, send your complete e-mail address as password.
 ---> PASS <somestring>
 230 Guest login ok, access restrictions apply.
 ---> PWD
 257 "/" is current directory.
 ---> TYPE I
```

```
200 Type set to I.
---> CWD pub
250 CWD command successful.
---> PWD
257 "/pub" is current directory.
---> PORT 198,112,209,17,4,4
200 PORT command successful.
---> RETR Index
150 Opening BINARY mode data connection for Index (1426 bytes).
#
Got 1426 bytes (1426 bytes/sec)
226 Transfer complete.
---> QUIT
221 Goodbye.
```

Check the FTP transaction log if you didn't get the file you want. Maybe you mis-typed a pathname or you were denied access to the archive.

We knew that the *Index* file was plain text, but we didn't ask Ftpmail to use *mode ascii*. That usually isn't needed with plain UNIX text files. You need *mode binary* for binary or compressed files.

The next few sections describe the Ftpmail commands in more detail. Items in brackets (`[]`) are optional. When you use an optional item, don't include the brackets.

26.1.2 Using a Different Address

When this command is used, it must be first in the message.

`reply-to` *`email-address`*

Tells Ftpmail that the results should not be mailed to the "Reply-to:" or "From:" address in the message header; this command sets another address. Use this if your email program sets an incorrect address or if you want Ftpmail to send the results to someone else.

26.1.3 Overall Session Commands

These commands choose the operation Ftpmail will perform: get help, request an FTP session, or cancel a previous Ftpmail request.

`help`

Sends a help message with a list of commands, default settings, limits, and examples

`delete` *`jobid`*

When Ftpmail receives a job request, it mails a reply with a job ID number and the number of previous jobs in the queue. To cancel a queued Ftpmail job, you mail a `delete` command to Ftpmail with the job ID number that Ftpmail sent you.

`open [`*`site`*` [`*`user`*` [`*`password`*`]]]`

To prepare to get files by FTP, use the `open` command.

Each Ftpmail server has a default FTP site; if the *site* isn't given, Ftpmail uses its default. The default user is usually *anonymous* (for anonymous FTP). The default password is typically the sender's complete email address from the *reply-to* command or the mail message header. To find a server's defaults (set in its *config.pl* file), send it a *help* command.

It might not be wise to access anything but an anonymous FTP site with Ftpmail. The password is mailed in clear text. Anyone who sees the email message can see the password. The password may be stored on backup tapes of email on any site along the way.

There's a fairly safe way to make private files available by anonymous FTP. The files can be "hidden" in the anonymous FTP area behind a system of unreadable directories and subdirectories with unusual names. Only people who have the exact pathname of the hidden subdirectory can get the files. See Section 6.3.3.

26.1.4 File Transfer Commands

If a message starts with an *open* command, it can include one or more of the commands listed in the following sections. Each Ftpmail server limits the number of commands that it accepts in one message. To find the limit, send a *help* command.

26.1.4.1 Moving through the archive

These commands change the FTP directory and send listings of what's in a directory.

`cd` *`pathname`* Change directory.

`ls` [*`pathname`*] Get a short listing of the files (and directories) in the current directory or *pathname.*

`dir` [*`pathname`*]

Get a long listing of the files (and directories) in the current directory or *pathname.* This may tell you the sizes of the files. (On some sites, there is no difference between *ls* and *dir.*)

26.1.4.2 Compressing files

If the person who requests a file from Ftpmail has the *uncompress* or *gunzip* utilities, the following Ftpmail commands might be useful. They can compress the file into a shorter binary file. But Ftpmail also has to use *uuencode, btoa,* or MIME format to encode the binary file into ASCII that can be transferred by email; these formats make the mail message bigger. In general, though—and especially for longer files—compression and ASCII encoding together make the mail message shorter. Also, encoding with *btoa* or MIME can make file transmission more reliable through different networks and gateways. MIME, especially, was designed to avoid transmission problems that *uuencode* can have in some cases.

`compress` Use *compress* on files and directory listings before mailing them. Takes effect until the end of the mail message or until a *gzip* or *no compress* command.

`gzip` Use *gzip* on files and directory listings before mailing them. Takes effect until the end of the mail message or until a *compress* or *no gzip* command.

`no compress` Turn off compression.

`no gzip` Turn off *gzip*ping.

26.1.4.3 Binary encoding

Binary files (with nonprintable characters) can't be mailed safely unless they're encoded. Ftpmail supports three different kinds of encoding. The default, *uuencode* format, requires the `uudecode(1)` utility to process the message received from Ftpmail. The *btoa* encoding may work better, but the recipient needs the `atob(1)` utility, which isn't as widely installed as *uudecode.* Finally, *mime* encoding may be the best of all, but the user needs the MIME/Metamail utilities to use it. (For example, *mmencode –u* decodes binary MIME files sent by Ftpmail.)

`uuencode` *uuencode* binary files.

`btoa` Use *btoa* on binary files.

`mime` Text is sent as a MIME-format message "text/plain charset=US-ASCII". Nontext is sent as "application/octet-stream". If the file is split into parts, it is sent as a MIME "message/partial".

`force uuencode`
Force all files and directory listings to be *uuencode*d.

`force btoa` Force all files and directory listings to be processed with *btoa.*

`force mime` Force all files and directory listings to be sent as type "application/octet-stream".

`no uuencode` Turn off *uuencode*ing.

`no btoa` Turn off *btoa* processing.

`no mime` Don't send MIME messages.

26.1.4.4 Splitting messages

Many system mailers limit the maximum size of each mail message. The Ftpmail *size* command makes Ftpmail split big files and send each piece in a separate mail message. Any file over 15 megabytes (set by the `$max_processing_size` variable) isn't sent; the job aborts. Otherwise, if the file is more than `$max_file_size`, it is split and each piece mailed separately.

`size num` Set maximum message size to `numK` (kilobytes, thousands of bytes) or `numM` (megabytes, millions of bytes). For example, use `size 64K` to make sure no message is more than 64 kilobytes long.

26.1.4.5 File transfer modes

These modes should be set as if the recipient were using the *ftp* command on a UNIX host. (That's because *Ftpmail* runs on a UNIX host. Give the commands that would make the file appear correct if you were running the UNIX *ftp* program on a UNIX host.) The default is *mode binary*.

For example, to transfer a program or a *tar* file from a UNIX computer to another UNIX computer, *mode binary* is the right choice. But for transferring a plain text file, especially from a non-UNIX FTP server, *mode ascii* is probably right. It enables translation between the non-UNIX server's ASCII format and the format used on the Ftpmail server.

`mode binary` Transfer characters with no translation. Ftpmail also processes files through *uuencode*, *btoa*, or *mmencode* (MIME), as described in Section 26.1.4.2. The default is *uuencode*.

`mode ascii` Transfer files as ASCII text.

26.1.4.6 Transferring files and quitting

After you set the modes with the commands listed above, use this command to get the files. Note that Ftpmail can't "put" files from a mail message to the remote FTP server.

`get pathname` Get a file and email it.

`quit` If a mail message has other text (like a "signature") after the Ftpmail commands, the *quit* command makes Ftpmail ignore the following lines.

26.2 Installing Ftpmail

Here's an overview of what you need to install Ftpmail:

- The Ftpmail archive file. As of this printing, you can get it by anonymous FTP from sites in three countries:
  - In the U.K., from *src.doc.ic.ac.uk* in the directory */packages/ftpmail*
  - In France, from *grasp1.univ-lyon1.fr* in the directory */pub/unix/mail/tools/ftpmail*
  - In the U.S., from *ftp.sterling.com* in the directory */mail/ftpmail*

  On all these sites, the file is stored in GNU *gzip* format. But if you don't have *gunzip*, don't worry: all these sites' FTP servers can also convert the file to *compress*ed format, too. Read the online instructions.

An older version of Ftpmail was posted to the Usenet newsgroup *comp.sources.misc*, volume 37.

- *mmencode*, *perl*, *btoa*, *uuencode*, *compress*, and *gzip*. The *mmencode* utility is part of the Metamail package; the latest version is on *thumper.bellcore.com* in the directory */pub/nsb* in a file named something like *mmN.N.tar.Z*. (As of this writing, the filename is *mm2.7.tar.Z*.) You can get the other utilities at many anonymous FTP sites; just ask Archie. One place that you can get them from is *ftp.uu.net*; we found the file */languages/perl/perl.tar.gz*, the directory */systems/unix/bsd-sources/usr.bin/uudecode*, the directory */usenet/comp.sources.unix/volume18/btoa*, the file */compress.tar* and the file */gzip.tar*.

  Note that old versions of *btoa* use a different encoding than version 4.0 and above. The archive listed above has *btoa* version 5.2.

Here are the installation steps:*

1. Create an account named *ftpmail*. Its home directory will hold the scripts and all of the queued files. Put it on a filesystem with plenty of free space.
2. If you don't have Perl and all of the other packages listed above, install them.
3. Set up the *ftpmail* account and home directory. Now you can **su ftpmail**; most of the rest of the installation doesn't need to be done as the superuser.
4. Make a temporary directory (or, if you want to keep the sources, make a permanent directory in your source tree). Get the Ftpmail *tar* file and extract it into this directory:

   ```
   % gzcat ftpmail-1.23.tar.gz | tar xvf -
   ```

   (If your command for unzipping *gzip*ped files is called *zcat*, use it instead. On System V systems, use **tar xovf** instead.)
5. Read the *README* file. If your system uses Solaris version 2.x, read the note about *socket.ph*: you *may* need to change your Perl setup.
6. Edit the *config.pl* file for your site. This file is read by the Perl interpreter; it needs to be valid Perl syntax. If you don't know Perl, that shouldn't be a problem; just follow the examples and replace the values you want to change. You'll definitely want to change the `$hostname` and `$managers_email` variables.

* Although we show a step-by-step procedure here, we can't promise that the following steps are exactly what you need for your computer. Your system might be different. You may have a different version of Ftpmail than the one we installed. Please use these steps as a *guide* only.

7. Edit the *auth* file to set the addresses that will be allowed to connect to the Ftpmail server. For example, to allow only educational institutions from the U.S.A. and your friend *joe* at *foo.com*, put these two lines in the file:

   ```
   .*@.*.edu
   joe@foo.com
   ```

   You also can add three other types of lines:

   - A line with the word `localhost` lets local users (on the host that runs the Ftpmail server) use Ftpmail too.
   - A line without the character `@` is treated as a literal hostname, not a regular expression. To allow access to all users on the host *foo.com*, add the single line `foo.com` to the *auth* file.
   - A line that starts with the word `not` will block access from the user or host listed on that line. So, for example, to allow access from all hosts (the regular expression `.`) but not from *badguy@a.b.fi*, use these two lines:

     ```
     .
     not badguy@a.b.fi
     ```

8. The Ftpmail scripts all assume that Perl is in */usr/bin/perl*. If that's not true, edit the first line of *inst.pl*, *req.pl*, *killfm.pl*, *q.pl*, and *dq.pl* to have the right paths.
9. The default *config.pl* file has this line:

   ```
   $gzip = '/usr/local/bin/gzip -9';
   ```

   The *gzip –9* option makes the file as small as possible—but it can be slow, especially on big files and busy computers. To speed things up (at the expense of slightly larger files), remove the option—or, to make *gzip* even faster, use the *–0* (zero) option.
10. When you run *inst.pl*, Perl variables in the *help_english* file are interpreted; then the file is copied into a new *help* subdirectory. That file contains the help message that's sent in response to a *help* command or an error. There are two reasons you may want to edit *help_english* before you install Ftpmail:

    - It shows examples for files that probably aren't on your default system. It also shows examples of opening FTP sessions to other hosts, but you may restrict Ftpmail to only your local site; this can confuse users. Editing the help message can make it more "real-life" for your particular installation.
    - On our system, the columns in the help file look a little jagged and some lines are a bit too long. Also, the help file assumes that the user's display has tabstops set every eight columns; that may not be true. You can run the file through the UNIX *expand* or *pr –t –e* utility to change the tab characters to spaces, then use a text editor to neaten the columns.

11. Run the *inst.pl* script. It makes the directories you named in the *config.pl* file and copies other files into the *ftpmail* home directory.

12. Next, set up a way for the system MTA to run *q.pl* for each incoming email message.

    If your site uses *sendmail*, copy the file *sendmail_forward* (from the Ftpmail distribution) into a *.forward* file in the *ftpmail* home directory. (Or you can make an alias in the *sendmail aliases* file.) You'll need to edit the *.forward* file to have the absolute pathname of your *q.pl* file. When *sendmail* delivers mail for *ftpmail*, it starts the *q.pl* script:

    ```
    "|/usr/local/ftpmail/q.pl || exit 75"
    ```

    The `|| exit 75` means that if the system has trouble running *q.pl* (if the filesystem is down, for example), the incoming message will be deferred instead of being returned to the sender.

    If your site uses MMDF, copy the *mmdf_mailforward* file (from Ftpmail) into the *.mailforward* file. Edit it to set the pathname of your *q.pl* file:

    ```
    default * pipe A "/usr/local/ftpmail/q.pl"
    ```

    Otherwise, use a setup that will start *ftpmail* and feed each incoming mail message to its standard input.

13. Arrange for *dq.pl* to be run periodically.

    The Ftpmail developer runs *dq.pl* every half hour from his *crontab* file—in case the daemon dies for some reason. This also starts an Ftpmail daemon within half an hour of the time the computer is rebooted. If *dq* is already running, the new one started by the *cron* job should quit right away (and add a message to the log like "queue already locked by *pid*").

    We use the following entry in the *ftpmail crontab* file:

    ```
    15,45 * * * * exec ./dq.pl >> dq.pl.log 2>&1
    ```

    Because *cron* starts personal *crontab* jobs from an account's home directory, the *crontab* entry doesn't need absolute pathnames. (Because the current directory isn't in the shell's search path, we use the pathname `./dq.pl` to start the daemon.) The *exec* command is optional; it replaces the shell started by *cron* with the daemon's Perl process (the shell doesn't do much except wait for the Perl daemon to die). The Bourne shell operators in the rest of the command line (`>> dq.pl.log 2>&1`) catch any output from the daemon and write it into a log file named *dq.pl.log*.

    Without the log-file setup shown above, you won't see any errors output by *dq.pl* until the daemon exits and *cron* sends mail to the user *ftpmail*. Worse, that error mail can cause other problems: mail sent to *ftpmail* can be reprocessed by Ftpmail as a user request. This will fail and send mail to *root*. Unless you want it to work that way, use a log file!

If your system doesn't have a *crontab* file for each account, run *dq.pl* from the system *crontab* file. Run it as the user *ftpmail*. If you can't name the user in the system *crontab*, one of the following two entries should do the job. Because */bin/su* starts a login shell, you need to use the right redirection syntax for the *ftpmail* account login shell. Use the first one if the login shell of the *ftpmail* account is a Bourne-like shell. The second entry works for shells like the C shell. Type all of the entry you choose on one line:

```
15,45 * * * * exec /bin/su ftpmail -c "exec /usr/local/ftpmail/dq.pl
   >> /usr/local/ftpmail/dq.pl.log 2>&1"   sh or ksh

15,45 * * * * exec /bin/su ftpmail -c "exec /usr/local/ftpmail/dq.pl
   >>& /usr/local/ftpmail/dq.pl.log"      csh
```

As before, each exec saves an extra shell; it's optional.

26.3 Testing Your Installation

Run a few basic tests to be sure that Ftpmail can receive and send mail. Then, try it as a user. Test the queueing by sending several large jobs quickly in separate mail messages.

A good way to test Ftpmail is with the *sendmail –v* (verbose) switch; it shows you what's happening. In case something is set up incorrectly, it's a good idea to have a superuser shell ready to do some fast cleanup.

Start by getting the help message:

```
% /usr/lib/sendmail -v ftpmail
/usr/local/ftpmail/.forward: line 1: ftpmail...
  forwarding to "|/usr/local/ftpmail/q.pl || exit 75"
help
^D
"|/usr/local/ftpmail/q.pl || exit 75"... Connecting to via prog...
"|/usr/local/ftpmail/q.pl || exit 75"... Sent
%
```

You should receive the help message shown in Section 26.1.1. Be sure the variable parts of the help message (like your hostname) have been set okay.

We had a problem with our site's Perl installation. The error was in the *dq.pl.log* file:

```
Can't locate sys/socket.ph in @INC (did you run h2ph?) at ftp.pl line 52.
```

The *socket.ph* library file had been clobbered. Replacing it fixed the problem.

Assuming you get the help message, send a simple request to your Ftpmail server:

```
% Mail ftpmail
Subject:
open
cd pub
get Index
^D
%
```

We configured our Ftpmail (in *config.pl*) to connect to *ftp.ora.com* by default. You'll receive the three messages that were shown in Section 26.1.1. The first one shows the job submitted. Here's the interesting part:

```
Ftpmail has received the following job from you:
   reply-to jerry
   open ftp.ora.com anonymous ftpmail/jerry@ora.com
   cd pub
   get Index
```

Notice that Ftpmail has fleshed out the *open* command by inserting its default site, anonymous, and your email address as the password.

The next message has the file we asked Ftpmail to get. Because the file was a plain text file, it was sent as-is, with no encoding. We won't show it again here.

Finally, you'll get a mail message to show the FTP transaction:

```
Date: Wed, 7 Sep 1994 00:44:41 PDT
From: ftpmail (ftpmail server)
To: jerry
Subject: ftpmail job completed

  ...
The ftp log contains:
  ...
 ---> RETR Index
 150 Opening BINARY mode data connection for Index (2037 bytes).
 #
 Got 2037 bytes (2037 bytes/sec)
 226 Transfer complete.
  ...
```

The FTP transaction looks correct.

Next, we send a request to check the MIME encoding for binary files:

```
% Mail ftpmail
Subject:
open
cd pub/power_tools
mime
get ls-lR.Z
^D
```

We get the MIME-encoded reply:

```
Date: Wed, 7 Sep 1994 01:29:59 PDT
From: ftpmail (ftpmail server)
To: jerry
Subject: ftp.ora.com:/pub/power_tools/ls-lR.Z mmencoded (get ls-lR.Z)
Mime-Version: 1.0
Content-Type: application/octet-stream;
 name="ls-lR.Z"
Content-Transfer-Encoding: base64
```


```
H52QdN7QCcMGhAwFLeTcSbhQTosWIEDEAKGmjBw5eSJq3BgRBogpZeBEtGFQho4YHtnMacFG
igstCsgoxKNwjkM8EWVQtIiR48YaMXQGqXMGxAyPMW7omDGxjcA0ZmLOrHkz586LGX1GBCoU
jhyjSGks1VnHTRo8ChQ4pQNVh4KAAwvSsJEjB0KFDBM+jDiRTBg7acj4xBF0xowaIIyUEcOX
b90ZIPC0odMihgsYLgbKeXm3YcO9EkH4BSx4YwygMXIATbzYIA3HOSBLpmzZsmbOefE6hBh6
dGCOMmDAwFHjMIihRWWQjDFDx9zIkyu7kJE5zGaYuT/z7vv3N0cap2EkPU50q0QYOmp4nC1d
hpgyA6tf75wbNHfSWlEaxkE++fLmz7EnRRFBENFEEWmVdZZbcBEEAl306WbfVT35dAMMNYB3
nFdgSSSWDPzVAQcdLrRhXWzycQY=
```


We also get the usual confirmation messages, which we won't print here.

If you've added restrictions (in the *config.pl* file)—for instance, you've set the `$ftp_permitted` variable—you may want to test these to be sure they're working the way you want them to.

26.4 Managing Ftpmail

The Ftpmail system is simple:

- A Perl script called *q.pl* is run by your system MTA (mail transport agent) for each new message that comes in. It checks the message and (unless it's rejected) adds it to the Ftpmail queue.
- Another Perl script, *dq.pl*, runs as a daemon. It checks the Ftpmail queue directory and processes any jobs there. (If you configured *config.pl* to do so, there may be several *dq* daemons. We don't recommend that unless your server gets a lot of use and your host has plenty of network capacity.)
- The *auth* file controls who is allowed to use this Ftpmail server. The file has one or more lines of Perl regular expressions that are compared to the "reply-to" mail address in the message (or the *reply-to* command, if any, in the message body). If the address doesn't match any of the expressions in the file, the request is rejected. UNIX regular expressions for the `ed`(1) editor work fine here, but you can also use Perl's extended regular expressions.
- If you make a file named *motd*, the text in it is included at the start of each email message that Ftpmail sends. You can use this for standard disclaimers, announcements, and so on.

- The log file keeps track of what Ftpmail does. The `$log` variable in *config.pl* sets the log name. It's a good idea to review the file every day (for problems like ignored mail) and truncate it periodically.
- The *dq_stats* file contains information used by *dq.pl*. You don't need to maintain it; *dq.pl* does that.

The following sections describe the routine checks you should do to maintain Ftpmail, and how to restrict which FTP sites Ftpmail can access and which people can use your Ftpmail server.

26.4.1 Routine Checks

Here are some routine checks we do to make sure Ftpmail is operating properly:

- Use *ps* to check for processes owned by the *ftpmail* user. Be sure there's just one daemon running (and that the daemon hasn't died).
- Check the size of the queue directory with *du* and the room on the filesystem with *df*.
- Watch the size of the mail queue, especially during the day when your network and server are probably busiest. If the queue fills up and doesn't empty until the evening, think about adding time restrictions.
- If you think there are problems, read your MTA's log file, looking at the mail sent to and from Ftpmail. (Use a pager like *more* or *less* and search for the string `ftpmail`.) Be sure that the incoming messages are marked "sent" and that the usual confirmation and replies are mailed to the user later.

  Failed mail may be left in a *dead.letter* file in the *ftpmail* home directory. Watch for mail returned to the sender instead of being delivered to *q.pl*.

26.4.2 Restricting Ftpmail

Here are some ideas for handling Ftpmail on systems that are busy or have busy networks.

The Ftpmail server usually sends out much bigger messages than it receives. If a lot of your users are offsite over a slow network, using Ftpmail to transfer files from a local FTP area, the slow network may not be able to transfer requests out as quickly as they come in. In that case, your mail queue will tend to fill up.

If the amount of queued mail grows during the day, you may be able to set the `$time_restrictions` variable. But note that although this variable is in the *config.pl* file, it doesn't seem to be supported in Ftpmail version 1.23.

If your system gets busy at the same time the network does, you can try making the *dq.pl* daemon "nice." That gives it less CPU time and makes it empty the queue more slowly (the queue still fills as quickly because that's handled by *q.pl*). For instance, here's a *crontab* entry to start the *dq.pl* daemon at a higher "nice level" and give it less CPU time:

```
15,45 * * * * /bin/nice -5 ./dq.pl >> dq.pl.log 2>&1
```

The -5 sets the nice level; see the nice(1) manual page. Your system's *cron* may already "nice" jobs that it runs, so be careful: the extra *nice -5* can make the *dq.pl* daemon so nice that it never does anything while the system is busy.

The most severe restriction is to shut down the daemon during your system's busy hours. To do that, create the file named in the $ftpmail_scan_end variable (by default, *scan-end*). If this file exists when the daemon wakes up to check the queue, *dq.pl* exits (and, therefore, stops processing all requests). Before you restart the daemon, remove the file. Here are some sample entries in the Ftpmail *crontab* to shut down the daemon between 9 A.M. and 6 P.M. on weekdays:

```
# Disable daemon between 0900-1800 weekdays:
0,30 0-8,18-23 * * 1-5 /bin/rm -f scan-end; exec ./dq.pl >> dq.pl.log 2>&1
58 8 * * 1-5 /bin/touch scan-end
# Run daemon 24 hours on weekends:
0,30 * * * 0,6 /bin/rm -f scan-end; exec ./dq.pl >> dq.pl.log 2>&1
```

As before, if your system doesn't have personal *crontab* files, run these from the system *crontab* and use full pathnames. Also, the execs are optional.

26.4.3 Ignored Mail

The $dont_reply_to variable is a regular expression that lists addresses which shouldn't be replied to—for example, the addresses on a bounced mail message. The default pattern looks like this:

```
$dont_reply_to = '(ftpmail|postmaster|mmdf|mailer-daemon|...deleted...).*@';
```

That expression won't match local addresses (addresses without an @ character). It also doesn't list all of the system addresses, like *root* and *gopher*, that might send mail which *ftpmail* shouldn't process. To fix those problems, we added a few new addresses. We also changed the end of the pattern from .*@ (zero or more characters followed by an @) to @? (zero or one @).

```
$dont_reply_to = '(ftpmail|...deleted...|daemon|gopher|root)@?';
```

We made those changes because we felt that the old .* wasn't restrictive enough (see below); also, the new @? matches an @ only if there is one.

This is a brute-force approach to mail filtering. Any mail from addresses containing these strings doesn't get any acknowledgment or rejection; the mail is just ignored. One problem we've seen is real users whose login names contain one of those strings—for instance, a person named Bernie Root. His system uses the last name as the login name, but that name was taken ;-). So his login name was *broot*. And our system ignored his mail.

`$dont_reply_to` is a sophisticated Perl regular expression, so you can tweak it quite a bit. But be careful: mail addresses can come in lots of different formats: *root@somehost*, *@relayhost:root@somehost*, *systema!root@systemb*, and so on. Leaving this expression fairly loose is the safest way to stop mail loops. Check the Ftpmail log file regularly for problems with ignored mail.

26.5 The Ftpmail Developer's Mailing List

If you want to help develop Ftpmail and fix bugs in it, you can join the mailing list *ftpmail-workers@doc.ic.ac.uk*. To subscribe, send email like this:

```
To: ftpmail-workers-request@doc.ic.ac.uk
Subject: add me

subscribe ftpmail-workers Your Full Name Here
```

In this Chapter:
- *What Is a Firewall?*
- *Types of Firewalls*
- *Hurdles for Information Providers*
- *Firewall Software*
- *Locating Servers*
- *Solutions for Various Clients*
- *For More Information*

27

Firewalls and Information Services

With each new company that connects to the "Information Superhighway," new frontiers are created for crackers to explore. Site administrators have found it necessary to implement various security measures to protect their internal networks. One of these is *xinetd*, covered in the next chapter. A more general solution is to construct a guarded gateway called a firewall that sits between a site's internal network and the wild and wooly Internet (see Figure 27-1). In fact, about one-third of all Internet-connected machines are already behind firewalls. So most information services have to deal with getting out through a local firewall or helping customers get to your service through their firewall.

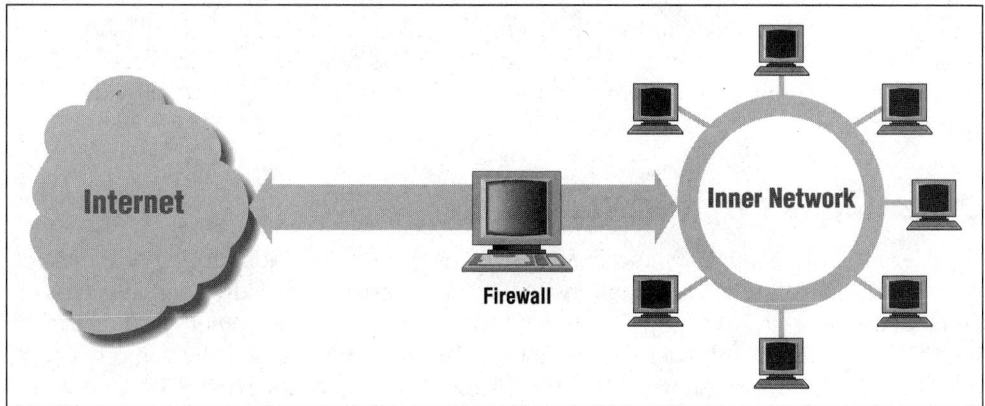

Figure 27-1. An Internet connection with firewall

This chapter is an introduction to the issues that firewalls raise for information service providers, and mentions some solutions. It does not provide a guide on how to set up

This chapter was written by Jeff LaCoursiere.

a firewall. Also, it mentions, but doesn't show how to use, the various free software packages available for dealing with firewalls.

27.1 What Is a Firewall?

The main purpose of a firewall is to prevent unauthorized access between networks. Generally this means protecting a site's inner network from the Internet. If your site has a firewall, decisions have been made as to what is allowed and disallowed across the firewall. These decisions should stem directly from your site's security policy. When planning to offer services from within your network, you need to be familiar with this policy, as it may dictate what options are available for configuring the service. If your site does not have a written policy, make good friends with the firewall administrator (this is probably a good idea anyway!). Chances are this person will have to be involved at some point to put your service into production.

A firewall basically works by examining the IP packets that travel between the server and the client. This provides a way to control the information flow for each service by IP address, by port, and in each direction.

A firewall embodies a "stance." The stance of a firewall describes the trade-off between security and ease-of-use. A stance of the form "that which is not expressly permitted is prohibited" requires that each new service be enabled individually. Conversely, the stance "that which is not expressly prohibited is permitted" has traded a level of security for convenience. It will be useful to know and understand the stance of your firewall when making design decisions.

A firewall has some general responsibilities. First and foremost, it must implement the site's security policy. If a particular action is not allowed by the policy, the firewall must make sure that all attempts to perform the action will fail. The firewall should log suspicious events. The firewall should alert internal administration of attempts to compromise the security policy. Some firewalls are in a prime position to provide usage statistics as well.

27.2 Types of Firewalls

In order to avoid headaches and head-scratching, it is a good idea to know the topology of your firewall and its limitations before attempting to provide a service across it. Discussed below are two popular firewall topologies. Although other types exist, the two below represent the basic forms; most other firewalls employ the same concepts and thus have the same limitations. Your firewall administrator should be able to tell you which model below fits your situation best.

27.2.1 The Dual-Homed Gateway

A dual-homed gateway is a firewall composed of a single system with at least two network interfaces (see Figure 27-2). This system is normally configured such that packets are not directly routed from one network (the Internet) to the other (the internal net). Machines on the Internet can talk to the gateway, as can machines on the internal network, but direct traffic between nets is blocked.

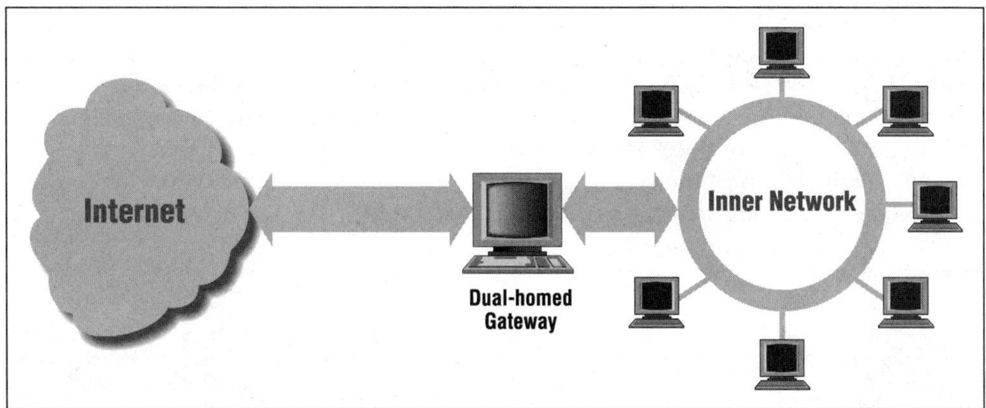

Figure 27-2. The dual-homed gateway

In discussing firewalls, it is generally accepted that you should think of your inner network as a medieval castle. The "bastions" of a castle are the critical points where defense is concentrated. It is typical to use this term when referring to the machine that is the critical point in your network security. In a dual-homed gateway topology, the dual-homed host itself is called the **bastion host**.

The main disadvantage of a dual-homed gateway is the fact that it blocks direct IP traffic in both directions.* Any programs running on the inner network that require a routed path to external machines will not function in this environment. A service on the internal network does not have a routed path to clients on the outside. To resolve these difficulties, dual-homed gateways run programs called proxies to forward application packets between nets. A proxy controls the conversation between client and server processes in a firewalled enironment. Rather than communicating directly, the client and server both talk to the proxy, which is usually running on the bastion host itself. It is desirable for the proxy to be transparent to the users.

A proxy on the bastion host does not just allow free rein for certain services. Most proxy software can be configured to allow or deny forwarding based on source or destination addresses or ports. Proxies may also require authentication of the requestor using encryption- or password-based systems.

* This disadvantage is from the viewpoint of the users of the network and anyone attempting to offer services to external users from the inner network.

The use of proxy software on the bastion host may mean that the firewall administrator has to provide replacements for the standard networking clients. This can be a great burden for administrator and user alike, especially in heterogeneous environments.* In general, any service that must pass through a dual-homed gateway is required to use a proxy.

27.2.2 The Screened Host Gateway

A screened host gateway is a firewall consisting of at least one router and a bastion host with a single network interface (see Figure 27-3). The router is typically configured to block (screen) all traffic to the internal net such that the bastion host is the only machine that can be reached from the outside. Unlike the dual-homed gateway, a screened host gateway does not necessarily force all traffic through the bastion host; through configuration of the screening router, it is possible to open "holes" in the firewall to other machines on your internal net.

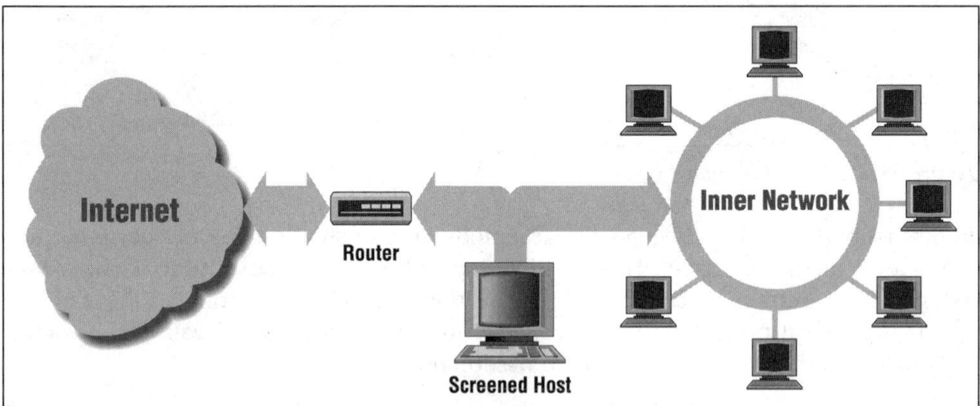

Figure 27-3. The screened host gateway

The bastion host in a screened host firewall is protected from the outside net by the screening router. The router is generally configured to only allow traffic to specific ports on the bastion host. Further, it may allow that traffic only from specific external hosts.† Many sites configure their router such that any connection (or a set of allowed

* Heterogeneous environment refers to a site with many different operating system platforms. Most large sites at least contain a smattering of PC's, workstations from Sun, IBM, DEC, and HP, to name a few. The replacement utilities must run on all in-house platforms to simulate direct IP connectivity.

† For example, the router may allow Usenet news traffic to reach the bastion host *only* if the traffic originated from the site's news provider. Granted, this filtering is relying on the IP address of a remote machine which can be forged. But this type of attack is very difficult.

connections) initiated from the inside net is allowed to pass.* This ability allows users on the internal net to use all the standard network utilities to communicate with the external net without a proxy service.

As was mentioned, this design also allows "holes" to be opened in the firewall for machines on the internal net. This can be very useful for providing services to the outside net on an internal machine. But be careful! In doing so you have increased your "zone of risk" to now include both the bastion host and the machine offering the service. It is then necessary to ensure that the service machine is at least as secure as the bastion host itself, if not more so. By offering services to a public network, attention may be drawn to the service machine as a potential weak point in your network security.

Many services (such as Web servers) are fairly new and probably still contain security-related bugs. By allowing full access to such a service on an internal machine, you may be offering an easy back door to your internal network. Even services that have been around for a long time have made the headlines as crackers discover a new hole (*sendmail* is a good example). The rule of thumb is "big is bad"; the bigger the package, the more chance that it has security-related bugs.

27.2.3 Other Firewall Topologies

The dual-homed gateway and screened host are probably the most popular, but by no means the only, firewall topologies. Other configurations include the simple screening router (no bastion host), the screened subnet (two screening routers and a bastion host), as well as many commercial vendor solutions. If you are interested in learning more about firewall topologies, a good place to start is Marcus Ranum's paper "Thinking About Firewalls" (available via anonymous FTP from *ftp.tis.com* in the file */pub/firewalls/firewalls.ps.Z*).

27.3 Hurdles for Information Providers

This list is an overview of what you need to learn and do to set up a service in the presence of a firewall:

- First, follow the security policy of your site. A good security policy keeps administrators from shooting themselves in the foot. Keep this in mind when considering addendums to the security policy simply to support your service.
- Learn how your service communicates with its clients. In which direction is each connection made? What protocol is used for communication? Does either the server or the client open additional connections during communication? Specific services will be examined later in this chapter that illustrate the use of this

* This is done by examining the SYN and ACK bits of TCP packets. The "start of connection" packet will have both bits set. If this packet's source address is internal, the packet is allowed to pass. Not all router vendors implement this feature.

information. Figure 27-4 shows the possible communication paths between servers and their clients.

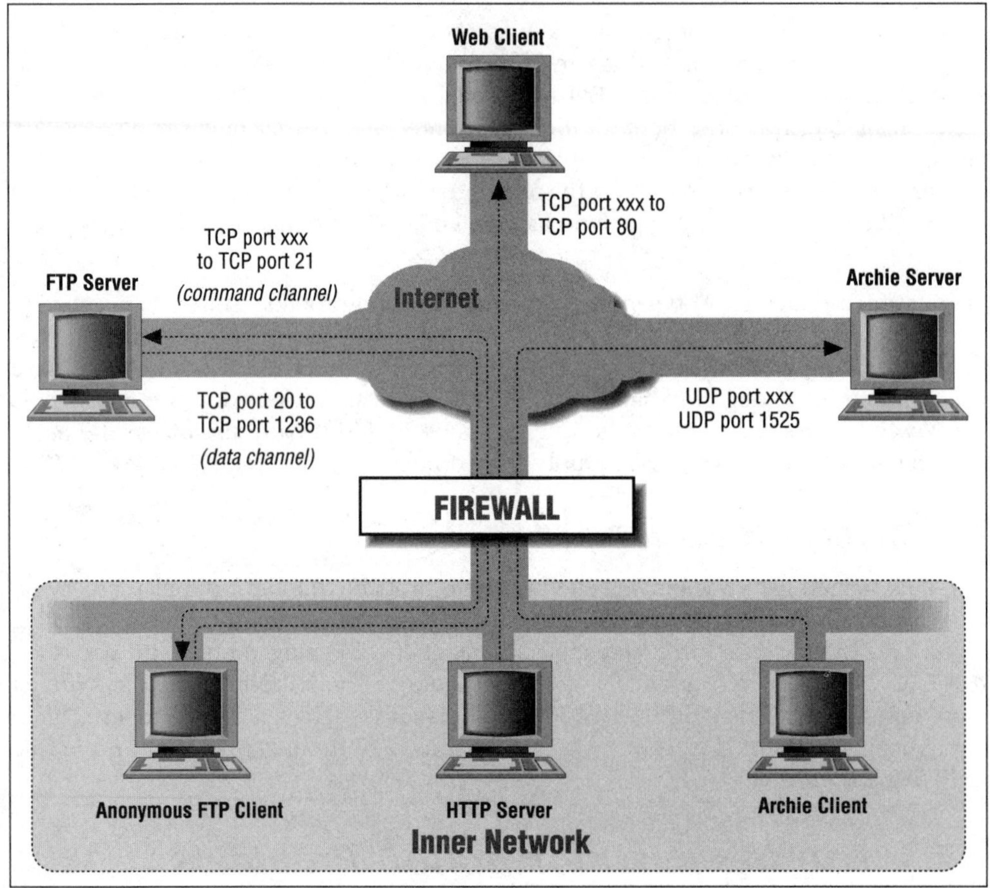

Figure 27-4. Possible communication paths

- Decide on a good location for your service. You must first have answered the questions about client/server communication. You must understand how your firewall topology affects this communication. You must understand the possible locations for your service with respect to the firewall topology (see Figure 27-5).
- Decide who should have access to the service. In many cases, the firewall can be configured to support your access restrictions. In a dual-homed gateway, the proxy supporting your service may be used to restrict access based on user, machine, or network. In a screened subnet, the screening router can be used in a similar manner (but not based on user, because routers generally work at the network level).

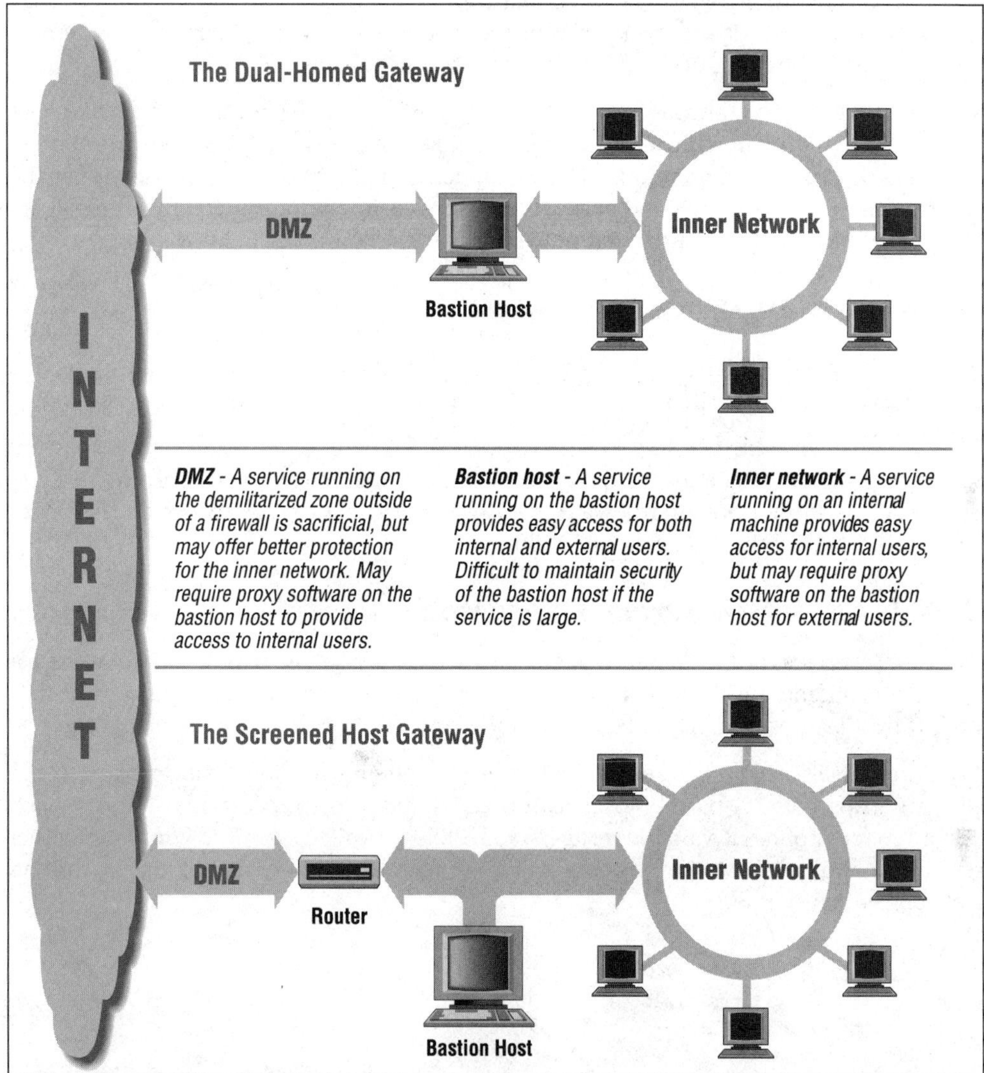
The Dual-Homed Gateway
DMZ
Bastion Host
Inner Network
I N T E R N E T
DMZ - A service running on the demilitarized zone outside of a firewall is sacrificial, but may offer better protection for the inner network. May require proxy software on the bastion host to provide access to internal users.
Bastion host - A service running on the bastion host provides easy access for both internal and external users. Difficult to maintain security of the bastion host if the service is large.
Inner network - A service running on an internal machine provides easy access for internal users, but may require proxy software on the bastion host for external users.
The Screened Host Gateway
DMZ
Router
Inner Network
Bastion Host

Figure 27-5. Possible locations for service

- If you have decided on a location for your service inside the firewall, make sure you know the risks involved. Ensure that some form of logging is being performed in a secure manner; ideally the logs should be collected on another internal machine not accessible from the Internet. It is a good idea to have an automated process scan the logs regularly, trapping suspicious information and notifying appropriate personnel.

- Plan for failure. If your logs detect intrusion, have a plan of action ready that may include shutting down the service or the machine running the service. Policy may also dictate shutting down the link to the Internet.
- Test your service thoroughly. If you have restricted access in any way, make sure the restrictions are functioning. Don't blindly trust your routing software, access lists, or proxy configurations! This is especially important if the service is on the internal net. Keep in mind that if your service is compromised, the firewall no longer protects the rest of your network.

27.4 Firewall Software

Because firewalls restrict traffic going directly from clients inside a firewall to servers outside, some software often runs on the firewall to allow and control that transition.

Before we go into the possible locations, we need to introduce some of the software solutions that allow clients inside a firewall to communicate with servers outside. Three of the most popular freeware packages are the CERN Web server (in proxy mode), SOCKS, and the TIS Firewall Toolkit.

27.4.1 CERN Web Server Proxy Mode

The CERN Web server has a "proxy mode," in which the server handles all requests for remote documents (and local documents, if required) from browsers inside the firewall. It handles not only HTTP, but also all the other protocols that Web clients use.

The server itself makes the remote connections, passing the information back to the clients transparently. X-based Mosaic can be configured for proxy mode simply by setting a few environment variables. Here's a shell script called */usr/local/bin/mosaic* that sets them and starts Mosaic, assuming the proxy-mode server is set up to run on *web.foo.com* on port 80:

```
#!/bin/csh -f
setenv http_proxy "http://web.foo.com:80/"
setenv ftp_proxy "http://web.foo.com:80/"
setenv gopher_proxy "http://web.foo.com:80/"
setenv wais_proxy "http://web.foo.com:80/"
setenv file_proxy "http://web.foo.com:80/"
/usr/local/bin/Mosaic-2.4 -home http://web http://web
```

These specific variables are used by NCSA's X-based Mosaic client; other browsers may have a different syntax or procedure for configuring proxy mode.

Proxy mode can work well because only the proxy server makes external requests instead of every client on every machine in your inner net. In addition, the CERN Web server has caching capabilities that can greatly reduce your Internet bandwidth usage. Imagine pulling just *one* copy of the latest Dr. Fun cartoon per day!*

* Dr. Fun is a daily cartoon available via the WWW. Once this server is discovered by your internal users, your non-cached Internet bandwidth is used up quickly!

27.4.2 SOCKS

The SOCKS package includes a proxy server that runs on the bastion host of a firewall. The proxy server relays TCP streams from the client (usually inside the firewall) to hosts on the Internet and back. With a bit of planning and effort, it is also possible to use SOCKS to relay from clients on the Internet to servers on the inner net. SOCKS is freeware and is available for anonymous FTP from *ftp.nec.com* in the file */pub/security/socks.cstc/socks.cstc.4.2.tar.gz.*

To use SOCKS, the client must undergo some minor source code changes and be linked with the SOCKS library. The SOCKS library includes replacements for standard IP socket calls such as `connect()`, `getsockname()`, `bind()`, `accept()`, `listen()`, and `select()`. The replacement routines allow the client to transparently use the SOCKS server to communicate with an external host. Currently, the software is bundled with pre-SOCKSified (all source modifications already done) versions of *ftp*, *telnet*, *finger*, and *whois*. Many people have contributed SOCKSified source to *ftp.nec.com*; sources for Mosaic, the CERN Web server, *ping*, *archie*, *gopher*, and many others are widely available. The package includes the library, which can be used to SOCKSify your own networking applications.

27.4.3 The Firewall Toolkit

The Firewall Toolkit contains several proxy servers that do not require client modification. *tn-gw* (a Telnet proxy), *ftp-gw* (an FTP proxy), and *plug-gw* (a socket-to-socket plugboard) handles a few of the basic networking clients. The price for the ability to use nonmodified clients is a two-step process. To Telnet to external hosts, the user must first Telnet to the bastion host (where *tn-gw* runs), receive the proxy prompt (`tn-gw>`), and type **`connect remotehostname`**. The FTP proxy is similar. You have traded transparency (with SOCKS) for the ability to proxy unmodified clients.

The toolkit contains many useful tools for building firewalls, in addition to the proxy servers. **netacl** can be used in *inetd.conf* to check incoming requests against an access table before spawning services such as *ftpd*, *httpd*, or other *inetd*-capable daemons. **smap** and **smapd** are scaled-down mail handlers that accept mail and store it away in a `chroot()`ed area of your filesystem for processing (possibly by *sendmail* running as a nonprivileged user). The toolkit also contains a scaled-down daemon that has the FTP proxy built into it. It is possible to use this daemon to support both anonymous FTP on the bastion host, as well as proxying internal requests to external FTP servers on the same port. This is important for those internal clients that cannot handle non-standard FTP server ports.

The Firewall Toolkit is available for anonymous FTP from *ftp.tis.com* in the file */pub/firewalls/toolkit/fwtk.tar.Z.*

27.5 Locating Servers

Here we discuss Web and FTP servers to illustrate the issues involved in deciding where, in relation to the firewall, to run information services.

Usually, when you set up a service, you want people outside on the Internet and people on your internal net to be able to reach the service. How your internal net gets access to other services on the Internet is also relevant to locating your service, because you want the same browsers or techniques to work for your service and other services.

27.5.1 Web Servers

Web URLs specify various communication protocols, including HTTP, Gopher, FTP, News, WAIS, and Telnet. However, only the browser deals with all these protocols. The NCSA Web server speaks only HTTP.*

27.5.1.1 Locating a Web server in a dual-homed gateway topology

The main consideration concerning topology is the location of the service. In most cases, three locations are possible with respect to the firewall (see Figure 27-5): in front of the firewall (between the firewall and the Internet, sometimes called the *DMZ*),† on the bastion host, or behind the firewall.

With dual-homed gateways, the DMZ location may not be practical. A standard dual-homed gateway would have the Internet feed plugged directly into one network interface. For most networks, this is not an Ethernet segment, but more likely a V.35 serial (for 56K, T1) or RS-232 (high-speed dial-up) connection. In this case, in front of the firewall would mean in your connection provider's machine room!‡

A location on the bastion host can be advantageous. Internal and external browsers have direct IP access to the bastion host (albeit through different interfaces), so there shouldn't be any problem reaching the Web server. Proxy software is necessary to forward internal browsers' requests to external Web servers, so a proxy-capable Web server (such as CERN's) is an elegant solution. It is difficult to trust the security of any large program, however. Were an intruder to exploit a bug in the Web server to gain access to the bastion host, it is very likely he would be able to subvert the firewall entirely, and your inner net would be at risk. Although this option has many advantages, it is not considered a secure configuration.

Finally, one could decide to place the service on an internal machine. Internal clients would certainly have no trouble accessing the server, but providing access for external

* The CERN web server in proxy mode speaks all the protocols on behalf of the browser.

† A special type of screened host gateway called the "screened subnet" contains an area often called the DMZ, or "demilitarized zone." By placing your service on this subnet, your inner net is protected from possible exploitation of the machine running the service.

‡ One of O'Reilly & Associates' *Global Network Navigator* (*GNN*) Web servers is set up this way.

clients would be difficult. Some method of proxying requests in the opposite direction than usual would be necessary. The SOCKS proxy software will accomplish this through *very* careful configuration. Unfortunately this solution requires that the external clients be built to specifically access *your* SOCKS server. This is probably not a viable solution for serving the public at large, although it may work for specific applications.

27.5.1.2 Locating a Web server with screened host topology

Options are slightly more open in a screened host gateway topology. A location in front of the firewall is usually possible and acceptable. The service machine can be placed on the same Ethernet segment as the bastion host; in this case the router would be configured to allow communication from the outside *only* to the port used by the Web server. This configuration works best if two routers are involved (the "screened subnet" topology) and communication from the Web server machine to the internal net is blocked by the internal router. In this setup, the Web server is accessible only to outside users, but the possible damage is limited if the machine is broken into from the outside. With a decent set of access-list capabilities, the internal router could be configured to allow only connections initiated from the inside to your Web server machine and still block access to your inner net from shells on the server. This is probably the most secure configuration possible for externally accessed Web services.

As with the dual-homed gateway, a location on the bastion host itself is an elegant solution for providing both internal and external access. A proxy-capable Web server on the bastion host can help reduce the number of holes in your screening router access lists, because all Web clients can be configured to use the proxy server rather than attempting external connections on their own. This solution trades security (running large software on the bastion host) for simplicity and elegance.

An internal location is identical to the "in front of" configuration described above when only one router is used. This configuration is considered fairly secure as long as *all* traffic from external sources is blocked except HTTP traffic. This should limit access to one port only—the port your Web server is listening on. The security of your inner network now depends (in large part) on the security of the Web server you run.

27.5.2 Anonymous FTP

FTP sessions (see Figure 27-6 for a sample session) are troublesome for firewalls, as they involve connections established in both directions. The initial connection is opened by the client to the server. This control connection is used for the login to the server, directory changes, and plain *ls* commands. The fun begins when any file-transfer command, such as *get* or *put*, is sent, causing the server to open a separate data connection back to the client to be used for one specific file transfer. TCP is used for both connections.

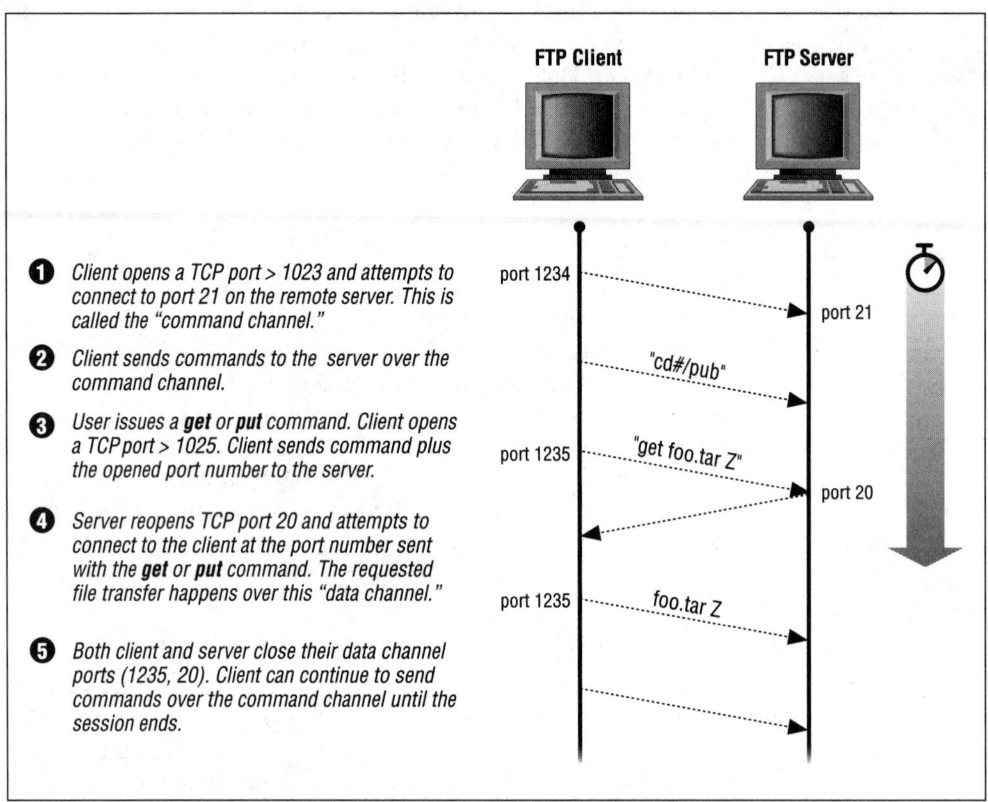

FTP Client
FTP Server
1 Client opens a TCP port > 1023 and attempts to connect to port 21 on the remote server. This is called the "command channel."
2 Client sends commands to the server over the command channel.
3 User issues a **get** or **put** command. Client opens a TCP port > 1025. Client sends command plus the opened port number to the server.
4 Server reopens TCP port 20 and attempts to connect to the client at the port number sent with the **get** or **put** command. The requested file transfer happens over this "data channel."
5 Both client and server close their data channel ports (1235, 20). Client can continue to send commands over the command channel until the session ends.
port 1234
port 21
"cd#/pub"
port 1235
"get foo.tar Z"
port 20
port 1235
foo.tar Z

Figure 27-6. Sample FTP session

27.5.2.1 Locating anonymous FTP with dual-homed gateways

A location in front of the firewall may be difficult (or impossible) with a dual-homed gateway topology, for the same reasons as discussed with Web servers. There is the possibility of locating your service on your connection provider's machine. Many connection providers offer disk space on their existing FTP sites for a fee. Much of the management (and risk) are then taken over by the connection provider.

Because of the difficulty in proxying connections from your provider's machine to internal hosts (in that special *ftp* clients are necessary), the best location for your *ftpd* is on the bastion host. The risks of running such a large and potentially buggy application on your bastion host can be minimized by running the *ftpd* in a `chroot()`ed area, and running it as a nonprivileged user (as recommended in this book). Since the service will be running on your bastion host, external *ftp* clients should have no difficulty with either connection. Likewise for internal clients.

27.5.2.2 Anonymous FTP with screened host gateways

Screened host gateways offer a bit more flexibility than dual-homed gateways. Implementing the service in front of the firewall is desirable. As with Web servers, the most secure method is to install a second router to shield the inner network from possible breaches of security on the service machine. The issue of how to allow access to the service from clients inside your network is problematic, however, because of the data connection from the server to the client. This problem can be avoided by using the proxy (PASV) mode of *ftp* (both the client and the server must support this mode). In this mode, the client opens both the command and the data channels, thus eliminating the need for allowing inward connections from the FTP server.

An FTP server can be elegantly implemented on the bastion host in the same manner as on a dual-homed gateway. The screening router must allow incoming connections on port 21 (the control channel) and outgoing connections from port 20 (the data channel) The risks of running a large application on the bastion host still hold.

If possible, use some authentication software to execute your FTP server. Several public-domain packages, such as *xinetd* or *netacl*, examine the source addresses/ports of requests and apply rule-based filters to decide whether or not to execute the service.

27.5.3 General Internal Location Concerns

If you decide to run your service from an internal machine, special attention should be paid to host-based security. As with the bastion host, it is best to strip the internal service machine of all special inner-net privileges in *hostp.equiv* or *.rhosts*. No internal machine should trust the server machine. The networking clients (*telnet*, *ftp*, *rlogin*, *rsh*, etc.) should all be removed. NFS (and NIS support on Sun platforms) should be disabled in the kernel. The kernel should not forward (route) IP packets. Disable all services in *inetd.conf* that are not used for maintenance of the service. Now, if your server is somehow used to obtain a shell on your server machine, it will be difficult to use the shell to gain access to other machines on your internal net. Some other good ideas:

- Leave traps for the unsuspecting attacker. Replace networking clients such as *telnet* and *ftp* with programs that appear to execute like their namesake, but actually email or page an administrator. Have your command simulate network delays or spit out random error messages. Keep him interested long enough to catch him in the act.*
- Run software that verifies the integrity of your filesystem. Several public-domain utilities exist that build a database of encryption "signatures" of all your files. A quick check run every few hours can catch possible Trojan horses before they

* For a highly detailed account of the effectiveness of this method, read Bill Cheswick's paper, "An Evening with Berferd In Which a Cracker is Lured, Endured, and Studied." It is available by anonymous FTP from *ftp.research.att.com* in */dist/internet_security/berferd.ps.*

become a problem. The public-domain package *tripwire* covers this well. It is available for anonymous FTP from *ftp.cs.purdue.edu.*

- Consider running the Web server in a `chroot()`ed environment (using a shell wrapper or possibly *netacl*). This may make the machine easier to maintain, as access will be constrained into the `chroot()`ed area (even if the server somehow delivers shell access).

27.6 Solutions for Various Clients

You may be called on to help local users inside the firewall access services on the Internet. Or you may get questions from remote users trying (unsuccessfully) to access your service from inside their firewall.

27.6.1 Telnet

From a communications point of view, *telnet* is a simple client. It utilizes the TCP protocol to communicate with its server counterpart, *telnetd. telnetd* can be configured (through *inetd.conf*) to answer on any network port on the host machine, but the standard port is 23. The initial connection is initiated by the client; there is never a connection attempted in the other direction.

There are several ways for an internal user to establish a *telnet* session through a firewall. In a screened host environment, the access lists in the router can be configured to allow outgoing connections. In a dual-homed gateway environment, a proxy can be used to relay packets between the client and server. SOCKS requires specially compiled clients. Other proxies allow the user to use a standard *telnet* client to connect to the bastion host (which runs the proxy), at which point the user is prompted for the remote machine name. Upon supplying a valid remote machine name, the proxy makes the remote connection and continues to relay packets between client and server.

27.6.2 Archie

Since we don't cover Archie in this book, this is a bit of a digression, but it's an interesting one.

archie is simple client that uses the UDP protocol for communication with its server. Archie servers listen on port 1525. Like *telnet* clients, *archie* clients initiate the connection by opening a random port greater than 1023 on the client machine. Packets are then sent to port 1525 on the remote server.

UDP protocols are more difficult to pass through firewalls. UDP conversations are not sequenced (like TCP streams), thus they do not have a "start of connection" packet. It is this "start of connection" packet that allows routers to distinguish the direction of an attempted connection with TCP. The lack of this packet is unfortunate, as the simple method of configuring the screening router to allow outgoing connections does not function with UDP-based clients.

Archie is a special case, however, that allows an approach that may not be viable for other UDP client/server applications. At the time of writing, approximately 20 Archie servers exist in the world. Because there are so few, one can be fairly certain that they are all used heavily. Assume the screening router is configured to allow all UDP traffic from any of the 20 Archie servers, provided that the originating port is 1525. An attack on the firewall would have to come from one of these 20 heavily used ports.* Such an attack would be very difficult, as any interruption of service (by a cracker attempting to attack your network or perhaps to install a Trojan horse that would attack your network) would be instantly noticed and, hopefully, corrected. The risk of a successful attack in this manner is probably very low.

In a dual-homed gateway environment, a proxy is required for internal machines to run an *archie* client. One such proxy, *udprelay*, is available for anonymous FTP from *ftp.wang.com*. SOCKS only proxies TCP-based packets. Another option is to allow user accounts on the bastion host. Users could log into the bastion host from an internal machine and run *archie* there. Having user accounts on the bastion host is generally considered insecure, as was mentioned earlier.

It should be noted that *archie* can be used to automatically retrieve files that were the object of the search. Some *archie* clients accomplish this by running (externally) the *ftp* client. The *ftp* client available on the machine running *archie* needs to have the ability to pass the firewall as well.

27.6.3 FTP

Two-channel FTP communication was explained in Section 27.5.2. The fact that the server initiates a connection back to the client poses problems for passing the firewall. Newer versions of the *ftp* client and server support an internal proxy mode where the client initiates both the command and data channels. This may be a good solution for text-based *ftp* clients, but may be difficult to configure in GUI clients that don't fully support the FTP specification. A slightly different syntax is used in the text-based *ftp* clients to support this feature; your users have to be informed of this.

In a screened host environment, holes in the screening router's access filters can be configured to allow the outgoing command channel. Unless FTP is being used in proxy mode, the data channel will still be blocked. It is possible to open the access filters to allow connections from any external host if the source port is 20 and the destination port is greater than 1023. This can be dangerous, however. Anyone who has supervisor privileges on an external machine could easily send packets from port 20. A number of well-known services listen on ports above 1023 (NFS, X Window System,

* It is also possible for a cracker to locate himself physically somewhere along the route between your network and the *archie* server, where he may attempt to "spoof" your firewall into believing he is the *archie* server. This type of attack is technically difficult.

database servers, etc.). It should be noted that proxy services can be run on screened host firewalls, as well as dual-homed gateways. In some situations (such as *ftp*), this is a more sensible solution.

In a dual-homed gateway environment, a proxy is required. SOCKS is distributed with the source for SOCKSified *ftp* client, which can be used in place of the vendor-provided client to work transparently through the firewall. The alternative exists, as with *archie* and *telnet*, to allow user accounts on the bastion host where normal vendor-supplied clients can be used directly. This is not recommended.

27.6.4 Mosaic

NCSA Mosaic is an interesting client, because it uses several protocols, each on a different port. This means you have more to worry about with respect to the firewall. If you are not operating a proxy Web server on the firewall, each protocol must be dealt with individually. See the previous two sections for allowing FTP and Telnet through your firewall.

A link of the type `telnet:` causes Mosaic to execute a separate *telnet* client on the client machine. X-based Mosaic opens an *xterm* window and spawns a *telnet* session inside it. Other than *telnet*, Mosaic handles all other protocols internally.

In a screened host environment, holes in the access filters may be used to allow the initial TCP connection from Mosaic to any of its remote servers. The servers (except FTP servers) do not attempt a connection in the opposite direction, so simply allowing outgoing connections should suffice.

In a dual-homed gateway environment, a proxy is required on the bastion host. It is elegant (although probably less secure) to run a proxy CERN Web server on the bastion host to serve as the proxy for Mosaic. This also allows for internal and external access to any Web services you may wish to make available. SOCKS also makes a fine proxy for Mosaic and all its related clients, although this requires recompiling the source for your clients with the SOCKS library and distributing them to the user base. SOCKSified source for Mosaic comes with SOCKS. As with the other clients discussed here, the alternative exists to allow user accounts on the bastion host. Mosaic could be run from there with the `DISPLAY` environment variable set to an internal machine. Besides the insecurity of this option, any files fetched by `ftp:` hyperlinks end up on the bastion host's filesystem, rather than on the machine where Mosaic is being used.

27.6.5 Solutions for Various DOS/Windows/Mac Clients

To this point, only UNIX–based clients have been discussed. Many Internet-connected networks contain MS-DOS or Microsoft Windows–based PC and Macintosh machines with IP networking functionality. Telnet, FTP, Mosaic, and other useful utilities are available from a number of vendors for these two platforms, but not many take firewall topologies into account in their design (yet). All is not lost.

In a screened host environment, holes in the access filters can solve most of your problems in the same manner as with the UNIX-based clients. FTP will still be troublesome, although some vendor-supplied *ftp* clients support PASV mode, as discussed above.

A dual-homed gateway environment is more problematic. Proxies must exist on the bastion host to pass connections between the PC and Mac machines and external servers. Most vendor-supplied clients do not ship with UNIX-based proxy server support. One exception is the "PC Socks Pack," a collection of networking clients for use on MS Windows–based PCs. This package is currently available from *ftp.nec.com* and includes SOCKS-ready *telnet*, *ftp*, and *finger*. You also need a *winsock.dll* file to support the TCP functionality of these clients from MS Windows. NCSA has SOCKS support for their Windows Mosaic clients starting at version 2.0 alpha2. This client also supports the CERN proxy Web server, if you are running one. Current versions of NCSA's Macintosh Mosaic client also support SOCKS and the CERN proxy Web server.

Attempts are being made to create a SOCKSified *winsock.dll* to handle proxying for any MS Windows networking client. Peter Tattam has a SOCKSified version of his Trumpet *winsock* (shareware, not freeware) in beta. For information on progress, contact *John.Miezitis@its.utas.edu.au.*

The fact that most PC and Mac software does not ship with source code makes it very difficult to add proxy support to your favorite applications (like you can SOCKSify UNIX-based client source code). SOCKS is quickly becoming a standard proxy for dual-homed gateway environments. If your network uses SOCKS, show your support for freeware by writing, calling, or threatening your PC and Mac vendors and suggest they add SOCKS support to their software.

27.7 For More Information

If you haven't found the answer to your deepest firewall-related problems here, you can ask the experts directly. Firewall-related topics are discussed daily on an automated mailing list dedicated to firewalls and Internet security. To join the list, send a message to *majordomo@greatcircle.com.* You will get a message back with instructions on joining the mailing list. Make sure you read the FAQ (Frequently Asked Questions) document (on *ftp.greatcircle.com* in */pub/firewalls/FAQ*) before posting your question to the list. This helps keep the same question from being asked every day. The automated response from Majordomo should explain how to retrieve the FAQ.

In this Chapter:

- *What xinetd Does*
- *How to Get xinetd*
- *Building xinetd*
- *Installing xinetd*
- *Configuring xinetd with xinetd.conf*
- *Managing xinetd*
- *How to Spot Security Break-Ins or Attempts*

28

xinetd

inetd, the Internet services daemon that we've mentioned throughout this book, doesn't take security any further than allowing individual services to be enabled or disabled. There's no middle ground. If, for example, you have an FTP or Telnet server enabled to support employees working from home over the Internet, then anybody can try to login using these services.

xinetd, a freely available enhanced replacement for *inetd*, provides you with a finer granularity of control. You can allow just those particular users to have FTP or Telnet access, without opening up access to the world.

Note that *xinetd* can only protect the system from intrusion by controlling initial access to most system services and by logging activities so that you can detect break-in attempts. However, once a connection has been allowed to a service, *xinetd* is out of the picture. It cannot protect against a server program that has security problems internally. For example, the *finger* server had a bug several years ago that allowed a particularly clever person to overwrite part of its memory. This was used to gain access to many systems. Even placing *finger* under the control of *xinetd* wouldn't have helped. The culprit could have been identified after the fact, by examining the log files, but *xinetd* could not have prevented the assault from being successful.

If you picture your secured firewall system as a fortress wall, each service that is enabled for incoming connection can be viewed as a door or window in your wall. Each must have a secure and reliable lock. The more openings you make available, the more opportunities for the trespasser.

This chapter was written by Greg George and Craig Strickland.

28.1 What xinetd Does

xinetd, the extended Internet services daemon, is a drop-in replacement for the standard system *inetd* daemon. It listens to all enabled service ports and permits only those incoming connection requests that meet authorization criteria.

xinetd can be configured to:

- Accept connections from only certain IP addresses, address ranges, or hostnames. This can limit the locations from which an attack can be launched.
- Accept connections only from authorized users. For example, a firewall system could permit only a small list of administrators to have access to *rlogin*.
- Reject connections outside of authorized hours. This can protect your network when you aren't there to keep an eye on things.
- Log selected services when connections are accepted or rejected. The authorization criteria can be quite sophisticated. Information that can be captured includes:
  - Remote HOST address
  - User ID of remote user (in some cases)
  - Time when access was granted, as well as exit time and status
  - Service-specific information, such as the terminal type for the login service. Services supported include *login*, *shell*, *exec*, and *finger*.

  The logging support can provide statistics on network gateway usage, as well as showing who is doing what to your security measures.

Until you enable the extended features of *xinetd*, it behaves exactly like the *inetd* that it replaces.

28.1.1 Understanding inetd's Role in Security

On any UNIX–based system, *inetd* listens for client requests on behalf of a large number of service daemons. To get an idea of just how many there are, try the following:

```
% netstat -a
Proto RcvQ SndQ  Local Addr     Foreign  (state)
tcp      0    0  *.echo         *.*      LISTEN
tcp      0    0  *.time         *.*      LISTEN
tcp      0    0  *.printer      *.*      LISTEN
tcp      0    0  *.exec         *.*      LISTEN
tcp      0    0  *.shell        *.*      LISTEN
tcp      0    0  *.login        *.*      LISTEN
tcp      0    0  *.telnet       *.*      LISTEN
tcp      0    0  *.ftp          *.*      LISTEN
tcp      0    0  *.733          *.*      LISTEN
```

```
tcp        0      0  *.730          *.*       LISTEN
tcp        0      0  *.725          *.*       LISTEN
```

The output includes all of the system's active connections, both inbound and outbound (for example, users connected through the network), as well as all of the servers. As you can see, there are a lot of services.

Each service is potentially an opening for a clever trespasser to gain access to your network. Most vanilla systems have nearly all of these services enabled right out of the box. Many of the services are needed for routine daily use of your systems, and it's not as easy as simply shutting them all off.

For example, if you want to be able to log in to your firewall system remotely (perhaps for after-hours monitoring), you have to permit Telnet or *rlogin* service. Without *xinetd*, this would allow a patient intruder to start trying passwords. But, having an idea of which services you need, and which are more likely to be vulnerable than others, is a big step in protecting your network. There are a few services which tend to be the most frequent targets of simple attacks. These include the following:

- FTP
- Telnet
- *login* (*rlogin*)
- *shell* (*rcmd*)
- *exec*

There are other services that could also be targeted by a more sophisticated intruder, including:

- *mount*
- *tft*
- *finger*
- NFS (Network File System)
- DNS (Domain Name Service)

Some of these (for example, *tftp* or *mount*) could allow the user to get access to information directly, while others (such as DNS) could give the intruder additional information about the system, the network, or other components of the network. This information might help direct the interloper toward other, more vulnerable, systems.

However, there are some security-related issues particular to a few of these services. For example, SMTP (*sendmail*), by default, accepts a message from any incoming connection. The "sender" of such a message can appear to have originated anywhere. The sender's claim of identity is accepted. Thus, a message's originator can be forged. While this isn't strictly a violation of system security, it can lead to it. A naive recipient could take the sender's claim at face value and send sensitive information to the "return address" provided. Thus, security can be at risk through the enlistment of an unwitting inside accomplice. Part of any secure environment must include some education of your user community to the potential risks involved.

28.2 How to Get xinetd

xinetd is freely available on the Internet. It was developed by Panagiotis Tsirigotis (*panos@cs.colorado.edu*), and enhancements and bug fixes are ongoing. Generally, the latest source can found on *mystique.cs.colorado.edu* and can be downloaded via anonymous FTP.

It's always a good idea to download only from an archive site known to be safe. Unscrupulous system crackers have been known to upload bogus versions of security-related tools, in hopes that they'll be downloaded and installed. This can open a customized back door into firewall systems.

The file *xinetd-2.1.4.tar* can be extracted using *tar*. Create a directory in which you'll build the *xinetd* program from the sources, and extract the *tar* file.

```
% tar xvf xinetd-2.1.4.tar
```

Consult the README file for the latest information about building and installing *xinetd*.

28.3 Building xinetd

On a platform running SunOS 4.1.x or Ultrix 4.x, it is a trivial matter to build *xinetd*. Inside the *xinetd* directory, you need to run the command:

```
% compile-src
```

This command automatically sets up the compile flags if you are running on SunOS or on Ultrix. After you type in the command, it asks you what system to compile for:

```
I need to know the operating system you are using and the version.
I know about
   SunOS 4.x (sunos4)
   Ultrix 4.x (ultrix4)
If your OS is among these, use the name in the parentheses, otherwise
just hit <return> and I will try to figure out how to properly
configure xinetd for your system -->sunos4
```

In this case we type in **sunos4** (for a Sun4 platform) and press return; the program then builds the libraries and executables.

On other platforms, it may be necessary to edit the *Makefile* and the C source and header files to get things to work properly. Depending on the operating system you're building for, the changes are generally not difficult, they're just time-consuming to identify. As this package evolves, it's likely that the configuration and compilation procedures will support more platforms.

28.4 Installing xinetd

Because network services will be interrupted when *xinetd* replaces *inetd*, the system should be in single-user mode. New requests for service, including remote logins, will not work once *inetd* is killed.

Before any work is done, it is a good idea to make backup copies of *inetd* and *inetd.conf*. After the backups are made, copy *xinetd* and *itox* to the */etc* directory. If *ftp* is used to transfer the copies to a different machine, execute permissions need to be added to both executables after the transfer. If *xinetd* is not executable and the system is rebooted with *xinetd* handling network services, no network access will be granted.

Edit the *inetd.conf* file and enable all network services. This modified version of *inetd.conf* is used to create a complete *xinetd* configuration that logs attempts to connect to all services; this is useful for detecting people trying to break in. It also creates an *xinetd.conf* file with entries for every service, in case you want to turn more services on later. After the conversion, you'll disable (except for logging) all services you don't want to provide (using the default entry described later).

With all services uncommented in the *inetd.conf* file, run *itox* on *inetd.conf* and put the output into *xinetd.conf*. The *itox* program acts like a filter, as follows:

```
% itox </etc/inetd.conf >/etc/xinetd.conf
```

Once *itox* has been run, all subsequent changes should be made to the *xinetd.conf* file. Do not run the *itox* command again, as you will lose any changes you've made to the file.

The format of *xinetd.conf* is considerably different than *inetd.conf*, but the same information is still provided. At this point in the installation, no extra security has been established; *xinetd* behaves exactly like *inetd* until we reconfigure it in the next section. With the *xinetd.conf* file created, it is now necessary to put an entry into your */etc/rc* (or */etc/netlinkrc* on HP-UX, or */etc/rc.tcpip* on AIX) and make copies of the existing lines that launch *inetd*. Comment out the code that has *inetd* in it and put *xinetd* into the copied code, as shown below.

A Sun */etc/rc* file entry looks like this:

```
# Inetd has been commented out to put xinetd in its place
#if [ -f /usr/etc/inetd ]; then
#       inetd;                  echo -n ' inetd'
#fi
# Xinetd replaces inetd, giving us more control over security
if [ -f /etc/xinetd ]; then
        xinetd -filelog /usr/adm/xinetd.log;      echo -n ' xinetd'
fi
```

An HP-UX */etc/netlinkrc* file entry looks like:

```
#
# Start the Internet daemon.
#
#[ -x /etc/inetd ]  &&  /etc/inetd -l &&  /bin/echo "inetd -l #STATUS=$?
#if [ ! $STATUS -eq 0 ]
#then
#   net_init=1
#fi
# Xinetd replaces inetd, giving us more control over security
[ -x /etc/xinetd ]  &&  /etc/xinetd -filelog /usr/adm/xinetd.log &&▶▶▶
▶▶▶ /bin/echo "xinetd STATUS=$?
if [ ! $STATUS -eq 0 ]
then
   net_init=1
fi
```

An AIX */etc/rc.tcpip* file looks like:

```
# Start up socket-based daemons
# start /etc/inetd "$src_running"
# Xinetd replaces inetd, giving us more control over security
start /etc/xinetd -filelog /usr/adm/xinetd.log "$src_running"
```

The log file specified on the command line shows when *xinetd* is started or restarted and also shows what services are up and running. See Section 28.6.1 for more information.

Don't actually reboot until you've put a few security precautions in place, as described in the next section.

28.5 Configuring xinetd with xinetd.conf

xinetd.conf is the configuration file that determines both the services provided and the security attached to each service.

The format of *xinetd.conf* is much different than the format of *inetd.conf*, but the same information (and more) is supplied. If you try to run *xinetd* without creating an *xinetd.conf* file either by hand or with *itox*, your system will have no network services in place.

The file contains entries, one per service, of the form:

```
service <service_name>
{
        <attribute> <assign_op> <value> <value> ...
}
```

Here's an example of a service entry:

```
service login
        {
            socket_type         = stream
            protocol            = tcp
            wait                = no
            user                = root
            server              = /usr/etc/in.rlogind
            instances           = UNLIMITED
        }
```

In this example, the socket connection type is *stream*; protocol type is *tcp* (indicating that this service uses the TCP connection-oriented protocol); specifying `wait=no` prevents *xinetd* from waiting for the server to complete before again listening on the login service port; the program to be run when handling a request to this service port address is */usr/etc/in.rlogind*, to be executed as user *root*; and there's no limit on the number of concurrent login sessions that *xinetd* can start. The `instances` field can be set to the desired maximum number of current sessions to limit the load. This also cuts down on the impact of an assault aimed at loading down the server by saturating it with hundreds of concurrent requests.

28.5.1 The Default Entry

Optionally, the first entry in *xinetd.conf* can be a default, taking the form:

```
defaults
{
        <attribute> <assign_op> <value> <value> ...
}
```

This sets up default values for attributes common to all services. The format is similar to a normal service entry. Here's an example:

```
defaults
        {
            log_type            = FILE /var/log/servicelog
            log_on_success      = PID
            log_on_failure      = HOST RECORD
            only_from           = 128.138.193.0 128.138.204.0
            only_from           += 128.138.252.1 128.138.209.0
            instances           = 10
        }
```

This example specifies how we want to log attempts and connections, what to log on success and on failure, where connections should be allowed from, and how many simultaneous instances of each service should be allowed. The += operator allows you to split long lines into multiple lines. The purpose of each attribute and more details on what values can be used for each is presented in the next two sections.

In addition to the attributes shown in the example above, you can also use the *passenv*, *env*, *no_access*, and *disabled* commands in the default section.

All attributes in the default entry except `log_type` and `instances` can have values specified both in the defaults section and in a service entry; the two values are combined (even if both use the = operator, not just +=). The `log_type` and `instances` values specified in a service entry override the defaults value.

28.5.2 Access Restrictions

There are three directives used in *xinetd.conf* for primary access control. They control what hostnames or IP addresses have access at what times and which ones don't:

`only_from`
: Determines which hosts can access a particular service. Its value is a list of host names or IP addresses, which are specified in the "dotted decimal" IP notation.

  Complete addresses or wildcard addresses can be specified. Complete addresses allow individual systems to have access to a service. For example, 192.9.200.10 allows only this system access to a service. A zero (0) in one of the octets of the address is treated as a wildcard. If an address of 192.9.200.0 were used, then all systems in the 192.9.200.xxx network would have access to the service. This allows groups of systems to use the network services.

  A "factorized" address in the form of 192.9.200 or even 192.9, leaving out the remaining portions of the address, tells *xinetd* to fill in zeros for the missing octets, granting wildcard access to those networks. With this method, it is easier to scan the *xinetd.conf* file and see exactly who has access to each service.

`no_access`
: This attribute determines which hosts do not have access to a particular service. It can contain hostnames, IP addresses, and wildcards, just like `only_from`.

`access_times`
: This determines when a service is available. The format is HH:MM-HH:MM where HH are hours in 24-hour (military) format, and MM is minutes. As an example, to grant access only during normal business hours, put the following attribute in the service line:

```
access_times    08:00-17:00
```

  If this is not used and individual systems are not put in, then all hosts are allowed to use the service.

`disabled`
: This totally turns off a service and logging of attempts. Use of the `disabled` directive is not recommended, since you should at least log attempts, even of services you don't intend to print.

All these attributes can be specified on multiple lines. As an example, you can use multiple *only_from* lines in one service entry as shown in the previous section. This makes it easier to edit *xinetd.conf* since there won't be gigantic long commands.

28.5.3 Controlling Logging

Many break-ins require several attempts before a security "hole" is discovered. By logging all incoming attempts, even from systems you do not plan to give access to, you'll have advance warning about what is being tried, and where it's coming from. This can be of tremendous value. Many security break-ins could have been deterred if the administrators only knew that someone had been relentlessly trying for days or weeks leading up to the breach.

The general rule of thumb to follow is that all services of interest should be enabled, with the restriction that the only system authorized to connect is the local host (the firewall system itself). Therefore, any other system will receive a "connection refused" error, but some identifying information from the TCP/IP packet will be logged.

Three attributes control logging: `log_type`, `log_on_success`, and `log_on_failure`.

The `log_type` attribute determines where the service log output is sent. There are two possible formats:

`SYSLOG` The log output is sent to *syslog* at the specified facility. Possible facility names include: *daemon*, *auth*, *user*, and *local0-7*.

`FILE` The log output is appended to the specified file, which is created if it does not exist.

The `log_on_success` attribute determines what information is logged when a server is started successfully. Any combination of the following arguments may be specified:

`PID` This logs the server process ID. This is usually only useful for debugging a server.

`HOST` This logs the remote host address along with the service name.

`USERID` This tries to log the user ID of the remote user, using the RFC 1413 identification protocol. If either your system or the user's system does not support this RFC, no user ID is printed to the log file.

`EXIT` This logs the fact that a server exited. Along with the message, the return or exit code of the server is also printed. If a signal was sent to the server that caused it to close down, that signal ID is also logged. If the PID option is used, the PID of the server is placed in the EXIT line.

`DURATION` This logs the amount of time a particular service was used by a particular user. The amount of time logged is in minutes. Note that if you don't enable EXIT for logging, DURATION does not work.

The `log_on_failure` attribute determines what information is logged when a server cannot be started (either because of a lack of resources or because of access control restrictions). Any combination of the following values may be specified.

`HOST` Logs the remote hostname (or IP address if the hostname is not known to either the Domain Name Server or your */etc/hosts* file). This is useful for determining if someone is breaking into your system. If you have names for all authorized remote systems in the */etc/hosts* file, then any IP addresses appearing in the log file should be viewed with suspicion.

`USERID` Logs the user IDx of the remote user as per RFC 1413 as discussed above.

`ATTEMPT` Logs the fact that a failed attempt was made and why the attempt failed. An attempt is considered failed if the host or IP address is listed in a *no_access* line, or is not listed in any *access_only* line, or the time of connection is outside of the *access_time.* The name of the service is included in the log file (the service number is used if no name is in the */etc/services* file), along with the reason for failure.

`RECORD` Records information about the remote end in case the server could not be started. This is the companion to the ATTEMPT command. This allows further monitoring of attempts to use the service. For example, the login service logs the local user, remote user, and terminal type.

28.5.4 Setting Environment Variables

There are two attributes that allow you to specify environment variables to be set when *xinetd* invokes a service:

`env` Allows environment variables to be set up for the server before execution. The value of this attribute is a list of strings of the form `name=value`. These variables are made available to the server through the *passenv* command.

`passenv` The value of this attribute is the list of environment variables from *xinetd*'s environment that get passed to the server. This allows individual variables to be sent and not the entire environment inherited from the *xinetd* daemon. An empty list implies passing no environment variables to the server.

We don't use this feature in our configuration.

28.6 Managing xinetd

The day-to-day operation of *xinetd* doesn't require much attention other than checking the log files. Generally, the only other activity occurs when new services need to be added to the system or additional hosts need to be granted access to existing services.

28.6.1 Logging

Four kinds of logs are useful in monitoring *xinetd*'s operation, service usage and security; *xinetd*'s log specified on the command line, *xinetd*'s log specified in *xinetd.conf*, individual service logs, and the System log file.

28.6.1.1 The command-line specified log

The file pointed to from the command line shows when *xinetd* is started or restarted and what services are up and running:

```
94/7/6@08:11:47 xinetd[181]: NOTICE: Started working: 20 available services
94/7/6@09:03:15 xinetd[181]: NOTICE: Starting soft reconfiguration
94/7/6@09:03:20 xinetd[181]: NOTICE: readjusting service ftp
94/7/6@09:03:20 xinetd[181]: NOTICE: readjusting service telnet
94/7/6@09:03:20 xinetd[181]: NOTICE: readjusting service name
94/7/6@09:03:20 xinetd[181]: NOTICE: readjusting service shell
94/7/6@09:03:20 xinetd[181]: NOTICE: readjusting service login
94/7/6@09:03:20 xinetd[181]: NOTICE: readjusting service exec
94/7/6@09:03:20 xinetd[181]: NOTICE: readjusting service comsat
94/7/6@09:03:20 xinetd[181]: NOTICE: readjusting service talk
94/7/6@09:03:20 xinetd[181]: NOTICE: readjusting service netstat
94/7/6@09:03:20 xinetd[181]: NOTICE: readjusting service time-stream
94/7/6@09:03:20 xinetd[181]: NOTICE: readjusting service time-dgram
94/7/6@09:03:20 xinetd[181]: NOTICE: readjusting service echo-stream
94/7/6@09:03:20 xinetd[181]: NOTICE: readjusting service echo-dgram
94/7/6@09:03:20 xinetd[181]: NOTICE: readjusting service mountd
94/7/6@09:03:20 xinetd[181]: NOTICE: readjusting service rexd
94/7/6@09:03:20 xinetd[181]: NOTICE: readjusting service rquotad
94/7/6@09:03:20 xinetd[181]: NOTICE: readjusting service sprayd
```

28.6.1.2 The xinetd.log file

xinetd logs messages about all connections to the file specified with `log_type` in *xinetd.conf*. Each contains a timestamp and indicates the nature of each event. Exactly what is logged depends on how you set the log attributes in *xinetd.conf*. Primarily, the log entries consist of pairs of messages, indicating the start and end of a particular connection. Here's a sample:

```
94/7/18@13:05:29: START: www from=192.9.7.97
94/7/18@13:05:30: START: www from=127.0.0.1
94/7/18@13:05:30: EXIT: www status=202 duration=0(sec)
94/7/18@13:05:30: EXIT: www status=202 duration=1(sec)
94/7/18@13:05:43: START: socks from=192.9.11.21
94/7/18@13:05:45: EXIT: socks status=3 duration=2(sec)
94/7/18@13:05:50: START: socks from=192.9.11.21
94/7/18@13:05:50: START: www from=192.9.7.97
94/7/18@13:05:52: EXIT: www status=202 duration=2(sec)
94/7/18@13:06:10: START: www from=192.9.7.97
94/7/18@13:06:17: EXIT: www status=202 duration=7(sec)
94/7/18@13:06:19: EXIT: socks status=3 duration=29(sec)
94/7/18@13:06:44: EXIT: socks status=3 duration=118(sec)
94/7/18@13:06:47: EXIT: socks status=3 duration=149(sec)
94/7/18@13:08:47: EXIT: socks status=3 duration=223(sec)
```

For *xinetd* to be useful in maintaining system security over the long term, it's not enough to simply reject unauthorized connection attempts. That keeps the intruder out for a while, but it doesn't let you know about the attempted transgressions. It's not unlike having a disconnected phone number. The caller gets an error message, and the intended recipient (you) never even knows the call was placed.

In order to get detailed information about who may be trying to crack system security, you need to enable logging for the system services. This is like letting the phone call ring through and examining the Caller ID information. Since *xinetd* is listening to the service port, it receives information about the caller attached to the incoming service connection request, which can be logged.

28.6.1.3 System and service log files

Several of the system services routed through *xinetd* also create log entries, which can be correlated with *xinetd*'s logs. In particular, the *sendmail*, *ftpd*, and *socks* logs should be watched closely. These logs are usually found in one of these files:

- */usr/adm/messagesi*
- */var/log/syslogi*
- */usr/logs/syslog*
- */usr/spool/mqueue/syslog*

By altering the configuration of *syslogd* you can change where messages are logged. You can also route error messages into email and notify users elsewhere on your network of security violations.

28.6.2 Reconfiguration

When you alter the configuration information for *xinetd*, you can keep existing connections in place, or kill them all. Usually it's desirable to keep existing connections in place.

xinetd is notified to reread *xinetd.conf* without killing connections with the SIGUSR1 signal:

```
# ps -ax | grep xinetd
  175 ? IW    0:11 xinetd -filelog /usr/adm/xinetd.log
# kill -SIGUSR1 175
```

NOTE

Be sure not to use the SIGHUP signal (or the command *kill −1*), as you may be accustomed to for other daemons and servers. *xinetd* uses SIGHUP to terminate the daemon and uses SIGUSR1 to reconfigure it. This is by design. Anyone attempting to break in by "reconfiguring" *xinetd* itself is likely to try *kill -1 pid*, which causes a fatal error and core dump.

To force all existing connections to be terminated when a reconfiguration is performed, the signal SIGUSR2 can be used. *xinetd* kills off all servers it has started, rescans the *xinetd.conf* file, and then reinitializes itself.

28.6.3 Debugging

Once the configuration is in place and has stabilized, you'll often find the complaints that arise are simply caused by the restrictions that are in place. Since *xinetd* tends to "work until you break it," you may forget what some of the restrictions are. Then, when a user complains that a file cannot be browsed across the firewall system, you may not notice that it's outside the authorized time of day (for example).

Considerable time can be saved by always checking the log files as the first step. Any errors that arise due to authorization restrictions will be apparent in the logs. Since access to each service can be controlled independently, things can easily get confusing if restrictions are not maintained consistently. Allowing access to FTP during different hours of the day than Telnet could mean that time is wasted tracking down the cause of a user complaint.

You can generally identify the cause of most problems by logging everything. Looking through the log will give clues about which attempts were rejected and which were granted. If you encounter messages showing that a connection was honored, but you didn't get the desired results, a frequent cause is an improperly configured service daemon (not an *xinetd* problem). Often, either a bad pathname has been entered in the configuration for the service, in which case the service never gets launched, or the command-line arguments don't notify the server that the connection has already been established by *xinetd*. The server must not attempt to begin listening for inbound connections. It must be configured to service the single connection that is handed off from *xinetd* and then exit.

xinetd can be forced to generate a core dump by sending a SIGHUP signal. This can be useful in post-mortem debugging. It's unlikely that this feature will be needed, since *xinetd* has proven to be very robust in operation. But, since you have access to the source code, additional debugging information can be added if extreme measures are required.

28.7 How to Spot Security Break-Ins or Attempts

The log files should be checked every day and scanned for possible breakins or break-in attempts. Scanning for the string FAIL will catch nearly all messages of interest:

```
# grep "FAIL" /var/log/xinetd.log
94/8/9@18:10:22: FAIL: www time from=159.97.8.41
94/8/16@13:34:51: FAIL: socks address from=159.97.11.20
94/8/19@16:27:38: FAIL: telnet address from=199.227.15.16
94/8/19@16:27:46: FAIL: ftp address from=199.227.15.16
94/8/22@13:33:54: FAIL: telnet address from=129.171.32.32
```

Any suspicious messages should be investigated, to determine if there was a security breach. A periodic visual spot check should occasionally be done, looking in the log file for any evidence of tampering. Since it is possible for knowledgeable prowlers to alter the logs to cover their tracks, it's important to poke around intermittently.

A visual scan of the log files can uncover inconsistencies, such as large time gaps in log entries. This could indicate that a block of entries has been deleted from the log. Another sign could be a connection from a workstation known to be idle at that time (perhaps late at night, when the office is empty). This could be evidence of an outside system acting as an impostor to gain access to the network.

Creating a script using *grep*, *awk*, or *perl* that will periodically search through the log file and send you notification of suspicious log entries can save you some time. It can also help keep you apprised of problems and keep you from forgetting to check the logs on a regular basis.

28.7.1 Tracking Down a Culprit

The first thing to remember about invasions of your security is that the information that has been obtained by *xinetd* might have been forged. It all depends on how clever the aggressor is. For starters, though, you can identify the IP address where the attempt originated.

By using *whois*, you can find the "contact" person for the organization from which the intruder allegedly launched his attack. This will usually produce information like that below, including a technical contact person. You can call or send email, notifying them of the incident, and providing the information you obtained. This will assist someone at their end in tracking down the breach. Frequently, these attempts originate on college campuses, where security is fairly lax and it's relatively easy for a knowledgeable interloper to "hide" among multitudes of subnets and workstation addresses.

For example, the IP address of an intruder might be 198.112.208.89. Here's how to find out where that is:

```
% telnet rs.internic.net
Connected to rs.internic.net.
Escape character is '^]'.

SunOS UNIX (rs) (ttyqb)

InterNIC > whois 198.112.208
Connecting to the rs Database . . . . . .
Connected to the rs Database
NEARNET (NETBLK-NEARNET-C198)  NEARNET-C-BLOCK  198.112.0.0 -198.115.255.0
O'Reilly & Associates, Inc. (NETBLK-ORA) NETBLK-ORA▶▶▶
▶▶▶198.112.208.0 -198.112.211.0
```

This provides information about the IP address, indicating that it is `netblk-ora`, owned by O'Reilly & Associates. Further inquiry about `netblk-ora` will provide more detailed information about the company and who to contact for further information:

```
Whois: netblk-ora
O'Reilly & Associates, Inc. (NETBLK-ORA)
   90 Sherman Street
   Cambridge, MA 02140

   Netname: NETBLK-ORA
   Netblock: 198.112.208.0 - 198.112.211.0

   Coordinator:
      Herlick, Tanya  (TH55)  tanya@RUBY.ORA.COM
      (617) 354-5800 (617) 499-7459 (FAX) (617) 661-1116

   Domain System inverse mapping provided by:

   RUBY.ORA.COM                    198.112.208.25
   NIC.NEAR.NET                    192.52.71.4
   NOC.CERF.NET                    192.153.156.22

   Record last updated on 17-Feb-94.
```

Depending on the network address class, higher levels in the address hierarchy may produce results when the original attempt doesn't reveal anything.

One common technique for concealing identity is to obtain the IP address of a legitimate workstation during normal hours. Then, late at night, when that workstation is known to be powered-off (or disconnected from a dialup PPP link), a different node on the network can be configured to use the counterfeit IP address. To everyone on the network, it will appear that the "legitimate" user is active.

In this Chapter:
- *What's Allowed on the Internet?*
- *Intellectual Property Rights and Responsibilities*
- *Other Publishing Pitfalls*

29 Legal Issues

Managing an Internet information service of any kind is considered publishing from most legal standpoints. Whether or not you plan to publish on the Internet for profit, you should understand the legalities of general publishing, and some issues particular to Internet publishing. Here we cover only U.S.A. laws. If you're in another country, or are in the U.S., but will be serving information to other countries, what we say here may not apply.

In general, the laws provide some protection, and they impose responsibilities. For instance, publishing on the Internet, like publishing on paper, is speech, protected under the First Amendment to the U.S. Constitution. But there are limits: untrue malicious statements may be considered libel. Original work you produce is covered under copyright law, but those laws also require you to be careful when publishing other people's work, even work they have previously given away on the Internet. Copyright protection may be insufficient given the ease of copying electronic documents, so you may want to use encryption. But using encryption may involve issues such as patents, licensing fees, and strict export controls.

Even if you run a service where you allow people to supply information to other people but provide none of the information yourself, you may have some responsibility for assuring that the users break none of the above laws.

We're not pretending this single chapter is going to tell you all you need to know to protect yourself. We're not lawyers, and even if we were, much of the "law of the Internet" has yet to be written or decided by the courts. We hope to give you at least enough awareness of the law, though, so that you know when you're in potentially perilous legal territory and then can seek the advice of an attorney.

If you'd like more information on the legal issues surrounding electronic publishing, we highly recommend Lance Rose's *Syslaw*, (published by PC Information Group, Inc.) which primarily covers the issues that relate to bulletin board systems, but is still an excellent resource.

29.1 What's Allowed on the Internet?

Since the Internet is nothing but a confederation of many smaller networks, each of those networks can determine a policy for what is and is not allowed. These are usually called Acceptable Use Policies (AUPs). You can pick up a few of them via anonymous FTP from *nic.merit.edu* in */acceptable.use.policies.*

The problem is that the Internet is a dynamically routed network, so there is no way to control the path between your service and its customers. So, strictly speaking, the only way to honor all AUPs is to restrict your activities to what's allowed on the strictest network. Just finding out what that would mean is difficult–every AUP is worded differently.

In practical terms, the AUP that applies to you directly is the one determined by the company or organization that supplies your Internet connection. We think you should remind your customers that it is their responsibility to make sure that using your service would not violate the AUP of their connection provider.

The only other AUPs that are important to you are those of the major backbones of the Internet, the large networks that carry most of the traffic. Although there are already other competing commercial backbone networks like ANS and PSI, the NSFNET is the biggest; it is publically subsidized through National Science Foundation grants. Use of the NSFNET is governed by an AUP intended to restrict use of the network to that consistent with NSF's goals (research and education).

But the NSFNET backbone won't be around much longer. The Internet is already in the middle of a transition that will replace the NSFNET with a number of privately run "backbone suppliers." These will interconnect the various regional Internet providers to continue to provide full network connectivity. The NSFNET will be gone and with it the NSFNET AUP. The transition is due to be complete by May 1995, but most regional networks are expected to switch to using private backbone suppliers by November 1994.*

So as of May 1, 1995, there will be no U.S. government constraints on commercial traffic on almost all parts of the Internet. Even by November 1994, commercial traffic will be allowed on most parts of the Internet, and as a practical matter, no one is likely to be prosecuted for commercial use on any part during the transitional period.†

* The NSF still plans to fund a new part of the Internet to link scientific sites at very high speed, and the AUP will still apply on those links, but this new network won't be generally accessible.

† We're talking about responsible commercial use here. Egregious violations have been punished by cutting off network access. For example, an immigration lawyer posted an ad for his services in every newsgroup on the Internet. The message traversed every network including NSFNET, and clearly violated the NSFNET AUP. His network provider cut off his service. The lawyer and his provider also received a huge volume of complaints, suggesting that activities pushing the boundaries of acceptable use may give you a bad reputation in the Internet community.

While the NSFNET AUP looks like it prohibits use of the network for profit, it is actually interpreted more liberally. Stephen Wolff of the NSF explains that "the touchstone is utility to the research and education community. It doesn't matter if you charge for your service: you're charging not for the NSF-funded facilities which are provided to both you and your clientele, but rather for the value you have added to those facilities." So if your service is of potential use and interest to the research and education community, then its transport over the NSFNET backbone is sanctioned. If you'd like to see the NFSNET AUP, use anonymous FTP to go to *nic.merit.edu* and look in */acceptable.use.policies/nsfnet.txt.*

29.2 Intellectual Property Rights and Responsibilities

Even a free service could break the law if you give away other people's intellectual property without permission. Conversely, you may want to take steps to protect your own intellectual property. This section describes the kinds of legal protection that are available and how to use them.

The next chapter describes some of the non-legal means of protecting intellectual property.

29.2.1 Types of Intellectual Property Protection

There are four major types of intellectual property protection in the U.S.: patents, trade secrets, copyrights, and trademarks. Three of these have at least some bearing on a prospective Internet publisher. Trademarks won't affect many publishers, so we won't cover them here.

- Patents are chiefly used to protect new ideas: novel designs for rocket engines, better mousetraps, and the like. Since patents are in the public record at the U.S. Patent Office, you won't need to worry about divulging the contents of someone's patent.

  The one aspect of patent law that may be relevant is that some encryption algorithms that are useful in publishing are patented (in particular, the RSA public-key algorithm). Even though there are free implementations of RSA on the Internet, you can't use them for profit-making purposes without a license. We'll have more on using encryption to protect intellectual property in Chapter 30, *Protecting Intellectual Property.*

- Basically, trade secrets are information and processes, known only to you or your company, that give you competitive advantages over others. You don't have to file any forms or include any legal declarations to get a trade secret designated. It's enough to take precautions to ensure that your secret isn't compromised. If you do a reasonably good job of protecting your secret, you can sue Bad Guys who steal or acquire and try to use your secret.

If you're in the business of publishing information, there's an aspect of trade secrets that you should be conscious of: making sure you don't reveal other people's secrets. If, in publishing information gained or gleaned from another company or an employee of another company, you come across a particularly valuable tidbit, make sure that it isn't a trade secret. Even if the employee willingly put pen to paper and turned the secret over to you, an implied or actual contract between the employee and his employer could keep you from publishing it.

- Copyright is the form of intellectual property protection most useful to you as a publisher. Copyright gives the author of an original work the sole right to copy the work and sell it, adapt it, and display it. We'll say more about copyrights in Section 29.2.3.

The way to make sure you don't run afoul of any of these laws is to have a legal agreement with the source of your information.

29.2.2 The Publishing Agreement

It's a good idea for any publisher to have a written agreement with people providing information (authors or other sources) in which the authors certify that they have the right to publish the material they submit. Here is the type of paragraph you might use:

> *The author warrants and represents that the work is original; that the author is either its sole author, or that he or she has the legal power to make this agreement if there are co-authors and that he or she has notified the co-authors of this agreement; and that the work doesn't impair anyone else's rights of any kind. The author agrees to indemnify O'Reilly & Associates, and its officers, employees, agents, and licensees and distributees, against loss or damage (including reasonable attorney's fees) arising out of any claim alleging a breach of these warranties and representations.*

The agreement should have other clauses spelling out who owns the copyright and exactly what publishing rights are being assigned and for how long.

29.2.3 Copyrights

If you're writing wonderful short stories and selling them over the Net, then copyright protection is what prevents your customers from legally emailing duplicates to their friends and relatives.

The following sections describe how to protect your own copyrights and honor those of others.

29.2.3.1 Creation of a copyright

A copyright is automatically created at the time you create an original work. There's no extra effort necessary: you write it, you own the copyright. There are certain exceptions to this, though. A work produced as part of your obligation to an employer, called a "work-for-hire," becomes the property of the employer. And, of course, a contract may affect the ownership: if your consulting contract with Some Enormous Faceless Transnational, Inc., stipulates that any output you produce as a result of your work under the contract is their intellectual property; they own the copyright.

Though the creation of a copyright is automatic, there are useful measures to take to protect your copyright. One of the most familiar is to include a copyright notice in a prominent place in your work. That copyright notice alerts others to the existence of your copyright and warns them against duplication or other use of your work without your consent. The form of a standard copyright notice is pretty simple: you begin with the word "Copyright," followed by the familiar © symbol (the letter c in a circle), then the year of publication and your name.* If there are multiple authors, their names should all be included. If a company owns the copyright, use the company's name. To ensure protection under certain countries' copyright laws, you should also include the phrase "All Rights Reserved" after the copyright notice. Here's an example:

```
Copyright © 1994 O'Reilly & Associates Inc. All rights reserved.
```

Copyright law is even generous enough to provide copyright protection for your work if you forget to include a copyright notice. As long as you make a good-faith effort to remedy the situation by trying to update all the copies of the work that snuck out without the notice and by registering the copyright within five years of the sneaking, your copyright is still valid. However, folks who violated the copyright because their copies of the work didn't have the appropriate notice probably won't be liable for their violations.

If you use a copyright notice on a work, you must submit two copies of that work to the U.S. Copyright Office within three months of the date of first publication. These copies go into the public record and can be very useful in proving later copyright violations. (Particularly if you submit copies *before* publication, since this proves without a doubt that you own the copyright, and aren't some clever miscreant dashing off to copyright some unknowing publisher's latest work.)

29.2.3.2 Lifetime of a copyright

New copyrights last until 50 years after the author's death (or 50 years after the last author's death, if there are multiple authors). If the copyright is owned by a company, the copyright lasts 75 years from the work's first publication or 100 years from the work's creation, whichever is shorter. That's a long time.

* Actually, either the © or the word "Copyright" or even the abbreviation "Copr" should be sufficient to indicate your copyright, but to gain full copyright protection under the Universal Copyright Convention, use © and "Copyright." This will make your copyright easier to enforce in foreign countries.

29.2.3.3 Registering copyrights

To gain maximum protection for your work, you should register your copyright. Registration is actually a surprisingly simple process. You've already done half the work if you've submitted the required two copies of your work to the Copyright Office. What's left is to fill out the appropriate form and submit it to the Copyright Office. The form you need depends on the type of work you want to register. Pick up a good book on registering copyrights at the bookstore or library for detailed instructions, or write the Copyright Office for the form and for instructions.

What does registering your copyright buy you? Primarily, it allows you to sue someone for infringing upon your copyright. Unless you register it, you can't protect or enforce your copyright, even though the copyright exists from the time you wrote the work. You can actually wait until someone violates your copyright to register and then sue, but there are advantages to registering early. If you register within three months of your work's publication, you can sue for statutory damages and legal fees. If you miss the deadline, you can only sue for actual damages, which can be more difficult to prove in borderline cases. The following documents might be helpful to you:

Copyright Basics (Circular 1)
Copyright Law of the United States of America (Circular 92)
Copyright Notice (Circular 3)
Copyright Registration for Automated Databases (Circular 65)
Copyright Registration for Computer Programs (Circular 61)
Copyright Registration for Multimedia Works (Circular 55)
Duration of Copyright (Circular 15a)
International Copyright Conventions (Circular 38c)
International Copyright Relations of the United States (Circular 38a)

The Library of Congress has an Internet Gopher server that makes quite a few of these circulars available. Point your Gopher client at *marvel.loc.gov* or aim your Web browser at the URL *gopher://marvel.loc.gov/11/copyright* to get them.

The address of the Copyright Office, for requesting forms and the circulars listed above, is:

Copyright Office
Information and Publications Section
Library of Congress
Washington, DC 20559

29.2.3.4 Respecting other's copyrights

As a broker of information, it's also critically important that you respect other people's copyrights. Make sure that the material you make available isn't copyrighted, or, if it has a clear copyright notice, take care to get written permission to use the material. Heck, on the Internet, publishing is still such a novelty—and people who pay attention to copyrights even more so—that many authors would probably be thrilled just to have you ask permission.

Even if there is no copyright notice in something given away free on the Internet, ask for permission.

29.2.3.5 Fair use

Some of you may be familiar with the concept of "Fair Use" in copyright law. Some people misconstrue "Fair Use" to mean that they can make use of a work as long as they don't use too much of it, or attribute the portion they use, or paraphrase part of the work.

Actually, "Fair Use" is very limited. Essentially, "Fair Use" allows educators to make copies of certain works for instructional purposes without expressed permission from the copyright holder and lets critics quote works in commentary. It normally doesn't apply to commercial use of copyrighted material.

29.3 Other Publishing Pitfalls

If you provide a service that allows members of the public to provide information to each other, it's a gray area whether or not you can be held liable for the contents. For example, if you host a moderated discussion group, you need to make sure you don't "publish" libelous statements. By moderating that discussion, you have perhaps taken on partial responsibility for its content. If you run an FTP archive that allows anyone to anonymously upload information (for others to download), you should watch out for pornography, bootlegged commercial software, or encryption software.

29.3.1 Libel

Libel is not a potential problem for every Internet publisher: you may have no interest in writing an Internet gossip column or in becoming the next hypermedia Geraldo. Still, the penalties for libel are severe enough to warrant a brief mention of them here.

Libel is defamation in writing. Unfortunately, libel is an area where new court opinions are constantly changing the legal landscape. But there are key elements to proving libel. The first requirement to proving a libel case is proving that the alleged libelous statements are false. Unless they're false, there's no case. The statements must also be damaging, not just embarrassing or infuriating to the subject. And the statements must also be published, rather than simply written down in your notes.

The law also treats public figures and public officials differently than private persons where libel is concerned. In the case of alleged libel against public figures, such as celebrities or public officials, like governors or presidents, many courts demand that you prove that the publisher was actually aware that what he published was false when he published it, or at least was grossly negligent in not verifying the facts.

As a publisher, you should exercise caution in what you print when there's the potential that it will cause another harm. At the very least, make sure your sources are good and your facts straight.

29.3.2 Pornography

Pornography is illegal in certain states and countries. In particular, child pornography has a high likelihood of getting you in trouble, even if someone else places such pictures on your archive and you have nothing to do with it. Know what's in your archive.

29.3.3 Bootlegged Commercial Software

Similarly, people may try to use your public FTP site to distribute illegal copies of commercial software. You need to keep an eye out for bootlegging and prohibit it at your FTP site.

29.3.4 Encryption Software

The U.S. government considers Internet publishing to be equivalent to export if you allow people to transfer files from your machine to overseas machines. As we'll explain later, export of most encryption software from the U.S. is illegal, even though the same software may be freely available overseas. If you need to have such software in your archive, you should take precautions to assure that users know about the law; you might even want to require preregistration. Precautions like these are possible (although in some cases cumbersome) with the security mechanisms many of the information servers we describe provide.

In this Chapter:
- *Non-Cryptographic Approaches*
- *Cryptographic Approaches*
- *Export Controls on Encryption*

30

Protecting Intellectual Property

Protecting your intellectual property is important, especially if you're running a service for profit. But it's a thorny problem. Most copyright law was established when duplication of a work was a tedious process (think of monks transcribing the Great Works for posterity, or at least the old offset printing process used to produce books), not worth the trouble when you could get a legitimate copy of the work by purchasing it. In the late days of the twentieth century, though, when duplicating someone's online ASCII copy of *Ulysses* takes a dozen keystrokes, it's trivial to make copies of copyrighted material and much cheaper than acquiring that material through legitimate means.

Not only is illegal copying easy, but the reach and breadth of the Internet make it very difficult to enforce copyrights and other legal rights. If someone in Taipei or Bangalore swipes a copy of your precious database and starts offering it up for free, you may have very little recourse but to mail out nastygrams and lobby to get them ostracized from the Internet community. Good luck getting the local authorities to shut them down. Copyright enforcement is notoriously weak in some parts of the world. Just understanding the laws in all countries worldwide is a huge endeavor.

There are several approaches to solving these problems. We'll divide them up into those that don't use cryptography and those that do.

30.1 Non-Cryptographic Approaches

Sometimes the best way to deal with the difficulty in enforcing your copyright is not to rely on the law. After all, the services you offer are not equivalent to the data you broker. In most cases, you provide value in the organization of the data—the links in your hypertext documents, the structure of your menus, or the description files you created to help index your binary files. Even if someone swipes most of your data, you can make it difficult to steal the "meta-information" that describes and organizes your data.

If your data is intended for a small audience who will pay a lot for it, they will guard it themselves. Or if the part of your data that an individual customer gets is small and specialized enough, you may have no problem with redistribution. For example, the commercial database services, like DIALOG, while stating that redistribution is copyright infringement, charge enough to cover the inevitable redistribution of the small pieces of data customers can afford to download. No one could afford to download the entire database piece by piece. However, this forces them to charge a high price for their service, and consequently, their market is limited—only businesses can afford it. The commercial services also have the advantage that businesses try to follow the rules to avoid legal complications.

The currency and timeliness of your data make it valuable, too. If the useful life of your data is very short (measured in minutes or hours), you may be able to distribute it more freely. Anything longer than that and Internet distribution can have it all over the planet. Say you live near the freeway and don't get out much, so you decide to offer up-to-the-minute traffic updates over the Internet. That data isn't worth much if it's more than fifteen minutes old (longer in L.A.), so it probably won't hurt much if some miscreant buys one traffic report and tries to pawn it off to the Internet underground. By the time it hits the streets, it'll be old news.

You can also add value by offering enhanced functionality that users can't get from standard servers. Plexus, for example, a Web server written in Perl, is easy to customize and extend to handle new data types, offer custom searching, and more. The NCSA *httpd* lets you write custom scripts to provide new functionality. While a would-be knock-off artist might snag your HTML files and other data, he can't get your custom server.

That said, you *can* try to sue someone for copyright infringement on the Internet, and in fact, you may feel like you deserve to if you went to the trouble of adding appropriate notice to your works and registering your copyright. Our best advice here is to seek out the counsel of a lawyer with a solid understanding of intellectual property law to advise you on your options.

30.2 Cryptographic Approaches

Cryptography offers a technical approach to copyright protection. Strong cryptographic algorithms can help an electronic publisher regain the edge that the printing press publishers had before copy machines: they can make it more convenient for the customer to purchase a work than purloin it. And that's really all that's necessary—the encryption used need not be unbreakable, just difficult enough so that the cost of breaking it exceeds the cost of acquiring the data through legitimate means.

First, we'll give you some background on encryption. This will be useful both in deciding how to protect your intellectual property, and in understanding the future developments in commercial use of Internet services. Various companies are now incorporating encryption into commercial versions of some Internet services.

30.2.1 Some Background on Encryption

There are two basic kinds of cryptography: secret-key and public-key. These and the "hash function" are the concepts you need to know to understand how cryptography works.

Secret-key cryptography relies on the sender and receiver of a message knowing and using the same secret key: the sender uses the secret key to encrypt the message, and the receiver uses the same secret key to decrypt the message. One example of a secret-key algorithm is DES, the U.S. government's Data Encryption Standard. There are many secret-key algorithms, and code for lots of them is available free on the Internet (although with U.S. government-imposed export restrictions).

The generation, transmission, and storage of keys is called *key management*. Key management is central to the security of all cryptosystems, since divulging a secret key can compromise encrypted data. A major problem with secret-key encryption systems is allowing the sender and receiver to exchange a secret key without anyone else discovering the key. If the sender and receiver are in separate physical locations, they must trust a phone system (or a courier or the Internet) not to disclose the secret key being communicated. Anyone who overhears or intercepts the key in transit can later read all messages encrypted using that key.

Public-key cryptography solves the transmission part of the key management problem. Each person generates a pair of keys, called the public key and the private key. Each person's public key is published, while the private key is kept secret. The sender and receiver don't need to share secret information: all communication involves only public keys. It isn't necessary to trust a communications channel to be secure against eavesdropping. Anyone can send a confidential message just using public information, but it can only be decrypted with a private key that is in the sole possession of the intended recipient.

Public-key encryption is a patented technology with code available free on the Internet for non-commercial use. For commercial use, however, you need a license from RSA Data Security, Inc. "RSA" is also the name of one public-key encryption algorithm they license. PGP, for "Pretty Good Privacy," is software that implements the RSA algorithm *and* is free under the GNU Public License. But PGP may violate RSA's intellectual property rights, because it uses RSA-patented technology without a license.* PEM (Privacy Enhanced Mail) is a free (for non-commercial use) implementation of the MH mail handling system, modified to support public-key encryption and digital signatures. Commercial users must license PEM from Trusted Information Systems, Inc.

The way people talk about public-key encryption, you'd think it cured the common cold. While it is an essential technology for building a commercial infrastructure on the Internet, it's not by itself the whole infrastructure. As mentioned above, its security

* The latest version of PGP, 2.6, may solve this problem. MIT, which with Stanford originally licensed the RSA public-key algorithm, produced this version expressly for non-commercial use by U.S. citizens. For more information, see O'Reilly & Associates' *PGP: Pretty Good Privacy.*

depends on the security of the generation and storage of keys, both of which tend to depend on the security features built into computer operating systems (which have various weaknesses). Also, for widespread use it requires a bureaucracy to certify that a particular public key is the one used by a particular person (this is called a Certificate Authority).* For Certificate Authorities to be reliable, you need another level of bureaucracy to certify the authorities. These Certificate Authorities are operating on a very small scale at present. In addition, you need a system for cancelling the validity of any public key (by notifying the world) when a private key's secrecy is breached (such as after a computer break-in). Also, keys must expire periodically to avoid the possibility of someone's cracking a private key using supercomputers. Many of these capabilities are technically difficult to implement without opening additional security holes.

Most importantly, public-key cryptography doesn't replace secret-key cryptography. Here are some of the reasons:

- Public-key cryptography's only advantage is avoiding key transmission. There are many applications where this isn't an issue. The book browser application, described later, is a good example.
- Public-key cryptography is 100 times slower than secret-key algorithms (10,000 times when both are implemented in hardware). That's why practical systems use public-key cryptography to exchange a secret key, then use secret-key cryptography to pass bulk messages.
- Public-key has the same key-storage vulnerability as secret-key.
- Public-key encryption software is never exportable. You can get export permission for some types of secret-key encryption.
- For commercial use, public-key requires licensing. There are many free secret-key algorithms.

Both kinds of cryptography can also be used for authentication: verifying that people are who they say they are. MIT's Kerberos system, for example, uses secret-key encryption to provide strong authentication.

But public-key cryptography can also be used to create digital signatures. A digital signature is like a written signature in concept, in that it proves your identity, except that if someone gets your private key they can forge it perfectly. Legally binding digital signatures depend on the Certificate Authorities and cancellation systems mentioned earlier, and additional infrastructure including a secure digital timestamping service and solutions to other time-based problems. (How do you verify a signature that was based on a key that expired 15 years ago? In that much time, a computer might have cracked the code and created a perfect forgery.)

You'll also see mention of "hash" functions. Digital signatures and some practical encryption systems depend on the ability to combine a large amount of information

* Otherwise I could create a key pair, send them around pretending to be you, then wait for someone to use the fake public key.

into a small number called a "hash." The hash is always the same size regardless of the amount of source information. A cryptographic hash function does this in such a way that you can't recover any of the information from the hash, and it is impractical to find any other text which hashes to the same value. A hash is used the same way at both ends of a secure transmission, basically as a fancy checksum, to assure that data has not been modified somewhere en route. The most common free hash function is MD5. It is considered secure enough that RSA digital signatures are based on it. Hash functions are useful in generating keys to enable particular customers to open encrypted documents only on a particular system.

30.2.2 A Practical Example of Encryption Issues

The publisher of this book, O'Reilly & Associates (ORA), has been working on a way to present its books online. Since the online product hasn't been released yet, the approach we describe may not be the final approach used, and there may be unforeseen problems with it. Nonetheless, it provides a good touchstone for discussing the issues.

O'Reilly books are an example of data that have a high value and don't change very quickly. They may be read in a networked environment where there might be hundreds or thousands (and if put on the Internet, millions) of people who can access a single copy of the books. Therefore, O'Reilly needs a means of charging based on some measure of the number of people who use a book.

ORA wants users to use a browser with World Wide Web capabilities for book reading, so that updates and associated documents and services can be linked in. However, because the books are big—megabytes each including figures—direct access through an Internet WWW server isn't an option. It would take far too long to load an entire book, or even a chapter, and moving around in a book that way would be painfully slow on all but the fastest Internet links. So due to the size problem, distribution can be by CD-ROM or over the Internet, but viewing will be off the CD-ROM or local disk. Providers of less voluminous data can use the same procedure, except they should be able to provide the encrypted data directly from an Internet WWW server.

Some of the goals for the access-control technique are that it:

- Work for files on disk, CD-ROM, or data off the Internet
- Provide good performance
- Be suitable for general publishing
- Be convenient to install and administer
- Be legally exportable from the U.S., if at all possible
- Support PCs and Macs in the future

As we said before, the mechanism need not be impregnable: just good enough that it's more convenient to comply than to cheat.

We considered various forms of honor-system licensing. The Simple License Manager used by Pure Software, Inc., logs uses of the product to a file and the administrator reads this file to determine how many licenses should be purchased. But Pure Software has only three products selling for thousands of dollars each; O'Reilly has at least 75 books selling for very little each. It is too much to expect of the administrator to monitor the changing demands for each O'Reilly book. But the most compelling disadvantages are simply that honor licensing isn't secure enough and doesn't allow the flexibility of distribution that encryption allows. With encryption, ORA can provide free trial access to encrypted copies of the books if it desires. UNIX computer manufacturers could include encrypted copies of O'Reilly books on CD-ROM or on disk. The manufacturers could buy access to certain books for their customers by providing coupons exchangeable for keys. ORA could also make the encrypted books available for FTP on the Internet.

Commercial software license managers are also available. However, we judged them not suitable without modification, because licensing a program is actually quite different from licensing a book. The difference is that a program is either allowed to run or not allowed to run. A book browser must be able to run anytime, but only allow the opening of books (actually, the many files that comprise a book) for which licenses have been purchased. Also, book licensing demands faster decryption than software licensing, since users open and close book chapters more often than they start licensed programs.

Those were the considerations that led us to encryption. However, there were more questions to answer: which kind of encryption should we use, and how? How widely could we use it? As an Internet publisher, you'll need to understand these issues, too.

30.2.3 Encryption in a Book Browser

The encryption and reading of an electronic book could work something like this. O'Reilly encrypts the documents using secret-key encryption. For optimal performance the user copies the documents off the Internet (or a CD) onto her local disk (the files are still encrypted after installation).

The user calls O'Reilly (or sends email) to purchase access to a book on the disk. The user must tell O'Reilly some piece of machine-readable information that identifies her system or location. We'll assume for now this is the DISPLAY variable for the X server on which the books will be viewed. It could also be any machine-readable data like a username or hostname.

The O'Reilly customer-service person (or email-response program) runs a program to mathematically combine this DISPLAY variable, the book codes of the desired books, and the secret key to generate a password. The process of combining the information employs a cryptographic hash function like MD5, so that the secret key can't be extracted from the password even when the other information is known. After payment by credit card, the customer is given this password to store in a file. One password may represent one book, or a set of books, and one DISPLAY or a whole list of DISPLAY variables.

Books are viewed in a World Wide Web browser (such as Mosaic), modified to include decryption features. The browser is allowed to run normally, and read normal WWW documents freely. But when it opens a file with the ORA book header, it checks the password (read from the password file) to see if this book is licensed. (It performs the same password-generation calculation that the O'Reilly customer-service program did and compares results.) If the license is valid, it decrypts the book and presents it in the viewer. Some features of the viewer are disabled to prevent dumping of the entire decrypted book text to a file.

With the addition of a separate network license manager program (modified to support book licensing), a customer can buy an "N simultaneous user" license instead of the DISPLAY license. In this case, the license manager reads the password file.

The encryption algorithm O'Reilly has chosen is MDC, a public-domain algorithm developed by Peter Gutmann. It is very fast, secure, a free implementation is available, and it supports variable key size, which is useful for getting export permission.* It is based on MD5, the hash algorithm on which RSA digital signatures are based. According to the book *Applied Cryptography* by Bruce Shneier, it is as secure as MD5. Another possibility is RC4, which can be licensed from RSA. The advantage of RC4 is that RSA has arranged for simplified export approval procedures, while the disadvantage is that it requires license fees. DES was another possibility, but was deemed too slow.

There are two major weaknesses to the scheme described above. One is that the browser has the secret key in it (although hidden), which a good programmer could find by decompiling and reverse-engineering the code. The second is that after decryption, raw text is used by the browser. A programmer may be able to modify the program to dump this to a file.

The actual encryption, therefore, is not the difficult part of this system to develop. What's crucial is the implementation of the security features in the browser.

30.3 Export Controls on Encryption

We've already mentioned exportability as an issue with many encryption algorithms; it's time to give you some of the nasty details. Most encryption algorithms, like the U.S. government's Data Encryption Standard (DES), are prohibited from export outside of the U.S. without the government's approval. Even though the DES algorithm has been *published* by the U.S. government in a Federal Information Processing Standard publication and many implementations are floating around the Internet in places like Finland, it's still considered illegal to export an implementation of DES. (Does this sound

* You're more likely to be able to export an algorithm that uses a small key size, since encryption with small keys is easier for the National Security Agency to break.

like locking the barn door after the horses are all gone?) In fact, exporting an implementation of an encryption algorithm is legally equivalent to exporting munitions, which means that the penalties are severe.

What can you do? Well, first of all, export of encryption software from the U.S. is possible if you apply to the Department of State's Office of Defense Trade Controls or the Department of Commerce's Bureau of Export Administration. Depending on the facts of the case, like how the encryption is being used, you'll deal with one or the other. And it's not impossible to gain the government's approval for the export of software that includes encryption functionality for certain applications. For example, some use of encryption algorithms for authentication only (that is, no encryption, just proving you are who you say you are) has been approved for export. If your code can only be used to decrypt documents you've encrypted, and won't function as a general-purpose encryption and decryption engine that a hostile foreign power could use to hide their evil thoughts and deeds from Uncle Sam's watchful eye, then you may have a strong argument for export. Some encryption algorithms with small key sizes are routinely approved for export. Our best advice is this: before exporting *anything*, seek the advice of an attorney familiar with export controls.

In this Appendix:
- *Defaults*
- *The Options—an Overview*
- *The Options—Explained*

gopherd Options

Chapter 11, *Gopher: Managing the Server*, describes the command-line option combinations that most sites should use. This appendix lists all of the options for reference, including some not mentioned in the chapters. First, we'll take a quick look at the options and then we'll go into a detailed explanation of each one.

The syntax of *gopherd* is as follows:

```
gopherd [-CcDI][-o optionfile] [-L loadavg] [-l logfile] [-o optionfile]
        [-u userid] [-U uid] Datadir Port
```

A.1 Defaults

If *gopherd* is run without any options, here are the effects:

Table A-1: gopherd Default Options

Option	Description	Default
-C	Directories cached	Yes
-c	`chroot()`ed	Yes
-D	Debugging enabled	No
-I	Running from *inetd*	No
-L loadavg	Load average maximum	Default compiled in (if enabled)
-l logfile	Logfile	None
-o optionfile	Configuration file	Default compiled in
-u, -U user	Run as user	User *gopherd* was started as, normally *root* (bad!)
Datadir	Data directory	Default compiled in
Port	Port number	Default compiled in

A.2 The Options—an Overview

–c Tells *gopherd* not to `chroot()` the Gopher data directory

–C Disables the server's directory caching

–D Enables debugging output

–I Needed if *gopherd* is started from *inetd*

–l logfile
Specifies a file to which *gopherd* logs every connection

–L loadavg
Specifies the load average at which *gopherd* stops serving data

–o optionfile
Specifies an alternate *gopherd* configuration file

–u login-name
Runs *gopherd* as the user specified by the given login name

–U uid Runs *gopherd* as the user specified by the given numeric user ID. Note: this feature has been removed from Gopher 2.x.

data-directory
Specifies an alternate Gopher data directory

port-number
Specifies an alternate Gopher port number

A.3 The Options—Explained

It's time to go into the gory details of each option. Here we go...

A.3.1 Disable chroot() (-c)

The *–c* option disables the server from `chroot()`ing at the Gopher data directory. Not recommended for public access Gopher servers.

By default (without *–c*) *gopherd* uses the `chroot()` system call to force the Gopher data directory to become the root directory for the *gopherd* process. This is a major security feature. When `chroot()`ed, it is impossible for the Gopher server to access any files outside of the Gopher data directory. This way, if there are any unknown bugs in *gopherd*, the bug will not allow the intruder access to any directories other than the Gopher data directory.

A.3.2 Disable Directory Caching (-C)

By default, *gopherd* caches directories. It works like this: when the server gets a request for a directory, it checks for a file named *.cache* in that directory. This cache file is only good for a specific length of time. With Gopher 1.x, this amount of time is specified by the `CACHE_TIME` setting in the *conf.h* file and is compiled into the server. With Gopher 2.x, it's specified by the `cachetime` token in the *gopherd.conf* file. If it finds that the cache file is less than `CACHE_TIME` seconds old, it sends the data in the file to the client. If the cache is older than `CACHE_TIME` seconds, or if a *.cache* file doesn't exist, it parses the contents of the directory, sends its information to the requester, and stores the newly gathered data in the *.cache* file for future use.

The *–C* option forces the server *not* to use existing cache files and forces it *not* to create any new cache files. It's useful to turn off caching when testing or adding data to your server. With caching turned off, you don't have to wait for cache files to expire before seeing changes you've made to any menu items.

A.3.3 Enable Debugging Output (-D)

The *–D* option enables some debugging output from the server. The *–D* option is useful for testing purposes, if you're stuck trying to figure out what's gone wrong. It's the most useful when you're trying to figure out problems related to indexing, FTP links, and host access.

A.3.4 Running Under inetd (-I)

If you're running *gopherd* from within *inetd*, then you *must* use this flag. It tells *gopherd* that it should run as a one-time process, rather than starting itself up as a daemon to listen to the Gopher port and spawn children to deal with connections. *inetd* will be listening and spawning *gopherds* instead.

Make sure that the *inetd* flag is *first* on the command line. Once *gopherd* knows that it's running from *inetd*, it won't spit out any of the warnings and information that it normally does upon startup. If the *–I* isn't placed first, startup text from *gopherd* gets sent to the *gopher* client, confusing the client to no end.

A.3.5 Log to a File (-l logfile)

When using the *–l* flag, *gopherd* logs each and every connection made to it in the specified file. Note that the log file must be writable by the user that *gopherd* was started as. Under Gopher 2.x, if `cwsyslog` is specified as the *logfile*, then logging is done via *syslog*, to the `daemon.info` logging facility. We recommend against using this feature, as many other system daemons log information to *syslog*'s `daemon.info` facility. It would be fairly cumbersome to extract the Gopher log information from the *syslog* file.

Logs can often be handy in figuring out what people like the most about your Gopher service. Several log analyzers are available; see Section 11.5.1.

Note that even if you're running *gopherd* `chroot()`ed, the `logfile` is still relative to the root of your normal filesystem. *gopherd* opens up the log file for appending before it `chroot()`s the server.

A.3.6 Load Average (-L loadavg)

If you've compiled *gopherd* with the LOADRESTRICT option enabled, then setting this switch sets the load at which *gopherd* stops serving data (overriding the value compiled in with the MAXLOAD variable in *conf.h*). When it reaches the maximum load, it sends the error message "System Load Too High" to the client instead of sending the requested data. See Section 10.2.1.2 for more information about compiling load restrictions into the server.

A.3.7 Alternate gopherd Configuration File (-o optionfile)

By default, *gopherd* uses the configuration file *gopherd.conf* that's stored in the *SERVERDIR* directory (as specified in *Makefile.config*). This command-line option lets you override the default, selecting an alternative *gopherd* configuration file. This is handy if you run more than one Gopher server with different access permissions on the same machine—you can have a unique configuration for each one.

A.3.8 Run As a Specific Login-name (-u login-name)

When using this option, *gopherd* runs as the user you specify. This option can only be used when the server is started as *root*. A good candidate for use with this option is the user *nobody*. Alternatively, you may decide to create a new user (perhaps with the login name *gopher*) and run the server under this login.

It's important to understand the difference between *starting* the daemon as *root* and *running* the daemon as *root*. Once the daemon has bound to the Gopher port, it can change to a different user if you use the *-u* or *-U* option.

This option is a security feature. Letting *gopherd* run as *root* is *not* a good idea. If there are any bugs in *gopherd* that might let an intruder have access to files other than the Gopher data files, it would be better to let a nonprivileged user, such as *nobody*, browse around, rather than the user *root*!

A.3.9 Run Under Specific User ID (-U uid)

This option has the same effects as the *-u* option, except that instead of using a login name, you use a UID (User ID). The UID is generally the third field in a password file entry. You should use either the *-u* or *-U* option, not both. Note: this feature has been removed from Gopher 2.x.

A.3.10 The Data Directory (data-directory)

You can override the default data directory that was compiled into *gopherd* by specifying the directory on the command line after all command-line options. Note that this directory (like all other Gopher subdirectories) must be both readable and executable by the user that *gopherd* runs as.

A.3.11 port-number

You can override the default Gopher port that was compiled into *gopherd* by specifying an alternative port number on the command line after the *data-directory*. In order to use an alternative port, you *must also* specify the *data-directory* on the command line. In order to use port numbers 1024 or less, the server must be started as *root*. These ports are considered "privileged," and can only be accessed by the user *root*. If you cannot start the server as *root*, then you have to specify a port above 1024 to use.

In this Appendix:
- *Setting an FTP gateway*
- *Client Security Options*
- *Setting Client Commands*
- *Using Downloading in the Client*

Gopher: Client Compilation Options

This appendix describes some variables in the *conf.h* configuration file that may need to be modified to use the Gopher curses client correctly.

B.1 Setting an FTP gateway

+ The two lines that read:

```
#define AFTP_HOST "gopher-gw.micro.umn.edu"
#define AFTP_PORT 70
```

are used to set an FTP gateway. Normally, they should be set to your Gopher server's hostname and port number. This allows the client to use the *f* command, enabling the user to open an anonymous FTP session to a host that they specify. This client feature is fairly powerful—Gopher can be used to access anonymous FTP sites instead of the normal (cumbersome) UNIX *ftp* client.

B.2 Client Security Options

+ There are two client security options that can be defined. These are the *DELETE_BOOKMARKS_ONLY* and *SECURE_MAPS_GLOBALRC_ONLY* options; both of these security features only come into use if the client is started in secure mode.

The bookmarks security feature makes the client only able to delete bookmarks and not menu items (menu-item removal does *not* actually remove the physical file—it just removes the item from the current client's menu). This feature is handy if the client is available for public use.

The *SECURE_MAPS_GLOBALRC_ONLY* only allows the client to set its application-viewers from the *globalrc* file (usually */usr/local/lib/gopherglobal.rc*). The client cannot add or change viewers. In version 2.016, this feature is broken.

B.3 Setting Client Commands

The majority of the rest of the *conf.h* file is dedicated to setting commands that the *gopher* client executes to process data it receives. Each command name set here should include the full pathname of the command. If you don't specify full pathnames, then the user's search path is used to locate the command. This could have undesirable effects. For instance, if your IMAGE_COMMAND is set to *xv* (an image viewer) and the user running the Gopher client doesn't have a program called *xv* in his path, he'll never be able to view images. So, if you're going to use the program *xv* as your image viewer, your IMAGE_COMMAND variable should be set to */usr/local/bin/xv* (or whatever the full pathname of the *xv* command is). This way, you're assured that the correct program is run every time. If a command does not exist on the system, *gopher* complains when it tries to execute the command:

```
sh: xv: No such file or directory
```

However, this flies by so quickly that it's hard to catch. Make sure that you have these commands on your system.

+ In the Gopher 2.x version, there is a whole section of the *conf.h* file dedicated to client commands on a VMS system. Make sure to skip over this section unless you're compiling Gopher on a VMS system.

Here is a list of the command variables in *conf.h* and when they're used:

PAGER_COMMAND
: Used to display text files one page at a time. With Gopher 2.x, you can set this to *builtin* to use a pager that's compiled into the *gopher* client, instead of calling an external pager command. This is recommended for public Gopher clients, since external pagers like *more* and *less* allow shell escapes, which are a security risk.

MAIL_COMMAND
: Used to mail text files from within the Gopher client. Beware—some operating systems have more than one *mail* command. For example, SunOS and Solaris have both */bin/mail* and */usr/ucb/mail*. On Suns and most other systems, you want to use */bin/mail*—the version of *mail* that does *not* interpret ~ (tilde) escapes. The reason is that if you use a version of *mail* that interprets tilde escapes, and you happen to serve any files that have a tilde as the first character on a line, the *mail* program tries to interpret the line as a tilde escape sequence.

TELNET_COMMAND
: Used to Telnet to remote hosts

TN3270_COMMAND
: Used to connect to a host using IBM tn3270 emulation. This is very rarely used on the Internet. If you don't have a tn3270 emulator, don't sweat it.

PRINTER_COMMAND
Used to print text files

PLAY_COMMAND
Used to play sound files. If you have a machine that can play sound files, substitute the sound-player command for */bin/false*, which is the current default.

There are a number of machines with speakers and programs that can play sounds. Here are some of them, with the appropriate PLAY_COMMAND commands.

Suns running SunOS 4.1.x
The correct PLAY_COMMAND is */usr/demo/SOUND/play -v 40 -*. Note that you must have the "demo" portion of the operating system installed in order for this *play* command to be available.

Suns running Solaris 2.x
The correct PLAY_COMMAND is */bin/playaudio -v 40 -*.

NeXTs
Compile the program *play* in the *misc/NeXT* directory in the Gopher 1.x distribution. Install it in a public directory and use *play -v 40 -* as the PLAY_COMMAND.

Silicon Graphics
Unfortunately, there is no one-step command to get sounds to work correctly on an SGI. You need to create your own shell script (name it something like *play_sound*) with the following commands in it:

```
#!/bin/sh
cat > /tmp/audio.$$
/usr/sbin/sfplay -i mu-law chan 1 rate 8000 end /tmp/audio.$$
rm /tmp/audio.$$
```

Make sure that it's executable and then put it in a directory that's in your users' path (such as */usr/local/bin*). Make your PLAY_COMMAND the name of the shell script.

Hewlett Packard machines running HP/UX 9.0
You need a shell script on HPs too. Call it *play_sound* or something similar:

```
#!/bin/sh

AUDIO=$DISPLAY
export AUDIO

SPEAKER=${SPEAKER:-E}
export SPEAKER
cat > /tmp/audio.$$
```

```
/usr/audio/bin/send_sound /tmp/audio.$$
rm /tmp/audio.$$
```

Make sure that it's executable and then put it in a directory that's in your users' path (such as */usr/local/bin*). Make your PLAY_COMMAND the name of the shell script.

MIME_COMMAND
: Used to display MIME (multimedia mail) messages

IMAGE_COMMAND
: Used to display pictures on graphical terminals

+ HTML_COMMAND
: Used to view HTML (World Wide Web) documents

Most of the default options are OK. However, there are a few commands listed as defaults that may not be installed on your machine. The *MIME_COMMAND* (*metamail –P*), the *IMAGE_COMMAND* (*xloadimage –fork*), and an *HTML_COMMAND* don't come installed with most operating systems.

MIME isn't used very much in Gopher 1.x, but is supported on Gopher 2.x. MIME stands for Multipurpose Internet Mail Extensions, a proposed standard for multimedia mail on the Internet. Unless you're extremely interested in viewing MIME messages, there's really no reason to spend the time compiling it (although it's pretty neat!). If you'd like to compile the latest MIME package, you can get it via anonymous FTP from *thumper.bellcore.com*, in the */pub/nsb* directory. The file is named *mm*`x.y`*.tar.Z*, where `x.y` is the most recent version number.

If you have a graphical display, you'll probably want to get a program that can display pictures (if you don't have one already!). The *xloadimage* and *xv* viewers are both pretty nice. *xv* also includes image tools that allow you to manipulate images and convert between different image types. *xv* is available via anonymous FTP from *ftp.cis.upenn.edu* in the */pub/xv* directory and *xloadimage* is available on *ftp.uu.net* in the */pub/window-sys/X/contrib* directory.

+ A good *HTML_COMMAND* is *lynx –force_html %s*, which uses the *lynx* line-mode World Wide Web browser. *lynx* is available via anonymous FTP from *ftp2.cc.ukans.edu* in the *pub/WWW/lynx* directory.

+ One thing to note about the Gopher 2.x client is that it *only* uses these *COMMAND*s when retrieving non-Gopher+ items. For Gopher+ items, it looks in the *gopher.rc* file to map the item's Gopher+-type to the command needed to view the file. See the *gopherrc* manual page and the *gopher.rc* file for details.

+ Lastly, *REMOTERC* defines the location of the client's *rc* file for remote (serial-connection) users.

B.4 Using Downloading in the Client

If the user is using a dialup connection from home and wants to be able to download files to his personal computer directly from within the Gopher client, you need to have *kermit*, *xmodem*, *ymodem*, and *zmodem* installed. *kermit* can be found via anonymous FTP on *cs.columbia.edu* in the */archive/kermit* directory as the file *cku189.tar.gz*. This file is compressed with the *gzip* program, which is available on *prep.ai.mit.edu* in the */pub/gnu* directory as the file *gzip-1.2.4.tar*. *x/y/zmodem* can be found on *ftp.uu.net* in the */networking/terms* directory as the file *zmodem.tar.Z* (this *zmodem* distribution also contains *xmodem* and *ymodem*). Once compiled, the binaries are named *kermit*, *sz*, *sb*, and *sx*. Unfortunately, there is no configuration variable that lets you set the exact location of these programs. They need to be installed in a directory that is in your users' path, such as */usr/local/bin*.

C

Gopher Tools and Gateways

The following is an alphabetical list of Gopher tools and gateways which may help you administer your Gopher server. A good place to look for additions to this list is the Gopher FAQ file, posted periodically in the newsgroup *comp.infosystems.gopher.*

Name: *Alcuin*
FTP: *feenix.metronet.com*
Location: */pub/perl/scripts/gopher/tools*
Alcuin is a Perl script used to organize WAIS indexes in a Gopher server's data directory.

Name: *Fwgstat*
FTP: *feenix.metronet.com*
Location: */pub/perl/scripts/gopher/tools*
Fwgstat is heavily based on the much better-written xferstats, which is packaged with the WU Archive FTP daemon. Fwgstat is capable of parsing the usage files for FTP, Gopher, WAIS, and HTTP; it also writes a nice usage report.

Name: *GEE*
FTP: *feenix.metronet.com*
Location: */pub/perl/scripts/gopher/tools*
Gee is a tool for Gopher administrators that allows quick and easy inspection of, and changes to, the Gopher archive. It uses a paged display, like the *gopher* client itself and displays files one directory at a time. Gee is compatible mostly with older Gopher servers, but works well with the Gopher+ server's *.name* files. Doesn't work with gn, but it could.

Name: *GLA*
FTP: *boombox.micro.umn.edu*
Location: */pub/gopher/Unix/GopherTools*
A Gopher Log Analyzer that lists who accessed your server, when, and what they retrieved. Hostnames and IP addresses are stripped of the most specific portion to

This appendix was compiled by Danny Iacovou.

ensure privacy. There are five sections in the GLA report: Hostnames in alphabetic order, hostnames in order of frequency, filenames in alphabetic order, filenames in order of frequency, and overall statistics. Any section can be eliminated with a command-line option. In addition, the number of hosts or files reported can be limited using a command-line option.

Name: *GLASS*
FTP: *boombox.micro.umn.edu*
Location: */pub/gopher/Unix/GopherTools*
Glass is a shell script that looks at the Gopher *logfile* and produces one of 22 reports. Glass uses *awk* and other commands to separate the specified data from the *logfile* and present it in an intelligible fashion.

Name: *GLOG*
FTP: *boombox.micro.umn.edu*
Location: */pub/gopher/Unix/GopherTools*
Gopher Log Analyzer allows you to analyze your Gopher log files, supplying you with useful reports/plots/histograms.

Name:
Gmail/Gmailcal
FTP: *boombox.micro.umn.edu*
Location: */pub/gopher/Unix/GopherTools*
Gmail is a Perl script that interprets an incoming mail message and, if it is acceptable, uses it to manipulate data in a Gopher data tree.

Gmailcal is a Perl script that organizes a calendar of events submitted via the mail-to-Gopherspace interface gmail.

Name: *GMV*
FTP: *boombox.micro.umn.edu*
Location: */pub/gopher/Unix/GopherTools*
GMV moves Gopher documents along with their *.cap* files to a new directory.

Name: *Go4gw*
FTP: *boombox.micro.umn.edu*
Location: */pub/gopher/Unix/GopherTools*
Go4gw is a daemon written in Perl that can handle many different Gopher gateways. It should be started from *inetd*. The package comes with the following gateways: *g2archie*, *g2finger*, *g2ftphack*, *g2netfind*, *g2nntp*, *g2snmp*, *g2webster*, *g2whois*, and *g2shield*.

Name: *Go4zgate*
FTP: *boombox.micro.umn.edu*
Location: */pub/gopher/Unix/gopher-gateways*
Go4zgate is a Gopher+-to-Z39.50 version 2 gateway.

Name: *Gofinger*
FTP: *feenix.metronet.com*
Location: */pub/perl/scripts/gopher/tools*
Gofinger allows someone to do a *finger* under a Gopher server.

Name: *Goform*
FTP: *boombox.micro.umn.edu*
Location: */pub/gopher/Unix/GopherTools*
Goform is a Telnetable Gopher form-fillout daemon.

Name: *Gonnrp*
FTP: *feenix.metronet.com*
Location: */pub/perl/scripts/gopher/tools*
Gonnrp is a Gopher-to-nnrp gateway (*nov*-threaded). *nnrp* is the newsreading part of *nntp* in INN. Gonnrp does not need the *tin* index files like gonntp did. Note that it will work without *nov* or with regular *nntp*, but it will be slower, as it threads with *xhdr* commands and INN with *nov* has a very fast response to *xhdr*.

Name: *Gopher2FTP*
FTP: *boombox.micro.umn.edu*
Location: */pub/gopher/Unix/gopher-gateways*
This is the third incarnation of a Gopher-to-FTP gateway. Running this daemon on a UNIX box gives folks running *gopher* clients access to all that good stuff available out there for anonymous FTP.

Name: *Gopher2mbox*
FTP: *boombox.micro.umn.edu*
Location: */pub/gopher/Unix/GopherTools*
Gopher2mbox gathers data about Gopher items and dumps them into a file which can later be read using a mail reader. Here is a sample file:

```
>From gopher2mbox Mon Aug  8 11:11:13 CDT 1994
From: 70 (1/computer)
Subject: Computer Information
Computer Information
is a nontext item in Gopher. To access this item, try
gopher -p "1/computer" spinaltap.micro.umn.edu 70
For reference, the "bookmark" for this Gopher item is:
        Name=Computer Information
        Type=1
        Port=70
        Path=1/computer
        Host=spinaltap.micro.umn.edu
```

Name: *Gopherclone*
FTP: *boombox.micro.umn.edu*
Location: */pub/gopher/Unix/GopherTools*
Gopherclone allows you to clone other Gopher servers.

Name: *Gopherdist*
FTP: *boombox.micro.umn.edu*
Location: */pub/gopher/Unix/GopherTools*
Gopherdist is a script that generates a link file on standard output for a given Gopher host/port/directory.

Name: *Gophreport*
FTP: *feenix.metronet.com*
Location: */pub/perl/scripts/gopher/tools*
Gophreport reports Gopher usage based on: days, time, files, hosts, and errors. It prints different types of summaries.

Name: *Gophersoc*
FTP: *quantum.Berkeley.EDU*
Location: */pub/gophersoc.dist*
Gophersoc is a set of Perl scripts that implement a Gopher server that allows relational searches to be performed on a schedule of classes, using simple to fairly complex queries such as:

> A class from a department containing "phy" (like Geography or Physics) that doesn't meet on either Tuesdays or Thursdays, that doesn't start before 10 A.M. or between 12:00 and 12:59 P.M., that has less than 3 units and meets in Bechtel Hall.

Name: *GopherSQL*
FTP: *boombox.micro.umn.edu*
Location: */pub/gopher/Unix/gopher-gateways*
Gophersql is a program which accepts Gopher requests and translates them into SQL requests. It should be started from *inetd.* It currently can talk to either a Sybase or Oracle Database Server.

Name: *Gophertree*
FTP: *boombox.micro.umn.edu*
Location: */pub/gopher/Unix/GopherTools*
Gophertree prints pretty indented listings of a Gopher menu tree.

Name: *Gophtech*
FTP: *boombox.micro.umn.edu*
Location: */pub/gopher/Unix/gopher-gateways/techinfo*
This is a one-way gateway from Gopher protocol to TI protocol. When a *gopher* client connects to this server and makes a request, this program connects to a TechInfo server and gets the appropriate information, sends the response to the client, and then closes.

Name: *Guestbook*
FTP: *boombox.micro.umn.edu*
Location: */pub/gopher/Unix/GopherTools*

Guestbook is a program which allows Gopher users to directly offer (through *telnet*) comments to that server's administrators.

Name: *Index2cap*
FTP: *feenix.metronet.com*
Location: */pub/perl/scripts/gopher/tools*
Index2cap is a way of making an archive that is accessed by both FTP and Gopher easier to maintain. It starts at the beginning of an archive (or part of an archive) searching for index files and then rewrites them into *.cap* entries with a "Name" field, which *gopherd* uses instead of the filename.

Name: *InstGopher*
FTP: *feenix.metronet.com*
Location: */pub/perl/scripts/gopher/tools*
InstGopher is a Perl script developed to make the process of installing documents into Gopher easier for non-UNIX types.

Name: *Jughead*
FTP: *ftp.cc.utah.edu*
Location: */pub/gopher/GopherTools*
Jughead is a tool for getting menu information from various Gopher servers; it is an acronym for "Jonzy's Universal Gopher Hierarchy Excavation And Display."

Name: *Linkmerge*
FTP: *feenix.metronet.com*
Location: */pub/perl/scripts/gopher/tools*
Linkmerge creates a "subject tree" of Internet resources categorized by subject area. It merges carefully selected subdirectories of other sites's subject-area trees. The result is a union of several trees, into which you are allowed to put your own local resources to create a superset tree.

Name: *Logger*
FTP: *boombox.micro.umn.edu*
Location: */pub/gopher/Unix/GopherTools*
Logger supports:

- Logfile rotation up to a maximum number of days to be kept
- A "guestbook" that tracks sites that hit on your server and the number of hits
- A primitive usage database that shows what files are getting hit
- A mailed report of "newbies" (i.e., new sites that have hit your server since the last report) that is sent to the system administrator

Name: *Metaclone*
FTP: *boombox.micro.umn.edu*
Location: */pub/gopher/Unix/GopherTools*
Metaclone allows you to clone other Gopher servers.

Name: *MHtogoph*
FTP: *feenix.metronet.com*
Location: */pub/perl/scripts/gopher/tools*
MHtogoph is a filter that is piped to by the Mail Handler system (MH); the resulting files get put into the appropriate Gopher directory along with a *.cap* file.

Name: *Newitems*
FTP: *feenix.metronet.com*
Location: */pub/perl/scripts/gopher/tools*
Newitems provides a listing of new/recently changed items in a Gopher server. It generates a link file, so the listing is a directory, not a flat file.

Name: *Secure Gopher*
FTP: *boombox.micro.umn.edu*
Location: */pub/gopher/Unix/GopherTools*
The Secure Gopher package contains sources for the *more* and *telnet* programs used by the Gopher-server software. These versions do not include the ability to shell-escape from the *gopher* client.

Name: *Shepherd*
FTP: *boombox.micro.umn.edu*
Location: */pub/gopher/Unix/GopherTools*
Shepherd is a utility that monitors standalone information servers like Gopher, WAIS, WWW, Jughead, and Submit to make sure they are responding. If they don't respond, they are restarted automatically. It is intended for UNIX systems, since it uses */etc/rc.local* to get a list of servers to check, and should be run by *cron* every 5 or 10 minutes. It works great!

Name: *Snooper*
FTP: *boombox.micro.umn.edu*
Location: */pub/gopher/Unix/GopherTools*
Snooper checks hosts and their ports to see what servers are still responding. When it finds a server is down, it pages you (literally) in order to bring it to your attention.

Name: *Techinpher*
FTP: *boombox.micro.umn.edu*
Location: */pub/gopher/Unix/gopher-gateways/techinfo*
Techinpher provides a gateway from Internet Gophers to TechInfo Services.

Name: *Traveller*
FTP: *boombox.micro.umn.edu*
Location: */pub/gopher/Unix/GopherTools*

The Traveller programs help users find their way around Gopher servers, by enabling them to search for a title (much like Veronica) and to know what is new in a Gopher graph (much like *whatsnewd*). The information is updated automatically, which poses some limitations to the tool: if part of the Gopherspace is updated very often, it tends to shadow the less-frequent updates to other parts of the Gopherspace.

Name: *Ts/Tb*
FTP: *boombox.micro.umn.edu*
Location: */pub/gopher/Unix/GopherTools*

The Ts/Tb package consists of several simple programs that allow you to create and search a keyword index of the user-visible titles in your Gopher server.

Name: *Veronica*
FTP: *futique.scs.unr.edu*
Location: */veronica-code*

Veronica is a service that maintains an index of titles of Gopher items and provides keyword searches of those titles. A Veronica search originates with a user's request for a search, submitted via a *gopher* client. The result of a Veronica search is a set of Gopher-type data items, which is returned to the client in the form of a Gopher menu. The user can access any of the resultant data items by selecting from the returned menu.

Name: *Whatsnewd/Findwhatsnew*
FTP: *boombox.micro.umn.edu*
Location: */pub/gopher/Unix/GopherTools*

When a user gives a date (e.g. "1 day ago") or enters a dated bookmark (generated by a previous query), he or she gets a Gopher menu of the Gopher items that are new or changed since that date.

The generated bookmarks allow a user to see just those items that have been created or changed since his or her last query.

Name: *Xferstats.gopher*
FTP: *feenix.metronet.com*
Location: */pub/perl/scripts/gopher/tools*

This is a modified xferstats (a program that analyzes data from *wuarchive*'s *ftpd* program) to also handle Gopher logfiles. It only provides statistics on Gopher file transfers (not on directory requests).

In this Appendix:
- *Common HTML Tags*
- *HTML Tags for Forms*

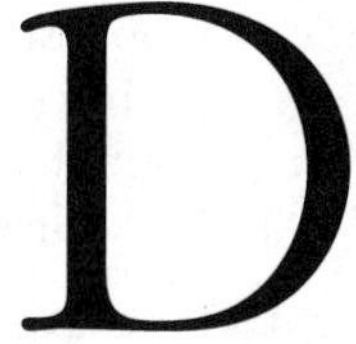

Web: More HTML Tags

This appendix lists and describes all the HTML tags not described in Chapter 19, *Authoring for the Web*. The first section describes regular tags valid anywhere in HTML, and the second section describes tags that are only valid within Forms.

D.1 Common HTML Tags

There are several other common HTML tagging pairs:

Break: `<BR>`
: This tag breaks the autoflow of a paragraph and starts the next line back at the left margin. It is similar to `<P>`, but is rendered without a blank line. This is useful for creating citations, specifications, or addresses where you do not want a blank line.

Preformatted: `<PRE>`*`lines-of-text`*`</PRE>`
: The preformatted tagging pair tells the Web browser to turn off autowrapping and autoflowing for the text between the beginning and ending tags. In HTML version 2.0 there are no tags for formatting tables. So each table is usually preformatted and put inside a `<PRE>` pair. You can embed hyperlinks in preformatted text.

Quote: `<BLOCKQUOTE>`*`quote-text`*`</BLOCKQUOTE>`
: This tagging pair is used to identify quotes or abstracts. It is rendered indented from both the left and right margins of the display.

Italics: `<I>`*`text`*`</I>`
: The `<I>` tag is used to mark specific text to be italicized on a graphical display. On a character-mode display, italicized text is underlined. In general, generic emphasis with the `<EM>` tag is preferred.

Strong Emphasis: `<STRONG>`*`phrase`*`</STRONG>`

The <STRONG> tag is used to indicate that something should be strongly emphasized. <STRONG> is a companion tag to <EM>. Both are used for generic emphasis.

Bold: `<B>`*`text`*`</B>`

The <B> tag is used to mark specific text to be bolded on a graphical display or reverse video on a character-mode display. In general, generic emphasis with the <STRONG> tag is preferred.

Comment: `<!/****`*`text`*`****/>`

This tag is used to place comments in HTML documents. Comments are ignored by Web browsers. The text can be anything except other HTML tags.

D.2 HTML Tags for Forms

There are four HTML tags used for defining forms; <FORM>, <INPUT>, <SELECT>, and <TEXTAREA>. However, these four tags have so many different options, it is useful to look at the different combinations by function.

D.2.1 <FORM>

Every form must use the <FORM> HTML tagging pair. There can be multiple forms in the same HTML document, but forms cannot be nested.

Forms Definition: `<FORM METHOD="`*`method`*`" ACTION="`*`URL`*`"> ... </FORM>`

method is the HTTP/1.0 method used to submit the filled-out form to your Web server. Although you can use the GET method discussed in Section 20.1, get in the habit of using the POST method. The POST method causes the filled-out form contents to be sent to the Web server in the data body instead of being appended to the end of the URL as with the GET method. Using POST is particularly important if you are going to allow users to send large amounts of information back to your Web server or you expect to someday receive encoded (private) form input from your users.

ACTION specifies the URL of the Web server to which the filled-out form contents will be submitted; if this attribute is absent, then the current document URL is used.

Forms are not visually different than the rest of an HTML document. We recommend using the <HR> tag before and after a form to differentiate it from the rest of the HTML document.

D.2.2 <INPUT>

The `<INPUT>` tag creates several types of input devices. The `<SELECT>` and `<TEXTAREA>` tags create other types. The following variations of the `<INPUT>` are important:

Text-entry field: `<INPUT TYPE="`*`text`*`" NAME="`*`name`*`" SIZE=`*`size`*`>`

The text-entry field is a standalone HTML tag. *name* becomes the variable name that is submitted to the Web server. *size* dictates the text-box length in characters. You typically include descriptive HTML text either before or after the text-entry field to clarify meaning.

Password field: `<INPUT TYPE="password" NAME="`*`name`*`" SIZE=`*`size`*`>`

The password field operates just like the text-entry field, but the user's keystrokes are replaced with asterisks.

Checkbox: `<INPUT TYPE="checkbox" NAME="`*`name`*`" VALUE="`*`value`*`">`

The checkbox is a standalone HTML tag. *name* becomes the variable name that is submitted to the Web server with the associated value only if the user clicks on the checkbox.

You can also optionally insert the `CHECKED` keyword if you want to indicate that the default condition is activated. You typically include descriptive HTML text either before or after the checkbox to clarify meaning.

Radio button: `<INPUT TYPE="radio" NAME="`*`name`*`" VALUE="`*`value`*`">`

The radio button operates much like the checkbox. The only difference is that by grouping multiple radio buttons with the same *name*, you can indicate a one-of-many button grouping. When the user clicks on one radio button in the group, all other buttons in the group are deactivated.

You can optionally insert a `CHECKED` phrase to indicate the default button among the group to be activated.

Submit push button: `<INPUT TYPE="submit" VALUE="`*`button-text`*`">`

The submit push button is a standalone HTML tag. The *button-text* is displayed in the button box. When clicked, this button terminates the form processing and sends all of the value names and associated data back to the Web server using the `METHOD` indicated on the `<FORM>` HTML tag.

You may not need to associate descriptive HTML text before or after the submit push button, because the *button-text* can carry the meaning of the button.

Reset push button: `<INPUT TYPE="reset" VALUE="`*`button-text`*`">`

The reset push button is a standalone HTML tag. The *button-text* is displayed in the button box. When clicked, this button resets the form—clearing and resetting all text fields, as well as reconfiguring the default conditions on checkboxes, radio buttons, pop-up menus, and scrollable lists.

You may not need to associate descriptive HTML text before or after the reset push button, because the `button-text` can carry the meaning of the button.

Note that all of the TYPE fields associated with the <INPUT> HTML tag must be lowercase.

D.2.3 <SELECT>

The <SELECT> tagging pair is used to construct pop-up menus and scrollable lists:

Pop-up menu: `<SELECT NAME="name"> <OPTION SELECTED> option-text </SELECT>`

Pop-up menus are built with the <SELECT> tagging pair, which is used to enclose multiple <OPTION> tags. *name* becomes the variable name that is submitted to the Web server. The <OPTION> tags are used to identify the options that are displayed as part of the pop-up menu. One of the <OPTION> tags can have a SELECTED clause that is used to identify the default option to be displayed. If the SELECTED clause is omitted, the first option on the list is the default. *option-text* cannot contain HTML tags.

Scrollable list:

```
<SELECT NAME="name" MULTIPLE SIZE=rows> <OPTION SELECTED> option-text</SELECT>
```

Scrollable lists are built with the <SELECT> tagging pair, which is used to enclose multiple <OPTION> tags. MULTIPLE is optional and is used to indicate that multiple options can be selected by the user. *rows* indicates how many rows should be displayed on the scrollable list. A *rows* value greater than one is what turns a pop-up menu into a scrollable list. *name* becomes the variable name that is submitted to the Web server. The <OPTION> tags are used to identify the options that are displayed as part of the scrollable list. With MULTIPLE specified, any number of the <OPTION> tags can have a SELECTED clause. When MULTIPLE is not specified, only one <OPTION> tag can have a SELECTED clause. If the SELECTED clause is omitted on all options, there are no default selections. *option-text* cannot contain HTML tags.

D.2.4 <TEXTAREA>

The <TEXTAREA> HTML tagging pair is used to implement a scrollable text area:

Scrollable text area:

```
<TEXTAREA NAME="name" ROWS=size COLS=size> optional-text</TEXTAREA>
```

The scrollable text area is a standalone HTML tag. The *name* becomes the variable name that is submitted to the Web server. *size* dictates the dimensions of the text area in characters. *optional-text*, if included, is used to initialize the scrollable text area. If omitted, the scrollable text area will be empty.

You typically include descriptive HTML text either before or after the scrollable text area to clarify meaning.

E

Web: httpd.conf Directives

This appendix lists all the directives that are valid for the *httpd.conf* configuration file. It explains each directive's options and defaults. The directives are in alphabetical order.

`AccessConfig` *`filename`*

The `AccessConfig` directive specifies the location of the global ACF (Access Control File). *`filename`* is either a partial pathname relative to `ServerRoot` or a full pathname. This configuration file is used to control access to your whole Web server or to individual directories. See Chapter 21, *Web: Access Control and Security*, for more detailed information about controlling Web server access.

Only one `AccessConfig` directive is allowed in the *httpd.conf* configuration file. If omitted, the default is:

```
AccessConfig conf/access.conf
```

`ErrorLog` *`filename`*

The `ErrorLog` directive specifies the filename of the error log file (either a partial pathname relative to `ServerRoot` or a full pathname). *httpd* logs the following error information:

- Clients that time out
- Scripts that produce no output
- *.htaccess* files that attempt to override global ACF settings without permission
- Server bugs that produce a segmentation violation or bus error
- User Authentification configuration problems

Only one `ErrorLog` directive is allowed in the *httpd.conf* configuration file. If omitted, the default is:

```
ErrorLog logs/error_log
```

`Group [ name | number ]`

The `Group` directive indicates the group ID to be used when running *httpd* as a standalone server. May be specified numerically by placing a # (pound sign) before the number, otherwise it must be a valid system group. Whichever you choose to use, the important thing is that the specified *name* or *number* exists in */etc/group.*

Note that this does not override the group that the original *httpd* runs in, but is used to control which group any child processes run under. The *httpd* server must be started as *root* in order to use this directive.

Only one `Group` directive is allowed in the *httpd.conf* configuration file. If omitted, the default is:

```
Group #-1
```

`IdentityCheck [ on | off ]`

The `IdentityCheck` directive determines whether or not the identity of the remote user is logged to the file defined by the `TransferLog` directive. For this logging to actually work, the system supporting the remote user must be running an RFC 931–compliant Identity daemon. It should not be trusted, but is useful for rudimentary usage tracking. If you do not plan to use this information, keep this directive set to off. Setting `IdentityCheck` on will adversely affect your Web server's performance.

Only one `IdentityCheck` directive is allowed in the *httpd.conf* configuration file. If omitted, the default is:

```
IdentityCheck off
```

`PidFile filename`

The `PidFile` directive specifies where (relative to `ServerRoot`) to write the server's process ID. The `PidFile` is only meaningful when running the *httpd* server standalone; it is used when you kill your Web server or send the server a signal to reboot.

Only one `PidFile` directive is allowed in the *httpd.conf* configuration file. If omitted, the default is:

```
PidFile logs/httpd.pid
```

`Port num`

The `Port` directive defines the port number your *httpd* server listens to. It can be any number from 0 to 65536, but remember that most of the ports below 1024 are reserved. You should run your server on port 80, which is the HTTP default port. To do this, you must start *httpd* as *root.* Before you consider using a non-standard HTTP port, remember that many of the Web browsers running behind firewalls (through proxy servers) can only access the default HTTP port. By configuring it any other way, you are limiting access to your Web server.

Only one `Port` directive is allowed in the *httpd.conf* configuration file. If omitted, the default is:

```
Port 80
```

`ResourceConfig` *`filename`*

The `ResourceConfig` directive identifies the location of the resource configuration file. *`filename`* is either a partial pathname relative to `ServerRoot` or a full pathname. Most of the options described in the resource configuration file deal with how the *httpd* server handles automatic directory indexing.

Only one `ResourceConfig` directive is allowed in the *httpd.conf* configuration file. If omitted, the default is:

```
ResourceConfig conf/srm.conf
```

`ServerAdmin` *`address`*

The `ServerAdmin` directive is used to specify the administrator's email address that is given to users when runtime problems occur with your Web server. Use your *webmaster* alias here.

Only one `ServerAdmin` directive is allowed in the *httpd.conf* configuration file. If omitted, there is no default.

`ServerName` *`hostname`*

The `ServerName` directive defines the *`hostname`* that the *httpd* server returns when creating redirection URLs. For example, if your server runs on a host that is actually called *mysystem.fredonia.edu*, but you want to reference your Web server at *http://www.fredonia.edu/* then you should place *www.fredonia.edu* as the *`hostname`* and also set up the appropriate CNAME.

Only one `ServerName` directive is allowed in the *httpd.conf* configuration file. If omitted, the *httpd* server retrieves the actual *`hostname`* through system calls.

`ServerRoot` *`directory`*

The `ServerRoot` directive defines the absolute path to the root directory where the *httpd* binary is located. At startup time, the *httpd* server expects to find the server configuration file in *conf/httpd.conf* relative to the `ServerRoot`.

Only one `ServerRoot` directive is allowed in the *httpd.conf* configuration file. If omitted, the default is:

```
ServerRoot /usr/local/etc/httpd
```

`ServerType [ inetd | standalone ]`

The `ServerType` directive defines whether you run the *httpd* server from the *inetd* process or as a standalone daemon. If you anticipate heavy usage, you will probably want to run it standalone.

Only one `ServerType` directive is allowed in the *httpd.conf* configuration file. If omitted, the default is:

```
ServerType standalone
```

`TimeOut` *`time`*

The `TimeOut` directive defines the amount of time (in seconds) the *httpd* server waits for a Web browser to send its request once connected, or the time the server waits for a Web browser to accept information. Before you make this number smaller, remember that Web browsers with slow Internet connections will need all of the time they can get before your Web server terminates the connection.

Only one `TimeOut` directive is allowed in the *httpd.conf* configuration file. If omitted, the default is:

```
TimeOut 1800
```

`TransferLog` *`filename`*

The `TransferLog` directive defines the filename of the transfer log file (either a partial pathname relative to ServerRoot or a full pathname). This is the log file that records file access from your *httpd* server by host, date, and filename.

Only one `TransferLog` directive is allowed in the *httpd.conf* configuration file. If omitted, the default is:

```
TransferLog logs/access_log
```

`TypesConfig` *`filename`*

The `TypesConfig` directive identifies the location of the MIME-type configuration file. *`filename`* is either a partial pathname relative to `ServerRoot` or a full pathname. The MIME-type configuration file is used to control how the *httpd* server maps filename extensions to MIME types when it returns this information to HTTP/1.0 Web browsers. Normally there is no need to edit this file.

Only one `TypesConfig` directive is allowed in the *httpd.conf* configuration file. If omitted, the default is:

```
TypesConfig conf/mime.types
```

`User [` *`name`* `|` *`number`* `]`

The `User` directive defines the user ID to be used when running as a standalone server. This may be different from the user ID at startup. *`number`* may be specified numerically by placing a `#` (pound sign) before the digit; otherwise, *`name`* must be a valid system account. Many people like to use *http* or *httpd* as the name. Whichever you choose to use, the important thing is that the specified `name` or `number` exists in */etc/passwd.*

Only one `User` directive is allowed in the *httpd.conf* configuration file. If omitted, the default is:

```
User #-1
```

F

Web: srm.conf Directives

This appendix lists all of the directives that are valid for the *srm.conf* configuration file. It explains each directive's options and defaults. The directives are in alphabetical order.

`AccessFileName` *`filename`*

The `AccessFileName` directive controls the filename used for directory-specific access control.

Only one `AccessFileName` directive is allowed in the *srm.conf* configuration file. If omitted, the default is:

```
AccessFileName .htaccess
```

`AddDescription` *`descriptive-text file-id`*

The `AddDescription` directive associates a descriptive text phrase with a particular type of file. The text appears to the right of the file name when the file is located in a directory that is being indexed. The *`descriptive-text`* must be surrounded by quotes and be fairly short—more like a line than a paragraph. *`file-id`* is either a filename extension (like *.doc*, *.txt*, *.dat*, or *.html*), a filename, a full pathname to a file, or a wildcard pattern. Here's an example of `AddDescription`:

```
AddDescription "(gzip compressed tar archive)" *.tar.gz
```

You can have as many `AddDescription` directives in the *srm.conf* configuration file as are required. If omitted, there is no default.

`AddEncoding` *`type extension`*

The `AddEncoding` directive adds unique encoding directives for the client/server handshake. *`type`* is the encoding type for the document. *`extension`* defines what file type(s) should use the new encoding.

This directive is often used to flag files that are compressed, so they can be uncompressed on the client side. For example, if you have compressed PostScript files in your document tree hierarchy, you should use the following directives:

```
AddEncoding x-compress Z
AddEncoding x-gzip gz gzip zip
```

In order for this to be used effectively, the clients must support the given encoding method.

You can have as many `AddEncoding` directives in the *srm.conf* configuration file as required. If omitted, there is no default.

`AddIcon` *icon-path name1 name2 ...*

The `AddIcon` directive indicates which icon should be displayed for a given document type by filename. *icon-path* identifies a virtual path to an *.xbm* icon file. There is an alternative syntax that you can use to identify text to display (instead of an icon) for non-graphics Web browsers:

AddIcon (*text,icon-path*) *name1 name2 ...*

Table F-1 shows the possible values for the `AddIcon` directive. The first two values are used exactly as shown and the last four are just examples.

Table F-1: AddIcon Values

Type	Value
For directories	`^^DIRECTORY^^`
For the blank icon	`^^BLANKICON^^`
Any file extension	*.html*
Any partial filename	..
Any wildcard expression	*PR*.txt*
Any complete physical pathname	*/docs/cs/org-chart.txt*

You can have as many `AddIcon` directives in the *srm.conf* configuration file as required. There are no defaults if `AddIcon` is omitted, but the initial *srm.conf* configuration file identifies:

```
AddIcon /icons/movie.xbm .mpg .qt
AddIcon /icons/binary.xbm .bin
AddIcon /icons/back.xbm ..
AddIcon /icons/menu.xbm ^^DIRECTORY^^
AddIcon /icons/blank.xbm ^^BLANKICON^^
```

`AddIconbyEncoding` *icon-path type1 type2 ...*

The `AddIconbyEncoding` directive is similar to the `AddIcon` directive, except that it associates icons with documents according to encoding information. There is an alternative syntax that you can use to identify text (instead of an icon) to display for non-graphical Web browsers:

```
AddIconbyEncoding (text,icon-path) name1 name2 ...
```

name is a wildcard expression specifying the content encoding for which to display this icon.

You can have as many `AddIconbyEncoding` directives in the *srm.conf* configuration file as required. If omitted, there is no default.

`AddIconType` *`icon-path type1 type2`* ...

The `AddIconType` directive is similar to the `AddIcon` directive except that it associates icons with documents by MIME type, as opposed to filename. There is an alternative syntax that you can use to identify text (instead of an icon) to display for non-graphical Web browsers:

AddIconType (*text,icon-path*) *name1 name2* ...

name can be any of the standard MIME *type/subtype* combinations.

You can have as many `AddIconType` directives in the *srm.conf* configuration file as required. There are no defaults if the directive is omitted, but the initial *srm.conf* configuration file identifies:

```
AddIconByType (TXT,/icons/text.xbm) text/*
AddIconByType (IMG,/icons/image.xbm) image/*
AddIconByType (SND,/icons/sound.xbm) audio/*
```

`AddType` *`type/subtype extension`*

The `AddType` directive allows you to override MIME-type definitions found in the *mime.types* configuration file.

You can have as many `AddType` directives in the *srm.conf* configuration file as required. The default MIME-type definitions are found in the MIME-type configuration file (*mime.types*).

`Alias` *`virtual path`*

The `Alias` directive creates a virtual name or directory on your server. The `Alias` directive is particularly appropriate if you are supporting multiple organizations on your Web server and each wants a short URL.

`virtual` identifies a path to a file or directory that you want remapped to a different location on your system. *`path`* is the absolute pathname to a file or directory that is used to satisfy the request.

You can have as many `Alias` directives in the *srm.conf* configuration file as required. There are no defaults if omitted, but the initial configuration file specifies:

```
Alias /icons/ /usr/local/etc/httpd/icons/
```

`DefaultType` *type/subtype*

The `DefaultType` directive is used to establish a default MIME type to be returned to the Web browser if the mappings found in the *mime.types* configuration file are not adequate. *type* and *subtype* can be any of the standard MIME combinations.

Only one `DefaultType` directive is allowed in the *srm.conf* configuration file. If omitted, the default is:

```
DefaultType text/html
```

`DefaultIcon` *path*

The `DefaultIcon` directive specifies the icon to be displayed when `FancyIndexing` is on and there is no icon associated with a given file type. Icons are in XBM format and are contained in the */icon* directory of your NCSA HTTP kit.

If you know the types of file extensions that are in your directory structure, you may not have to worry about surprise file types that need a default.

Only one `DefaultIcon` directive is allowed in the *srm.conf* configuration file. There is no default if omitted, but the initial *srm.conf* configuration file identifies:

```
DefaultIcon /icons/unknown.xbm
```

`DirectoryIndex` *file*

The `DirectoryIndex` directive specifies the file that is returned when a URL identifies a directory on your Web server. This is usually thought of as a prewritten index file for a directory, but could be any file.

Only one `DirectoryIndex` directive is allowed in the *srm.conf* configuration file. If omitted, the default is:

```
DirectoryIndex index.html
```

`DocumentRoot` *absolute-directory-path*

The `DocumentRoot` directive sets the directory from which *httpd* serves files. If you need to serve files from outside of this directory, you can use the `Alias` directive or create symbolic links.

Only one `DocumentRoot` directive is allowed in the *srm.conf* configuration file. If omitted, the default is:

```
DocumentRoot /usr/local/etc/httpd/htdocs
```

`FancyIndexing [ on | off ]`

The `FancyIndexing` directive is provided for backwards compatibility with NCSA HTTP V1.0. If you are setting up a new Web server with NCSA V1.3 or later, you should use the `IndexOptions FancyIndexing` instead. Although obsolete, the initial *srm.conf* configuration file has `FancyIndexing` initialized to be `on`.

`HeaderName` *filename*

The `HeaderName` directive identifies the *filename* that is used as the directory header during automatic directory indexing. The *httpd* server automatically includes the file at the start of the HTML directory-listing stream. *httpd* first tries to open and include `filename.html` and then, if unsuccessful, just `filename` (with no extension), encapsulated with the <PRE>...</PRE> HTML tagging pair. If neither is found in the directory, no action is taken.

Only one `HeaderName` directive is allowed in the *srm.conf* configuration file. There is no default if omitted, but the initial configuration file specifies:

```
HeaderName HEADER
```

`IndexIgnore` *`pattern1 pattern2`* ...

The `IndexIgnore` directive is used to identify any files that should be ignored during directory processing. *`pattern`* is a file extension or filename that should be ignored. When your Web server is processing a directory, it tries to match each of these strings to the righthand side of the entry's string and, if they match, it ignores that entry in its directory index. If *`pattern`* is a wildcard expression, *httpd* matches the filename against the given expression.

You can have as many `IndexIgnore` directives in the *srm.conf* configuration file as required. If omitted, the only file ignored by default is the `.` file. However, the initial *srm.conf* configuration file specifies:

```
IndexIgnore */.??* *~ *# */HEADER* */README*
```

This causes directory processing to ignore the default `HeaderName` and `ReadmeName`, hidden files, *emacs* autosave files, and *emacs* backup files.

`IndexOptions` *`option1 option2 option3`*

The `IndexOptions` directive specifies whether you want fancy directory indexing (with icons and file sizes) or standard directory indexing, and which options you want active for indexing. The options are:

`FancyIndexing`
: Turns FancyIndexing on

`IconsAreLinks`
: Makes the icons part of the anchor for the filename

`ScanHTMLTitles`
: Causes the description field of any unknown HTML document to be scanned from its <TITLE> HTML tagging pair

`SuppressLastModified`
: Do not print the last date of modification in index listings.

`SuppressSize`
: Do not print the size of the files in index listings.

`SuppressDescription`
: Do not print descriptions for any files.

Only one `IndexOptions` directive is allowed in the *srm.conf* configuration file. If omitted, all options default to the `off` condition.

`OldScriptAlias` *`virtual path`*

The `OldScriptAlias` directive is provided for backwards compatibility with NCSA HTTP V1.0 and its pre-CGI script interface. If you are setting up a new Web server with NCSA V1.2 or later, this directive can be ignored.

`ReadmeName` *`filename`*

The `ReadmeName` directive is the companion directive to the `HeaderName` directive. The only difference is that it identifies the trailer information to be included at the bottom of an automatic directory index.

Only one `ReadmeName` directive is allowed in the *srm.conf* configuration file. There is no default if omitted, but the initial *srm.conf* configuration file specifies:

```
ReadmeName README
```

`Redirect` *`virtual URL`*

The `Redirect` directive is used to map an existing document path and file on your server to a new URL. *`virtual`* is a partial pathname after URL translation. *`URL`* is the URL of a new document (perhaps on a different system).

You can have as many `Redirect` directives in the *srm.conf* configuration file as required. There is no default.

`ScriptAlias` *`virtual path`*

The `ScriptAlias` directive creates a virtual name or directory on your server for scripts. It is used in the mapping of gateways to the actual CGI scripts. *`virtual`* is the name given out externally as part of the URL. *`path`* is the absolute pathname of the directory that contains CGI server scripts which fulfill the request.

You can have as many `ScriptAlias` directives in the *srm.conf* configuration file as required. There are no defaults if omitted, but the initial *srm.conf* configuration file specifies:

```
ScriptAlias /cgi-bin/ /usr/local/etc/httpd/cgi-bin/
```

You should always place a trailing `/` after `ScriptAlias` directives that reference directories, to prevent similar entries from conflicting with each other.

`UserDir` [*`directory-path`* | DISABLED]

In addition to files in the document tree, you can also let users make directories off their own home directory available for HTTP access. You can use the `DISABLED` keyword to turn this feature off, if you are not going to allow users to serve files from their personal directory hierarchy.

Only one `UserDir` directive is allowed in the *srm.conf* configuration file. If omitted, the default is:

```
UserDir public_html
```

G

Web: access.conf Directives

This appendix lists all the directives that are valid for the *access.conf* configuration file. It explains each directive's options and defaults. The directives are in alphabetical order.

`allow from` *`host1 host2`*...

The `allow` directive affects which hosts can access a given directory with a given method. *`host`* is one of the following:

`domain-name`

A domain name, like *.fredonia.edu.* Only hosts from that domain are permitted access

`host-name`

A full hostname

`full-IP-address`

An IP address of a host

`partial-IP-address`

The first 1–3 bytes of an IP address, for subnet restriction

`all`

This means that all hosts will be denied access.

There can be only one `allow` directive per `Limit` section. If omitted, there is no default.

`AllowOverride` *opt1 opt2 ...*

The `AllowOverride` directive controls the extent to which you allow local per-directory access control files to override the global access defaults defined by the *access.conf* configuration file. Valid entries are:

`None`
: ACFs are not allowed in this directory.

`All`
: ACFs are unrestricted in this directory.

`Options`
: Allow use of the `Options` directive.

`FileInfo`
: Allow use of the `AddType` and `AddEncoding` directives.

`AuthConfig`
: Allow use of these directives: `AuthName`, `AuthType`, `AuthUserFile`, `AuthGroupFile`.

`Limit`
: Allow use of the `Limit` section directive.

The `AllowOverride` directive can only be used for global ACF. If omitted, the default is:

```
AllowOverride All
```

`AuthGroupFile` *path*

The `AuthGroupFile` directive sets the file to use as a list of user groups for user authentication. *path* is the absolute path of the group file to use in this directory.

The `AuthGroupFile` directive must be accompanied by `AuthName`, `AuthType`, and `AuthUserFile` directives in order for user authentication to work properly. This directive applies to both global ACF and per-directory ACFs. If omitted, there is no default.

`AuthName` *name*

The `AuthName` directive sets the name of the authorization realm for this directory. This realm is a name given to users so they know what username and password to send. *name* is a short name describing this authorization realm; it can contain spaces.

The `AuthName` directive must be accompanied by `AuthType`, `AuthUserFile`, and `AuthGroupFile` directives in order for user authentication to work properly. This directive applies to both global ACF and per-directory ACFs. If omitted, there is no default.

`AuthType` *`type`*

The `AuthType` directive sets the type of authorization used in this directory. *`type`* is the authentication type to use for this directory. In NCSA HTTP V1.3 only `Basic` is currently implemented.

The `AuthType` directive must be accompanied by `AuthName`, `AuthUserFile`, and `AuthGroupFile` directives in order for user authentication to work properly. This directive applies to both global ACF and per-directory ACFs. If omitted, there is no default.

`AuthUserFile` *`path`*

The `AuthUserFile` directive specifies the file that contains a list of users and passwords for user authentication. *`path`* is the absolute path of a user file created with the *htpasswd* support program.

The `AuthUserFile` directive must be accompanied by `AuthName`, `AuthType`, and `AuthGroupFile` directives in order for user authentication to work properly. This directive applies to both global ACF and per-directory ACFs. If omitted, there is no default.

`deny from` *`host1 host2`* ...

The `deny` directive affects which hosts are denied access to a directory. *`host`* is one of the following:

`domain-name`
: A domain name, like *.fredonia.edu*. Hosts from that domain are denied access.

`host-name`
: A full hostname

`full-IP-address`
: An IP address of a host

`partial-IP-address`
: The first 1–3 bytes of an IP address, for subnet restriction

`all`
: This means that all hosts are denied access.

There can only be one `deny` directive per `Limit` section. If omitted, there is no default.

`<Directory` *`dir`*`>`

The `Directory` directive is a sectioning directive (with corresponding opening and closing tags) that identifies the directory or directories to which other access-control directives apply. *`dir`* is the absolute pathname of that directory.

You can also use the `*` and `?` wildcard characters as part of the *`dir`* expression to identify a set of directories you wish to protect. These act just as they do when used as shell wildcard patterns. Every `Directory` directive must be closed with a corresponding `</Directory>` directive.

The `Directory` directive is only valid as part of the global ACF. If omitted, there is no default.

`</Directory>`
: This closing directive is required with a corresponding `Directory` directive.

`<Limit` *`method1 method2`* ...`>`
: The `Limit` directive is a sectioning directive that identifies which clients can access a directory. This directive applies to both the global ACF and per-directory ACFs. *`method`* is one of the following:

  `GET`
  : Allows clients to retrieve documents and execute scripts.

  `POST`
  : Allows clients to use POST scripts.

  Only the `order`, `deny`, `allow`, and `require` directives are allowed inside of the `Limit` sectioning directive.

`</Limit>`
: This closing directive is required with a corresponding `Limit` directive.

`Options` *`option-list`*
: The `Options` directive controls the degree of advanced features that you allow on your Web server. Valid entries are:

  `None`
  : No features are enabled in this directory.

  `Indexes`
  : Allows users to request indexes in this directory. Disabling this option disables only the server-generated indexes. It does not stop the server from sending any precompiled index file it may find in there.

  `Includes`
  : Server-side include files are enabled in this directory.

  `IncludesNoExec`
  : This enables server-side includes in the directory, but disables the exec feature.

  `ExecCGI`
  : Execution of CGI scripts is allowed in this directory.

`FollowSymLinks`
: The server follows symbolic links in this directory.

`SymLinksIfOwnerMatch`
: The server only follows symbolic links for which the target file/directory is owned by the same user ID as the link.

`All`
: All features are enabled in this directory.

The `Options` directive can be used in both the global ACF and in per-directory ACFs. There can be only one `Options` directive per `Directory` directive segment. If omitted, the default is:

```
Options All
```

`order` *`ord`*
: The `order` directive affects the order in which deny and allow directives are evaluated within a `Limit` section. This directive is only available within Limit sections, but can be used on a global ACF or per-directory ACF basis. *`ord`* is one of the following:

`deny,allow`
: `deny` directives are evaluated before `allow` directives.

`allow,deny`
: `allow` directives are evaluated before `deny` directives.

There can only be one `order` directive per `Limit` section. If omitted, the default is:

```
order deny,allow
```

`require` *`entity name1 name2`* ...
: The `require` directive affects which authenticated users can access a given directory with a given method. *`entity`* is one of the following:

`user`
: Only the named users can access this directory with the given methods.

`group`
: Only users in the named groups can access this directory with the given methods.

`valid-user`
: Only users listed in the `AuthUserFile` are allowed access upon providing a valid password.

`name` is a specific name in the context of the entity type. If the *`entity`* is `user`, *`name`* is a user name. If *`entity`* is `group`, *`name`* is a group name. Multiple names are separated by spaces. There can be only one `require` directive per `Limit` section. If omitted, there is no default.

In addition to these directives, the following directives can also be used within the global ACF and per-directory ACFs as indicated:

`DefaultType`
: Only per-directory ACFs

`AddEncoding`
: All ACFs

`AddDescription`
: Only per-directory ACFs

`AddIcon`
: All ACFs

`IndexIgnore`
: All ACFs

`DefaultIcon`
: All ACFs

`ReadmeName`
: All ACFs

These directives are a subset of those allowed in *srm.conf*, and are described in detail in Appendix B, *Gopher: Client Compilation Options*.

In this Appendix:
- *World Wide Web FAQ*
- *Newsgroups*
- *Mailing Lists*
- *Examples of Web Servers*
- *GNN's Best of the Net Servers*
- *Online Conference Proceedings*

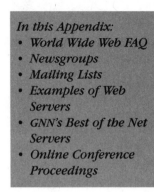

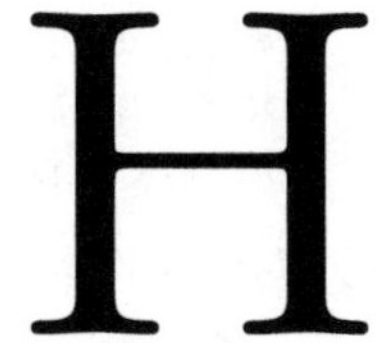

Web: For More Information

These sources of information should be helpful in your quest to learn more about the Web than this book provides.

The first three sections are listed in the order you should go to them.

H.1 World Wide Web FAQ

Your first line of defense is the World Wide Web FAQ edited by Thomas Boutell, *boutell@netcom.com*. In addition to being posted every four days to many of the newsgroups listed below, an HTML version of the FAQ is available on the Web at:

```
http://siva.cshl.org/~boutell/www_faq.html
```

If you want an ASCII text version, the most recently posted version of the FAQ is also available on the *news.answers* FTP archive:

```
ftp://rtfm.mit.edu/pub/usenet/news.answers/www/faq
```

H.2 Newsgroups

The Web-related newsgroups should be considered your next source for resolving questions about the World Wide Web. You can draw on the experiences of others.

comp.infosystems.www.providers (unmoderated)
: Discussion of Web server software and the use of that software to present information to users. General server design, setup questions, server bug reports, security issues, HTML page design and other concerns of information providers are among the likely topics found in this group. This is the newsgroup to read if you are setting up a Web server.

comp.infosystems.www.users (unmoderated)
: Discussion of Web client software and its use for accessing various Internet information sources. New-user questions, client-setup questions, client bug reports, and

resource-discovery questions on how to locate information on the Web that can't be found by the means detailed in the FAQ, as well as comparison between various client packages are among the acceptable topics for this group.

comp.infosystems.www.misc (unmoderated)
: Discussion of Web-related topics that are NOT covered by the other newsgroups in the *comp.infosystems.www* hierarchy. This includes discussions of the Web's future, politicking regarding changes in the structure and protocols of the Web that affect both clients and servers, etc.

comp.infosystems.announce (moderated)
: Although used to announce everything from mailing lists to gopher servers, this newsgroup should be followed to keep abreast of new Web servers coming online. Remember that each new Web server that comes online presents a new resource that could add value to your Web server (with the appropriate hyperlinks.)

alt.hypertext (unmoderated)
: Discussion of hypertext concepts and tools. This is a good newsgroup to get ideas about presenting information in different ways to add clarity and understanding.

H.3 Mailing Lists

Beyond newsgroups, CERN sponsors a number of mailing lists that you may want to follow to keep up with recent developments on the Web.

www-announce
: This is the mailing list to follow if you want to keep current on new Web servers and software tools.

  To join the list, send email to *listserv@info.cern.ch* with this line in the body:

```
subscribe www-announce your name
```

www-talk
: This is the discussion list used by the developers of the various Web browsers and Web servers discussed in this chapter. It is generally used to debate the merits of new HTTP and/or HTML features.

  To join the list, send email to *listserv@info.cern.ch* with this line in the body:

```
subscribe www-talk your name
```

www-html
: This mailing list is for technical discussions of HTML and future versions. It is for design discussions only, not introductory questions.

To join the list, send email to *listserv@info.cern.ch* with this line in the body:

```
subscribe www-html your name
```

www-rdb

This mailing list is for those interested in the development and deployment of CGI gateways between the Web and relational databases.

To join the list, send email to *listserv@info.cern.ch* with this line in the body:

```
subscribe www-rdb your name
```

H.4 Examples of Web Servers

Many Web browsers have predefined starting points for exploring the World Wide Web. To get to Mosaic's starting points, pull down the Navigate pulldown menu and click on Internet Starting Points. To get to Lynx's starting point, type *i* for index.

In addition to the URLs referenced in this chapter, some other interesting Web servers that you may want to check out include:

CERN's list of Web servers by continent and country:

```
http://info.cern.ch/hypertext/DataSources/WWW/Servers.html
```

City of Palo Alto, California:

```
http://www.city.palo-alto.ca.us/home.html
```

Commercial sites on the Web:

```
http://tns-www.lcs.mit.edu/commerce.html
```

Computer companies on the Web:

```
http://www.digital.com/
http://www.hp.com/http://www.sgi.com/http://www.sun.com/
```

Non-profit sites on the Web:

```
http://www.ai.mit.edu/people/ellens/non.html
```

What's new on the Web:

```
http://www.ncsa.uiuc.edu/SDG/Software/Mosaic/Docs/whats-new.html
```

H.5 GNN's Best of the Net Servers

O'Reilly & Associates' *Global Network Navigator* recently recognized twelve destinations on the World Wide Web as the "Best of the Net." Each represents a unique value-added server to the Web community. As you develop your Web server, consider visiting each of these to get a feel for how others have set up their servers:

ArtServe:

`http://rubens.anu.edu.au/`

The Currency Converter:

`http://www.ora.com/cgi-bin/ora/currency`

Edupage Newsletter:

`http://www.ee.surrey.ac.uk/edupage/edupage/`

The Paleontology Server:

`http://ucmp1.berkeley.edu/welcome.html`

International Teletimes:

`http://www.wimsey.com/teletimes.root/teletimes_home_page.html`

Internet Underground Music Archive:

`http://sunsite.unc.edu/ianc/`

Science Fiction Resource Guide:

`ftp://gandalf.rutgers.edu/pub/sfl/sf-resource.guide.html`

New Zealand Information:

`http://www.cs.cmu.edu:8001/Web/People/mjw/NZ/MainPage.html`

Taxing Times:

`http://www.scubed.com:800I/tax/tax.html`

US Census Information Server:

`http://www.census.gov/`

Hypertext USENET FAQs:

`http://www.cis.ohio-state.edu/hypertext/faq/usenet/FAQ-list.html`

Xerox PARC Map Viewer:

`http://pubweb.parc.xerox.com/map`

H.6 Online Conference Proceedings

First International World Wide Web Conference, Geneva, Switzerland, May 25-27, 1994:

```
http://www1.cern.ch/WWW94/Welcome.html
```

ACM European Conference On Hypermedia Technology (ECHT 94), Edinburgh, Scotland, September 18-23, 1994:

```
http://www.njit.edu/Professional_Society/SIGLINK.html
```

Second International WWW Conference '94: Mosaic and the Web, Chicago, Illinois, October 17-19, 1994:

```
http://www.ncsa.uiuc.edu/General/Announce/MosaicConf.html
```

Index

absolute URLs, 332
 definition, 286
 syntax of, 332
 versus relative, 333
absolute_dir variable type, 460
absolute_file variable type, 460
abstract (Gopher)
 attributes of, 210
 definition, 155
 example, 156
Acceptable Use Policies (AUPs)
 obtaining, 532
access control
 by delegating management of Web document tree, 310
 denying to selected accounts, 89
 domain-level, 382-384
  concommitant with user authentication, 388
  definition, 381
  directives for, 383
  general and unrestricted, setting up, 383
  general, unrestricted versus individual authentication, 386
  local-domain only, setting up, 383
  multi-organization access only, setting up, 384
 file for, 304
 for WAIS server, 125
 in FTP archive, 102-105
 limiting number of users via ftpaccess, 78
 on FTP archive, facilitating, 95-102
 on Gopher server, based on load, 167
 on Internet, 2-5
 per-directory versus server-wide, 381
 security and, 389
 to Gopher server via access token, 180
 to Web servers, 381-388
  two methods for, 381
 via encryption
  goals for, 543
 via ftpaccess, 75-81, 102-103
 via user authentication (Gopher 2.1), 276
 via xinetd.conf, 522
access control files (ACF)
 global versus per-directory, 381
 (see also access.conf file)
access method, 332
access token
 using to control reading, searching and browsing, 180
access.conf file
 as global access control file, 381
 directives, 585-590
 disabling symbolic links via, 388
 editing
  for local domain access only, 383
  for multi-organization access only, 384
  to give access to individual users, 385
  to protect personal HTML directories,

access.conf file, editing (cont'd)
389
to set up group user authentication, 387
enabling automatic directory indexing in, 321
enabling server-side includes in, 320
setup of, 304
AccessConfig directive, 573
AccessFileName directive, 579
accessing WAIS from World Wide Web, 376-380
access_times directive, 522
ACF file (see access.conf file; access control files)
ACM European Conference On Hypermedia Technology (ECHT), proceedings of, 595
AddDescription directive, 579
AddEncoding directive, 579
AddIcon directive, 580
AddIconbyEncoding directive, 580
address tag (HTML), 329
addresses
IP, 8
mail
associated with sendmail, 413
types of, 409
(see also local addresses (users) of mail)
AddType directive, 581
admin token, 182
adminemail token, 182
administrivia variable, 461
admin_passwd variable, 461
ADMIT1 Protocol, 275
advertise variable, 461, 467
AFTP_HOST variable, 553
AFTP_PORT variable, 553
Alcuin, 559
alias command, 87, 96
Alias directive, 581
aliases
domain names and, 13
facilitating navigation via, 96
for list owners, 455
for sendmail, 414
Majordomo, 437
local network and, 416
mail, 398
setting owner- to -request, 419
standard for FTP maintainer, 57
starting with owner-, 441
using as FTP domain name, 56
webmaster, for mail to Web server, 311
aliases file
adding list aliases to, 441
for large mailing lists, 415-416, 437
for small mailing lists, 414
shared, workarounds for, 416
aligning images in HTML documents, 337
allow command, 90
allow directive, 383, 585
in unrestricted access versus local domain access, 383
AllowOverride directive, 586
ALT option to image tag (HTML), 339
alternate gopherd configuration file
option for gopherd, 550
anchor tag (HTML), 331
anchor tagging pair, 330
anchors, definition, 285
Andreessen, Marc, 279
anonymous FTP, 507
accessing Blue-Skies via, 49
converting into Gopher hierarchy, 221
default user for Ftpmail, 484
definition, 20, 51
description, 52
directory structure, creating, 58
dual-homed gateway and, 508
Firewall Toolkit, address for, 505
kermit, 557
restricting access via chroot(), 55
screened host gateway and, 509
SOCKS, address for, 505
standard files for, 99
anonymous user class (ftp)
definition, 76
ANS (Advanced Networks and Services), 532
approve command, 456
approve program
description, 431
approve script, 430, 469
approve_passwd variable, 461
approving subscriptions, 469
without approve, 471
APPSDIR variable, 117

Archie
facilitating navigation on FTP archive, 99-102
firewalls and, 510
to-do checklist before adding files to, 101
archive maintainer (see data librarian)
archive servers, 19
definition, 19
archive2.pl program
description, 431
archives subdirectory (Majordomo), 435
ArtServe, 594
ASCII text to HTML tool, 349
+ASK attribute, 263
Ask Blocks
adding
checkboxes to, 268
default values to, 267
multiline input to, 268
radio boxes to, 267
debugging checklist, 273
example of, 265
filename of, 264
(see also Gopher+ Forms)
ASK forms
supported by GopherApp, 161
using to register Gopher server, 202
AskL query type for Gopher+ Forms, 268
attributes of menu items (Gopher)
definition, 155
example, 158
forms and abstracts (Gopher+), 210
how client fetches, 158
mapping to file extensions, token for (Gopher+), 185
AuthGroupFile directive, 586
AuthName directive, 586
authoring for the Web, 325-356
tools, 347-350
AuthType directive, 587
AuthUserFile directive, 587
auto lists (mail)
definition, 430
setting with subscribe_policy, 466
autoflowing, definition, 326
autogroup command, 80
automated list server
definition, 392
(see also list servers)
automatic directory indexing, 321-323
autowrapping, definition, 326

backslash (\)
in regular expressions, 468
backup copies
of inetd and inetd.conf, 519
banner command, 82, 99
banners
ideas for WU Archive FTP, 98
BASE tag (tag), 366
bastion host, 500, 507, 509
definition, 499
Beginner's Guide to HTML, 341
BibTeX to HTML tool, 349
bin directory
FTP permission and ownership, 59
binary files
encoding commands for Ftpmail, 485
BITFTP, xxxii
blank lines
inserting into HTML documents, 329
blockext token (Gopher+), 185
Blue-Skies, 49
Gopher client for Macintosh, 161
body tag (HTML), 327
bold tag (HTML), 568
bookmarks security feature, 553
bool variable type, 460
bootlegged commercial software, 538
bounce program, description, 431
bounce script (Majordomo), 430
to unsubscribe users for mailing lists, 478
bounced messages, 399, 411, 494
handling, 417
minimizing, 420
bounces mailing list (Majordomo), 476-478
setting up, 439
breaking lines
in xinetd.conf, 521
browsers
book, encryption in, 544
Lynx, 44, 289
Mosaic, 22-23
Web, 286, 288-292

browsers (cont'd)
display capabilities of, 325
use with inline images, 339
BSDI, 27
btoa command
in Ftpmail, 485
bug reports
sending to Majordomo, 454
sending via Mosaic, 28
building
WAIS, 112-118
WU Archive FTP daemon, 72
xinetd, 518
bummermsg token, 183
business cards (electronic), 281

cachetime token (Gopher+), 186
caching
files in Gopher server, 170
of directories
disabling gopherd option, 549
of inline images, 338
Can't open the logfile error message, 194
Can't Set UID! log error message, 198
canned_reply, 393-398
complete script, 393-396
installing, 393
mail file server, 392
reply files, 397
changing default directory of, 396
Cannot Access Directory error message, 244
Cannot change to data directory! error message, 194
.cap directory, 208
description, 207
.cap files, 563
enabling in Gopher server, 168
for script queries, 250
moving via GMV, 560
using to incorporate WAIS index, 240
captured shells
as login shells, 44
starting X clients in, 45-47
caret (^)
in regular expressions, 468
catalog (.cat) file, 135
option for creating, 146
catalogs
available on Internet, 26
CC variable, 113
cd command, 87
CERN Line Mode Browser
description, 292
CERN Web server
description, 293
proxy mode, 504
CERN World Wide Web Servers list, 312
CFLAGS variable, 114
CGI (see Common Gateway Interface)
CGI scripts, 370
debugging, 373
location, 390
trapping metacharacters in, 390
CGI variables, 340
cgi-bin directory
contents of, 358
making additional, 367
Chapman, Brent, 427
paper on Majordomo, 434
checkboxes
adding to Gopher+ Forms, 268
adding to World Wide Web forms, 373
Chimera
description, 292
choose query type for Gopher+ Forms, 267
chroot()
disabling, gopherd option, 548
hypertext links and, 95
restricting access
to FTP archive via, 55
to Gopher data directory, 187
sublogins and, 62
symbolic links in Gopher and, 219-221
class command, 76
Clearinghouse for Networked Information Discovery and Retrieval, 110
clickable image maps, 295, 350-356
enhancement to HTML, 295
HTML tag for, 354
planning, 351
testing, 354
Client Went Away log error message, 197
client/server
definition, 7

clients
as login shells, 43
definition in client/server, 7
role of in WAIS, 111
DOS, Mac, and Windows, security and, 512
UNIX, security and, 510-513
closed lists (mail)
definition, 427, 430
setting with subscribe_policy, 466
CNAME alias record, 311
colormaps
in HTML documents, 337
command line
specified log, 525
comment tag, 568
comments
in Gopher files, 167
in mailing list configuration files, 458-459
effect of writeconfig on, 461
comments CGI script, 370
comments variable, 461
CommerceNet, 298
Common Gateway Interface (CGI), 358-361
definition, 358
required prefix, 358
sample gateways and test scripts, 358
scripts
description, 360
prompting for input, 361
comp.infosystems.announce newsgroup, 312
compile-src command, 518
compiling
Gopher client and server, 174-176
Gopher server, 163-177
WU Archive FTP daemon, 70-72
compress command
in Ftpmail, 485
compressed files
Gopher, 217
compressing files
in Ftpmail, 484
compression programs
file formats and (table), 94
computational load, 33
Computer Emergency Response Team, 35
conf.h file
editing, 169
to configure Gopher server, 170
specifying default server and port number, 171
config command, 457
#config command, 341
configuration files
access.conf, 304, 320-321, 383-385, 388-389, 585-590
alternate, gopherd option, 550
cg-bin, 367
conf.h, 169
date_info variable, 456
for mailing lists, 456-468
changing, 457-468
comments in, 458
description, 457
sample, 457
variable types (table), 460
variables in, 458, 460-468
for NCSA Web server, 302-305
ftpaccess, 70, 75-81, 87-89, 96, 98
ftpconversions, 70, 73
ftphosts, 70, 89
gopherd.conf, 179, 217, 278
httpd.conf, 303, 315, 573-577
inetd.conf, 41, 120
FTP startup via, 54
inetd.file, 12
.mailcap, 319
mime.types, 319
srm.conf, 304, 321, 323, 579-584
WU Archive FTP daemon, 69
xinetd.conf, 519
configuring
waisserver, 124-131
Web server for site, 302-305
WU Archive FTP daemon, 75-81
config_parse.pl program
description, 432
connection provider
definition, 2
Connection Refused error message, 193

conventions
for announcing new Web server, 311
for public access to Web server, 311
cool links, 229-236
definition, 229
copyrights, 533-537
creating, 534
duration, 535
registering, 536
respecting others, 536
Couldn't Open Grep Command log error message, 198
cover.abstract file, 211
creating
aliases in WU Archive FTP daemon, 87
HTML documents, 325-356
Internet database server with WAIS, 109-131
moderated mailing lists, 469
CSO Phone Book Server, linking to, 227
Currency Converter, 594
curses gopher client, 205
ABSTRACT attribute and, 211
using to locate link, 225
customized login and no login services, 47
CyberLeaf, 349

daemons
starting as root versus running as root, 550
usefulness of, 12
WU Archive, 69-92
dash
meaning of to Majordomo, 429
dash format, 139
data architecture
of Gopher server, 211-214
data directory
option for gopherd, 551
Data Encryption Standard, 541, 545
data librarian
attributes of, 35
creating WAIS sources, 133-150
duties, 34
meaning of icon, 6
preparing information for Gopher, 205-221
role in linking services into Gopher server, 223-236
role in maintaining FTP archive, 93-107
database files (waisindex), 135
database security file (WAIS), 127
databases
Genera, gateway for, 367
searching capabilities, 237-256
DATA_SEC file, 127
date_info configuration file variable, 456
date_info variable, 461
debug variable, 462
debugging
enabling output, gopherd option for, 549
FTP archive, 64-68
decoder token (Gopher+), 186
dedicated line to Internet, 2
DefaultIcon directive, 582
DefaultType directive, 582
defining user classes in WU Archive FTP daemon, 75
definition lists (HTML), 334
delete command for Ftpmail, 483
DELETE_BOOKMARKS_ONLY variable, 553
delivery of electronic mail, 408-411
Denied Access for Host log error message (Gopher+), 198
deny command
ftaccess file, 77, 102
ftphosts file, 89
deny directive, 383, 587
in unrestricted access versus local domain access, 383
deny from all directive, 383
denying access
to FTP archive, 102
to WU Archive FTP daemon, 77
description variable, 462
device-independent TeX output format, 139
df
checking room on filesystem, 493
dial-up
access to Internet, 4
connection to Internet, 4
DIALOG database services, 540
dictionary (.dct) file, 134

digest program
description, 431
digested mailing lists (see mail digests)
digests subdirectory, 435
digest_issue variable, 462
digest_name variable, 462
digest_volume variable, 462
digital signatures, 296, 542
Direct User Access Terminal System, 21
directives for access control, 383
directories
automatic indexing of, 321-323
.cap, 207
cgi-bin, making additional, 367
creating aliases for in WU Archive FTP daemon, 87
disabling caching of, option to gopherd, 549
dist, 61
Gopher link to, example, 226
hidden, 104, 238
HTML, personal, 389
indexing entire tree via waisindex, 145
optional FTP, 61
overriding of default Gopher data, 551
permission and ownership for FTP, 59
restricting access to Gopher data, 187
searching FTP archive via cd command, 87
structure of, moving, 313
Directory directive, 587
directory tree (see document tree (HTML))
directory-of-servers.src
definition, 144
DirectoryIndex directive, 582
disable chroot(), option for gopherd, 548
disable directory caching, option for gopherd, 549
disabled directive, 522
disk space
on server, 33
saving via waisindex option, 146
displaying messages in WU Archive FTP daemon, 98
dist directory, 61
distributing mailing lists to other hosts, 423-425
dl databases
description, 167
switch for compiling in Gopher, 167
document (.doc) table, 134
document formats
example, in Gopher+, 156
Gopher
adding new types, 185
registering new types, 185
handling multiple in Gopher+, 155
how waisindex handles multiple, 149
document tree (HTML)
delegating control of, 310
links outside, 388
moving, 313
updating, 312
documentation, tool for installing in Gopher, 563
DocumentRoot directive, 305, 311, 582
setting up top of document tree via, 304
dollar sign ($)
in regular expressions, 468
domain name servers
description, 13
Domain Name System (DNS)
description, 13
domain names
setting for Gopher server, 168
$dont_reply_to variable, 494
dot directories (see hidden directories)
dot, single
having sendmail ignore, 418
dotted-octet notation, 8
downloading in the client, 557
du
checking size of queue, 493
dual-homed gateways, 499
locating a Web server in, 506
Mosaic and, 512
DUATS (Direct User Access Terminal System)
service for pilots, 21
duplicating Web documents and servers, 314-315
dvi format, 139

#echo command, 340
editing files with medit, 451
Edupage Newsletter, 594

EM tag (HTML), 327, 329
Emacs
HTML mode, 348
World Wide Web browser, description, 290
email (see mail)
email file servers
definition, 393
(see also mail file servers)
email information server
definition, 392
emphasis tag (HTML), 327, 568
employee directory
handling electronically, 27
enable debugging output
option for gopherd, 549
encryption
as means of protecting property rights, 540
background, 541
example of issues, 543-544
federal export controls on, 545
MDC algorithm, 545
private key, 542
public key, 541
software, 538
end command
Majordomo, 429
enum variable type, 460
envelope data, definition, 408
envelope recipient, definition, 408
envelope sender
address
checking (Majordomo), 447
for bounced message, 417
set to owner-, workaround for, 419
definition, 408
option for setting, 419
environmental variables
for use with server-side includes, 340
for xinetd, 524
equal sign (=)
for storing in variables, 458
equals (=) key
differences in Gopher and Gopher+, 156
ErrorLog directive, 315, 573
Errors-to: message header field, 421
etc directory
FTP permission and ownership, 59
/etc/passwd file
setting up ftp user, 55
creating guest users via, 80
ethics
electronic mail and, 405
example programs
obtaining, xxx
#exec command, 341
exec link type, 232
exec: links
combining with shell indexes, 252-255
Executed Script log message (Gopher+), 197
executing scripts via links, 232-236
exploders
list (see list exploders)
export controls on encryption, 545
ext token (Gopher 1.x), 183
extensions
.abstract, 211
.ask, 211
configuring recognition of in Gopher, 183-185
file formats and (table), 94
for HTML documents, 284
ftp processing of files according to, 73
ftp types in Gopher 1.x (table), 231
gopher file types and (table), 183
standard, in FTP archive, 94
supported by Gopher (table), 216
external images, 336, 338
external services
list of, 27

FAIL string, 527
fancy indexing of Web server directories, 321-322
FancyIndexing directive, 582
FAQs (Frequently Asked Questions)
about firewalls, 513
Gopher, 162
World Wide Web, 591
federal export controls on encryption, 545
feedback form, 370
fields in inetd.conf entry, 12
FIFOs, 39
file extensions (see extensions)

file formats
creating WAIS index with multiple, 149
extensions and (table), 94
Gopher 1.x types and (table), 183
Gopher+ menu items in multiple, 210
how HTTP supports, 288
overriding default Gopher, 217
recognized by Gopher via extension, 183-185
supported by Gopher, 215-219
table of, 216
understood by waisindex, 138
file transfer commands, 484-486
file transfer modes
ascii, 486
binary, 486
file transfer protocol (see FTP)
file types (see file formats; extensions)
file= tag (HTML), 340
filename (.fn) table, 134
filename format, 139
files
.cap, 240
conf.h, 169
editing with medit, 451
finding on FTP archive, 99
ftpgroups, 81
ftpusers, 71
Gopher link to, example, 226
group, 58
image map, 351
imagemap.conf, 354
.links, 211, 223-225
ls-lR files, 99-102
.names, 208, 211, 217-218
passwd, 58, 62
permission and ownership for FTP, 59
SERV_SEC, 125
(see also configuration files)
financial rewards
obstacles to, 28
find command
using with waisindex, 146
to avoid indexing unwanted Gopher data, 242
Finger, 20
trick for updating, 39
uses for, 38
weather reports and, 21
.fingerrc script, 38
Firewall Toolkit, 505
firewalls
definition, 498
for WAIS, 128-131
guidelines for setting up, 501
information services and, 497-513
questions about, 513
screened subnet, 501
server location and, 506
simple screening router, 501
software for, 504
CERN Web server proxy mode, 504
Firewall Toolkit, 505
SOCKS, 505
types of, 498
First Amendment to the U.S. Constitution, 531
First International World Wide Web Conference, proceedings of, 595
first_line format, 139
#flastmod command, 340
float variable type, 460
FORM tag
description, 369
FORM tag (HTML), 568
forms
for Web server (see World Wide Web forms)
Gopher+ (see Gopher+ Forms)
forward-path (RFC 821), 408
forwarding capabilities of WAIS
to circumvent firewalls, 128
FrameMaker, 348
freeWAIS, 28, 110
security features of, 125
upcoming fixes to SERV_SEC, 126
(see also WAIS (Wide Area Information Servers))
Frequently Asked Questions (FAQs)
firewall questions, 513
Gopher, 162
World Wide Web server, 591
From: mail message header field
Ftpmail command, 483
security and, 402
versus From message header field , 418"
#fsize command, 340

FTP
- avoiding legal problems, 53
- computational load on server, 33
- description, 20
- example programs, obtaining, xxxi
- firewalls and, 511
- Gopher2FTP gateway, 561
- mail (see Ftpmail)
- transaction log, 483
- user FTP (see user FTP)
- weaknesses, 20

ftp access token, 180

FTP archive
- alias for system maintainer, 57
- components, 53
- connecting to, 65
- example of ORA's, 97
- facilitating navigation, 95-102
- filesystem (see FTP filesystem)
- finding files on, 99
- hypertext links for, creating, 95
- linking to from Gopher, 229-232
- maintaining, 93-107
- optional directories, 61
- populating, 93-95
- server (see FTP server)
- setting up, 51-68
- sublogins to, definition, 62
- SUNOS and Solaris and, 60
- testing and debugging, 64-68
- using for the first time, 67
- (see also WU Archive FTP daemon)

FTP filesystem, 58-63
- anonymous FTP, setting up for, 58
- directories, optional, 61
- passwd and group files, 58

ftp format, 139

FTP gateway setting, 553

ftp link type, 229

FTP server, 53-57
- command-line options, 56
- domain naming, 56
- firewalls and, 507
- inetd configuration and, 53-55
- types of access provided by, 51
- user ID of ftp
  - login directory, 59
  - setting up, 55

FTP types
- recognized by Gopher 1.x (table), 231

ftp-admin alias, 57

ftp-gw, 505

ftpaccess file, 70, 75-81, 96, 98
- navigation and, 87
- uploading files, controlling, 88-89

ftpconversions file, 70, 73

ftpcount utility program, 90

ftpd (see FTP server)
- logs, 526

ftpgroups file, 81

ftphosts file, 70, 89

Ftpmail, xxxi, 479-495
- binary encoding, 485
- changing directories in, 484
- commands, 483-486
- compressing files, 484
- description, 480-486
- file transfer commands, 484-486
- installing, 486-492
- listing files and directories in, 484
- mail command limits, 484
- mailing list for, 495
- managing, 492
  - ignored mail, 494
  - restricting, 493
  - routine checks, 493
- sample session, 480
- sending mail to server, 480
- testing your installation, 490

ftpshut utility program, 91

ftpusers
- contrasted with ftphosts, 89

ftpusers file, 71

ftpwho utility program, 91

Fwgstat, 559

gateways, 358-367
- definition, 357
- developing custom WAIS, 377
- dual-homed, 499, 506
- FTP, 277
  - setting, 553
- Go4gw, 560
- Go4zgate, 560
- Gonnrp, 561
- Gopher2FTP, 561
- Gophtech, 562

gateways (cont'd)
imagemap, 355
list of, 366
samples in NCSA Web server kit, 358
screened host, 500
simple search, creating, 362
simple search, example, 364
Techinpher, 564
URLs in HTML documents returned by, 366
Web to WAIS, 377
GEE, 559
Genera gateway, 367
geog token, 182
get command
for Ftpmail, 486
Majordomo, 429
GET method
definition, 358
used by Web-to-WAIS gateways, 377
getstats
description, 317
gif format, 139
gindexd
invoking gopherd as, 195
serving WAI and NeXt indexes with, 246-249
syntax, 248
GLA, 559
(see also Gopher Log Analyzer)
GLASS, 560
global access control file (ACF) (see access.conf)
global attributes of Gopher+ server, 182
Global Network Navigator (GNN), 27, 297
Best of the Net servers, 593
electronic magazine, 280
GLOG, 560
(see also Gopher Log Analyzer)
Gmail, 560
Gmail/Gmailcal, 560
Gmailcal, 560
GMV, 560
gn server, 160
Go4gw, 560
Go4zgate, 560
Gofinger, 561
finger-like tool for Gopher, 561
Goform, 561
Gonnrp, 561
Gopher
client software, 161
description, 21
directory protocol
meaning of fields in, 153
enhancements to in Gopher+, 155
FAQs, 162, 559
forms
Goform tool, 561
gateways, 559-565
how protocol works, 152-154
interaction of client and server, 151-154
introduction to, 151-162
limitations, 22, 152, 155
menu items
as displayed by client, 151
as displayed by server, 153
learning about, contrast with Gopher+, 156
servers, versions of software, 159
tools, 559-565
usage report, 562
Gopher 2.0.16, features of, 275
Gopher 2.1
FTP gateway, 277
user authentication, 276
Gopher 2.x
(see Gopher+)
Gopher client
compilation options, 553-557
compiling with server, 174-176
excluding certain files from, 185
installing, 176
menu items
characters for denoting files and directories, 205
security options, 553
setting commands, 554-556
software for, 161
Gopher links
as represented in menu, 223
examples of different types, 226
Gopher Log Analyzer, 198-200, 559
Gopher MOO, 162
Gopher server
cloning, tool for, 561, 564
communication with client, example, 14
compile-time options for, 167

Gopher server (cont'd)
compiling, 163-177
with client, 174-176
with NeXT indexing, 172
with WAIS indexing, 172
computational load on, 33
configuring, 179-186
converting existing FTP structure into, 221
data architecture of, 211-214
directory tree, examining, 213
menus, 211
data directory, 169
database search capability, 237-256
effect of chrooting on WAIS query, 241
NeXT indexes, incorporating, 244-246
using gindexd (Gopher 1.x), 246-249
WAIS indexes, incorporating, 237-244, 559
default port number, 169
directories and files used by Makefile.config, list of, 166
document length and format, 212
domain name setting, 168
file types
overriding default, 217
recognized by, 215-219
finger-like tool, 561
gindexd server, 246-249
gn server for World Wide Web and, 160
indexing script, 276
installing, 176
invoking, 187-191
as gopherls or gindexd, 195
preparing data directory prior to, 187
problems, 192-195
recommended command-line options, 188
standalone, 188
under inetd versus standalone, 187, 189
using inetd, 189
Jughead, 259-262
linking services, 223-236
CSO Phone Book Server, 227
FTP archives, 229-232
Telnet, 228
via scripts, 232-236
linking to data on another, 225
.links files, 223-225
keywords for, 224
logging, 196-201
managing, 179-204
menu items
importance of precise names, 212
naming, ordering, and attributes of, 206-211
naming host, 179
options for gopherd, 547-551
precompilation configuration, 165-174
optional, 171
prefixes and file types (table), 226
registering, 202-204
example, 203
root, starting as, option for, 550
setting system load, 550
setting up information and directories, 205-221
software for, 159
source code for, 163-165
main files and directories, 164
special files, 217-219
specifying default, 171
testing, 191-195
updates, learning about, 564-565
using inetd
option for, 549
Veronica, 257-259
avoiding registration with, 258
registering with, 258
Gopher+, 155-161
attributes, setting, 182
cache timeout setting for server, 170
client options not in Gopher 1.x, 168
concurrent sessions, limiting, 181
features, 155-157
forms (see Gopher+ Forms)
licensing terms of server, 160
.links files, 211, 224
menu items
multi-format, 210
learning about, 156
.names file, 211, 217-218
.names file, alternative to .cap, 208
new features, 275-278
protocol, 158-159
server options not in Gopher 1.x, 167

Gopher+ (cont'd)
- source code not in Gopher 1.x server, 165
- special characters
  - denoting client request for menu item attributes, 158
  - denoting support by menu items of, 158, 225
- tokens, 180-181, 185-186
- version number, 160

Gopher+ Forms, 263-275
- attributes of, 210
- debugging Ask Blocks, 273
- naming form definition (Ask Block) and script files for, 264
- query types for, 263
- returning non-text types, 271
- saving output of, 270
- script for returning non-text types, 272-273
- simple example of, 265
- (see also Ask Blocks)

gopher-type
- used with ext token, 183

Gopher2FTP, 561
Gopher2mbox, 561
GopherApp, 161
Gopherclone, 561
gopherd command
- command-line options for, 188
- Gopher+ Forms and, 271
- options for, 547-551
- using to create script querying type, 250-255

gopherd.conf file, 278
- editing to override default file format, 217
- location, 179
- setting global attributes in, 182
- specifying alternate, 189

Gopherdist, 562
gopherindex command, 276
gopherls, invoking gopherd as, 195
Gophersoc, 562
GopherSQL, 562
gophertree script, 213, 562
Gophreport, 562
Gophtech, 562
graphical formats understood by waisindex, 139
graphics, 336-339
grep indexes, 249
group file (hypertext), 386-387
group files, 58
guest user class
- definition, 76
- setting up, 80

Guestbook, 563
guestgroup command, 80
gwstat
- description, 317

gzip command
- in Ftpmail, 485

hash functions
- encryption and, 542

hash mark (#)
- comments in mailing list configuration files, 458

HEAD tag (HTML), 327
header level tag (HTML), 329
HeaderName directive, 582
headers
- displayed after directory index, 322
- mail (see mail message headers)

headline (.hl) table, 135
help command
- Majordomo, 429
- Ftpmail, 483

Hewlett Packard
- sound programs and, 555

hidden directories, 104, 238
hierarchy
- of DNS names, 13

home pages
- including webmaster alias on, 311
- setting up, 309

home.html, 309
hostalias token, 179
hostdata file, 247
hostname command, 168
hosts response, checking for, 564
HoTMetaL, 348
hotspots, 295, 351
- definition, 351
- mapping in image map files, 351

HR (horizontal rule) tag (HTML), 329

HREF tag (HTML), 330
.htacess file, 381
htget script, 314-315
.htgroup file, 386-387
HTML (HyperText Markup Language)
  enhancements to, 294
  for World Wide Web forms, 368
  generating directory contents in, 321-323
  indexing files for, 141
  introduction, 284
  use by World Wide Web, 22
  versions of, 294
HTML documents
  authoring tools, 347-350
  autoflowing, 326
  autowrapping, 326
  conversion tools and filters, 349
  degree of hypertext linking, issues about, 342
  graphics in, 336
  how Web server recognizes, 320
  information design, 341-346
    example, 344
  linking to points within, 331
  mirroring, 314-315
  modularity, 341
  overview, 325-341
  returned by gateways, URLs in, 366
  sample, 327
  structure of, 327
  style guidelines, 344
  updating, 312
HTML tages
  syntax of, 326
HTML tags, 567-571
  for addresses, 329
  for anchors, 331
  for blank lines, 329
  for bold, 568
  for clickable image maps, 354
  for comments, 568
  for email address of owner, 328
  for emphasis, 568
  for forms, 568
  for glossary definitions, 335
  for headers, 329
  for horizontal rules, 329
  for input devices, 569
  for inserting images, 328
  for italics, 567
  for links, 330
  for lists, 334
  for paragraphs, 567
  for pop-up menus, 570
  for preformatting, 343, 567
  for quotes, 567
  for scrollable lists, 570
  for scrollable text area, 570
  for sections, 344
  for tables, 567
  for titles, 328
  standalone, 327
  used in pairs, 327
htmltext, 347
HTML_COMMAND command, 556
.htpasswd file, 385
  managing, 385
htpasswd program, 385-386
HTTP (HyperText Transfer Protocol)
  description, 287
  security enhancements to, 296
  versions, 287
httpd (HTTP daemon) (see NCSA Web server)
httpd command, 540
  command-line options for, 305
httpd.conf file
  changing location and names of Web log files via, 315
  configuring to run server under inetd, 307
  directives, 573-577
  making logs writable, 305
  setup of for standalone server, 303
human requirements for running an information service, 34
hyperlinking (see hypertext links)
hypertext group file, 386-387
hypertext links, 330-331
  automatic versus manual, 343
  clickable image maps, 350-356
  creating for FTP archive, 95
  definition, 330
  degree of, issues about, 342
  description, 22, 283
  hotspots, 351

hypertext links (cont'd)
- selecting, 286
- to points within documents, 331

hypertext username/password file, 385-386
Hypertexted USENET FAQs, 594
Hytelnet gateway, 366

icons
- associated with filename, how treated, 321
- data librarian, 6
- displaying for Web browsers, 580

IdentityCheck directive, 574
If All Else Fails . . . error message, 195
ignore token, 185
ignored mail, 494
ignore_patt token (Gopher+), 186
[IMAGE]
- default display in Web browser, overriding, 339

image map files
- mapping hotspots in, 351

image maps, clickable
- (see clickable image maps)

image tag (HTML), 328
imagemap program, 355
imagemap.conf, 354
images, 336-339
- aligning, 337
- colormap issues, 337
- external, 336, 338
- inline (see inline images)
- inserting in HTML documents, 328, 330, 337

IMAGE_COMMAND command, 556
img tag (HTML), 328, 330
#include command, 340
include files (see server-side includes)
include statements
- in HTML documents, 340

INCLUDES variable, 117
index, Gopher link to (example), 226
index command
- Majordomo, 429
- variable for, 465

index files, 133-136
- controlling operation of waisindex on, 145
- rewriting into .cap files, 563
- updating, 144, 148-149

index.html, 307
Index2cap, 563
indexer (WAIS component), 111
IndexIgnore directive, 583
indexing directories automatically, 321-323
indexing text files (see Wais (Wide Area Information Servers))
IndexOptions directive, 583
inetd
- information services based on, 40-42
  - security, 43
- running
  - FTP server under, 53-55
  - Gopher server under, 189-191
  - undergopherd option, 549
  - waisserver under, 120-121
  - Web server under, 307

inetd server
- description, 11
- (see also xinetd)

inetd.conf file, 41, 120
- backing up before installing xinetd, 519
- description, 12
- FTP startup via, 54

info command
- Majordomo, 429
- variable for, 465

Information Only type (Gopher), 276
information servers, communication with clients, 14
information services
- based on Finger, 37-40
- entrepreneurship and, 28
- Finger-based, 37-40
- firewalls and, 497-513
- Gopher, 21
- human requirements, 34
- inetd-based, 40-42
- Internet concepts, 1-15
- linking to Gopher server, 223-236
- mail-based, 18-19
- offered externally, 27
- offered internally, 26
- overview of Internet, 18-36
- restricting access to, 522
- setting attributes of xinetd.conf, 521
- suggested use of, 26-29

information services (cont'd)
- system and network requirements, 29-34
- targets of trespassers, 517
- Telnet-based, 42-50
- WAIS, 24
- World Wide Web, 22
- (see also Internet services)

inline images, 337
- caching of, 338
- thumbnails, 338
- using translucent backgrounds with, 337
- with character-based Web browsers, 339
  - overriding default display of, 339

input device tag, 569
INPUT tag, 370
inserting blank lines (HTML), 329
inserting images in HTML documents, 330
install command, 176
INSTALLDIR variable, 117
installing
- Ftpmail, 486-492
- Gopher client and server, 176
- Majordomo, 432-439
- WAIS, 118-122
- xinetd, 519-520

InstGopher, 563
integer variable type, 460
intellectual property rights, 533-538
- cryptographic methods, 540
  - background, 541
- non-cryptographic methods, 539
- protecting, 539-546
- types of protection, 533

Interleaf to HTML tool, 350
internal services, list of, 26
Internet
- definition, 1
- domain address, basis of access control, 382
- inetd server, 11
- multimedia mail, 556
- names of computers on, 13
- number of users, 6
- organizations connected to, 6
- overview of appeal, 5-7
- TCP/IP, 8-11
- ways of accessing, 2

Internet provider, definition, 1
Internet services
- concepts, 1-15
- Finger, 20
- FTP, 20
- overview, 18-36
- suggested use of, 26-29
- Telnet, 20

Internet Underground Music Archive (IUMA), 594
inverted (.inv) file, 134
IP
- addresses, 8
  - defining user class via, 76
  - denying access to FTP archive via, 89
  - denying access to selected, 77
  - format, 522
  - using to control access to xinetd, 522
  - using to track culprit, 528
- description, 8-10
  - of full-time connection, 2

ISDN (Integrated Services Digital Network), 5
ISINDEX tag (HTML), 361
ISMAP tag (HTML), 354
italics tag, 567
iterative searches, 24
itox command, 519
ixBuild command, 244-245

Jughead, 259-262, 563
- building a search table and index, 261
- creating a search table for, 260
- description, 259
- invoking, 261
- linking to from Gopher, 262

kermit, 557
key management, 541

language token, 182
LaTeX to HTML tool, 350
legal issues, 531-538
LFLAGS variable, 117
libel, 537
LIBS variable, 117
licensing of Gopher+ server, 160
limit command, 78, 103
Limit directive, 588
limiting access to FTP archive, 103

limiting number of WU Archive FTP daemon users, 78
link tag (HTML), 328
linking
files via waisindex, 142
NeXT index into Gopher server, 245
services to Gopher server, 223-236
to points within HTML documents, 331
WAIS index into Gopher server, 239
Linkmerge, 563
links
Gopher (see hypertext links)
hypertext
.links files, 223-225
creating script queries via (Gopher+), 250
generating, 562
making Gopher+ Forms return non-text types via, 271
setting a menu item's abstract in, 211
list exploders, 423-425
description, 423
setting up, 423
list members file
format for, including in aliases file, 415
sorting, 415
using, 415-416
list owners
aliases for, 455
approving messages to moderated lists, 475-476
commands for (Majordomo), 456
definition, 399, 430
duties, 401
moderating process, 473
receiving copy of configuration file, 457
role in creating mailing list (Majordomo), 440
scripts for (Majordomo), 430
security and, 403
setting up account for (Majordomo), 451
types of messages received by, 430
view of list server, 401
list servers, 399-403
definition, 392, 399
disadvantages of, 401
feature comparison with each other and MTA, 403-405
Majordomo, 427-454
list tags (HTML)
definition, 334
nested, 335
ordered, 334
unordered, 334
LIST variable, 170
list-managers mailing list, 408
obtaining archives of, 408
subscribing to, 408
listname alias, 423
editing to create listname-digest, 445
listname-approval alias, 430, 442, 455
types of messages received from Majordomo, 469
listname-digest alias, 444
listname-outgoing alias, 442
listname-request address
definition, 414
listname.info file
description, 456
ListProcessor
example of use, 399
features of, 398
V6.0c compared with Majordomo and MTA, 404
lists command
Majordomo, 429
lists subdirectory (Majordomo), 435
listserv, 393
load average
option for gopherd, 550
loc token, 182
local addresses (users) of mail
definition, 409
mail from, 419
sending copies of messages to, 418
(see also addresses, mail)
local URLs, 334
log commands command, 85
log files, enabling
gopherd option, 549
log to a file
option for gopherd, 549
log transfer command, 86
logger tool, 563
logging
four kinds of logs, 524

logging (cont'd)
FTP's syslog and xferlog, monitoring, 106
Gopher, 196-201
analyzer program, 198-200, 559-560
enabling client's syslog, 168
rotating files, 201
summarizing data, 198-200
mail messages, 423
Majordomo, 452
waisindex, options for, 145
Web server, 315-318
managing files for, 313
WU Archive FTP daemon, 85
Xferstats.gopher program, 565
xinetd, 524-526
checking files, 527
controlling via attributes in, 523
role in security, 523
login directory, user ID of ftp, 59
login services, customizing, 47
login shells
Telnet, 43-50
captured shells as, 44
clients as, 43
security problems with, 43
logs directory, defined in httpd.conf, 305
log_on_failure attribute, description, 523
log_on_success attributes, description, 523
log_type attributem description, 523
log_type directive, 523
ls-lR files, 99-102
Lynx
description, 289
using as Web login program, 44

Macintosh clients for Gopher, 161
mail, 182
addresses
types of, 409
aliases, 311
for Majordomo list owners, 430
bounced messages
handling (Majordomo), 476-478
resending, 417
delivery process, 408-411
error messages
owner-listname address and, 414
ethics, 405
Ftpmail, 479-495
gateway for, 561
reading, 107
services and networks
avoiding mail loops, 406
easing load on, 406
spool file, Gopher, 219
to HTML document owner, 334
mail alias, 398
mail archives
definition, 398
listing files in, 429
managing (Majordomo), 453
reply traffic on servers, 32
sending files from, 429
setting up (Majordomo), 440
mail digests, 460
definition, 398
expanding text of all messages in, 463
setting up (Majordomo)
description, 444
testing, 450
variables for, 462
mail file servers
canned_reply, 393-398
requirements of, 407
mail hub
setting up list alias for, 416
mail loop, definition, 406
mail message headers
controlling where errors are sent
by manual editing, 420
via manual editing, 421
via scripts, 421
Errors-to: field in, 421
From versus From:, 418
Precedence: field, 421
treatment by MTA, 420
mail messages
approved by moderator, 427
bounced, 494
handling bounced, 417
handling returned (Majordomo), 476-478
how sendmail returns errors, 414
logging, 423
minimizing bounced, 420
splitting, 485

mail messages (cont'd)
to moderated lists, sending and delivering, 473
mail servers
BITFTP, xxxii
disk space requirements, 33
Ftpmail, xxxi
mail services
advantages and disadvantages of, 391
overview of, 391-411
mail to HTML tool, 350
mail transport agent (MTA), 398, 408-411
compared with list servers, 403
description, 409
role in starting Majordomo, 432
(see also MMDF mail transport agent systems)
mail user agent (MUA), 408
description, 408
mail-based archives
computational load on, 33
mail-based services on Internet, 18-19
.mailcap files, 319
waisindex and, 141
mailing digests, 457
variables for, 462
mailing lists
advertising, 461
approving subscriptions to, 469
automatic, 466
bounced messages, 417, 420
bounces (Majordomo), 439
changing administrative password (Majordomo), 456
closed, definition, 430
computational load of server, 33
configuration files
changing (Majordomo), 457
copying, 457
correspondence about, 414
creating own, 27
definition, 19, 392
digested (see mail digests)
distributing (see list exploders)
exploders (see list exploders)
features, 392
for announcing new Web server, 311
for World Wide Web, 592
getting added to, 19
how to handle shared alias file for, 416
large, option for queueing messages to, 418
list-managers, 408
logging messages, 423
majordomo-users, 454
managing, 398-399
moderated, 427, 469
alias for requests to approve messages, 430
setting up, 469
testing, 449
without approve script, 473
open, definition, 430
private, 466
public, 466
publicity, 467
reply traffic on servers, 32
security, 402
setting up, 413-416
setting up for use with Majordomo, 440-445
archived, 440, 442
digested, 444
simple (MTA), 413-425
using aliases for smaller, 414
using list members file for larger, 415-416
MAIL_COMMAND command, 554
mail_digest format, 139
mail_or_rmail format, 139
maintaining
FTP archive, 93-107
log files, 106
Web server, 312-318
Majordomo, 28, 427-454
administrator
alias, 438
day-to-day duties, 451-454
definition, 431
Brent Chapman's paper on, 434
common problems with, 443
compared with ListProcessor and MTA, 404
description, 427
disabling temporarily for maintenance, 453
features of, 398
installing, 432-439

Majordomo (cont'd)
configuring majordomo.cf, 436
home directory, 434-435
Makefile, editing, 434
requirements, 432
list owners
commands for, 456
scripts for, 430
logs, 452
managing archives, 453
overview, 428-432
programs and files, description, 431
secure version, obtaining, 428
sending bug reports to, 454
sendmail V.8 and, 419
subscription commands, 428
testing installation of, 446-451
versus majordomo program, 428
majordomo program
description, 431
determining if list is publicized, 461
mailing configuration file to, 460
regular expressions in, 467
majordomo-announce mailing list, 454
majordomo-users mailing list, 454
majordomo-workers mailing list, 454
majordomo.cf file
configuring, 436
logging and, 452
managing archives via, 453
majordomo.cf program
description, 432
Makefile for WAIS (Wide Area Information Servers), 113
Makefile.config (Gopher)
definition, 165
directories and files installed by, 166
editing, 165-169
Malformed Hostdata File log error message, 197
maltshop
creating local links to Veronica server via, 259
man2html gateway, 366
managing xinetd, 524-529
map files (see image map files)
maxlength variable, 463
MAXLOAD variable, 170
McLoughlin, Lee, 479
MDC, public-domain encryption algorithm, 545
MecklerWeb
for NetWorth, 298
medit
program description, 431
script, 451
memory
saving via waisindex option, 146
menus (Gopher) (see Gopher server, menu items)
message command, 83, 98
message facility of WU Archive FTP daemon, 82-85
message headers (see mail message headers)
messages
approving, 475-476
bounced mail, 411
denying access, 77
displaying for WU Archive user, 98
Gopher
access denied to Gopher server, 183
error upon incorporating WAIS index, 243
error upon invoking, 192-195
log, 196-197
log error, 197
mail (see mail messages)
mail error (see bounced messages)
undeliverable (see returned mail messages; bounced messages)
upon connecting to FTP archive, 65
message_footer variable, 463
message_fronter variable, 463
message_headers variable, 464
metacharacters
trapping in interactive shells, 390
understood by regular expressions, 467-468
Metaclone, 564
MH mail handler, 471
MHtogroph, 564
MidasWWW
description, 289
MIME (Multipurpose Internet Mail Extensions) protocol, 556
adding types to Web server, 318-320
encoding, 491

MIME (Multipurpose Internet Mail Extensions) protocol (cont'd)
in Ftpmail, 485
how HTTP supports data types via, 288
types understood by waisindex, 141
mime.types file, 319
MIME_COMMAND command, 556
mindexd, 255
mirroring Web documents and servers, 314-315
mkdigest command, 457
MMDF mail transport agent systems, 438, 441, 444, 489
mode ascii, 483, 486
mode binary, 483, 486
modem access to Internet, 2, 4
moderate variable, 464
moderated lists
definition, 427
(see also mailing lists, moderated)
moderating with approve, 469
moderator of mailing list
definition, 398
monitoring log files, 106
moog, Gopher client, 161
Mosaic, 22-23
associating files in, 142
decryption features, 545
description, 290
direct access to WAIS server, 376
dual-homed gateway and, 512
firewalls and, 504, 512
history of development, 279
hotlist to HTML tool, 350
proxy mode configuration, 504
screened host gateway and, 512
sending bug reports via, 28
starting points, 593
waisindex and, 141
X-based, 504
MTA (see Mail Transport Agent)
multimedia mail, 556
Multipurpose Internet Mail Extensions, 556
(see also MIME (Multipurpose Internet Mail Extensions) protocol)
mungedomain variable, 464

name tag (HTML), 330
named pipes 39
.names file
displaying name-only menu items in Gopher), 276
editing to override default file type, 217-218
setting a menu item's abstract in, 211
naming Gopher menu items, 207-208
naming scheme of DNS, 13
navigating
FTP archive, facilitating, 95-102
hypertext links
definition, 283
WU Archive FTP daemon, facilitating, 87
NCSA Web server
compiling NCSA HTTP source, 300
configuring, 302-305
guidelines for, 302
description, 293
installing, 305
precompiled HTTP daemon, 299
maintaining, 312-318
platforms supported, 299
precompiled binaries, contents of, 300
samples gateways in, 358
setting up, 299-312
standalone startup
configuring for, 303
invoking, 306
rebooting server, 306
starting, 305-307
under inetd, 307
netacl, 505
netnews format, 139
Network Information Service (NIS)
how to handle shared alias file, 416
network requirements
connection type, 30
for Internet services, 29-34
load, 30
query sizes, 30
New Zealand Information, 594
new-list program
description, 431
newaliases command , 414
newconfig command, 457
newinfo command, 456
Newitems, 564

newsgroups
for World Wide Web (WWW), 591
NeXT
enabling indexing on Gopher server, 172
sound programs and, 555
Web browser, 291
NeXT indexes
incorporating in Gopher server, 244-246
served by gindexd (Gopher 1.x), 246-249
no login services
customizing, 47
no-break shells, 44
noadvertise variable, 461, 464, 467
nobody alias
substitute for, 420
Nothing Available error message, 243
no_access directive, 522
NSFNET, 532

OldScriptAlias directive, 584
on the Internet
definition, 2
one_line format, 139
only_from directive, 522
open command
file transfer and, 484
for Ftpmail, 483
open lists (mail)
definition, 430
setting with subscribe_policy, 466
Options directive, 588
ORACLE gateway, 367
order directive, 383
ordered lists (HTML), 334
org token, 182
Other Gopher and Information Servers directory, 202
override the default Gopher port
option for gopherd, 551
overriding default Gopher data directory, 551
owner- alias, 419
owner-listname address
definition, 414
owner-listname alias, 430, 455
owner-Majordomo alias, 438
owner-owner alias, 438
ownership of FTP files and directories, 59

PAGER_COMMAND command, 554
Paleontology Server, 594
paragraph tag (HTML), 326, 567
PARC Map Viewer, 594
partial URLS (see relative URLs)
passwd command, 456
passwd files, 58
setting up for sublogins, 62
passwd-check command, 79
passwords
changing for mailing list, 456
changing the backup administrative, 456
for authenticating user of Web server, 384
patents, 533
path-filter command, 89
pathnames
filtering in FTP archive, 89
in WU Archive FTP daemon, 70
pbmplus package, 337
PC Gopher clients, 162
PEM (Privacy Enhanced Mail), 391, 541
Perl library, 47
Perl scripts
Alcuin, 559
approve, 470
canned_reply, 393
complete script, 393-396
comments CGI, 370
creating a captured shell for login, example, 44
for analyzing Gopher log data, 198
for developing custom WAIS gateway, 377
for listing Gopher data tree, 213
for managing Ftpmail, 492
for obtaining HTML noninteractively, 314-315
for running Gopher+ Forms, 265, 270
for starting X client on remote display, 45
Fwgstat, 559
GEE, 559
GLA, 559
GLOG, 560
Gmail, 560
Gmailcal, 560

Perl scripts (cont'd)
GMV, 560
Gonnrp, 561
Gopher tools, 559-562
Gophersoc, 562
InstGopher, 563
maltshop, 259
MHtogroph, 564
to avoid security problems with shell index and exec: links, 255
perlWWW, description, 291
permissions
changing for security on FTP archive, example, 104
for FTP files and directories, 59
personal HTML directories, 389
PGP (Pretty Good Privacy), 541
phone book server (CSO)
linking to, 227
pict format, 139
PidFile directive, 574
pids_directory token (Gopher+), 186
pilots, service for, 20
.plan file, 37
replacing with FIFO, 39
PLAY_COMMAND command, 555
Plexus, 540
description, 294
plug-gw, 505
+= operator, 521
pmake
using to compile Gopher server, 175
pop-up menu tag, 570
populating FTP archive, 93-95
pornography, 538
Port directive, 574
port numbers
changing waisserver's, 124
default for Gopher server, 169, 171
default Web, 306
definition, 10
for Web server, 287
overriding default Gopher, 551
protocols and (table), 32
UDP, 11
using in a URL, 333
Possible Security Violation log error message, 198
PostScript format, 139
PostScript to HTML tool, 350
PPP (Point-to-Point Protocol) connection, 5
pre tag (HTML), 343
precedence variable, 465
Precedence: message header field, 420-421
adding, 465
prefixes, and Gopher file types (table), 225
preformatting tag, 567
press releases available on Internet, 26
primary access control, 522
directives for, 522
PRINTER_COMMAND command, 555
private key encryption, 541
private_get variable, 465
private_index variable, 465
private_which variable, 465
private_who variable, 465
privileges, running sendmail from local host with own, 419
procmail (mail filter) program, 452
product information, 27
protocols
Gopher, 152-154
ports and (table), 32
services provided by, 8-11
proximity (waisindex)
definition, 137
enabling searches by, 145
proxy software, 506
ftp-gw, 505
netacl, 505
plug-gw, 505
role in firewalls, 499
tn-gw, 505
udprelay, 511
ps
checking for processes owned by ftpmail user, 493
format, 139
PSI, 532
pub directory, 61
FTP permission and ownership, 59
public access to Web server, 311
public FTP (see anonymous FTP)
public key encryption, 541
versus private key encryption, 542
publishing agreement, 534
publishing on the Internet, 531-538
purge_received variable, 465

queries
building for WAIS server, 111
script, 250-255
sizes of, 30
types for Gopher+ Forms, 263
queueing messages to large mailing list, 418
quit command
for Ftpmail, 486
quotes tag, 567

radio boxes
adding to Gopher+ Forms, 267
RANLIB variable, 113
reading mail, 107
Readline: Timed out! log error message, 198
readme command, 84
README file, trick for accessing, 20
ReadmeName directive, 584
READTIMEOUT variable, 170
real user class (ftp), definition, 76
Redirect directive, 584
regexp variable type, 460
registering Gopher server, 202-204
regular expressions
definition, 467
for advertise and noadvertise variables, 467-468
using to check for valid keystrokes, 363
using to split a document (Gopher 2.1), 278
relative URLs
definition, 286
using BASE tag in document containing, 366
versus absolute, 333
relevance feedback, 30
definition, 24
relevance ranking, by waisindex, 136
remote addresses (users) of mail
definition, 409
reply files, 397
editing default directory, 396
Reply to: mail message header
Ftpmail command, 483
reply traffic (see responses)
reply_to variable, 465
-request address
used for correspondence about mailing list, 414
-request alias, 419, 448
request-answer program, 436, 443, 447
description, 431
require directive, 589
resending bounced messages, 417
resend_host variable, 465
RESOLVER variable, 117
resolvers
description, 13
ResourceConfig directive, 575
responses
formula for sizes of, 31
restricting access (see access control)
restricting Ftpmail, 493
restrict_post variable, 465
restrict_post variable type, 460
Retrieved Binary log message, 197
Retrieved Directory log message, 197
Retrieved File log message, 197
Retrieved FTP Host log message, 197
Retrieved Maildir log message, 197
Retrieved Sound File log message, 197
returned mail messages, 476-478
definition, 430
reverse-path (RFC 821), 408
Root Connection log message, 197
root, starting daemon as root versus running as, 550
router, definition, 2
RSA Data Security, 541
run as a specific login-name
option for gopherd, 550
run under specific user id
option for gopherd, 550
running under inetd
option for gopherd, 549

sample programs, obtaining, xxx
saving output of Gopher+ Forms, 270
Science Fiction Resource Guide, 594
screened host gateway, 500
Mosaic and, 512
screened subnet, 501
script queries, 250-255
ScriptAlias directive, 367, 584

scripts
developing for simple search gateways, 362
security problems with, 363
simple example, 364
executing via links, 232-236
within a chrooted server, 234-236
.fingerrc, 38
for CGI gateways, 360-361
for editing mail message headers, 421
problems caused by, 422
for indexing Gopher server, 276
to handle Web form input, 370
scrollable list tag, 570
scrollable text areas in Web forms
tag for, 370, 570
Search Database for Keywords log message, 197
search paths, facilitating navigation via, 96
searches
altering with cd command, 87
Gopher keyword index, 565
locating via Gopher log, 200
of multiple indexes, 255
on WAIS, 24, 118
via links, 236
relational, using Gophersoc, 562
using search gateways, 362
via Jughead, 259-262
via Veronica, 257-259
Second International WWW Conference '94, proceedings of, 595
section tags (HTML), 344
Secure Gopher, 564
Secure HTTP specification, 296
SECURE_MAPS_GLOBALRC_ONLY variable, 553
security
access control and user authentication and, 389
achieving by limiting access to FTP archive, 104
Archie and, 510
avoiding problems
in FTP passwd file, 58
when invoking gopherd, 188
bogus versions of xinetd
problems caused by, 518
Computer Emergency Response Team, 35
concerns with shell indexes and exec: links, 254
ensuring on Web servers, 388-390
for Telnet and inetd services, 43
host-based, 509
maintaining via xinetd.log, 525
Majordomo
log files and, 452
problems with, 35
of mailing lists, 402
security options for Gopher clients, 553
personal HTML directories and, 389
problems
created by user FTP, 51
introduced by CGI scripts, 363
with xinetd, 516
provided by HTTP, 296
server-side includes and, 390
trapping breakins, 509
xinetd, spotting break-ins, 527-529
security firewalls (see firewalls)
Select query type for Gopher+ Forms, 268
sender variable, 466
sendmail, 393, 398
aliases file
running command on after editing, 414
syntax, 414
workarounds for shared, 416
associated addresses, 413
envelope sender address, setting in V.8, 419
invoking for small mailing list, 409
logging messages and, 423
logs, 526
option
to ignore line with single dot, 437
to queue messages for handling one at a time, 418
to send copy of message to local users, 418
to set envelope sender address, 437
to set set envelope sender, 419
to test Ftpmail installation, 490
option to
ignore line with single dot, 418

sendmail (cont'd)
problem with owner-xxx alias in V.8, 438
starting new process for each bounced message, 417
verbose switch, 490
sendmail.cf
when to define list alias in, 416
sequence numbers (TCP), 10
server (WAIS component), 111
server format, 140
server-side includes, 339, 390
description, 320
ServerAdmin directive, 575
ServerName directive, 575
ServerRoot directive, 575
servers
computation load of, 33
definition in client/server, 7
disk space on, 33
standalone, 12
ServerType directive, 576
service log files, 526
service resource configuration file (see srm.conf)
SERV_SEC file, 125
upcoming fixes to , 126
setting up
digested mailing lists, 444
FTP archive, 51-68
mailing lists (Majordomo), 440-445
SGML (Standard Generalized Markup Language), 285
Document Type Definition (DTD), 294
shell access to Internet, 2
shell indexes
combining with exec: links, 252-255
shell metacharacters
in Web forms, trapping, 390
shell scripts
GLASS, 560
Gopher and, 219
shells (see login shells)
Shepherd, 564
shutdown command, 84
signature file
HTML, 280
signatures
digital, 542
Silicon Graphics
sound programs and, 555
simple screening router, 501
site gpass command, 81
site group command, 81
size command
in Ftpmail, 485
SIZRETTYPE variable, 170
SLIP (Serial Line Internet Protocol) connection, 5
SMTP (Simple Mail Transfer Protocol)
basic concepts of, 409
port number, 11
security and, 517
Snooper, 564
SOCKS, 505-506, 512
logs, 526
telnet and, 510
software
bootleg commercial, 538
encryption, 538
Sorry Dude . . . error message, 195
Sorry, This Isn't a Wais Index error message, 243
sorting Gopher menu items, 208
sorting ist members file, 415
sound files
Gopher and, 219
sound programs
commands and, 555
source description (.src) file, 135
example, 136
finding on Internet, 144
(see also WAIS source)
SOURCE.syn file for waisindex synonyms, 147
special characters
denoting Gopher directories and files, 205
splitting mail messages, 485

SQL requests
tool for translating Gopher requests into, 562
.src files
Gopher and, 219
linking to WAIS from Gopher, 236
srm.conf file, 308
adding special MIME extensions to, 319
directives, 579-584
enabling automatic directory indexing in, 321
directives for, 323
making additional cg-bin directories via, 367
setting UserDir directive in, 310
setup of, 304
standalone servers
inetd and, 12
waisserver, 121-122
stock prices
available on Internet, 26
example of providing, 40
stoplist.c, 147
stopwords
adding to stoplist, 147
definition, 146
string variable type, 460
strip variable, 466
structure of Gopher menus, 211
Style Guide for Online Hypertext, 344
subject_prefix variable, 466
sublogins (FTP), 62-63
subnets
definition, 9
subscribe command
Majordomo, 429
subscribers
listing, 429
making a list of (Majordomo), 440
of mail services, definition, 392
on open and closed lists, 430
unsubscribing, 478
variables for, 465
view of list server, 399
subscribe_policy variable, 466
subscriptions
address (Majordomo), 442
approving, 456, 469-476
commands
for Majordomo, 429
syntax of, 400
non-routine, definition, 471
notification of Majordomo administrator of, 432
notification of successful, to Majordomo list owner, 430
removing, 478
request for, 414
requests to majordomo-users mailing list, 454
types, variables for, 466
suffixes (see extensions)
surfing (see navigating hypertext links)
Sybase databases
gateway for integrating into World Wide Web, 367
symbolic links
disabling to prevent use outside HTML document tree, 388
in Gopher, chroot() and, 219-221
synonyms
setting for waisindex, 147
syslog, 106
logging uploads and downloads, 85
message upon connecting to FTP archive, 65
using output to determine mail traffic, 32
syslogd
specifying location of log messages, 526
system administrator
role in compiling Gopher server, 163-177
role in managing Gopher server, 179-204
token for setting name and mail address, 182
system connections
monitoring, 517
reason for keeping in xinetd, 526
system load
enabling restriction in Gopher server, 170
limiting access to Gopher server based on, 167
mail traffic, easing, 406

system load (cont'd)
System Load Too High log error message, 197
system log files, 526
system requirements
for Internet services, 29-34
responses, 31

table tag (HTML), 567
Taxing Times, 594
TCP
description, 10
TCP/IP (Transmission Control Protocol/Internet Protocol)
definition, 8
Techinpher, 564
Telnet, 20, 42-50
as interface for starting X clients, 45-47
connecting to Gopher via, example, 152
example of using, 41
firewall and, 510
gateway for sites, 366
replacing server's login procedure, 47
using to test Web browser, 309
telnet link type, 228
TELNET_COMMAND command, 554
term weight, definition, 137
terminal emulation
effect on Internet connection, 4
testing
installation of Majordomo, 446-451
WAIS, 118-124
waisserver, 122-124
Web server, 309
Texinfo to HTML tool, 350
text entry fields in Web forms
tag for, 370
text files
indexing (see Wais (Wide Area Information Servers))
text format, 139
TEXTAREA tag, 370
Thinking Machines, Inc., 109
This isn't a NeXT ... Is It? error message, 243
thumbnail images, 338
tiff format, 139
timecards
handling electronically, 27
TimeOut directive, 576
timeouts, setting for Gopher server, 170
title tag (HTML), 328
TkWWW Broswer/Editor for X11
description, 292
tn-gw, 505
TN3270_COMMAND command, 554
tokens
for identifying Gopher types by file extensions, 183-186
for managing Gopher server, 179-186
TOP variable, 114
trade secrets, 533
trademarks, 533
traffic (see responses)
TransferLog directive, 315, 576
transluscent backgrounds in HTML documents, 337
Traveller, 565
tripwire, 510
troff to HTML tool, 350
trusted users of mail
sendmail and, 418
workaround for sendmail option, 419
Ts/Tb, 565
TurboGopher, 161
TypesConfig directive, 576

UDP protocol, 11
udprelay, 511
UM-WEATHER service, 49
uncompressing files
setting command for via Gopher 1.x variable, 171
via ftpconversions file, 73
Universal Resource Citation (URC), 297
Universal Resource Name (URN), 296
UNIX
approve script, 469
curses gopher client, 205
uucp command, xxxii
file transfer modes, 486
Gopher clients, 161
Internet platform of choice, 6
mail system
From versus From:, 418
components, 408

UNIX, mail system (cont'd)
- major Gopher servers for, 159
- regular expressions, 467
- versions of in this book, xxx

Unknown Index Type error message , 243
unordered lists (HTML), 334
unsetting variables
- in mailing list configuration files, 459

unsubscribe command
- Majordomo, 429

unsubscribing mail users, 478
updating document tree (HTML), 312
updating index files
- existing files only, 144
- rebuilding, 148
- two methods for, 148

upload command, 88
uploading files
- controlling via ftpaccess, 88-89
- FTP, 51

URL datatype
- form building headline files formatted as URLs, 376

URL format, 140
URL redirection
- definition, 358

URLs
- absolute (see absolute URLs)
- relative (see relative URLs)

URLs (Uniform Resource Locators), 331-334
- absolute, 286
- absolute versus relative, 333
- appending search phrase to, 362
- as part of a hyperlink, 338
- connecting image map file to, 353
- description, 285
- disadvantages of, 296
- Emacs World Wide Web browser, 290
- for A Beginner's Guide to HTML, 341
- for ACM European Conference On Hypermedia Technology (ECHT) proceedings, 595
- for ArtServe, 594
- for ASCII text to HTML tool, 349
- for BibTeX to HTML tool, 349
- for CERN Line Mode Browser, 292
- for CERN Web server, 293
- for CGI library for Perl, 363
- for CGI test script, 360
- for Chimera, 292
- for CommerceNet, 298
- for Currency Converter, 594
- for DEC's home page, 310
- for Edupage Newsletter, 594
- for Emacs HTML mode, 348
- for First International World Wide Web Conference proceedings, 595
- for FrameMaker authoring, 348
- for FTP archive at O'Reilly & Associates, 332
- for Genera gateway, 367
- for getstats, 317
- for GNN, 297
- for Gopher server at University of Minnesota, 332
- for HoTMetaL, 349
- for HTML conversion tools, 349
- for HTML enhancements, 295
- for htmltext, 347
- for Hypertexted USENET FAQs, 594
- for Hytelnet gateway, 366
- for Interleaf to HTML tool, 350
- for International Teletimes, 594
- for Internet Underground Music Archive (IUMA), 594
- for LaTeX to HTML tool, 350
- for list of Web browsers, 289
- for list of Web servers, 286
- for Lynx, 289
- for mail to HTML tool, 350
- for man2html gateway, 367
- for master list of Web servers, 332
- for MecklerWeb, 298
- for MidasWWW, 289
- for Mosaic, 290
- for Mosaic hotlist to HTML tool, 350
- for NCSA Web server, 293
- for NCSA Web server binaries, 300
- for New Zealand Information, 594
- for NeXT, 291
- for ORACLE gateway, 367
- for Paleontology Server, 594
- for PARC Map Viewer, 594
- for perlWWW, 291
- for Plexus, 294
- for PostScript to HTML tool, 350
- for Science Fiction Resource Guide, 594

URLs (Uniform Resource Locators) (cont'd)
  for Second International WWW Conference '94 proceedings, 595
  for Secure HTTP specification, 296
  for server-side includes, 341
  for Style Guide for Online Hypertext, 344
  for Taxing Times, 594
  for Texinfo to HTML tool, 350
  for TkWWW Broswer/Editor for X11, 292
  for transluscent backgrounds, 337
  for troff to HTML tool, 350
  for US Census Information Server, 594
  for ViolaWWW, 291
  for w3-mode extension, 290
  for WAISgate, 379
  for Web-to-WAIS gateways, 377
  for World Wide Web FAQ, 591
  for wusage, 317
  for wwwstat, 317
  format understood by waisindex, 140
  in HTML documents returned by gateways, 366
  inclusion in Gopher+, 156
  local, 334
  location in mail messages, 312
  mapping to document, 307
  relative, 286
  tag for including in Web form, 369
  using a port number in, 333
US Census Information Server, 594
user authentication, 384-388
  concommitant with domain-level access control, 388
  definition, 381
  group, 386
    compared to individual, 387
  in Gopher 2.1, 276
  individual, 385
    compared to general, unrestricted access, 386
    on a directory-level basis, 386
  security and, 389
user classes
  defining in ftpaccess, 75
  displaying number of users per, 90
User directive, 576
user FTP
  definition, 51
UserDir directive, 584
username
  creating .htpassed file for, 386
  for authenticating user of Web server, 384
username/password file (see .htpasswd file)
UUCP, xxxii
uucp command, xxxii
uuencode
  use with mail messages, 393
uuencode command
  in Ftpmail, 485

variable types
  in Majordomo configuration files, 460
variables
  for building WAIS for X clients, 117
  in Majordomo configuration files, 460-468
  set in Gopher conf.h file, 170
  setting and unsetting in mailing list configuration files, 458
  setting WAIS, 113
Veronica, 257-259, 565
  avoiding registration of Gopher server with, 258
  description, 257
  registering Gopher server with, 258
  running locally, 258
  updates, learning about, 258
VeronicaIndex: no token (Gopher+), 258
viewext token (Gopher+), 184
ViolaWWW
  description, 291
virtual directory
  defining in srm.conf, 308
virtual documents (Gopher 2.1), 277
virtual name of document
  when to append to URL, 308
virtual= tag (HTML), 340

w3-mode extension, 290
WAIS (Wide Area Information Servers)
  accessing from World Wide Web server, 376-380
    comparison of methods, 379
  building, 112-118

WAIS (Wide Area Information Servers) (cont'd)
- components, 111
- customizing top-level Makefile, 113
- database security, 127
- database, using, 110
- description, 24, 109-112
- disk space requirements, 33
- firewalls and, 128-131
- forwarding capabilities of, 128
- Gopher server
  - enabling indexing on, 172
  - links incorrect when compiling, 175
- limitations, 25
- obtaining source, 112
- running server
  - standalone, 121-122
  - under inetd, 120-121
- searching, via link from Gopher, 236
- security, 125-131
- setting up, 109-131
- testing and installing, 118-122
- (see also freeWAIS)

WAIS indexes
- creating, issues about, 238
- incorporating into Gopher server, 237-244
  - effect of chrooted server, 241
  - errors, 243
  - placement of data, 237
  - via .cap file, 240
  - via Alcuin, 559
  - via link, 239
  - via WAIS source file, 240
- served by gindexd (Gopher 1.x), 246-249

WAIS source
- containing documents of multiple types, 149
- definition, 118
- exporting, 144
- naming, 143
- registering, 144
- (see also source description (.src) file)

WAISgate, features, 378

waisindex command, 118

waisindex program
- associating files, 142
- avoiding indexing of unwanted Gopher data
  - syntax and example, 242
- command-line options
  - table of, 138
  - description, 143-146
- creating WAIS sources with, 133-150
- customizing operation of, 146
- default indexing, overriding, 145
- document formats understood by, 138
- effect of -T and -t options on index incoporated into Gopher server, 238
- files created by, 134
- format specified on command line, 133
- handling documents of many types, 149
- how it builds index files, 133-136
- indexing entire directory tree option, 145
- indexing selected files via find, 146
- logging option, 145
- relevance ranking, 136
- saving disk space option, 146
- source
  - exporting option, 144
  - naming option, 143
  - registry option, 144
- synonyms, setting up, 147
- setting up direct Web server access via, 376
- updating existing index files option, 144, 149
- using with MIME types understood by Mosaic, 141
- words to ignore, selecting, 147

WAISMAXHITS variable, 170

waisq command, 377

waissearch command, 118, 122

waissearch program
- ws, front-end for, 119

waisserver
- configuring, 124-131
- dictionary file and, 134
- inverted file and, 134
- run-time configuration, 124
- running
  - as non-root user, 125

waisserver, running (cont'd)
- standalone, 121-122
- under inetd, 120-121
- testing, 122-124

waissrc link type, 236
Warning! You really shouldn't run the server as root error message, 194
Warning! You should run the server with the -u option! error message, 194
weather reports, obtaining via DUATS, 20
Weather Underground, 47-49
- source, 48

Web (see World Wide Web)
webmaster alias, 311
weighting algorithm of waisindex, 136
whats-new mailing list, 312
Whatsnewd/Findwhatsnew, 565
which command
- Majordomo, 429
- variable for, 465

who command
- Majordomo, 429
- variable for, 465

whois, using to track interloper, 528
Wide Area Information Servers (see WAIS)
Wolff, Stephen, 533
word density, definition, 137
word pairs, disabling indexing of, 145
word variable type, 460
word weight, 134
- definition, 136

World Wide Web (WWW)
- authoring, 325-356
- basic concepts, 282-288
- Best of the Net (GNN), 593
- browsers (see World Wide Web browsers)
- commercial sites on, 593
- commercialization, 297
- computer companies on, 593
- description, 22
- FAQ, 591
- future of, 294-298
- gn server for Gopher and, 160
- history of development, 279
- introduction to, 279-298
- list of servers, 593
- mailing lists, 592
- newsgroups, 591
- non-profit sites on, 593
- online conference proceedings, 595
- purposes of, 280-281
- security enhancements, 296
- server (see World Wide Web servers)
- showing links to associated Gopher document, 156
- sources of information about, 591-595
- URLs, uniform naming of, 296
- using CERN and Lynx browsers as login programs, 44
- What's New page, 593

World Wide Web browsers, 288-292
- CERN Line Mode Browser, 292
- Chimera, 292
- Emacs, 290
- Lynx, 289
- MidasWWW, 289
- Mosaic, 290
- NeXT, 291
- perlWWW, 291
- TkWWW Broswer/Editor for X11, 292
- types of, 288
- using, 286
- ViolaWWW, 291

World Wide Web forms, 368-376
- definition, 357
- handling input to, scripts for, 370
- HTML for, 368
- maintaining state between multiple, 375
- shell metacharacters in, trapping, 390
- valid constructs in, 370

World Wide Web servers, 292-294, 320
- access control, 381-388
- accessing WAIS from, methods for, 376-380
  - comparison of, 379
- adding MIME types to, 318-320
- announcing new, 311
- automatic directory indexing, 321-323
- CERN, 293
- communication with client, 15
- compiling NCSA HTTP source, 300
- computational load on, 33
- configuring, 302-305
  - guidelines for, 302
- delegating document tree management, 310
- description, 287

World Wide Web servers (cont'd)
- examples of, 593
- firewalls and, 504-506
- gateways, 358-367
- how it recognizes HTML file, 320
- installing, 305
- installing precompiled HTTP daemon, 299
- log files and analysis, 315-318
- log files on, 313
- maintaining, 312-318
- mapping URLs to documents, 307
- mirroring, 314-315
- NCSA, 293
  - platforms supported by, 299
- Plexus, 294
- screened host firewall and, 507
- security, ensuring, 388-390
- setting up, 299-312
- standalone startup
  - effect on logging, 313
  - invoking, 306
  - rebooting server, 306
- starting, 305-307
- startup under inetd, 307
  - effect on logging, 313
- statistics for, 317
- testing, 309
- user authentication on, 384-388

wrapper program, 441
- description, 431

writeconfig command, 457, 461

writing HTML documents, 325-356

ws (front-end for waissearch), 119, 122

WU Archive FTP daemon, 69-92
- aliases for easier navigation, creating, 87
- building, 72
- command-line options, new, 73
- compiling, 70-72
- configuration files, 69
- configuring, 75-81
- defining user classes, 75
- denying access to, 77
  - selected accounts, 89
- features, 69
- group membership, controlling access via, 80
- limiting number of users, 78
- logging facility, 85
- message facility, 82-85
- messages for user, displaying, 98
- password checking, 79
- pathnames settings, 70
- restricting use of conversions and commands, 78
- shutdown, 84, 91
- uncompressing files, 73
- updates to, finding out about, 92
- utility programs, 90
- (see also FTP archive)

wusage
- description, 317

WWW (see World Wide Web)

www
- prefix for Web server name, 311

www-announce mailing list, 312, 592

www-html mailing list
- www-talk, 592

www-rdb mailing list, 593

www-request mailing list, 312

www-talk mailing list, 592

wwwstat, description, 317

X clients
- freeWAIS distribution, 116
- starting via captured shell, 45-47

xferlog, 106

Xferstats.gopher, 565

xgopher, 161

xinetd, 515-529
- building, 518
- configuring via xinetd.conf, 520-524
- debugging, guidelines for, 527
- description, 516-518
- installing, 519-520
- logging, 524-526
  - role in security, 523
- managing, 524-529
- obtaining, 518
- security, 516
  - spotting breaks in, 527
- setting environmental variables for, 524
- (see also inetd)

xinetd.conf file, 519-524, 526
- breaking long lines in, 521
- configuring out of inetd.conf, 519
- contrasted with inetd.conf, 519
- default entry, example of, 521

xinetd.conf file (cont'd)
reconfiguring, 526
sample, 520
specifying log attributes in, 525
xinetd.log file, 525
role in security, 525
xloadimage, 556
xv, 353, 556

You should run without root perms error message, 194

Z39.50 protocol, 109
z3950 port, 124-125
ZCATCMD variable, 171

About the Authors

Cricket Liu matriculated at the University of California's Berkeley campus, that great bastion of free speech, enlightened liberalism, unencumbered UNIX, and cheap pizza. For two summers during school, and ever since, Cricket has worked for Hewlett-Packard. He was hostmaster@hp.com (manager of the hp.com domain) from right after the Loma Prieta earthquake until May 1993, when he left to join HP's external consulting arm, the Professional Services Organization. Currently, Cricket consults with HP customers on TCP/IP networking and UNIX, including network security and the Domain Name System, which he will never escape (Cricket co-authored the Nutshell Handbook *DNS and BIND*).

Cricket has had his nickname since he was a baby and his dad decided he looked like Jiminy Cricket. His real name is a pain to pronounce. He and his wife Paige live in Colorado with their cat, Sydney, and their dog, Dakota, who aspires to be an O'Reilly cover animal. They fly trapeze (yes, really—well, not the dog and cat) nearly every Wednesday and Friday night.

Jerry Peek has used UNIX since the early 1980s. He has a B.S. in electronic engineering technology from California Polytechnic State University. In the years since, Jerry has worked as a user consultant for UNIX and VMS, developed and taught UNIX courses, administered a VAX 11/780 running BSD UNIX, and hacked Bourne Shell and C language code. He's now the Online Services Manager for O'Reilly & Associates, Inc. In his copious :-) free time, he hikes and bicycles the California coast and travels to obscure places in Latin America.

Russ Jones is the Internet Program Manager for Digital Equipment Corporation. He manages Digital's Web server when not advocating and coordinating Internet use across the company. Before joining Digital, Russ managed a software development group at McDonnell Aircraft Company. It was there that Russ developed his first hypertext system in 1983. Of course, he didn't realize it until he started working on *Managing Internet Information Services*. Russ is a graduate of Purdue University's computer science program. When not wandering cyberspace, Russ enjoys current events, architecture, cooking, and history. He and his wife Linda live in Palo Alto, California. Although close enough to his office that he *could* ride his bicycle, Russ prefers the bus.

Bryan Buus quietly kickstarted O'Reilly & Associates' online efforts in 1992 by creating ORA's Gopher server. He received his bachelor's degree in computer science from Boston University in 1992. He graduated the following year from Boston University with his master's degree in computer science, specializing in Internet information services. He then packed up all his stuff and ventured to Boulder, Colorado.

Bryan currently works at XOR Network Engineering as a System Administrator and Information Services Specialist, developing their Internet Plaza. His interests include Net surfing (for fun and profit), skiing (all types), zymurgy, and a little trapeze (thanks Cricket and Paige!).

Adrian Nye is a developmental editor at O'Reilly & Associates. He is the author or editor of several volumes in the X Window System Series from O'Reilly & Associates.

Adrian has worked as a programmer writing educational software in C and as a mechanical engineer designing offshore oil spill cleanup equipment. He has interests in the environment and the impact of people and technology. He graduated from the Massachusetts Institute of Technology in 1984 with a B.S. in mechanical engineering.

Colophon

Our look is the result of reader comments, our own experimentation, and feedback from distribution channels. Distinctive covers complement our distinctive approach to technical topics, breathing personality and life into potentially dry subjects. UNIX and its attendant programs can be unruly beasts. Nutshell Handbooks® help you tame them.

The animals featured on the cover of this book are bobacs, or Asian marmots. Close relatives of the marmot family include squirrels and gophers. There are eight species of marmot in Eurasia and six in North America. The bobac was prominent in the European Soviet Union before being pushed out by agriculture, and it now lives primarily in Central Asia.

Marmot's bodies are designed for digging, having muscular shoulders, widely set forelegs, and thick, blunt claws. Up to 90 percent of a marmot's life is spent in the underground lodges they build and maintain through generations. Because marmots don't like to stray far from the safety of their lodges, they build extensive networks of entrances and tunnels to the main lodge. They leave their lodges for only a few hours each day, and much of that time is spent sunbathing on the mounds of dirt their digging creates by the tunnel entrances.

Marmots eat mainly green plants, but they will, on occasion, eat animal flesh. A young marmot can eat up to 30 percent of its body weight each day throughout the summer. Adults eat 11-13 percent of their body weight daily. By summer's end marmots often gain so much weight that they can barely move. This apparent gluttony is necessary to survive the winter's hibernation. Depending on the species of marmot, hibernation lasts from three to nine months.

Edie Freedman designed this cover and the entire UNIX bestiary that appears on other Nutshell Handbooks. The beasts themselves are adapted from nineteenth century engravings from the Dover Pictorial Archive. The cover layout was produced with Adobe Photoshop 2.5 and QuarkXPress 3.3 for the Macintosh, using the ITC Garamond font. The inside layout was designed by Edie Freedman and Jennifer Niederst.

Text was prepared in SGML using the DocBook 2.1 DTD. The print version of this book was created by translating the SGML source into a set of gtroff macros, using a filter developed at ORA by Norman Walsh. Steve Talbott designed and wrote the underlying macro set on the basis of the GNU gtroff –gs macros; Lenny Muellner adapted them to SGML and implemented the book design. The GNU groff text formatter version 1.08 was used to generate PostScript output. The figures were created in Aldus Freehand 4.0 by Chris Reilley and Hanna Dyer. Screenshots were processed using Photoshop 2.5. This colophon was written by Clairemarie Fisher O'Leary.

INTERNET
Books from O'Reilly & Associates, Inc.
FALL/WINTER 1994-95

The Whole Internet User's Guide & Catalog

By Ed Krol
2nd Edition April 1994
574 pages, ISBN 1-56592-063-5

The best book about the Internet just got better! This is the second edition of our comprehensive—and bestselling—introduction to the Internet, the international network that includes virtually every major computer site in the world. In addition to email, file transfer, remote login, and network news, this book pays special attention to some new tools for helping you find information. Useful to beginners and veterans alike, this book will help you explore what's possible on the Net. Also includes a pull-out quick-reference card.

"An ongoing classic."
—*Rochester Business Journal*

"The book against which all subsequent Internet guides are measured, Krol's work has emerged as an indispensable reference to beginners and seasoned travelers alike as they venture out on the data highway."
—*Microtimes*

"*The Whole Internet User's Guide & Catalog* will probably become the Internet user's bible because it provides comprehensive, easy instructions for those who want to get the most from this valuable electronic tool."
—David J. Buerger, Editor, *Communications Week*

"Krol's work is comprehensive and lucid, an overview which presents network basics in clear and understandable language. I consider it essential."
—Paul Gilster, *Triad Business News*

!%@:: A Directory of Electronic Mail Addressing & Networks

By Donnalyn Frey & Rick Adams
4th Edition June 1994
662 pages, ISBN 1-56592-046-5

This is the only up-to-date directory that charts the networks that make up the Internet, provides contact names and addresses, and describes the services each network provides. It includes all of the major Internet-based networks, as well as various commercial networks such as CompuServe, Delphi, and America Online that are "gatewayed" to the Internet for transfer of electronic mail and other services. If you are someone who wants to connect to the Internet, or someone who already is connected but wants concise, up-to-date information on many of the world's networks, check out this book.

This is the fourth edition of this directory, now in a simplified format designed to allow more frequent updates.

"The book remains the bible of electronic messaging today. One could easily borrow the American Express slogan with the quip 'don't do messaging without it.' The book introduces you to electronic mail in all its many forms and flavors, tells you about the networks throughout the world...with an up-to-date summary of information on each, plus handy references such as all the world's subdomains. The husband-wife team authors are among the most knowledgeable people in the Internet world. This is one of those publications for which you just enter a lifetime subscription."
—Book Review, *ISOC News*

The Mosaic Handbooks

Mosaic is an important application that is becoming instrumental in the growth of the Internet. These books, one for Microsoft Windows, one for the X Window System, and one for the Macintosh, introduce you to Mosaic and its use in navigating and finding information on the World Wide Web. They show you how to use Mosaic to replace some of the traditional Internet functions like FTP, Gopher, Archie, Veronica, and WAIS. For more advanced users, the books describe how to add external viewers to Mosaic (allowing it to display many additional file types) and how to customize the Mosaic interface, such as screen elements, colors, and fonts. The Microsoft and Macintosh versions come with a copy of Mosaic on a floppy disk; the X Window version comes with a CD-ROM. All three books come with a subscription to The Global Network Navigator (GNN)™, the leading WWW-based information service on the Internet.

The Mosaic Handbook for Microsoft Windows

By Dale Dougherty & Richard Koman
1st Edition October 1994
230 pages, ISBN 1-56592-094-5
(two diskettes included)

The Mosaic Handbook for the X Window System

By Dale Dougherty, Richard Koman & Paula Ferguson
1st Edition October 1994
288 pages, ISBN 1-56592-095-3
(CD-ROM included)

The Mosaic Handbook for the Macintosh

By Dale Dougherty & Richard Koman
1st Edition October 1994
198 pages, ISBN 1-56592-096-1
(diskette included)

Internet In A Box

Produced by Spry, Inc.
Available late September 1994
UPC 799364 01100
(sold only in the US and Canada)

Internet In A Box™ is the first shrink-wrapped package to provide a total solution for PC users to get on the Internet. *Internet In A Box* provides instant connectivity, a multimedia Windows interface, a full suite of applications, and a complete online guide to the Internet. The box contains:

- Two ways to connect to the Internet: five-minute automated connection via SprintLink or manual connection to any PPP provider in the US and Canada.
- A subscription to the Global Network Navigator (GNN)™, an online interactive guide to the Internet.
- Software: The Air Series applications, including Mosaic, electronic mail, Usenet news reader, drag-and-drop file transfer, gopher, and telnet.
- Three books that clearly describe how to use these resources: a special edition of Ed Krol's bestselling *The Whole Internet User's Guide & Catalog*, a *Getting Started* guide, and an *Install* guide.

Connecting to the Internet

By Susan Estrada
1st Edition August 1993
188 pages, ISBN 1-56592-061-9

This book provides practical advice on how to get an Internet connection. It describes how to assess your needs to determine the kind of Internet service that is best for you and how to find a local access provider and evaluate the services they offer.

Knowing how to purchase the right kind of Internet access can help you save money and avoid a lot of frustration. This book is the fastest way for you to learn how to get on the Internet. Then you can begin exploring one of the world's most valuable resources.

"A much needed 'how to do it' for anyone interested in getting Internet connectivity and using it as part of their organization or enterprise. The sections are simple and straightforward.... If you want to know how to connect your organization, get this book."
—Book Review, *ISOC News*

Learning the UNIX Operating System

By Grace Todino, John Strang & Jerry Peek
3rd Edition August 1993
108 pages, ISBN 1-56592-060-0

If you are new to UNIX, this concise introduction will tell you just what you need to get started and no more. Why wade through a 600-page book when you can begin working productively in a matter of minutes? It's an ideal primer for Mac and PC users of the Internet who need to know a little bit about UNIX on the systems they visit.

This book is the most effective introduction to UNIX in print. The third edition has been updated and expanded to provide increased coverage of window systems and networking. It's a handy book for someone just starting with UNIX, as well as someone who encounters a UNIX system as a "visitor" via remote login over the Internet.

"If you have someone on your site who has never worked on a UNIX system and who needs a quick how-to, Nutshell® has the right booklet. *Learning the UNIX Operating System* can get a newcomer rolling in a single session. It covers logging in and out; files and directories; mail; pipes; filters; backgrounding; and a large number of other topics. It's clear, cheap, and can render a newcomer productive in a few hours."
—*;login*

Smileys

By David W. Sanderson
1st Edition March 1993
93 pages, ISBN 1-56592-041-4

From the people who put an armadillo on the cover of a system administrator book comes this collection of the computer underground hieroglyphs called "smileys." Originally inserted into email messages to denote "said with a cynical smile" :-), smileys now run rampant throughout the electronic mail culture.

"For a quick grin at an odd moment, this is a nice pocket book to carry around :-) If you keep this book near your terminal, you could express many heretofore hidden feelings in your email ;-) Then again, such things may be frowned upon at your company :-(No matter, this is a fun book to have around."
—Gregory M. Amov, *News & Review*

TCP/IP Network Administration

By Craig Hunt
1st Edition August 1992
502 pages, ISBN 0-937175-82-X

TCP/IP Network Administration is a complete guide to setting up and running a TCP/IP network for administrators of networks of systems or lone home systems that access the Internet. It starts with the fundamentals: what the protocols do and how they work, how to request a network address and a name (the forms needed are included in an appendix), and how to set up your network.

Beyond basic setup, the book discusses how to configure important network applications, including sendmail, the r* commands, and some simple setups for NIS and NFS. There are also chapters on troubleshooting and security. In addition, this book covers several important packages that are available from the Net (such as *gated*). Covers BSD and System V TCP/IP implementations.

"*TCP/IP Network Administration* provides a great service to network managers. Any network manager responsible for TCP/IP networking should keep a copy of this inexpensive reference nearby."
—*Network Computing*

Managing Internet Information Services

By Cricket Liu, Jerry Peek, Russ Jones, Bryan Buus & Adrian Nye
1st Edition Winter 1994/95 (est.)
400 pages (est.), ISBN 1-56592-062-7

This comprehensive guide describes how to set up information services to make them available over the Internet. It discusses why a company would wnat to offer Internet services, provides complete coverage of all popular services, and tells how to select which ones to provide. Most of the book describes how to set up email services and FTP, Gopher, and World Wide Web servers.

"*Managing Internet Information Services* has long been needed in the Internet community, as well as in many organizations with IP-based networks. Although many on the Internet are quite savvy when it comes to administering these types of tools, MIIS will allow a much larger community to join in and perhaps provide more diverse information. This book will be a welcome addition to my Internet shelf."
—Robert H'obbes' Zakon, MITRE Corporation

sendmail

By Bryan Costales, with Eric Allman & Neil Rickert
1st Edition November 1993
830 pages, ISBN 1-56592-056-2

Although sendmail is used on almost every UNIX system, it's one of the last great uncharted territories—and most difficult utilities to learn—in UNIX system administration. This book provides a complete sendmail tutorial, plus extensive reference material. It covers the BSD, UIUC IDA, and V8 versions of sendmail.

"The program and its rule description file, sendmail.cf, have long been regarded as the pit of coals that separated the mild Unix system administrators from the real fire walkers. Now, sendmail syntax, testing, hidden rules, and other mysteries are revealed. Costales, Allman, and Rickert are the indisputable authorities to do the text."
—Ben Smith, *Byte*

DNS and BIND

By Cricket Liu & Paul Albitz
1st Edition October 1992
418 pages, ISBN 1-56592-010-4

DNS and BIND contains all you need to know about the Internet's Domain Name System (DNS) and the Berkeley Internet Name Domain (BIND), its UNIX implementation. The Domain Name System is the Internet's "phone book"; it's a database that tracks important information (in particular, names and addresses) for every computer on the Internet. If you're a system administrator, this book will show you how to set up and maintain the DNS software on your network.

"At 380 pages it blows away easily any vendor supplied information, and because it has an extensive troubleshooting section (using nslookup) it should never be far from your desk—especially when things on your network start to go awry :-)"
—Ian Hoyle, BHP Research, Melbourne Laboratories

MH & xmh: E-mail for Users & Programmers

By Jerry Peek
2nd Edition September 1992
728 pages, ISBN 1-56592-027-9

Customizing your email environment can save time and make communicating more enjoyable. *MH & xmh: E-Mail for Users & Programmers* explains how to use, customize, and program with the MH electronic mail commands available on virtually any UNIX system. The handbook also covers *xmh*, an X Window System client that runs MH programs.

The second edition added a chapter on mhook, sections explaining under-appreciated small commands and features, and more examples showing how to use MH to handle common situations.

"The MH bible is irrefutably Jerry Peek's *MH & xmh: E-mail for Users & Programmers*. This book covers just about everything that is known about MH and *xmh* (the X Windows front end to MH), presented in a clear and easy-to-read format. I strongly recommend that anybody serious about MH get a copy."
—James Hamilton, *UnixWorld*

Practical UNIX Security

By Simson Garfinkel & Gene Spafford
1st Edition June 1991
512 pages, ISBN 0-937175-72-2

Practical UNIX Security tells system administrators how to make their UNIX system—either System V or BSD—as secure as it possibly can be without going to trusted system technology. The book describes UNIX concepts and how they enforce security, tells how to defend against and handle security breaches, and explains network security (including UUCP, NFS, Kerberos, and firewall machines) in detail. If you are a UNIX system administrator or user who deals with security, you need this book.

"Timely, accurate, written by recognized experts...covers every imaginable topic relating to Unix security. An excellent book and I recommend it as a valuable addition to any system administrator's or computer site manager's collection."
—Jon Wright, *Informatics* (Australia)

O'Reilly & Associates—

GLOBAL NETWORK NAVIGATOR

The Global Network Navigator (GNN) ™ is a unique kind of information service that makes the Internet easy and enjoyable to use. We organize access to the vast information resources of the Internet so that you can find what you want. We also help you understand the Internet and the many ways you can explore it.

In GNN you'll find:

Navigating the Net with GNN

The *Whole Internet Catalog* contains a descriptive listing of the most useful Net resources and services with live links to those resources.

The *GNN Business Pages* are where you'll learn about companies who have established a presence on the Internet and use its worldwide reach to help educate consumers.

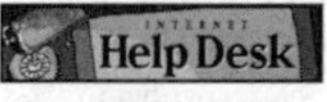

The *Internet Help Desk* helps folks who are new to the Net orient themselves and gets them started on the road to Internet exploration.

News

NetNews is a weekly publication that reports on the news of the Internet, with weekly feature articles that focus on Internet trends and special events. The Sports, Weather, and Comix Pages round out the news.

Special Interest Publications

Whether you're planning a trip or are just interested in reading about the journeys of others, you'll find that the *Travelers' Center* contains a rich collection of feature articles and ongoing columns about travel. In the *Travelers' Center*, you can link to many helpful and informative travel-related Internet resources.

The *Personal Finance Center* is the place to go for information about money management and investment on the Internet. Whether you're an old pro at playing the market or are thinking about investing for the first time, you'll read articles and discover Internet resources that will help you to think of the Internet as a personal finance information tool.

All in all, GNN helps you get more value for the time you spend on the Internet.

The Best of the Web

GNN received "Honorable Mention" for "**Best Overall Site**," "**Best Entertainment Service**," and "**Most Important Service Concept**."

The *GNN NetNews* received "Honorable Mention" for "**Best Document Design**."

Subscribe Today

GNN is available over the Internet as a subscription service. To get complete information about subscribing to GNN, send email to **info@gnn.com**. If you have access to a World Wide Web browser such as Mosaic or Lynx, you can use the following URL to register online: `http://gnn.com/`

If you use a browser that does not support online forms, you can retrieve an email version of the registration form automatically by sending email to **form@gnn.com**. Fill this form out and send it back to us by email, and we will confirm your registration.

AUDIOTAPES

O'Reilly now offers audiotapes based on interviews with people who are making a profound impact in the world of the Internet. Here we give you a quick overview of what's available. For details on our audiotape collection, send email to **audio@ora.com**.

"Ever listen to one of those five-minute-long news pieces being broadcast on National Public Radio's 'All Things Considered' and wish they were doing an in-depth story on new technology? Well, your wishes are answered." —Byte

Global Network Operations

Carl Malamud interviews Brian Carpenter, Bernhard Stockman, Mike O'Dell & Geoff Huston
Released Spring 1994
Duration: 2 hours, ISBN 1-56592-993-4

What does it take to actually run a network? In these four interviews, Carl Malamud explores some of the technical and operational issues faced by Internet service providers around the world.

Brian Carpenter is the director for networking at CERN, the high-energy physics laboratory in Geneva, Switzerland. Physicists are some of the world's most active Internet users, and its global user base makes CERN one of the world's most network-intensive sites. Carpenter discusses how he deals with issues such as the OSI and DECnet Phase V protocols and his views on the future of the Internet.

Bernhard Stockman is one of the founders and the technical manager of the European Backbone (EBONE). EBONE has proven to be the first effective transit backbone for Europe and has been a leader in the deployment of CIDR, BGP-4, and other key technologies.

Mike O'Dell is vice president of research at UUNET Technologies. O'Dell has a long record of involvement in data communications, ranging from his service as a telco lab employee, an engineer on several key projects, and a member of the USENIX board to now helping define new services for one of the largest commercial IP service providers.

Geoff Huston is the director of the Australian Academic Research Network (AARNET). AARNET is known as one of the most progressive regional networks, rapidly adopting new services for its users. Huston talks about how networking in Australia has flourished despite astronomically high rates for long-distance lines.

The Future of the Internet Protocol

Carl Malamud interviews Steve Deering, Bob Braden, Christian Huitema, Bob Hinden, Peter Ford, Steve Casner, Bernhard Stockman & Noel Chiappa
Released Spring 1994
Duration: 4 hours, ISBN 1-56592-996-9

The explosion of interest in the Internet is stressing what was originally designed as a research and education network. The sheer number of users is requiring new strategies for Internet address allocation; multimedia applications are requiring greater bandwidth and strategies such as "resource reservation" to provide synchronous end-to-end service.

In this series of eight interviews, Carl Malamud talks to some of the researchers who are working to define how the underlying technology of the Internet will need to evolve in order to meet the demands of the next five to ten years.

Give these tapes a try if you're intrigued by such topics as Internet "multicasting" of audio and video, or think your job might one day depend on understanding some of the following buzzwords:

- IPNG (Internet Protocol Next Generation)
- SIP (Simple Internet Protocol)
- TUBA (TCP and UDP with Big Addresses)
- CLNP (Connectionless Network Protocol)
- CIDR (Classless Inter-Domain Routing)

or if you are just interested in getting to know more about the people who are shaping the future.

Mobile IP Networking

Carl Malamud interviews Phil Karn & Jun Murai
Released Spring 1994
Duration: 1 hour, ISBN 1-56592-994-2

Phil Karn is the father of the KA9Q publicly available implementation of TCP/IP for DOS (which has also been used as the basis for the software in many commercial Internet routers). KA9Q was originally developed to allow "packet radio," that is, TCP/IP over ham radio bands. Phil's current research focus is on commercial applications of wireless data communications.

Jun Murai is one of the most distinguished researchers in the Internet community. Murai is a professor at Keio University and the founder of the Japanese WIDE Internet. Murai talks about his research projects, which range from satellite-based IP multicasting to a massive testbed for mobile computing at the Fujisawa campus of Keio University.

Networked Information and Online Libraries

Carl Malamud interviews Peter Deutsch & Cliff Lynch
Released September 1993
Duration: 1 hour, ISBN 1-56592-998-5

Peter Deutsch, president of Bunyip Information Services, was one of the co-developers of Archie. In this interview Peter talks about his philosophy for services and compares Archie to X.500. He also talks about what kind of standards we need for networked information retrieval.

Cliff Lynch is currently the director of library automation for the University of California. He discusses issues behind online publishing, such as SGML and the democratization of publishing on the Internet.

European Networking

Carl Malamud interviews Glenn Kowack & Rob Blokzijl
Released September 1993
Duration: 1 hour, ISBN 1-56592-999-3

Glenn Kowack is chief executive of EUnet, the network that's bringing the Internet to the people of Europe. Glenn talks about EUnet's populist business model and the politics of European networking.

Rob Blokzijl is the network manager for NIKHEF, the Dutch Institute of High Energy Physics. Rob talks about RIPE, the IP user's group for Europe, and the nuts and bolts of European network coordination.

Security and Networks

Carl Malamud interviews Jeff Schiller & John Romkey
Released September 1993
Duration: 1 hour, ISBN 1-56592-997-7

Jeff Schiller is the manager of MIT's campus network and is one of the Internet's leading security experts. Here, he talks about Privacy Enhanced Mail (PEM), the difficulty of policing the Internet, and whether horses or computers are more useful to criminals.

John Romkey has been a long-time TCP/IP developer and was recently named to the Internet Architecture Board. In this wide-ranging interview, John talks about the famous "ToasterNet" demo at InterOp, what kind of Internet security he'd like to see put in place, and what Internet applications of the future might look like.

John Perry Barlow
Notable Speeches of the Information Age

USENIX Conference Keynote Address
San Francisco, CA; January 17, 1994
Duration: 1.5 hours, ISBN 1-56592-992-6

John Perry Barlow—retired Wyoming cattle rancher, a lyricist for the Grateful Dead since 1971— holds a degree in comparative religion from Wesleyan University. He also happens to be a recognized authority on computer security, virtual reality, digitized intellectual property, and the social and legal conditions arising in the global network of computers.

In 1990 Barlow co-founded the Electronic Frontier Foundation with Mitch Kapor and currently serves as chair of its executive committee. He writes and lectures on subjects relating to digital technology and society and is a contributing editor to *Communications of the ACM*, *NeXTWorld*, *Microtimes*, *Mondo 2000*, *Wired*, and other publications.

In his keynote address to the Winter 1994 USENIX Conference, Barlow talks of recent developments in the national information infrastructure, telecommunications regulation, cryptography, globalization of the Internet, intellectual property, and the settlement of Cyberspace. The talk explores the premise that "architecture is politics": that the technology adopted for the coming "information superhighway" will help to determine what is carried on it, and that if the electronic frontier of the Internet is not to be replaced by electronic strip malls, we need to make sure that our technological choices favor bi-directional communication and open platforms.

Side A contains the keynote;
Side B contains a question and answer period.

O'Reilly on the Net—
ONLINE PROGRAM GUIDE

O'Reilly & Associates offers extensive information through our online resources. If you've got Internet access, we invite you to come and explore our little neck-of-the-woods.

Online Resource Center

Most comprehensive among our online offerings is the O'Reilly Resource Center. Here, you'll find detailed information and descriptions on all O'Reilly products: titles, prices, tables of contents, indexes, author bios, CD-ROM directory listings, reviews... you can even view images of the products themselves. We also supply helpful ordering information: how to contact us, how to order online, distributors and bookstores around the world, discounts, upgrades, etc. In addition, we provide informative literature in the field, featuring articles, interviews, bibliographies, and columns that help you stay informed and abreast.

The Best of the Web

The *O'Reilly Resource Center* was voted "**Best Commercial Site**" by users participating in "Best of the Web '94."

To access ORA's Online Resource Center:

Point your Web browser (e.g., `mosaic` or `lynx`) to:

`http://gnn.com/ora/`

For the plaintext version, `telnet` or `gopher` to:

`gopher.ora.com`

(telnetters login: `gopher`)

FTP

The example files and programs in many of our books are available electronically via FTP.

To obtain example files and programs from O'Reilly texts:

`ftp` to:

```
ftp.uu.net
cd published/oreilly
```

or

`ftp.ora.com`

Ora-news

An easy way to stay informed of the latest projects and products from O'Reilly & Associates is to subscribe to "ora-news," our electronic news service. Subscribers receive email as soon as the information breaks.

To subscribe to "ora-news":

Send email to:
listproc@online.ora.com

and put the following information on the first line of your message (not in "Subject"):
subscribe ora-news "your name" **of** "your company"

For example:
subscribe ora-news Jim Dandy of Mighty Fine Enterprises

Email

Many other helpful customer services are provided via email. Here's a few of the most popular and useful.

Useful email addresses

nuts@ora.com
For general questions and information.

bookquestions@ora.com
For technical questions, or corrections, concerning book contents.

order@ora.com
To order books online and for ordering questions.

catalog@ora.com
To receive a free copy of our magazine/catalog, "ora.com" (please include a snailmail address).

Snailmail and phones

O'Reilly & Associates, Inc.
103A Morris Street, Sebastopol, CA 95472
Inquiries: **707-829-0515, 800-998-9938**
Credit card orders: **800-889-8969**
FAX: **707-829-0104**

O'Reilly & Associates—
LISTING OF TITLES

Internet

!%@:: A Directory of Electronic Mail Addressing & Networks
Connecting to the Internet: An O'Reilly Buyer's Guide
Internet In A Box
MH & xmh: E-mail for Users & Programmers
The Mosaic Handbook for Microsoft Windows
The Mosaic Handbook for the Macintosh
The Mosaic Handbook for the X Window System
Smileys
The Whole Internet User's Guide & Catalog

System Administration

Computer Security Basics
DNS and BIND
Essential System Administration
Linux Network Administrator's Guide (Fall 94 est.)
Managing Internet Information Services (Fall 94 est.)
Managing NFS and NIS
Managing UUCP and Usenet
sendmail
Practical UNIX Security
PGP: Pretty Good Privacy (Winter 94/95 est.)
System Performance Tuning
TCP/IP Network Administration
termcap & terminfo
X Window System Administrator's Guide: Volume 8
X Window System ,R6, Companion CD (Fall 94 est.)

Using UNIX and X

Basics

Learning GNU Emacs
Learning the Korn Shell
Learning the UNIX Operating System
Learning the vi Editor
SCO UNIX in a Nutshell
The USENET Handbook (Winter 94/95 est.)
Using UUCP and Usenet
UNIX in a Nutshell: System V Edition
The X Window System in a Nutshell
X Window System User's Guide: Volume 3
X Window System User's Guide, Motif Ed.: Vol. 3M
X User Tools (with CD-ROM) (10/94 est.)

Advanced

Exploring Expect (Winter 94/95 est.)
The Frame Handbook (10/94 est.)
Making TeX Work
Learning Perl
Programming perl
sed & awk
UNIX Power Tools (with CD-ROM)

Programming UNIX, C, and Multi-platform

Fortran/Scientific Computing

High Performance Computing
Migrating to Fortran 90
UNIX for FORTRAN Programmers

C Programming Libraries

Practical C Programming
POSIX Programmer's Guide
POSIX.4: Programming for the Real World (Fall 94 est.)
Programming with curses
Understanding and Using COFF
Using C on the UNIX System

C Programming Tools

Checking C Programs with lint
lex & yacc
Managing Projects with make
Power Programming with RPC
Software Portability with imake

Multi-Platform Programming

Encyclopedia of Graphics File Formats
Distributing Applications Across DCE and Windows NT
Guide to Writing DCE Applications
Multi-Platform Code Management
Understanding DCE
Understanding Japanese Information Processing
ORACLE Performance Tuning

Berkeley 4.4 Software Distribution

4.4BSD System Manager's Manual
4.4BSD User's Reference Manual
4.4BSD User's Supplementary Documents
4.4BSD Programmer's Reference Manual
4.4BSD Programmer's Supplementary Documents
4.4BSD-Lite CD Companion
4.4BSD-Lite CD Companion: International Version

X Programming

Motif Programming Manual: Volume 6A
Motif Reference Manual: Volume 6B
Motif Tools
PEXlib Programming Manual
PEXlib Reference Manual
PHIGS Programming Manual (soft or hard cover)
PHIGS Reference Manual
Programmer's Supplement for R6 (Winter 94/95 est.)
Xlib Programming Manual: Volume 1
Xlib Reference Manual: Volume 2
X Protocol Reference Manual, R5: Volume 0
X Protocol Reference Manual, R6: Volume 0 (11/94 est.)
X Toolkit Intrinsics Programming Manual: Vol. 4
X Toolkit Intrinsics Programming Manual, Motif Edition: Volume 4M
X Toolkit Intrinsics Reference Manual: Volume 5
XView Programming Manual: Volume 7A
XView Reference Manual: Volume 7B

The X Resource

A Quarterly Working Journal for X Programmers

The X Resource: Issues 0 through 12 (Issue 12 available 10/94)

Business/Career

Building a Successful Software Business
Love Your Job!

Travel

Travelers' Tales Thailand
Travelers' Tales Mexico
Travelers' Tales India (Winter 94/95 est.)

Audiotapes

Internet Talk Radio's "Geek of the Week" Interviews

The Future of the Internet Protocol, 4 hours
Global Network Operations, 2 hours
Mobile IP Networking, 1 hour
Networked Information and Online Libraries, 1 hour
Security and Networks, 1 hour
European Networking, 1 hour

Notable Speeches of the Information Age

John Perry Barlow, 1.5 hours

O'Reilly & Associates—

INTERNATIONAL DISTRIBUTORS

Customers outside North America can now order O'Reilly & Associates books through the following distributors. They offer our international customers faster order processing, more bookstores, increased representation at tradeshows worldwide, and the high quality, responsive service our customers have come to expect.

EUROPE, MIDDLE EAST, AND AFRICA

(except Germany, Switzerland, and Austria)

INQUIRIES

International Thomson Publishing Europe
Berkshire House
168-173 High Holborn
London WC1V 7AA
United Kingdom
Telephone: 44-71-497-1422
Fax: 44-71-497-1426
Email: ora.orders@itpuk.co.uk

ORDERS

International Thomson Publishing Services, Ltd.
Cheriton House, North Way
Andover, Hampshire SP10 5BE
United Kingdom
Telephone: 44-264-342-832 (UK orders)
Telephone: 44-264-342-806 (outside UK)
Fax: 44-264-364418 (UK orders)
Fax: 44-264-342761 (outside UK)

GERMANY, SWITZERLAND, AND AUSTRIA

International Thomson Publishing GmbH
O'Reilly-International Thomson Verlag
Attn: Mr. G. Miske
Königswinterer Strasse 418
53227 Bonn
Germany
Telephone: 49-228-970240
Fax: 49-228-441342
Email: gerd@orade.ora.com

THE AMERICAS, JAPAN, AND OCEANIA

O'Reilly & Associates, Inc.
103A Morris Street
Sebastopol, CA 95472 U.S.A.
Telephone: 707-829-0515
Telephone: 800-998-9938 (U.S. & Canada)
Fax: 707-829-0104
Email: order@ora.com

ASIA

(except Japan)

INQUIRIES

International Thomson Publishing Asia
221 Henderson Road
#05 10 Henderson Building
Singapore 0315
Telephone: 65-272-6496
Fax: 65-272-6498

ORDERS

Telephone: 65-268-7867
Fax: 65-268-6727

AUSTRALIA

WoodsLane Pty. Ltd.
Unit 8, 101 Darley Street (P.O. Box 935)
Mona Vale NSW 2103
Australia
Telephone: 61-2-979-5944
Fax: 61-2-997-3348
Email: woods@tmx.mhs.oz.au

NEW ZEALAND

WoodsLane New Zealand Ltd.
21 Cooks Street (P.O. Box 575)
Wanganui, New Zealand
Telephone: 64-6-347-6543
Fax: 64-6-345-4840
Email: woods@tmx.mhs.oz.au